Learner Experience and Usability in Online Education

Imed Bouchrika
University of Souk Ahras, Algeria

Nouzha Harrati
University of Souk Ahras, Algeria

Phu Vu
University of Nebraska at Kearney, USA

A volume in the Advances in Educational Technologies and Instructional Design (AETID) Book Series

IGI Global
DISSEMINATOR OF KNOWLEDGE

Published in the United States of America by
IGI Global
Information Science Reference (an imprint of IGI Global)
701 E. Chocolate Avenue
Hershey PA, USA 17033
Tel: 717-533-8845
Fax: 717-533-8661
E-mail: cust@igi-global.com
Web site: http://www.igi-global.com

Library of Congress Cataloging-in-Publication Data

Names: Bouchrika, Imed, editor. | Harrati, Nouzha, editor. | Vu, Phu, 1979- editor.
Title: Learner experience and usability in online education / Imed Bouchrika, Nouzha Harrati, and Phu Vu, editors.
Description: Hershey PA : Information Science Reference, [2018]
Identifiers: LCCN 2017030383| ISBN 9781522542063 (hardcover) | ISBN 9781522542070 (ebook)
Subjects: LCSH: Web-based instruction. | Internet in education. | Human-computer interaction. | User interfaces (Computer systems)
Classification: LCC LB1044.87 .L428 2018 | DDC 371.33/44678--dc23 LC record available at https://lccn.loc.gov/2017030383

This book is published in the IGI Global book series Advances in Educational Technologies and Instructional Design (AETID) (ISSN: 2326-8905; eISSN: 2326-8913)

British Cataloguing in Publication Data
A Cataloguing in Publication record for this book is available from the British Library.

For electronic access to this publication, please contact: eresources@igi-global.com.

Advances in Educational Technologies and Instructional Design (AETID) Book Series

Lawrence A. Tomei
Robert Morris University, USA

ISSN:2326-8905
EISSN:2326-8913

Mission

Education has undergone, and continues to undergo, immense changes in the way it is enacted and distributed to both child and adult learners. From distance education, Massive-Open-Online-Courses (MOOCs), and electronic tablets in the classroom, technology is now an integral part of the educational experience and is also affecting the way educators communicate information to students.

The **Advances in Educational Technologies & Instructional Design (AETID) Book Series** is a resource where researchers, students, administrators, and educators alike can find the most updated research and theories regarding technology's integration within education and its effect on teaching as a practice.

Coverage

- Web 2.0 and Education
- Classroom Response Systems
- Digital Divide in Education
- Instructional Design
- Adaptive Learning
- Online Media in Classrooms
- Hybrid Learning
- K-12 Educational Technologies
- Collaboration Tools
- Game-Based Learning

IGI Global is currently accepting manuscripts for publication within this series. To submit a proposal for a volume in this series, please contact our Acquisition Editors at Acquisitions@igi-global.com or visit: http://www.igi-global.com/publish/.

The Advances in Educational Technologies and Instructional Design (AETID) Book Series (ISSN 2326-8905) is published by IGI Global, 701 E. Chocolate Avenue, Hershey, PA 17033-1240, USA, www.igi-global.com. This series is composed of titles available for purchase individually; each title is edited to be contextually exclusive from any other title within the series. For pricing and ordering information please visit http://www.igi-global.com/book-series/advances-educational-technologies-instructional-design/73678. Postmaster: Send all address changes to above address.

Titles in this Series

For a list of additional titles in this series, please visit: www.igi-global.com/book-series

Enhancing Social Presence in Online Learning Environments
Michael Marmon (University of North Texas, USA)
Information Science Reference • copyright 2018 • 317pp • H/C (ISBN: 9781522532293) • US $185.00 (our price)

Digital Technologies and Instructional Design for Personalized Learning
Robert Zheng (University of Utah, USA)
Information Science Reference • copyright 2018 • 391pp • H/C (ISBN: 9781522539407) • US $195.00 (our price)

Curriculum Development for Gifted Education Programs
Jessica Cannaday (Azusa Pacific University, USA)
Information Science Reference • copyright 2018 • 284pp • H/C (ISBN: 9781522530411) • US $175.00 (our price)

Curriculum Internationalization and the Future of Education
Semire Dikli (Georgia Gwinnett College, USA) Brian Etheridge (Georgia Gwinnett College, USA) and Richard Rawls (Georgia Gwinnett College, USA)
Information Science Reference • copyright 2018 • 360pp • H/C (ISBN: 9781522527916) • US $195.00 (our price)

Handbook of Research on Integrating Technology Into Contemporary Language Learning and Teaching
Bin Zou (Xi'an Jiaotong-Liverpool University, China) and Michael Thomas (University of Central Lancashire, UK)
Information Science Reference • copyright 2018 • 626pp • H/C (ISBN: 9781522551409) • US $265.00 (our price)

Technology Management in Organizational and Societal Contexts
Andrew Borchers (Lipscomb University, USA)
Information Science Reference • copyright 2018 • 365pp • H/C (ISBN: 9781522552796) • US $195.00 (our price)

Engaging Adolescent Students in Contemporary Classrooms Emerging Research and Opportunities
Prathiba Nagabhushan (St. Mary MacKillop College, Australia)
Information Science Reference • copyright 2018 • 216pp • H/C (ISBN: 9781522551553) • US $135.00 (our price)

Impact of Learning Analytics on Curriculum Design and Student Performance
Manoj Kumar Singh (Mekelle University, Ethiopia) Zenawi Zerihun (Mekelle University, Ethiopia) and Neerja Singh (Ram Manohar Lohia Avadh University, India)
Information Science Reference • copyright 2018 • 215pp • H/C (ISBN: 9781522553694) • US $175.00 (our price)

IGI Global
DISSEMINATOR OF KNOWLEDGE

701 East Chocolate Avenue, Hershey, PA 17033, USA
Tel: 717-533-8845 x100 • Fax: 717-533-8661
E-Mail: cust@igi-global.com • www.igi-global.com

List of Reviewers

Gary L. Ackerman, *Windsor (Vermont) School, USA*
Hesham Alomyan, *University of Petra, Jordan*
Jason Bader, *Mt. San Jacinto College, USA*
Amir Benzaoui, *University of Boumerdes, Algeria*
Amar Ranjan Dash, *Berhampur University, India*
Samia Drissi, *University of Souk Ahras, Algeria*
Nouredine Gasmallah, *University of Souk Ahras, Algeria*
Lijia Lin, *East China Normal University, China*
Zohra Mahfouf, *University of Souk Ahras, Algeria*
Desislava Paneva-Marinova, *Bulgarian Academy of Sciences, Bulgaria*
Monica Rysavy, *Goldey-Beacom College, USA*
Laila Shoukry, *Technical University of Darmstadt, Germany*
Matthias Teine, *Paderborn University, Germany*

Table of Contents

Detailed Table of Contents

There is an abundant amount of literature on visual design principles, graphic design theory, and media theory. Yet very little is discussed, at least in a systematic way, about the process of making online courses aesthetically pleasing. A major obstacle to gaining such knowledge is the lack of understanding of applied definitions, conceptual ideas, and methods of creating online learning interfaces. In this chapter, the authors seek to clarify the process of using visual design to improve the online learning experience. The chapter concludes with strategies on how colleges and universities can help faculty and instructional designers learn visual design skills through the creation of a design studio.

Our economies and societies are changing, with significant effects on each individual, as they have to cope with increasingly complex and unpredictable working lives. Therefore, innovative digital learning applications that respond to their end user's needs and desires become inevitable. Whilst relying on user-centered design structures, the participatory design methodology provides a promising approach towards the creation of such a new generation of digital learning applications. After thoroughly outlining the research undertaking's rationale and following to a theoretical discussion, the author gives insights into the results of problem-centered interviews with digital learning and user experience experts that build the basis for the creation for a prototypical participatory design process. These findings primarily confirm the recent literature and provide, complemented by the created process, a sound basis for further theory-oriented, scientific discussions but application in practice as well.

Anyone is free to use open source software without the need to purchase the right to install it. Despite its appeal to school and technology leaders in rural communities, they are less likely to install it than others. In this chapter, three cases in which open source technology was installed to support teaching and learning in three rural communities are described. In each, the systems were deployed and refined using decision-making grounded in educational design research. The projects are detailed, and the method of technology planning is assessed. Unanswered questions are also addressed.

This chapter describes how the researchers at a small private Master's level college examined how different delivery modes—face-to-face (F2F), hybrid, and online instruction—may impact first-year students' perceptions of their information literacy (IL) skills compared to their test-assessed information literacy skills using the students perception of information literacy-questionnaire (SPIL-Q) and information literacy assessment (ILA) instruments. These instruments were developed and deployed to international graduate business students in two previous studies: Michalak and Rysavy and Michalak, Rysavy, and Wessel. The students (n=161) in this study were enrolled in a first-year English composition course in the Spring 2017 semester. This iteration achieved an overall response rate of 87.04% (n=141). Overall, results demonstrated the greatest achievement were demonstrated by students in hybrid course sections.

In this chapter, the topic of evaluating learner experience in serious games is discussed with respect to four different dimensions: gaming, learning, using and context with a special focus on using multimodal data. After reviewing relevant research fields, the steps involved in a serious games evaluation process is investigated and relevant evaluation studies are reviewed with emphasis on the use of different modalities for recording and assessing in-game interactions. Finally, a theoretical framework (LeGUC) is proposed defining parameters related to the four dimensions discussed which can be observed during evaluation studies of serious games and how they relate to logged in-game interactions. The framework is based on relevant literature as well as a conducted observational user study.

Virtual worlds can be considered immersive e-learning environments, whose characteristics of interactivity, immersion, and collaboration can be applied in different areas of teaching, such as in the field of sciences. In this way, this chapter presents the construction of a virtual world to aid in the teaching of sciences in which different types of learning materials and simulations were developed in the OpenSim platform. A group of sixth grade students used the immersive environment for a semester, being evaluated their learning through a pre- and posttest applied together with an analysis of their learning styles, being realized a correlation between the results obtained. Added to this, usability assessments with interviews about the environment was applied. The results demonstrated the potential of virtual worlds to contribute to the adaptation of the different learning styles in a class and their contribution to the improvement of the learning process.

This chapter presents solutions for personalized observation and enhanced learning experience in digital libraries (DLs) by special smart educational nooks. Main factors related to the DLs user experience and content usability issues are considered. During the user experience design, the users' needs, goals, preferences, and interests have been carefully studied and have become the starting point for the new DLs functionality development. This chapter demonstrates several educational nooks or their components, such as learning tools in a digital library for fashion objects, a smart learning corner in an iconographical art digital library, an ontology of learning analysis method, and some educational games for art and culture in which authors are co-developers.

With the increase in number of electronic services being delivered through web portals, a lot of emphasis is being given to ensure the quality of web portals in terms of contents and associated design aspects. This has led to studies investigating various requirements of web users and to guidelines for quality enhancement in order to make web portals accessible to all irrespective of one's age, physical challenges, ethnicity, and level of literacy. In this chapter, the authors address the accessibility issues of web portals based on ongoing research. They analyze the accessibility in three levels (i.e., at the levels of authoring tool, web component, and user-agent). The contents of this chapter can throw light on the design aspects of web portals, web browsers, and media players to make them more suitable for users in general.

Preface

In a modern society, the use of online technology has become ubiquitous and integral part of our daily life from education to entertainment. This is mainly due to the proliferation of the use of computers and smart devices combined with the availability and affordance of internet connectivity in most places. As technology has progressed so much that geographical gap is virtually bridged with the deployment of tools that make people collaborate and interact together remotely with the feeling that they are inside the same room. The use of e-Learning in schools and corporations gained popularity mainly due to the perceived advantages of flexibility around fitting the students' time requirements and overcoming the issue around the geographical restrictions. Because of the ubiquity of e-learning and vital influence for engineering the educational process, it is no surprise that many research studies are conducted to explore different aspects covering the use of e-learning in higher education. The assessment and evaluation aspects are considered arguably the most influential part for measuring the success and effectiveness of e-learning experience. This research publication would serve as an authoritative reference for the state of the art research on the design, implementation and evaluation of user experience aspect for online learning systems. Positive user experience is of prime importance for online systems playing vital role for technology acceptance as well as the continuous success of uptake of e-learners systems.

This research handbook seeks to provide the latest research and technological developments on exploring the user experience, ease of interactivity and engagement level of students for using online learning system. Different tools, approaches and systems proposed into the research literature to determine the user experience of learners through online learning systems, will provide guidance and state of the art resource for university researchers as well as industry professionals from different disciplines including human computer interaction, education and behavioral science. Although, there are many research books published on appropriate practices in online education or usability, but few merge the theory and practice of user experience when it comes to online education. The main objective of the book is to deepen and broaden the practical use of well-established user experience aspects and educational theories to aid the incorporation and enhancement of online learning. The foremost benefit of this research project is that publication would serve as a resource to online lecturers and instructors in addition to software developers and user experience consultants for how to best design, implement and evaluate online learning systems and pedagogical contents. This is believed to have a positive impact in the field of online education in numerous ways including mainly improving the uptake of e-learning technological systems and learners' engagement.

In spite of the widespread use of e-learning systems and the substantial investments in purchasing, developing and maintaining learning management systems, there is no consensus yet on devising a standard framework or taxonomy for evaluating the quality and effectiveness of e-learning systems. The dearth of conventional e-learning system quality models is in stark contrast compared to the considerable body of work on software quality assurance. Positive user experience is of prime importance for online systems playing vital role for technology acceptance as well as the continuous commercial success of software companies. Considerable research within the human-computer interaction literature concerns the analytical quantification of the various factors that determine and shape software usability. Positive user experience emerges as an important pillar for the adoption of educational learning systems. This is mainly because the availability of technological infrastructures and systems is not adequate to enforce the uptake of new educational approaches from both sides of the teachers or the learners. Because of the ubiquity of e-learning and vital influence for engineering the educational process, it is no surprise that many research studies are conducted to explore different aspects covering the use of e-learning in higher education. This includes for instance the learning models, software interactivity and human behaviors. The assessment and evaluation aspects are considered arguably the most influential part for measuring the success and effectiveness of e-learning experience. In fact, considerable criticism regarding the quality of existing e-learning systems are being cited by a number of studies in addition to further issues including low performance, poor user experience and customizability. Furthermore, online education has been further criticized as not supporting a student-centred learning but replicating the traditional face-to-face teaching paradigm.

For the first chapter of the book, Bader *et al* clarified the process of using visual design to improve the online learning experience. This is because of the scarcity for research studies for making online courses aesthetically pleasing. A major obstacle to gaining such knowledge is the lack of understanding of applied definitions, conceptual ideas, and methods of creating online learning interfaces. The chapter concludes with strategies on how colleges and universities can help faculty and instructional designers learn visual design skills through the creation of a design studio. In the second chapter, Teine *et al* have given insights into the results of problem-centered interviews with digital learning and user experience experts that build the basis for the creation for a prototypical participatory design process. These findings primarily confirm the recent literature and provide, complemented by the created process, a sound basis for further theory-oriented, scientific discussions but application in practice as well.

In Chapter 3, Ackerman discussed the use of open online learning in rural communities. Despite their appeal to school and technology leaders in rural communities, they are less likely to install it than others. In the chapter, three cases in which open source technology was installed to support teaching and learning in three rural communities are described. In each, the systems were deployed and refined using decision-making grounded in educational design research. The projects are detailed and the method of technology planning is assessed. Unanswered questions are also addressed. In the fourth chapter, Rysavy *et al.* have describe how the researchers at a small private master's level college examined how different delivery modes: face-to-face (F2F), hybrid, and online instruction—may impact first-year students' perceptions of their information literacy (IL) skills compared to their test-assessed information literacy skills using the Students Perception of Information Literacy-Questionnaire (SPIL-Q) and Information Literacy Assessment (ILA) instruments. In Chapter 5, Shoukry *et al* have discussed the topic of evaluating learner experience in Serious Games with respect to four different dimensions: Gaming, Learning, Using and Context with a special focus on using multimodal data. After reviewing relevant research fields, the steps involved in a serious games evaluation process is investigated and relevant evaluation studies are reviewed with emphasis on the use of different modalities for recording and assessing in-game interactions. Finally, a theoretical framework (LeGUC) is proposed defining parameters related to the four dimensions discussed which can be observed during evaluation studies of Serious Games and how they relate to logged in-game interactions. Nunes *et al* discussed the concept of virtual words for area of e-learning in Chapter 6. A group of sixth grade students used the immersive environment for a semester, being evaluated their learning through a pre- and posttest applied together with an analysis of their learning styles, being realized a correlation between the results obtained. Added to this, usability assessments with interviews about the environment was applied. The results demonstrated the potential of Virtual Worlds to contribute to the adaptation of the different learning styles in a class and their contribution to the improvement of the learning process.

In Chapter 7, Paneva-Marinova *et al* have presented solutions for personalized observation and enhanced learning experience in digital libraries (DLs) by special smart educational Nooks. Main factors, related to the DLs user experience and content usability issues are considered. During the user experience design, the users' needs, goals, preferences, and interests have been carefully studied and have become the starting point for the new DLs functionality development. This chapter demonstrates several educational nooks or their components, such as learning tools in a digital library for fashion objects, a smart learning corner in an iconographical art digital library, an ontology of learning analysis method and some educational games for art and culture, in which authors are co-developers. For the eighth chapter, Dash *et al.* have addressed the accessibility issues of web portals based on our ongoing research. The authors have analyzed the accessibility in three levels, viz. at the levels of authoring tool, web component, and user-agent. The contents of this chapter can throw light on the design aspects of web portals, web browsers, and media players to make them more suitable for users in general. Alomyan have reviewed and evaluated some issues related to Web-based learning in Chapter 9 where they stressed on the importance of using the Web in education. In the last chapter (10), Lin conducted an empirical study on the behavioral, emotional and cognitive engagement, as well as their learning, in a blended learning environment. The quantitative results showed that students' online login, the behavioral engagement indicator, had a positive impact on their learning, which was supported by qualitative findings. Further analysis revealed the mixture of students' engagement, such as confusion vs. interesting feelings to online discussions and frustration vs. not much effort using the online system.

Finally, It is our earnest wish and hope that this research book will be of benefit to various academic readers including instructors, teachers, students, policy makers as well as university researchers. This is because the scope of usability of e-learnings spans across different research community including human computer interaction, education and behavioral science.

Imed Bouchrika
University of Souk Ahras, Algeria

Nouzha Harrati
University of Souk Ahras, Algeria

Phu Vu
University of Nebraska at Kearney, USA

Chapter 1
Using Visual Design to Improve the Online Learning Experience:
A Synthesis of Research on Aesthetics

Jason D. Bader
Mt. San Jacinto College, USA

Patrick R. Lowenthal
Boise State University, USA

ABSTRACT

There is an abundant amount of literature on visual design principles, graphic design theory, and media theory. Yet very little is discussed, at least in a systematic way, about the process of making online courses aesthetically pleasing. A major obstacle to gaining such knowledge is the lack of understanding of applied definitions, conceptual ideas, and methods of creating online learning interfaces. In this chapter, the authors seek to clarify the process of using visual design to improve the online learning experience. The chapter concludes with strategies on how colleges and universities can help faculty and instructional designers learn visual design skills through the creation of a design studio.

INTRODUCTION

We see with our brains, and therefore the more visual an input, the more likely something will be recognized and recalled (Medina, 2008). Thus, vision is in many ways the most powerful tool humans have for learning (Medina, 2008). But while a great deal of time goes into designing modern education buildings and classrooms, both in terms of form and function, minimal effort is dedicated to the "look and feel" of online courses. This lack of visual design in online courses exists primarily because most educators, course designers, and developers have no background in visual communication design (Lohr, 2008; Metros, 2008; Braden, 1996). At the same time, though, even trained graphic designers—while underrepresented on most college campuses—struggle when designing for online learning environments (Malamed, 2009; Karabeg, 2003) that take place in predesigned or established interfaces, interfaces designed and developed by technologists. The lack of attention to the visual design of online courses is also

DOI: 10.4018/978-1-5225-4206-3.ch001

problematic because students make judgments about an institution or a course based on how a website looks (see Szabo & Kanuka, 1999). Further, aesthetics matter! Traditional practices of design—like architecture, graphic design, industrial design, and digital media design—focus on both the functional and the visual aspects of design. The authors contend that the field of instructional design and technology, and specifically online course design, has largely ignored the importance of aesthetics.[1] Aesthetics are what make creative experiences, inclusive of user-generated content and mass media, unique, personal, and memorable (Manovich, 2017; Margolin & Margolin, 2002).

While research on visual design and learning is nascent (Kimball, 2013; William & Stamitz, 2005), the authors posit that colleges and universities have a responsibility to focus on aesthetics and how online courses are visually designed if they are to improve the overall learning experience. In the following chapter, the authors synthesize literature on visual design, illustrate how these ideas can be used to improve the visual design of online courses, and conclude with strategies on how colleges and universities can help faculty and instructional designers learn visual design skills through the creation of a design studio.

PROBLEM

The first online course was offered over 30 years ago. For decades, though, online learning was just an extension of distance education used by a small minority of teachers and learners. During the past 5–10 years, however, this has all begun to change. Online learning is no longer a fringe activity in education taught only by early adopters. Today, to meet the increased demand, all types of teachers end up designing and teaching courses online, most with minimal technical or design experience. Recognizing this problem, colleges and universities have developed multiple approaches to train and support faculty to design online courses from an instructional perspective, but very little effort has focused on how to help faculty improve the visual design of online courses. Given this, the authors questioned, what are the essential activities and knowledge in graphic design that can be useful for learning skills in online course design? This chapter explores pertinent knowledge to support faculty in the development of visual design awareness for online courses.

DESIGN PROBLEMS

The two most basic components of any visual design are the functionality and the aesthetic of the product. Many designers consider the functionality the primary concern and the visual appeal a secondary concern, while others consider the two intertwined (this is discussed in more detail in the form follows function section), but all designers consider the activity of design as the development of a creative solution for heuristic experiences. In other words, all designers consider visual design as a process of solving ill-defined design problems, otherwise known as wicked problems.

Rittel and Webber (1973) define wicked problems as ill-formulated and complex problems that involve clients and decision makers with conflicting values. In many ways, online course design—especially visual design—involves solving extraordinarily wicked problems. However, adherence to established visual design theories, rules, and principles makes the process of solving these wicked problems more comprehensible. Figure 1 is a visual representation that compares simple and wicked problems. In a simple problem, the solutions will typically yield the same result. For instance, when letters and backgrounds have similar values they cannot be easily read. Creating more contrast between the background and text can easily solve this problem. The solution will have the same effect on all participants; they can now read the text. However, the contrast between black and white is binary and straightforward. If low contrast exists due to the values of two colors being similar, the solution becomes much more complicated. An adjustment of the hue without knowledge of color may adverse effects of creating a visually unappealing environment, color discord, unintended cultural implications, or color contrasts that make it difficult for color blind viewers. The decision of what color combinations to choose thus becomes a wicked problem.

While knowledge of design principles may transition the functional design problems from wicked to simple, the aesthetic development of visual design will always remain a wicked problem. Buchanan (1992) describes a wicked problem as a design problem that has "no special subject matter of its own apart from what a designer conceives it to be" (p. 16). In other words, designing visuals is not only about functionality; it is just as importantly about the human experience. Each experience of a single visual design can be unique for each individual who interacts with it. Table 1 compares every criterion of a wicked problem and relates it to an activity in the visual design process.

Facing wicked problems in any design is commonplace. The activity of design is to plan for events with unknown results. Usually, this type of planning happens in a process known as brainstorming.

Figure 1. A comparison of the application of visual design processes to simple and wicked problems and the respectively expected and unexpected results

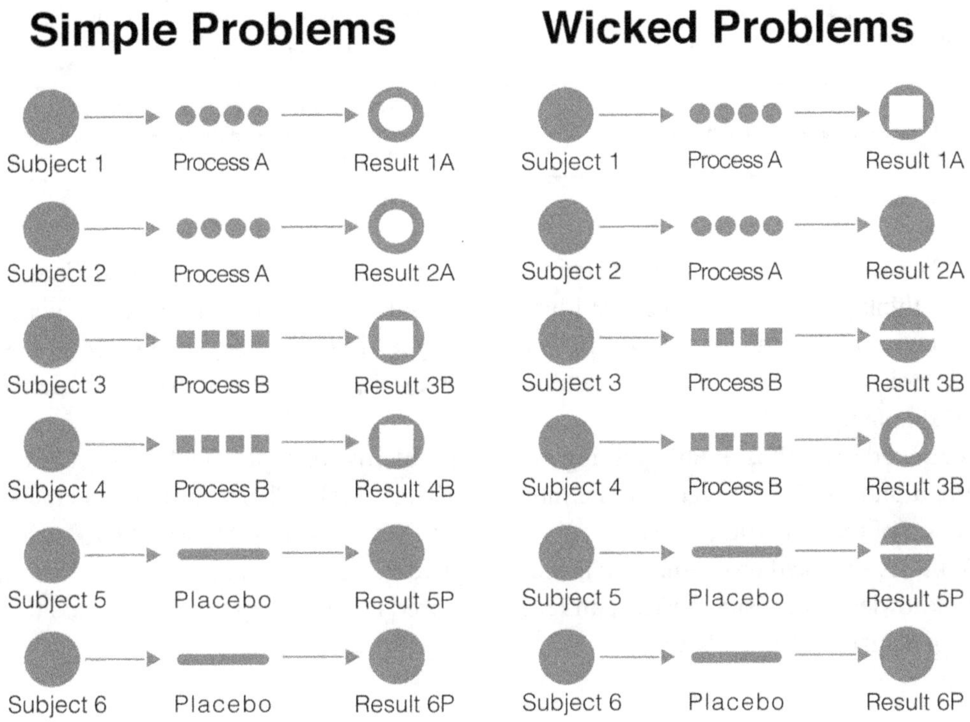

Table 1. Comparison of visual design to wicked problems

Wicked Problems (Rittel & Webber, 1973)	Visual Design
There are no definitive formulations of a wicked problem.	There is no defined visual design problem to solve. A solution needs to work visually, but what works in one context does not necessarily work in another.
Wicked problems have no stopping rules.	The visual design is never final; circumstances always resurrect the visual design process.
Solutions to wicked problems cannot be true or false, only good or bad.	The perception of a visual design solution is, "I like it." or, "It doesn't work for me."
There is no immediate and no ultimate test of a solution to a wicked problem.	There is no mechanism to verify if a visual design correctly functions, as there will always be subjective criteria by which to analyze a visual design solution. We can examine the perception or feelings that people get from a design, but even this cannot be standardized.
Every solution to a wicked problem is a "one-shot operation"; because there is no opportunity to learn by trial-and-error, every attempt counts significantly.	When a visual design is released to the public, only then can the result be analyzed for its actual intent. These results can vary significantly from those of focus groups.
Wicked problems do not have an enumerable (or an exhaustively describable) set of potential solutions, nor is there a well-described set of permissible operations that may be incorporated into the plan.	The methods that visual designers use to create ideas vary according to the designer's preference. Also, a number of drafts or final solutions presented to the client may change as well.
Every wicked problem is essentially unique.	The content, purpose, and audience of every visual design is unique.
Every wicked problem can be considered to be a symptom of another problem.	When using visual design within a scenario, new problems may arise. Information may not be communicated as intended. Technology may not work as planned.
The existence of a discrepancy representing a wicked problem can be explained in numerous ways. The choice of explanation determines the nature of the problem's resolution.	In the case of visual design, discrepancies may be explained in terms of the visual objects, principles, or properties used. For instance, users may choose not to read material because of typeface, line spacing, contrast, length of passage, lack of visuals, or any combination of these.
The wicked problem solver has no right to be wrong.	The visual designer is ultimately responsible for the success or the failure of the reception of the work. They are responsible for understanding the concepts needed to solve the wicked problem.

Robson (2002) associates the activities of brainstorming as conception or building up ideas with few or no limits (i.e., thinking outside the box). With wicked problems, designers may have a general idea of the problem, but a significant amount of time and effort goes into the analysis portion of design thinking (Beyer & Holtzblatt, 2009), including activities such as requirement gathering, problem definition, and problem shaping.

Online course design thus entails solving wicked problems. In a practical sense, the course must function serendipitously for navigation to be intuitive (Krug, 2000). There must be visual cues given to the organization of the material if the user is to be able to act (Austin & Doust, 2007; Norman, 1990). But because this is a wicked problem, even a well-designed visual does not guarantee consistent results; nonetheless, knowledge of visual design can reach a desired result in larger pool of users than an uninformed design decision.

DESIGN PROCESS

Experienced designers do not begin with a preconceived idea or solution (Rand, 1985). Rather, designers typically progress through a series of self-defined activities, which generally can be categorized as a process of looking, thinking, and doing (Pentak & Lauer, 2015). A typical design process involves redefining the problem, experimenting with media, generating graphic styles, adjusting the visual composition, revising the content, interpreting the visual results of prototyped outcomes generated during the design process (Noble & Bestley, 2016).

New designers, though, need to learn the typical or basic design process. Solving a visual design problem, or any design problem, typically requires a dynamic, iterative approach rather than a sequential, linear approach (Lauer & Pentak, 2016; Meinel & Leifer, 2011; Buchanan, 1992; Rittel & Webber, 1973). This design process usually involves looking, thinking, doing, and critiquing (Pentak & Lauer, 2016). Figure 2 illustrates the iterative design process. In theory, the process appears as a sequential cycle, but in practice, the design process is non-sequential.

Buchanan (1990) argues that the oversimplified linear outline of the design process is far from standard practice. Designers operate in an intricate social web, where individuals communicate in specialized terminologies and logic; this web is a product of the relationship between their areas of conceptual and technical expertise (Buchanan, 1990). Furthermore, designers also apply unique cultural or intellectual models that inadvertently inform (or elude) their perspective of a particular design situation (Manzini, 1989).

A designer operates using personal frameworks with a unique process model that influences all those involved with the design process (i.e., the design team, the clients, and the users). Furthermore, based upon the desired media output, the design process evolves towards the medium in which the designer operates. Table 2 presents an overview of conventional design methods that the authors have found in textbooks. Each textbook's related field heavily influences the proposed set of design activities. Despite

Figure 2. Visual mapping of the basic design process

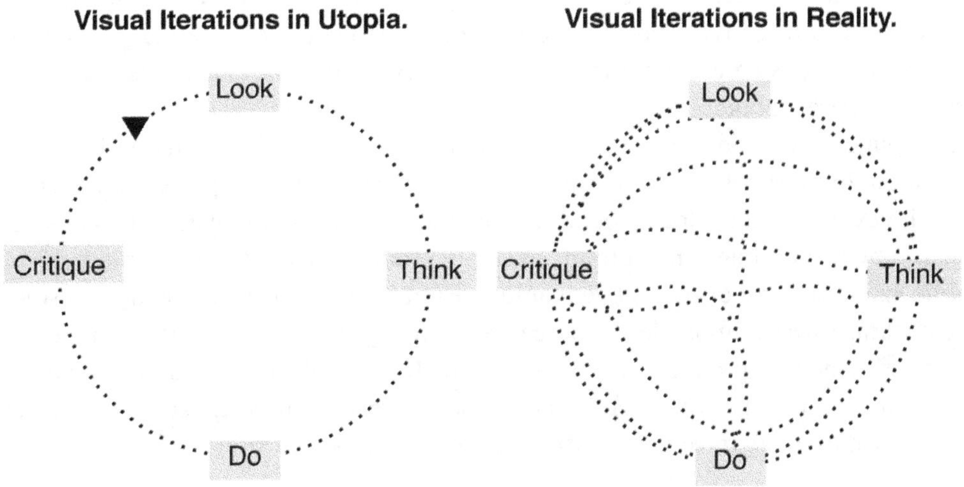

Table 2. Common design processes

Book	Design Process
Design Basics **(Pentak & Lauer, 2015)** Used in introductory studio art courses as a foundation for two-dimensional design, this is an extraordinary textbook to use in the development of a visual language for any visual discipline.	1. Looking 2. Thinking 3. Doing 4. Critiquing
The Design Method **(Karjaluoto, 2014)** This is a small personal reflective text that creates a discourse on functional design and application. It goes beyond the visual solutions and also discusses client relationships upon deployment of deliverables.	1. Discovery 2. Planning 3. Creativity 4. Application
Design thinking: Understand - improve - apply **(Plattner, Meinel, & Leifer, 2011)** This book describes the interactive environment that promotes learning, remarking on traditional learning design (as opposed to visual design) through rapid conceptual prototyping within technical and human aspects.	1. (Re)define the problem 2. Needfind and benchmark 3. Bodystorm 4. Prototype 5. Test
Graphic Design Basics **(Arntson, 2011)** This traditional textbook on the process of making graphic design solutions is geared towards the student in higher education. The projects described are grounded in real-world problems.	1. Research 2. Thumbnails 3. Roughs 4. Comprehensives 5. Presentation 6. Production/Distribution
New Media Design **(Austin & Doust, 2007)** This text summarizes the duties of a graphic designer who works in the field of new media, as opposed to print media. The focus of the book is primarily on the real-world operations of a practicing designer.	1. Strategy a. Experience Analysis b. Branding c. Market Research 2. Architecture a. Conceptualization b. Content Strategy 3. Design a. Visual Design/Prototype b. Style Guides 4. Production a. Front-End b. Back-End

this, one can see similarities between each of these design processes. For instance, planning and thinking primarily refer to the same activity. Pentak and Lauer's (2015) simplified verbiage describing steps of the design process remains an excellent foundation for new designers, since those activities (looking, thinking, and doing) are ambiguous enough to relate to any discipline.

Design disciplines also emphasize forms of collaborative design that focus on brainstorming, critique, and iteration. In most colleges and universities, these activities take place within a design studio, a workspace with extended time blocks for ad-hoc instruction. The learning activities in a design studio are characterized by one-on-one, small group, and large group work on design problems reinforced by a periodic public and individual critiques (Cennamo & Brandt, 2012). The typical design studio contains many people working toward similar design processes, so design becomes a heuristic process that enables practice in the refinement of production skills paired with the application of new knowledge and prior knowledge. In other words, this type of environment helps create well-designed products that are vetted by peers, as opposed to unorganized, uninformed, and random design solutions.

DESIGN THEORIES

Because the real-world application of design is categorized as an industrial practice, graphic design programs rarely have courses dedicated to theory (Blauvelt, 1998). Designers must consider the audience, the stakeholders, the methods, and other practicalities rather than relying on ambiguous theories (Crow, 2016; Noble & Bestley, 2016). However, Armstrong (2009) suggests that visual design methods focus on three domains—the process of conceptualization, the process of construction, and the process of context—that can help new designers think about design. Design theories drive the conceptualization, specifically its relationship to construction and context. Design theory is the answer to why humans make design decisions (Lupton & Miller, 2006). In the following section the authors describe the relevant theories, rules, and fundamentals that can help those involved in online course design. In each section, the authors also suggest possible studio questions. These questions are used to guide criticisms within each theory or principle.

The Bauhaus Philosophies

At the end of the 19th century, the Bauhaus School of Design sought to build aesthetically pleasing, functional designs due to Germany's industrialization having created poorly crafted, ugly, mass machine-produced utilitarian artifacts. Two theories sum up the functionalist Bauhaus movement, and they are still ubiquitous in all design disciplines: less is more and form follows function.

Less is more is a philosophy of minimalist design that emphasizes efficiency (Galitz 1997; Nielsen, 1993; Mullet & Sano, 1995; Norman, 1990; Schwier & Misanchuk, 1993). The early masters of design (e.g., Lissitzky, Rodchenko, Moholy-Nagy, and Beyer) perceived old art as egotistical works constructed for elitists (Lupton & Miller, 2006). They believed that subjective, bourgeois visions tarnished society. They instead explored the innovation of form that was "inspired by the machine—functional, minimal, ordered, and rational" (Armstrong, 2009, p. 9).

Schwartz (2004) argues that choices in society can be overwhelming and that the availability of more options does not equate to higher satisfaction; on the contrary, more options can lead to anxiety and stress that cause decision-making paralysis. Schwartz aptly advises that a social perspective on what is "good enough" should supersede what is "best" (p. 5), since always searching for something better can impinge upon other aspects of design like time management.

While human consciousness has an extraordinary ability to filter out extraneous information (Tufte, 1990), this does not mean that online courses should include copious amounts of data. The Online Course Workshop (n.d.) suggests that "talking too much or doing too much" and "assuming students should know that" are some of the worst things teachers do. In online learning, this creates a problem for the designer, as there must be enough information presented without it being overwhelming, making the idea of less is more a concept that any educator should consider when returning to the evaluation inflexion point of the design process.

[Less is More Studio Question: What can be removed without destroying the visual structure?]

Form follows function is a classic design theory. The original quote, "Form ever follows function" (Sullivan, 1896, p. 408), was intended to mean that in cases of life, function and form are inevitably intertwined, and neither can change without the other being changed. Many writers and designers have viewed this redacted aphorism in different philosophical perspectives. Some interpret form follows function in a verbatim and linear way. Husby (2014) describes the theory with this logical conclusion: a cup cannot perform as a cup unless shaped in a way to hold liquid, whereas if the cup cannot hold liquid, then it is not a cup. Karjaluoto (2014) argues that when a design looks good but the object does not achieve its objective, the design is a failure. In this case, the idea of form is a subset of the functionality. Figure 3 illustrates this literal definition of form follows function as a graph where there is a higher-order design at the point where the highest quality of form and function intersect.

There are some that offer a different viewpoint, arguing that within a design, the visual form drives function. Sullivan (1896) asserts, for instance, that architects manifest functionality from within the form (e.g., various levels of an office building can take on different uses). Following this logic of form follows function, an altered visual appearance can change the functionality of the design, creating a more sophisticated interpretation of form follows function. Rand (2014) points out that in an ideal case, visual appeal and utilitarianism are "mutually generative" (p. 10). Figure 4 represents Sullivan's elementary logic of form "ever" following function as a critical way of evaluating work: the best designs are the solutions that have both high style and high functionality, and the two design criteria are intertwined. Expanding on this logic, Dewey (2005) explained quite eloquently that to experience an object aesthetically is to experience such things as the application, utensil, and technology in the "degree of completeness of living" (p. 27). Functionality in design may be critical to the achievement of a particular output, but when the audience experiences the artistic interpretation of the designer, the designer furnishes an enriched life—a hidden, subconscious relationship between the audience and the ingenuity of the creator.

Even though philosophies differ, they all point to the need for any design to carry practical use, visual appeal, technical proficiency, and expressive qualities. Online courses, which are built for human interaction, would need to follow this same logic: the visual appearance of the course's navigational system, the content integration, the emotional tone, and the intuitive layout have a direct impact on the functionality of the course.

[Form Follows Function Studio Question: Do the design properties capture the essence of the content?]

Figure 3. Perspective of form follows function as functionality having priority

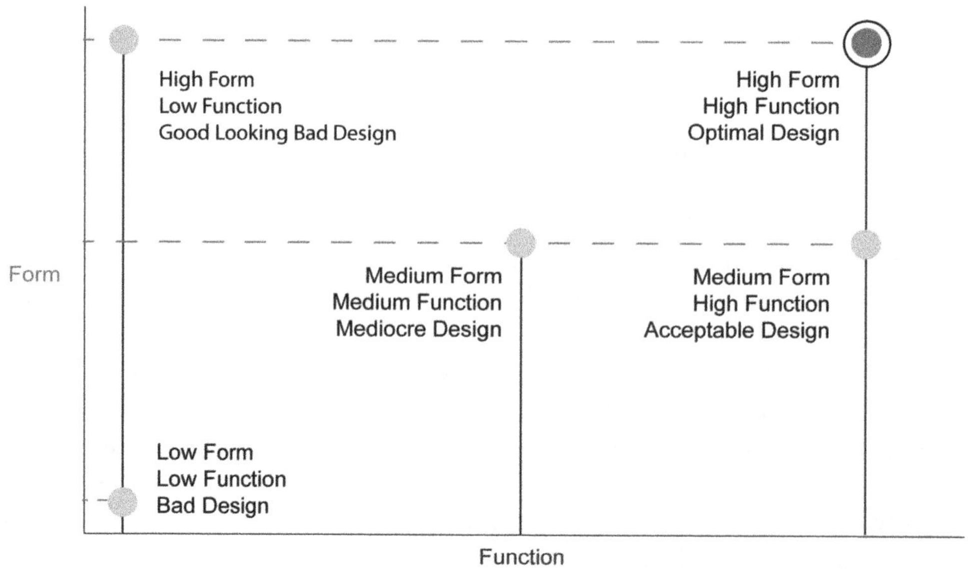

Figure 4. Perspective on form follows function as form and function interrelated

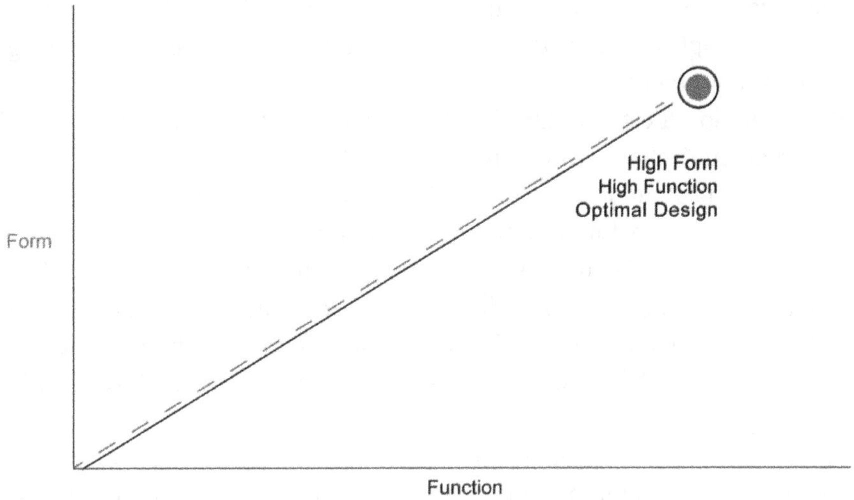

Design Thinking

Design thinking analyzes and questions both familiar and uncertain aspects of ongoing circumstances to uncover limitations and alternative possibilities that lead to desired outcomes. While the development of aesthetics is important, it takes much more than knowledge of beauty and refined style to create successful designs. The audience and the system must also be part of the plan. This section focuses on the heuristic and systematic components of design. Meinel and Leifer (2011) identified four rules related to this type of design thinking: the human rules, the ambiguity rules, the re-design rules, and the tangibility rules.

The human rules relate directly to ethnography in social activities, specifically in communication. As Ireland (2003) points out, design requires a "keen understanding of people, cultures, and belief systems that may seem completely foreign and unintelligible" (p. 22). In human-computer interaction, the primary purpose of design is for users to be able to achieve objectives intuitively and efficiently (Karjaluoto, 2014; Krug, 2000); however, when addressing issues of self-identity, culture, or expressiveness in design, another mindset is necessary (Shedroff, 2003).

While aesthetics make visual information emotional, beautiful, creative, and interesting, under certain conditions, culturally oriented aesthetics have the advantage of reaching into cognitive traits such as interpretive effects and accessibility (You, Kim, & Lim, 2016). *Cultural reflexivity* is the ideology, culture, and gender identity that drive visual preferences and interpretations (Armstrong, 2009; Mills, 2006); that is, designers must simultaneously express their self-identity while also creating a design that is accessible, inviting, intuitive, and efficient. In a multicultural space, like a web space, design objects and elements like colors are interpreted differently (Cyr, 2013; Smith et al., 2004; Marcus & Gould, 2000). The variance of perception or visual bias amongst different cultures makes critique of visual solutions from multicultural perspectives important.

[Human Rules Studio Question: Can the content be understood by the greatest number of people? Does the course design reflect a unique self-identity of the creator?]

The tangibility rules are the interaction between digital and physical worlds through the integration of computations within physical artifacts and environments (Shaer, Horn, & Jacobs, 2009). Conversely, this could be defined in the inverse as physicality within a digital realm, as guidelines that dictate how physical interactions become relevant in a virtual world. Shaer et al. (2009) concluded that "designing tangible interaction is a complex process that encompasses multidisciplinary knowledge including engineering, art, and the social sciences" (p. 260).

[Tangibility Rules Studio Questions: Do the chosen buttons, links, and navigational layout enable the proper action of interactivity? Is the content accessible?]

The re-design rules are profoundly rooted in efficiency. They are the result of individual modular components that make up a long-lasting functional design, rather than a finalized product with a single, limited use. Meinel and Leifer (2011) point to the continuing human needs of this rule; for instance, for online learning systems to be made more efficient, they must be recycled and redesigned. Even institutions are using templates in courses with multiple sections, enabling others to recycle the content en masse. Lowenthal and White (2009) refer to this as a standardized course design within an enterprise model of online learning.

It is easy to see how an enterprise model works from a visual design standpoint, but online learning can quickly become sterile without a human element to visual design. Duarte (2010) emphasizes the importance adding a human element to the system. Therefore, it is imperative that an online course design be refined on the first deployment of the course so that others can personalize the content without losing the course instructional design structure. In other words, there must be a middle ground between standardization and personalization.

[Re-design Rules Studio Questions: Will the design be able to be modified by others without losing its instructional essence? Will the design still be usable five or ten years from now on a different content management system?]

The ambiguity rules allow for various interpretations. In many fields, specifically learning theory and social interactions, there is support for complexity over simplicity (Rowland, 2003; Wilson, 1996). When an enterprise model for online learning is used, it may be common sense to believe that less ambiguity is better for learning interfaces, and this is true regarding the visual design for interaction. However, the design of course modules that allow for ambiguous relationships is more versatile than those with univocal relationships (Figure 5).

For instance, in a univocal relationship, module A depends on module B. When module B is modified, module A must also be modified similarly. Conversely, in an ambiguous relationship, if module B is modified, then module A will not need to be modified. From a standpoint of visual design, the introduction of a few design elements, like a two-color design, may bring about some advantages over a one-color design. In this case, adjusting the color within a single page will not violate the consistency of the visual design throughout the entire online course. The course author will not need to adjust the design elements on every page to match.

[Ambiguity Studio Question: Do the introductory title pages give enough design variance to allow subordinate pages to use varied design attributes?]

Remediation

Remediation, from a media theory perspective, is the idea that culture desires to expand its media while simultaneously erasing all traces of mediation (Bolter & Grusin, 1999). Thus, there are two logics of remediation: hypermediacy, where the technology is purposefully apparent, and immediacy, where the technology becomes transparent. It is interesting to note that with each new technology people become

Figure 5. Visualization of ambiguous relationships compared to univocal relationships

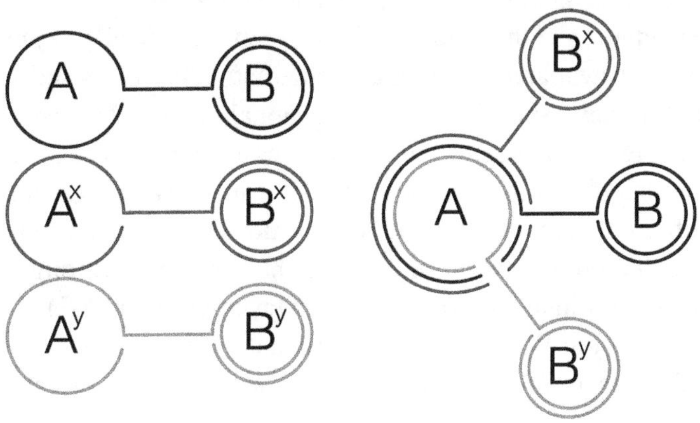

aware of the medium because they focus on the technology rather than just the content. In this case, the immediacy of the design manifests hypermediacy in the design. While media technologies incorporate networks that are specific to physical, social, aesthetic, and economic terms, humans and computers are not separate entities that control relationships. Rather, human-computer interaction is the result of human-human and human-computer relationships; whereby, human practices are cyclically shaped and shaped by these relationships (Bolter & Grusin, 1999; Verbeek, 2010). For instance, the desktop interface superseded the command line protocol for computing back in the 1990s. Conversely, the design of online courses hides the internal code, turning the process into what Seigel (2006) calls "the templated mind" (p. 116). Templates and toolbars force the developers of online courses to work within a constrained set of commands that limit the possibilities of design, negatively shaping the way in which online course designers can use creativity.

Moholy-Nagy, one of the professors at the Bauhaus, argued in his writings that artists of his day could find no active use for a man on a stage stating that, "artists and theorists still struggle to develop truly interactive—rather than only participatory" (Prager, 2006, p.202). Following Friedrich Kittler's dictum, Moholy-Nagy was aware of the profound effect of technology on society, arts, and pedagogy: "It is we who adapt to the machine. The machine does not adapt to us" (Latourelle, 2015, para. 2). Adapting to

Table 3. Examples of the process of remediation

Images	Engravings: Etching in stone Painting: Pigments on a surface Photography: Light on a surface Motion imagery: Light in a box Interactive images: Dynamic images in a virtual environment Augmented space: Dynamic images in a physical environment
Educational Media	Textbooks: Textual content with images and illustrations for the individual Transparencies: Static visual content coincided with lecture for the group Video: Dynamic visual content in linear form for the individual PowerPoint: Text, image, and movies coincided with lecture for the group Online: Text, image, and movies in an interactive interface for the individual Augmented: Text, image, and movies in an interactive format, anywhere.

new technology is a similar dilemma that instructors have today, as they become both designers and facilitators of blended and online courses. Educators must adapt pedagogical styles and content to the machine, as the learning management systems will not adapt to them.

There is a constant remediation of the practice of education, specifically in physical, social, aesthetic, and economic terms, with each available new media. Remediation in web-based applications has enabled most laymen to become designers, specifically in educational mediated spaces. Learning management systems in the early stages clearly involved hypermediacy as a navigation structure, using a navigational design that mimicked the interfaces of most websites. For instance, navigational bars were the focal point of interaction and human-computer interaction. In more modern iterations of LMSs, focus is on the linear layout of pages, thus containing immediacy in the experience through segmenting content by allowing the user to click a "continue" button (Clark & Mayer, 2016, p. 207).

[Remediation Studio Question: What can be done to make the experience more intuitive and transparent? What technical abilities, beyond the default tools, are there in the system or modify the visuals? How are they used?]

Gestalt

The phenomenon known as gestalt is a part of visual psychology and has a longstanding scientific and technical background in research studies, but it is also beneficial to the visual arts (Pentak & Lauer, 2015). Gestalt is a theory that directly drives some of the design principles like unity, where the brain attempts to find a coherent pattern. Under gestalt, the removal of extraneous information allows the viewer to process only the correct information (Malamed, 2009). Figure 6 shows that even with a minimal amount of visual information, an audience can subconsciously fill in the blanks through familiarity (Solomon, 1994).

A few of the Bauhaus faculty—Klee, Kandinsky, and Albers—attended lectures in an emerging science of gestalt psychology by gestalt theorists, including Rudolph Arnheim (Behrens, 1998). The correlation between the Bauhaus philosophies and gestalt is uncanny, but the two are not directly related (Boudewijnse, 2012). The teachings at the Bauhaus focused explicitly on the nature of objects, but gestalt focuses on the relationship of objects that determine the resulting object's function. Also, gestalt theorists were interested in perception of physical stimuli, whereas, the Bauhaus philosophy was interested in beauti-

Figure 6. Imagery that is still recognizable after removal or abstraction. (a.) Using abstract lines in a facial proportion. (b.) Distorting pieces of a photograph. (c.) Removal of letterforms.

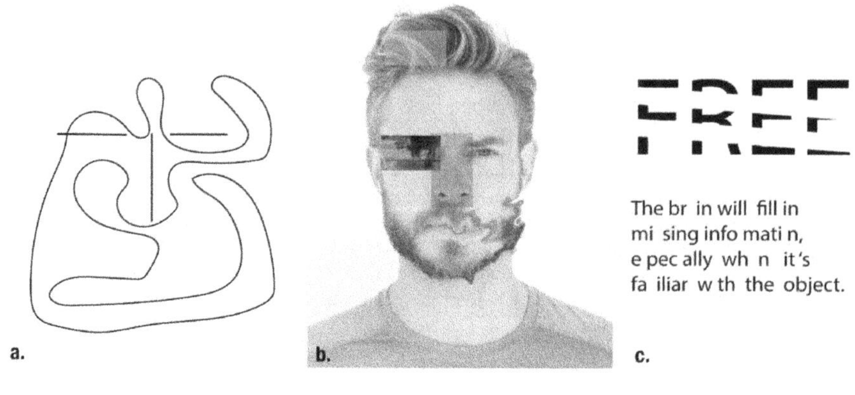

ful functionality (Boudewijnse, 2012; Lupton & Miller, 2006). While gestalt can be applied in multiple ways visually, Tufte's (1990) notion of 1+1 = 3 (Figure 7) is the simplest to understand.

In online learning, gestalt manifests in many parts of the design such as web pages, titles, infographics, and movies. The many unique parts that make up the image are consolidated down to a single sum or design, thus giving the viewer the maximum amount of ideas in a consolidated time and surface space (Tufte, 1990). Seven main visual ideas describe gestalt (Seeker, 2016):

1. **Similarity:** Assigning similar design properties to objects
2. **Proximity:** Placing objects close together.
3. **Continuity:** Aligning objects to follow one another
4. **Closure:** Creating a shape using the negative space and implied line
5. **Symmetry:** Creating sets of symmetrical objects and grouping them together
6. **Prägnanz:** Seeing the group in its simplest form
7. **Common Fate:** The brain anticipating movement through multiple images, or when objects move in simultaneous motion, like a flock of birds

The gestalt principle is useful in online interfaces for differentiating aesthetic properties through contrast while simultaneously unifying content. Figure 8 shows difference in shape yet perception through various techniques to regroup the objects by form, scale, or value. Gestalt when used correctly can create visually appealing, intuitive visual interfaces.

[Gestalt Studio Question: How can the content be simultaneously integrated and differentiated through the transformation of visual properties?]

Figure 7. The 1+1=3 visualization of the prägnanz gestalt theory using circles

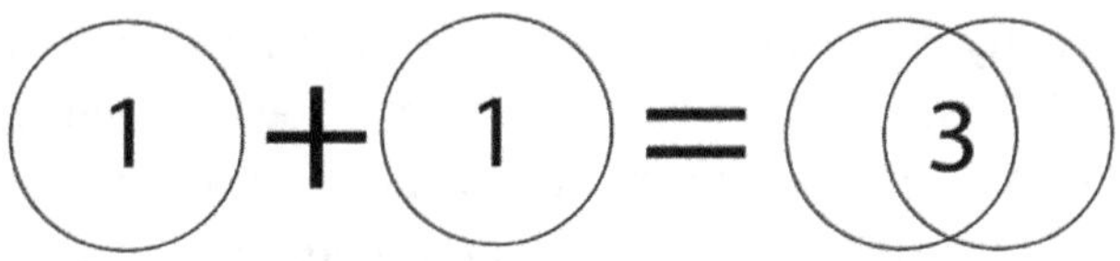

Figure 8. Gestalt principle of similarity using three different design properties

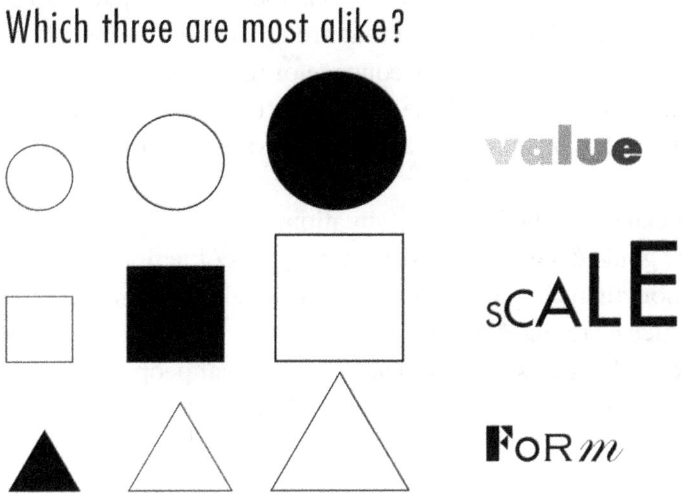

DESIGN FUNDAMENTALS

Online course designers should be aware of three fundamentals of design: design objects, design principles, and design properties. Design objects are ultimately the media used in an interface, design principles are the psychological result of the observed arrangement of the design objects, and design properties are the alterations of the appearance of the objects to make each instance unique. Each of these will be discussed in more detail in the following pages. The knowledge of the effects of each of these will help inform the studio questions generated from the design theories.

Design Objects

Any design object is a graphic representation of an idea; it is always an attempt on the part of the designer to make reality intelligible (Massironi, 1937/2010). Design objects related to online courses include font, image, and shape. Of course, the possibilities for fashioning design objects to integrate within the learning interface can seem overwhelming. A shape can take on many forms, such as a line, a square, a circle, an oval, or an organic splat. A square with an outline could contain typefaces in its interior, thus highlighting the type. Conversely, a long line could separate information into sections to chunk the information. An image can be an array of sizes, static, dynamic (video), interactive (link), transparent (background or texture), or opaque. The image can also act within a multitude of learning functions: decorative, interpretive, representative, organizational, or transformative (Lohr, 2008). Lastly, the font based on the chosen typeface is used for such things as body copy, titles, section heads, and hyperlinks (Bringhurst, 2002).

Design Principles

As Pentak and Lauer (2015) aptly note, design is "basically the arrangement of shapes" (p. 152), but the arrangement and treatment of those shapes, or design objects, does influence how the viewers perceive their relationships. Design principles are the way in which design objects interact with each other, the background, and the viewer. For instance, value and contrast are two different things. Value is a design property, while contrast is a design principle. A solid square, for example, is a design object that can increase or decrease darkness, a design property of value. Contrast is the result of the interaction between the square's value and its relationships to other objects in the working space. To describe this distinction, consider a black square on a black background that produces low contrast. This resulting similarity of value creates low or no contrast. It is the consequence of the value quality of black on black. If either the square or background has its value adjusted to white, the result would be high contrast. Kimball's (2013) research listed the following characteristics of a design principle (pp. 35-36):

- **Generalizable:** It can be applied to many situations
- **Heuristic:** It helps guide decisions and determine paths of action
- **Grounded:** It is more than simple preference; it is based on organized experience, whether developed through practice or research
- **Meaningful:** It helps designers communicate ideas to real people in rhetorically effective ways
- **Contingent:** Its application depends on local conditions

Using these guidelines, the authors traverse through Kimball's frequency list (Kimball, 2013, p.11) and categorize design principles and design properties that pertain only to the visual design for online courses. For instance, conventional graphic design verbiage like perspective, radiation, and ascension are likely not relevant to the visual design of most online courses. Table 4 shows a consolidated list of relevant terms in which the authors have identified design principles and, by association, the regularly taught design properties in the field of visual design that are also related to online course design, namely, structure, rhythm, unity, hierarchy, contrast, and gestalt. Duplicated terms that are associated conceptually have been consolidated into single terms for simplicity (e.g., difference, similarity, and contrast have been combined into the single term contrast).

Structure

Structure refers both to the container and to how the content is held together. Three key terms of structure are framing, balance, and alignment. A web browser or device usually predetermines the framing, but static framing is possible using tables whose size is defined by pixels. Most might argue against using a table to frame the content, as the content management system is built to handle various devices, each with a unique aspect ratio to display content, for example, iPad (4:3), iPhone (3:2), and widescreen display (16:9). This concept shows the need for prototyping the result on multiple systems to see the various ways that a final layout is structured. Checking the final view on a computer screen, tablet, and cell phone will usually cover the range of possible devices that a viewer would use.

Balance is an interesting concept of structure because designers typically consider horizontal page balance; however, in the case of web pages, balance is also vertical. In a single page, placement of all resource videos at the top and the supporting text below can create asymmetry. In this case, it is a good practice to balance all media objects logically and coherently. This method of consistent layout should also properly align media. There is one suggestion that the authors can associate with the alignment of type: Do not use the center command unless necessary. Centered text is difficult to read due to the eye needing to find the start point of each line. The only text that should be centered is short bits of information for an aesthetic purpose, like a header or a pull quote (Bringhurst, 2002; Lupton, 2009; Williams, 1996).

Rhythm

Rhythm in visual design describes repetition of visual elements either on the same page or throughout multiple pages. In music, rhythm comes from an equal timing of beats; in poetry, rhythm is apparent in a cadence of the constant flow or sounds of syllables. In online learning, this concept is highly relevant. Chunking, for instance, is a form of rhythm in which the learner experiences a limited amount of

Table 4. Design principles and properties relevant to online course design

Design Principles (Associative Terms)	Design Properties (Associative Terms)
Structure (Framing, Balance, Alignment) Rhythm (Chunking, Consistency) Unity (Proximity, Repetition) Hierarchy (Focal Point, Emphasis, Subordination) Contrast (Similarity, Difference)	Color (Hue, Saturation, Value) Form/Typeface (Scale, Shape)

content, so the brain is not overloaded (Clark & Mayer, 2016). Consistency is another term to associate with rhythm, as the design properties, objects, and actions need to be consistent throughout a CMS. Otherwise, the learners may become confused about how to act.

Unity

Unity creates a psychological congruity amongst the elements in the design; without unity a design becomes chaotic (Pentak & Lauer, 2015). It is essential that a designer compose design elements in a way that visually organizes the media. According to Pentak and Lauer (2015), there are four ways in which the online course designer can create unity, as demonstrated in Figure 9: (a) proximity, the closeness of the objects; (b) repetition, the repetition of the design properties; (c) continuation, an arrangement where objects are aligned from beginning to end; and, (d) continuity, the alignment of the objects.

Hierarchy

Hierarchy dictates how a viewer will navigate a page visually and understand what information is primary, secondary, and tertiary (Landa, 2014). Typically, the designer chooses what will be the focal point of the content, after which the developer applies design properties that emphasize the focal point, simultaneously using subordination techniques to the surrounding objects. A good way to evaluate hierarchy in the design studio is do the following: (1) identify the information that is important for viewers to see, (2) order the information from most important to least important, (3) observe the designed space, (4) order the observed points of information from most important to least important, and (5) analyze the important content values with the observed design values.

Contrast

Contrast is a continuum that exists from low to high and speaks to how similar or different the contrasted objects are; however, there are many design properties, each with its unique continuum, that affect the contrast level. Figure 8 illustrates this possible dilemma. What aspects of contrast make the most difference?

The most common design properties in which course designers control contrast are scale, value, color, and form. The scale is the size that ranges from small to large or in the case of a line, thick to thin. Value describes the level of lightness and darkness, with white on one end of the continuum, black on the other, and 50% grey right in the middle. Color has unique properties of contrast that the authors

Figure 9. Ways to create unity with multiple objects

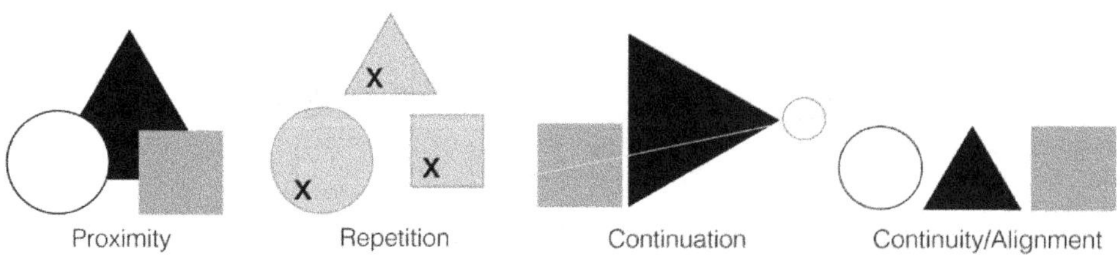

discuss below, but for the purposes of this paper, saturation is the most evident in contrast of color. A pure hue exists on one end of the continuum, while a desaturated hue, which results in a grey, exists on the other end. The form that shapes an object is a little more complex: an organic form will contrast with a geometric form, a rectilinear form will contrast with a circular form, and sans-serif typefaces with vertical stress will contrast with old-style typefaces with diagonal stress. It is important for a designer to control contrast because if there are too many contrasting elements, both hierarchy and unity can be destroyed, and the viewer experience will be chaotic.

Design Properties

Within each design object there usually exist ways to modify it; these modifiable characteristics are the design properties. For instance, in shapes the color, size, shape, texture, rhythm can be altered in almost infinite ways. In fonts, multiple type families and properties can be selected.

Form

In art class, the term form only means shape, but it can also more broadly refer to color, texture, and composition (Pentak & Lauer, 2015). When it comes to online learning, the term form also relates to the visualization of information: images, tables, illustrations, and infographics (Lohr, 2007; Lupton, 2016). These characteristic properties are controlled as shape, scale, and position. But the most ubiquitous use of a form in online courses is fonts. Font families, or typefaces, are designed in visually different shapes, weights, x-heights, and the like, and are therefore considered form.

Typography

Online courses can be best thought of as interactive documents. The inherent nature of a website includes a modular grid that generates content layout resembling magazines. In print, the modular grid system systematically arranges images, graphics, and typography, but for the web, the system gives objects the extra ability to be dynamic and interactive. In both print and web, the correct use of typography is highly multimodal (Lupton, 2014; Norgaard, 2009; Van Leeuwen, 2006). While LMSs may not have the range of fonts that are at the disposal of the designer, they can still manipulate the typefaces' properties in ways that communicate clear ideas and directions to the user. For instance, a blue underlined typeface would indicate that it links to further information or an interactive command. A declaration of a header <H2> tag with a bold, larger, or modified typeface may indicate a new section of text.

The computer has changed typography from a unique craft to one of a designer's necessary skills (Heller & Fernandez, 1999). While there are still people making a career of creating fonts (Heller & Fernandez, 1999), the use in practice now falls under the purview of the creator of a digital or printed artifact. Typographers always aim to maximize the two primary uses of text, readability and legibility (Williams, 1996). These are the functional aspects of textual communication: readability applies to how smoothly the body copy reads, and legibility applies to the clarity of the section titles. Lupton (2015) lists the uses for screen-based type as body copy, heads, block quotes, lists, and captions; it would be prudent to add hyperlinks to this list. Educators in a dynamic classroom typically must make design decisions for these instances of typographical uses. "It is important to make each function distinct through the choice of type styles but not so far as the digital classroom loses its cohesiveness" (Bader, 2015, para. 8). Van

Leeuwen (2006) infers that the majority of us, as producers of text, only see binary choices of typeface manipulation: bold or regular. Limiting the selection of design properties makes creating an aesthetically pleasing experience challenging, but when typographical elements are varied too much, unity within the meaning of letterforms erodes (Bringhurst, 2002; Garfield, 2010; Lupton, 2014; Lupton, 2010; Williams, 1996). Too many changes to typographical properties within a document can make it more difficult for the reader to associate typographical elements with one another; however, Macario (2009) suggests that combining opposite typefaces with dissimilar form between headlines and body copy helps to enhance hierarchy in the content. For example, Constantin (2013) showed that most online news sources selected sans-serif fonts for headlines and fonts with serifs for body copy, but as Lupton (2014) says, "At the end of the day, these judgments are more subjective than scientific" (p.20).

According to Williams (1996), extensive studies have shown that today in our society, typefaces with serifs are easier to read, but many others have stated that the typeface does not matter (Carter, 2014; Norgaard, 2009). But most critics agree that certain fonts or unusual arrangements of letters can be difficult to read. For example, bold fonts, very few words per line, too many words per line, script fonts, grunge fonts, extra-small typefaces, inconsistently spaced words, and other arrangements can be difficult for the eye (Lupton, 2010, Williams, 1996).

Some research has shown that certain fonts under certain circumstances have a higher reading efficiency. For instance, Bernard et al. (2002) looked at the reading speed of online fonts and found that Arial and Times were read about 10% faster than Courier, Schoolbook, and Georgia; however, Georgia received a 4 out of 6 in attractiveness while Arial received 3 out of 6 (Bernard et. al, 2002). Is the difference in reading speed great enough to warrant using a particular font, like Arial over Georgia? If a white shirt gives the most significant amount of heat resistance on a hot day, why do people wear shirts of various colors or patterns instead of plain white shirts? The likely answer to this rhetorical question goes back to the form follows function theory, as the slight increase in heat is worth the aesthetic appearance of the chosen outfit or, most likely, people do not even consider the problem.

The limitations of fonts in the LMS interfaces also limit possible mistakes in type, but they also make it harder to create aesthetically unique typography experiences. Figure 10 demonstrates one such experience, the creation of emotion or feeling through the form of the typeface (Bringhurst, 2002; Lupton, 2010). In this case, the typeface is used as semiotics. (Which version of "Warning" would scare you

Figure 10. Using a typographic image as semiotics to show emotion

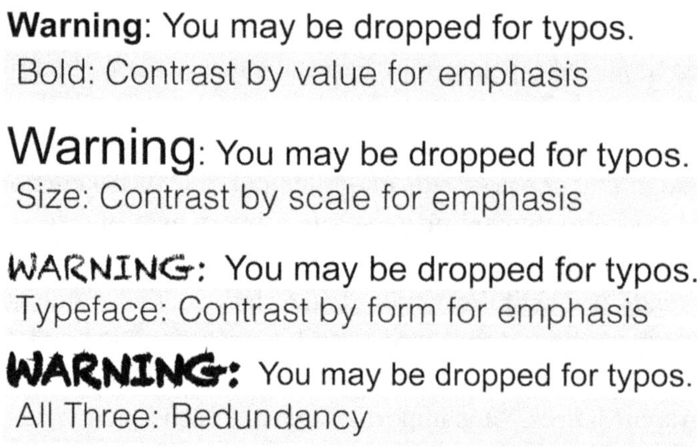

the most?) It is possible to both create aesthetically unique typography experiences and create emotion through the form of the typeface in a learning management system. Typefaces can be exported as images and placed into the online learning system; however, this may destroy accessibility based upon available technology, since some programs rely on inline tags (H1, H2, etc.), which determine hierarchy for the visually impaired. Since display fonts would require conversion into an image, the image alt tag may be functional enough to make the decision viable without hindering accessibility, as shown in this image tag: <img src="warning.png" alt="Warning in a psychotic killer typeface">.

Non-designers who design are going to ask what font works best. Unfortunately, there are not any studies that show definitively what font works best for every situation. In a class exercise on leading and kerning, students would adjust a font's size, tracking, and leading to determine what settings were necessary to make fonts more readable for print and more readable on the screen. Out of over two hundred observations, no two students returned the same settings between sets, meaning that the nuancing of font settings is subjective. But Bringhurst (2002) suggests creating a textual layout using many suggested rules; here are the most relevant to content management system pages layouts:

1. Be aware of the typeface's intended medium. Consider fonts that were designed to be read on screen and that scale appropriately with various devices and window sizes. Simply choosing fonts that have traditionally worked in printed texts may not be best.
2. Change one design property at a time. If the body text is set in 12pt Arial, it is not necessary to change size, weight, and style to 24pt bold italic all at once. Choose and change only one of the three.
3. Restrain the foreground from hogging line space. Within the body copy, use bold only for what should be bolded, and no more; that is, do not make such things as commas and periods bold. Consider other possible solutions like italics or small caps instead of bold. "Get my **pencil**, **paper**, and **crayons**" is correct; "Get my **pencil, paper, and crayons**" is incorrect; "Get my PENCIL, PAPER, and CRAYONS" is optimal.
4. Make the introductory page a dignified symbol of the typography. This may be the place to identify the structure of your typographical systems. Also, the content fills a blank page that exists within a LMS. Preserving some background space is a good thing. Nobody likes a space hog.
5. Do not permit the text to be overwhelmed by titles. The titles should point to the hierarchy to the text, not be a point of emphasis in the design. Beware of the level of contrast that is applied. When changing a property, it may be prudent to set one property in the inverse of the other. For instance, **TITLE** (Bold, 100% grey) could be diluted to **TITLE** (Bold, 70% grey).
6. Set titles and headings using design properties that conform to and support the overall design. Design properties should associate with the rest of the system. They should *never* be randomized choices. If they are random and work, then make the design properties a part of the system by using them elsewhere so that they belong.
7. Only use levels of headings that are absolutely necessary: no more, no less. This follows the less is more and gestalt theories, making the organization of text concise and clear.

Color

The choice of color is not only one of the most subjective choices, but also one of the most destructive. Landa (2014) states that the designer has two challenging responsibilities for any given design solution: selecting color and composing color. There is some truth to Landa's logic. But after the designer understands how color works visually, the larger choice typically boils down to preference, especially if the work is with color as a visual representation, as opposed to symbolic or emotional meaning (Pentak & Lauer, 2015). This statement does not mean that colors should be selected at random. There must be knowledge of how the colors operate and interact.

Color can be broken down into three components: hue, saturation, and value. The hue is the placement on the color wheel; the saturation is the purity of the color, and the value is the lightness or darkness that is added to the color. Also, colors are wavelengths, so improper mixtures can create discordant experiences (Albers, 2006). Color schemes that are discordant can create a lively, energetic, tense aesthetic (Pentak & Lauer, 2015; Pentak & Roth, 2003) or vibrating boundaries, where two colors become three (Albers, 2006). While color can create lively experiences, improper use of color creates visual distractions that can be disastrous (Tufte, 1990). Colors are typically used for three artistic purposes: visual, emotional, or symbolic (Pentak & Roth, 2003). It is highly unlikely that the design of online courses will demand the use of color with an emotional or symbolic approach, so this section is only dedicated to the visual use of color. Color helps us separate visual cues (Malamed, 2009; Thompson, 1994; Tufte, 1990); however, to separate visuals by color, the design principle of color contrast must be understood. According to Itten (2004/1961), there are seven types of contrast, each being unique in aesthetic and expressive effect:

1. **Hue:** The difference of pure colors
2. **Light-Dark:** The difference of the value of the colors
3. **Cold-Warm:** The difference of the temperature of the colors
4. **Complementarity:** The difference of colors opposite from each other on the color wheel
5. **Simultaneity:** A dull tone surrounded by an intense hue slightly changes the hue of the dull tone
6. **Saturation:** The dilution of the hue with white, black, or grey
7. **Extension:** The relative power of a certain hue to dilute contrast when the correct proportion is used

Aside from contrast, colors can create unity in content through "systematic color relationships capable of serving as a basis for composition" (Itten, 2003/1961, p. 72). These systems are known as color schemes or color harmonies, all determined by relationships of colors on the color wheel. Currently, there are many applications on the web that help a designer determine a color palette using color schemes; however, due to the complexity of choosing colors the authors suggest and give examples of the following order of color schemes in online learning:

1. **Monochromatic (1 hue):** Green, dark green, and light green
2. **Complimentary (2 hues):** Purple, yellow
3. **Analogous (many hues):** Orange paired with any hue between red and yellow
4. **Triadic (3 Hues):** Red, yellow, and blue
5. **Split-Complementary (3 Hues):** Yellow, red-purple, and blue-purple (purple split into two hues) or purple, yellow-orange, and yellow-green (yellow split into two hues)

SOLUTION: ONLINE COURSE DESIGN STUDIO

The authors have identified design process, theory, and fundamentals that can help improve the visual design of online courses. The question remains, what is the best way for faculty and online course designers to learn how to apply these principles? The authors posit that the answer lies in the design studio.

A design studio is not just a place where students learn how to do things; rather, it is a conceptual and theoretical workshop for solving visual design problems. It pushes the boundaries of each participant's ideas of what is technically possible, and it offers multiple perspectives on the contextual interpretation of the design process and a reflection on the final product. The design studio will optimally lead to a learning space that promotes an individual's visual identity through aesthetic while simultaneously providing instruction in technique. Using a rigorous visual design process like one shown in Figure 11 is a procedure that would be best developed in a design studio, which provides maximum feedback at every stage of thought.

Development Process in Studio

While the authors have analyzed many processes that contribute to design and have found that the design process itself is incredibly dynamic, they believe that there can be some rigor to the process. When repetitive inflexion points of evaluation are used at each step, with practical ways of prototyping the result, the

Figure 11. The studio process of creating a visually appealing online course

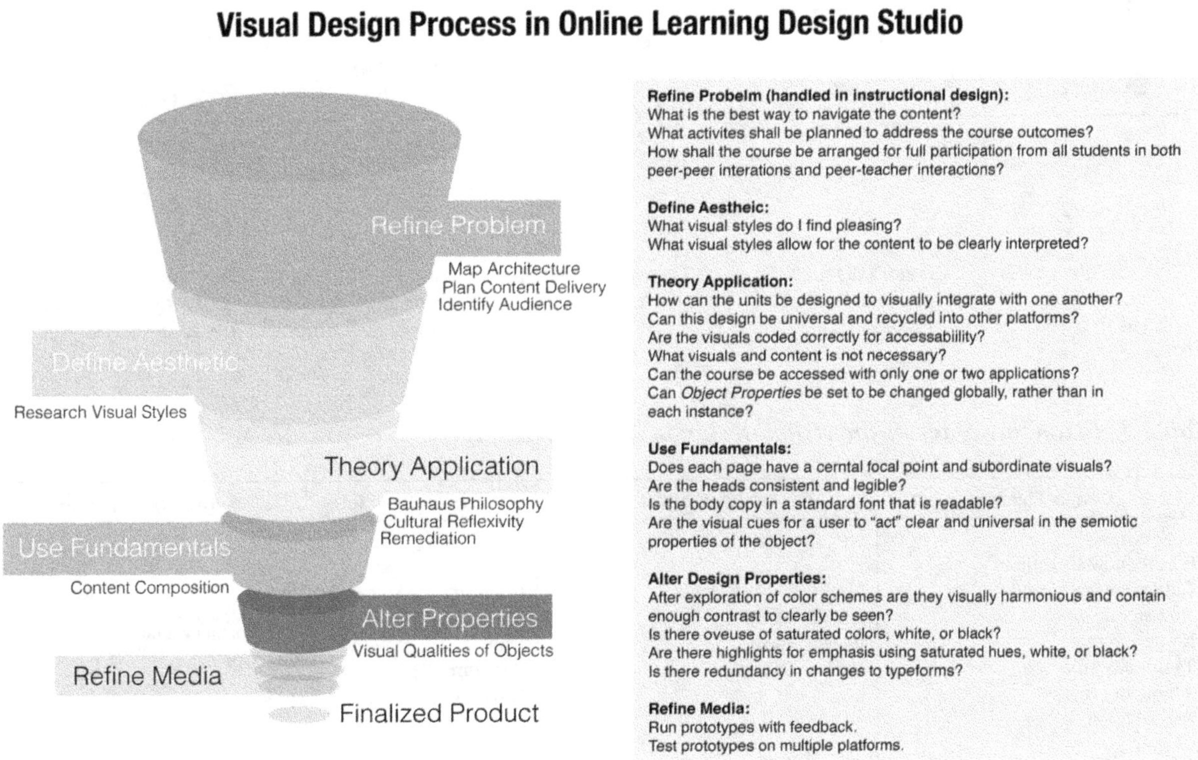

final design will excel both functionally and visually. Borrowing from Pentak and Lauer (2015), which outlines the most basic process of design, the authors have developed an example of ordered studio activities for creating online learning environments, as shown in Figure 12.

It has been suggested that non-designers who attempt to design should follow four primary rules: contrast, repetition, alignment, and proximity (Lohr, 2008; Williams, 2004). Kimball (2013) argues that these are oversimplifications because there are many other elements to consider by saying:

Design principles can also guide the development of subsequent prototypes. Sometimes the results from usability testing a prototype can give us only a hazy sense of direction; design principles allow us to explore that direction efficiently, by developing another prototype—or three—and testing them quickly. (p. 37)

A synthesis of the important terminologies relative to online learning is listed in Table 5; it is apparent these terminologies extend well beyond CARP (which focuses primarily on design composition using design principles). Within each solution, the following aspects should be part of the language that justifies the decision of how to compose media through visual design.

Figure 12. Studio-based learning process for online course visual design

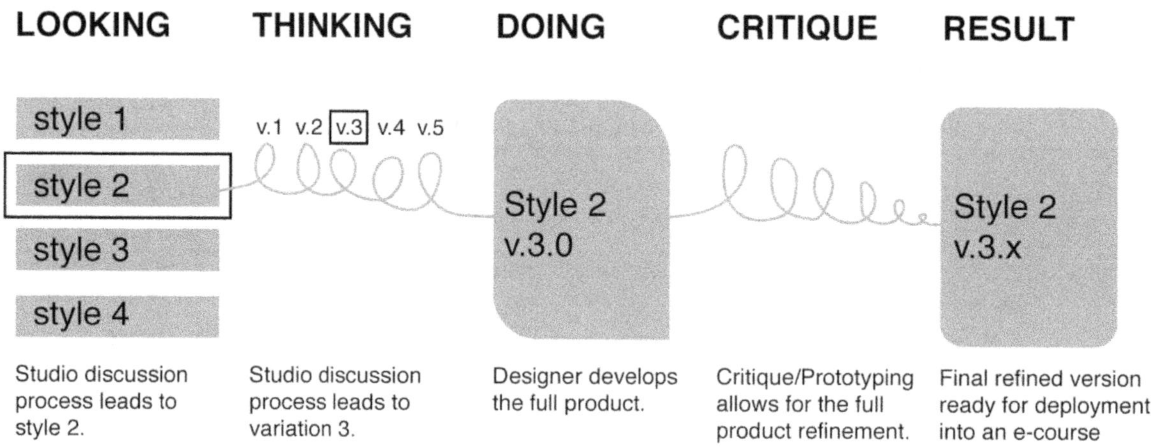

Table 5. Taxonomy of terms for visual design in online learning

Design Theories	Design Objects	Design Principles	Design Properties
Less is more Form follows function Cultural reflexivity Human rule Re-design rule Tangibility rule Ambiguity rule Remediation Gestalt	Font/Paragraph Image/Video Vector/Animation	Contrast Hierarchy Unity Structure Rhythm	Form/Typeface Color

A design studio serves as an integral part of the design process, enabling participants to understand both what design is and how design can contribute to the process of research, collaboration, and enlightenment of alternative perspectives, especially through culture (Niederhelman, 2001). By facilitating the application of the looking-thinking-doing-critiquing process of design, the studio becomes a suitable space to build rigorous and appropriate solutions. To demonstrate the power of the design studio, Table 6 shows a cross reference of each inflexion point of the looking-thinking-doing-critique process with the infusion of research, collaboration, and culture.

Conceptual Research (Looking)

Research in solving visual problems is radically different from traditional research but still boils down to a process of analysis and synthesis (Nobel & Bestley, 2016). While a designer must be able to operate under an ontological philosophy, considering infinite solutions in design problems using design objects, the developer must simultaneously practice pragmatism, ultimately deciding what works (Karjaluoto, 2014). Creswell (2013) states that the pragmatist's philosophy of methodology uses multiple forms of research and ultimately chooses one that best suits their inquiry. One of the most effective ways to plan a design is to integrate familiar design objects into conceptual ideas. As Noble and Bestley (2016) point out, to make a design innovative is not to create something unique, yet it is to construct intimate visual relationships and use them in fresh and exciting ways. In this case, innovation of visual systems is another form of remediation.

Part of using pragmatism to solve wicked problems is the realization that the problems cannot be permanently or universally solved. Any solution is at best provisional; however, this shows the need for persistent visual research to improve design. The researcher must be aware that the well-constructed beautiful visual designs can become undesirable over time. Even more frustrating is implementing what would seem to be a well-thought-out solution when the actual results are not what was anticipated. Rittel

Table 6. the integration of the design studio properties and the design process at each inflexion point as displayed in Figure 2

Process	Research	Collaboration	Culture
Looking	Discover what is possible and what is aesthetically pleasing.	The information that one person finds may be relevant to another collaborator's idea.	Varied perceptions that would be impossible for one designer to see based upon their background, e.g., hidden cultural knowledge of information design (You, Kim, & Lim, 2016)
Thinking	Plan how the user will use the design; also, explore new stylistic possibilities and possibly reinterpret the design.	Reflection on plans may cause alternative thoughts that result in combination, reworking, innovation, and new ideas.	A clearer picture of the socio-cultural "complexification" (Findeli, 2001, p. 11)
Doing	Learn how to complete technical tasks or experiment with new ways to get things done.	A collection of technical knowledge makes the affordance of possibilities larger in scope within the system.	An alternative perspective on making or shared making, "concurrent design" (Julier, 2008, p. 33)
Critique	Collect feedback from the users and develop a new iteration of the product.	Sharing multiple instances of results creates a larger picture of feedback from users and designers.	Well-rounded discourse on the epistemological nature of human-made, social, and symbolic world views

and Webber (1984) explain that sometimes in wicked problems the researcher cannot validate results unless the solution is applied to the real-world scenario and that application is the only way to investigate a solution's usefulness. Real-world testing means that design research operates within the framework of social constructivism which requires methodologies such as interviewing, observing, and analyzing narratives (Creswell, 2013). A critical method for the application of the social constructivist framework as research is the analysis of visual design in the studio prior to deployment.

Exploring Variations (Thinking)

Since the focus of the studio for research is the deconstruction and analysis of the designed artifacts (Noble & Bestley, 2016), prototyping is used widely in the studio as a form of testing ideas or iterations of design that are close to being finalized. New media systems and software allow the creation of multiple versions of the same object (Manovich, 2000). This process makes it possible to discover what may work or not work or possibly be used in some other application. Schön (1984) creates a discourse on the necessity of reflection in education and industrial practice, specifically mentioning the complementary roles of reflection in action and reflection on action. Analyzing variations is important to the analysis of wicked problems, as variations create a vicious circle in which the planner must continually reflect on their process and those affected by it at all points throughout plan and implementation. Reflection in action is an evaluative process in which the planner considers available information for in-the-moment decisions; on the other hand, reflection on action is deliberate action, as the director formally scrutinizes an implemented experience or process (Schön 1984, 1987).

Prototyping helps the designer make decisions that cannot be described within design parameters through (a) decision making from instant feedback using educated choices from others aware of similar problems and criteria, (b) focus on feedback of all senses through real experience of the design, and (c) parallelism that links the many aspects of the design process in which even initial brainstorming could be evoked and new ideas, unthought-of earlier in the process, are reconsidered (Cao, 2015; Van Allen, 2011). Prototyping can sit on a continuum of low to high fidelity, where the low fidelity versions focus primarily on the user experience of the interface. In high fidelity prototyping, the iterations focus on the aesthetics, semiotics, and content interactions. Conversely, in low fidelity prototyping, obvious mistakes like a lack of contrast between a title and a background, or missing learning objectives within an assignment as required by administration, can be gauged.

Technical Execution (Doing)

Part of the studio process of doing is the development of the ability to execute a task. People are not born with an innate ability to code HTML, compose pages using design principles, or even manage files properly. The ability or inability to construct a solution may move the designer back to the thinking or looking inflexion points; however, a designer must work within their technical limitations or expand their skills. Fortunately, the systematic approaches and experimentation in the studio environment fosters such an expansion of production ability, thus, opening new visual design potential. Noble & Bestley (2016) use the phrase form follows technology, summarizing that new technological capabilities enable new aesthetic possibilities for the designer; however, it should be noted that design options can also be limited. Designers are at the mercy of the possibilities or the limitations of the software that they use. The range of options that a construct offers is its affordance (Gibson 1979). Most learning management systems, for instance, do not allow the visual flexibility of cascading style sheets (CSS) that is available in HTML. The design properties or styles are limited in learning management systems making construction within a design studio an enlightening experience. Leaders and peers in the workshop can positively affect technical skills through advice in the possibilities and affordance of their institution's LMS.

It is important to note that affordance is not just limited to the technological aspects of the system: the perception of the user must also be considered (Noble & Bestley, 2016; Norman, 1990). The concept of affordance in online learning relates to the user's interaction with hyperlinks. Figure 13 demonstrates the way a user could traverse through an interactive timeline: the NEXT button moves the user forward, the BACK button to the previous page, the ASSIGNMENTS button to a list within the system, and the hyperlinks to entirely different web spaces that have relevant information.

A counterpart of affordance is accessibility, which allows affordance for those with disabilities; however, according to Lidwell, Butler, and Holden (2010), the implementation of accessible designs became beneficial for everyone. For institutions that require accessible content, the parameters can be confusing. The studio would allow discourse on the development of content that is compliant to code or law through an informal, open setting instead of a mandated evaluation.

Evaluating (Critique)

The process of criticism is integral to the design studio and the larger practice of design. Within the design studio, it becomes possible to critique action to generate a more mature and efficient process of action (Barnett, 1997). When a plan that is part of the looking and thinking process materializes into a tangible product or multiple prototypes, it is constructed. The critique is the antithesis of the construction process; it is the deconstruction.

Feldman's model of critique is a common framework for the critique process of art, and it comprises four activities: description, analysis, interpretation, and judgment (Pentak & Lauer, 2015). While formulated for art, these activities can be useful in an online learning studio. A description is an inventory of what is there, listing the pages of a course and the elements on each page. An analysis is an observation on what the designer has done to compose the course, for example, the navigation, the arrangement, the media, the styles, and the coding. Interpretation is the use of an interpretive lens to determine the affordance, effectiveness, and beauty of the course. Finally, judgment is the final reflection to how good or bad the course is; it allows for suggestions to better the final solution based upon the synthesis of design theories and fundamentals that the observer understands. Having knowledgeable peers in the critique can strengthen everybody's work, which makes the studio a mutually beneficial, collaborative space.

EXTERNAL CONTEXTS

When piecing together a usable and aesthetically relevant learning experience, the designer must consider the audience or end users (Fogg, 2003). The authors offer no research to support this claim, but

Figure 13. Buttons that exhibit the concept of affordance

this situation is analogous to marketing strategies: certain audiences have very different preferences that require varying visual solutions. It is likely that interface and visual design preferences for science majors are very different from those of art majors. Due to the dynamics of visual and usability preferences, it is important to address design issues within end-user surveys. Research in the online digital culture is complex. Svensson (2003) suggests some salient features that embody the shared space and so need to be understood: cyberspace, online communication, virtual social communities, hypertext, interfaces, digital art, and immersion. Getting a physical snapshot of the learners is a strategy for defining end-user demographics that allows for the development of solutions that address personal needs (Don & Pettrick, 2003). Conversely, serving the needs of the majority is not the typical educational institution's plan. Part of the strategy of online learning is to serve students who may be atypical or those who might not have the ability to attend a physical location.

Accessibility

Research from the 2008–2009 academic year shows there were approximately 707,000 disabled students enrolled in postsecondary institutions (NCES, 2011). According to Edmonds (2004), higher education institutions online courses sometimes neglect disabled students' needs. Burgstahler (2004), suggests that external programs for accessibility are not enough; individual courses should provide accessibility as well. Content within courses that is not accessible to students with disabilities creates additional barriers to participation (Burgstahler, 2004). There are many types of disabilities, but Crow (2008) divides them all into four categories: visual, auditory, mobility, and cognitive. This chapter has already mentioned the idea of affordance, and instructional design focuses on image tags and other features for those with hearing and cognitive disabilities. To not deviate from the topic, this section will only focus on some examples of visual disabilities and where shared knowledge in the design studio can positively affect online content.

A designer, by nature, never creates solutions for a single group; they attempt instead to reach the greatest possible number of people. Visual design for accessibility is not a frequent topic in higher education graphic design curricula. Fortunately, there are many conceptual suggestions with functionally sound visual approaches to be found on the web. Many people have common misconceptions about the effects of impairment. For instance, most consider those who are visually impaired to be blind; however, there are other types of visual impairments, like color blindness and low vision (WebAIM, 2013). Babich (2017) suggests that color blindness comes in various types anomalous conditions; therefore, materials designed for use by color blind individuals must create contrast through means other than different hues. Using color as the sole design property to distinguish data in charts and graphs is thus a poor design choice. The addition of texture or pattern along with color makes the data separable by those who are color blind. Changing too many design properties may seem at odds with the principle of design redundancy, but under the circumstances, in this case, altering more than one design property is a justified design choice.

According to Marks (2016), there is a push from Apple, Google, and Twitter to lower the contrast ratio between the background and the foreground of text. Extreme contrast within design properties is usually not aesthetically pleasing, creating as it does the appearance that the creator used default properties instead of putting thought into the design. Conversely, choosing low contrast levels, which may be useful to those without visual impairments, can make it impossible for those with a moderate vision

Figure 14. An illustration of the contrast ratio using achromatic text

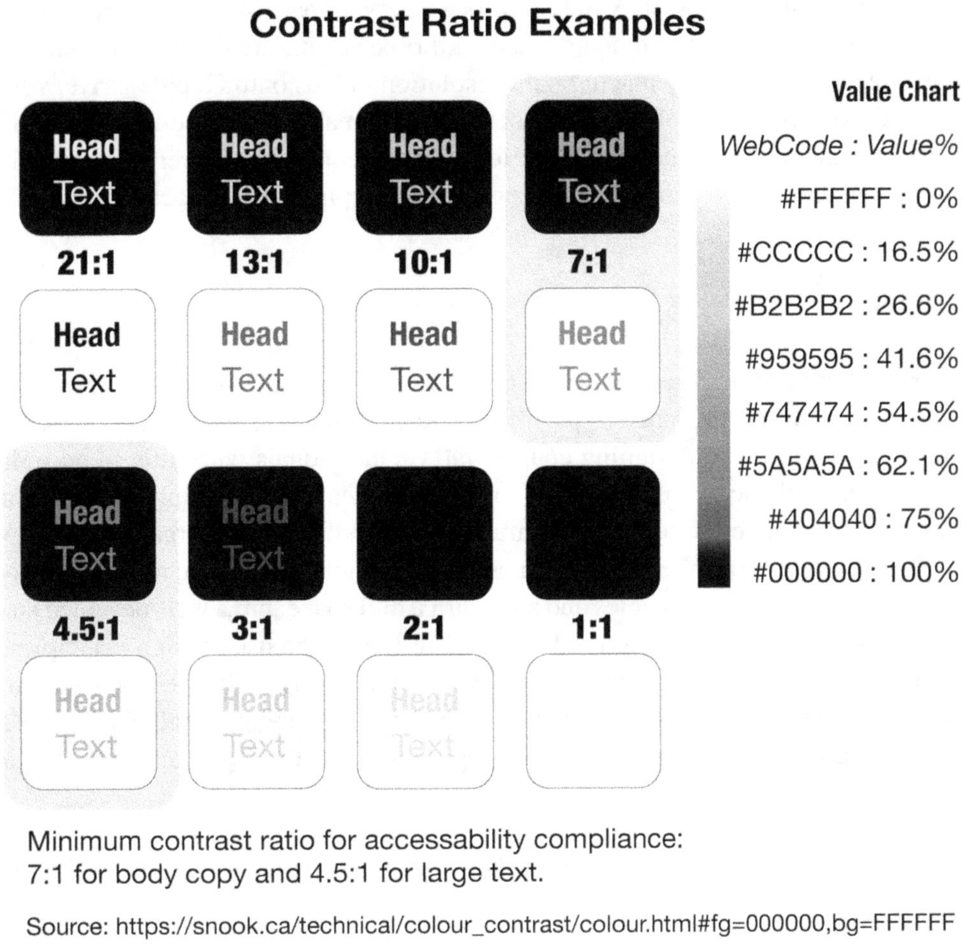

impairment. Marks (2016) and Babich (2017) cite a W3C guideline that gives a contrast ratio of 4.5:1 as minimum, 7:1 for those with disabilities. Therefore, a design decision should be made to never use a contrast ratio below 7:1 so that a greater number of people can access the textual information.

FUTURE TRENDS

Predicting the status of online learning and the future is difficult at best, but design trends are typically defined by innovation and needs. Svensson (2003) envisioned online education as teachers producing information and the students receiving it, but fifteen years after this statement, the authors would argue that online education is more complex. Teachers are the composers of information that embodies a virtual social environment for the students. As with any technological system, it is important to push the boundaries with new ideas, but constraints are also needed to ensure efficiency. Experimentation and constraint provide an optimal solution for the studio: new ideas are explored, prototyped in the studio, and then evaluated with summative surveys.

Sometimes the most inconspicuous things will become larger concerns to the learners. One institution placed its instructional videos on YouTube to save server space, but YouTube's algorithms had compressed the videos to where the students had a hard time seeing the finer detail in the videos. The institution remedied the situation by placing high-resolution videos onto Google Drive, where the students could download them. This solution was not necessary in all courses: some wicked problems are individualized to specialized course content. Therefore, future trends will uncover themselves in the studio though discussion, updating of technology, and regular prototyping with the actual users, the students.

CONCLUSION

Few institutions are hiring trained graphic designers to help build online course interfaces for individualized LMSs. Trained graphic designers typically have a BFA degree, spending at least four years in formal training, yet the duties of designing courses fall on individuals with little to no training in the graphic arts. Without aesthetic forms, LMS designs become impersonal, insipid, and uninspiring. The LMS interface is also in danger of becoming confusing, misleading, and unorganized.

Kimball (2013) identifies a proficient designer as a person with the ability to justify decisions through rationalization of applied design principles and so to turn a dull space into a well-designed space. Figure 14 shows two prototypes of visual design in Canvas. The left image uses design principles: hierarchy in type with minor adjustments to typefaces, an emphasis on learning objectives by isolation, and unity of textual signifiers by repetition. The right image ignores design principles and places content into the page with perceived arbitrary decisions in design properties, thus creating a sense of disorganization.

Figure 15. A comparison of two canvas pages with the use (left) and avoidance (right) of design principles

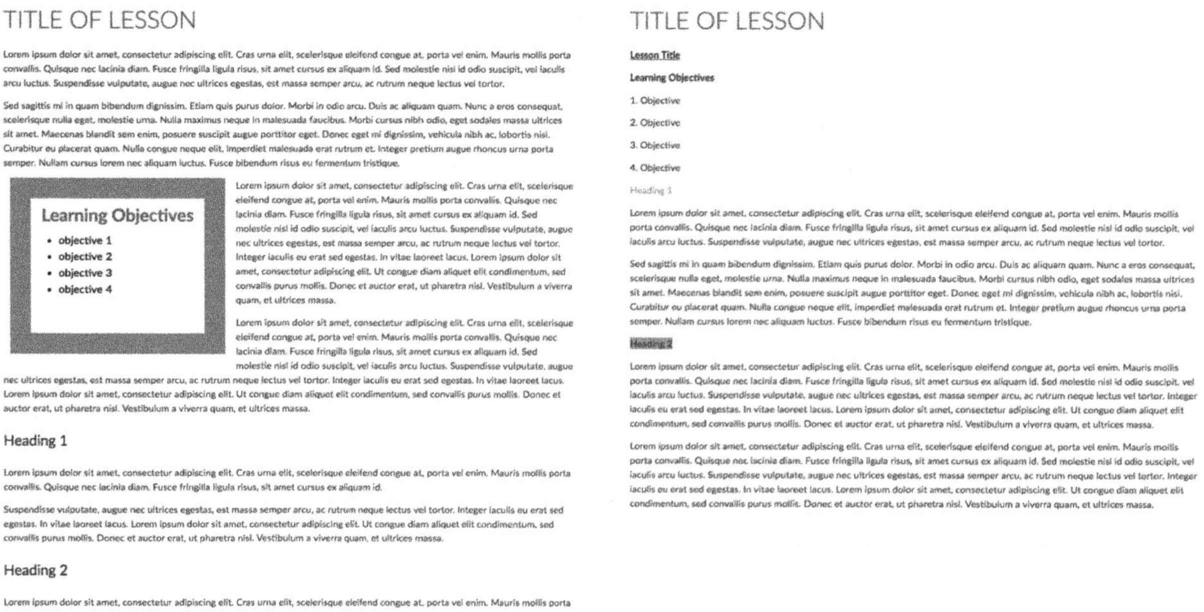

There is a need for designers to make ambiguous choices as they use design objects and apply design properties; that is, they must have technical skills that apply specifically to LMSs. The authors believe that the design studio provides the optimal setting for instructors and instructional designers to meet that need and to conduct the further research that can describe the effect of applied theories and principles. The most common strategies for improving visual design are case studies that describe experiences, art-based research to rationalize critical analysis, and grounded theory to develop principles. Any of these strategies can be implemented in an open studio with developers or in the field among end users. Furthermore, to describe effects of practice, both practical action research within the studio setting and design-based research are viable methods for raising the standards of aesthetics in online learning.

REFERENCES

Albers, J. (2006). *Interaction of color*. New Haven, CT: Yale University Press.

Armstrong, H. (2009). *Graphic design theory: Readings from the field*. New York: Princeton Architectural Press.

Arntson, A. E. (2011). *Graphic design basics*. Fort Worth, TX: Harcourt Brace College Publishers.

Austin, T., & Doust, R. (2007). *New media design*. London, UK: Laurence King Publishing.

Babich, N. (2017). *Accessibility for visual design*. Retrieved from http://www.uxbooth.com/articles/accessibility-visual-design/

Bader, J. (2015). *Functional e-learning design*. Unpublished manuscript, Boise State University.

Barnett, R. (1997). *Higher education: A critical business*. Maidenhead, UK: Open University Press.

Behrens, R. (1998). Art, design and gestalt theory. *Leonardo*, *31*(4), 299–303. doi:10.2307/1576669

Bernard, M., Lida, B., Riley, S., Hackler, T., & Janzen, K. (2002). *A comparison of popular online fonts: Which size and type is best?* Retrieved from http://goo.gl/7uiHk2

Beyer, H., & Holtzblatt, K. (2016). *Contextual design: Defining customer-centered systems* (2nd ed.). San Francisco: Morgan Kaufmann.

Blauvelt, A. (1998). Remaking theory, remaking practice. In S. Heller (Ed.), *The education of a graphic designer* (pp. 71–77). New York: Allworth Press.

Bolter, J. D., & Grusin, R. A. (1999). *Remediation: Understanding new media*. Cambridge, MA: MIT Press.

Boudewijnse, G. (2012). Gestalt theory and Bauhaus: A correspondence. *Gestalt Theory*, *34*(1), 81–98.

Braden, R. A. (1996). Visual literacy. In D. H. Johanssen (Ed.), *Handbook of research for educational communications and technology* (pp. 491–520). New York: Simon & Schuster.

Bringhurst, R. (2002). *The elements of typographic style*. Point Roberts, WA: Hartley & Marks.

Buchanan, R. (1992). Wicked problems in design thinking. *Design Issues*, *8*(2), 5–21. doi:10.2307/1511637

Buchanan, R., Manzini, E., Vanlaethem, F., & Ambasz, E. (1990). Metaphors, narratives, and fables in new design thinking. *Design Issues*, *7*(1), 78–82. doi:10.2307/1511474

Burgstahler, S. (2004). *Real connections: Making distance learning accessible to everyone*. Retrieved from https://goo.gl/aQ2DaP

Cao, J. (2015, January 26). *How & why prototypes are mandatory for good design*. Retrieved from https://goo.gl/NdGVZR

Carter, M. (2014). *My life in typefaces* [Video file]. Retrieved from https://www.ted.com/talks/matthew_carter_my_life_in_typefaces

Cennamo, K., & Brandt, C. (2012). The "right kind of telling": Knowledge building in the academic design studio. *Educational Technology Research and Development*, *60*(5), 839–858. doi:10.100711423-012-9254-5

Clark, R. C., & Mayer, R. E. (2016). e-Learning and the science of instruction: Proven guidelines for consumers and designers of multimedia learning. Hoboken, NJ: Wiley.

Constantin, J. (2013, May). Typographic design patterns and current practice. *Smashing Magazine*. Retrieved from https://www.smashingmagazine.com/2013/05/typographic-design-patterns-practices-case-study-2013/

Creswell, J. W. (2013). *Qualitative inquiry and research design: Choosing among five approaches* (3rd ed.). Thousand Oaks, CA: Sage.

Crow, D. (2016). *Visible signs: An introduction to semiotics in the visual arts* (3rd ed.). London: Bloomsbury.

Crow, K. L. (2008). Four types of disabilities: Their impact on online learning. *TechTrends*, *52*(1), 51–55. doi:10.100711528-008-0112-6

Cyr, D. (2013). Website design, trust and culture: An eight country investigation. *Electronic Commerce Research and Applications*, *12*(6), 373–385. doi:10.1016/j.elerap.2013.03.007

Dewey, J. (2005). Art as experience. New York: Berkley.

Don, A., & Petrick, J. (2003). User Requirements. In B. Laurel (Ed.), *Design research: Methods and perspectives* (pp. 70–80). Cambridge, MA: MIT Press.

Edmonds, C. D. (2004). Providing access to students with disabilities in online distance education: Legal and technical concerns for higher education. *American Journal of Distance Education*, *18*(1), 51–62. doi:10.120715389286ajde1801_5

Findeli, A. (2001). Rethinking design education for the 21st century: Theoretical, methodological, and ethical discussion. *Design Issues*, *17*(1), 5–17. doi:10.1162/07479360152103796

Fogg, B. (2003). Conceptual designs. In B. Laurel (Ed.), *Design Research: Methods and Perspectives* (pp. 201–211). Cambridge, MA: MIT Press.

Galitz, W. O. (1997). *The essential guide to user interface design: An introduction to GUI design principles and techniques* (3rd ed.). Medford, MA: Wiley.

Garfield, S. (2010). *Just my type*. New York: Gotham.

Gibson, J. J. (1979). *The ecological approach to visual perception*. Boston: Houghton Mifflin.

Heller, S., & Fernandez, T. (1999). *Becoming a graphic designer*. New York: Wiley.

HusbyO. (2014). *The function utopia*. Retrieved from http://www.oysteinhusby.com/function-utopia-form-follows-function/

Ireland, C. (2003). The changing role of research. In B. Laurel (Ed.), *Design research: Methods and perspectives* (pp. 22–29). Cambridge, MA: MIT Press.

Itten, J. (2003). *The elements of color*. New York: John Wiley and Sons.

Itten, J. (2004). *The art of color: The subjective experience and objective rationale of color*. New York: John Wiley and Sons.

Julier, G. (2008). *The culture of design*. Los Angeles, CA: Sage.

Karabeg, D. (2003). Designing information design. *Information Design Journal*, *11*(1), 82–90. doi:10.1075/idj.11.1.12kar

Karjaluoto, E. (2014). *The design method: A philosophy and process for functional visual communication*. San Francisco: New Riders.

Kimball, M. A. (2013). Visual design principles: An empirical study of design lore. *Journal of Technical Writing and Communication*, *43*(1), 3–41. doi:10.2190/TW.43.1.b

Krug, S. (2000). *Don't make me think!: A common sense approach to Web usability*. Indianapolis, IN: New Riders.

Landa, R. (2014). *Graphic design solutions*. Boston: Wadsworth.

Latourelle, R. (2015). *Sensing the future: Moholy-Nagy, media and the arts* [e-flux online editorial]. Retrieved from http://goo.gl/Jg9Gt3

Lidwell, W., Butler, J., & Holden, K. (2010). Universal principles of design: 125 ways to enhance usability, influence perception, increase appeal, make better design decisions, and teach through design. Beverly, MA: Rockport.

Lohr, L. (2008). *Creating graphics for learning and performance: Lessons in visual literacy*. Columbus, OH: Pearson.

Lowenthal, P. R., & White, J. W. (2009). Enterprise model. In P. Rogers, G. Berg, J. Boettcher, C. Howard, L. Justice, & K. Schenk (Eds.), Encyclopedia of distance and online learning (2nd ed., pp. 932-936). Hershey, PA: IGI Global. doi:10.4018/978-1-60566-198-8.ch130

Lupton, E. (2009). Forward. In H. Armstrong (Ed.), *Graphic design theory: Readings from the field* (pp. 6–7). New York: Princeton Architectural Press.

Lupton, E. (2010). Thinking with type: A critical guide for designers, writers, editors, & students. New York: Princeton Architectural Press.

Lupton, E. (2014). *Type on screen: A guide for designers, developers, writers, and students*. New York: Princeton Architectural Press.

Lupton, E., & Miller, J. A. (2006). *The ABC's of ▲■ ●: The Bauhaus and design theory*. London: Thames and Hudson.

Macario, J. W. (2009). *Graphic design essentials: Skills, software, and creative solutions*. Upper Saddle River, NJ: Pearson.

Malamed, C. (2009). *Visual language for designers: Principles for creating graphics that people understand*. Beverly, MA: Rockport Publishing.

Manovich, L. (2000). *The language of new media*. Cambridge, MA: MIT Press.

Manovich, L. (2017). Aesthetics. In L. Ouellette & J. Gray (Eds.), *Keywords for media studies* (pp. 9–11). New York: NYU Press.

Manzini, E. (1989). *The materials of invention: Materials and design*. Cambridge, MA: MIT Press.

Marcus, A., & Gould, E. W. (2000). CROSSCURRENTS. Cultural Dimensions and Global Web-User Interface Design. *Interaction*, *7*(4), 32–46. doi:10.1145/345190.345238

Margolin, V., & Margolin, S. (2002). A "social model" of design: Issues of practice and research. *Design Issues*, *18*(4), 24–30. doi:10.1162/074793602320827406

Marks, K. (2016). How the web became unreadable. *Wired Magazine*. Retrieved from https://www.wired.com/2016/10/how-the-web-became-unreadable/

Massironi, M. (2010). *The psychology of graphic images: Seeing, drawing, communicating*. Mahwah, NJ: L. Erlbaum. (Original work published 1937)

Medina, J. (2008). *Brain rules: 12 principles for surviving and thriving at work, home, and school*. Seattle, WA: Pear Press.

Meinel, C., & Leifer, L. (2011). Design thinking research. In H. Plattner, C. Meinel, & L. Leifer (Eds.), *Design thinking: Understand - improve - apply* (pp. xiii–xxi). Berlin: Springer. doi:10.1007/978-3-642-13757-0

Metros, S. E. (2008). The educator's role in preparing visually literate learners. *Theory into Practice*, *47*(2), 102–109. doi:10.1080/00405840801992264

Mills, M. (2006). Appendix: Gender of the universal. In E. Lupton & J. A. Miller (Eds.), *The ABC's of ▲■ ●: The Bauhaus and design theory* (pp. 46–49). London: Thames and Hudson.

Mullet, K., & Sano, D. (1995). *Designing visual interfaces: Communication oriented techniques*. Englewood Cliffs, NJ: Prentice Hall.

Neilsen, J. (1993). *Usability engineering*. Boston: Academic Press.

Niederhelman, M. (2001). Education through design: Review of the "Re-inventing design education in the university" conference. *Design Issues*, *17*(3), 83–87. doi:10.1162/074793601750357222

Noble, I., & Bestley, R. (2016). *Visual research: An introduction to research methods in graphic design*. London: Bloomsbury.

Norgaard, N. (2009). The semiotics of typography in literary texts: A multimodal approach. *Orbis Litterarum, 64*(2), 141–160. doi:10.1111/j.1600-0730.2008.00949.x

Norman, D. A. (1990). *The design of everyday things*. New York: Doubleday.

On Course Workshop. (n.d.). *The 67 worst teaching mistakes*. Retrieved from http://oncourseworkshop.com/table-contents/67-worst-teaching-mistakes/

Parrish, P., Wilson, B. G., & Dunlap, J. C. (2011). Learning experience as transaction: A framework for instructional design. *Educational Technology, 51*(2), 15–22.

Parrish, P. E. (2009). Aesthetic principles for instructional design. *Educational Technology Research and Development, 57*(4), 511–528. doi:10.100711423-007-9060-7

Pentak, S., & Lauer, D. (2015). *Design basics* (9th ed.). Thousand Oaks, CA: Wadsworth.

Pentak, S., & Roth, R. (2003). *Color basics*. Thousand Oaks, CA: Wadsworth.

Prager, P. (2006). Back to the future: Interactivity and associational narrativity at the Bauhaus. *Digital Creativity, 17*(4), 195–204. doi:10.1080/14626260601073195

Rand, P. (1985). *Paul Rand, a designer's art*. New Haven, CT: Yale University Press.

Rand, P. (2014). *Thoughts on design*. San Francisco: Chronicle Books.

Rittel, H. W. J., & Webber, M. M. (1973). Dilemmas in a general theory of planning. *Policy Sciences, 4*(2), 155–169. doi:10.1007/BF01405730

Robson, M. (2002). *Problem-solving in groups*. Aldershot, UK: Gower.

Rowland, G. (2003). *A little ambiguity can go a long way*. Presented at Association for Educational Communications and Technology Annual Conference, Anaheim, CA.

Schön, D. A. (1984). *The reflective practitioner: How professionals think in action*. New York: Basic Books.

Schön, D. A. (1987). *Educating the reflective practitioner: Toward a new design for teaching and learning in the professions*. San Francisco: Jossey-Bass.

Schwartz, B. (2004). *The paradox of choice: Why more is less*. New York: Ecco.

Schwier, R., & Misanchuk, E. (1993). *Interactive multimedia instruction*. Englewood Cliffs, NJ: Educational Technology Publications.

Seeker. (2016, September 25). *How your brain simplifies complex reality* [Video file]. Retrieved from https://www.youtube.com/watch?v=YmDqJniyK6U

Seigel, D. (2006). Designing Our Own Graves. In H. Armstrong (Ed.), *Graphic design theory: Readings from the field* (pp. 115–118). New York: Princeton Architectural Press.

Shaer, O., Horn, M., & Jacob, R. J. K. (2009). Tangible user interface laboratory: Teaching tangible interaction design in practice. *Artificial Intelligence for Engineering Design, Analysis and Manufacturing, 23*(03), 251–261. doi:10.1017/S0890060409000225

Shedroff, N. (2003). Research methods for designing effective experiences. In B. Laurel (Ed.), *Design research: Methods and perspectives* (pp. 155–163). Cambridge, MA: MIT Press.

Smith, A., Dunckley, L., French, T., Minocha, S., & Chang, Y. (2004). A process model for using cross-cultural websites. *Interacting with Computers, 16*(1), 63–91. doi:10.1016/j.intcom.2003.11.005

Solomon, G. (1994). *Interaction of media, cognition and learning*. Mahwah, NJ: Lawrence Erlbaum.

Sullivan, L. H. (1896). *The tall office building artistically considered.* Retrieved from https://archive.org/details/tallofficebuildi00sull

Svensson, P. (2003). Interdisciplinary design research. In B. Laurel (Ed.), *Design Research: Methods and Perspectives* (pp. 193–200). Cambridge, MA: MIT Press.

Szabo, M., & Kanuka, H. (1999). Effects of violating screen design principles of balance, unity, and focus on recall learning, study time, and completion rates. *Journal of Educational Multimedia and Hypermedia, 8*, 23–42.

Thompson, M. E. (1994). Design considerations of visuals. In D. M. Moore & F. M. Dwyer (Eds.), *Visual literacy: A spectrum of visual learning* (pp. 165–182). Englewood Cliffs, NJ: Educational Technology Publishing.

Tufte, E. R. (1990). *Envisioning information*. Cheshire, CT: Graphics Press.

U.S. Department of Education, National Center for Education Statistics, Institute of Education Sciences. (2011). *Learning at a distance: Undergraduate enrollment in distance education courses and degree programs (NCES 2012–154).* Retrieved from http://nces.ed.gov/pubs2012/2012154.pdf

Van Allen, P. (2011). *Prototyping for interaction design*. Retrieved July 14, 2017, from https://www.slideshare.net/pvanallen/prototyping-for-interaction-design

Van Leeuwen, T. (2006). Towards a semiotics of typography. *Informational Design Journal & Document Design, 14*(2), 139–155. doi:10.1075/idj.14.2.06lee

Verbeek, P. P. (2015). Beyond interaction: A short introduction to mediation theory. *Interaction, 22*(3), 26–31. doi:10.1145/2751314

WebAIM. (2013). *Visual disabilities.* Retrieved from http://webaim.org/articles/visual/

Williams, B., & Stimatz, L. R. (2005). The origins of graphic screen design principles: Theory or rhetoric? *International Journal of Instructional Media, 32*, 181–194.

Williams, R. (1996). *Beyond the Mac is not a typewriter*. Berkeley, CA: Peachpit Press.

Williams, R. (2004). *The non-designer's design book: Design and typographic principles for the visual novice*. Berkeley, CA: Peachpit Press.

Wilson, B. G. (Ed.). (1996). *Constructivist learning environments: Case studies in instructional design.* Englewood Cliffs, NJ: Educational Technology Publications.

You, S., Kim, M., & Lim, Y. (2016). Value of culturally oriented information design. *Universal Access in the Information Society*, *15*(3), 369–391. doi:10.100710209-014-0393-9

KEY TERMS AND DEFINITIONS

Bauhaus: A German school of art (1919–1933) that instituted workshops to create utilitarian objects that were both functional and beautiful. The school laid the curricular foundation for the majority of the commercial arts today.

Contrast: The difference between two extremes of a design property.

Cultural Reflexivity: Using design to exhibit the self through aesthetics; this includes ideology, culture, and gender identity.

Design Object: The media used for content.

Design Principle: The effect based upon the interaction of chosen design objects and the chosen design properties.

Design Property: The visual appearances of the design object that can be adjusted: size, color, thickness, shape, texture, opacity, and value.

Gestalt: The sum of the parts that equal a visual whole or an image that is not physically drawn but is optically created through the interaction of the parts.

Remediation: The replacement of an old technology with a new medium that serves the same purpose.

Similarity: The closeness of two extremes of a design property.

Typography: The art of making letters readable, legible, and aesthetically pleasing.

Wicked Problem: A problem that is extraordinarily complex, where a solution for one problem will not apply successfully to the problem as a whole. They are usually judged on their success based upon how good or bad the solution is.

ENDNOTE

1 Parrish (2009) is perhaps the one notable exception, though Parrish does not focus solely on online course design. Also see Parrish, Wilson, & Dunlap (2010).

Chapter 2
A Prototypical Participatory Design-Process:
Bringing Digital Learning and User Experience Together

Matthias Teine
Paderborn University, Germany

ABSTRACT

Our economies and societies are changing, with significant effects on each individual, as they have to cope with increasingly complex and unpredictable working lives. Therefore, innovative digital learning applications that respond to their end user's needs and desires become inevitable. Whilst relying on user-centered design structures, the participatory design methodology provides a promising approach towards the creation of such a new generation of digital learning applications. After thoroughly outlining the research undertaking's rationale and following to a theoretical discussion, the author gives insights into the results of problem-centered interviews with digital learning and user experience experts that build the basis for the creation for a prototypical participatory design process. These findings primarily confirm the recent literature and provide, complemented by the created process, a sound basis for further theory-oriented, scientific discussions but application in practice as well.

LEARNING IN THE 21ST CENTURY

We are living in the 21st-century, the so-called Information Age which is characterized by transformations towards information societies and their accompanying knowledge-based economies (Korucu & Alkan, 2011, p. 1925; Becla, 2012, p. 125; Pârgaru, Gherghina, & Duca, 2009, p. 646). As the unprecedented technological advancement particularly in the field of information and communication-technology (ICT) causes this transformation (Rana, Singh, & Lal, 2014, p. 20; Akilli, 2007, p. 2), it is still in its early development, as Becla (2012) outlines thoroughly (p. 125). Technical, economical, and societal change thereby dominates our society and leads continuously to ever-changing, increasingly more complex, unpredictable challenges for corporations but any individual as well. Thus, the transformation affects

DOI: 10.4018/978-1-5225-4206-3.ch002

our lives in all its different facets and shapes the way of how people live and think (Pârgaru et al., 2009, p. 646; Galarneau & Zibit 2007, p. 62; Rana et al., 2014, p. 20).

In an information society, knowledge (which is in this notion represented by information) becomes a factor of economic and social development (Vali, 2013, pp. 388-389). It is, i.a., the dominating production factor, connected to innovation and thereby competition, and (as the importance of knowledge-based work and the service sector gains importance) the biggest contributor to the gross national product (Becla, 2012, p. 126). This requires individuals to acquire the latest knowledge, to build up new skills and competences, to be mentally agile, and to be willing to try out new ways of doing things (Galarneau & Zibit, 2007, pp. 61, 82). Otherwise, they could not adapt continuously and successfully to the demands of the society/ economy. The term '21st-century skills' summarizes such skills that are inevitable to succeed in an ever-changing knowledge-based economy, including critical thinking, teamwork and collaboration, problem solving, facility with technology, information literacy, communication, and others (Galarneau & Zibit, 2007, p. 61; Schrader & McCreery, 2012, p. 11). Moreover, the individual's creative potential, its ability to build-up knowledge, and its utilization to innovation is as important for the individuals and corporations to stay successful like it has never been before (Pârgaru et al., 2009, pp. 646, 648).

Therefore, a society's educational system becomes a key component of change and its quality becomes a prerequisite of cultural and economic success (Pârgaru et al., 2009, pp. 646-648). Here, Barik and Karforma (2012) outline that "technology has changed the current scenario of education system drastically" (p. 51). However, according to Akilli (2007) "The field of education is not an exception in the permeation of technology. On the contrary, education has always been considered as potentially one of the most productive breeding-grounds for technology, where it would perhaps find its finest resonances and lead to revolutionary effects." (p. 2). Thus, for the one, technological advancement is a catalyst for change and requires us to face demanding challenges. Contrastingly, it is a hotbed for technology-solutions that help us to master the continuing transformation process, and to utilize it for realizing economic growth and social development. Solutions that make use of the advancements on the field of ICT to address the aforementioned educational needs are thereby of utmost importance. This reasons why modern e-learning systems gain importance and popularity (Rana et al., 2014, p. 20). Blumschein & Fischer acknowledged already in 2006: "e-learning acquired a tremendous educational potential" (p. 39), but also that "e-learning is not a panacea for all existing problems" (p. 39). Given the technological advancement of the recent years, these statements are valid like they have never been before.

'E-learning' refers according to Arnold, Kilian, Thillosen, & Zimmer (2011) to a polymorphic, objective, and organizationally arrangement of electronic respectively digital media, used for individual or collaborative learning, competence development, and other education purposes (p. 18). This term, however, seems to be outdated meanwhile. Given the variety of possibilities to use digital media for educational purposes with all of them covered by the term of 'e-learning', there is no clearly distinguishable definition of this term anymore (Kerres, 2016, pp. 1, 7). Against the background of the pervasive digitalization of the whole educational system, penetrating all processes, places, and formats of educational work, it therefore makes sense to use the much broader term of 'digital learning' (p. 9). 'Digital learning application' thereby takes a broader variety either of learning arrangements and formats (e.g. web-based trainings, serious games, ...) or technical systems that support educational processes (e.g. course management, document upload) into account, whilst 'e-learning' originally refers to the concrete learning and teaching processes, supported by electronic or digital media, only.

Nowadays, as technology is not a limiting factor even for the development of innovative approaches anymore (Pechuel & Beutner, 2013, p. 931), there is a vast amount of digital learning applications for actual any educational problem available with many of them of lacking didactical quality. Thereby, in contrast to former years, the focus should be on the development of didactical concept that utilize the given technical potentials (p. 931). In addition, Garetta-Domingo & Mor (2007) outline that a well-designed human-computer interaction must fall under consideration as well: "As e-learning systems grow and more people are accessing them, it is necessary to consider (…) the diverse needs and characteristics users have. This allows building systems that people can use easily, efficiently, and effectively, where the learning process leads to a good user experience and becomes a good learning practice." (p. 1). By saying that, they implicitly advocate the use of approaches such like user-centered and participatory design in the context of digital learning applications. These approaches base on the philosophy to design products that respond to the end users' needs, and promise increased usability, user experience, user satisfaction, user acceptance, and high adoption rates which shall lead, in consequence, to valuable learning experiences, higher learner satisfaction, and thus, better learning achievement (Garetta-Domingo & Mor, 2007, pp. 1-2; Cheock, & Wong, 2015, p. 76). The findings of an empirical study by Eon, Wen, and Ashill (2006) support this claim. Based on a survey with 397 students that participated in the universities' web-based courses they found that user satisfaction is a highly significant predictor for perceived learning outcomes (Table 3).

In this light, there is interest in comprehensive but easy to apply instruments that facilitate the design of products like digital learning applications meeting the mentioned criteria. The unmanageable number of popular scientific, heterogeneous, primarily practice-oriented but expedient instruments supports this concern (e.g. Hagen et al., 2012). Simultaneously, comparatively technic-oriented processes such like the ISO standard on human-centered design or theoretical discussions of certain methodologies (e.g. Spinuzzi, 2005) might be too abstract than that they could guide practice. Thus, instruments that base on empiric research and that bring recent theoretical discussions as well as state-of-the-art practices together into a practicable approach are missing. The purpose of this chapter is therefore to outline an evidence-based prototypical participatory design process, which aims to provide researchers with a sound basis for future discussions in this field, but also to serve practitioners as a valuable instrument.

Taking the rationale and research purpose into account, the following structure applies to this chapter:

- General discussion of usability, user experience, user-centered design, and participatory design.
- Brief literature review on the status quo of user-centered and participatory design approaches in the context of digital learning.
- Outline of the research design, including a description of the applied methodologies in general, and its actual application by the author in particular.
- Presentation of the research results and consequently the evidence-based prototypical participatory design process.
- General remarks and conclusion followed up by an outlook on future research directions.

USER-CENTERED AND PARTICIPATORY DESIGN IN DIGITAL LEARNING

The following provides, for the one, an understanding of Usability and User Experience in general. On the other hand, it discusses how user-centered and participatory design approaches provide the methodical basis for the development of products like digital learning applications that meet these quality attributes. Thereby it builds the theoretical underpinning of the later research activities.

A Story From Usability and User Experience

Usability is a quality attribute of user interfaces, which refers to its learnability, efficiency of use, memorability, handling of errors, and the user satisfaction of a product (Liang, Chou, Hsu, & Yang, 2009; p. 71, Garreta-Domingo & Mor, 2007, p. 2). The focus is thereby on effectivity and efficiency (Geis, T., 2010a, para. 3) or, to say it differently, on supporting the user in achieving his/ her tasks more efficiently and effectively. As user satisfaction refers to the user's perceptions and responses when using a product, system or service, it relates closely to User Experience (Bevan, 2009, p. 1).

According to Hassenzahl, Burmester, & Koller (2008) the mentioned concept of User Experience slowly replaces Usability (p. 78), although it is not to see as a substitute (Geis, T. 2010b, para. 7). User Experience focuses on the end user's perceptions, feelings, and interactions resulting from the anticipated, actual or reflected interaction (use) with a product, system, or services (Garreta-Domingo & Mor, 2007, p. 2; Geis, T., 2010a, para. 3; Geis, T., 2010b, para. 2). In concrete, according to ISO 9241-210, it refers to the "users' emotions, beliefs, preferences, perceptions, physical and psychological responses, behaviors, and accomplishments that occur before, during, and after use" (as cited in Bevan, 2009, p. 3). Thereby, User Experience complements and enhances the concept of Usability (Geis, T., 2010b, para. 7) by explicitly adding the before use and after use perspectives.

Given this difficultness to separate Usability and User Experience, Law, Roto, Hassenzahl, Vermeeren, & Kort (2009) outline that usability „focuses primarily on user cognition and user performance in human-technology interactions" whilst user experience shifts "the focus to user affect, sensation, and the meaning as well as value of such interaction in everyday life." (p. 719). Thereby, a differentiation by the focus of the actual concepts (cognition and performance against affect and value in everyday life) seems more reasonable than a differentiation by perspective (during against before, during, and after use) (Bevan, 2009, p.1).

Origin and Understanding of User-Centered and Participatory Design

Reasoned by the aforementioned interest in user interfaces, software, and systems (products) with a high degree of usability respectively user experience, methodological approaches such like user-centered design and participatory design, which consider the user's perspectives during the design and development process, arose. A thorough discussion of the application of such approach is subject to the following paragraphs.

User-Centered Design

User-Centered Design approaches base on the philosophy that the needs, wants, and limitations of a product's end user are the focus at each design/ development process-stage (note: following the author will use design/ development and designer/ developer to stress both components if not indicated differently). Their overall purpose is thereby to design systems that are not only user-friendly, but also "rooted in the practices of people using them." (Greenbaum, 1993, p. 30) Typically, this means studying documents or descriptions of e.g. work arounds or tasks to extrapolate the context of use. However unfortunate, such formal descriptions often differ from the actual (best) practice, which is why Burmester & Hassenzahl (2013) claim that the end-user should be involved actively at each process stage (para. 6, 9). This allows end user feedback on their experiences with the system, which is valuable to ensure that the product responds to the user's needs (Garreta-Domingo & Mor, 2007, p. 1).

To safeguard this, the international standard *ISO 9241-210 Ergonomics of human-system interaction* (part 210: human-centered design for interactive systems, "DIN EN ISO 9241-210," n.d.) refers to the following six basic principles in the context of the so-called user-centered usability engineering (Geis, T., 2010a, para. 2):

1. The design bases on a holistic understanding of the user, his/ her tasks, and work environment. Here, Burmester & Hassenzahl (2013) recommend an empirical analysis (para. 9).
2. Users participate in the design and development processes. With the switch from a usability-perspective to a user experience-perspective, this does also mean losing objectivity – which has, in this context, a positive connotation (Hassenzahl et al., 2008, p. 78).
3. Continuous refinement and adjustment of mock-ups/ prototypes based on user-centered evaluations respectively end-user feedback. Here, an early visualization helps to make ideas become vivid, and each evaluation is to understand as testing a hypothesis about the perfect design (Burmester & Hassenzahl, 2013, para. 21, 28).
4. The process foresees iterations.
5. Consideration of a holistic understanding of user experience during the design process (e.g. Jetter & Gerken, 2007).
6. The design team brings multiple professions and perspectives together.

Additionally, DIN EN ISO 9241-210 outlines a process towards user-centered design of interactive systems, as shown in Figure 1.

This figure also visualizes iterations as the central element of user-centered design process. This means that reworking takes place, until it matches the quality criteria as outlined in the initial phase (Burmester & Hassenzahl, 2013, para. 42-44).

Burmester & Hassenzahl (2013) describe the different phases as outlined following:

- **Planning the User-Centered Design:** Focusses the need of carrying out a user-centered design process. This means, that it is necessary to proof to which extent the user interacts with the system, and how critical this interaction is. Moreover, this step includes the definition of the system's quality criteria (para. 7, 43).

Figure 1. User-centered design process for designing usable interactive systems, acc. to DIN EN ISO 9241-210:2010

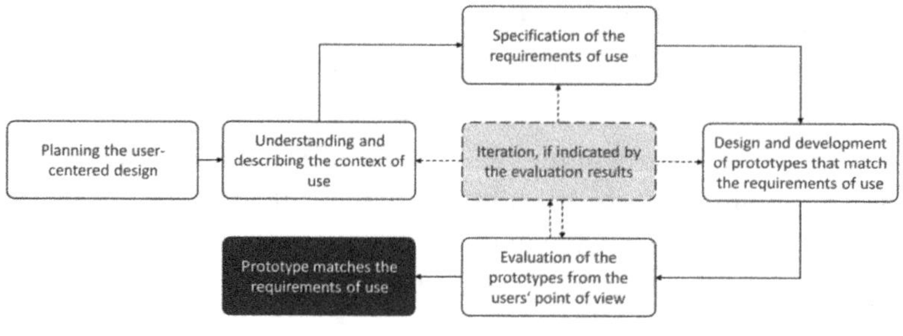

- **Understanding and Describing the Context of Use:** Typically requires an empirical analysis of the users, their (workplace) objectives, tasks and routines, the equipment of their workplace, but also their physical and social environment. Analyses of documents that e.g. formally describe the concrete tasks can support the empirical work. Inaccurate analyses of the context of use or relying on formal descriptions only might result in lacking user acceptance and a missing match with the user requirements (para. 8-9).
- **The Specification of the Requirements of Use:** Bases on the interpretation of the aforementioned analyses. Here, the focus is on deriving concrete system requirements. According to Standard IEEE P1233/D3, the formulation of the requirements should be abstract, unambiguous, traceable, and checkable (para. 12-13). A revision of this specification takes place during the prototyping and evaluation processes, and thereby they find their way into new prototypes (para. 42).
- **Design and Development of Prototypes:** The translation of outlined requirements into a concrete software system respectively user interface. The design and development actions typically base on prototyping approaches (para. 15-27).
- **Evaluation:** A prototype is to understand as a hypothesis about the optimal design of a user-interface within a given context of use. Testing this hypothesis is part of the evaluation. Based on the evaluation findings, reworking actions take place (para. 33-34).

However, although the participation of users in the design and development process is already part of the user-centered design approach, they are not fully involved yet and the process is typically "not participatory in and on itself" (Greenbaum, 1993, pp. 27, 31) – in contrast to participatory design, which will be in focus following.

Participatory Design

Often misunderstood as a design approach, particularly in the field of human-computer interaction of technical systems, participatory design actually is a research methodology with its roots in participatory action research (Bratteteig, Bødker, Dittrich, Mogensen, & Simonsen, 2013, p. 117). According to Spinuzzi (2005), "As the name implies, the approach is just as much about *design* – producing artifacts, systems, work organizations, and practical or tacit knowledge – as it is about *research*. In this methodology, design *is* research." (p. 164). Therefore, it also has its own methods and techniques such like ethnographic observations, interviews, analysis of artifacts, and others of minor relevance. These "methods are always used to iteratively construct and elicits the research results as co-interpreted by the designer-researchers and the participants who will use the design." (p. 164). Thus, the applied methods aim to let the users participate in the design and decision-making processes actively (Bratteteig et al., 2013, p. 117; Bonsignore, Ahn, Clegg, Guha, & Yip, 2013, p. 549). In consequence, the designed artifacts reflect the research results whilst simultaneously building the basis for further development and refinement activities within an iterative design-research process. Concurrently, they supports gaining a better understanding of the actual problem (Spinuzzi, 2005, p. 164). Broken-down to a common denominator, such an iterative design consists of the following phases (p. 167):

1. **Initial Exploration of Work:** Here, the focus is on bringing the system developers (or: designers) together with the users with the aim to familiarize the designers with the user's work, which

technologies they use, what workflows, tasks, and routines exists, but other work-related aspects as well.

2. **Discovery Process:** Has a focus on understanding the users' work, their visions, but also to "clarify the users' goals and values and to agree on the desired outcome of the project." (p. 167).
3. **Prototyping:** Iterative development of technological artifacts that meet the defined users' needs. Different users participate in the creation process, and test it on-the-job to evaluate its functionality.

A unique characteristic of Participatory Design is, "the democratic ideal that the people who are effected by a decision or event should be given the opportunity to influence it" (Bonsignore et al., 2013, p. 549). This does not only imply a full and active participation of the end users, but a shift in power relations as well (Greenbaum, 1993, p.29). Formerly, an 'expert' or 'manager' examined the end users' work, tasks, and routines to break them down into small, easy to handle pieces. Typically, designers and developers had to build a system based on these information pieces then, with the aim to make work more efficiently and effectively. Such an approach, however, completely denies the tacit craft skills and knowledge of the actual system users. Participatory design, in contrast, acknowledges the situatedness of knowledge in artifacts, practices, or interactions. Thereby, it aims to uncover this tacit knowledge and to reflect on it, to bring it together with the more abstract and analytical knowledge of the designer-researchers. Applying participatory design means to hand over such a responsibility to the workers, and to let them determine how they accomplish their tasks best. Consequently, the tacit knowledge of the future system users becomes the objective of study within participatory design research, although most of it will always remain invisible. Such an approach, however, ensures that the system supports the workers in the best way possible and that it preserves and fits into existing knowledge (Spinuzzi, 2005, pp. 164-166).

However, the mentioned shift in power relation does also mean that the system developers "move into uncharted water" (Greenbaum, 1993, p. 28), as the overall idea of this approach is to let future system users participate in decisions that affect the system they will use and be working with in future. This "Movement from involving users in design to full participatory design means encroaching on some decisions that have traditionally been considered the prerogative of management." (p. 29). By fully involving users in the design process, system developers can learn from their daily experiences, as they know best about their task requirements. Such an involvement requires one the one hand, an environment in which the users feel free to express their ideas (p. 31). On the other hand, however, it requires the system developers to take an active role in helping users becoming involved into the design process, as participatory design bases on the belief that the communication barriers between technical specialists and the people using the systems "need to be broken down in order to build effective communication during the design process." (Greenbaum, 1993, p. 27; Spinuzzi, 2005, p. 166; Robertson & Simonsen, 2013, p. 2)

However, although participatory design promises a mindset change regarding end-user involvement and centricity, the methodology also comes with limitations, such like the following (Spinuzzi, 2005, pp. 168-169):

- Participatory design typically leads to evolutionary instead of revolutionary changes.
- There is the tendency to focus too narrowly on the design artifact instead of the overall work.
- It is difficult to maintain the focus on democratic empowerment.
- Designer-researcher tend to apply the research methods too loosely.
- "It takes an enormous amount of time, resources, and institutional commitment to pull off." (p. 169).

- Participatory design projects suffer from little structure and deadlines, which is why participants might lose commitment to, e.g., show up on workshops.

This above-standing, concise overview illustrated the user-centered core of participatory design (Bonsignore et al, 2013, p. 550). However, whilst 'user-centered design' refers to a clearly defined structure of a design and development process, 'participatory design' refers to a research methodology and principles that underlie such a process (Robertson & Simonsen, 2013, p. 3; Bratteteig et al., 2013, p. 117).

Participatory Design Approaches in E-Learning and Digital Learning

For digital learning applications, classic user-centered design approaches enjoy a more or less widespread acceptance for various target groups and contexts (Teine & Beutner, 2016; Ngampornchai & Adams, 2016; Liang et al., 2009; Valtolina, Barricelli, Mesiti, & Ribaudo, 2012). Anyhow, when it comes to participatory design, education experts such like instructional designers show reluctance. According to Yip (2017), they probably fear faulty conceptualizations that do not meet the end-user requirements, as the end-users themselves do not know e.g. about strategies that match their own learning best (p. 202). The following shall provide a concise overview about the application of participatory design in digital learning. The author picked studies that are no older than five years, cover a variation of (exceptional) target groups and application contexts, and that show different ways of what participatory design could actually look alike in practice:

Bonsignore et al. (2013) explore how participatory design might augment design-based research approaches in the context of learning, and how a design-based research framework might incorporate the participatory design approach (p. 549). Based on a thorough literature review, the authors criticize that only a low number of studies on computer supported collaborative learning environments integrated participatory design techniques. Exposing results from practically oriented studies (1997-2012), they nevertheless issue a promising report regarding the beneficially and value of approaches that incorporate the active participation of learners (such like design thinking) in the design and development process of virtual environments, game-based learning solutions, drawing applications, and others (p. 550). They moreover outline that working with different target groups requires flexible design techniques (p. 551), and that children ranging from pre-school age to teenagers can act as critically reflecting co-designers and developers that contribute valuably (p. 551-553). They also give proof about the validity of their findings for learners with autism (p. 554). Methodology wise they outline, "that comparing two sets of co-designers allows for triangulation and insights into complementary design ideas that can be optimized for the design of learning technologies." (p. 553)

Huang (2015) presents the results of a project that aimed to gap the digital divide in rural Taiwan by delivering ICT education courses to elderly in rural areas. Therefore, tech affine young adults drive with technology-equipped vans into rural areas, to teach curricula that take the needs of the respective community and the elderly into account. The elderly co-designed the curriculum that supports the participants with creating a Blog to stay informed about ICT education. The author had a strong methodological focus that also shows how participatory design derived from participatory action research (pp. 52-54).

Gros (2016) takes a theoretical point of view and focuses on so-called smart learning environments that, e.g. predict the learner's needs in terms of content. Thereby, learner feedback is crucial for designing personalized learning experiences, as "users are an important resource and can be partners in the design process to ensure that technology is useful and usable." (p. 8) Discussion, reflection, and critique are key characteristics of iterative and collaborative design, and as designers/ developers can barely know about the particular (contextual) needs and preferences of learners, participatory design is the methodology of choice (pp. 2-3, 8). Nevertheless, as the involved learners do typically not have a proper theoretical understanding of this field, this approach involves the danger to "not address the deeper issues in learning. Therefore, researchers in learning and instructional design still need to utilize their own expertise into the design but be able to listen and work with learners." (Yip, 2017, p. 206).

Santa-Rosa (2012) outlines the results of a study that aimed to find out whether the learners participation in the development of a virtual learning environment led to higher acceptance by the students, or not. Noteworthy is, that the students were elderly people enrolled to a histology course. However, after their participation in user research and prototyping activities, the research findings show that the frequency of use was low at first, but "that the adoption [of the] virtual environment by teachers is a determining factor of use by students" (p. 1159).

The outlined studies show that researchers, designers, and developers apply participatory design to a variety of problem contexts, target groups, and with varying success. Nevertheless, the examples generally stress the beneficiary of this approach in the context of digital learning.

RESEARCH DESIGN

Against the primarily theoretically oriented body of literature on participatory design, it is the author's claim to contribute to this discussion with sound empirical findings. Therefore, the applied research process followed a clearly determined qualitative-hermeneutic research approach. According to Hussy, Schreier, & Echterhoff (2013) the focus of qualitative research is on the exploration of new fields of research and research questions (pp. 9-10). Therefore, the author conducted Problem-Centered Interviews (Witzel, 2000) and applied Qualitative Content Analysis (Mayring, 2000) for data analysis purposes.

Altogether, the author conducted four problem-centered interviews. The author picked the interviewees carefully and with the aim to bring different expertise and experience together. All participants are German citizens, hold a University degree and are professional contacts of the author. The lengths of the interviews ranged between 50 minutes and two hours, with all of them covering the whole interview guideline questions. The final sample had the following structure:

P1: Ph.D. student, strong research experiences and practical experience with the conceptualization and development of innovative digital learning applications.

P2: User Experience-coach, responsible for the management of a learning portfolio in an internationally acknowledged, industrial leading company.

P3: User Experience-coach, consults software development projects (also in the context of digital learning), manifold experience as a User Experience designer in different worldwide acknowledged and industrial leading companies.

P4: User Experience-designer, responsible for user-centered design projects within an industrial leading company, more than a decade of experience in worldwide-acknowledged companies.

Data Generation: Semi-Structured, Problem-Centered Interviews

Focusing on the data generation at first, according to Witzel (2000), problem-centered interviews "aim to gather objective evidence on human behavior as well as on subjective perceptions and ways of processing social reality" (para. 1). Thereby, they have a theory-generating character, and base furthermore on the following three principles:

1. **Problem-Centered Orientation:** The interviewer makes use of his/ her comprehensive expertise related to the research field to understand the interviewees' statement and explanations. This allows him a targeted, problem-centered questioning and re-questioning. Due to this character, the interviews produce broad and differentiated data at first. As the interviewer starts to understand the interviewees' point of view, the questions become more oriented towards the actual research problem (para. 4).
2. **Object-Orientation:** Emphasizes methodological flexibility, meaning that the applied methodology needs to adapt to the observed object. Thus, problem-centered interviews do neither prescribe a process nor any frame conditions the researcher needs to adhere (para 5).
3. **Process Orientation:** Meaning that an interview is to see as a communication situation in which the respondent needs to feel accepted, secure, and taken seriously. Otherwise, the respondents will not open-up, unfold their point of view, speak unprotected, correct earlier statements, show different perspectives, or reflect on themselves in general (para. 6).

Short socio-demographic questionnaires, interview guidelines, tape recordings, and postscripts support the interview process, with the interview guidelines being the most crucial instrument. These guidelines provide a framework of orientation for the interviewer, and ensure comparability of interviews (Witzel, 2000, para. 8). This character also reasons why the author carried out the interviews as so-called *semi-structured interviews*. These "(…) are simply conversations in which you know what you want to find out about – and so have a set of questions to ask and a good ideas of what topics will be covered – but the conversation is free to vary, and is likely to change substantially between participants." (Fylan, 2005, p. 65). This flexibility makes semi-structured interviews well suited to explore complex fields of research and to find out about reasons and arguments respectively the "Why?" (p. 66). Thereby, this approach matches well with the basic principles of problem-centered interviews and with the so-called structure laying technique as well (Scheele & Groeben, 1988, p. 47; Christmann, Groeben, & Schreier, 1999, pp. 141-142). The *structure laying technique* is actually a dialogue-hermeneutic method that primarily serves for *communicative validation purposes* following to an interview phase (Scheele & Groeben, 2017). Therefore, its focus is on visualizing subjective theories and complex relationships by applying a set of rules, structuring criteria, and pre-defined steps to data such like interview transcripts or content analysis results (Flick, 2014; Klemme & Siegemann, 2006, p. 64). The author adapted this approach as follows:

- For each interview session, the author pinned cards with the central process steps taken from the user-centered design cycle on a pin board.
- The interviewees had the logical operators +/-, a straight arrow, and dotted-arrows to visualize relationships and conditions.
- Empty cards provided the opportunity to add process (sub) steps, stakeholders, etc., and the interviewees were free to re-arrange or change the process to their liking.

- An explanation sheet with descriptions of the different operators and an exemplary process guided the interviewees during their process modification.

Thus, based on their answers, the interviewees modified the process, which, in consequence, encouraged deep reflection processes and argumentation structures. Moreover, the modifications built the basis for further questioning.

However, the interview guidelines covered three different types of questions, which are typically associated with the so-called structure laying technique (Flick, 2014; Scheele & Groeben, 1988, pp. 35-37; Christmann et al., 1999, pp. 141-142):

1. Open questions aim to provide the interviewee with the opportunity to explicate his/ her immediately available knowledge, such like his/ her understanding or definitions of a topic. Further questions shall then help to concretize his/ her subjective theories.
2. Hypothesis-directed questions orient on the scientific literature or the researcher's theoretical presuppositions, and aim to make the interviewees' implicit knowledge explicit. "The assumptions in these questions are designed as an offer to the interviewees, which they might take up or refuse according to whether they correspond to their subjective theories or not" (Flick, 2014).
3. Confrontational questions are competing alternatives that stand in thematic opposition to the theories presented by the interviewee. They function to initiate re-examination processes and, in conclusion, to explicate, complement, and specify subjective theories conscientiously.

For asking the questions, the author followed a story-telling approach, meaning that he arranged the order of questions as it suits best to drive the interviewee's story forward. Therefore, questions typically start by referring to a former answer. Additionally, redundant questioning elicits new formulations of answers or the expression of individual ambivalences. This, in consequence, facilitates interpretation and helps to reduce errors (Witzel, 2000, para. 6, 22). In sum, the author's interview guideline consisted of seven questions covering the main topics of interest, complemented by 23 for specification purposes.

Before the actual interview started, the author read a standardized introduction text to all interviewees. Following Witzel (2000, para. 13-16), Christmann et al. (1999, p. 142), and Flick (2014) the author herein

- Requested the interviewee's allowance to record the interview,
- Ensured anonymity of the interview transcripts and to black company names out,
- Assured that the interviewee's will receive a copy of the interview transcripts, and that the participants will have the change to retroactively decline the processing of their data,
- Explained the study's context and its leading questions,
- Stressed the participants position as an experts, and that his/ her understanding is valuable for research, and
- Described the structure laying technique and three types of questions, based on examples.

Altogether, the four conducted interviews led to about 90 pages of transcripts to which the author then applied a qualitative content analysis.

Data Analysis: Qualitative Content Analysis

In context of the data analysis, problem-centered interviews do not prescribe any data analysis approach, as this depends on the research interest and topic (Witzel, 2000, para. 22). A matching methodology is the qualitative content analysis, "an approach of empirical, methodological controlled analysis of texts within their context of communication, following content analytical rules and step by step models, without rash quantification." (Mayring, 2000, para. 5). The object of analysis can be any recorded communication, such like transcripts of interviews.

A so-called category system, which consists of different categories and sub-categories, stands in centrum of this methodology. During the analysis process, the researcher carefully assigns particular statements, passages, or remarks to one of such categories. Each category consists of a name, a definition, an example taken from the analysis material, and so-called coding rules. The coding rules determine under which circumstances such an analysis item belongs to a category (Mayring, 2000, para. 4, 21).

The category development can either follow a deductive, inductive, or deductive-inductive approach. Deductive category development "works with prior formulated, theoretical derived aspects of analysis bringing them in connection with the text. The qualitative step of analysis consists in a methodologically controlled assignment of the category to a passage of text." (Mayring, 2000, para. 20). Thus, the categories and their definition already exist before the actual analysis starts, and might represent the structure of an interview guideline. In contrast, the process of inductive category development is less clear, although Mayring (2000, Fig. 1) outlines a step model for the inductive category development. Here, the category development starts with the preliminary definition of a particular analysis item as exemplary for a new category and outlining preliminary coding rules as well. Based on an ongoing process with several feedback-loops the researcher continuously defines and redefines categories. Given an existing, deductive system, the actual analysis might lead to the necessity to redefine these categories, to delete them, or to add new.

Here, the author used a deductive-inductive approach as well. Figure 2 shows the final category system (code system) with the number of assigned analysis item. Altogether, the author worked 265 analysis items out of the transcripts. The below-standing paragraphs provide a comprehensive overview about these findings.

RESEARCH RESULTS

The focus for the presentation of the research results shall be on the actual design and development process. Extracts of results that relate to the importance of user experience in the context of digital learning application, the basic principles of participatory design, and user involvement complement this view.

For the interpretation of the results please acknowledge that, e.g., the shortcut 'P1, para. 86' means that the displayed content relates to Paragraph 86 from within the interview transcript of P1. Moreover, please be informed that the author translated the German interview results to English, and that the original research data is accessible upon request.

Figure 2. Code system with number of paragraphs attributed to each category

- Codesystem — 265
  - User Experience — 0
    - Definition, characteristics & differentiation — 4
    - Importance in general — 4
    - Importance in the context of learning — 8
  - Participatory design — 0
    - Preconditions — 19
    - Definition and general understanding — 8
    - User involvement — 0
      - Necessity of user involvement — 4
      - Sampling — 13
      - Regularity and intensity — 7
      - Biases — 0
        - Subjectivity — 1
        - Highest-Paid Opinion — 5
        - Self-affirmation — 8
        - Slowdown of the process — 2
        - Dissapointment — 2
        - My-Baby effect — 1
    - Democratic principle — 14
    - Roles within the process — 17
    - Evolution vs. Innovation — 11
    - Frame conditions — 18
    - Stakeholder — 8
  - Design and development process — 0
    - Process characteristics — 6
    - Process phases — 4
      - Perception of a problem — 3
      - User Research — 14
      - Development aims and standards — 13
      - Definition of application context — 10
      - Definition of usage requirements — 6
      - Idea generation and synthesis — 5
      - Prototyping — 17
      - Evaluation — 18
      - Final product/ release — 8
    - Generalizability — 4
    - Process stop without results — 3

User Experience in the Context of Digital Learning

User Experience has different component such like joy of use, ease of use, aesthetics, and image of use – and all of them are highly relevant in the context of (corporate) learning (P3, para. 53, 95). Against the design / development context and the planned product, these components vary in their weigh (P3, para. 53). Although cognitive components such like ease of use (usability) base on measurable heuristics, it is difficult to measure user experience as a whole. This is because other components are more affective and thereby less selective. Individuals have a subjective sensitivity for aesthetics, joy of use, and possibly also for image of use (P3, para. 47, 51). Following a user-centered design/ development approach becomes thereby inevitable. This is, because the User's will experience the product anyways. "You cannot not have user experience." Given the importance of User Experience, it thereby becomes the aim to allow worthy experiences (P3, para. 53). According to P2, a good user experience is an inherent part of any

Figure 3. Prototypical participatory design process

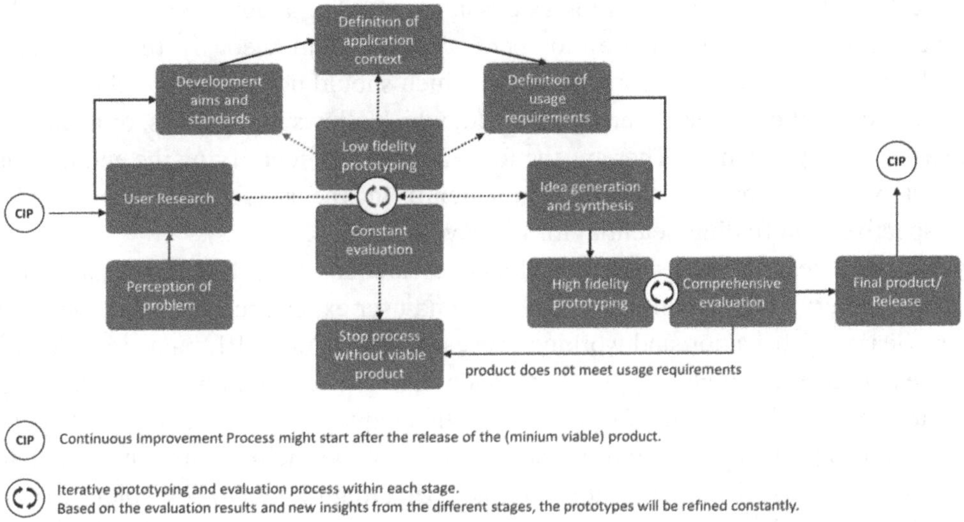

qualitative product, and is particularly important to stand a chance against market competitors (para. 94). In contrast to a high usability only (high pragmatic quality), user experience fosters the end user's desire to make use of a product (hedonic quality) (P4, para. 51). A high degree of both qualities thereby drives the end user's motivation to use a product (e.g. a digital learning application) continuously (P4, para. 47; P2, para. 94).

User experience is about serving the end user's needs and desires. Thereby, the individual's perceived relevance of the learning content and its desire to acquire certain knowledge or competencies and serving different learning styles build user experience-components as well (P2, para. 102, 104; P3, para. 95).

In consequence, end user orientation and user experience affect the learning outcome. The better the user experience, the higher the expected learning outcomes (P2, para. 98-99, 102; P3, para. 96-97). Summarizing, good user experience leads to learners that are enthusiastic to use a digital learning application, they become intrinsically motivated to steer their learning, and this affects the learning outcome positively (P1, para. 65).

Participatory Design and Development Process

In essence, the participatory design and development process is an iterative, reflexive prototyping process, in which the focus is on a continuous evaluation and improvement of a product until it matches the defined requirements (P1, para. 171, 173, 167-169; P4, para. 31; P3, para. 101-103). Thereby, it typically follows a rapid prototyping approach (P4, para. 120). Each iteration cycle should cover all process phases (P2, para. 121-122), whereby the orientation on the process phases intensifies as the development activities progress (P4, para. 31). In practice, as the research findings show, a clear differentiation of the process phases and their systematic application is difficult (P4, para. 29). However, Figure 3 represents the consolidated research findings in form of a prototypical participatory design and development process.

The initial perception of a (potential) end user problem or a product idea starts the actual design/ development process, and motivates the following user research phase (P3, para. 30-31; P2, para. 42, 48).

In general, the focus of the User Research is on finding out about the end users' 'pain points' (P3, para. 57) and gathering as many information as possible regarding a desired product or solutions (P2, para. 46), given the respective design/ development context. Simultaneously, the user research builds the basis for defining a design/ development scope, which should not be too broad or too narrow (P3, para. 25, 29). The context could be either a greenfield, which allows innovations, or an already existing system that seeks for improvement. Thereby, the focus is either on identifying the end user needs to get an estimation of "where the journey leads us", or on identifying the users' problems and challenges with the system respectively on finding potential for improvements (P4, para. 5).

To carry out their research, the designer/ developer-researchers apply different research methodology including surveys, interviews, (preliminary) usability and user experience tests, and the observation of daily routines, (learning) behavior, and working processes (P4, para. 5; P1, para. 15). Complementary, literature and external professionals typically provide valuable information about the target group's problems, desires, and needs (P1, para. 7). Approaches that request the end users to ideate potential solutions for their outlined problems or to build first, rough prototypes help to infer on the actual, probably hidden problems and needs. "It is that what you think at first might seem to be a solution, but it actually uncovers that the real problem is different to what you thought it is." (P3, para. 21). Methodologies like engaging the end users into an informal talk or dialogue are less controlled but lead to valuable insights as well (P1, para. 145).

With a focus on user interviews, P3 states that they make use of strongly methodologically controlled questioning techniques to uncover the end users problems (para. 23). Open questions such like "What do you need?" or "What is your problem?" are useful to get a first understanding of the end user needs, whilst more targeted and specific questions such like "Why is this a problem for you?" help to uncover the real problems (P2, para. 27; P3, para. 23).

Clustering and analyzing the user research findings is necessary to draw conclusions that lead the actual design/ development process activities (P2, para. 48). Given the mentioned greenfield, such a conclusion could also be not to start any design/ development activities, or, for the other case, to stop ongoing activities (P1, para. 25).

P1 distinguishes in-between development aims and development standards (set target dimensions for any product) such like User Experience, Didactical Quality, and Profitability (para. 87, 105, 115, 119). Setting such development aims and standards for a product/ project requires defined frame conditions and a clear scope for solutions (P3, para. 91). In general, the development aims take the respective user research findings into account (P1, para. 13) and call for answers in form of so-called *target states* to, amongst others, the following questions (P3, para. 29, 91)

- What are we doing?
- Why are we doing it?
- Where are we doing it?
- For whom are we doing it?
- How are we doing it?
- Is there any similar or contrasting project?
- What is the project's scope of solutions?
- What is the intended degree of innovativeness (evolution or revolution)?

In the context of digital learning applications, the development aims also derive from the didactical intention and the learning subject matter (P1, para. 61). The defined target states, e.g. the intended degree of innovativeness, act as an internal benchmark for the final product, and thereby as a driver of the design and development activities (P1, para. 46-47).

A well-planned and conscientiously carried out user research provides information on the end users, their working or learning situation, the support they need, and other tools they use. Thereby, it builds the basis for understanding and defining the context of application correctly (P3, para. 29). P4 suggest to, e.g., conduct Design Thinking-Workshops or to engage the end users into dialogues that help to understand their problem (para. 31). An initial specification of the application context bases on the consequent findings (P3, para. 33), and consists, at least, in form of a user story-list (P4, para. 87). This specification might become subject to further re-defining by taking creative and rationale elements as artifacts of the progressing prototyping activities into account (P1, para. 173). This depends on the creativity of the involved participants and the intended degree of innovativeness (P4, para. 87; P1, para. 46-47).

According to P1, the definition of the application context is a facet of the previous phase (para. 164-165).

The definition of usage requirements is the final step towards the ideation and synthesis phase (P2, para. 50-52) which is also why first design and development activities might already run in parallel (P4, para. 84), although the consequent outcomes are not to see as final solutions (P3, para. 45). The performed actions and outcomes of this phase include the following:

- End user-Stakeholder-Interaction Map and Touch-Point Map (P4, para. 78).
- Concise concept catalogues and books, based on the user research (P2, para. 42).
- Sketches of ideas – not yet solutions or finalized (P3, para. 43).

As the latter mentioned bullet-point shows, the idea generation and synthesis phase interweaves partly with the definition of user requirements (P3, para. 57). Considering the user research findings, the focus is on a creative process (P4, para. 81), for which P1 suggest to make use of different creativity methods that help to reconsider the status quo (para. 113). The aim of this process, however, is to generate a bandwidth of potential solutions without getting in too much detail (P3, para. 57; P4, para. 81). For one, these ideas build the basis for the following prototyping activities (P3, para. 57). On the contrary, they actually are low-fidelity prototypes (P4, para. 81). P4 describes, "You can start with an ideation, to develop ideas early in the process. You can synthesize [consolidate] these ideas to get via another ideation phase into the prototyping. The direction of this cycle is not pre-defined. (…) This is actually prototyping at an early stage…" (para. 81). The high-fidelity prototyping, in contrast, focuses on further developing one specific idea (para. 81).

Prototyping in general, irrespective of its degree of fidelity, is to understand as a trial-and-error process driven by both arguments and creativity (P1, para. 25). An early and intense prototyping phase and end user involvement safeguards the design/ development of a product that matches the end users' needs and desires. Their early feedback helps to significantly decrease adjustment costs (P1, para. 19), and "I am convinced that there is always something you can show, whatever form it has" (P2, para. 17). During the prototyping process, the stakeholders and particularly the involved end users act as a corrective. Their feedback and responses initiate reflection and reconsideration processes which, in consequence, drives the design/ development process and thereby the further development of prototypes (P1, para. 25). Assuming a conscious user research and analysis phase, such an evaluative approach that seeks for continuous and fast feedback, complemented by a multidisciplinary team, builds the basis for innovative approaches and solutions (P1, para. 45). Within the different process phase, prototyping can take different shapes.

Drawn visualizations and low-fidelity sketches of first ideas or the user requirements actually are first paper prototypes (P4, para. 31; P2, para. 17). They provide a basis to engage the end users into a discussion, to receive valuable feedback, and thereby to verify or redefine the requirements (P2, para. 13). In consequence, re-worked visualizations and sketches become more reliable and build the basis for prototypes of higher fidelity (P3, para. 57).

However, the end users do not only provide valuable feedback but could and should be involved into the actual prototype-development and creation process as well. Taking the context of hardware development as an example, P4 states, "this established German manufacturer developed a bicycle-system, a speedometer, and during the development process they build prototypes out of Styrofoam in different versions (…). Here, the end users had the chance to participate and to build their own prototype." (para. 9). The development of different prototypes that vary in certain characteristics (also their visionariness) occurs naturally, as it is typically not possible to synthesize the bandwidth of generated ideas into one consistent prototype (P3, para. 58-59). Such a variation of prototypes and their evaluation is valuable, and provides the opportunity to get a differentiated picture of the prototype's advantages and disadvantages (P3, para. 61). Following, on the one hand, a synthesis of the advantages (Cherry picking) might lead to the development of the best possible product. Given the necessary capacity and budget, on the other hand, further developing different prototypes might lead to new projects (P3, para. 63). However, building visionary prototypes with a high degree of innovativeness, and that do not represent the 'obvious' solution based on the user research findings comes with benefits. The end users do not necessarily know about their desires due to different reasons, like lacking information on the feasibility of technical solutions – and an early end user involvement would lead to a fast verification or falsification anyways (P4, para. 93-95). As the prototypes become more reliable, the user feedback will do so as well. "Better results lead to better feedback lead to better ideas." (P4, para. 98).

From an overall perspective, a 'fail fast, fail cheap'-approach safeguards the development of products and solutions that match the end user's needs (P2, para. 23; P1, para. 20-21). Lastly, dependent from the product, the market release of a minimum viable product leads to important feedback and therefore information for improving the product (P1, para. 19).

The essence of evaluation is a systematic approach to gathering and analyzing feedback with the objective to determine a product's – and thereby a prototype's – value (P3, para. 105). Within a feedback-driven prototyping approach, the evaluation activities closely follow the design/ development activities (P1, para. 25) - they build an inseparable dyad, based on rapid feedback, reflections of assumptions, and small but continuous improvements (P2, para. 52; P1, para. 17). Thereby, for the one, the evaluation's purpose is to determine continuously whether a certain status of prototype matches the defined user requirements, or not. Thereby, it allows early adjusting and corrections (P1, para. 23) that might also become necessary due to misunderstandings or wrong interpretations of the user research findings (P2, para. 19). On the other hand, the evaluation results provide a precise picture of needs for improvement and further development (P3, para. 105).

In general, the focus of the evaluation is on the end users' perspective (P2, para. 112), although malfunctioning prototypes or those who did not reach a minimum viable level to a certain point might be evaluated internally at first (P2, para. 110). The more the design/ development activities progress the more end users and stakeholders are involved (P1, para. 23). It is important to involve the end-users actively and intensely, and to confront them with the prototypes that reflect the analyzed user research findings and made assumptions (P4, para. 17). For the case that different prototyping activities run in parallel, a sufficient number of involved end users is crucial. At best, a certain group of end users participates in the evaluation of one prototype only (P3, para. 50).

To carry out evaluations, the designer/ developer-researchers make use of different standardizes tools on the one hand, and adapts or develops measures bespoke to the application context and user requirements on the other hand. Dependent from the design/ development process phase and the planned budget, standardized measures that mostly base on heuristics such like Usability or User Experience questionnaires provide valuable information and insights (P3, para. 50-51). Sophisticated methodologies such like user interviews, dialogues, and observations allow inquiring into the end users' actual behavior (P2, para. 15). Strictly methodologically controlled testing scenarios primarily apply to high-fidelity prototypes (P4, para. 31).

Within such scenarios, end users perform exemplary actions, e.g. within a clickable HTML-based prototype under laboratory conditions (P4, para. 31, 33). Therefore, the investigators derive guidelines from the user requirements, define a standardized test flows, and a screener carefully builds a sample that represent the end user's profiles (P4, para. 25, 33). Analyses of the subject's performance give evidence whether the prototype suits the user requirements, or not (P4, para. 33). Moreover, e.g. when applying the think aloud methodology within the testing scenario, the subjects often provide alternative solutions that might improve the prototype's quality within following design/ development phases (P4, para. 23). As already mentioned, such a comprehensive evaluation under laboratory conditions builds the decision-basis for the product's market release.

A somewhat special evaluation results might be stop the design/ development process without market-ready product. Due to different reasons, evaluation results might indicate that the prototyped product is neither beneficial nor valuable for the end users. In such a situation, it is important to weight whether it makes sense to take a step back and start a new design/ development process, or if the activities should stop completely. Stopping the design/ development activities might be the perfectly fine decision. This is particularly the case at early development stages, as fast failures reduce later adjusting costs (P1, para. 25, 173; P2, para 54).

Determining the correct moment for a product's market release is difficult. The term minimum viable product describes the status at which a product is beneficial enough to reach the user's acceptance and their willingness to wait for further update whilst simultaneously allowing an early market release. An early market release, in consequence, allows gathering feedback on the product's quality. This, however, is a critical threshold, as a too early market release will result in negative feedback only (P4, para. 41). Therefore, P1 recommends reaching the status of a system that runs stable in standard operation mode (para. 114, 177). Following, a continuous optimization can be either evolutionary or revolutionary, taking the end user's feedback and experiences into account (P1, para. 181).

P3 goes a step further and states, "Revolutions should be as perfect as possible. Obviously, it should not be a 50% solution. Maybe it is a 90% solution only, but 90% is pretty good" (para. 114). This is particularly because design/ development projects do not aim to deliver perfect solutions anymore. Budget and capacity constraints but also time pressure typically require the release of product that seeks for further improvement (P3, para. 115-118).

Thereby, the research findings show that it is difficult to find the right moment for a product release. Releasing too early might lead to negative feedback and, in consequence, bad reputation. Contrastingly, waiting too long might give competitors the opportunity to move first which affects the business negatively as well (P4, para. 112).

Democratic Principle

A main philosophy behind participatory design is that it follows a democratic approach, meaning that neither role nor hierarchy should influence the design and development process. According to P1, arguments might overrule democracy and hierarchy (para. 33, 187). He outlines that "there might be a small group of people that reasons well why a particular solutions might make sense, or not" (para. 35) whilst the majority might not accept such a solutions because of its novelty. Therefore, it is the designers/ developers task to weigh arguments whilst having the overall project in mind (para. 35). Given the iterative prototyping approach, the users will nevertheless make the final decision whether they accept a certain functionality, or not (P3, para. 17). However, experts should have the opportunity to overrule the end-users when it comes to decisions in their particular field of expertise (P1, para. 183). Thus, experts such like pedagogues or technicians have the overall responsibility and make decisions, whilst the end-users have a limited voice (para. 183).

P3 has a similar understanding and states that it is difficult to have a democratic decision-making in a process in which people from different disciplines, with different experiences, and different expertise come together. Experts are able to solve problems within their field of expertise with better quality than non-experts can, and therefore their voice should have a higher weight (para. 15, 77). P4, in contrast, states that the end-users can overrule the experts as well. When the majority of the involved end-users would solve a task equally different to the expert, this approach to solving a certain problem must find its way into the future system (para. 25). P1 has a similar opinion here. Although the designers have "the power of decision at several points, they nevertheless have to take seriously what the end-users are saying." (para. 37). Albeit such statements break with the democratic principle at some points, P4 stresses that the final system needs to respect respectively include the highest prioritized user requirements respectively functionalities. Otherwise, end-user involvement would not make sense at all (para. 55).

User Involvement

It is not the experts but the end users who know best about their needs and the qualities of a desired product (P2, para. 94). Thus, an early end user involvement is crucial to safeguard successful and valuable design/ development processes (P2, para. 57-58). Without such an involvement, the chance of matching the end user's needs and desires is "one-in-a-million" (P3, para. 17). However, a conscientious sample design considers the following:

- The more end user (and stakeholder) involvement the costlier the decision-making (P4, para. 61). Nevertheless, a sample must represent all target groups and stakeholders (P1, para. 8-9).
- The sample must reach a sufficient size, appropriate to the estimated number of end users (P2, para. 90). Too narrowly defined samples lose crucial diversity, objectivity, and openness (P3, para. 67).
- Different samples should represent the targeted end users equally appropriate, although variations regarding socio-demographic characteristics might make sense for uncovering systematic differences (P3, para. 71, 77; P4, para. 11).
- Working with consistent/ fixed samples brings the advantage to evaluate progress, and how a product developed compared to its predecessor. In contrast, sample participants might peg to their imagination of the future product. Thereby, new participants might bring new insights/ perspec-

tives and ideas (P1, para. 27; P3, para. 65; P2, para. 47). Hence, a mixed-approach seems valuable (P2, para. 19).

- Working with consistent/ fixed samples is costly, and difficult to manage (P4, para. 11).
- A sample must represent worldwide and cross-cultural differences. "The user behavior of an Asian in America is different to the user behavior of an Asian in China." (P4, para. 71).

If it is not possible to work with real sample that represent the actual end user's, P2 recommends making us of so-called Personas (para. 116).

P1 proposes for a constant involvement of experts and end users (para. 149, 153), although such a regular and intense involvement is costly (P4, para. 11). Thus, an intense involvement at crucial phases such like the user research and early prototyping seems reasonable, whilst high-fidelity prototyping requires the involvement of experts (P4, para. 17). This is, because later stages require an end user involvement primarily for evaluation purposes. Thereby, the regularity and intensity depends on the evaluation design, the available budget, and the number of developed prototypes.

The research findings show that different biases or undesired effects might occur caused by the democratic approach of participatory design but end user and stakeholder involvement as well. The interviewees referred to the following biases and effects:

- **Disappointment:** During the process, the involved end users articulate their needs, desires, and expectations on the future product. They moreover give suggestions on the design/ development activities. If the finalized future product does not match with their expectations, they might not feel taken seriously. Thereby, they become critics rather than promoters of the product (P4, para. 53; P2, para. 21). To avoid such effects, a transparent communication and decision-making is crucial (P2, para. 21).
- **Highest-Paid Opinion:** Often, sponsors or taskers of a design/ development project bring in their personal, strongly defended opinion about the future product and its specifications. They expect the designers/ developers to take their opinion as granted, although it might contradict user research findings and overall design/ development principles (P4, para. 57; P1, para. 29, 33). This leads in consequence to undesirable, faulty products. Here, P4 proposes to confront the sponsor/ tasker with the user research findings early in the user requirement-phase, and to outline that his/ her single-opinion is not valid (P4, para. 57).
- **My-Baby Effect and Subjectivity:** Especially at later stages, evaluation results might indicate to discard or rework certain functionalities - despite significant (time) investments (of a single designer/ developer) (P2, para. 86). This is also a valid point from the involved end user's point of view, which, in consequence, might lose objectivity (P3, para. 67). Relying on clearly defined principles and transparent communication might help to handle such a conflictual situation.
- **Self-Affirmation:** It is difficult for designers/ developers to concentrate on user research findings, and what others said rather than their own opinion (P2, para. 78). Thus, they tend to hasty interpretations of (an unreliable basis of) user research findings, to affirm their own opinion or solutions/ product designs they already had in mind – they seek for self-affirmation (P3, para. 33; P2, para. 80-82). By missing deep reflections of the user research, they oversee the actual problem, which leads in consequence to faulty products (P3, para. 33-35). To reduce this bias, P4 proposes to carry out prototype evaluations by others than the designers/ developers (para. 25-27). Additionally,

they must, for the first, become aware of their role and task, and, for the other, develop the necessary mindset that helps them to focus on solutions that lead to user acceptance (P1, para. 29).

- **Process Slowdown:** Involving a certain amount of end users and stakeholders in the design/ development process is time consuming – and thereby costly (P3, para. 17, 19).

REMARKS, CONCLUSION, AND FUTURE WORK

The thoroughly outlined rationale of this research undertaking undoubtedly showed the need for a new generation of digital learning applications. Such applications consider the actual end user needs and preferences, and they base on diligent user research and iterative prototyping rather than on assumptions derived from theory or results of infrequent, incomprehensive evaluations. Thereby new design/ development approaches like user-centered and participatory design continue to gain significance. For both educational professionals and software designers/developers it thereby becomes crucial to redefine their professional roles and build new competences. In future, their success is heavily dependent on (basic) research expertise, multidisciplinary knowledge, the ability to orchestrate the expert's work, and skills in stakeholder management. It is their task, to safeguard that digital learning applications support the learners in coping with the complex and unpredictable tasks and challenges of an increasingly fast economic and societal transformation. Here, the literature review presented only little ongoing participatory design/ development activities in the context of digital learning, but the identified undertakings showed widespread foci, which is a promising and, hopefully, trend-setting tendency.

The author's empirical research findings confirmed the relevance of user experience respectively learner experience in the context of (digital) learning, but also that participatory design is primarily a topic of theoretical discussions up to now. Thereby, future research should focus on practically oriented projects, as there is the need for strong empirical findings on well-functioning *user involvement methodologies* including shortcomings and frame conditions, *applying the democratic principle* successfully, and the creation and characteristics of the necessary *mindset of involved researchers, developers and stakeholders*. Such empirical data about the proven practice might make participatory design easier to grasp and apply for practitioners – which is a precondition for realizing its true potential. Moreover, although user-centered and participatory design rely on end user-involvement, literature recently lacks findings on their perspective, e.g. regarding their experiences with certain involvement methodologies or their actual motivation to participate in prototyping processes.

Considering the aforementioned, future research on the role of user experience and participatory design in digital learning should focus rather on improving practice than driving elaborated scientific discussions that are too abstract for practitioners to apply. This requires research activities such like projects within different fields of application, with varying target groups, and under different frame conditions. Else, it would neither be possible to draw a detailed picture of the strengths/ limitations of participatory design with all its different facets nor to outline, e.g. applicable frameworks. Here, from the author's point of view, it is also crucial not to apply participatory design too rigid. The research findings show that although all participants referred to the standard user-centered design process implicitly, they somewhat varied in how they apply it. Good practice rarely follows processes rigidly, but orients on processes and adapts its structure the way it is beneficial to the specific problem context. Systematical and occasional variations in applying processes might help to become aware of new ways of doing, and thereby to improve the status quo of good practice. This might also reason the variation within the currently available instruments. However, the outlined, generally applicable prototypical participatory design process will provide a valuable basis for researchers and practitioners, as it combines empirical findings with experiences from good practice.

REFERENCES

Akilli, G. K. (2007). Games and Simulations: A New Approach in Education? In D. Gibson, C. Aldrich, & M. Prensky (Eds.), *Games and simulations in online learning. Research and development frameworks* (pp. 1–20). Hershey, PA: Information Science Publishing. doi:10.4018/978-1-59904-304-3.ch001

Arnold, P., Kilian, L., Thillosen, A., & Zimmer, G. (Eds.). (2011). *Handbuch E-Learning. Lehren und Lernen mit digitalen Medien*. Bielefeld, Germany: Bertelsmann.

Barik, N., & Karforma, S. (2012). Risks and Remedies in E-Learning System. *International Journal of Network Security & Its Applications*, *4*(1), 51–59. doi:10.5121/ijnsa.2012.4105

Becla, A. (2012). Information Society and Knowledge-based Economy – Development Level and the Main Barriers – some Remarks. *Economia e Sociologia (Evora, Portugal)*, *5*(1), 125–132.

Bevan, N. (2009). *What is the difference between the purpose of usability and user experience evaluation methods.* Paper presented at UXEM'09Workshop, INTERACT 2009, Uppsala, Sweden.

Blumschein, P., & Fischer, M. (2006). *Didactic Design of E-Learning Measures. E-learning in Vocational Education and Training.* Bonn, Germany: Capacity Building International, on behalf of Federal Ministry for Economic Cooperation and Development.

Bonsignore, E., Ahn, J., Clegg, T., Guha, M. L., & Yip, J. C. (2013). Embedding Participatory Design into Design for Learning: An Untapped Interdisciplinary Resource? In CSCL 2013 Proceedings (pp. 549-556). Madison, WI: Academic Press.

Bratteteig, T., Bødker, K., Dittrich, Y., Mogensen, P. H., & Simonsen, J. (2013). Participatory Design: an introduction. In J. Simonsen & T. Robertson (Eds.), *Routledge international handbook of participatory design* (pp. 117–144). New York, NY: Routledge.

Burmester, M., & Hassenzahl, M. (2013). *Benutzerzentrierte Softwaregestaltung*. Retrieved March 25, 2017, from http://www.ergo-online.de/site.aspx?url=html/software/software_entwicklung_prototyp/benutzerzentrierte_softwarege.htm

Cheock, M. L., & Wong, S. L. (2015). Predictors of E-Learning Satisfaction in Teaching and Learning for School Teachers: A Literature Review. *International Journal of Instruction*, *8*(1), 75–90. doi:10.12973/iji.2015.816a

Christmann, U., Groeben, N., & Schreier, M. (1999). Subjektive Theorien: Rekonstruktion und Dialog-Konsens. *Siegener Periodikum zur Internationalen Empirischen Literaturwissenschaft: SPIEL*, *18*(1), 138–154.

DIN EN ISO 9241-210. (n.d.). In *Standards of NA 023*. Retrieved from http://www.din.de/en/getting-involved/standards-committees/naerg/standards/wdc-beuth:din21:135399380

Eom, S. B., Wen, H. J., & Ashill, N. (2006). The Determinants of Students' Perceived Learning Outcomes and Satisfaction in University Online Education: An Empirical Investigation. *Decision Sciences Journal of Innovative Education*, *4*(2), 215–235. doi:10.1111/j.1540-4609.2006.00114.x

Flick, U. (Ed.). (2014). *An Introduction to Qualitative Research* (5th ed.). Los Angeles, CA: Sage Pub.

Fylan, F. (2005). Semi-structured interviewing. In D. Miles & P. Gilbert (Eds.), *A Handbook of Research Methods for Clinical and Health Psychology* (pp. 65–78). New York: Oxford University Press.

Galarneau, L., & Zibit, M. (2007). Online Game for 21st Century Skills. In D. Gibson, C. Aldrich, & M. Prensky (Eds.), *Games and simulations in online learning. Research and development frameworks* (pp. 59–88). Hershey, PA: Information Science Publishing. doi:10.4018/978-1-59904-304-3.ch004

Garreta-Domingo, M., & Mor, E. (2007). *User Centered Design in E-Learning Environments: from Usability to Learner Experience.* Retrieved March 13, 2017, from https://www.researchgate.net/publication/43669285_User_Centered_Desing_in_E-Learning_Environments_from_Usability_to_Learner_Experience

Geis, T. (2010a). Neue ISO 9241-210 "Prozess zur Gestaltung gebrauchstauglicher Systeme" ersetzt die ISO 13407. Retrieved March 3 from http://www.procontext.com/aktuelles/2010/03/iso-9241210-prozess-zur-entwicklung-gebrauchstauglicher-interaktiver-systeme-veroeffentlicht.html

Geis, T. (2010b). Usability und User Experience unterscheiden. Retrieved March 31 from http://www.procontext.com/aktuelles/2010/03/usability-und-user-experience-unterscheiden.html

Greenbaum, J. (1993). A design of One's Own: Towards Participatory Design in the United States. In D. Schuler & A. Namioka (Eds.), *Participatory Design: Principles and Practices* (pp. 27–40). Hillsdale, NJ: Lawrence Erlbaum Associates, Inc., Publishers.

Gros, B. (2016). The design of smart educational environments. *Smart Learning Environments*, *15*(3). doi:10.118640561-016-0039x

Hagen, P., Collin, P., Metcalf, A., Nicholas, M., Rahilly, K., & Swainston, N. (2012). *Participatory Design of evidence-based online youth mental health promotion, prevention early intervention and treatment.* Melbourne: Young and Well Cooperative Research Centre.

Hassenzahl, M., Burmester, M., & Koller, F. (2008). Der User Experience (UX) auf der Spur: Zum Einsatz von attrakdiff.de. In H. Brau, S. Diefenbach, M. Hassenzahl, F. Koller, M. Peissner, & K. Röse (Eds.), *Usability Professionals 2008* (pp. 78–82). Stuttgart, Germany: German Chapter der Usability Professionals Association.

Huang, Y.-T. (2015). Participatory Design to Enhance ICT Learning and Community Attachment: A Case Study in Rural Taiwan. *Future Internet*, *7*(1), 50–66. doi:10.3390/fi7010050

Hussy, W., Schreier, M., & Echterhoff, G. (Eds.). (2013). *Forschungsmethoden in Psychologie und Sozialwissenschaften für Bachelor* (2nd ed.). Berlin: Springer. doi:10.1007/978-3-642-34362-9

Jetter, H.-C., & Gerken, J. (2007). A Simplified Model of User Experience for Practical Application. In *Proceeding of 2nd COST294-MAUSE International Open Workshop* (pp. 106-111). Oslo, Norway: Academic Press.

Kerres, M. (2016). E-Learning vs. Digitalisierung der Bildung: Neues Label oder neues Paradigma? In A. Hohenstein & K. Wilbers (Eds.), *Handbuch E-Learning (61. Ergänzungslieferung)*. Köln, Germany: Fachverlag Deutscher Wirtschaftsdienst.

Klemme, B., & Siegmann, G. (Eds.). (2006). *Clinical Reasoning. Therapeutische Denkprozesse lernen.* Stuttgart: Georg Thieme Verlag.

Korucu, A. T., & Alkan, A. (2011). Differences in m-learning (mobile learning) and e-learning, basic terminology and usage of m-learning in education. *Procedia: Social and Behavioral Sciences, 15*, 1925–1930. doi:10.1016/j.sbspro.2011.04.029

Law, E. L.-C., Roto, V., Hassenzahl, M. Vermeeren, A. P. O. S., & Kort, J. (2009). Understanding, Scoping and Defining User eXperience: A Survey Approach. In *Proceedings of the 27th International Conference on Human Factors in Computing Systems, CHI 2009* (pp. 719-728). Boston, MA: Association for Computing Machinery (ACM). 10.1145/1518701.1518813

Liang, C., Chou, W.-S., Hsu, Y.-L., & Yang, C.-C. (2009). A User-Centered Design Approach to Develop a Web-Based Instructional Resource System for Homeland Education. *Knowledge Management & E-Learning: An International Journal, 1*(1), 67–80.

Mayring, P. (2000). Qualitative Content Analysis. *Forum Qualitative Social Research, 2*(1). Retrieved from http://www.qualitative-research.net/index.php/fqs/article/view/1089/2385

Ngampornchai, A., & Adams, J. (2016). Students' acceptance and readiness for E-learning in Northeastern Thailand. *International Journal of Educational Technology in Higher Education, 13*(34). doi:10.118641239-016-0034-x

Pârgaru, I., Gherghina, R., & Duca, I. (2009). The role of education in the knowledge-based society during the economic crisis. *Annales Universitatis Apulensis Series Oeconomica, 11*(2), 646–651.

Pechuel, R., & Beutner, M. (2013). Task based authentic Serious Game in vocational and further education and the PVEC – Paderborn Vocational Education Concept for e-learning: The Copy Job – A Bid Comparison of Suppliers. *Proceedings of E-Learn: World Conference on E-Learning in Corporate, Government, Healthcare, and Higher Education, 2013*, 931–939.

Rana, H., Singh, R., & Lal, M. (2014). E-learning: Issues and Challenges. *International Journal of Computers and Applications, 97*(5), 20–24. doi:10.5120/17004-7154

Robertson, T., & Simonsen, J. (2013). Participatory Design: an introduction. In J. Simonsen & T. Robertson (Eds.), *Routledge international handbook of participatory design* (pp. 1–18). New York, NY: Routledge.

Santa-Rosa, J. G. (2012). Participatory design in the project of virtual learning environments of histology. *Work (Reading, Mass.), 41*(Suppl. 1), 1157–1159. doi:10.3233/WOR-2012-0296-1157 PMID:22316875

Scheele, B., & Groeben, N. (1988). *Dialog-Konsens-Methoden zur Rekonstruktion Subjektiver Theorien: die Heidelberger Struktur-Lege-Technik (SLT), konsensuale Ziel-Mittel-Argumentation und kommunikative Flußdiagramm-Beschreibungen von Handlungen*. Tübingen, Germany: Francke.

Scheele, B., & Groeben, N. (2017). *Dialog-Konsens-Methodik*. Retrieved June 6, 2017, from https://portal.hogrefe.com/dorsch/dialog-konsens-methodik/

Schrader, P. G., & McCreery, M. (2012). Are All Games the Same? In D. Ifenthaler, D. Eseryel, & X. Ge (Eds.), *Assessment in game-based learning. Foundations, innovations, and perspectives* (pp. 11–28). New York: Springer. doi:10.1007/978-1-4614-3546-4_2

Spinuzzi, C. (2005). The Methodology of Participatory Design. *Technical Communication (Washington), 52*(2), 163–174.

Teine, M., & Beutner, M. (2016). Conceptualizing an M-Learning System for Seniors. In *Proceedings of the 12 International Conference on Mobile Learning 2016* (pp. 85-88). Academic Press.

Vali, I. (2013). The role of education in the knowledge-based society. *Procedia Social and Behavioral Sciences, 76*, 388-392. doi: 101016/j.sbspro.2013.04.133

Valtolina, S., Barricelli, B. R., Mesiti, M., & Ribaudo, M. (2012). User-Centered Design of E-Learning Tools for Users with Special Needs: The VisualPedia Case Study. *Interaction Design and Architecture(s). Journal, 13-14*, 47–55.

Witzel, A. (2000). The Problem-Centered Interview. *Forum Qualitative Social Research, 1*(1). Retrieved from http://www.qualitative-research.net/index.php/fqs/article/viewArticle/1132/2521

Yip, J. (2017). Participatory Design. In A. A. Carr-Chellman & G. Rowland (Eds.), *Issues in Technology, Learning, and Instructional Design. Classic and contemporary dialogues* (pp. 202–209). New York: Routledge.

KEY TERMS AND DEFINITIONS

Digital Learning: Derives from the term of e-learning, and refers to the digital pervasion of learning and education as a whole.

Participatory Design: Research-based design methodology with a democracy-ruled design and development process as its core.

Problem-Centered Interview: Interview technique that has a primarily theory-generating character, not following a rigid structure but main principles that allow adaptation to the research objective.

Prototyping: Iterative design and development of a product until it matches the end users' needs or a predefined quality.

Qualitative Content Analysis: Research data analysis technique, following a structured approach, aiming to categorize findings.

User Experience: Quality attribute of a product, as it refers to a product user's affections before, during, and after its use.

User-Centered Design: Design and development process that focuses on the end user's needs rather than formal descriptions of tasks or routines, heavily relying on iteration and evaluation.

Chapter 3
Open Source Online Learning in Rural Communities

Gary L. Ackerman
Windsor (Vermont) School, USA

ABSTRACT

Anyone is free to use open source software without the need to purchase the right to install it. Despite its appeal to school and technology leaders in rural communities, they are less likely to install it than others. In this chapter, three cases in which open source technology was installed to support teaching and learning in three rural communities are described. In each, the systems were deployed and refined using decision-making grounded in educational design research. The projects are detailed, and the method of technology planning is assessed. Unanswered questions are also addressed.

INTRODUCTION

Educational communities face many challenges as they seek to prepare students for the technology-rich future in which they will live and work. Educators must create curriculum that reflects rapidly changing content expectations (Dede, 2010; Susskind & Susskind, 2015) and that reflects emerging and incompletely understood economic, political, and cultural norms (Miller, 2011; Wokurka, Banschbach, Houlder, & Jolly, 2017). In addition, school leaders must support teachers as they create classrooms that reflect new discoveries from the learning sciences (Benassi, Overson, & Hakala, 2014; Sawyer, 2008). All of these changes can be traced, at least in part, to rapidly evolving information and computer technology and its effects on the creation and dissemination of information (Benkler, 2006). For rural communities, these challenges are exacerbated by several factors (Beeson, 2001). Rural schools tend to be smaller, thus they lack the economy of scale that can provide greater resources for larger populations (Tholkes & Sederberg, 1990). Because they are more widely dispersed, travel time between rural schools can limit the responsiveness of professionals who are shared among multiple sites. Because they serve small populations, rural educators frequently teach outside their area of specialty (Miller, 2012).

Advocates suggest the technology used to deliver online learning can be adapted to address many problems faced by educators and school leaders. For example, school leaders can use online learning to

DOI: 10.4018/978-1-5225-4206-3.ch003

expand opportunities for students (Dabrowski & Lodge, 2017), facilitate teachers' professional learning (Baran & Correia, 2014), and support authentic learning and assessment (Herrington, Reeves, & Oliver, 2006). Platforms for online learning are available from both proprietary publishers and from open source communities; open source platforms can be obtained and installed at no cost to the user. Ostensibly, open source tools will have wide appeal to school and technology leaders in rural communities because of the minimal costs. Despite this, there is evidence rural schools are less likely than suburban and urban schools to use open source tools to manage information and to promote learning (Kimmons, 2015). In this chapter, the author describes three projects in which open source distance learning technologies were applied to the professional needs of educators working in rural communities in the northeast United States; the planning and decision-making that focused the projects were grounded in educational design research (McKenny & Reeves, 2012).

Open Source Technology

A growing community produces open source software and open educational resources (OER) communities have grown and their products have begun to compete with and complement commercial products. They are also increasingly used in both K-12 and higher education. Baker (2017) suggested open resources are defined by dimensions of transparency and freedom, and these characteristics can be traced through the information products created by educators for many generations. Transparency is that characteristic of open resources that allows users to access and modify the original works; freedom is that characteristic that allows use of the products without the need to purchase or license the work. More importantly, however, freedom entails the rights to create and distribute derivative works.

The software used in these projects is published and licensed under the GNU General Public License (Free Software Foundation, 2016); the Apache License, Version 2.0 (Apache Software Foundation, 2017); or the Creative Commons Attribution-ShareAlike 3.0 Unported License (Creative Commons, n.d.). All of these licenses fit Baker's (2017) dimensions of transparency and freedom. In the cases described in this chapter, school and technology leaders obtained copies of open software, installed it per the conditions of the license, and customized it using the options available in the software. In no case did the author or any other individuals involved with the projects vary the source code of the software or create derived works.

Educational Design Research

This chapter describes both the software used to support virtual teaching and learning as well as the planning decisions and processes that led to changes in the ways the technology was configured and used. In these cases, the school and technology leaders followed a multi-step process grounded in educational design research (McKenny & Reeves, 2012) Educational design research is a variety of user-based research (Stokes, 1987) in which researcher-practitioners seek to simultaneously understand phenomena and to design interventions that meet human needs. McKenny and Reeves (2014) described educational design research as "the iterative development of solutions… to practical and complex educational problems" which leads to "new knowledge that can inform the work of others" (p. 133). The iterative processes are undertaken for three distinct phases (see Figure 1), and each phase finds researcher-practitioners consuming (or creating) literature for the wider community and also reconciling the literature with the local circumstances.

Figure 1. Phases of educational design research
Adapted from McKenny & Reeves (2012).

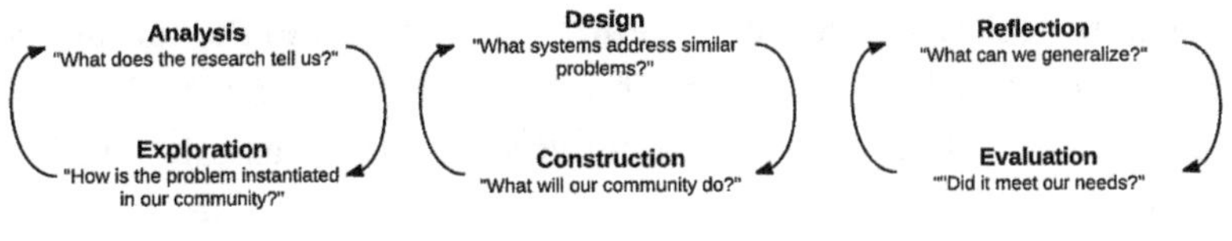

Analysis/ exploration comprises both literature review and deconstructing local situation to clarify the problem and identify relevant factors that are unique to local the instantiation; this work leads to deeper understanding of the problem. The product that emerges from this phase is a description of the problem and the nature of the anticipated solution. Design/ construction includes the development of interventions; existing technology and practices become the basis for the initial designs and further iterations improve them according to the local circumstances. Evaluation/ reflection finds researcher-practitioners both determining the degree to which the intervention met local needs and articulating new knowledge that can be applied to other problems and that can be used by other researcher-practitioners.

PURPOSES

Qualitative data are provided for two purposes. The first is to illustrate the iterative analysis/ exploration and design/ construction phases of educational design research (McKenny & Reeves, 2012) and to describe how the process influenced planning decisions and outcomes. The second is to articulate several generalizations about the practice of using open source online learning platforms in rural schools that appear to be supported by this data.

METHODS

As part of the author's duties as either an internal or external consultant, he facilitated projects to use open source online learning technologies in six schools between 2013 and 2015; planning and decision making followed the generic model of educational design research (McKenny & Reeves, 2012). During analysis/ exploration, the author engaged school leaders in a two-part semi-structured interview (Drever, 2006) held in a single session; the interview was focused by the prompts, "tell me about the situation you seek to improve" and "tell me what you want students and teachers to experience." The author summarized these into a problem statement and a statement of anticipated outcomes; these were revised with the leader or leaders until they were satisfied it accurately summarized the situation. These statements gave direction to the groups convened to begin design/ construction of interventions to solve the problem.

Once the leader deemed the problem was sufficiently understood and the expected outcomes accurately defined; other professionals (including licensed and non-licensed teachers and educational technology professionals) engaged with the author to develop an initial intervention. From the beginning, it was made clear to those involved with design/ construction that the work would be iterative so the interventions would be redesigned and reconstructed based on observations made and feedback gathered during the process. Participants understood also they would keep journals that would be used as data to research the projects.

The primary role of the author in the design/ construction phase was investigating open source solutions that appeared to solve the identified problem and that were compatible with extant information technology systems. In some cases, the author installed and configured the initial open source solution, then provided training while it was first deployed. The author also provided technical advice and support for expanding the open source solutions and refining configurations as the iterative phases of design/ construction proceeded.

In 2016, the author contacted the schools in which these interventions had been deployed. In three cases, the leaders who initiated the projects were still employed and the project was still active. In those three cases, transcripts and summaries of the original exploration/ analysis interviews with leaders, agendas and minutes from planning meetings, and journals kept by participants during the design/ construction phase were reviewed to describe the work. These descriptions were composed by reviewing minutes that recorded meetings to identify decisions that were made, then analyzing participants' research journals and other documents to describe the situations that led to the decisions. Finally, the leaders reviewed the descriptions and marked any sections they identified as potentially inaccurate; those were rewritten after the leader and the author reviewed and agreed on the meaning of the original documents.

The leaders who initiated the three cases described in this chapter were also interviewed in 2016. These two-part interviews were conducted via video conference; each was scheduled for thirty minutes and the two sessions separated by about one week. The first session was focused on the degree to which the project had solved the original problem and the second focused on generalizations about the process and project. In addition, a school leader who initiated a fourth project, which had been abandoned, was interviewed. Transcripts of these interviews were analyzed using the constant comparative method (Glaser, 1965); the author and another researcher who was enrolled in a graduate level education research course at the time coded the transcripts. The themes that were common to both reviewers are elucidated in the findings.

THE PROJECTS

The three projects described in this chapter were undertaken by school leaders and professionals working in public schools located in rural areas of New England. The schools are all members of larger organizations that provide a similar range of clerical and administrative support, including technology support, to member schools. In this chapter these organizations will be called "alliances," and schools in the same organization will be "allied" schools. One case occurred in a single school with no alliance to other schools in the study; one case included several allied schools, and the third case comprises data from two different communities of allied schools that deployed similar solutions and that found professionals from non-allied schools collaborating.

Replacing and Expanding a Learning Management System

Northern Middle and High School enrolls approximately 300 students in grades seven through 12. Most students who attend Northern attend one of two allied elementary schools. Three years prior to the initiation of this project, Northern had begun a one-to-one initiative, so it was undertaken in the first year that each student in the high school grades (nine through 12) had access to a laptop computer.

Coincident with the beginning the one-to-one initiative, teachers started using a proprietary learning management system (LMS). The version of the LMS used by the school was free to use, but had limited functions; it was not transparent, thus is was not open source (Baker, 2017). The principal articulated the coincident goals of the LMS and one-to-one initiatives, "with the one-to-one computers, teachers will use [the LMS] post materials so we can replace textbooks. They can lead discussions and share files for creative purposes, and move towards online materials and collaboration." He recognized, however, this had not been realized. The LMS had been adopted by about half of the faculty, but it served primarily as a digital drop box for and a file repository. The principal recorded a conversation during which "students said their online classroom was 'like a big filing cabinet for handouts' and they usually printed files from the site or they uploaded files the teacher printed out to grade." The principal further pointed to questions posed when broken copier which also served as a scanner broke; teachers asked, "How are we supposed to get out handouts online if we can't scan them?" For the principal, the LMS should, "be a space where students and teachers interact and collaborate, but this is not happening." It was clear the LMS was being used, but not in the intended manner.

It was not clear from the documents available if the limited use of the LMS by teachers was the result of the limited functionality of the version they were using or if the functions were available, but unused. The decision to replace the free version of the propriety LMS was motivated the discovery that an online classroom had become corrupted and work was lost. Because they were using the free version of the LMS, there was neither a backup copy of the course nor was the school entitled to technology support from the provider. After that incident the principal reported, "we need a more professional system so this does not happen again." In replacing the LMS, the principal insisted "it be flexible so teachers can do more things with students online, plus they need to be able to share assessment rubrics with others, and we need backups to prevent loss of work." It was clear the cost of subscribing to the proprietary LMS at the level necessary for support and flexibility was beyond the budget, so the principal accepted the recommendation that and open source solution be deployed.

A design/ construction committee comprising two teachers who had been using the proprietary LMS, the technology coordinator for the allied schools, and the author was convened to recommend a replacement LMS. At the first meeting, the technology coordinator resigned from the group reasoning, "I have no time, budget, or server resources to dedicate to this project, and other projects need my attention this year." He did recommend to the group, "Get a web hosting service that meets the system requirements, install the LMS you want, and have teachers manage it all." The reduced committee advised the principal to purchase space on a virtual private server (VPS) with storage, bandwidth, and processing that exceeded the estimated need and that fell within the budget identified by the principal. The committee also

reviewed the features of several open source learning management systems. The demonstration sites all appeared to provide the features we want and could be installed on the VPS service we recommend. The committee suggests we install Moodle, because the three people on the committee all have experience using it.

Within one week, the principal had secured space on a virtual private server, and the author had installed Moodle (Version 2.7) (Moodle, 2014), an open source learning management system that is widely used in both K-12 and higher education, and configured the database. As an initial test, committee members confirmed: a) the Moodle site was available from the school's network, b) it was available off-campus, c) teachers could create courses, d) several users could administer the site. Once the initial test was successful, the two teachers on the design/ construction committee began using Moodle with their students. Within days of learning it was available, three teachers (who were still using the proprietary LMS) requested access to Moodle. This was granted, so the test installation and the committee participating in its development quickly expanded.

The design/ construction committee now comprised five teachers, and they recorded observations of Moodle before reconvening to "discuss changes to Moodle before extending the pilot project any further." The first recommendations focused on navigation and appearance. The teachers reported that students complained about the appearance of the site and found it "hard to use," but those complaints dissipated as students became familiar with the interface. One teacher observed, "I can't see the menus without scrolling and I can't see the names of students who posted in the discussions" The committee was able to resolve the navigation problems by changing the theme which controlled the appearance of the site (including the behaviors of menus and discussion boards).

The committee also recognized Moodle allowed more sophisticated grading than the replaced propriety LMS. While teachers wanted to use those features, they felt unprepared, so they shared a word processing document on which they recorded the steps to filter submissions, display a single individual's assignments, update grades for multiple students at once, and otherwise manage grades. One teacher also described a feature she had used at another school that allowed teachers to add comments to portable document format (PDF) files that students had uploaded. The plugin that added the PDF mark-up functionality was located and the author installed and configured it.

Less than one month after the initial test of Moodle, the first redesign/ reconstruction iteration was complete. By deploying a different theme, the committee improved navigation of Moodle for all users within minutes by editing the settings that were provided by the producers. Using advanced grading features was developed over several days and included both the deployment of a new plugin (a technology solution) and effort by teachers to share new learning (a non-technology solution).

About four months into the project, it had expanded to a total of eight teachers and over 100 students who were enrolled in more than 20 sections. It was nearing the end of the school year, so the principal asked for recommended next steps. The teachers described the minor changes that had been made to the installation of Moodle during the first iteration. When asked directly about the original goals of using more advanced features of the LMS, the teachers shared examples of threaded discussions, embedded media, and examples of PDF assignments with comments; none of which had been used on the replaced LMS. Convinced it was used for more types of activities than the previous LMS, the principal charged the committee with "rolling this out so the whole school can use Moodle when we return to school at the end of summer."

Meeting minutes indicated the committee members were satisfied the functionality of Moodle met the previous uses of the LMS (a drop box and a collection of shared files) and advanced features were sufficiently understood and supportable that the Moodle could be "promoted to teachers as the 'new and improved' online platform." The committee noted, however, "students have too many usernames and passwords—the network, their email, the student information system, and now Moodle", so it recommended, "a single sign-on is necessary so students do not have to remember another username and password, and teachers don't have to know how to reset them." It further recommended, "allowing self-enrolling in Moodle courses, so teachers don't have to 'do all of that clicking' to get students in their courses."

Both of those recommendations were incorporated into the next design/ construction iteration. Another plugin was added to Moodle to allow users to log on using their Google Applications for Education accounts, which were already used for other purposes by both teachers and students. To address security concerns, only accounts controlled by Northern Middle and High School were allowed to be used to log on to Northern's installation of Moodle. The configuration of Moodle was also changed to allow authenticated users to self-enroll in courses; when teachers returned for the start of school, they were given directions on how to utilize this feature.

At the same time the LMS replacement was underway, the faculty was undertaking a separate initiative to add authentic learning (Herrington, Oliver, & Reeves, 2013) into the curriculum. Associated with that initiative was the decision to replace the existing electronic portfolio platform. A group of faculty who were working on the authentic learning initiative met with the Moodle committee. The first meeting of this combined committee found the team returning to the explore/ analyze phase of educational design research. The combined committee articulated the goal of "designing a single online space where students' work could flow easily between the online classroom and the online portfolio."

During the initial design/ construction iteration, the team identified Mahara (Mahara, n.d.) as an open source portfolio platform that that could be installed on the same virtual private server use to host Moodle. Once the system was installed and configured, the combined committee spent time "sandboxing, so the teachers can determine it Mahara fits the assessment and data collection needs of the authentic learning initiative." After they concluded Mahara provided the necessary portfolio functions, the combined committee directed the author to configure Mahara so that students and teachers could use their Moodle accounts, which were actually users' GAFE accounts, to authenticate into Mahara. This configuration also allowed for documents and portfolios to be shared between the two platforms.

Northern Middle and High School's full development of the Moodle/ Mahara system began with an initial decision to replace the proprietary LMS, this decision was made to improve the performance of the technology and to provide more flexible teaching and learning. Several iterations of design/ construction based on users' feedback made the LMS easier to use and expanded its functionality while easing management. Further design/ construction iterations resulted in the LMS and the electronic portfolio system being integrated so that they appeared to be a single system. In each step, the combined Moodle/ Mahara complex more closely reflected the teaching and learning goals the principal had originally articulated.

Algebra 1 at a Distance

Dan is the principal at Crossroads Elementary School which enrolls just over 100 students in grades K-8. More than half of the students who attend the school live in the village that extends about one mile in each direction from the intersection where the school is situated. Most of the other students live on the farms that are scattered throughout the town. He recognized, "the community takes great pride in nurturing young people and providing excellent opportunities, but the tightening budget and some personnel changes have made continuing that tradition very challenging."

One particular problem was providing Algebra 1 for the students who were ready to take that course for high school credit. Dan explained the process recently adopted by the allied high school, "students can take Algebra 1 in their home school, but they take the same final exam as the high school students. If they pass, they get credit, if not they take it again." In the letter that explained the new policy, the principal of the allied high school and the chairperson of the mathematics department had explained, "we need more control over who enrolls in advanced mathematics courses."

Dan further described the situation in which he found his faculty, "We have one science and math teacher for our middle school. Her schedule was full and we had three kids who were ready for Algebra, but we had no teacher." When Dan learned an allied K-8 schools had hired a new part-time math teacher who was very experienced, he contacted the principal and asked how his students might be able to access that teacher. With the cooperation of the curriculum coordinator who was shared among the allied K-8 schools and the high school, Dan arranged for the schools to teach eighth grade math at a time that coincided with the Algebra 1 class taught by the new math instructor. At Crossroads Elementary, the instructional problem was summarized as, "Providing Crossroads students access to a highly qualified Algebra teacher who teaches at a location other than our school," and the "instruction is to be synchronous."

The first solution to having remote students participate in the Algebra 1 course was to set up a web camera in the classroom where the teacher was and to use a free, but proprietary, video chat tool to connect the teacher with students at Crossroads and the other schools. It was clear during the first session, however, it was not an adequate solution. Dan observed the first session and noted, "all of the students agree they cannot see the board well enough and there is little chance for them to ask questions. Plus, the teacher had his back to the students much of the time." The technology integration specialist employed by the allied K-8 schools observed the session from a different remote site and confirmed students at that site had the same experience. Dan noted, "this solution will not work for our students. We need another way for kids to work with [the Algebra teacher]." The initial design/ construction iteration in this case was deemed a failure; so it was immediately abandoned.

Dan convened a group (the composition of which is unclear) to reopen the analysis/ understanding of the problem of, especially to reexamine the need for Algebra to be taught via synchronous meetings. That group asked the author and the technology integration specialist to "test other technology systems that will resolve the connections between the teacher and the remote sites, specifically: a) unclear transmission of visuals, b) unclear transmission of spoken information, and c) lack of two-way communication between the remote sites to the location of the teacher." It was proposed that sites be connected through a video conferencing tool rather than simply a camera, and the author and the technology integration specialist suggested, "screen sharing, an open audio channel between the sites, and reliable chat between the sites will improve interaction."

The next iteration of the design/ construction of the video conferencing link connecting the K-8 schools found a group of people at each location for a "test activity in which we will try to replicate an Algebra lesson, but with a focus on refining the system rather than learning math." At each site, one of the students taking the Algebra course, along with the school's principal, connected to a video conference that was initiated by the Algebra teacher from his school. The technology integration specialist was at the site with the teacher and the author was at Crossroads. The connection was established using a free to use version of a proprietary video conferencing platform. Further, the remote Algebra teacher had constructed a system whereby a digital camera pointed at the whiteboard where he wrote.

Upon completion of the trial, Dan and the student at his school concurred, "this is a much better system. We could see and hear what was said and written and we could ask questions by both chat and speaking." The individuals who participated at all of the sites further concurred that several practices needed to become standard for the course, including "a) sites need to mute their microphones unless they are speaking, b) the teacher needs to watch for chat requests, and c) there needs to be a seamless method for switching between the white board camera and the camera on the computer." While the video conferencing platform was deemed an improvement over the web camera, the arrangement of the digital camera and whiteboard was determined to need further improvement before the system was used for teaching and the limits placed on users of the freemium software were deemed to pose a significant obstacle to its effective use. Prior to using the system to teach Algebra again, the author and the technology integration specialist along with the teacher completed a second design/ construction phase in which two changes were implemented.

First, the team (in collaboration with the technology coordinator employed by the allied school) deployed Jitsi (n.d.), an open source video conferencing platform. Tests of this platform determined it appeared to resolve the video, audio, and interaction problems that prompted the decision to abandon the original web camera solution. Second, the video transmission of the visuals drawn on the whiteboard were improved by devising a method whereby a camera was poised over a whiteboard on a table where the teacher wrote and drew. The method of viewing the whiteboard through the video conference was even adopted by the students in the room where the teacher taught, so they would connect to the same video conference and watch the same whiteboard presentations as the students at the remote sites. The teacher also reported the students in the classroom with him began using the same chat channels to interact as the remote students, as well.

Unlike the case of Northern Middle and High School, in which the feedback that led to design/ construction decisions were largely informed by students and teachers who were actively using the systems for their work and which took place over weeks, Crossroads and its allied schools made decisions based on small groups of users who tested the system prior to its being deployed again. Dan noted, "the web camera thing was terrible, we needed to fix all of it before we tried it again." In the notes he kept as the system was used in the following months, Dan further noted, "as the teacher got better at using it, the lessons seemed to flow much better and students and got better at asking questions using the chat feature."

Two unpredicted outcomes arose from this project. First, the chairperson of mathematics department at the allied high school attended some distance Algebra classes by connecting to the video conference, so it had more oversight by the high school mathematics department than had been reasonable previously. She noted, "We did not want to be intrusive, but we wanted to be sure student were getting what they needed because we were essentially giving credit for what happened in those schools. It worked well, and we even had some of our students participate in some of the sessions." Second, the teacher began recording parts of the sessions and those became a resource for several purposes including a collection of worked examples and posted them for students and parents to use as a reference during homework and they became a focus of professional development for the mathematics teachers at the high school.

Supporting New Teaching via Online Classrooms

Peter is the assistant superintendent for an alliance of six schools that extends "more than 25 miles from end to end," and Joan is a part-time technology coordinator working in an adjoining alliance of four schools including three small elementary schools. In each of those jurisdictions, curriculum initiatives were underway. Peter was engaged in an initiative to increase problem-based learning in all grades, but especially in the secondary grades. Joan was engaged in an initiative to refresh technology-based teaching and learning to coincide with the arrival of new Chromebooks in the elementary schools. This project started when the two began to collaborate with the author to support teachers' learning.

Both Peter and Joan sought to include teacher-leaders to provide leadership to their peers. One of the teacher-leaders from Joan's schools described the problem and her motivation as "finding technology resources that are appropriate for my students, we have been inheriting old technology from the high school. Now, we get new stuff and we want to show what we can do." Joan explained that most of the computers in the district's elementary schools had been "hand-me-downs from the high school, but a new superintendent insisted the elementary students get better technology to use." A teacher-leader in Peter's high school said he had been motivated by "the excessive focus on standardized testing, and the need to give students the chance to dig deeper into our subjects." These two projects had similar goals as they both sought to support teachers who were developing previously untaught curricula and using unfamiliar methods and tools; the support was to include both access to instructional materials and collaborative development of teaching methods.

Peter's district had been using Moodle to provide online classrooms for students; Peter explained,

most of our teachers were at least familiar with Moodle and used it for at least some things. Middle school and elementary teachers less so than high school, and we wanted them to use it more, so we decided to start an online classroom dedicated to project-based learning and we enrolled all of the teachers in it.

Joan described her decision to follow a similar approach to Peter's, "when I heard what they were doing, I decided to steal the idea, and Peter's 'tech guy' was very helpful in helping me get Moodle up running much quicker than I could have because I am only part-time." For the teachers in Joan's schools, this would be the first and only use of Moodle in their professional lives; she noted, "when this was introduced at a faculty meeting, no one said they had used Moodle before. Some younger teachers have done some online courses in college, but it was very limited." The first iteration of the design/ construction phase concluded when Joan's schools had Moodle installed and teachers could access a classroom for teachers to "explore how the Chromebook can help you teach and share ideas."

Because Joan's teachers were using Chromebooks, many of the materials they shared on Moodle were links to web sites. One problem they soon encountered was reported in an email sent to one of the teachers-leaders; "the sites are great, but the list is getting too big and it is kind of disorganized. It takes too long to scroll through them and it would help if we could keep some notes on them, so we know how to find the ones we need." Teachers in Peter's schools encountered a similar problem. A teacher recorded, "We share good sites, like [an art museum's] online collection, but it would be more useful if we could see just the stuff we need for our classes." Joan and Peter identified "finding an easy method of organizing the materials on the Moodle site, so users can quickly find what they need" as a problem that needed to be resolved through design/ construction. Peter and Joan each assigned one teacher-leader to collaborate to find a solution. That pair of teacher-leaders met with the author to explore different options for categorizing or filtering materials in Moodle. The group prepared three different options; specifically, they demonstrated a) adding tags to items using that feature which is part of Moodle, b) organizing materials into folders, and c) organizing resources with a wiki. Screen recordings of each method were posted on the World Wide Web and teachers in both jurisdictions were invited to review the methods. One week later, the teacher-leaders hosted an afterschool meeting in two locations (one in each jurisdiction and connected via a video conference tool) at which teachers discussed the method they preferred.

In the report to Peter and Joan that followed that session, the teacher-leaders noted, "The teachers recommend tagging as the preferred method for organizing resources. The primary reason was the ease for teachers—they just type the words they want to use or they select from existing tags." In addition, the group had expressed concern over the potential of a teacher deleting items added by others. The teacher-leader from Peter's schools met with the technology coordinator who served those allied schools, and who had the greatest experience administering Moodle of anyone in the group, to discuss the concern about teachers editing or deleting items. The teacher-leader reported, "solutions were possible, but we concluded any changes were too much work to develop and test. Basically, we just need to be careful, and if [accidental deleting] becomes a problem, then we can worry about preventing it."

In the weeks after tagging was introduced as a strategy for organizing resources, the pair of teacher-leaders worked within their schools to ensure teachers knew how to tag; concurrently, they asked teachers to cull and tag the remaining resources. One of the teacher-leaders recorded, "Mrs. Smith was a teacher who was overwhelmed by the disorganized resources, but she is now using tags and is always reminding others to add tags. The site is much more useful to her now." Although there are no other data regarding teachers' perceptions of the process or the value it added to the collection in either jurisdiction, in October 2016 Joan and Peter tallied the 50 most recent additions to the Moodle site he or she manages and at least 45 on each had been tagged with at least one term.

As project-based learning was becoming a focus of teaching in his schools, Peter had led many in-person curriculum development workshops to introduce the method and to provide teachers with experience in preparing materials. As the initiative entered its third year (which was the first year that Moodle was introduced to support the work) teachers were becoming increasingly independent in the work and found others' input on their ideas helped, but the face-to-face sessions seemed less important. Peter observed, "teachers are impatient with the time to schedule face-to-face reviews, so they wanted to move that work online." Peter described how "teachers started a forum where they posted projects they were thinking about and they gave each other feedback and found connections between the projects in one subject areas and those in another."

Because Joan and Peter communicated frequently on this work, Joan decided to add forums to her installation of Moodle as well. Joan sent an email to teachers indicating she had added a "forum for questions and answers about how to use the Chromebooks in classrooms." About a month after the forum was added to Moodle, Joan noted there were fewer than five posts on the forums and none had responses. Peter observed a similar situation when his schools first deployed forums to Moodle, "three of our teachers were absent from the forums. It turns out they were unsure of what to do. But after a tutoring session, they were participating along with the others." Using this as a cue, Joan decided to provide a brief in-person training session in how to use forums for teachers in her schools. Immediately afterwards, she noted far greater participation in the forums, with teachers posting suggestions, asking questions, and answering others' questions.

In the case of online professional development in these two jurisdictions, several iterations of design/ construction led to an improved online environment for teaching and learning. The decision to adopt Moodle for professional development purposes by Joan and her school was largely informed by the similar decision made by Peter and the collaborative relationship Joan and Peter had established. In the same way improvements to the LMS at Northern Middle and High School were made in response to feedback from individuals who were actively using the system, Joan and Peter convened groups to design/ construct solutions in response to the feedback from active users. Using that feedback to identify deficiencies in the configuration or the manner of professionals' use of the system, decisions were made and improvements were deployed.

FINDINGS

This final phase of educational design research (McKenny & Reeves, 2012) is evaluation/ reflection. This finds researcher-practitioners evaluating the work to determine if the intended outcomes were realized and also to articulate generalizations that can inform their further work in the field, that can be applied by others in other settings, or that can be applied to different problems. The data from these cases support generalizations with regard to the use of educational design research as a strategy to inform planning decisions and also the application of open course technologies to the support of teaching and learning in rural schools.

Educational Design Research as Technology Planning

Educational design research (McKenny & Reeves, 2012) is simultaneously a research methodology and a method for designing interventions. In the semi-structured interviews conducted with the school leaders who initiated these projects that were conducted in 2016, the leaders where asked about educational design research as a method of designing interventions. In each case, the leaders differentiated these planning processes from those they typically employed. They identified these as more satisfactory than others and described specific aspects of educational design research that appeared to contribute to the value of the interventions. There is evidence the improvement are grounded in the iterative nature of the process and in the clearly defined roles of different individuals in the process.

Understanding Improvement

Researchers adopt an objective stance towards the measurements they make and the data they analyze and interpret; through objective analysis, they seek to use evidence to support and elucidate theories that accurately predict and explain observations. In contrast, designers of interventions adopt a subjective stance towards data; designers seek to achieve outcomes that are defined by the designers or others, and data is interpreted to ascertain the degree to which the outcomes were achieved. While there appears to be a contradiction in these two approaches to data and evidence, there is a tradition of applying research methods, including sophisticated data collection and analysis procedures, to the design of interventions.

Bereiter (2002) described progressive discourse as a planning method that is simultaneously grounded in a research and intended to improve conditions. For Bereiter, progressive discourse depends on a shared understanding of activity that will constitute the intended outcome (simply agreeing on language is insufficient), and interventions are defined and refined so that what is observed more closely resembles what the planners want to observe. Like progressive discourse, educational design research (McKenny & Reeves, 2012) is intended to be iterative and improving; planners deploy an intervention, observe its effect, then refine and redeploy it so that its performance improves according to the designers' perceptions.

Dan, the principal who initiated the Algebra at a distance project, contrasted the planning he was taught as a graduate student to the planning he experienced in this project. "I was taught planning was a step-by-step process. Once you have a goal, you plan to meet it, then decide if you met it. It is step at a time and slow," but he observed in this project "we failed at first, we quickly went back to much quicker planning than I am used to." Dan further described how the iterative processes were connected, and the first failure helped to revise his understanding.

I knew we wanted 'a good way to have our students take the class, but I didn't really know what that meant... I thought I did... but it wasn't until I saw how bad our first solution was that I could break it into the parts.

For Dan, the lens of the failure was essential to defining improvement, "Once I saw the bad images on the screen, I knew what we needed to improve."

It became immediately clear to Dan what would constitute improvement, but for other leaders, the improvements were less obvious at first. The principal at Northern admitted the problem was originally unclear in his school; "using online courses to replace textbooks and the authentic learning stuff we were doing were both good ideas—teachers were on board the community was too—but we really didn't know what it was going to look like." Because the initiatives were unfamiliar to most faculty, there was little agreement about the technology capacity and functionality necessary. "For us," he said, "we moved from non-technology to technology," and he clarified that with the example of electronic portfolios,

we talked about what we did [previously] and what we wanted to do with portfolios to document learning, then we looked to the tech people who were on the committee to build it. Our work then became better organized as we followed the procedures for using the technology.

In Northern Middle and High School, the activity of compiling portfolios to document students' authentic learning was improved by the process of designing a technology solution for that work; specific improvements included more teachers documenting more work than had been done previously.

Iterations

The iterative nature of planning the followed educational design research (McKenny & Reeves, 2012) also changed the approach to planning experienced by these school leaders. The principal at Northern described how iterations were essential to the progress and improvements that he observed as the proprietary LMS was replaced and as the open source LMS was configured to provide better service. He noted, "Our school had a long history of making technology decisions, but then never revisiting them. The response from the technology coordinator was always, 'I built what you asked for, it is your problem you didn't ask for the right thing.'" The principal described a sense of relief when that technology coordinator removed himself from the LMS planning process, "the committee had permission to keep working and keep fixing until it was right which is important in education, because you can't always know what you will need until you are using it with students."

For Peter, also, the explicit nature of planning that followed educational design research led to iterative and continuous planning. "Too often, we try to change things all at once in education and that can be uncomfortable for teachers," Peter said. He contrasted that with how the Moodle classrooms had been refined in his schools. "We started with one step, and when it got to where it wasn't working the question we asked was, 'how do we improve what we have?' rather than 'what do we replace [Moodle] with?'" Joan concurred with the view of the manner in which Moodle was implemented and she described the approach as "a slow process, but it never restarted. Once teachers were comfortable, we took the next step. It is unusual to improve professional development slowly with each step 'a step up' from where we were."

The Need for Expertise

The open source technology solutions deployed in these cases were all designed to improve the use of technology for teaching and learning. Educational technology is a multidimensional aspect of school planning and it requires expertise in multiple areas to be effectively deployed. In each of these cases, technical expertise was needed to identify and initially evaluate then install and configure open source software. Much of the feedback that informed the iterative design/ construction cycles originated in observations and criticisms from teachers or others who lacked the technical expertise to reconfigure the technology, but whose experience using it was deeply connected to how it was configured. In these cases, effective open source solutions resulted from systems that were properly configured by those with technical expertise and appropriately configured to reflect the needs of teachers and learners.

The lack of sufficient technical expertise appears to be an impediment to the improvements that were illustrated in these cases. The one principal who was interviewed, but who abandoned the project she had initiated fewer than 18 months previously noted, "we used Moodle for curriculum development work and it was great. Our part-time technology person made some changes to it, but something went wrong. He found a full-time job, and he wasn't able to fix it before leaving." She did contrast managing content and courses with configuring Moodle; "we had a teacher who had been doing lots with Moodle try to fix the problems but there was a setting that he could not figure out, so we switched our work over to Google Drive so we could get better technology support." For that principal, access was limited by the expertise necessary to perform the duties; she was unable to secure an individual with the necessary knowledge given the time and salary limits of her budget.

Access to technology expertise is also a challenge to Joan's initiative, but the access appears to have been in time, not knowledge. She observed,

Working with [the technology coordinator from Peter's schools], I have learned how to manage Moodle. It was not much different from the work I have done for years as a web master for schools, but I just don't have the time to tend to problems in a timely manner.

These data also appear to confirm the need for greater levels of technological expertise in communities using open source tools compared to those using proprietary tools (Kimmons, 2015). Budgets limit the level of expertise that can be hired in some rural communities; while in others, individuals with sufficient expertise have other duties or reduced schedules which limit the degree to which their expertise can be used.

Collaboration Among Experts

Stefaniak (2015) noted the tendency to perceive educational technology to be primarily technical in nature, so projects and improvements are assigned to technical experts. Once technologists assume responsibility for a project, there tends to be a sharp boundary separating educators from technologists who receive little oversight from school leaders. This can contribute to a challenging situation in schools where the individual with the greatest expertise in implementing technology changes are the individuals with least experience using it with students, so the systems they build or the changes they make can pose an obstacle to students' use of technology. Wegner, White, and Smith (2009) observed the most effective technology leaders are often those whose experience is based in the operation of the organization. As was demonstrated in these cases, effective technology was designed only with the input of both educators and technologists.

When the faculty in Peter and Joan's schools identified the need to organize resources on the LMS, a small number of teachers with greater than usual technical skill collaborated with the author (who served as a technology expert) to develop three potential solutions. After the potential solutions had been tested, they were presented to the full faculty to make the final decision. In this way, there was a division of labor that led to improvement, but the division was collaborative as the final decision was made by the teachers and it was further refined following their feedback. The committee that met to develop those options was charged with "bring to the committee multiple methods of organizing the things teachers add to the site, so the teachers can agree on the one that seems best." Peter recorded, "the resulting collaboration worked—people with tech expertise built [the solutions], but the teachers selected the best one." These are examples of how collaboration between educators and technologists produced a solution that was both easy and effective for the teachers and easy to deploy for the technologists.

The principal at Northern recorded a similar observation early in the planning of the initial LMS project. "It is probably good that [the technology coordinator] is not on the team. He is known to build what we first say we want, but then to react badly when the plan changes." The principal compared the typical progress with technology projects with sharp divisions of labor to the work that led to the Moodle-Mahara system, "We needed both tech people and teachers to get this to work… and they needed to listen to each other and to change their thinking based on what the others were saying." At Northern, the iterative and collaborative nature of the planning allowed for an effective solution to be developed by excluding an individual who had avoided collaboration in the past; the principal noted, "when [the technology coordinator] resigned from the committee before it even met, his excuse was [a lie,] but it was good that he understood he would not do well on that team."

In these cases, the decision that led to new cycle of design/ construction decisions were informed by educators who sought to improve or expand the function of the technology systems. Technologists were largely responsible for configuring the systems to reflect the design/ construction decisions, then the solutions were evaluated by educators before they were deployed for all users. The role of the teacher-leaders whose recommendation led to organizing resources in the Moodle installations deployed by Peter and Joan via tagging explained, "School administrators left it to us, as long as it worked, they wanted 'hands-off.' We sat with [the author] to research options on the Moodle site, then configure them, but if teachers didn't like it, we would fix it."

Open Source Technology in Rural Communities

The projects undertaken for this study were designed to improve technology-rich teaching and learning in schools located in rural areas. Because the solutions made us of open source technologies, which are available at no cost to users, the findings regarding the successful development of the tools are of particular interest to educators in rural areas. The decision to use these tools is likely to alleviate some of the financial challenges faced by school and technology leaders in rural areas. Further, the nature of the technology use and the changes in educators' interaction with these tools indicate educators may become more sophisticated users of technology if they are deployed in a collaborative and iterative manner.

Technology Acceptance

Technology acceptance model (Davis, 1989) was first elucidated to identify the factors positively associated with the decision to use technology; it was later combined with eight other theories the predict technology use into the unified theory of acceptance and use of technology (UTAUT) (Venkatesh, Morris, Davis, & Davis, 2003). In general, technology acceptance predicts tools that are perceived to be easy to use (high effort expectance), effective (high performance expectancy), and that is used by others (high social expectancy) are more likely to be used than tools that do not demonstrate these characteristics.

Two decisions captured in this data support the observation that effort expectancy is influenced redesign decisions. In the case of Northern Middle and High School, the selection of Moodle (and then the subsequent decision to install Mahara) was motivated by the fact that the systems could be connected to students' existing accounts on the Google domain already managed by the school technologists and used daily by the students. The principal described his observations of students' work in classes using the replaced LMS, "before we rolled this system out, I watched teachers spend 20 minutes getting passwords reset because they forgot them, and it was a system not everyone used—in part because of the password problems." Although there is no evidence that his "20 minutes" assessment is accurate, it does capture effect that using a single-sign on exerted on increasing effort expectancy, thus improving the system.

Ease of use also contributed to expanded use project-based learning and other authentic learning activities at Northern. Some resistance from teachers to incorporating authentic assessments was that grounded in the perception that documenting it was too much work and it was done inconsistently by teachers. The principal described how authentic learning was documented prior to the Moodle-Mahara system,

we used to take pictures of projects, but some teachers put them on a server, others used [Google Drive,] and still others did who knows what. When we had students try to compile a portfolio, it was a mess trying to find everything they needed.

Dan described how ease of use affected the distance-based Algebra course at Crossroads Elementary School, as well.

One of the challenges we faced as the course progressed was testing. We started out scanning tests to the teacher, but that was a very slow process. The Algebra teacher worked with some of his former colleagues to learn how to use the free version of [a propriety learning management system] for online tests. It was much easier to have students just go take tests online, but we kept scanning the projects and more challenging problems he had them do.

The decision to recommend tagging as a means of organizing content in the LMS's provided for professional development in the schools led by Peter and Joan also supports the observation that perceived effort expectancy is associated with the intention to use technology. The primary decision to adopt tagging was made because it was going to be the easiest of the three options for the teachers, and Joan noted, "one of our teachers who was reluctant to use the site at first now introduces it to new teachers and she tells them all the time how easy it is to use."

A second factor associated with increased use of technology according to UTAUT (Venkatesh et al., 2003) is performance expectancy; that factor is grounded in several characteristics including job fit. The principal at Northern described a situation in which the technology influenced teachers' curriculum decisions in a manner that was perceived as improvement by school leaders. He observed "teachers can have students create portfolio pages, then hand them in on Moodle, so there seems to be a stronger connection between the projects in portfolios and the content of the courses." With the greater amount of authentic learning being compiled in the system, the principal observed, "we are taking it more seriously, and finally having conversations about broad learning expectations that go across all courses," and he also noted, "we seemed to be struggling with both authentic learning and using the online classrooms, but once both were built and connected, there has been increased use of each."

UTAUT (Venkatesh et al., 2003) further posits that use of technology is increased in those instances in which there are strong social influences. Specifically, one is more likely to use technology used by others whose opinions are valued. In these cases, this was illustrated in the active role of teacher-leaders in Norther Middle and High School and in Joan's and Peter's schools. When asked about the quick spread of the initial tests of Moodle in his school, the principal at Northern said,

looking back, that was important, the few teachers who started using Moodle were really mentors to others, and they just started sharing without me or anyone else telling them to. Others saw what they were doing and wanted to join the club.

Joan noted the importance of the teacher-leaders in the wide adoption of the Moodle site to support Chromebook-based teaching in her schools as well. "I knew I could not be the full time leader and principals were all too busy, so I thought carefully about the teachers who I asked to be leaders." Joan detailed the characteristics she wanted in the teacher-leaders, "They needed to be perceived as strong teachers, have technical skill, and be able to work with colleagues in a patient manner."

Teo (2011) observed, "teachers spend much of their planning time to consider how technology could be harnessed for effective lesson delivery and assessment" (p. 1). In these cases, there appears to be support for the conclusion that planning can be more efficacious and solutions perceived to be improving if they are designed to increase factors associated with technology acceptance.

Participatory Cultures

In 2009, Jenkins and his colleagues defined participatory cultures as those "with relatively low barriers to artistic expression and civic engagement, strong support for creating and sharing creations, and some type of informal mentorship whereby experienced participants pass along knowledge to novices" (p. xi). While Jenkins' participatory culture is largely understood to be a phenomenon of younger generations, scholars have identified an increasing expectation that users of digital information assume a more active role in creating and consuming information compared to those generations that experienced only print media and electronic mass media (Deuze, 2006). One of the defining characteristics of participatory cultures is the collaborative nature of the creative processes (Halverson, 2012). The interventions described in each of the cases in this chapter were produced by collaborative interactions among the professionals. All school leaders in the schools described this chapter played an active role in both initiating the projects and ensuring they were adequately supported. Their active support included scheduling time for professionals to meet, arranging for the purchase of necessary materials and technologies, and ensuring other professionals participated as appropriate. Teachers ensured that the interventions were tested under appropriate situations and they gave focused and informative feedback to those with technological expertise who configured and reconfigured the open source technology to provide necessary functions.

Two of the cases described in this chapter appear to have contributed to on-going consumption and creation of open educational resources by the teachers who were initially engaged in them. The Algebra 1 teacher who taught remotely for students at Crossroads became interested in other remote teaching. Dan explained the teacher originally wanted to put recordings of his lectures online but the teacher decided against that; "he saw there was plenty of other good lectures online already, so he shifted his focus." Dan noted as well the Algebra course has shifted "from a traditional course just taught via video conference to a problem solving course." The teacher has created a web site to show students how to work problems," and "the video conferences have become students talking about complex problems and sharing their own solutions." In addition, the students are "using some new tools to show off their own solutions." In effect, Dan noted, "we have transitioned away from using the technology to deliver the content to using the technology as a place where students explore the content."

In addition, Dan described how the experience with Algebra 1 motivated him, along with the principals of the allied schools, to explore the use of the distance learning infrastructure for other projects. "We had a virtual science fair before the actual science fair, [students] discussed their projects before we all got on a bus and took the displays boards to [an allied school]" and "teachers get students together to discuss books on Jitsi." At Crossroads and the allied schools, the distance learning activities tended to be for specific projects, and each teacher adopted the platforms for single projects rather than as the primary method of instruction. Dan noted, "last year students did maybe five or six distance learning activities in different units in different classes. Teachers have shared the load without overdoing it, but students use distance learning in many contexts."

The teachers in Peter's schools discovered that textbooks were a weak resource for the authentic learning projects they sought to include in the curriculum; textbooks often did not provide sufficient coverage to meet students' needs when they researched topics of their own interest. In response, two of the teacher-leaders in Peter's schools began to explore open educational resources (OER) and to include resources from several open providers in their classes. Peter noted, "one science and one English teacher have become leaders in our expanded use of open educational resources." Their participation in the OER communities has expanded as well. While presenting workshops for their colleagues these two teachers illustrated the similarities between our use of Moodle and their participation in the extended OER communities.

Peter further described what he had observed in these teachers' classrooms, "the students were writing their own materials to repost to the OER site." According to Peter, this project appeared to be engaging students on multiple levels. "Some students were double-checking their materials against the novel to make sure details were accurate, but other students were working as copy editors." Peter also recounted the conversation he had with the teacher after the lesson, "he told me that students had become heavily invested in the work once someone downloaded an early draft of one piece [from the OER site] and they got some critical feedback."

DISCUSSION

Data reported in the chapter illustrate the use of decision-making processes grounded in educational design research (McKenny & Reeves, 2012) to develop and deploy open source technology solutions. The schools in which these projects were undertaken were rural, and demonstrated many of the characteristics of rural schools, including difficulties in staffing and limited access to support staff. These appear to have been limiting factors in previous school planning initiatives. Among the effects of these limiting factors were terminal interruptions to efforts toward school improvement. In these cases, there appears to be evidence that school leaders perceived interventions designed through educational design research (McKenny & Reeves, 2012) to have improved technology-rich teaching and learning, the improvements include both results that more closely reflect the intended outcomes and more sustained efforts to continue the improvements compared to previous planning strategies.

In addition to illustrating the application of design as an effective planning strategy, the data reported in this chapter appear to support several generalizations the are consistent with other findings. Hew & Bush (2007) observed technology integration, which they described as the use of computer and information technologies for instructional purposes, is a practice that is affected by many and interconnected factors. According to Hew & Bush, overcoming these barriers, and improving the level of technology integration is accomplished when barriers are identified and there is a strategy for overcoming them. Further, the strategy must be informed by a clear vision for technology which gives "school leaders and teachers an avenue to coherently communicate how technology can be used as well as a place to begin, a goal to achieves, and a guide along the way" (p. 234).

This research suggests that a vision is insufficient to completely support technology integration. In this data, there is evidence that the school leaders had a vision, but the iterative nature of this planning led them to clarify the vision and to guide not only the beginning place but also a strategy and framework that encouraged refining the vision and the improving the practices as technology was deployed. In addition to clarifying the problem, and contributing to effective evaluation of efforts, the method allowed school leaders to identify needs that previously would have remained hidden to them. The planning strategies provided a framework for how the work would proceed so the vision could be realized. In this way, the planning and decision-making described in this chapter supports the conclusion that iterative planning in which observation of activity is the data that informs further decisions leads to improved performance of the systems.

Davis (1989) observed that white collar workers did not always use technology that was available to facilitate their work. When originally elucidating technology acceptance model, he found that the intention to use technology was affected by several factors, especially the degree to which the user perceived the technology to be easy to use and to be useful. In 2003, Venkatesh, Morris, Davis, & Davis combined eight theories that had been used to predict technology use into the unified theory of acceptance and use of technology (UTAUT). UTAUT posits that technology perceived to be easy to use (high effort expectancy), useful (high performance expectancy), and used by others (high social expectancy) is more likely to be used than other technologies. While originally designed to predict and explain decisions to use technology in setting other than education, there is growing evidence that it describes the use of technology in these populations (Holden & Rada, 2010; Hu, Clark, and Ma, 2003; Smarkola, 2007) and also that efforts to increase technology acceptance can improve the degree to which technology is used in K-12 schools (Ackerman, 2017; Straub, 2009). These data further support the applicability of technology acceptance as a heuristic for predicting and explain technology use in schools. Educators in rural schools tend to adopt multiple roles, and those school tend to have fewer resources to support professional development. When planning increased technology acceptance, the systems tend to be easier to use, thus reducing the need for training, so these data describe planning that will reduce the need for this already limited resource in rural schools.

A final conclusion that appears to be supported by this data describes the changing nature of educators' engagement with educational technology. Blumenfeld, Kempler, and Krajik (2006) define autonomy to include the "perception of a sense of agency" (p. 477), which arises from awareness and understanding of problems and solutions, as well as capacity and authority to implement solutions. The conclusion that educators exerted greater than usual autonomy in these planning efforts arises from the observation that the iterative process led to deeper understanding of the problem and the solutions than other planning efforts. Further, there is evidence in each case that the educators who were participating in the process had been given authority to make decisions. In these case of Northern Middle and High School's adoption of Moodle, there were budgetary limits placed on the decision to purchase space on a web server to host Moodle. In the decision to adopt tagging in Joan's schools, the teachers were given choice of limited options. In these examples, the authority to make decisions was limited by school leaders' decisions, but within those limits authority was given. There is evidence that teachers may exert limited autonomy with regards to regarding instructional practices (Range, Pijanowski, Duncan, Scherz, & Hvidston, 2014), however, so additional research in the emerging role of autonomy is necessary.

LIMITATIONS

The school leaders associated with these cases articulated differences between these planning methods and those used in other activities. Despite these observations, it cannot be determined from these data if those perceptions were the result of the planning methods or other factors. There are no data available to compare these planning efforts with those envisioned by the leaders when they identified differences. There is also no evidence that the problems solved in these cases would not have been solved using different planning methods. In each case, the problem was perceived to be real and efforts of multiple professionals were focused on solving it, so a sufficient solution might have emerged from any planning processes. Given the perceptions that educational design research was effective because it recognized improvement of students' and teachers' experiences as a worthy outcome, it was iterative, and it focused the work of the various types of experts in the design/ construction of technology-rich interventions; it appears those aspects of planning grounded in educational design research deserve additional inquiry.

This research also did not gather data regarding the application of planning methods derived from educational design research (McKenny & Reeves, 2012) to other planning problems encountered by the participants in this research. Schools are places where leaders constantly seek to make improvements. If this approach to planning was perceived to be more effect than other approaches, then it would be reasonable to expect these school leaders to have applied these methods to other aspects of school management. This study gathered no data to investigate other planning; it is also reasonable to expect evidence of this approach to school planning would be observed in other areas of school planning if the school leaders did find it more effective than other methods.

The data appear to support the conclusion that teaching and learning was improved in these cases. Improvement is a very difficult construct to define as it is based in individuals' perceptions, thus the same situation can be perceived differently by different people (Rittel and Weber, 1973). In these cases, improvements were judged only from the perspective of the school leaders who were both involved with the projects and were interviewed many months after the project began. It is unknown if the improvements were manifest in any other data sources or if the improvements were perceived to be improvements by other stakeholders.

The three cases described in this chapter are a subset of projects begun between 2013 and 2015; the author began collecting data for six projects when they were initiated, but only three met the inclusion criteria of being still active and under the original leaders. This research leaves unanswered questions regarding the sustainability of projects developed using educational design research. The three cases described in this chapter are still active, but they appear to have evolved since they were initiated. This research does not indicate what factors affected continuation and modification decisions. Data were collected from one of the projects that was abandoned, and it appears to suggest the lack of sufficient technical expertise contributed to that decision. It is unclear what other factors might cause a leader to abandon a project that was begun using planning grounded in educational design research. It is not known if the projects continued beyond the tenure of the leaders who initiated the project.

CONCLUSION

As illustrated in these cases, iterative planning undertaken to understand how a problem is instantiated and to design and deploy technology solutions appears to be and effective strategy for school and technology leaders. For professionals working in these rural communities, open source technology was deployed and efforts to improve instruction through sustained iterative planning were demonstrated.

REFERENCES

Ackerman, G. (2012). *Measuring technology acceptance: Adapting an instrument.* Paper presented at the New England Educational Research Organization Annual Conference, Portsmouth, NH.

Ackerman, G. (2017). Strategies to increase technology acceptance. In M. Grassetti & S. Brookby (Eds.), *Advancing next-generation elementary teacher education through digital tools and applications.* Hershey, PA: IGI Global, Inc. doi:10.4018/978-1-5225-0965-3.ch001

Apache Software Foundation. (2017). *Licenses.* Retrieved March 28, 2017, from https://www.apache.org/licenses/

Baker, F. (2017). An alternative approach: Openness in education over the last 100 years. *TechTrends, 61*(2), 130–140. doi:10.100711528-016-0095-7

Baran, E., & Correia, A.-P. (2014). A professional development framework for online teaching. *TechTrends, 58*(5), 95–101. doi:10.100711528-014-0791-0

Beeson, E. (2001). Rural schools: Facing unique challenges. *Principal, 8*(1), 22–24.

Benassi, V., Overson, C., & Hakala, C. (2014). *Applying science of learning in education: Infusing psychological science into the curriculum.* Retrieved from the Society for the Teaching of Psychology web site: http://teachpsych.org/ebooks/asle2014/index.php

Benkler, Y. (2006). *The wealth of networks: how social production transforms markets and freedom.* New Haven, CT: Yale University Press.

Bereiter, C. (2002). *Education and mind in the knowledge age.* Mahwah, NJ: L. Erlbaum Associates.

Blumenfeld, P., Kempler, T., & Krajcik, J. (2006). Motivation and cognitive engagement in learning environments. In R. Keith Sawyer (Ed.), *The Cambridge Handbook of Learning Science* (pp. 475–488). New York: Cambridge University Press.

Creative Commons. (n.d.). *Creative Commons — Attribution-ShareAlike 3.0 Unported — CC BY-SA 3.0.* Retrieved March 28, 2017 from https://creativecommons.org/licenses/by-sa/3.0/

Dabrowski, A., & Lodge, J. (2017). Pedagogy, practice, and the allure of open online courses: Implications for schools and their students. In A. Marcus-Quinn & T. Hourigan (Eds.), *Handbook on digital learning for K-12 schools* (pp. 443–454). Cham, Switzerland: Springer International Publishing. doi:10.1007/978-3-319-33808-8_27

Davis, F. (1989). Perceived usefulness, perceived ease of use, and user acceptance of information technology. *Management Information Systems Quarterly*, *13*(3), 319–340. doi:10.2307/249008

Dede, C. (2010). Comparing frameworks for 21st century skills. In J. Bellanca & R. Brandt (Eds.), 21st century skills: Rethinking how students learn (pp. 51-76). Bloomington, IN: Solution Tree Press.

Deuze, M. (2006). Participation, Remediation, Bricolage: Considering Principal Components of a Digital Culture. *The Information Society*, *22*(2), 63–75. doi:10.1080/01972240600567170

Drever, E. (2006). *Using semi-structured interviews in small-scale research: a teacher's guide.* Glasgow, UK: The SCRE Centre.

Free Software Foundation. (2016, November 18). Retrieved March 28, 2017, from https://www.gnu.org/licenses/gpl.html

Glaser, B. (1965). The constant comparative method of qualitative analysis. *Social Problems*, *12*(4), 436–445. doi:10.2307/798843

Halverson, E. (2012). Participatory media spaces: A design perspective on learning with media and technology in the 21st Century. In C. Steinkuehler, K. Squire, & S. Barab (Eds.), *Games learning & society: Learning and meaning in a digital age* (pp. 244–270). New York: Cambridge University Press. doi:10.1017/CBO9781139031127.020

Herrington, J., Oliver, R., & Reeves, A. (2013). Authentic learning environments. In Handbook of research on educational communications and technology (4th ed., pp. 401-412). New York, NY: Springer New York.

Herrington, J., Reeves, T. C., & Oliver, R. (2006). Authentic tasks online: A synergy among learner, task, and technology. *Distance Education*, *27*(2), 233–247. doi:10.1080/01587910600789639

Hew, K., & Brush, T. (2007). Integrating technology into K-12 teaching and learning: Current knowledge gaps and recommendations for future research. *Educational Technology Research and Development*, *55*(3), 223–252. doi:10.100711423-006-9022-5

Holden, H., & Rada, R. (2011). Understanding the influence of perceived usability and technology self-efficacy on teachers' technology acceptance. *Journal of Research on Technology in Education*, *43*(4), 343–367. doi:10.1080/15391523.2011.10782576

Hu, P., Clark, T., & Ma, W. (2003). Examining technology acceptance by school teachers: A longitudinal study. *Information & Management*, *41*(2), 227–241. doi:10.1016/S0378-7206(03)00050-8

Jenkins, H. (2009). *Confronting the challenges of participatory culture: media education for the 21st century*. Cambridge, MA: The MIT Press.

Jitsi [Computer Software]. (n.d.). Retrieved from https://jitsi.org/

Kimmons, R. (2015). Open online system adoption in K-12 as a democratising factor. *Open Learning: The Journal of Open. Distance and E-Learning*, *30*(2), 138–151. doi:10.1080/02680513.2015.1077109

Mahara [Computer Software]. (n.d.). Retrieved from https://mahara.org/

McKenney, S., & Reeves, T. (2012). *Conducting educational design research*. New York: Routledge.

McKenney, S., & Reeves, T. (2014). Educational design research. In J. M. Spector, M. D. Merrill, J. Elen, & M. J. Bishop (Eds.), *Handbook of research on educational communications and technology* (pp. 131–140). New York, NY: Springer New York. doi:10.1007/978-1-4614-3185-5_11

Miller, L. (2012). Situating the rural teacher labor market in the broader context: A descriptive analysis of the market dynamics of New York state. *Journal of Research in Rural Education*, *27*(13), 1–31.

Miller, V. (2011). *Understanding digital culture*. Los Angeles, CA: SAGE.

Moodle [Computer Software]. (2014). Retrieved from http://www.moodle.org

Range, B., Pijanowski, J., Duncan, H., Scherz, S., & Hvidston, D. (2014). An analysis of instructional facilitators' relationships with Teachers and Principals. *Journal of School Leadership*, *24*(2), 253.

Rittel, H., & Webber, M. (1973). Dilemmas in a general theory of planning. *Policy Sciences*, *4*(2), 155–169. doi:10.1007/BF01405730

Sawyer, K. (2008). Optomising learning: Implications of learning sciences research. In *Innovating to learn, learning to innovate* (pp. 45–65). Organisation for Economic Co-operation and Development Publishing. doi:10.1787/9789264047983-4-en

Smarkola, C. (2007). Technology acceptance predictors among student teachers and experienced classroom teachers. *Journal of Educational Computing Research*, *37*(1), 65–82. doi:10.2190/J3GM-3RK1-2907-7U03

Stefaniak, J. (2015). Promoting learner-centered instruction through the design of contextually relevant experiences. In B. Hokanson, G. Clinton, & M. W. Tracey (Eds.), *The design of learning experience* (pp. 49–62). Cham, Switzerland: Springer International Publishing. doi:10.1007/978-3-319-16504-2_4

Stokes, D. (1997). *Pasteur's quadrant: basic science and technological innovation*. Washington, DC: Brookings Institution Press.

Straub, E. (2009). Understanding technology adoption: Theory and future directions for informal learning. *Review of Educational Research, 79*(2), 625–649. doi:10.3102/0034654308325896

Susskind, R., & Susskind, D. (2015). *The future of the professions: how technology will transform the work of human experts*. Oxford, UK: Oxford University Press.

Teo, T. (2011). Technology acceptance research in education. In T. Teo (Ed.), *Technology acceptance in education: Research and issues* (pp. 1–5). Rotterdam, The Netherlands: Sense Publishers. doi:10.1007/978-94-6091-487-4_1

Tholkes, R., & Sederberg, C. (1990). Economies of scale and rural schools. *Journal of Research in Rural Education, 7*, 9–15.

Venkatesh, V., Morris, M., Davis, G., & Davis, F. (2003). User Acceptance of Information Technology: Toward a Unified View. *Management Information Systems Quarterly, 27*(3), 425–478. doi:10.2307/30036540

Wenger, E., & White, N., Smith, J. (2009). *Digital habitats: Stewarding technology for communities.* Portland. OR: CPSquare.

Wokurka, G., Banschback, Y., Houlder, D., & Jolly, R. (2017). Digital culture: Why strategy and culture should eat breakfast together. In G. Oswald & M. Kleinemeir (Eds.), *Shaping the Digital Enterprise* (pp. 109–120). Springer International Publisher. doi:10.1007/978-3-319-40967-2_5

Chapter 4
Information Literacy Education for First-Year Composition Students:
A Case Study of Three Deployment Modes

Monica D. T. Rysavy
Goldey-Beacom College, USA

Russell Michalak
Goldey-Beacom College, USA

Kevin Hunt
Goldey-Beacom College, USA

ABSTRACT

This chapter describes how the researchers at a small private Master's level college examined how different delivery modes—face-to-face (F2F), hybrid, and online instruction—may impact first-year students' perceptions of their information literacy (IL) skills compared to their test-assessed information literacy skills using the students perception of information literacy-questionnaire (SPIL-Q) and information literacy assessment (ILA) instruments. These instruments were developed and deployed to international graduate business students in two previous studies: Michalak and Rysavy and Michalak, Rysavy, and Wessel. The students (n=161) in this study were enrolled in a first-year English composition course in the Spring 2017 semester. This iteration achieved an overall response rate of 87.04% (n=141). Overall, results demonstrated the greatest achievement were demonstrated by students in hybrid course sections.

BACKGROUND

The researchers at a small private master's level college examined how different delivery modes: face-to-face (F2F), hybrid, and online instruction—may impact first-year students' perceptions of their information literacy (IL) skills compared to their test-assessed information literacy skills using the Students

DOI: 10.4018/978-1-5225-4206-3.ch004

Perception of Information Literacy-Questionnaire (SPIL-Q) and Information Literacy Assessment (ILA) instruments. These instruments were developed and deployed to international graduate business students in two previous studies: Michalak and Rysavy (2016) and Michalak, Rysavy, & Wessel (2017). The students (n=161) in this study were enrolled in a first-year English composition course in the Spring 2017 semester. This iteration achieved an overall response rate of 87.04% (n=141).

Librarians have utilized a variety of measurement tools to assess undergraduate and graduate students' basic information literacy skills that follow the information literacy guidelines set forth by the American College and Research Libraries (ACRL). For example, some academic librarians have utilized pre- and post-tests in short-term and longitudinal studies to capture, measure, and assess students' information literacy skills (Kiel, Burclaff, & Johnson, 2015; Hsieh, Dawson, Hofmann, Titus, & Carlin, 2014; Fain, 2011; Gross and Latham, 2007; Trail, Gutierrez, & Lechner, 2006). However, few academic librarians have measured students' test-assessed information literacy skills along with their perceived information literacy skills in the same study (Michalak et al., 2017; Michalak and Rysavy, 2016; Gross and Latham, 2012; Gross and Latham, 2007; Ivanitskaya, Laus, & Casey, 2004).

The researchers could not locate any studies that discussed utilizing a Learning Management System (LMS), Course Management Software (CMS), or any proprietary software tools (such as Adobe Captivate/Connect or Office Mix) to assess college students' perceived information literacy skills along with their test-assessed information literacy skills in the same research instrument. The absence of cases that utilize eLearning tools to assess students' perceived skills versus actual IL skills led the IL team to explore the potential benefits and challenges of doing so through the creation and deployment of IL assessments and training modules with Office Mix.

This current work describes how students' information literacy skills have been assessed in the past and highlights research conducted with IL online training modules to date. This research, conducted at the authors' present institution, is offered as an addition to the information literacy training literature.

RESEARCH PROBLEM

The purpose of this study was to examine how different delivery modes: face-to-face (F2F), hybrid, and online instruction—may impact first-year students' perceptions of their information literacy (IL) skills compared to their test-assessed information literacy skills using the Students Perception of Information Literacy-Questionnaire (SPIL-Q) and Information Literacy Assessment (ILA) instruments.

INFORMATION LITERACY ASSESSMENT (ILA) INSTRUMENT: PILOT ITERATION

In 2015, the information literacy (IL) team developed the first iteration of their information literacy skills assessment instrument - the Information Literacy Assessment (ILA) instrument (see Appendix 1). The ILA was used by the IL team to learn about the college's international graduate business students' IL skills. This internally developed tool and multiple-choice quiz has six assessment topics:

1. Develop a Topic
2. Locate Information

3. Access Information
4. Evaluate Information
5. Write
6. Cite

This iteration of the ILA followed the Association of College and Research Libraries' (ACRL, 2004) five standards for information literate students:

1. The information literate student determines the nature and extent of the information needed.
2. The information literate student accesses needed information effectively and efficiently.
3. The information literate student evaluates information and its sources critically and incorporates selected information into his or her knowledge base and value system.
4. The information literate student, individually or as a member of a group, uses information effectively to accomplish a specific purpose.
5. The information literate student understands many of the economic, legal, and social issues surrounding the use of information and accesses and uses information ethically and legally.

Each standard correlated directly to a topic, that is,

Develop a Topic questions addressed ACRL Standard #1. One exception to this was with standard #5, which was separated into two assessment topics (#5-Write and #6-Cite). To ensure inter-rater reliability, two library staff members, an English faculty member, two college staff members, and four undergraduate library student workers reviewed the ILA instrument and tested it for question clarity, terminology, and format. The IL team selected student workers based on the criteria that they had had one or more business information literacy instruction sessions or a first-year basic IL instruction session during the previous academic year. (Michalak and Rysavy, 2016, p. 156).

For the first phase of the project, the IL team examined other institutions' internally developed online instruments. The IL team reviewed three instruments including Stanford University's SKIL (Stanford's Key to Information Literacy) test (The Board of Trustees of the Leland Stanford Junior University, 2009), Clark College's IRIS (Information, Research and Instruction Suite) quiz (Clark College Libraries, 2015), and Madonna University's TIP (Tutorial for Info Power) quiz (Madonna University Library, 2014). After careful examination, the IL team modeled the outline of their test after SKIL to ensure in-depth coverage of ACRL's five IL standards so that their instrument fit within six modules.

To ensure inter-rater reliability of the ILA, two library staff members, an English faculty member, two college staff members, and four undergraduate library student workers reviewed the ILA instrument and tested it for question clarity, terminology, and format. The IL team selected student workers based on the criteria that they had had one or more business BIL instruction sessions or a first-year basic IL instruction session during the previous academic year.

The institutional purpose of the ILA instrument was two-fold; to collect internal benchmark data and to create a personalized tool that would enable the college to gather data to build an internal benchmark of students' IL skills and their perceived knowledge. The research purpose of this instrument was to identify students' level of content mastery with the five ACRL standards for information literate students.

INFORMATION LITERACY SKILLS QUESTIONNAIRE (SPIL-Q)

Also during the first phase of the project, the IL team developed a secondary instrument, the Students' Perceptions of their Information Literacy Skills Questionnaire, also known as the SPIL-Q instrument. The SPIL-Q began with identifying questions, asking students to provide the following personal details:

- First and last name
- College e-mail address
- Age range (18–24, 25–34, 35–44, 45 or older)
- Gender
- Current major or program concentration(s).

Collecting identifying information was useful for later data analysis so that potential trends could be analyzed (such as exemplary content mastery or content deficiencies amongst groups that the institution targets programming for, e.g. "Commuter Students", "Residential Students", or "Student Athletes").

In the next portion of the questionnaire, students responded to what extent they agreed with the following six statements, under the heading of "Perceptions of Information Literacy Skills":

1. I feel I have the skills necessary to select a relevant topic for any written papers required in my graduate classes at the college.
2. I feel I have the skills necessary to locate relevant research on my chosen research topic using a variety of resources, including the Library, online databases, and online resources.
3. I feel I have the skills necessary to select appropriate keywords, Boolean searching, and connector words to find relevant research when searching online databases and websites.
4. I feel I have the skills necessary to evaluate reference resources for relevance to my topic and accuracy of content.
5. I feel I have the skills necessary to write my research papers. I am familiar with note taking and outlining as methods to help layout the structure of my papers.
6. I understand the difference between paraphrasing and quoting authors. I know when I should paraphrase an author versus when I should quote, and I am comfortable using both methods when referencing existing work.

Students selected one response for each statement, along a 5-point Likert-type scale from 1 (strongly disagree) to 5 (strongly agree). The IL team selected those statements because the descriptors directly corresponded with the six areas assessed by the ILA instrument.

ILA/SPIL-Q INSTRUMENT UPDATES

Since the development of the ILA and SPIL-Q instruments in 2015, the IL team continued to refine and develop the instruments. While slight wording changes were made for clarity, the instrument questions remained primarily the same and the method of deployment was improved over the course of five deployments:

Deployment 1 (Summer 2015): All International graduate students enrolled at time of deployment (n=932); assessments completed by students in Google Forms and scored by Flubaroo, a free Google Forms plugin; instructional content provided through LibGuides (static content website).

Deployment 2 (Fall 2015): All full-time students (n=1,851) enrolled at time of deployment; assessments and instructional content packaged within online training modules completed by students in Office Mix modules (a free eLearning plugin for PowerPoint). It is possible that some students who completed Deployment 2 also completed Deployment 1, however, as this deployment represented a dramatic change in research design, data collected from this deployment was treated as pilot data and not published external to the institution.

Deployment 3 (Fall 2015): One professor elected to utilize the Office Mix modules in a first-year composition class as optional supplemental resources (n=33).

Deployment 4 (Summer 2016): Students in the bridge program (n=17), Boot Camp, completed the modules as part of their computer applications course. Assessment questions and training modules in Office Mix.

Deployment 5 (Spring 2017): This study; 10 sections of first-year composition class sections (n=161), described in this paper. SPIL-Q and ILA questions in Qualtrics, training modules in Office Mix.

INFORMATION LITERACY STANDARDIZED TESTS

Standardized tests that assess information literacy (IL) skills exist, but higher education institutions have not accepted any one assessment as the standard tool to utilize (Thomson, Sharun, Knoch, & Goebel, 2014; Gross and Latham, 2012). Saunders (2009) pointed out

Assessment of information literacy skills continues at low levels. Although teaching faculty are more conscious of integrating these skills into their courses, they typically do not test for or assess these competencies separately from other course-related skills. Standardized assessment tests for information literacy (SAILS, TILT, EST, and so on) are not implemented on a large scale. (p. 111)

Furthermore, Lindauer (2004) made the case for expanding traditional measures of information literacy, stating

Traditional measures of information literacy assessment focus primarily on student learning outcomes, but student learning outcomes are not the only important arena of assessment. It is equally important to measure and document personal experiences that directly contribute to the development of information literate individuals, such as specific indicators that capture the quality of the learning environment and learner self-assessment of skills and instruction/learning satisfaction ratings. (p. 123)

THE INFORMATION LITERACY RESEARCH DIVIDE: PERCEPTIONS, COMPETENCY, AND/OR INSTRUCTION

Studies regarding students' information literacy competence and/or perceptions of their information literacy competence tend to be categorized in three ways: studies that examined only student competence, studies that examined only student perceptions, and studies that examined both competence and perceptions. The literature is limited in the area that this work focuses on – a joint study on competence and perceptions in the hybrid, online or face-to-face format.

Studies have discussed the utilization of pre- and post-tests to assess information literacy skills in combination with online instructional tutorials (Kiel et al., 2015; Hsieh et al., 2014; Fain, 2011; Gross and Latham, 2007; Trail et al., 2006). For example, in Samson and Granath's (2004) study at the University of Montana, Missoula, they "implemented and analyzed pre- and post-tests, the use of online instruction modules, literature cited analyses, grade comparisons, and varied instructional opportunities in an effort to identify and assess effective pedagogy for research instruction provided to entry-level students" (p. 149). They pointed out that the pre- and post-tests were randomly administered to "six sections of English Composition" (p. 150). However, they did not deploy an instrument to assess students' self-perceptions of their information literacy skills.

Ivanitskaya et al. (2004) developed an online tool at Central Michigan University (CMU), the Research Readiness Self-Assessment (RRSA) "that assesses how student research attitudes and perceptions correlate to their actual research skills in order to educate them about state-of-the-art library resources and prepare them to write high-quality research papers" (p. 167). They asserted that the RRSA "is a versatile tool that can easily be adapted to specific disciplines and to different levels of students. Since it measures skills and attitudes, it can be readily used as a pretest and posttest" (p. 180-181). They pointed out RRSA had "three classes of assessment: (1) multiple choice questions, (2) skill-based problems, and (3) measures of students' attitudes" (p. 172). This instrument was deployed to "Health Professions students [n=26] and [to] a diverse group of students [n=95], most of whom specialized in Administration or Education" (p.174) across all CMU off-campus centers. The CMU study was one of the few that combined both perceptions and research skills in the same deployment.

Another example of one of the few studies that combined perceptions and skills is Gross and Latham's (2007) study that surveyed "students [n=58] representing the top and the bottom 25% of the incoming class (based on high school GPA and SAT/ACT scores) at Florida State University who were participating in summer session" (p. 338). They utilized James Madison University's (JMU) Information Literacy Test (ILT)—a computer-based multiple-choice instrument—to measure students' tested information literacy skills (p. 388). Their "findings reveal that the relationship between information literacy skills and self assessments predicted by competency theory are evident in the domain of information literacy" (p. 332).

In their follow-up study, Gross and Latham (2012) tested the validity of the Dunning-Kruger effect, or competency theory, by comparing it to information literacy proficiency (Ehrlinger, Johnson, Banner, & Kruger, 2008; Kruger and Dunning, 1999). They deployed a pre-test and post-test survey to assess first-year college students' IL skills and "their self-estimates of their IL skills" (p. 576). This iteration included an expanded population as they delivered it to 577 freshmen students from two community colleges. Students were asked to complete "two short surveys, one administered before the ILT was taken and one after the ILT was completed" to assess their self-views for two-and-a-half years (p. 576). The results of their study concluded that students "tend to believe that they have above-average IL skills, when, in fact, an objective test of their ability indicates that they are below proficient in terms of their actual skills" (p. 574).

In their previous research, Michalak and Rysavy (2016) examined the test-assessed information literacy skills of international graduate business students (n=172) as compared to their perceived information literacy skills. They found there was a wide discrepancy in results between how information-literate the students perceived themselves as being and how much they actually knew, as assessed by one of their instrument questionnaires. The majority of students surveyed felt confident in their abilities in all six of the ILA-topic areas; however, they scored below the college's passing standard of 70% on the assessment questions for these same six areas.

ONLINE TRAINING MODULES

Literature about the utilization of eLearning tools such as Office Mix, or similar products like Adobe Captivate and Connect, to deliver tests with online instruction tutorials for information literacy assessment or any other assessment to evaluate instruction in higher education is limited. Researchers such as Germek (2011) pointed out "further research is required that examines ways in which tutorials work with LMS to capture and examine online assessment and support information literacy initiatives" (p. 92). His research revealed both Adobe Captivate and Connect to be effective eLearning tools, and commented that "librarians can modify their work and publish updated learning tutorials instantaneously without LMS administrator involvement due to Adobe Connect's ability to function as an LMS" (p. 90). Singh and Hardaker (2014) concurred that research in this area is inadequate, stating that this oversight is "a significant exclusion and one which clearly calls for further research" (p. 105). Similarly, Lyons and Warlick (2012) called for further research in this area with their study of CMS environments, stating that "assessment practices of online library instruction need additional attention to provide a more robust approach" (p. 770).

While there are some studies in which academic librarians have integrated a quiz or test into an LMS or CMS to assess students' information literacy skills, those studies did not assess students' perceptions of their information literacy skills. In these studies, students were required to watch an online instructional tutorial, which was oftentimes reinforced by in-class instruction or face-to-face instruction, e.g. blended learning (Chaiyama, 2015; Lowe, Booth, Tagge, & Stone, 2014). For example, Lowe et al. (2014) at the Claremont Colleges Library adapted an open-source tutorial, "Start Your Research", from the University of California, Irvine Libraries. The authors noted

[b]y providing an LMS-connected means of assessing student IL skills, a number of pedagogical, learning, and assessment goals have been achieved through course-integration of the tutorial and quiz module: faculty are able to gain insight into student research skills, librarians are able to determine a baseline of students' abilities in order to tailor instruction to their needs, and students receive a self-paced online learning opportunity that reinforces in-class IL instruction. (p. 116)

There have been efforts by academic librarians to incorporate IL tutorials with information literacy instruction in the literature (Lapidus, Mccord, Mccloskey, & Kostka-Rokos, 2012; Gustavson, Whitehurst, & Hisle, 2011; Kellum, Mark, & Riley-Huff, 2011; Weiner, Pelaez, Chang, & Weiner, 2011; Tronstad, Phillips, Garcia, & Harlow, 2009; Ganster and Walsh, 2008; Lindsay, Cummings, Johnson, & Scales,

2006; Armstrong and Georgas 2006; Kendall, 2005; Ondrusek, Dent, Bonadie-Joseph, & Williams, 2005; Bracke and Dickstein, 2002; and Getty, Burd, Burns & Piele, 2000), but each lacked course-based assessment and integration within an eLearning tool. Other studies have discussed integrating a pre- and post-test in an LMS (Dennis, Murphey, & Rogers, 2011; Smale and Regaldo, 2009), but not in conjunction with an online tutorial or tutorials.

Lowe et al. (2014) found two examples of IL tutorial use within learning management systems: "Cook (2002) who utilized Blackboard for the tutorial and Sliver [sic] [& Nickel] (2007) who used Blackboard for both the tutorial and the quiz/assessments" (p. 117). Cook delivered an online tutorial in Blackboard with an instrument comprising multiple-choice and nine open-ended questions about information literacy skills to 200 students at Shippensburg University of Pennsylvania (p. 186). Prior to the delivery of the survey in the pilot project, he found "that the quiz creation module of BlackBoard caused difficulties" (p. 182). Since the most recent version of Blackboard at that time would not permit Cook "to mix 'Presentations' and 'Quizzes' in the same folder", his team alternatively "used an off-line assessment product called Respondus", which permitted them to create and upload quizzes (Cook, 2002, p. 182). The online tutorial was developed and delivered in PowerPoint (Cook, 2002, p. 186).

Furthermore, Silver and Nickel (2007) delivered a pre- and post-test to assess psychology students' (n=295) information literacy skills and one survey instrument to assess students' confidence levels after receiving library instruction at University of South Florida—Tampa campus. The survey that tested their confidence level was delivered once after the students received library instruction, but before they took the post-test (Silver and Nickel, 2007, p. 393). They pointed out that "[t]he tutorial itself is comprised of multiple modules, including sections on searching, evaluating, etc. All modules are animated, interactive, and include voice narration as well as on-screen messages that correspond with the voice" (p. 391). They concluded students' confidence level increased in both groups who took online instruction and face-to-face instruction. Except for these studies, the literature is very sparse in this area.

ONE-SHOT LIBRARY INSTRUCTION (FACE-TO-FACE)

Wang (2016) described one-shot library instruction as "course-specific single class visits" (p. 619) that are a "long-established form of library instruction" (p. 619) on information literacy and research-related topics. Robinson, a librarian, and professor of mathematics at the University of Rochester in New York, was considered to be the pioneer of course-related library instruction. He succeeded in "getting at least half his faculty, a large part of the students, and sometimes even the president, into the library to help students use the collections effectively" (Lockwood, 1979, p. 8). The one-shot model of librarian instruction has become common place in higher education, as Jaguszewski and Williams (2013) noted, "the one-shot model is familiar and easy for faculty to incorporate into the syllabus" (p. 7).

BLENDED AND EMBEDDED INFORMATION LITERACY INSTRUCTION

Researchers have explored the potential of blended and/or embedded information literacy instruction. Garrison and Kanuka (2004) defined blended learning as "the thoughtful integration of classroom face-to-face learning experiences with online learning experiences" (p. 96). Shumaker (2012) defined embedded librarianship as a "distinctive innovation that moves the librarians out of libraries and creates a new model of library and information work" (p. 4).

Oakland University library faculty followed the blended and embedded approach to IL instruction with their Rhetoric 160 course by combining online tutorials in their institution's LMS – WebCT – and in-class teaching sessions (Kraemer, Lombardo, & Lepkowski, 2007). In their study of twelve sections of this course (n=224) they compared three deployment methods: online, live instruction, and hybrid (a combination of online and live). Results from this study led the authors to conclude that "contact with a librarian is an important component of student learning" (p. 339) and that the "hybrid group showed the greatest improvement in performance" (p. 339). Overall, each of the deployment groups (online, live, and hybrid) experienced gains from pre- to post-test.

In contrast to the Kraemer et al. study (2007), Nichols, Shaffer, & Shockey (2003), who conducted a similar study (both an embedded and blended approach), found "no significant difference in either student satisfaction or performance regardless of instruction format" (p. 379). The results from the Nichols et al. study indicated that "students learn as much from an online tutorial as from traditional in-class instruction and that they are satisfied with online instruction" (p. 385). Similarly, Anderson and May (2010) found in their study of 103 students in an Introduction to Communication first-year course that the "method of instruction (online vs. FTF vs. blended) does not influence students' retention of IL skills" (p. 498).

SELF-EFFICACY

Researchers have applied the psychological construct of self-efficacy to assess students' perceptions of information literacy and ability. Bandura (1977) defined self-efficacy as a measure of peoples' belief in their ability to accomplish tasks, and he demonstrated that self-efficacy effects people's decisions about the task they perform and the effort they put forth to accomplish the task, and how it effects their attitude about the task (p. 193). Essentially, the higher a person's self-efficacy, the more effort and persistence the person will put forth to accomplish a challenging task.

Kurbanoglu (2010) pointed out that "the necessity for the measuring self-efficacy for information literacy relates to the impact information literacy is having on many aspects of life and in particular on lifelong learning," (p. 4) and found that accurate self-efficacy measures provided a useful means of identifying students in need of assistance. To measure self-efficacy for information literacy skills, Kurbanoglu, Addoynlu, & Umay (2006) in another study developed a 28-item assessment that used a 7-point Likert-type scale in seven categories: "A. Defining the need for information, B. Initiating the search strategy, C. Locating and accessing the resources, D. Assessing and comprehending the information, E. Interpreting, synthesizing, and using the information, F. Communicating the information, G. Evaluating the product and process" (p. 733). They concluded the 28-item assessment "is of reasonable length and should prove to be a useful tool for researchers who are interested in measuring individual's self-efficacy levels for information literacy" (p. 737).

METHODOLOGY

This research follows design-based research principles popularized by Allan Collins (1990) and Ann Brown (1992) and included a pre-test (ILA and SPIIL-Q instruments), online training modules, a post-test (ILA instrument), and faculty interviews. The purpose of the pre-test instrument was to establish a baseline of participating students' understanding of the ILA concepts and to measure their perceptions regarding their perceived abilities. Online training modules were provided to two of the three deployment modes (hybrid and online) as experimental academic interventions. The post-test contained the same IILA questions as the pre-test (no SPIL-Q). Faculty interviews were conducted throughout the program as regular feedback was solicited and at the end of the semester for a debriefing session to learn what worked well and what should be improved for future iterations.

SURVEY DESIGN AND DEPLOYMENT

ILA Program: Current Iteration

After the initial development of the ILA and SPIL-Q instruments, a new set of standards regarding information literacy competency was adopted by the ACRL in January 2016 – the Framework for Information Literacy for Higher Education (Framework). According to the ACRL, this new framework grew "out of a belief that information literacy as an educational reform movement will realize its potential only through a richer, more complex set of core ideas" (ACRL, 2016, p. 2). The updated framework represented the first major revision to the information literacy standards since the publication of the Information Literacy Competency Standards for Higher Education fifteen years earlier. As stated by the ACRL, the six concepts of the new framework are as follows:

- Authority is constructed and contextual
- Information creation as a process
- Information has value
- Research as inquiry
- Scholarship as conversation
- Searching as strategic exploration.

According to Farkas (2017), the new Framework "recognizes that information literacy comprises not just skills but also dispositions and habits of mind, and that librarians should not be the only ones teaching information literacy. The American Association of School Librarians' Standards for the 21st-Century Learner also includes dispositions that would be impossible to foster in a single instruction session" (p. 54). With this in mind, the IL team developed this study with the intent of determining how to best incorporate both librarian-led instructional sessions and online information literacy tutorials into a course that most closely aligned with the topics addressed by the ILA modules.

The IL team decided to pilot an embedded deployment of the ILA program within the traditional research curriculum in the second of the college's two-course first-year composition sequence. Historically, the curriculum was structured to achieve learning outcomes created by the Council of Writing

Program Administrators (WPA), which is "a national association of college and university faculty with professional responsibilities for (or interests in) directing writing programs" (Council of Writing Program Administrators). The WPA outcomes are designed to provide guidance on "the writing knowledge, practices, and attitudes that undergraduate students develop in first-year composition" (Council of Writing Program Administrators), and form the basis of curriculum design for first-year composition programs in the United States. The outcomes promote a process-based approach to critical thinking, reading, and writing, particularly in regard to the process of conducting college-level research.

Although the WPA outcomes focused on the research curriculum of first-year composition, they paralleled the overall intent of the ACRL's Framework for Information Literacy for Higher Education, and the ACRL's recommendation to structure courses that "create student-centered learning environments where inquiry is the norm, problem solving becomes the focus, and thinking critically is part of the process" (Association of College and Research Libraries, p. 5). For example, the WPA's outcomes of students understanding how to "[l]ocate and evaluate (for credibility, sufficiency, accuracy, timeliness, bias and so on) primary and secondary research materials" and to "compose texts that integrate the writer's ideas with those from appropriate sources" parallel the ACRL's standard specifying that "[t]he information literate student evaluates information and its sources critically and incorporates selected information into his or her knowledge base and value system" (p. 11).

To facilitate the WPA outcomes, the research curriculum in the college's composition course involved engaging students in a series of project tasks and stages that included asking questions, finding and evaluating a variety of texts and their rhetorical contexts, analyzing information from the texts as a means of answering or reformulating the initial questions, integrating information and ideas from texts with those of the writer, and applying appropriate citation conventions. The project culminated in the completion of an 8-10 page research paper.

Despite the parallels between the WPA outcomes and the ACRL's Information Literacy Framework, and despite the central role that information literacy practices play in the research process in the college's first-year composition curriculum, the overall approach to the research process was the province of composition instructors versed in writing instruction, with cursory guidance drawn from the college's librarian and library resources at a discrete point within the process. For example, rather than integrating the librarian and library resources into the entire research process, the librarian typically enlisted a presentation on the technical details of using library databases after students had established a working research question and were beginning their search for sources in earnest.

Typically, a librarian would provide an orientation (often referred to as "one-shot instruction") to the college's proprietary databases and a demonstration of how to use the databases, including performing keyword searches, using search filters, and using the databases' built citation tools. In the past, the orientation and demonstration sessions took place either in a standard classroom—with the librarian projecting the databases from the instructor's podium in the front of the room—or in a computer lab-- projecting the databases from computer screen onto the student's screen using LAN School. If the orientation and demonstration took place in a computer classroom, then after receiving the overview and orientation, students were given time to perform their own database searches. However, in both venues, the orientations did not involve the students in extensive active learning.

ILA Program: Deployment Modes

With this pilot of the embedded ILA program, the team elected to deploy three distribution modes during the Spring 2017 semester: face-to-face (F2F), hybrid, and online, with a total enrollment of 162. Table 1 illustrated the breakdown of enrollment by deployment method (Face-to-Face, Hybrid, and Online). F2F sections (3), taught by Dr. Habib (full-time associate professor), would have the typical "one-shot" librarian instructional session–one fifty-five-minute session on developing a topic presented by the library director–during the beginning of the semester and no online tutorials. Figure 1 describes the participation model of students in F2F courses–from pre-test, one-shot librarian instruction, to post-test.

Hybrid course sections (3), taught by Ms. Booth (adjunct faculty), would have one librarian instructional session and online training modules. Appendix 2 describes the participation model of students in hybrid courses–from pre-test (ILA and SPIL-Q), one-shot librarian instruction, online training modules, and post-tests (ILA). Training modules are both animated and interactive, and include voice narration. Furthermore, these modules used on-screen messages with voice prompts to guide students through each module.

Online course sections (4), taught by Mr. West and Dr. Steel, would have online training modules and no librarian instructional sessions. Appendix 3 describes the participation model of students in online courses– from pre-test (ILA and SPIL-Q), online training modules, and post-tests (ILA).

For this iteration, the ILA and SPIL-Q instruments were deployed using the online survey tool, Qualtrics, along with training modules designed and deployed with Office Mix. Deployment steps for each of the three distribution modes are as follows.

Face-to-Face (F2F) Sections Deployment

Three sections of the first-year composition course, taught by Dr. Habib (the English department chair), completed the ILA program in the face-to-face format, with a total enrollment of 49 students. The ILA program was administered to the F2F students as follows:

Figure 1. Participation model of students in F2F course sections

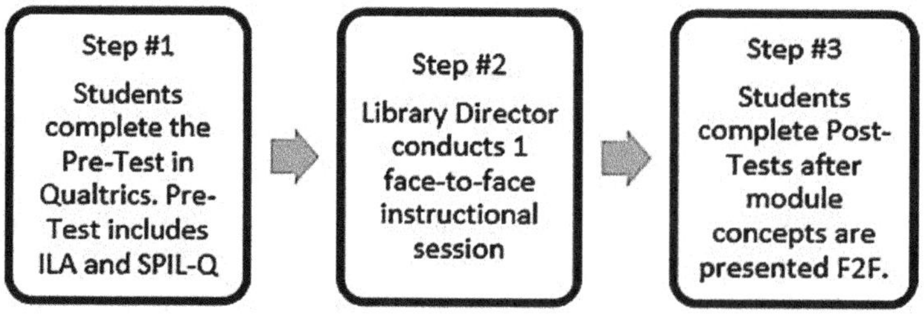

Table 1. Population of enrolled students

	F2F	Hybrid	Online	Total
# of Students Enrolled	49	52	61	162

Week 1: Distribute pre-test survey link via email and/or post it in LMS
Week 2: Remind students to complete the pre-test
Week 3: Face-to-face one-shot librarian instructional session (55 minutes)
Weeks 3-13: Cover the six information literacy topics throughout course per normal curriculum planning
Week 14: Distribute the post-test survey link via email and/or posted in LMS
Week 15: Remind students to complete the post-test

Hybrid Sections Deployment

Three sections of the first-year composition courses, taught by Ms. Booth (who strictly followed Dr. Habib's course outline), completed the ILA program in the hybrid format, with a total enrollment of 52 students. The ILA program was administered to the hybrid students as follows:

Weeks 1 and 2: Distribute pre-test survey link via email and/or post it in LMS; Face-to-face one-shot librarian instructional session (55 minutes)
Weeks 3-15: For each training module (total of six), over the 15-week course, students complete the SPIL-Q in Qualtrics, training module in Office Mix, and post-test in Qualtrics.

Online Sections Deployment

Four sections of the first-year composition courses, taught by two instructors, Mr. Steel and Dr. West, completed the ILA program in the online deployment format, with a total enrollment of 61 students. Mr. Steel and Dr. West followed the course concepts but did not follow Dr. Habib's course outline. The four sections following the online deployment model for the ILA program followed slightly different schedules. Three of the four sections were taught by Mr. Steel, during the day, for 15-weeks. One of the sections was taught by Dr. West and was offered as an eight-week evening course. Mr. Steel followed the following schedule for ILA program deployment:

Weeks 1 and 2: Distribute pre-test survey link (Qualtrics) via email and/or post it in LMS
Weeks 3-15: For each training module (total of six), over the 15-week course, students complete the SPIL-Q in Qualtrics, training module in Office Mix, and post-test in Qualtrics.

Dr. West followed the following schedule for his 8-week evening course's ILA program deployment:

Week 1: Pre-test is distributed to students
Weeks 2-8: For each training module (total of six), over the 8-week course, students complete the SPIL-Q in Qualtrics, training module in Office Mix, and post-test in Qualtrics

RESULTS

This iteration achieved a response rate of 87.04% (n=141). Table 2 illustrates response rates by deployment mode.

Slightly more female students (n=76) than male students (n=65) participated in the ILA program. The average age of participating students was 20, with an age range of 17-42. Table 3 illustrates gender distribution by deployment mode.

As this iteration was deployed to students enrolled in a first-year composition course, 100% of enrolled and participating students were enrolled in the undergraduate division

F2F Results

Table 4 illustrates F2F students' participation and response rates in the ILA program by each component (Pre-Test and Post-Test).

F2F students were initially the most confident on the topic of M4 – Evaluating Information, as indicated by average SPIL-Q results (4.51). Comparison of F2F students' average pre- and post-test ILA module scores indicated increases in content mastery across all six ILA concepts. Students in F2F

Table 2. Response rates of enrolled students, by deployment mode

	F2F n	F2F %	Hybrid n	Hybrid %	Online n	Online %
# of Students Enrolled	45	91.84%	52	100%	44	72.13%

Table 3. ILA participating students, by gender, by deployment mode

Deployment Mode	F	M	Total
F2F	23	22	45
Hybrid	26	26	52
Online	27	17	44
Total	76	65	141

Table 4. Comparison of average SPIL-Q, pre-test, and post-tests for F2F courses

	SPIL-Q n	SPIL-Q AVG	Pre-Test n	Pre-Test %	Post-Test n	Post-Test %	% Change
M1	45	3.78	45	59.98%	43	62.79%	+2.81%
M2	45	4.16	45	49.56%	40	55.00%	+5.44%
M3	45	3.87	45	41.78%	41	45.12%	+3.34%
M4	45	4.51	45	46.89%	41	53.66%	+6.77%
M5	45	3.98	45	64.67%	39	73.85%	+9.18%
M6	45	2.56	45	60.44%	40	61.25%	+0.81%

modules had the highest post-test score with M5 – Write (73.85%). F2F students' lowest post-test score was on M3 – Accessing Information (45.12%). Module 5 (Write) experienced the greatest percentage gain between pre- and post-test of 9.18%. Module 6 (Cite) experienced the least percentage gain between pre- and post-test of .81%. The average percentage gain across all modules for F2F students was 4.73%

Comparison of F2F students' pre-tests, post-tests, and final course average (on a 4.0 scale) showed a slight percentage change gain from pre- to post-test of 4.70%. The average final course grade was 3.16, as illustrated in Table 5.

Hybrid Results

Table 6 illustrates hybrid students' perceptions of their skills as well as average pre- and post-test scores in the ILA program by each module.

Students enrolled in hybrid course sections were initially the most confident on the topic of M4 – Evaluating Information, as indicated by average SPIL-Q results (4.27). Comparison of hybrid students' average pre- and post-test ILA module scores indicated increases in content mastery across all six ILA concepts. Students in hybrid courses had the highest post-test score with M1 – Develop a Topic (84.78%). Hybrid students' lowest post-test score was on M4 – Evaluating Information (67.44%).

Module 3 (Accessing information) experienced the greatest percentage change gain between pre- and post-test of 26.67%. Module 5 (Writing) experienced the least percentage change gain between pre- and post-test of 12.50%. The average percentage change gain across all modules for hybrid students was 17.65%

Comparison of hybrid students' pre-tests, post-tests, and final course average (on a 4.0 scale) showed a percentage change gain from pre- to post-test of 17.60%. The average final course grade was 3.22, as illustrated in Table 7.

Table 5. Comparison of pre-test, post-test, and average course final grade for F2F courses

	n	Pre-Test AVG	Post-Test AVG	AVG Course Final Grade (4.0 Scale)
F2F	45	53.89%	58.61%	3.16

Table 6. Comparison of average SPIL-Q, pre-test, and post-tests for hybrid courses

	SPIL-Q n	SPIL-Q AVG	Pre-Test n	Pre-Test %	Training Completion n	Post-Test n	Post-Test %	% Change
M1	52	4.25	52	69.81%	46	46	84.78%	+14.97%
M2	52	4.13	52	57.31%	47	47	74.68%	+17.37%
M3	52	3.98	52	49.04%	35	35	75.71%	+26.67%
M4	52	4.27	52	49.04%	45	45	67.44%	+18.40%
M5	52	4.21	52	69.13%	43	43	81.63%	+12.50%
M6	52	2.35	52	57.12%	39	39	73.08%	+15.96%

Table 7. Comparison of pre-test, post-test, and average course final grade for hybrid courses

	SPIL-Q and Pre-Test n	Pre-Test AVG	Post-Test AVG	AVG Course Final Grade (4.0 Scale)
Hybrid	52	58.58%	76.22%	3.22

Online Results

Table 8 illustrates online students' perceptions of their skills as well as average pre- and post-test scores in the ILA program by each module.

Students enrolled in online course sections were initially the most confident on the topic of M5 – Write, as indicated by average SPIL-Q results (4.32). Comparison of online students' average pre- and post-test ILA module scores indicated increases in content mastery across all six ILA concepts. Students in online courses had the highest post-test score with M1 – Develop a Topic (80.00%). Hybrid students' lowest post-test score was on M4 – Evaluating Information (58.57%).

Module 5 (Write) experienced the greatest percentage change gain between pre- and post-test of 19.75%. Module 1 (Develop a Topic) experienced the least percentage change gain between pre- and post-test of 2.95%. The average percentage change across all modules for online students was 10.75%.

Comparison of online students' pre-tests, post-tests, and final course average (on a 4.0 scale) indicated a percent change gain from pre- to post-test of 10.8%. The average final course grade was 3.34, as illustrated in Table 9.

Table 8. Comparison of average SPIL-Q, pre-test, and post-tests for online courses

	SPIL-Q n	SPIL-Q AVG	Pre-Test n	Pre-Test %	Training Completion n	Post-Test n	Post-Test %	% Change
M1	44	4.18	44	77.05%	42	42	80.00%	+2.95%
M2	44	4.07	44	59.09%	39	39	66.41%	+7.32%
M3	44	4.16	44	53.86%	41	41	63.41%	+9.55%
M4	44	4.23	44	46.93%	14	14	58.57%	+11.64%
M5	44	4.32	44	60.00%	40	40	79.75%	+19.75%
M6	44	2.32	44	53.64%	36	36	66.94%	+13.30%

Table 9. Comparison of pre-test, post-test, and average course final grade for online courses

	SPIL-Q and Pre-Test n	Pre-Test AVG	Post-Test AVG	AVG Course Final Grade (4.0 Scale)
Online	44	58.43%	69.18%	3.34

Overall Comparison Results

Table 10 summarizes students' perceptions of their skills as assessed by the SPIL-Q across all modules across all deployment modes. Students were initially most confident on their skills with the topic of M4 – Evaluating Information, as indicated by average SPIL-Q results (4.62).

Table 11 summarizes students' pre- and post-test averages across all modules from all deployment modes.

Comparison of students' average pre- and post-test ILA module scores across all deployment modes indicated increases in content mastery across all six ILA concepts. The lowest pre-test average score was M4-Evaluating Information (47.70%). The highest pre-test average score was M1-Develop a Topic (68.93%). The lowest post-test average score was M4-Evaluating Information (60.55%). The highest post-test average score was M5-Write (78.52%).

Module 5 (Write) experienced the greatest percentage change gain between pre- and post-test of 13.66%. Module 1 (Develop a Topic) experienced the least percentage change gain between pre- and post-test of 7.1%.

Comparison of all students' pre-tests, post-tests, and final course average (on a 4.0 scale) indicated a percent change gain from pre- to post-test of 11.09%. The average final course grade was 3.24, as illustrated in Table 12.

Table 10. Overall comparison of average SPIL-Q

M1	M2	M3	M4	M5	M6
4.08	4.12	4.00	4.33	4.17	2.40

Table 11. Overall comparison of average pre-test and post-tests (%)

M1 Pre	68.93	**M1 Post**	76.03
M2 Pre	55.39	**M2 Post**	65.87
M3 Pre	48.23	**M3 Post**	60.68
M4 Pre	47.70	**M4 Post**	60.55
M5 Pre	64.86	**M5 Post**	78.52
M6 Pre	57.09	**M6 Post**	67.04

Table 12. Overall comparison of pre-test, post-test, and average course final grade

	SPIL-Q and Pre-Test n	Pre-Test AVG	Post-Test AVG	AVG Course Final Grade (4.0 Scale)
Overall	141	57.03%	68.12%	3.24

DISCUSSION

The purpose of deploying embedded modules was, in part, to address the new ACRL Framework's position that teaching information literacy concepts should not be isolated within one librarian-led instructional session. In partnership with the English department chair, the IL team selected first-year composition courses to deploy the ILA program (including the ILA and SPIL-Q instruments) using three deployment modes: F2F, hybrid, and online. Overall, on average, students enrolled in the ten sections of the first-year composition course improved their mastery of the information literacy skills taught to them through the ILA program in all deployment modes: F2F interaction, hybrid, and the online modules. Students enrolled in the hybrid deployment mode sections experienced the greatest achievement gains.

Overall, students (n=141) had the greatest content mastery gains between pre- (64.86%) and post-test (78.52%) for M5-Write (% change=13.66%). Students were initially fairly confident regarding their skills with this topic (4.17; Agree). Students were initially the most confident with the M4-Evaluating Information (4.62), but experienced a slightly smaller percentage gain in terms of mastery on this topic (12.85%). Overall, students achieved passing mastery according to the college's grade scale (65%+) for the post-test averages with four of the six topics: M1-Develop a Topic (76.03%), M2-Locate Information (65.87%), M5-Write (78.52%), and M6-Cite (67.04%). This finding of perceived skills being higher than actual skills is consistent with the findings of Gross and Latham's 2012 study, which tested the validity of the Dunning-Kruger effect. Michalak and Rysavy (2016) and Michalak et al. (2017) found the same results in their studies.

Students participating in F2F sections (n=45) were also the most confident on their skills for M4 – Evaluating Information prior to completing training (4.51). Similar to the overall results, these students also experienced the greatest percentage knowledge gains for M5-Write between pre-test (64.67%) and post-test (73.85%), of 9.18%. F2F students' average post-test score for M4-Evaluating Information was 53.66%, which represented a 6.77% gain from their pre-test average of 46.89%. F2F students achieved passing mastery for their post-test average score with one of the six topics, M5-Write (73.85%).

Dr. Habib, the instructor for the F2F sections, invited the library director, (a co-author on this paper), to conduct one face-to-face librarian-led instructional session in each of his sections. These sessions, approximately 55 minutes in length, focused on developing a topic, accessing databases, and citing. With the F2F deployment, students did not complete the training modules; however, Dr. Habib volunteered having his students complete the post-tests for each of the topics after he presented the content in class. This provided the post-test data presented in this paper as the researchers did not initially plan to collect post-test data for the F2F sections. Dr. Habib urged the researchers that moving forward "the modules need to be carefully and formally built into the structure of the course. Students need to be held accountable for the content (e.g., part of their course grade needs to be based on their scores on the modules)."

Similar to overall results and F2F students, students participating in hybrid sections (n=52) were also initially the most confident regarding their skills for M4-Evaluating Information prior to completing training (4.27). Hybrid students experienced the greatest percentage knowledge gains (26.67%) with M3-Access Information between their average pre-test score of 49.04% and average post-test score of 75.71%. Hybrid students' average post-test score for M4-Evaluating Information was 67.44%, which represented a 18.50% gain from their pre-test average of 49.04%. Hybrid students achieved passing mastery for their post-test average scores for all six of the ILA topics: M1-Develop a Topic (84.78%), M2-Locate Information (74.68%), M3-Access Information (75.71%), M4-Evaluating Information (67.44%), M5-Write (81.63%), and M6-Cite (73.08%).

Ms. Booth, the instructor for the hybrid courses, invited the library director, (a co-author on this paper), to conduct one face-to-face librarian-led instructional session in each of her sections. These sessions, approximately 55 minutes in length, focused on developing a topic and citing. Ms. Booth actively communicated with the researchers throughout the process with questions about the process and sought assistance when technological issues arose. In response to one email the researchers sent checking in regarding her experiences, Ms. Booth commented "Things are going well! Thanks for checking in! I did have some issues with modules 3 and 4. I informed [the library director] about these issues and we decided to have my students come in and take the rest of the modules in the library. I had assigned them to work on the modules at home as homework assignments but there were a few glitches with the links. There was a lot of back and forth through email so I decided this would be the way to go."

Students participating in courses experiencing the online deployment of the ILA program (n=44) were initially the most confident regarding their skills for M5-Write (4.32). Similar to students participating in the F2F deployment, online students experienced the greatest achievement gains between pre- (60%) and post-test (79.75%) with M5-Write (% change=19.75%). Online students' average post-test score for M4-Evaluating Information was 58.57%, which represented a 11.64% gain from their pre-test average of 46.93%. Online students achieved passing mastery for their post-test average scores with four of the six ILA topics: M1-Develop a Topic (80%), M2-Locate Information (66.41%), M5-Write (79.75%), and M6-Cite (66.94%).

Mr. Steel, one of the two instructors, shared praise of the ILA program deployed in the online mode for his course sections, stating, "This is an excellent way to reinforce what we teach in the classroom and to add a bit of formality to it. By completing the modules and doing pre- and post-tests, the students recognize that all this is done for a reason . . . to help them write quality research papers." Mr. Steel also reflected on ways he could improve the process for his students in future course sections, commenting, "I need to tie them in with milestones 1, 2, and 3 (the research process for writing the research essay) and make sure the links are correct so they can use the modules in conjunction with writing the research essay."

Mr. Steel initially struggled with technological aspects of the deployment, and shared links from a previous project (initially shared with instructors participating in this deployment to preview content they would be using in this iteration) with his students as opposed to the current iteration. This resulted in an initially low response rate until the issue was discovered and corrected. Ultimately, Mr. Steel had mainly positive comments about the ILA program, sharing "I love this stuff! And I think it really helps the students learn to apply the research process".

LIMITATIONS

The first limitation centers around the technology used to provide the online training modules - Office Mix - a free PowerPoint plugin. This tool is designed to be used by one developer, i.e. one designer publishes the training from his/her computer to his/her Office Mix account. There is not currently a way to share access to the Office Mix dashboard (where the analytics are housed) or Office Mix presentations because each account is for one person (there are no team accounts). This resulted in only one person having access to the data, which the researchers found to be burdensome and resulted in delays in sharing data due to other responsibilities of the researchers. Based on testing for other projects, the researchers have decided to utilize an alternative eLearning tool to publish future iterations of the ILA program, Knovio, as it permits sharing of both presentation modules and multi-user access to user analytics along with pre- and post-test results. Despite the limitations shared about Office Mix, it is a free tool, and many institutions have access to PowerPoint; therefore, it continues to be a tool worthy of consideration, particularly with departments facing budgetary constraints.

The second limitation, which will particularly impact small to mid-sized institutions, is the sheer volume of data that is collected and must be analyzed in similar deployments. Furthermore, in order to provide actionable data to faculty expediently so they can make decisions about their courses during the same semester, data must be analyzed and reported quickly. Due to the nature of the fairly rigorous deployment mode timelines, combined with the fact that this was the pilot deployment of this program, the researchers found the process to be, at times, very time consuming, particularly because the oversight, data management, and communication with all instructors was handled by two directors of the college with many other professional responsibilities. While the researchers would have typically utilized the assistance of their research assistants, for this iteration the assistant was part of the program so we did not utilize her due to potential conflict of interest.

Other institutions considering deploying such a program should consider that increased staffing may be necessary to deploy, analyze, and report on the data collected. Furthermore, institutions should consider how the program might be structured so that components of the ILA were significantly weighted in the overall grading scheme of the course to encourage student and faculty buy-in.

FUTURE RESEARCH

The results of this iteration of the ILA program led the researchers to conclude that the hybrid deployment was the most successful in terms of student participation and knowledge gains. Therefore, moving forward the researchers proposed to the college that this program continue to be embedded within the first-year composition course sections. The proposal was approved, so beginning with the Spring 2018 semester, the ILA program will be a permanent addition to this course, resulting in continuous data collection moving forward.

After presenting the results of the ILA program at a faculty meeting, professors expressed interest in utilizing the ILA program with their students. For example, an economics professor requested a partnership for the Fall 2017 semester and the researchers will embed the ILA program in a similar manner to this study with his courses.

Embedded deployment of the ILA program within the English capstone course is in progress. The researchers deployed the pre- and post-tests within this course during the Spring 2017 semester. Additionally, the institution has agreed for the researchers to oversee required completion of the ILA modules by all incoming graduate students to provide a baseline of skill competency prior to beginning coursework.

Furthermore, the college sponsors a bridge program known as “Bootcamp” for incoming first-year students who fall below the college’s expected SAT and/or GPA scores. The ILA program was piloted with this group of students during the Summer 2016 program and will now be a permanent fixture of this course moving forward to ensure continuous data collection from this population regarding their IL perceptions and test-assessed skills.

One minor issue was discovered with the pre-test instrument: a seven-point Likert-scale was inadvertently used for Question 9. This was discovered prior to analysis and student responses were recoded to fit the five-point scale utilized for all other questions that utilized a Likert-scale.

CONCLUSION

The purpose of this study was to examine how three different delivery modes of the ILA program–face-to-face (F2F), hybrid, and online instruction– may potentially impact first-year college students' perceptions of their IL skills as compared to their test-assessed IL skills using the ILA and SPIL-Q instruments (Michalak and Rysavy, 2016; Michalak et al., 2017). By deploying the ILA program during the Spring 2017 semester to 10 course sections of a first-year English composition course using the three deployment modes, the researchers could compare students' perceptions of their skills and their actual test-assessed skills, both within course sections and across deployment modes.

Results from this study indicated that students, on average, increased their IL skills across all six IL topics for all deployment modes, with an average percentage increase of 11.09%. Overall, students achieved passing mastery (according to the college's standard of 65% or higher) with four of the six IL topics (M1-Develop a Topic, M2-Locate Information, M5-Write, and M6-Cite). However, students in the hybrid mode experienced the greatest average gains from pre- to post-test, with an average percentage increase of 17.65%. Furthermore, students enrolled in hybrid sections achieved passing mastery with all six of the IL topics.

Despite overall increases of student mastery for ILA program content, it was important to note that there was clearly a disparity between final course grades (average of 3.08 / "B") and post-test average scores overall and across all deployment modes. Overall students, for example, achieved an average post-test score of 68.12% which aligns with the college's undergraduate grading scale as a "F", not a "B", which was the average final course grade overall for students. As mentioned within the limitations of this study, delayed delivery of student completion and performance scores data to participating instructors may have factored into this disparity. Future iterations of the program will incorporate distribution of student participation data at frequent intervals, as well as clear direction for instructors regarding how to incorporate ILA program elements into students' final course grades. While course grades clearly are a sensitive topic for faculty, the senior leadership team of the institution has decided to adopt the ILA program as a significantly weighted component of the first-year composition courses moving forward.

REFERENCES

ACRL. (2004). *Information literacy competency standards for higher education.* Retrieved fromwww.ala.org/acrl/standards/informationlit?PMU ?eracycompetency#ilassess

Anderson, K., & May, F. (2010). Does the method of instruction matter? An experimental examination of information literacy instruction in the online, blended, and face-to-face classrooms. *Journal of Academic Librarianship, 36*(6), 495–500. doi:10.1016/j.acalib.2010.08.005

Armstrong, A., & Georgas, H. (2006). Using interactive technology to teach information literacy concepts to undergraduate students. *RSR. Reference Services Review, 34*(4), 491–497. doi:10.1108/00907320610716396

Association of College & Research Libraries Board. (2016). *Framework for Information Literacy for Higher Education.* Retrieved from http://www.ala.org/acrl/standards/ilframework

Bandura, A. (1977). Self-efficacy: Toward a unifying theory of behavioral change. *Psychological Review, 84*(2), 191–215. doi:10.1037/0033-295X.84.2.191 PMID:847061

Bostick, S. L. (1992). *The development and validation of the library anxiety scale* (Order No. 9310624). Available from ProQuest Dissertations & Theses Global. (304002616)

Bracke, P. J., & Dickstein, R. (2002). Web tutorials and scalable instruction: Testing the waters. *RSR. Reference Services Review*, *30*(4), 330–337. doi:10.1108/00907320210451321

Brown, A. L. (1992). Design experiments: Theoretical and methodological challenges in creating complex interventions in classroom settings. *Journal of the Learning Sciences*, *2*(2), 141–178. doi:10.120715327809jls0202_2

Chaiyama, N. (2015). The development of blended learning management model in developing information literacy skills (BL-ILS Model). *International Journal of Information and Education Technology (IJIET)*, *5*(7), 483–489. doi:10.7763/IJIET.2015.V5.554

Clark College Libraries. (2015). *IRIS*. Retrieved from http://www.clark.edu/Library/iris/ index.shtml

Collins, A. (1990). *Toward a design science of education*. New York, NY: Center for Technology in Education. Retrieved from http://cct2.edc.org/ccthome/reports/tr1.html

Cook, D. L. (2002). Ship to shore: An online information literacy tutorial using BlackBoard distance education software. *Journal of Library Administration*, *37*(1), 177–187. doi:10.1300/J111v37n01_16

Council of Writing Program Administrators. (2008). *WPA outcomes statement for first-year composition*. WPA.

Dennis, M. R., Murphey, R. M., & Rogers, K. (2011). Assessing information literacy comprehension in first-year students. *Practical Academic Librarianship: The International Journal of the SLA, 1*(1), 1-15.

Ehrlinger, J., Johnson, K., Banner, M., & Kruger, J. (2008). Why the unskilled are unaware: Further explorations of (absent) self-insight among the incompetent. *Organizational Behavior and Human Decision Processes*, *105*(1), 98–121. doi:10.1016/j.obhdp.2007.05.002 PMID:19568317

Fain, M. (2011). Assessing information literacy skills development in first year students: A multi-year study. *Journal of Academic Librarianship*, *37*(2), 109–119. doi:10.1016/j.acalib.2011.02.002

Farkas, M. (2017). Information literacy toolkits: Creating better resources for instructors. *American Libraries*, *45*(5), 54.

Ganster, L. A., & Walsh, T. R. (2008). Enhancing library instruction to undergraduates: Incorporating online tutorials into the curriculum. *College & Undergraduate Libraries*, *15*(3), 314–333. doi:10.1080/10691310802258232

Garrison, D. R., & Kanuka, H. (2004). Blended learning: Uncovering its transformative potential in higher education. *The Internet and Higher Education*, *7*(2), 95–105. doi:10.1016/j.iheduc.2004.02.001

Germek, G. (2011). Empowered library eLearning: Capturing assessment and reporting with ease, efficiency, and effectiveness. *RSR. Reference Services Review*, *40*(1), 90–102. doi:10.1108/00907321211203658

Getty, N. K., Burd, B., Burns, S. K., & Piele, L. (2000). Using courseware to deliver library instruction via the Web: Four examples. *RSR. Reference Services Review*, *28*(4), 349–359. doi:10.1108/00907320010359678

Gross, M., & Latham, D. (2007). Attaining information literacy: An investigation of the relationship between skill level, self-estimates of skill, and library anxiety. *Library & Information Science Research, 29*(3), 332–353. doi:10.1016/j.lisr.2007.04.012

Gross, M., & Latham, D. (2012). What's skills got to do with it?: Information literacy skills and self-views of ability among first-year college students. *Journal of the American Society for Information Science and Technology, 63*(3), 574–583. doi:10.1002/asi.21681

Gustavson, A., Whitehurst, A., & Hisle, D. (2011). Laying the information literacy foundation: A multiple-media solution. *Library Hi Tech, 29*(4), 725–740. doi:10.1108/07378831111189796

Hsieh, M., Dawson, P., Hofmann, M., Titus, M., & Carlin, M. (2014). Four pedagogical approaches in helping students learn information literacy skills. *Journal of Academic Librarianship, 40*(3/4), 234–246. doi:10.1016/j.acalib.2014.03.012

Ivanitskaya, L., Laus, R., & Casey, A. M. (2004). Research Readiness Self-Assessment. *Journal of Library Administration, 41*(1/2), 167–183. doi:10.1300/J111v41n01_13

Jaguszewski, J., & Williams, K. (2013). *New Roles for New Times: Transforming Liaison Roles in Research Libraries.* Association of Research Libraries. Retrieved from the University of Minnesota Digital Conservancy, http://hdl.handle.net/11299/169867

Kellum, K., Mark, A. E., & Riley-Huff, D. A. (2011). Development, assessment and use of an on-line plagiarism tutorial. *Library Hi Tech, 29*(4), 641–654. doi:10.1108/07378831111189741

Kendall, M. (2005). Tackling student referencing errors through an online tutorial. *Aslib Proceedings, 57*(2), 131–145. doi:10.1108/00012530510589100

Kiel, S., Burclaff, N., & Johnson, C. (2015). Learning by doing: Developing a baseline information literacy assessment. *portal. Libraries and the Academy, 15*(4), 747–766. doi:10.1353/pla.2015.0049

Kraemer, E., Lombardo, S., & Lepkowski, F. (2007). The librarian, the machine, or a little of both: A comparative study of three information literacy pedagogies at Oakland University. *College & Research Libraries, 68*(4), 330–342. doi:10.5860/crl.68.4.330

Kruger, J., & Dunning, D. (1999). Unskilled and unaware of it: How difficulties in recognizing one's own incompetence lead to inflated self-assessments. *Journal of Personality and Social Psychology, 77*(6), 1121–1134. doi:10.1037/0022-3514.77.6.1121 PMID:10626367

Kurbanoglu, S. (2010). *Self-efficacy: An alternative approach to the evaluation of information literacy.* QQML 2009: Qualitative and Quantitative Methods in Libraries, *International Conference*, Chania, Greece.

Kurbanoglu, S., Akkoyunlu, B., & Umay, A. (2006). Developing the information literacy self-efficacy scale. *The Journal of Documentation, 62*(6), 730–743. doi:10.1108/00220410610714949

Lapidus, M., McCord, S. K., McCloskey, W. W., & Kostka-Rokosz, M. (2012). Combined use of online tutorials and hands-on group exercises in bibliographic instruction for pharmacy students. *Medical Reference Services Quarterly, 31*(4), 383–399. doi:10.1080/02763869.2012.724277 PMID:23092416

Lindauer, B. G. (2004). The three arenas of information literacy assessment. *Reference and User Services Quarterly*, *44*(2), 122–129.

Lindsay, E. B., Cummings, L., Johnson, C. M., & Scales, B. J. (2006). If you build it, will they learn? Assessing online information literacy tutorials. *College & Research Libraries*, *67*(5), 429–445. doi:10.5860/crl.67.5.429

Lockwood, D. L. (1979). *Library instruction: A bibliography*. Westport, CT: Greenwood Press.

Lowe, S. M., Booth, C., Tagge, N., & Stone, S. (2014). Integrating an information literacy quiz into the learning management system. *Communications in Information Literacy*, *8*(1), 115–130. doi:10.15760/comminfolit.2014.8.1.156

Lyons, S., & Warlick, T. (2012). Health sciences information literacy in CMS environments: Learning from our peers. *The Electronic Library*, *31*(6), 770–780. doi:10.1108/EL-06-2012-0063

Madonna University Library. (2014). *Tip quiz*. Retrieved from http://library. madonna.edu/pages/InfoLit-TipQuiz/generalform.cfm

Mellon, C. A. (1986). Library anxiety: A grounded theory and its development. *College & Research Libraries*, *47*(3), 160–165. doi:10.5860/crl_47_02_160

Michalak, R., & Rysavy, M. (2016). Information literacy in 2015: International graduate students' perceptions of information literacy compared to test-assessed skills. *Journal of Business & Finance Librarianship*, *21*(2), 152–174. doi:10.1080/08963568.2016.1145787

Michalak, R., Rysavy, M., & Wessel, A. (2017). Students' perceptions of their information literacy skills: The confidence gap between male and female international graduate students. *Journal of Academic Librarianship*, *43*(2), 100–104. doi:10.1016/j.acalib.2017.02.003

Moser, F. (2007). Faculty adoption of education technology: Educational technology support plays a critical role in helping faculty add technology to their teaching. *EDUCAUSE Quarterly*, *30*(1), 66–69.

Nichols, J., Shaffer, B., & Shockey, K. (2003). Changing the face of instruction: Is online or in-class more effective? *College & Research Libraries*, *64*(5), 378–388. doi:10.5860/crl.64.5.378

Oakleaf, M. (2009). The information literacy instruction assessment cycle. *The Journal of Documentation*, *65*(4), 539–560. doi:10.1108/00220410910970249

Ondrusek, A., Dent, V. F., Bonadie-Joseph, I., & Williams, C. (2005). A longitudinal study of the development and evaluation of an information literacy test. *RSR. Reference Services Review*, *33*(4), 388–417. doi:10.1108/00907320510631544

Resnis, E., Gibson, K., Hartsell-Gundy, A., & Misco, M. (2010). Information literacy assessment: A case study at Miami University. *New Library World*, *111*(7/8), 287–301. doi:10.1108/03074801011059920

Samson, S., & Granath, K. (2004). Reading, writing, and research: Added value to university first-year experience programs. *RSR. Reference Services Review*, *32*(2), 142–156. doi:10.1108/00907320410537667

Saunders, L. (2009). The future of information literacy in academic libraries: A Delphi study. *portal. Library and the Academy, 9*(1), 99–114. doi:10.1353/pla.0.0030

Shumaker, D. (2012). *Distinctive Roles: Engagement, Innovation, and the Liaison Model.* Medford, NJ: Information Today.

Silver, S. L., & Nickel, L. T. (2007). Are online tutorials effective? A comparison of online and classroom library instruction methods. *Research Strategies, 20*(4), 389–396. doi:10.1016/j.resstr.2006.12.012

Singh, G., & Hardaker, G. (2014). Barriers and enablers to adoption and diffusion of eLearning: A systematic review of the literature – a need for an integrative approach. *Education + Training, 56*(2/3), 105–121. doi:10.1108/ET-11-2012-0123

Smale, M. A., & Regalado, M. (2009). Using blackboard to deliver library research skills assessment. *Communications in Information Literacy, 3*(2), 142–157. doi:10.15760/comminfolit.2010.3.2.77

Taylor, L., & Atwong, C. (2008). Integrating information literacy into business education: A successful case of faculty-librarian collaboration. *Journal of Business & Finance Librarianship, 13*(4), 433–449. doi:10.1080/08963560802202227

The Board of Trustees of the Leland Stanford Junior University. (2009). *Stanford's key to information literacy.* Retrieved fromhttp://skil.stanford.edu/intro/index.html

Thomson, M. E., Sharun, S., Knoch, J., & Goebel, N. (2014). Institutions collaborating on an information literacy assessment tool. *Library Management, 35*(8/9), 538–546. doi:10.1108/LM-03-2014-0035

Trail, M. A., Gutierrez, C., & Lechner, D. (2006). Reconsidering a traditional instruction technique: Reassessing the print workbook. *Journal of Academic Librarianship, 32*(6), 632–640. doi:10.1016/j.acalib.2006.07.003

Tronstad, B., Phillips, L., Garcia, J., & Harlow, M. A. (2009). Assessing the TIP online information literacy tutorial. *RSR. Reference Services Review, 37*(1), 54–64. doi:10.1108/00907320910934995

Wang, R. (2016). Assessment for one-shot library instruction: A conceptual approach. *Portal (Baltimore, Md.), 16*(3), 619–648. doi:10.1353/pla.2016.0042

Weiner, S. A., Pelaez, N., Chang, K., & Weiner, J. (2011). Biology and nursing students' perceptions of a web-based information literacy tutorial. *Communications in Information Literacy, 5*(2), 187–201. doi:10.15760/comminfolit.2012.5.2.112

APPENDIX 1

Pre-Test

Q1 This semester students in ENG 176 courses will be completing surveys and training modules to help them learn more about the research process as part of the College's efforts to improve students' information literacy skills. Data collected from your responses may be shared for research purposes in articles, presentations, or public forums. However, your name, course section, e-mail address, or any other identifiable information will not be shared. Clicking on the "agree" button below indicates you voluntarily agree to have your data shared (without identifying details) in articles, presentations, or public forums. Clicking the "disagree" option means that you do not agree and that your data will not be shared outside the College. Thank you very much for your participation!

❍ Agree
❍ Disagree

Q2 First Name:

Q3 Last Name:

Q4 GBC Email:

Q5 Select your course section. Note: If you aren't sure, please visit your Course Schedule (LINK) in Campus Web to check. You will need to login with your GBC username and password.

❍ ENG 176 AB-Instructor Mr. Steel
❍ ENG 176 BB-Instructor Mr. Steel
❍ ENG 176 CB-Instructor Mr. Steel
❍ ENG 176 DB-Instructor Dr. Habib
❍ ENG 176 EB-Instructor Dr. Habib
❍ ENG 176 FB-Instructor Dr. Habib
❍ ENG 176 GB-Instructor Mrs. Booth
❍ ENG 176 HB-Instructor Mrs. Booth
❍ ENG 176 IB-Instructor Mrs. Booth
❍ ENG 176 WB-Instructor Dr. West

Q6 I feel I have the skills necessary to select a relevant topic for any written papers required in my classes at the college.

❍ Strongly disagree
❍ Somewhat disagree
❍ Neither agree nor disagree
❍ Somewhat agree
❍ Strongly agree

Q7 I feel I have the skills necessary to locate relevant research on my chosen research topic using a variety of resources, including the Library, online databases, and online resources.

❍ Strongly disagree
❍ Somewhat disagree
❍ Neither agree nor disagree
❍ Somewhat agree
❍ Strongly agree

Q8 I feel I have the skills necessary to select appropriate keywords, Boolean searching, and connector words to find relevant research when searching online databases and websites.

❍ Strongly disagree
❍ Somewhat disagree
❍ Neither agree nor disagree
❍ Somewhat agree
❍ Strongly agree

Q9 I feel I have the skills necessary to evaluate reference resources for relevance to my topic and accuracy of content.

❍ Strongly disagree
❍ Disagree
❍ Somewhat disagree
❍ Neither agree nor disagree
❍ Somewhat agree
❍ Agree
❍ Strongly agree

Q10 I feel I have the skills necessary to write my research papers. I am familiar with note taking and outlining as methods to help layout the structure of my papers.

❍ Strongly disagree
❍ Somewhat disagree
❍ Neither agree nor disagree
❍ Somewhat agree
❍ Strongly agree

Q11 I understand the difference between paraphrasing and quoting authors. I know when I should paraphrase an author versus when I should quote, and I am comfortable using both methods when referencing existing work.

❍ Strongly agree
❍ Somewhat agree
❍ Neither agree nor disagree
❍ Somewhat disagree
❍ Strongly disagree

Q12 Where is the best place to go if you are at the very beginning of a research project?

❍ College Library
❍ Google
❍ Web
❍ YouTube

Q13 What is the best source to use to find background information on a topic and key ideas, important dates or concepts?

❍ Google
❍ Magazines
❍ Newspapers
❍ Encyclopedias

Q14 Which of the following are effective strategies for choosing search terms:

❍ List abbreviations and alternate spellings of words
❍ Check a subject encyclopedia for ideas and concepts
❍ Brainstorm synonyms, broader terms, and narrower terms
❍ All of the above

Q15 What do you need to know how to do to be information literate in the 21st Century?

❍ Recognize when information is needed
❍ Find, critically evaluate, and effectively use information
❍ Use resources on the Web for your information needs
❍ Create and communicate information using various formats
❍ All of the above

Q16 What is the name of the Goldey-Beacom College's library?

❍ Goldey-Beacom College Library
❍ Jones Library
❍ Morris Library
❍ Hirons Library

Q17 You are writing a 15-page research paper about using social media in tourism marketing. Which of the following thesis statements is the strongest?

❍ It is a good idea to use online marketing to increase tourism.
❍ The FlipBoard app helped tourism for Hudiksvall, Sweden in 2012.
❍ In my opinion, the Internet has had a major impact on tourism marketing.
❍ The use of Web 2.0 tools in tourism marketing improves customer loyalty.

Q18 You have to write a 10-page research paper and the topic you want to explore is childhood obesity. Why might you want to start with a subject encyclopedia?

❍ To get an overview and keywords for your topic
❍ To put off doing the real research
❍ To get up-to-date news and statistics
❍ To read a primary source
❍ All of the above

Q19 You should use the following focus areas to NARROW your research topic EXCEPT:

❍ Choose more synonyms for your topic (related terms, broader terms)
❍ Choose a more specific period (Civil War, Iron Age, 1920s, 18th Century)
❍ Choose a more specific population to study (Age, race, gender, nationality, occupation)
❍ Choose a specific location (Europe, U.S., Denver, urban, eastern)

Q20 A thesaurus is a good place to find synonyms for your topic.

❍ True
❍ False

Q21 Background research has the following benefits:

❍ Leads to bibliographies which provide additional sources of information
❍ Can help you refine your topic
❍ Helps identify important facts
❍ All of the above

Q22 Which of the following statements best describes information in the library as compared to the Web?

- ❍ Information is in a permanent collection.
- ❍ Information is not well organized.
- ❍ Information is selected through a review process.
- ❍ Information can be ephemeral, and comes and goes quickly.

Q23 What source would you use to find an extensive amount of well-organized information on a topic, to put your topic in context with other important issues, or to find historical information?

- ❍ Newspapers
- ❍ Magazines
- ❍ Web
- ❍ Blogs
- ❍ Books

Q24 If you need to find scholarly articles on your topic and bibliographies that point to other relevant research, which of the following is the best source to use?

- ❍ Blogs
- ❍ Library catalog
- ❍ Newspapers
- ❍ Journals
- ❍ Web

Q25 What would you use to find out what books the library owns on your topic and where are they located?

- ❍ Newspaper
- ❍ Library catalog
- ❍ Books
- ❍ Google
- ❍ Journals

Q26 What is a periodical?

- ❍ A journal, magazine, or newspaper
- ❍ Online full text of the article you need
- ❍ A list of citations relevant to your topic
- ❍ A magazine that comes in microfilm
- ❍ None of the above

Q27 All general search engines return the same results.

- ❍ True
- ❍ False

Q28 A URL is a Web address that means Uniform Resource Locator.

- ❍ True
- ❍ False

Q29 Materials in the Hirons Library are organized with what classification system?

- ❍ Taxonomy
- ❍ Dewey Decimal
- ❍ Library of Congress
- ❍ None of the above

Q30 The latest news can be found using this source:
- ❍ Magazines
- ❍ Journals
- ❍ College library catalogs
- ❍ Web

Q31 What is the invisible Web?
- ❍ Pages done by government agencies
- ❍ Pages you can find on one search enginge, such as Yahoo, but not on another
- ❍ Pages in searchable, specialized electronic databases
- ❍ All of the above

Q32 A keyword search looks for words:
- ❍ in the title field only
- ❍ In the abstract field only
- ❍ In the subject field only
- ❍ In any field in the record

Q33 The record for an article in a periodical database will provide the following information: (Select 3)
- ❑ The date it was published
- ❑ The author's name
- ❑ The location of the publisher
- ❑ The name of the periodical in which the article appears

Q34 You would use a truncation symbol to:
- ❍ Search for various endings of a word
- ❍ Exclude words in a search
- ❍ Search in a specific database
- ❍ Substitute letters in the middle of a word
- ❍ All of the above

Q35 Here is your research topic: College students are under lots of stress today. Stress management is something that college students need to learn if they want to be successful students. What contributes to their stress and how do they handle it? Which of the following is the best set of keywords to use to search a library catalog or library databases?
- ❍ Stress and management
- ❍ College students and management
- ❍ College students and success and contribute
- ❍ College student and success
- ❍ Stress management and college students

Q36 Using the connector AND in a search:
- ❍ Searches for the word "and"
- ❍ Searches only these words
- ❍ Narrows your search
- ❍ Broadens your search

Q37 Imagine you are searching a database for articles about college students' jobs. Choose the best search strategy from the list below.
- ❍ college student(s) or employment
- ❍ work or employment or job or college or students

❍ students who work
❍ (work or employment or job) and college students

Q38 To refine your Web search results, you should: (select 2)
❑ Use the advanced search feature
❑ Limit your results to the first 10 pages
❑ Use only one search engine
❑ Use the built-in "Help" features

Q39 While searching in a research database, the use of Boolean operators "AND", "OR", and "NOT" can be useful in narrowing or widening your search results. Which word would you use to increase the items you will receive?
❍ NOT
❍ AND
❍ OR
❍ All of the above

Q40 Which is the BEST way to search for books on a given topic?
❍ Keyword or subject
❍ Author or title
❍ ISSN or ISBN
❍ Publisher or call number

Q41 You are looking for a book on how understanding child psychology can help parents. You search the library's book catalog for the terms CHILD PSYCHOLOGY and get back 549 titles. What's the best thing to do next?
❍ Add another term to make the search more specific
❍ Pick a title from the first screen
❍ Change the search to psychology child
❍ Start over and choose a new topic

Q42 How can you tell if you are looking at a popular magazine? (Select 2)
❑ Issues have few, if any, advertisements
❑ Issues generally have lots of photographs
❑ Articles are written for the general public
❑ Articles are in-depth and often have a bibliography

Q43 You are writing a paper on the history of the food industry. When evaluating resources, which of the following actions is the least important?
❍ Read the mission statement of a website.
❍ Find out if others have cited the resource
❍ Use only the most current resources
❍ Use resources that include different viewpoints
❍ Check the author's authority to write on the topic

Q44 When evaluating resources, which one is the LEAST important to consider:
❍ Author
❍ Publisher
❍ Document format
❍ Publishing date

Q45 The best sites always come up first in a search result
- ❍ True
- ❍ False

Q46 How do you know if someone is an authority on climate change?
- ❍ She uses technical jargon that most readers wouldn't understand
- ❍ Numerous peer-reviewed articles on global warming cite her work
- ❍ She has a PhD in political science
- ❍ She has her own web site

Q47 What would you assume is the primary purpose of the Centers for Disease Control and Prevention Vaccines and Immunizations (www.cdc.gov/vaccines) website?
- ❍ To sell vaccines to medical professionals
- ❍ To present personal opinions and experiences about vaccines
- ❍ To give an in-depth overview on the history of vaccines
- ❍ To disseminate authoritative research on vaccines so that it can be integrated into the practice of conventional medicine and inform the general public

Q48 Who would represent the target audience for the Journal Criminal Law & Criminology?
- ❍ Someone studying to become a bail bondsman
- ❍ Fans of the television show "Cops"
- ❍ Professors, researchers, and students in criminology
- ❍ People in trouble with the law

Q49 A primary source is
- ❍ An original document such as a diary, letter, etc.
- ❍ A collection of critical essays
- ❍ An article of book that extensively analyzes a topic
- ❍ The first book or journal article that is written on a topic
- ❍ All of the above

Q50 All of the following terms refer to academic journals EXCEPT:
- ❍ Scholarly
- ❍ Refereed
- ❍ Peer-Reviewed
- ❍ Industry

Q51 Which of the following is true about evaluating websites?
- ❍ You need to evaluate every website before using the information
- ❍ You do not need to evaluate sites that are from organizations
- ❍ Sites with a domain of ".edu" are from educational institutions and are all OK to use
- ❍ None of the above

Q52 What will be the starting point of your paper?
- ❍ Bibliography
- ❍ Conclusion
- ❍ Summary of a source
- ❍ Thesis statement

Q53 In your outline, the major points that support your thesis statement will be labeled as:
- ❍ Roman Numerals (I, II, III)
- ❍ Numbers (1, 2, 3)

❍ Capital letters (A, B, C)

Q54 Which note taking form can be used to capture information?

❍ Summarize
❍ Quote
❍ Paraphrase
❍ All of the above

Q55 In research papers you should quote from a source when you want the reputation of the author to lend authority and credibility to your point.

❍ True
❍ False

Q56 You should summarize or paraphrase when you:

❍ Find memorable or historically significant language
❍ Find the author's language so clear and concise you wouldn't be able to effectively make the same point in your own words
❍ Want the ideas presented in the source, but not the specific language used to express it
❍ Don't want the author's meaning to be lost or changed if you paraphrased or summarized

Q57 In researching school lunch nutrition, you look up your topic on the web and find an article in a personal blog that claims the amount of calories in school lunches increased by 15% in 2000. Your next BEST step is:

❍ Verify the statistic in another source, such as a reference book or journal article
❍ See if you can find another blog that has the same information
❍ Write down the information so you can cite this source in your paper
❍ None of the above

Q58 It is acceptable to copy and paste text from an abstract of an article without citing it.

❍ True
❍ False

Q59 Abstracts are a good place to begin your research when:

❍ You want to learn more about a topic
❍ You have run out of time and do not want to read the entire article
❍ You are confident you have enough information
❍ You need to find statistical information to validate your thesis statement

Q60 An outline of your paper can help you create:

❍ A more fluid paper
❍ A more focused paper
❍ A more balanced paper
❍ A more complete paper
❍ All of the above

Q61 When you need assistance to determine your keywords, you should ask: (Select 2)

❑ Grocer
❑ Professor
❑ Mother or father
❑ A librarian

Q62 All of the following are good ways to avoid plagiarism, EXCEPT:

- ❍ Document citations of items you use
- ❍ Change a couple of words from the original source rather than directly copying the words
- ❍ Use quotation marks or block quotes around exact quotations
- ❍ Take accurate notes where you found specific ideas

Q63 The type of information that you need for citing articles includes:

- ❍ Title of Journal
- ❍ Issue
- ❍ Author's Name
- ❍ Date
- ❍ All of the above

Q64 Some magazines contain in-depth articles which appear to be good sources for research papers but because they are not scholarly, you should not cite them.

- ❍ True
- ❍ False

Q65 Material on the Internet is in the public domain and not protected by copyright.

- ❍ True
- ❍ False

Q66 Of the following types of information, which one does NOT need to be acknowledged:

- ❍ A word-for-word quotation from The New York Times online about economic recovery
- ❍ A photograph of Rosa Parks that you found in Women in World History: A biographical Dictionary
- ❍ A paragraph you wrote summarizing information from a Newsweek article about bioengineered food
- ❍ A list of three most important things you think students can do to success in college

Q67 You only have to cite sources that you use in written papers.

- ❍ True
- ❍ False

Q68 You do NOT need to credit someone's ideas as long as you change some of their words.

- ❍ True
- ❍ False

Q69 When citing a book, which of the following would NOT be a part of your citation?

- ❍ Place of publication
- ❍ Title
- ❍ Author
- ❍ Number of pages

Q70 When citing a website, which of these should be part of your citation?

- ❍ Web address (URL)
- ❍ Webmaster's e-mail address
- ❍ Search engine used
- ❍ All of the above

Q71 APA and MLA style both refer to:

- ❍ Article indexes
- ❍ Formats for documenting the sources used for a paper

❍ Call numbers
❍ Library classification systems

Q72 Ethical Research Practices
Q73 See Table 13.
Q74 See Table 14.
Q75 What is your definition of plagiarism?
Q76 Students should be punished harshly when he/she plagiarizes.

❍ Never
❍ Once
❍ Rarely
❍ Occasionally
❍ Regularly
❍ Always

Q77 See Table 15.

Table 13. How often have you done the following without citing the source?

	Never	Once	Rarely	Occasionally	Regularly	Always
Used another author's ideas	❍	❍	❍	❍	❍	❍
Used another author's phrases	❍	❍	❍	❍	❍	❍
Used another author's sentences/paragraphs	❍	❍	❍	❍	❍	❍
Used entire document by another author	❍	❍	❍	❍	❍	❍

Table 14. How often do you think most students do the following, without citing the source?

	Never	Once	Rarely	Occasionally	Regularly	Always
Used another author's ideas	❍	❍	❍	❍	❍	❍
Used another author's phrases	❍	❍	❍	❍	❍	❍
Used another author's sentences/paragraphs	❍	❍	❍	❍	❍	❍
Used entire document by another author	❍	❍	❍	❍	❍	❍

Table 15. How serious an incident is each of the following?

	Not at All	Somewhat	Very
Using another author's ideas	❍	❍	❍
Using another author's phrases	❍	❍	❍
Using another author's sentences/paragraphs	❍	❍	❍
Using entire document by another author	❍	❍	❍

APPENDIX 2

Figure 2. Hybrid deployment workflow

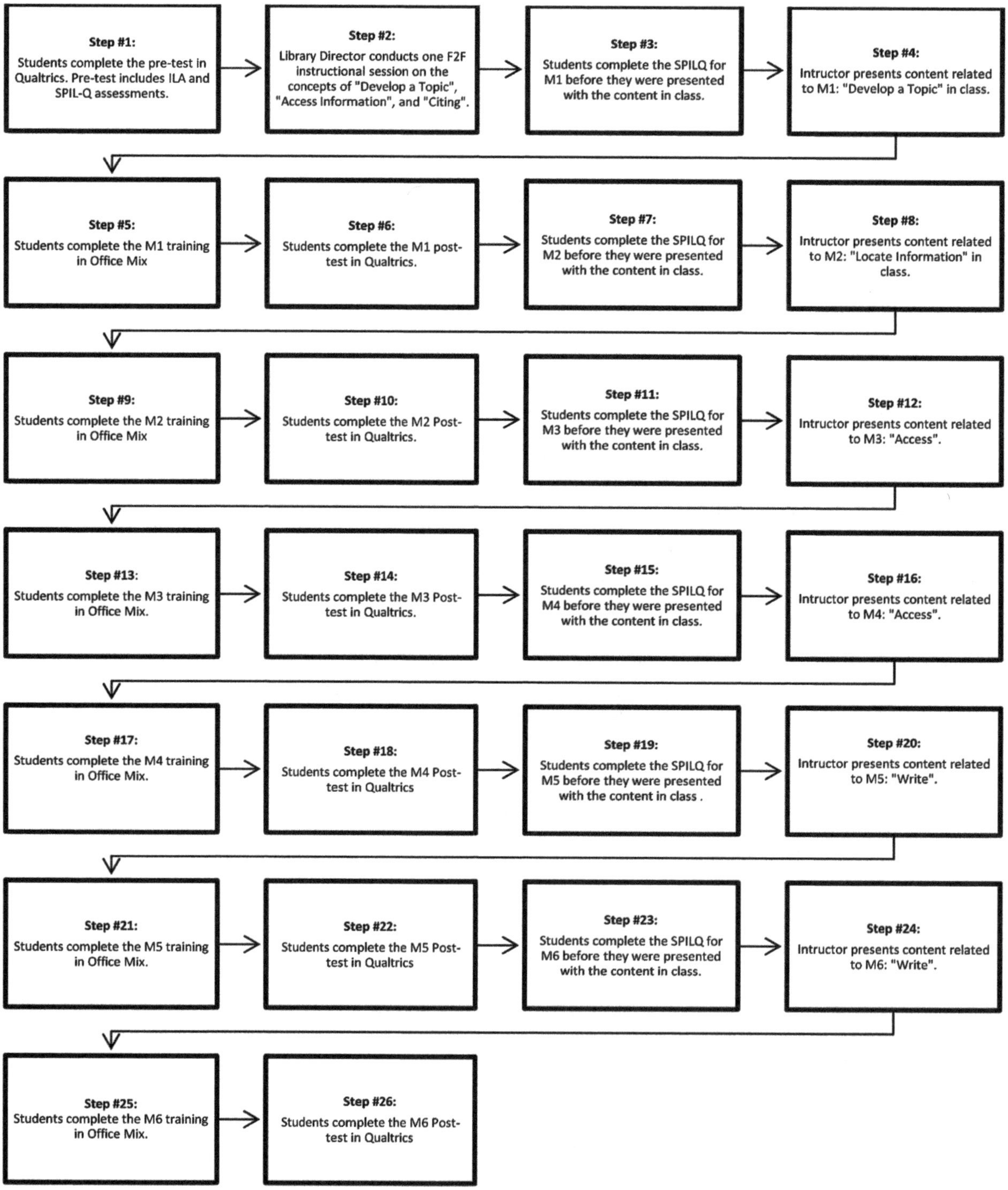

APPENDIX 3

Figure 3. Online deployment workflow

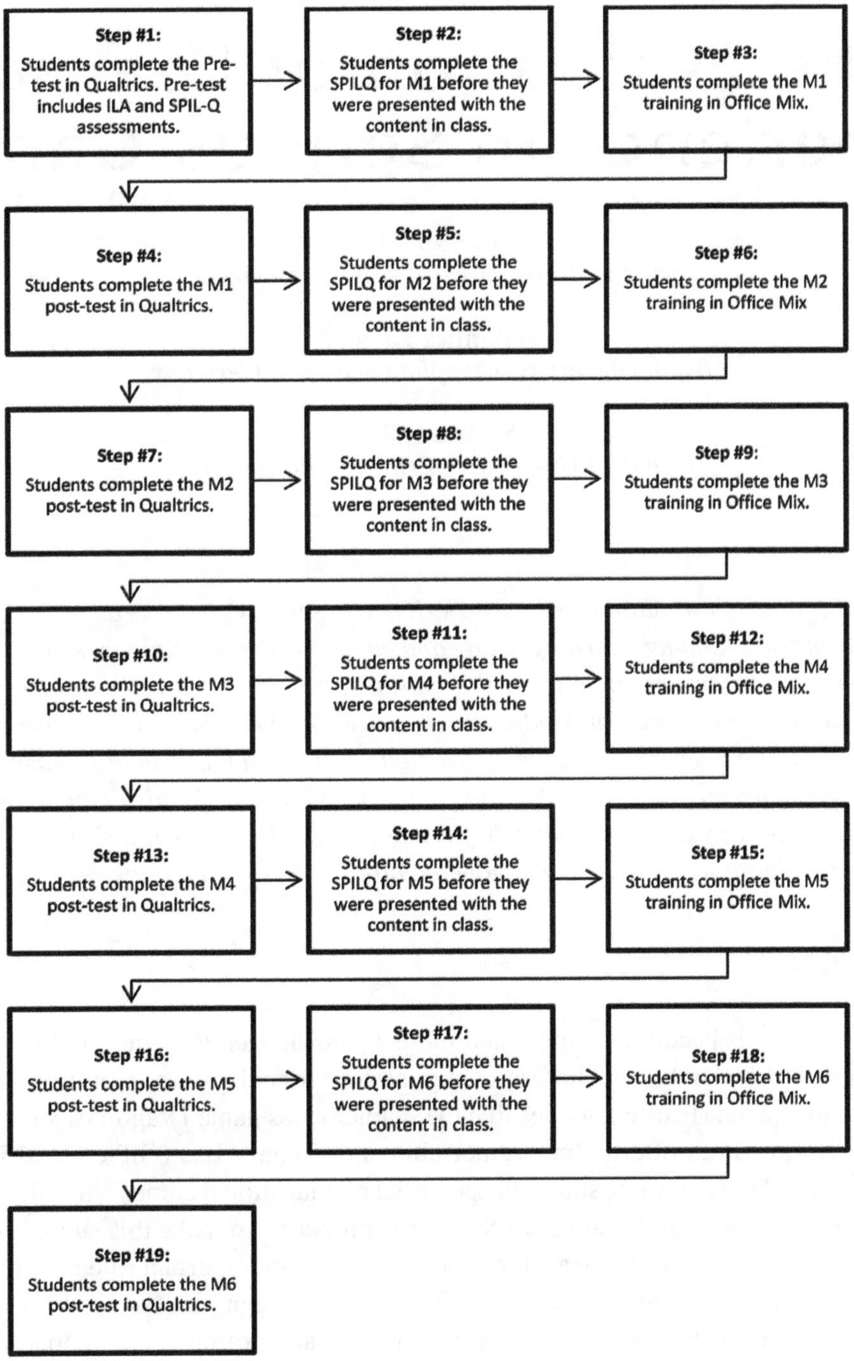

Chapter 5
The Evaluation of Learner Experience in Serious Games

Laila Shoukry
Technical University of Darmstadt, Germany

Johannes Konert
Beuth University of Applied Sciences, Germany

Stefan Göbel
Technical University of Darmstadt, Germany

ABSTRACT

In this chapter, the topic of evaluating learner experience in serious games is discussed with respect to four different dimensions: gaming, learning, using and context with a special focus on using multimodal data. After reviewing relevant research fields, the steps involved in a serious games evaluation process is investigated and relevant evaluation studies are reviewed with emphasis on the use of different modalities for recording and assessing in-game interactions. Finally, a theoretical framework (LeGUC) is proposed defining parameters related to the four dimensions discussed which can be observed during evaluation studies of serious games and how they relate to logged in-game interactions. The framework is based on relevant literature as well as a conducted observational user study.

INTRODUCTION

As game-based learning is becoming a more and more acknowledged learning field and with the rapid advancement in digital technologies, the use of digital educational games is on the rise. In the commercial games market, some learning games like the mathematics game Dragon Box on the Apple App Store even outperform games offering pure entertainment revenue-wise (Gilbert, 2015). Such a phenomenon, although still not common, shows the potential of educational games when designed properly, be it with the need of a practical definition of the word "properly" to make this success reproduceable. With assessment being integral to any learning process, it plays an important role in digital game-based learning, especially where the time-consuming and expensive design process needs extra justification. The features which make educational games more appealing and promising than non-gaming learning environments, for instance "intrinsic motivation" and "pleasurable frustration", are the same aspects

DOI: 10.4018/978-1-5225-4206-3.ch005

which make their design and, more so, evaluation, a challenging task (Mitgutsch & Alvarado, 2013). The lack of consensus regarding the best approach to combining gaming and educational theories and on methods to fully capture and analyze the rich and deep interaction experience with this interdisciplinary software makes it challenging to link certain product elements to its success or failure to improve further development cycles (Khine, 2011). Looking into established evaluation techniques of non-gaming learning environments or non-educational games adds to the confusion as they do not provide tailored methods which can be directly applied to evaluate the aspects which distinguish learning games from both product categories (Loh, Sheng & Ifenthaler, 2015). The need for more insight into the serious gameplay experience is further intensified with the emergence of novel interaction paradigms and modern educational theories and landscapes accompanying the digital revolution increasingly rendering classical evaluation methods insufficient (Mirza-Babaei *et al.*, 2014; Shoukry, Göbel & Steinmetz, 2014b; Bosch, Hall & Dame, 2015).This need for understanding naturalistic serious play experience has led to more and more research being conducted to use multimodal methods in the evaluation of serious games. A main focus of this chapter is to investigate the ways in which the field of Serious Games evaluation can benefit from multimodal methods by reviewing current trends as well as future potential. Although there are numerous reviews on Serious Games evaluation frameworks and techniques, they lack the focus on multimodality despite its many promises and challenges (Mitgutsch & Alvarado, 2013; Gee *et al.*, 2014; Kiili *et al.*, 2014). A main problem in providing such an overview is the variation in terminology, research background and objectives among different researchers when discussing similar topics. This can be facilitated by starting with locating this interdisciplinary research area and related terminology in the research landscape which is done in the first section of this chapter. Serious Games apply concepts of game technology in a broad application spectrum ranging from educational, training and simulation to persuasive and social impact games or games for health. In this chapter the term Serious Games will be used to refer to digital educational games, although this is one application area of Serious Games. Because of its interdisciplinarity, the evaluation of Serious Games lies in the intersection of and benefits from metrics and strategies from several different fields. Hence, it is important to review some important fields which are considerably related to this topic.

Learning Analytics

As the learning aspect is what Serious Games (here digital educational games) from regular games, the evaluation of Serious Games uses methods from the field of Learning Analytics. The assessment of learning in Serious Games, as in any other learning environment, can take place before, during and/or after the interaction with the game. Assessment of learning before using the game can inform the design of the game, help personalizing the game or serve as a pre-test for performance comparison. Assessment of learning during the game can be used to adapt the game on-line, to monitor learning progress by teachers or institutions, as self-assessment for learners to reflect on their learning and understanding, as part of the learning process to improve their memory recall or as a means to evaluate the design and effectiveness of a game level or module. Assessment of learning after finishing a game helps evaluate the effectiveness of the game, help learners know what they need to improve or, if used (merely) as an assessment tool, to assist instructors/institutions to assess learner achievements against intended outcomes. The field of Learning Analytics describes the "measurement, collection, analysis and reporting of data about learners and their contexts" to improve learning (Siemens George & Long, 2011). It establishes conceptual foundations as well as application-specific recommendations for making efficient and effective use of "information about learners' interactions with learning content and their learning progress". Metrics typically extracted in Learning Analytics include information about the learners (independent of their interaction with the learning environment) in addition to context-specific data extracted during interaction (Loh, Sheng & Ifenthaler, 2015). For the evaluation of Serious Games, Learning Analytics provide an objective and cost-effective approach for justifying the expense of using them in learning contexts. Hereby, the critical question is how to best collect academically meaningful information from learners without disrupting their game-flow. In addition, interacting with a Serious Game is usually more complex and produces larger datasets than interacting with a regular learning environment. In this regard, the field of Game Analytics and, more so, Serious Games Analytics provide suitable solutions.

Game Analytics

While Learning Analytics focuses on learning-relevant information, Game Analytics, as the term implies, focuses on gameplay interactions and gives enjoyment of the game experience the highest priority (Loh, Sheng & Ifenthaler, 2015). Metrics used in Game Analytics are also typically more profit-oriented and are used to inform business-intelligent decision-making and improve game development cycles (Loh, Sheng & Ifenthaler, 2015). Monitoring the effect of design updates on players is crucial for continuously improving and thus increasing revenue. These insights into real and dynamic data in huge amounts (also called game telemetry) has been made possible with the digital advances in recent years and thus the field of Game Analytics is relatively young. The term Game User Research also describes an emergent research field investigating the interaction between players and games (Seif El-Nasr *et al.*, 2012). In addition to general business data, Game Analytics trace players' actions inside the gaming environment in order to gain a better understanding of their preferences, detect crucial design flaws as well as identify best-gamers. However, although games offer rich information about players' progress, the game industry is not focusing on assessing competencies gained through the game as the games are not designed with this purpose (Loh, Sheng & Ifenthaler, 2015). Thus, pure Game Analytics cannot be directly applied to Serious Games which were not created for mere entertainment.

Serious Game Analytics

It would appear reasonable that combining metrics from the fields of Learning Analytics and Game Analytics would enable an effective way of evaluating Serious Games considering both their learning goals and their highly interactive nature. However, some metrics of the two fields are actually conflicting. For instance, failure associated with exploration inside a gaming environment contributes to the flow needed to stay captivated inside the game whereas failure is not typically a desired experience inside a learning environment and subsequently can be treated as a conceptual error. Another example is the time to complete a certain task: While in Games it is desired to make fast decisions and complete tasks in a short time, learning needs more time to allow reflecting and critical thinking. Users of Serious Games are players as well as learners, and are thus referred to as play-learners (Loh, Sheng and Ifenthaler, 2015) and need special metrics to measure their performance as well as evaluate the quality of their playing experience. This is where the field of Serious Games Analytics comes into play, tracing play-learners actions and behaviors and assessing their performance with the purpose of improving Serious Game Design. Figure 1 depicts the process of applying Analytics in Serious Games as described in (Shoukry, Göbel & Steinmetz, 2014a).

Figure 1. Process of applying learning analytic in serious Games as described in (Shoukry, Göbel and Steinmetz, 2014a).

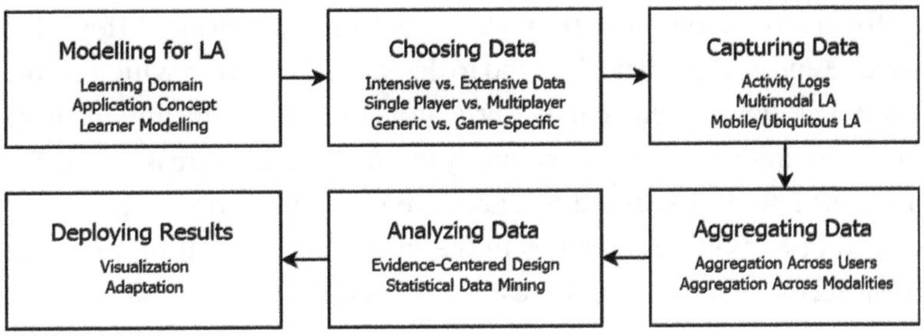

Multimodal Recognition

As Serious Games claim to offer learning content in a more "fun" environment, assessing User Experience is a crucial part of Serious Games Evaluation. As humans display their emotions and cognitive states through different channels, also using non-verbal communication elements like facial expressions, eye movements, body movements, tone of voice, posture and physiological reactions, pure textual data is not enough to fully capture the experience. In that context, researchers explore approaches to allow computers to detect and recognize changes in a person's affective state. This is the specialty of the field of Affective Computing which is largely applied in evaluating digital products as one application possibility (Picard & Daily, 2005). Using such multimodal data capturing and recognition techniques in the evaluation of Serious Games is the main focus of this chapter. This approach of applying multimodal recognition for assessing learning has been used in the field of Multimodal Learning Analytics (MMLA), particularly in "the analysis of natural rich modalities of communication during situated interpersonal and computer-mediated learning activities" (Oviatt, Cohen & Weibel, 2013).

Mobile Sensing

Reports of the Serious Games market point to the mobile sector as the dominant future direction, especially location-based learning games and mobile augmented reality games as new interaction paradigms (Insight, 2013). Along with new types of user-generated data, the use of smartphones offers new contexts in which learning occurs which should be taken into consideration when evaluating users' interactions and also have direct effects and pose new challenges on other evaluation aspects such as affect detection (Bosch *et al.*, 2015). This shift makes testing in traditional laboratory environments not only difficult but also not naturalistic as it ignores a large scope of the experience. As Learning Analytics based purely on logging of traditional interaction patterns becomes insufficient, it needs to be enriched with multimodal mobile sensing data in order to detect, for instance, that a learner is being distracted by environmental or social factors. The term Mobile Learning Analytics describes "the collection, analysis and reporting of the data of mobile learners, which can be collected from the mobile interactions between learners, mobile devices and available learning materials" (Aljohani & Davis, 2012). Thus, the field of Mobile Sensing, which is concerned with using mobile sensors to unobtrusively track users and their non-static environment, also started to play a growing role in the evaluation of Serious Games. The following are some smartphone sensors and their potential affective and cognitive measures listed in Shi and Ali (2012): Smartphone Cameras can be used for eye-tracking and facial feature recognition which can be useful for inferring information about attention, stress, learning patterns, different skills and emotions. Accelerometer, gyroscope and compass can be used to detect body motion which could be used to measure arousal. Finger pressure on touch screens can be indicators of stress, certainty of response and cognitive load. Voice recorded by the microphone can be analyzed to measure stress and other affective states.

Figure 2 shows an overview of discussed research areas and their intersections. Nowadays, the topic of multimodal evaluation of Serious Games lies in the intersection of all four discussed research fields. We call it "Multimodal Serious Games Analytics" (MSGA).

Figure 2. Topics and intersections of the discussed research areas

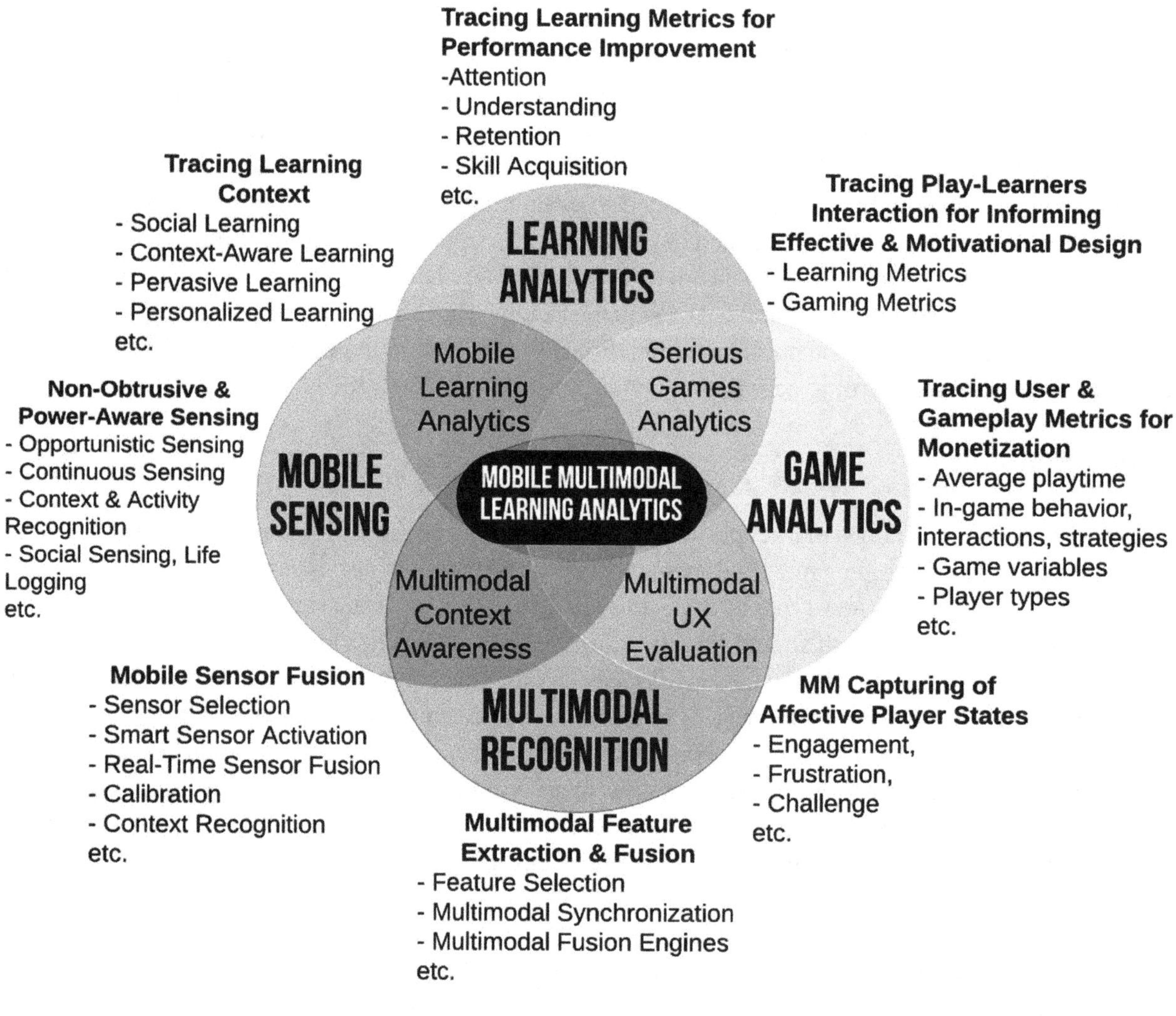

SERIOUS GAMES EVALUATION

Primary Objective of Evaluation: "Why to Measure?"

When reviewing research dealing with assessment in Serious Games, it becomes evident that, depending on the primary purpose and context of the studies, they are either directed towards assessing the learner or assessing the Serious Game. As discussed earlier, assessing the learner online can help in adapting the game or making predictions. This is also referred to as in-game analysis (Baalsrud Hauge *et al.*, 2014). Assessing the learner can also be useful, together with purchasing habits, for making recommendations. Integrated assessment in Serious Games, also referred to as "Stealth Assessment" (Shute, 2011), can serve teachers, institutions or the learner himself for monitoring learning. Using games as assessment tools in academic contexts is becoming more and more popular due to their interactive, non-invasive and engaging nature and the big amount of gameplay data they can offer. Assessing the Serious Game is typically done off-line, also referred to as posterior analysis (Baalsrud Hauge *et al.*, 2014)and has the aim of proving the fun and effectiveness of the game or uncovering possible shortcomings to be fed into further development cycles or new games. Although there is no common agreement on the best method to evaluate and improve the design of Serious Games, there are many assessment frameworks in literature which attempt to close this gap:

- Design, Play and Experience Framework (Winn, 2008),
- Educational games (EG) design framework: Combination of game design, pedagogy
- and content modeling (Ibrahim and Jaafar, 2009),
- Key criteria for Game Design A: Framework (Sanchez, 2011),
- What makes a good serious game (Göbel, Gutjahr and Steinmetz, 2011),
- "Serious Educational Game Rubric (SEGR)" (Annetta and Bronack, 2011),
- A Serious Game Design Assessment Framework (Mitgutsch and Alvarado, 2013),
- Assessing Serious Games: The GRAND Assessment Framework (Gee *et al.*, 2014),
- Flow framework for analyzing the quality of educational games (Kiili *et al.*, 2014)

Many studies using multimodal methods have the aim of responding to affective and cognitive states or adapting the environment accordingly. These studies can be classified to research areas such as Affective Learning, Affective Gaming or Intelligent Tutoring Systems. Other studies have the main purpose of comparing different serious games, a serious game with a non-gaming digital learning environment or different modalities for evaluating the same game. With further investigation, it was found that many studies did not really focus on assessment, but rather are exploratory attempting to discover relations and correlations to lay foundations which can benefit future research with different goals. Thus, in summary, the following four goals were found in literature:

- Evaluation for Design Improvement
- Adaptation/Personalization/Responding/Predicting
- Comparison of Products or Modalities
- Exploring Relationships/Categorization

These four categories will be used in Tables 1, 2 and 3 for categorizing the goals of presented studies.

Aspects to Evaluate: "What to Measure?"

By inspecting the name "Serious (or, in this case more precisely, Educational) Games", one can already derive two main dimensions of parameters which need to be considered in Serious Games evaluation: Learning and Gaming. However, by reviewing literature on Serious Games evaluation, a third dimension was found to also play an important role, even more for Serious Games than for other software categories: the dimension of Usability and User Experience. This is because usability issues can greatly hinder interactions with serious games, which directly has a negative effect on both learning and gaming, and may thus make all design and development efforts on the other two dimensions go in vain (Pinelle, Wong & Stach, 2008; Bernsen & Dybkjær, 2010; Mohamed & Jaafar, 2011, 2012; Olsen, Procci & Bowers, 2011; Moreno-Ger *et al.*, 2012; Perry *et al.*, 2012). As serious games development teams typically have a much lower budget than the entertainment game industry, not much is usually left for ensuring good usability which can explain the mostly inferior quality of experience. In addition, many users of Serious Games are not regular gamers and may thus need special measures concerning usability. The main difference to regular usability testing in Serious Games evaluation is that some obstacles to proceeding introduced in a game are necessary components for adding challenge while these could be considered as negative issues in a normal usability setting. The dimensions Learning, Gaming and Using as well as all data which can be captured for each category were investigated in more detail in our Reasons and Responses model described in (Shoukry & Gobel, 2017). All three dimensions: Learning, Gaming and Using are interdependent and thus there is a need to evaluating inter-dimension coherence in design. Different studies in this direction are concerned with finding mappings between learning and gaming design decisions (Arnab *et al.*, 2015). In addition to logging in-game interaction events during sessions, a common measure which was found to be integral in evaluating the in-game experience on all three dimensions: learning, gaming and using, is determining affective and cognitive states. Affect has been proven to be integral in any learning process, which makes it even more important for Serious Games as they claim to entertain and thus should directly consider affective factors.

In addition to the three dimensions concerned with interactions with the game, a fourth dimension is concerned with the context in which the interaction takes place (Fu & Yu, 2008; Van Staalduinen a& de Freitas, 2011; Marne *et al.*, 2012; Plass, Homer & Kinzer, 2014). Context is crucial not only for personalization but also for disambiguating and inspecting reasons behind in-game actions. For example, a response delay inside a game may be due to external factors such as an interruption by another person or event in the surrounding. Context aspects which can be captured can be related to the environment such as location, noise, illumination and weather, those related to the device (e.g. smartphone) can be orientation and shaking and those related to the user can be activity, mood and social interactions.

In-game event logging in addition to observing/recording/recognizing affective and cognitive states and context parameters was used in most studies to determine answers to the following questions:

- In how far did the game achieve its intended purpose?
- Which aspects/elements contributed to its success/failure?
- Which aspects/elements should be improved and how?
- Which aspects/elements should be improved/made more appropriate for a specific user/target audience/context?

Evaluation Methods: "How to Measure It?"

After determining what aspects about the serious game are required to be evaluated, it is time to decide for the appropriate evaluation procedure. For that, the evaluators, the time and place of the evaluation as well as the tools used are to be planned. Evaluators of a serious game can be real users or surrogate users who perform expert evaluation (Hasiah & Azizah, 2010). These can be educational, game design, interaction design and/or content experts. According to the time and place of the evaluation, different types of mechanisms can be differentiated. Ex-situ evaluation refers to remote data collection without the need for co-location (Loh, Sheng & Ifenthaler, 2015). In this case telemetry refers to remotely tracing the in-situ generated gameplay data from a gaming environment (Shoukry, Reuter & Mehm, 2014). In synchronous evaluation, the users and their actions are traced/analyzed in real-time whereas in asynchronous evaluation, gameplay data is reviewed any time after the evaluation session. Laboratory-based evaluation needs testers to be co-located which limits participation and the testing environment is controlled but artificial. Remote or mobile evaluation gives the possibility of employing testers from all over the world in their natural environments, without the need for special, expensive and obtrusive equipments but has the downside of having an uncontrolled and dynamic environment and may suffer hardware limitations. Thus, if the serious game to be tested is mobile and needs to be tested in a naturalistic setting, a remote evaluation may be appropriate. (Porayska-Pomsta *et al.*, 2013) reviews different elicitation methods for studying learners' affect in intelligent tutoring systems. Similarly, (Göbel, Gutjahr & Hardy, 2013) discusses different methods and modalities used in the evaluation of serious games. Static (user-independent) product aspects can be evaluated just by inspection or expert heuristic evaluation without the need for real users to do the testing (Shoukry, Sturm and Galal-Edeen, 2015). With real users, qualitative or quantitative methods can be used. Qualitative or manual evaluation methods include observation, think-alouds, pre-post-tests, self-reports, video analysis or surveys based on heuristic rules. Quantitative methods usually rely on game telemetry or automatic capture and analysis of multimodal data.

Data: "What Will Be Captured to Measure It?"

According to the aspects to be evaluated and the evaluation methods applied, the data to be captured will differ. Qualitative studies will result in questionnaire/interview responses, observation notes, think-aloud protocols and/or screen/video/audio recordings. Data from quantitative studies can also include video and audio recordings which are commonly used for detecting visual and audio features but will most probably include log files and recently also frequently rely on physiological and/or mobile sensing. For recording in-game interactions, log files are mostly used, while for detecting affective and cognitive states, visual and physiological features are mostly extracted, although many studies also attempt to do this using pure logging alone. For context, mobile sensors are usually used. In many recent evaluation studies, data from multiple modalities is used. As this indicates a recent trend in the evaluation of Serious Games, we will try to shed the light on it here. Studies found to be using multimodal data for the evaluation of Serious Games (see Table 1) did not cover all aspects and modalities. However, as serious games, in essence, can be evaluated by evaluating the three different dimensions of Table I independently, we have also surveyed studies evaluating non-gaming learning environments (see Table 2) as well as non-educational games (see Table 3). In addition, some studies using multimodal data for the evaluation of multimedia, like videos, pictures and ads are summarized in Table 4. The studies in all tables are ordered by date. By looking at the time range of the studies in the tables, one can recognize that most studies on multimodal evaluation of serious games are from recent years whereas non-educational games started earlier. Non-gaming learning environments started early to do affect recognition in the field of affective intelligent tutoring systems but we chose the recent ones to be comparable to the serious games studies. Most studies evaluating Serious Games, non-gaming learning environments and non-educational games using multimodal methods as seen in the tables focus on especially logging user actions and recognizing cognitive and affective states through different modalities, then combining both to examine aspects in the product assessed. By examining studies determining cognitive states, the order of modalities used according to the frequency of use in the listed studies is the following: Eye-tracking was found to be the most used modality for determining cognitive states, followed by physiological data and lastly audio. Other modalities like pressure exerted on mouse and seat also played a role in one study in determining cognitive states. As for automatically recognizing affective states for evaluation, it was found that facial expressions is the most frequently used feature in the listed studies, followed by physiological data, then posture, gesture and finally audio. Most studies focusing on user performance and strategies included logging with the other multimodal data in their evaluation. Above all, the tables show how multimodal data are playing an increasing role in the evaluation of learning and gaming aspects and in recent years, while still limited, in the evaluation of Serious Games.

Analysis: "How to Make Sense of Data?"

According to evaluation method and data captured, different analysis methods can be used. Qualitative data can be explored and annotated by experts manually to make conclusions (Shoukry *et al.*, 2014). Quantitative or automated evaluation methods can use data mining or unsupervised machine learning on logging and multimodal data. Hybrid methods use supervised machine learning or fuses self-reports with logging (Shoukry *et al.*, 2015).

Figure 3 summarizes steps in planning and conducting serious games evaluation.

LEARNER EXPERIENCE ASPECTS IN FIELD STUDIES OF SERIOUS GAMES

In this section we will introduce the LeGUC framework (Learning-Gaming-Using-Context) defining a concept for linking serious games log data with affective and cognitive states, user behavior and context data. It is initially based on a literature review on related models in the fields serious games, affective learning, context-aware mobile learning and user experience and then refined and expanded using a study carried out with 20 participants.

The theoretical construct was needed for evaluating learner experience in a mobile educational game for children teaching them the German "Artikel", the ArtikelGame – see Figure 4, to give insight for further development cycles. The game was created with StoryTec (Mehm, Göbel and Steinmetz, 2012), an authoring environment for creating scene-based serious games based on the NGLOB (Narrative Game-Based Learning Object) Model (Göbel *et al.*, 2009).

Most studies detecting affective and cognitive states within serious games interaction sessions were limited to a small number of traditional emotions (see Table 1) which do not cover all aspects related to the three dimensions learning, gaming and using in addition to the context dimension, which are, as discussed in this chapter, crucial for understanding learner experience in serious games (Olsen, Procci

Figure 3. Steps in planning and conducting serious games evaluation

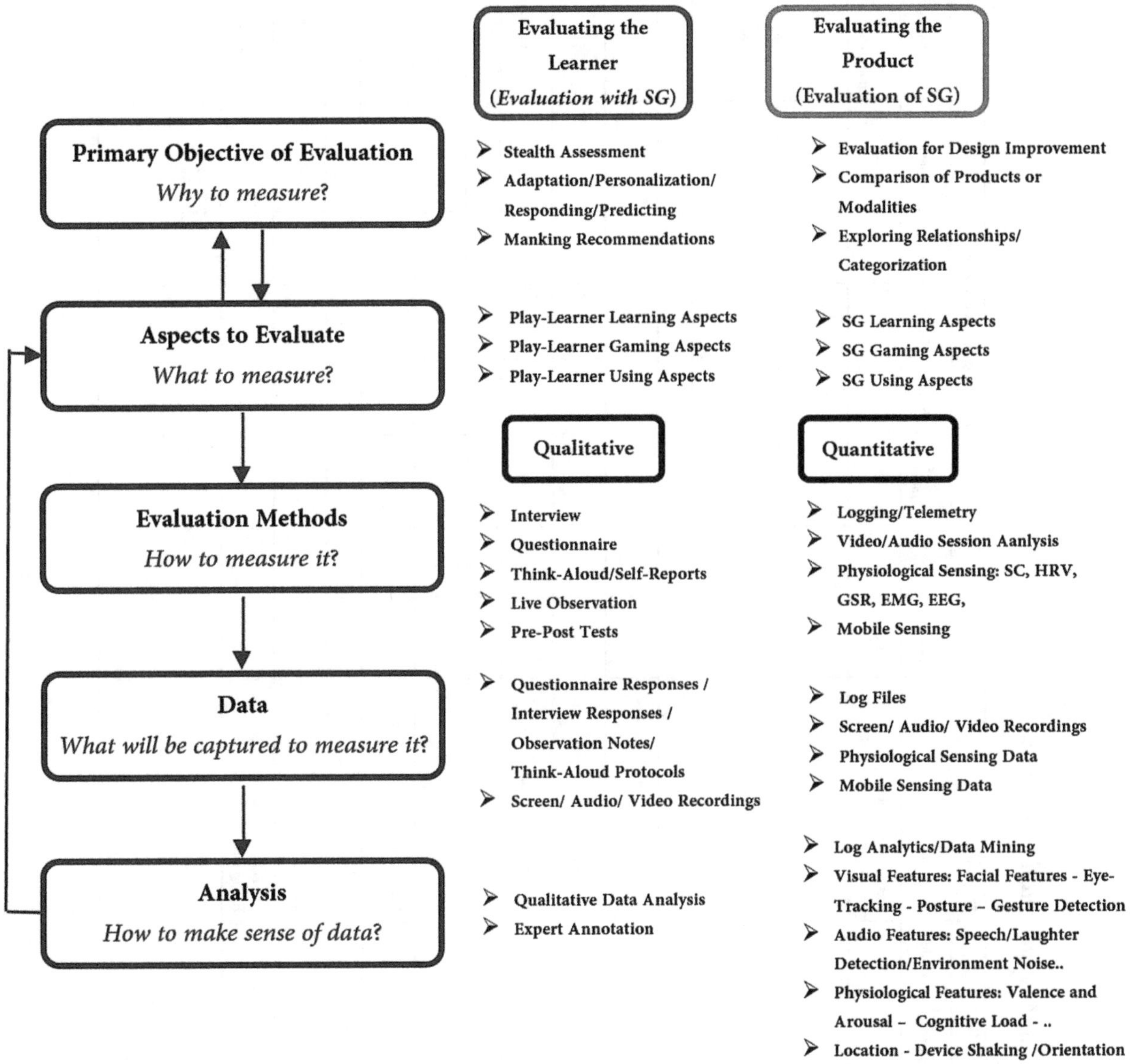

& Bowers, 2011). A more general approach was thus needed to include a reasonable set of states worth capturing during a serious games evaluation session in the field. This should consider aspects related to affect, cognition, behavior and context which are possible to encounter during an educational game session and related to the dimensions: learning, gaming, using and context. To do this, it will need to take into account measures originally defined for pure learning environments, others defined for games as well as measures defined for user experience evaluation. The focus of the study is not how to recognize these features using automated methods nor which modalities are best suitable for capturing the data but rather define which aspects need to be considered to gain a better understanding of the full experience.

As event logs typically capture interactions with the game environment, it needs in many cases to be enriched by user reactions and other context data to be more effectively analyzed. Consider a user

Table 1. A summary of serious games studies using multimodal data

Study	Goal				Aspects	Modalities/Features							
	Evaluation	Adaptation	Comparison	Relation		Logging	Facial	Eye Tracking	Posture	Gesture	Audio	Physiological	Qualitative
(Zain *et al.*, 2011)	X				Ineffective presentation and navigation	X		X					Questionnaires, think-aloud
(Rodrigo and Baker, 2011)			X		On- and off-task behavior and conversation, gaming the system, Affective states						X		Live annotation
(Muir and Conati, 2012)	X							X					
(Cowley, Ravaja and Heikura, 2013)				X								HRV, EMG	GT: pre-post tests, logging
(Patsis *et al.*, 2013)		X			Attention level	X	X					EEG	
(Gomes *et al.*, 2013)				X	Visual processing, problem-solving, attention	X		X					
(Kristian Kiili Harri Ketamo, 2014)	X				Attention-grabbing elements	X		X					
(Byun, Loh and Zhou, 2014)				X	Performance assessment			X					GT: questionnaire
(Li, Han and Liu, 2014)			X	X	pleasure							HRV	
(Bahreini, Nadolski and Westera, 2014a)		X			emotions		X						
(Keefe *et al.*, 2014)				X	Fixation transitions and learning outcomes			X					
(Cowley *et al.*, 2014)	X			X	Attention, motivation, vigilance							EEG	
(Paquette *et al.*, 2015)		X			affect	X			X				GT: Live observation using BROMP
(Bosch, Hall and Dame, 2015)			X		Boredom, confusion Engagement, frustration	X	X						GT: Live observation using BROMP
(Nesbitt *et al.*, 2015)	X				Pleasentness of game elements							Startle EyBlink (EMG)	
(Kai *et al.*, 2015)			X		Off-task behavior, Six affects	X	X						Live annotation

Table 2. A summary of non-gaming learning environments' studies using multimodal data

Study	Goal				Aspects	Modalities/Features								
	Evaluation	Adaptation	Comparison	Relation		Logging	Facial	Eye Tracking	Posture	Gesture	Audio	Physio-logical	Qualitative	Others
(Weber *et al.*, 2011)		X			Performance assessment, boredom, confusion, engagement, frustration	X	X		X				GT: annotation by learner, peer and judges	
(Banda and Robinson, 2011)		X			Emotions		X		X	X	X		GT: annotated dataset	
(Grafsgaard *et al.*, 2013)				X	Embodied affect in dialogue acts	X			X	X		SC	GT: dialogue act tags	
(Salmeron-majadas, Santos and Boticario, 2013)		X			valence	X	X						GT: expert annotation	
(Akputu, Seng and Lee, 2013)			X		Boredom, confusion, delight, engagement, frustration, disappointment		X						GT: annotation	
(Bahreini, Nadolski and Westera, 2014b)		X			Seven emotions		X				X			
(Grafsgaard *et al.*, 2014)		X			learning, engagement, frustration	X	X		X	X	X		GT: retrospective self-reports, pre-posttest	
(Salmeron-majadas, 2014)		X				X	X							Screen Recording
(Arroyo *et al.*, 2014)				X	Confidence, interest, frustration, excitement		X		X					Pressure on mouse, pressure on seat
(San Pedro, d Baker and Rodrigo, 2014)				X	Carelessness, affect	X							annotation	
(Brown and Howard, 2014)		X			Total time, response accuracy, proper function execution (on-task vs. off-task), engagement	X		X	X					
(Ezen-can *et al.*, no date)	X			X	Classifying dialogue acts	X			X	X	X		GT: annotation	
(Bahreini, Nadolski and Westera, 2015)		X			emotions						X			
(Chaouachi, Jraidi and Frasson, 2015)		X			Attention and workload							EEG	GT: debriefing	

Table 3. A summary of non-educational games' studies using multimodal data

Study	Goal				Aspects	Modalities/Features								
	Evaluation	Adaptation	Comparison	Relation		Logging	Facial	Eye Tracking	Posture	Gesture	Audio	Physio-logical	Qualitative	Others
(Ravaja *et al.*, 2006)	X				Valence and arousal							fEMG, SC, HR		Screen recording
(Mandryk and Atkins, 2007)	X				Boredom, challenge, excitement, frustration, fun							fEMG, GSR, HR, EKG	GT: self-reports	
(van den Hoogen *et al.*, 2008)		X			Player experience				X					Pressure patterns
(Drachen *et al.*, 2010)				X	Player experience							HR, EDA	GT: game experience questionnaire	
(Nacke, Stellmach and Lindley, 2010)	X				Boredom, immersion, flow			X				EEG		
(Shaker *et al.*, 2013)		X			Engagement, frustration, challenge					X			Sefl-Reports	
(Nunez Castellar, Oksanen and Van Looy, 2014)				X	Competence, flow, tension, challenge, positive and negative affect, immersion	X						HRV	GT: Questionnaire	
(Burelli, Triantafyllidis and Patras, 2014)				X	Attention, challenge, frustration, fun, anxiety, engagement						X			
(Paris Mavromoustakos Blom *et al.*, 2014)		X			Neutrality, happiness, anger		X							
(Nogueira *et al.*, 2014)	X	X			Valence and arousal	X						SC, HR, fEMG		
(Shaker and Shaker, 2014)		X			Happiness, sadness, anger, surprise		X		X	X				
(Marczak and Schott, 2015)				X	Play performance									Key graphical and sound gameplay feedback

Note: Abbreviations in the Tables: GT: Ground Truth, EEG: Electroencephalogram, EMG: Electromyography, fEMG: facial Electromyography, HR: Heart Rate, HRV: Heart Rate Variability, BCI: Brain-Computer Interface, BROMP: a protocol for Quantitative Field Observations of Student Affect and Behavior, GSR: Galvanic Skin Response, SC: Skin Conductance, EDA: Electrodermal Activity, EKG: Electrocardiogram

Figure 4. ArtikelGame: An educational game created with StoryTec for teaching children the German "Artikel"

Table 4. Evaluation states identified in literature to occur in interaction environments

Citation	Environment	Affective and Cognitive	Context	Behavior
(O'regan, 2003)	Online learning	Frustration, Anxiety, Shame, Excitement, Pride		
(Kort and Reilly, 2002)	Learning Activities	Frustration, Dispiritedness, Puzzlement, Confusion, Curiosity, Satisfaction, Hopefulness, Determination		
(Conati, 2004; Conati and Maclaren, 2009)	Educational Games	Joy, Regret, Admiration, Reproach, Pride, Shame		
(Baker *et al.*, 2004, 2010)	Intelligent Tutoring Systems	Boredom, Confusion, Delight, Engaged Concentration, Frustration, Surprise, Neutral		On-Task, On-Task Conversation, Off-Task Conversation, Off-task Solitary Behavior, Inactivity, Gaming the System
(Garris, Ahlers and Driskell, 2002)	Game-Based Learning	Interest, Enjoyment, Task Involvement, Confidence		
(Shen *et al.*, 2007)	e-learning	Interest, Engagement, Confusion, Frustration, Boredom, Hopefulness		
(Pekrun, 2006; Pekrun *et al.*, 2007, 2011)	Academic Settings	Enjoyment, Hope, Pride, Relief, Anger, Anxiety, Shame, Hopelessness, Boredom		
(Gutica and Conati, 2013; Conati and Gutica, 2016)	Educational Games	Boredom, Shame, Frustration, Confusion, Disappointment, Surprise, Neutral, Curiosity, Engaged Concentration, Delight, Excitement, Confidence, Pride		
(Bhaskar and Govindarajulu, 2008)	Mobile Learning		Location, Time, Weather, Temperature, Noise, Lighting, Day, Movement, Device Capabilities	
(Yau and Joy, 2010)	Mobile Learning	motivation	noise, busyness of the environment, temperature	
(Gómez *et al.*, 2014)	Mobile Learning		People, Hardware and Software Capabilities, Place, Time, Noise, Illumination	
(Economides, 2009)	Mobile Learning	Enthusiasm, Boredom, Happiness, Sadness, Satisfaction, Calmness, Anger, Anxiety, Frustration, Fear, Confusion, Hope, Pessimism, Expectancy, Astonishment, Sympathy, Disgust, Hate, Pride, Shame	Time, Location, Terrain, Weather, Neighbors Mobility, Device Capabilities	

being inactive for a remarkable time period inside a serious gaming session. The log data will capture the time elapsed before an interaction occurs but more data will be needed to disambiguate the reasons behind this behavior to properly determine the resulting design decision. The reasons for such a response delay can lie on the learning dimension if the user is found to be reflecting on the answer to a question or on the gaming dimension if the user is reflecting on the strategy to make the next game move, for example. Furthermore, the problem might be related to usability if the user is found to be confused on how to proceed with the navigation, for example. However, the reason might also be exterior to the whole gaming experience, as it might lie in the context: the user might have been distracted by an event in the environment which happens frequently in real-life situations or when testing in the wild. All these factors need to be taken into account for an ideal evaluation. For this, we will assume an observer watching the testing session and being able to take note of states related to these dimensions which can have influence on the experience at the moment they occur. This would be the ideal situation for capturing all relevant data which, in real testing scenarios, however, will naturally suffer from many limitations. Nevertheless, it can serve as the ultimate goal of recording the experience, whether doing this manually or automatically. Table 4 presents parameters of Affect, Cognition, Context and Behavior considered in different models investigating data in learning environments.

After reviewing the different parameters considered in literature, it was found that the best approach would be to carry out a study to determine which of the factors present in literature will be elicited during playtesting sessions of Serious Games carried out in the field. This would help decide which of the above listed models more precisely fits the evaluation of (mobile) educational games in natural environments on each of the three categories: Affective and Cognitive States, Context and Behavior.

Field Study

A field study carried out on three days with twenty children in total aged four to ten playing the Artikel-Game on different devices (laptop, tablet, smartphone) in a language learning center was carried out (see Figure 5). The researcher observed and took note of occurrences of different states related to the three categories (Affect and Cognition, Context and Behavior) during the playtesting sessions using a mobile app designed specifically for this purpose. In this app it was possible to record observations which are saved with timestamps at the moment they are annotated (see Figure 6).

RESULTS AND DISCUSSION

The main identified states are depicted in Figure 7. The Affective and Cognitive States elicited were: reflection (or concentration, thinking, workload,..), surprise (here positive, e.g. by funny game elements), confidence and confusion (or hesitance), pride and sadness (or disappointment, shame,.., e.g. when giving a wrong answer on a quiz), satisfaction and anger (e.g. anger mostly to usability), enjoyment (or excitement, engaged concentration) and boredom. Thus, our findings on this dimension closely resemble the affective and cognitive states identified in (Gutica and Conati, 2013; Conati and Gutica, 2016), where the author also identified the occurrence of these states using observation of participants playing an educational game.

Figure 5. Playtesting sessions

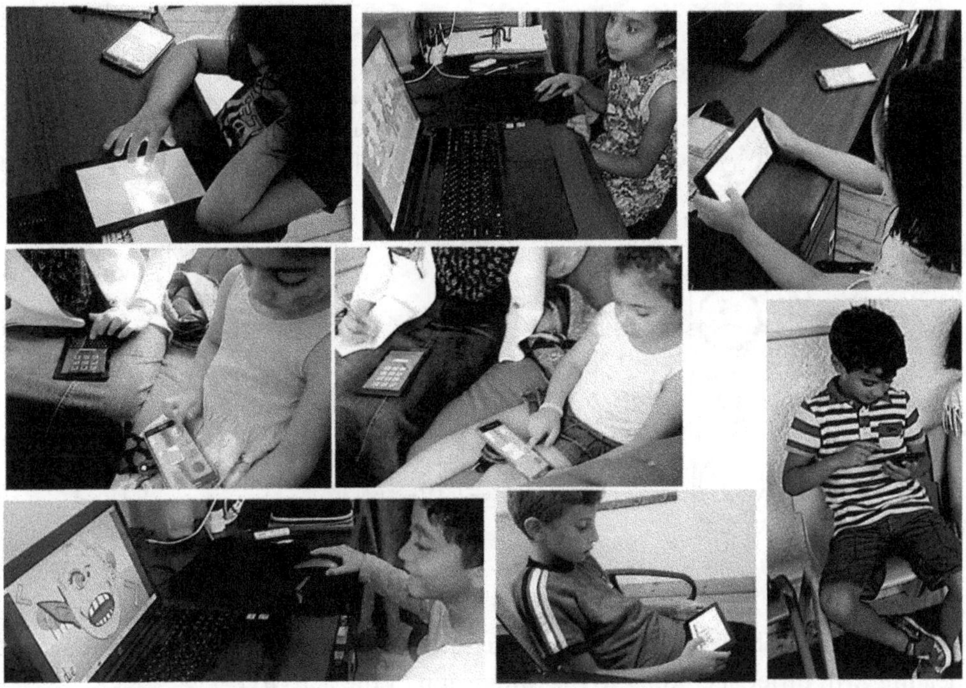

Figure 6. Observer app for recording notes and annotations with timestamps

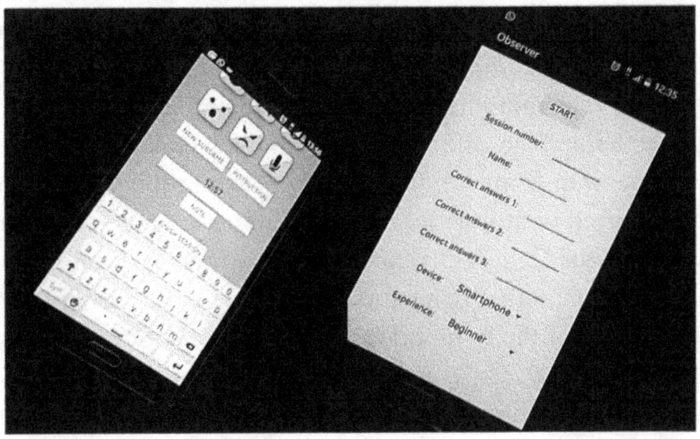

To better understand how these states can be linked to event logs recorded from the game, they were further categorized according to the time they took place related to in-game events on the three dimensions of learning, gaming and using. The results are depicted in Figure 9.

Categorizing affective and cognitive states according to their occurrence in relation to achievements is not a new concept and has been investigated in research, resulting in notions such as activity emotions, prospective and retrospective outcome emotions (Pekrun, 2006; Pekrun *et al.*, 2007, 2011). For the cur-

Figure 7. LeGUC features for evaluating experience in serious games testing sessions

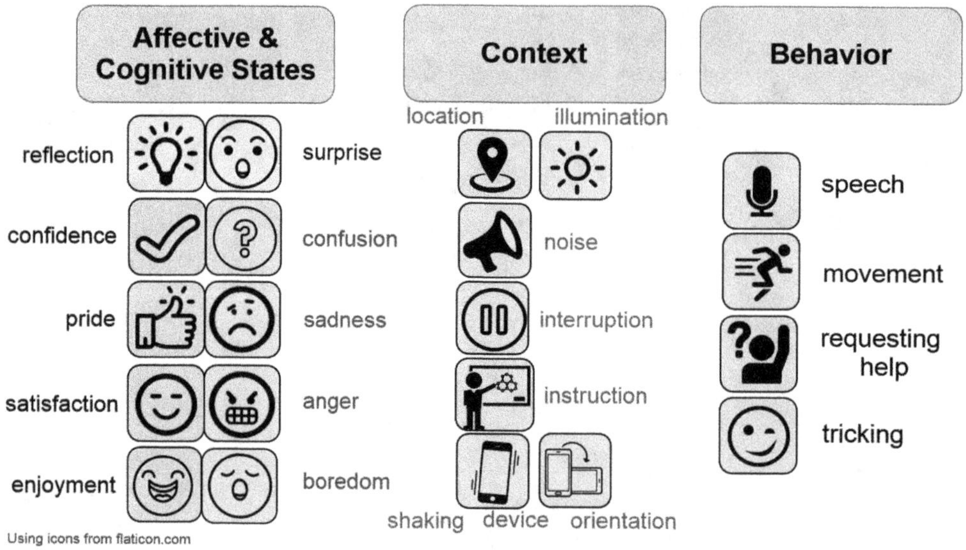

rent framework, they are more explicitly defined in relation to Serious Games evaluation and describing how their meaning will differ according to the dimension of the activity.

As for context states and events shown in Figure 7, the identified parameters related to environment were location (also indoors or outdoors), illumination (can influence ability to see game graphics clearly) and noise (can influence ability to hear game instructions). Those related to the device were shaking (may make it difficult to interact, e.g. putting the device on the lap and trying to hit an object) and orientation (landscape/portrait, flat/upright influence viewing angle and size). Other external events influencing the interaction are interruptions (e.g. a teacher opening the door and getting into the room) and instruction (the observer helped the student proceed in the game after s/he were stuck and asked for help, to prevent the testing session from stopping early or lasting longer than intended..). Most of the context states were also identified in mobile learning research as presented in Table 4 but were lacking or not precisely defined in Serious Games evaluation frameworks and studies found in literature.

In addition to affect and context, other behaviors expressed by the participants were observed which cannot be categorized under any of the two notions (see Figure 7). Some kids were speaking with the observer, speaking with friends, answering in-game questions verbally, singing (along with a song in the game or alone), laughing or thinking aloud. All this can be captured in a testing session using a microphone and are important for evaluation. This were grouped under the behavior: speech. Another behavior exhibited was movement: People (and especially children) tend to be moving a lot while engaged in activities and this was observed during the playtesting sessions. Sudden movements affect the device condition and also media captured during sessions such as recorded session videos. They can also lead to undesired game actions like accidentally touching the screen, especially when navigation buttons are placed near screen edges, which is considered a poor design decision for mobile apps. The behavior of requesting help from the facilitator was considered separately from the speech behavior as it can be used as an indicator of confusion or uncertainty but where the problem faced is explicitly verbalized, offering enormous help to evaluation. Taking note of this can help, for example, in highlighting this portion of speech, if recorded, as important to consider. Another behavior, which is actually related to interactions inside the game, but can be better recognized by observing reactions of a participant is the behavior of tricking or gaming the system. This occurred so frequently in our sessions that it deserved to be considered in the model: A participant is quickly clicking on random answers of a question instead of thinking about the answer until the correct answer is clicked. If during looking at the log data, the researcher only investigates where the user clicked and not how fast s/he clicked, s/he might miss to interpret this behavior and falsely assume a purposeful decision in choosing the answer. Thus recording this behavior can help explain strategies behind pure user event logs.

Icons similar to those from Figure 7 were then used as real-time annotating buttons in the new version of the observer app to be used for further playtesting sessions of Serious Games. Figure 8 shows occurrences of some behavioral, affective and context states recorded during the playtesting sessions.

Figure 8. Occurrences of cognitive, behavioral and context states during playtesting sessions

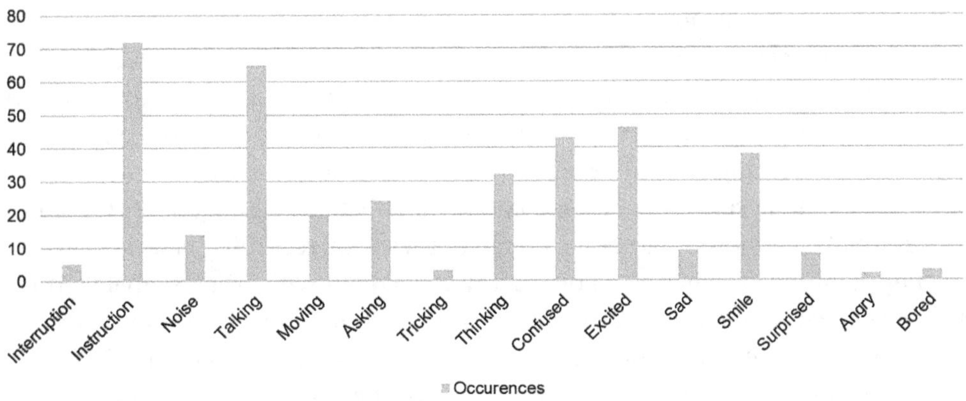

Figure 9. Timing of affective and cognitive states related to dimensions of in-game actions

Timing Related to Action	Aff./Cogn. State	Learning	Gaming	Using
Before Action		Thinking about answer	Thinking about strategy	
		Understands/confused by question	Understands/confused by mechanics	Understands/confused by presentation
During Action		Confident/hesitant in answer	Confident/hesitant in move	Confident/hesitant in interaction choice
After Action		Proud/sad about learning achievment	Proud/sad about game achievement	
		Helpful feedback?	Game responds as expected?	System responds as expected?
		Surprised by feedback element	Surprised by game element	
Anytime			Enjoying/ Bored	

Using icons from flaticon.com

CONCLUSION AND FUTURE RESEARCH DIRECTIONS

This chapter reviewed the topic of evaluating Learner Experience in Serious Games bringing together motivation, theoretical background, approaches and challenges. As this topic is an interdisciplinary one, related literature was found under different research directions and using varying terminology. For this reason the chapter started with a brief discussion of different research areas such as Learning Analytics, Game Analytics, Serious Games Analytics, Multimodal Recognition and Mobile Sensing and their intersections. Although evaluating Serious Games, as the term implies, combines methods from the different research fields, it was discussed how the nature of this category of products requires having guidelines of its own which led to developing more and more frameworks in recent years. However, these frameworks do not focus on multimodality despite the increasing number of studies using these methods and despite its many benefits discussed in this chapter. An overview over evaluation studies was needed to investigate which aspects of Serious Games were evaluated using multimodal methods, which modalities were used and which were combined together. As such studies were found not only in the field of Serious Games but in areas which started earlier in applying these methods, we have chosen the most related fields, namely the evaluation of non-gaming learning environments and non-educational games so as to reach a more thorough understanding of the landscape. As expected, studies with Serious Games were fewer in number and only more recent in publication dates than the other two areas. This shows that this field is emerging but can benefit from studies in adjacent fields to accelerate faster. The GeLU framework for linking serious games log data with affective and cognitive states, user behavior and context data was also proposed based on a literature review on recording emotions in serious games and other learning environments as well as on a study carried out with 20 participants. It is difficult to make conclusive statements about which multimodal data are more useful for evaluating which serious game elements. Every study only picked a method and an element without having a connection to other studies and cannot be generalized to other games. Another aspect which needs further research is how to facilitate closing the feedback loop and help developers infer recommended game-based learning design improvements from evaluation results. Although from the shown studies, multimodal data was captured mainly for measuring affective and cognitive states and thus cannot be directly used as a measure for learning outcomes, these states accompanying the learning process have been shown in learning theories to have a considerable effect on learning. In fact, the aim of using multimodal data is not to replace classical assessment of learning or even logging-based mechanisms of assessment but rather to enrich these methods where more data is needed and beneficial. More research is needed to determine when exactly adding more data adds value for the evaluation of Serious Games and when it is a waste of resources. Some studies in mobile sensing address these problems to adaptively switch on different sensors according to environmental, device and user conditions. This research area is especially promising as it helps develop efficient and effective multimodal mechanisms which add richness to evaluation processes. In addition, mobile sensor technology can help solve a problem which always existed in assessment which is the difficulty to gather naturalistic data over long periods of time. Allowing to track not only users interactions with the software but also the context in which these interactions take place along with tracking the progress for a longer period of time can be helpful in assessing learning outcomes. It can help developers update their software according to new trends and circumstances and help teachers track their students' achievements over time.

REFERENCES

Akputu, K. O., Seng, K. P., & Lee, Y. L. (2013). Facial Emotion Recognition for Intelligent Tutoring Environment. *2nd International Conference on Machine Learning and Computer Science (IMLCS'2013)*, 9–13. Available at: http://scholar.google.com.my/scholar?hl=en&q=oryina+Kingsley+Akputu&btnG=&as_sdt=1%252C5&as_sdtp=

Aljohani, N. R., & Davis, H. C. (2012). *Learning Analytics in Mobile and Ubiquitous Learning Environments*. Academic Press.

Annetta, L. A., & Bronack, S. (2011). *Serious Educational Game Assessment: Practical Methods and Models for Educational Games, Simulations and Virtual Worlds: Practical Methods and Models for Educational Games, Simulations and Virtual Worlds*. Springer Science & Business Media.

Arnab, S., Lim, T., Carvalho, M. B., Bellotti, F., Freitas, S., Louchart, S., ... De Gloria, A. (2015). 'Mapping learning and game mechanics for serious games analysis', *British Journal of Educational Technology. Wiley Online Library*, *46*(2), 391–411.

Arroyo, I., Woolf, B. P., Burelson, W., Muldner, K., Rai, D., & Tai, M. (2014). A Multimedia Adaptive Tutoring System for Mathematics that Addresses Cognition, Metacognition and Affect. *International Journal of Artificial Intelligence in Education*, *24*(4), 387–426. doi:10.100740593-014-0023-y

Baalsrud Hauge, J., Berta, R., Fiucci, G., Fernandez Manjon, B., Padrón-Nápoles, C., Westra, W., & Nadolski, R. (2014). Implications of learning analytics for serious game design. *Advanced Learning Technologies (ICALT), 2014 IEEE 14th International Conference on*, 230–232.

Bahreini, K., Nadolski, R., & Westera, W. (2014a). *Multimodal Emotion Recognition for Assessment of Learning in a Game-Based Communication Skills Training*. Springer International Publishing.

Bahreini, K., Nadolski, R., & Westera, W. (2014b). Towards multimodal emotion recognition in e-learning environments. In Interactive Learning Environments. Taylor & Francis.

Bahreini, K., Nadolski, R., & Westera, W. (2015). *Towards real-time speech emotion recognition for affective e-learning. In Education and Information Technologies* (pp. 1–20). Springer.

Baker, R., D'Mello, S. K., Rodrigo, M. M. T., & Graesser, A. C. (2010). Better to be frustrated than bored: The incidence, persistence, and impact of learners' cognitive--affective states during interactions with three different computer-based learning environments. *International Journal of Human-Computer Studies*, *68*(4), 223–241.

Baker, R. S., Corbett, A. T., Koedinger, K. R., & Wagner, A. Z. (2004). Off-task behavior in the cognitive tutor classroom: when students game the system. *Proceedings of the SIGCHI conference on Human factors in computing systems*, 383–390. 10.1145/985692.985741

Banda, N., & Robinson, P. (2011). Multimodal affect recognition in intelligent tutoring systems. *Affective Computing and Intelligent Interaction (ACII'11)*, 200–207. Available at: http://link.springer.com/chapter/10.1007/978-3-642-24571-8_21

Bernsen, N. O., & Dybkjær, L. (2010). Usability data analysis and evaluation. In *Multimodal Usability* (pp. 351–385). Springer. doi:10.1007/978-1-84882-553-6_16

Bhaskar, N. U., & Govindarajulu, P. (2008). Context exploration for requirements elicitation in mobile learning application development. *IJCSNS International Journal of Computer Science and Network Security*, *8*(8), 292–299.

Bosch, N., Chen, H., Baker, R., Shute, V., & D'Mello, S. (2015). Accuracy vs. Availability Heuristic in Multimodal Affect Detection in the Wild. *Proceedings of the 17th International Conference on Multimodal Interaction*. 10.1145/2818346.2820739

Bosch, N., Hall, F., & Dame, N. (2015). *Multimodal Affect Detection in the Wild : Accuracy*. Availability, and Generalizability. doi:10.1145/2818346.2823316

Brown, L., & Howard, A. M. (2014). *Assessment of Engagement for Intelligent Educational Agents: A Pilot Study with Middle School Students*. Georgia Institute of Technology.

Burelli, P., Triantafyllidis, G., & Patras, I. (2014). Non-invasive player experience estimation from body motion and game context. *Computational Intelligence and Games (CIG), 2014 IEEE Conference on*, 1–7. 10.1109/CIG.2014.6932871

Byun, J. H., Loh, C. S., & Zhou, T. (2014). 'Assessing play-learners' performance in serious game environments by using in situ data: Using eye tracking for Serious Game Analytics. In *Annual Conference of the Association for Educational Communications and Technology*. Jacksonville, FL: AECT. Retrieved from http://www. csloh. com/research/publications/

Chaouachi, M., Jraidi, I., & Frasson, C. (2015). MENTOR: A Physiologically Controlled Tutoring System. In *User Modeling, Adaptation and Personalization* (pp. 56–67). Springer. doi:10.1007/978-3-319-20267-9_5

Conati, C. (2004). *How to evaluate models of user affect? In Affective dialogue systems* (pp. 288–300). Springer.

Conati, C., & Gutica, M. (2016). Interaction with an Edu-Game: A Detailed Analysis of Student Emotions and Judges' Perceptions. *International Journal of Artificial Intelligence in Education*, *26*(4), 975–1010.

Conati, C., & Maclaren, H. (2009). Modeling user affect from causes and effects. *International Conference on User Modeling, Adaptation, and Personalization*, 4–15. 10.1007/978-3-642-02247-0_4

Cowley, B., Fantato, M., Jennett, C., Ruskov, M., & Ravaja, N. (2014). Learning When Serious: Psychophysiological Evaluation of a Technology-Enhanced Learning Game. *Journal of Educational Technology & Society*, *17*(1), 3–16.

Cowley, B., Ravaja, N., & Heikura, T. (2013). Cardiovascular physiology predicts learning effects in a serious game activity. *Computers & Education. Elsevier*, *60*(1), 299–309. doi:10.1016/j.compedu.2012.07.014

Drachen, A., Nacke, L. E., Yannakakis, G., & Pedersen, A. L. (2010). Correlation between heart rate, electrodermal activity and player experience in first-person shooter games. *Proceedings of the 5th ACM SIGGRAPH Symposium on Video Games - Sandbox '10*, 49–54. 10.1145/1836135.1836143

Economides, A. A. (2009). Adaptive context-aware pervasive and ubiquitous learning. *International Journal of Technology Enhanced Learning*, *1*(3), 169–192.

Ezen-can, A., Grafsgaard, J. F., Lester, J. C., & Boyer, K. E. (n.d.). *Classifying Student Dialogue Acts with Multimodal Learning Analytics Categories and Subject Descriptors*. Academic Press.

Fu, F.-L., & Yu, S.-C. (2008). Three layered thinking model for designing web-based educational games. *International Conference on Web-Based Learning*, 265–274. 10.1007/978-3-540-85033-5_26

Garris, R., Ahlers, R., & Driskell, J. E. (2002). Games, motivation, and learning: A research and practice model. *Simulation & Gaming*, *33*(4), 441–467. doi:10.1177/1046878102238607

Gee, D., Chu, M.-W., Blimke, S., Rockwell, G., Gouglas, S., Holmes, D., & Lucky, S. (2014). Assessing Serious Games: The GRAND Assessment Framework. *Digital Studies/Le champ num{é}rique*.

Gilbert, S. (2015). *Designing Gamified Systems: Meaningful Play in Interactive Entertainment, Marketing and Education*. CRC Press.

Göbel, S., de Carvalho Rodrigues, A., Mehm, F., & Steinmetz, R. (2009). Narrative game-based learning objects for story-based digital educational games. *Narrative*, *14*, 16. Available at: http://www.eightydays.eu/Paper/GdCMS09.pdf

Göbel, S., Gutjahr, M., & Hardy, S. (2013). *Evaluation of Serious Games*. Serious Games and Virtual Worlds in Education, Professional Development, and Healthcare.

Göbel, S., Gutjahr, M., & Steinmetz, R. (2011). What Makes a Good Serious Game--Conceptual Approach Towards a Metadata Format for the Description and Evaluation of Serious Games. *Proceedings of the European Conference on Games Based Learning*, 202–210.

Gomes, J., Yassine, M., Worsley, M., & Blikstein, P. (2013). Analysing Engineering Expertise of High School Students Using Eye Tracking and Multimodal Learning Analytics. Educational Data Mining 2013.

Gómez, S., Zervas, P., Sampson, D. G., & Fabregat, R. (2014). Context-aware adaptive and personalized mobile learning delivery supported by UoLmP. *Journal of King Saud University-Computer and Information Sciences*, *26*(1), 47–61.

Grafsgaard, J. F., Wiggins, J. B., Boyer, K. E., Wiebe, E. N., & Lester, J. C. II. (2013). Embodied affect in tutorial dialogue. *16th International Conference on Artificial Intelligence in Education, AIED 2013*.

Grafsgaard, J. F., Wiggins, J. B., Boyer, K. E., Wiebe, E. N., & Lester, J. C. (2014). *Predicting Learning and Affect from Multimodal Data Streams in Task-Oriented Tutorial Dialogue. In Proceedings of the 7th International Conference on Educational Data Mining* (pp. 122–129). EDM. Available at http://research.csc.ncsu.edu/learndialogue/pdf/LearnDialogue-Grafsgaard-EDM-2014.pdf

Gutica, M., & Conati, C. (2013). Student emotions with an edu-game: a detailed analysis. *Affective Computing and Intelligent Interaction (ACII), 2013 Humaine Association Conference on*, 534–539. 10.1109/ACII.2013.94

Hasiah, M. O., & Azizah, J. (2010). Challenges in the evaluation of educational computer games. *2010 International Symposium in Information Technology (ITSim)*, 15–17.

Ibrahim, R., & Jaafar, A. (2009). Educational Games (EG) design framework: Combination of game design, pedagogy and content modeling. *Electrical Engineering and Informatics, 2009. ICEEI'09. International Conference on*, 293–298. 10.1109/ICEEI.2009.5254771

Insight, A. (2013). *International eLearning Market Research*. Academic Press.

Kai, S., Paquette, L., Baker, R. S., Bosch, N., D'Mello, S., Ocumpaugh, J., ... Ventura, M. (2015). *A Comparison of Video-based and Interaction-based Affect Detectors in Physics Playground*. EDM.

Keefe, P. A. O., Letourneau, S. M., Homer, B. D., Schwartz, R. N., & Plass, J. L. (2014). *Computers in Human Behavior Learning from multiple representations: An examination of fixation patterns in a science simulation*. Academic Press.

Khine, M. S. (2011). *Learning to play: exploring the future of education with video games*. Peter Lang. doi:10.3726/978-1-4539-0084-0

Kiili, K., Lainema, T., de Freitas, S., & Arnab, S. (2014). Flow framework for analyzing the quality of educational games. *Entertainment Computing. Elsevier*, *5*(4), 367–377. doi:10.1016/j.entcom.2014.08.002

Kort, B., & Reilly, R. (2002). Analytical models of emotions, learning and relationships: towards an affect-sensitive cognitive machine. *Conference on virtual worlds and simulation (VWSim 2002)*.

Kristian Kiili Harri Ketamo, M. D. K.-R. (2014). Eye Tracking in Game-based Learning Research and Game Design. *International Journal of Serious Games*, 1.

Li, J.-S., Han, Y.-X., & Liu, S. (2014). Physiological Evaluation of the Players' Emotions in Different Educational Games. *American Journal of Educational Research*, *2*(9), 735–739.

Loh, C. S., Sheng, Y., & Ifenthaler, D. (2015). Serious games analytics: Theoretical framework. In *Serious Games Analytics* (pp. 3–29). Springer. doi:10.1007/978-3-319-05834-4_1

Mandryk, R. L., & Atkins, M. S. (2007). A fuzzy physiological approach for continuously modeling emotion during interaction with play technologies. *International Journal of Human-Computer Studies*, *65*(4), 329–347.

Marczak, R., & Schott, G. R. (2015). Audio visual analysis of player experience: feedback-based gameplay metrics. Game Research Methods, 207–230.

Marne, B., Wisdom, J., Huynh-Kim-Bang, B., & Labat, J.-M. (2012). The six facets of serious game design: a methodology enhanced by our design pattern library. *European Conference on Technology Enhanced Learning*, 208–221. 10.1007/978-3-642-33263-0_17

Mehm, F., Göbel, S., & Steinmetz, R. (2012). *Authoring of serious adventure games in storytec*. Springer. doi:10.1007/978-3-642-33466-5_16

Mirza-Babaei, P., Wallner, G., McAllister, G., & Nacke, L. E. (2014). Unified Visualization of Quantitative and Qualitative Playtesting Data. *Proceedings of CHI EA 2014*, 1363–1368. 10.1145/2559206.2581224

Mitgutsch, K., & Alvarado, N. (2013). Purposeful by Design? A Serious Game Design Assessment Framework. Academic Press.

Mohamed, H., & Jaafar, A. (2012). Analyzing critical usability problems in educational computer game (UsaECG). *Proceedings of the IASTED International Conference on Human-Computer Interaction, HCI 2012*, 162–168. 10.2316/P.2012.772-038

Mohamed, O., & Jaafar, A. (2011). Usability of Educational Computer Game Usa _ ECG: Applying Analytic Hierarchy Process. *Advances in Visual Informatics, 2011*, 147–156.

Moreno-Ger, P., Torrente, J., Hsieh, Y. G., & Lester, W. T. (2012). Usability Testing for Serious Games: Making Informed Design Decisions with User Data. *Advances in Human-Computer Interaction, 2012*, 1–13. doi:10.1155/2012/369637

Muir, M., & Conati, C. (2012). Understanding student attention to adaptive hints with eye-tracking. In *Advances in User Modeling* (pp. 148–160). Springer. doi:10.1007/978-3-642-28509-7_15

Nacke, L. E., Stellmach, S., & Lindley, C. (2010). Electroencephalographic Assessment of Player Experience: A Pilot Study in Affective Ludology. *Simulation & Gaming, 42*(5), 632–655. doi:10.1177/1046878110378140

Nesbitt, K., Blackmore, K., Hookham, G., Kay-Lambkin, F., & Walla, P. (2015). Using the Startle Eye-Blink to Measure Affect in Players. In *Serious Games Analytics* (pp. 401–434). Springer. doi:10.1007/978-3-319-05834-4_18

Nogueira, P. a., Aguiar, R., Rodrigues, R., Oliveira, E., & Nacke, L. E. (2014). *Fuzzy Affective Player Models: A Physiology-Based Hierarchical Clustering Method. In Proceedings of the Tenth Artificial Intelligence and Interactive Digital Entertainment Conference* (pp. 132–138). Aiide. Available at http://www.aaai.org/ocs/index.php/AIIDE/AIIDE14/paper/view/8947

Nunez Castellar, E., Oksanen, K., & Van Looy, J. (2014). Assessing game experience: Heart rate variability, in-game behavior and self-report measures. *Quality of Multimedia Experience (QoMEX), 2014 Sixth International Workshop on*, 292–296. 10.1109/QoMEX.2014.6982334

O'regan, K. (2003). Emotion and e-learning. *Journal of Asynchronous Learning Networks, 7*(3), 78–92.

Olsen, T., Procci, K., & Bowers, C. (2011). Serious games usability testing: How to ensure proper usability, playability, and effectiveness. *International Conference of Design, User Experience, and Usability*, 625–634. 10.1007/978-3-642-21708-1_70

Oviatt, S., Cohen, A., & Weibel, N. (2013). Multimodal learning analytics: Description of math data corpus for ICMI grand challenge workshop. *Proceedings of the 15th ACM on International conference on multimodal interaction*, 563–568. 10.1145/2522848.2533790

Paquette, L., Mott, B., Brawner, K., Rowe, J., Lester, J., Sottilare, R., ... Georgoulas, V. (2015). Sensor-Free or Sensor-Full: A Comparison of Data Modalities in Multi-Channel Affect Detection. *Proceedings of the 8th International Conference on Educational Data Mining*.

Paris. M. B., Bakkes, S., Tan, C. T., Whiteson, S., Roijers, D., Valenti, R., & Gevers, T. (2014). Towards Personalised Gaming via Facial Expression Recognition. *Proceedings of Tenth AAAI Conference on Artificial Intelligence and Interactive Digital Entertainment*, 30–36.

Patsis, G., Sahli, H., Verhelst, W., & De Troyer, O. (2013). Evaluation of attention levels in a tetris game using a brain computer interface. In *User Modeling, Adaptation, and Personalization* (pp. 127–138). Springer. doi:10.1007/978-3-642-38844-6_11

Pekrun, R. (2006). The control-value theory of achievement emotions: Assumptions, corollaries, and implications for educational research and practice. *Educational Psychology Review*, *18*(4), 315–341.

Pekrun, R., Frenzel, A. C., Goetz, T., & Perry, R. P. (2007). *The control-value theory of achievement emotions: An integrative approach to emotions in education*. Academic Press.

Pekrun, R., Goetz, T., Frenzel, A. C., Barchfeld, P., & Perry, R. P. (2011). Measuring emotions in students' learning and performance: The Achievement Emotions Questionnaire (AEQ). *Contemporary Educational Psychology*, *36*(1), 36–48.

Perry, G. T., Kulpa, C. C., Pinheiro, E. T., & Eichler, M. L. (2012). Lessons from an educational game usability evaluation. *International Journal of Interactive Mobile Technologies*, *6*(2).

Picard, R. W., & Daily, S. B. (2005). Evaluating affective interactions: Alternatives to asking what users feel. *CHI Workshop on Evaluating Affective Interfaces: Innovative Approaches*, 2119–2122.

Pinelle, D., Wong, N., & Stach, T. (2008). Heuristic evaluation for games: usability principles for video game design. *Proceedings of the SIGCHI Conference on Human Factors in Computing Systems*, 1453–1462. 10.1145/1357054.1357282

Plass, J. L., Homer, B. D., & Kinzer, C. K. (2014). *Playful Learning: An Integrated Design Framework*. White Paper.

Porayska-Pomsta, K., Mavrikis, M., D'Mello, S., Conati, C., & Baker, R. S. J. D. (2013). Knowledge elicitation methods for affect modelling in education. *International Journal of Artificial Intelligence in Education*, *22*(3), 107–140. doi:10.3233/JAI-130032

Ravaja, N., Saari, T., Salminen, M., Laarni, J., & Kallinen, K. (2006). Phasic emotional reactions to video game events: A psychophysiological investigation. *Media Psychology. Taylor & Francis*, *8*(4), 343–367. doi:10.12071532785xmep0804_2

Rodrigo, M. M. T., & Baker, R. (2011). 'Comparing learners' affect while using an intelligent tutor and an educational game. *Research and Practice in Technology Enhanced Learning*, *6*(1), 43–66.

Salmeron-majadas, S. (2014). Affective standards-based modeling in educational contexts from mining multimodal data sources State of the art. *CEUR Workshop Proceedings*.

Salmeron-majadas, S., Santos, O. C., & Boticario, J. (2013). Affective State Detection in Educational Systems through Mining Multimodal Data Sources. *Proceedings of the 6th International Conference on Educational Data Mining*, 348–349. Available at: http://www.educationaldatamining.org/EDM2013/papers/rn_paper_75.pdf

San Pedro, M. O. Z., Baker, R. S. J., & Rodrigo, M. M. T. (2014). Carelessness and Affect in an Intelligent Tutoring System for Mathematics. *International Journal of Artificial Intelligence in Education*, *24*(2), 189–210.

Sanchez, E. (2011). *Key criteria for game design. A framework*. Academic Press.

Seif El-Nasr, M., Desurvire, H., Nacke, L., Drachen, A., Calvi, L., Isbister, K., & Bernhaupt, R. (2012). Game user research. CHI'12 Extended Abstracts on Human Factors in Computing Systems, 2679–2682. doi:10.1145/2212776.2212694

Shaker, N., & Shaker, M. (2014). Towards Understanding the Nonverbal Signatures of Engagement in Super Mario Bros. In *User Modeling, Adaptation, and Personalization* (pp. 423–434). Springer. doi:10.1007/978-3-319-08786-3_38

Shaker, N., Shaker, M., Abuabdallah, I., Zonjy, M., & Sarhan, M. H. (2013). A Quantitative Approach for Modeling and Personalizing Player Experience in First-Person Shooter Games. *2013 Conference on User Modeling, Adaptation and Persolization*. Available at: http://citeseerx.ist.psu.edu/viewdoc/summary?doi=10.1.1.416.371

Shen, L., Leon, E., Callaghan, V., & Shen, R. M. (2007). Exploratory research on an Affective e-Learning Model. *Proceedings of Workshop on Blended Learning*, 267–278.

Shi, K., & Ali, K. (2012). GetJar Mobile Application Recommendations with Very Sparse Datasets. In *Proceedings of the 18th ACM SIGKDD International Conference on Knowledge Discovery and Data Mining*. New York, NY: ACM. 10.1145/2339530.2339563

Shoukry, L., Caserman, P., Göbel, S., & Steinmetz, R. (2015). Blitzmerker: learning idioms with a mobile game. *Joint International Conference on Serious Games*, 77–88. 10.1007/978-3-319-19126-3_7

Shoukry, L., & Gobel, S. (2017). *Reasons and Responses: A Multimodal Serious Games Evaluation Framework. IEEE Transactions on Emerging Topics in Computing.*

Shoukry, L., Göbel, S., Galal-Edeen, G. H., & Sturm, C. (2014). Conducting Evaluation Studies of Mobile Games with Preschoolers. *CEUR Workshop Proceedings*, *1227*, 262–269.

Shoukry, L., Göbel, S., & Steinmetz, R. (2014a). Learning analytics and serious games: Trends and considerations. *Proceedings of the 2014 ACM International Workshop on Serious Games*, 21–26. 10.1145/2656719.2656729

Shoukry, L., Göbel, S., & Steinmetz, R. (2014b). Towards Mobile Multimodal Learning Analytics. *Proceedings of the Learning Analytics for and in Serious Games Workshop at EC-TEL.*

Shoukry, L., Reuter, C., & Mehm, F. (2014). StoryTec and StoryPlay as Tools for Adaptive Game-Based Learning Research. In *Games for Training, Education, Health and Sports* (pp. 195–198). Springer. doi:10.1007/978-3-319-05972-3_21

Shoukry, L., Sturm, C., & Galal-Edeen, G. H. (2015). Pre-MEGa: A Proposed Framework for the Design and Evaluation of Preschoolers' Mobile Educational Games. In *Innovations and Advances in Computing, Informatics, Systems Sciences, Networking and Engineering* (pp. 385–390). Springer. doi:10.1007/978-3-319-06773-5_52

Shute, V. J. (2011). Stealth assessment in computer-based games to support learning. *Computer Games and Instruction*, *55*(2), 503–524. Available at: http://myweb.fsu.edu/vshute/pdf/shute

Siemens, G., & Long, P. (2011). Penetrating the Fog: Analytics in Learning and Education. *EDUCAUSE Review*, *46*(5), 30.

van den Hoogen, W. M., IJsselsteijn, W. A., de Kort, Y. A. W., & Poels, K. (2008). *Toward real-time behavioral indicators of player experiences: Pressure patterns and postural responses. In Proceedings of Measuring Behaviour 2008* (pp. 100–101). Citeseer.

Van Staalduinen, J.-P., & de Freitas, S. (2011). A game-based learning framework: Linking game design and learning. *Learning to play: exploring the future of education with video games*, *53*, 29.

Weber, B. G., John, M., Mateas, M., & Jhala, A. (2011). Modeling Player Retention in Madden NFL 11. IAAI.

Winn, B. (2008). The design, play, and experience framework. In Handbook of research on effective electronic gaming in education. IGI Global.

Yau, J. Y.-K., & Joy, M. (2010). An adaptive context-aware mobile learning framework based on the usability perspective. *International Journal of Mobile Learning and Organisation*, *4*(4), 378–390.

Zain, N. H. M., Razak, F. H. A., Jaafar, A., & Zulkipli, M. F. (2011). Eye tracking in educational games environment: evaluating user interface design through eye tracking patterns. In *Visual Informatics: Sustaining Research and Innovations* (pp. 64–73). Springer. doi:10.1007/978-3-642-25200-6_7

KEY TERMS AND DEFINITIONS

Game Analytics: Collecting gaming data for analyzing games.

Game-Based Learning: Learning through games.

Learning Analytics: Collecting and using learning data for analyzing and enhancing learning environments.

Mobile Learning Analytics: Collecting and using mobile learning data for analyzing mobile learning.

Multimodal Learning Analytics: Collecting and using data from different modalities for analyzing digital learning activities.

Serious Games: Computer games employed for more than just entertainment.

Serious Games Analytics: Collecting and using learning and gaming data for analyzing game-based learning.

Chapter 6
Analysis of Users in an Immersive Environment for Teaching Science

Felipe Becker Nunes
Federal University of Rio Grande do Sul, Brazil

Manuel Constantino Zunguze
Pedagogical University, Mozambique

Kelly Hannel
Military School of Porto Alegre, Brazil

Fabiano Ferreira Antunes
Military School of Porto Alegre, Brazil

Sérgio Roberto Kieling Franco
Federal University of Rio Grande do Sul, Brazil

José Valdeni De Lima
Federal University of Rio Grande do Sul, Brazil

ABSTRACT

Virtual worlds can be considered immersive e-learning environments, whose characteristics of interactivity, immersion, and collaboration can be applied in different areas of teaching, such as in the field of sciences. In this way, this chapter presents the construction of a virtual world to aid in the teaching of sciences in which different types of learning materials and simulations were developed in the OpenSim platform. A group of sixth grade students used the immersive environment for a semester, being evaluated their learning through a pre- and posttest applied together with an analysis of their learning styles, being realized a correlation between the results obtained. Added to this, usability assessments with interviews about the environment was applied. The results demonstrated the potential of virtual worlds to contribute to the adaptation of the different learning styles in a class and their contribution to the improvement of the learning process.

DOI: 10.4018/978-1-5225-4206-3.ch006

INTRODUCTION

The expansion of hardware and software resources in the last decades allowed a wide range of initiatives in different fields of knowledge, using specific tools and software. Education is one of these areas. The creation and adaptation of different types of systems and methodologies favored the incorporation of Information and Communication Technologies into the students and teachers' lives.

In this scenario, one of the teaching methods that has been adopted as alternative is e-Learning, which, according to Clark and Mayer (2011), can be defined as instructions delivered on a digital device (such as, desktop computers, laptops, tablets or smartphones), that is intended to support learning.

Among the alternatives that are included in the educational scenario, there is the approach of immersive e-Learning environments, also known as Metaverse or Virtual Worlds (VW). Bainbridge defined it as a persistent online environments (i.e., continue to exist even after users leave it and the changes made by them are in a permanent way) generated by computer, where people can interact, whether for work or leisure, comparable to the real world (BAINBRIDGE, 2010, p. 1).

Pardo et al. (2014) pointed out that some characteristics of the VW, such as the ease of use, collaborative nature and attractiveness found in the 3D resources, which provide a new and exciting sense of immersion to users. The creation of immersive environments focused on education requires several factors to be considered, e.g., educational goals and teaching strategies well defined, based on learning theories, user-friendly design and objects able to encourage interaction and collaboration between users (HERPICH et al., 2014). This autonomy provided to students can assist in developing their own actions and investigations about the concepts approached during an education activity, based on the features present in a 3D environment.

The use of different types of multimedia resources, such as videos, slides, texts, images, questions and links, opens a wide range of possibilities to apply these resources to educational activities in the VW. The communication using chat also fosters the exchange of information between users, and the settlement of doubts.

Nelson and Erlanderson (2012) understand that in a VW, the evaluation takes two ways, the first is the quality of the software associated with the user experience and the second is the student's way of learning regarding the use of VW. Aspects related to the Human-Computer interface need to be considered in the development of VW, since it is a highly interactive environment with large amount of information and 3D objects, which need to be analyzed and constructed properly so as not to cause cognitive overload to the users.

As explained by Bouda (2012), the development of the VW should have user-centered design, and should be built in such way, that highlights the most important information first, paying attention to avoid information's that diverts the user's attention from the goal to be achieved. At this point, the evaluation of usability and collection of quantitative and qualitative information from users becomes fundamental, so that a process of continuous improvement can be adopted.

Another point to take into consideration is the analysis of the user's individual preferences and how the process will be conducted during the interaction in the VW. The individual analysis of each student is essential for the identification of their learning trajectories, reinforcing the need to identify each student's learning styles.

Felder (1993) understands learning styles as dominant preferences and characteristics that each people have to receive and process information. For Felder and Henriques (1995), the ways, in which, an individual characteristically acquires, conserves, and retrieves information is collectively termed learning style. The analysis of the learning style of each participant has the potential to add a higher level of personalization and corroborate to a presumed enrichment of the teaching and learning processes.

In this context, an Immersive e-Learning Environment provides support to different types of multimedia materials, which results in several options of didactic activities to be implemented by the teacher in the environment. This total virtual immersion appears to challenge traditional approaches of learning and raises the question of whether traditional learning style classifications do indeed encompass those of the millennials in a virtual environment (Junglas et al., 2007).

The user's ability to interact with different types of learning materials provides a wide variety of options to be explored, taking into account the different learning styles that exist in a group of learners. This factor instigates the investigation of how users behave in this type of environment in relation to the interaction with teaching materials taking into account their learning styles.

Taking the basic assumptions about these topics, this book chapter aims to help the reader understand the process of development and user's analysis of the educational activities performed at the Immersive e-Learning Environment, aimed to teach Sciences in elementary education. The area of Sciences was chosen given it potential to develop simulations in the virtual world, besides of being an area of theoretical and practical studies, which corroborates with the characteristics of this type of environment.

Concrete cases of development of activities in the VW are presented in order to illustrate an immersive and collaborative learning process, which have the focus on interdisciplinary. Is presented in detail the construction of virtual laboratories in OpenSim, composed of a number of different types of resources (e.g. slides, videos, texts, questions, experiments, simulations), that is part of the set of activities performed by the students in this environment.

A group of sixth grade students used the immersive environment for a semester, being evaluated their learning through a pre and posttest applied together with an analysis of their learning styles, being realized a correlation between the results obtained. Added to this, usability assessments with interviews about the environment was applied.

This chapter is organized as follows: in the background section is presented the concepts, characteristics and other relevant information about the topic of virtual worlds applied in education, learning styles and usability in e-learning environments. In the next section is presented arguments related to the problems and difficulties involved in adopting this type of approach and what solutions have been developed within the scope of this research. The case of study applied to this research is also presented in detail, as well as the results from this experiment.

Subsequently, the section of future directions presents several arguments and applications that can be explored in new researches to be carried out, within the scope of this work. Finally, the conclusions regarding the study made in this experiment and assertions presented in the course of this chapter are discussed.

BACKGROUND

Immersive e-Learning environments make possible for teachers to plan activities that are more interactive and practical, in which, areas such as science, physics and chemistry can be explored to demonstrate content that often requires real or virtual labs to be better described. The possibility of carrying out the activities in the distance format, at the moment the student considers most appropriate (respecting the deadlines imposed for the task), allows the teacher to plan complementary activities to the topics seen in classroom or to plan an synchronous activities with the whole class using this type of virtual environment.

In this way, the opportunity of creating and using different types of teaching materials opens up the possibility of articulating different types of tasks, that take into account the different preferred learning styles that a group can have, seeking to satisfy in a more comprehensive way the needs of the students in a discipline. Added to this, the teacher can also apply questionnaires and interviews that aim to evaluate how the students are using the environment and to obtain a constructive feedback on its usability, so that aspects of design and organization of the resources can be constantly improved.

All of these aspects can be related to the student's performance in the assessments and analyze how the content is being learned for the whole class or individually. The following subsections present more comprehensively the main concepts related to the study carried out in this research.

Virtual Worlds

The virtual worlds were originally developed to be applied in different areas such as business, training, health, games, and education. Soto (2013) defines Virtual Worlds as being computerized simulations that offer a three-dimensional graphic space that represents a physical environment in which users can interact with each other and manipulate the environment with the creation and modification of objects. Nelson and Erlandson (2012) corroborate this definition, stating that they are computer-simulated three-dimensional spaces that can be explored in first or third person through a graphic representation called Avatar.

The avatar can be defined as the virtual representation of the user in the environment and can be customized according to their preferences. As described by Colin et al. (2010), users create their virtual representations through avatars that have a personal inventory associated with them, in which objects such as clothing, cars, buildings, and other types of elements may be contained. Such objects are 3D representations that can be located in any valid position of the virtual world, considering that this type of environment is formed by several earth spaces defined by its developer. Nelson and Erlandson (2012) explain that each object is located through three coordinate axes, since no object or avatar can be inserted or moved to a location that does not have a previously specified coordinate, for example, in a non-existent region within the Virtual World.

For Morgado (2011), virtual worlds platforms provide a virtual space shared by several users, providing content production tools focused on the characteristics or needs of the end users, not the experts, but are used by some experts for the production of complex spaces. Examples of virtual worlds generating platforms are Second Life, OpenSim and Open Wonderland.

According to Konstantinidis et al. (2010), Second Life can be considered an ideal environment for experiential learning, although it has not been created for educational purposes, several educational institutions have adopted this solution as a support tool for educational activities. Difficulties involving the collection and use of 3D objects and regions in this type of environment, in addition to the closed code, result in the decrease of users in recent years, although it still has a well-populated base.

With respect to Open Wonderland, it consists of a set of open source tools for creating collaborative 3D Virtual Worlds in which users can communicate using the chat channel and interact with shared and cooperative applications in areas such as educational, Social or business (Kotsilieris and Dimopoulou, 2013). However, some points are important to emphasize regarding the choice of use, for example, poor quality of graphics resolution when compared to Second Life and OpenSim, and it is still an emerging solution.

Such considerations in relation to these two environments make OpenSim, in the view of the authors of this work, become the most viable solution to be worked on in academic research. OpenSimulator or OpenSim is an open source, cross-platform, 3D application with shared user access that allows individuals and companies around the world to customize their Virtual Worlds based on their technology preferences (Kickmeier-Rust & Albert, 2013).

Because it is an open source environment, free of charge and with extensive documentation in the academic world, its choice becomes the most appropriate in this type of research. This choice is also based on the description of Banerjee et al. (2013) in which OpenSim is considered the best tool for educational content development since it is freely available and all files can be retrieved in "OAR" format, which can be shared and uploaded by the user anywhere.

For visualization and interaction with the Virtual World, it is necessary to install an application known as a viewer, in which the user can interact and perform his activities. This application must be installed on the user's computer and configured to access the desired virtual world. Some examples of viewers are the Singularity, Imprudence and Firestorm.

Johnson et al. (2009) argue that immersive environments can offer a new type of approach in which users move from a passive and observatory state to become active subjects within the Virtual World. Chow (2016) emphasizes that the benefits and resources of this environment allow people, places, and objects to become concrete and tangible in the Virtual World, stimulating the user's experiential perception.

This point of view becomes essential when applied in an educational field in which the resources provided by the environment, such as interactivity, immersion, collaborative, communicability and the realization of experiential actions are important for the student during his/her learning process. In this way, one of the alternatives to be adopted is the construction of laboratories of remote or virtual experimentation, in which the costs involving infrastructure and trained personnel are abstracted, in addition to the inherent risks that a real environment may have.

Machet and Lowe (2013) emphasize that laboratory work in education is recognized for bringing real benefits to students. One factor that can enhance these results is the interface used to contextualize laboratory activity, as in Virtual Worlds. Thus, within a region in the virtual world can be created one or more virtual labs, separated by content or areas, containing different types of learning materials such as slides, videos, audios, texts, simulations, and questions.

Simsek and Can (2016) corroborate this line of thinking, in that by giving students the freedom to choose the type of learning material to explore, this makes them active individuals in their learning process, thus developing the impression of authorship during this process. This approach allows students to choose different types of learning materials to visualize and interact, an aspect that is directly related to their learning styles.

However, given that individuals differ in terms of the ways they can effectively learn new concepts, it is important to investigate whether the performance of students in 3D educational environments depends on their learning style (Zaharias et al., 2010). The authors explain that, if any such dependency can be shown, further research about the design of future virtual worlds aspiring to provide effective support to the various learning styles, would be of great value to the educational research community (Zaharias et al., 2010).

In this way, the virtual world opens a wide field of research on the impact that the planning of didactic activities, based on different types of learning materials, can have to meet the different needs and preferences of learning styles in virtual worlds. Thus, the next section of this chapter seeks to present in more detail the aspects related to this area.

Learning Styles

A concern that should be at the center of teaching activities is the knowledge of the profile of each group of students in the school context, with the understanding of the preferences revealed by the students in the learning processes and their peculiar ways of learning scientific concepts (Flores et al ., 2013). Students should be at the center of teaching and learning processes, in which the teacher must take an investigative stance in order to identify and take into account individual needs, interests, abilities and styles in the course of the activities carried out.

In this context, Geller et al. (2004) have identified the importance of discovering which individual characteristics of learners influence the teaching and learning processes, in order to help the way teachers prepare the contents and the interaction between them, so that they can adapt to the Educational environments. The learning styles (LS) and cognitive styles (CS) are two integrating elements of the multiple individual characteristics that the student possesses, with broad and different definitions in the academic environment, being considered in this chapter as two different terms, although some authors do not make a clear distinction between them.

Witkin and Goodenough (1981) define cognitive styles as subtle and relatively stable ways used by the individual to perceive, solve problems, learn and relate to others. For Bariani (1998), cognitive styles are relatively stable structures and can be impacted by experiences lived during the years of schooling, including in the higher education stage.

Authors such as Messick (1984) and Riding and Rayner (1998) understand that individual differences in the properties of the cognitive structure, which may vary according to the life history and which will consequently determine the way in which experiences and information are organized and processed, as well as guide in problem-solving and decision-making, thereby influencing people's personality. Based on the recognition of these cognitive differences, it is possible to implement teaching strategies to improve the relationship between teachers and students, thus providing greater efficiency and quality in teaching and learning processes (Oliveira and Oliveira, 2012).

In this book chapter, we choose the adoption of learning styles to be worked together on the topics of Virtual Worlds. While cognitive styles are related to the particular way of perceiving information during teaching and learning processes (Ford and Chen, 2001), learning styles are focused on the preferred way of learning.

Based on the assumption that students learn in different ways, the availability of various didactic resources aims to satisfy the different profiles that may exist in a group of students, both in the classroom and in a distance-learning environment.

The learning styles are an important element in the method of mapping the learning trajectories of the students, in what concerns the identification of students' preferences with regard to the types of materials they wish to use. Ford and Chen (2001) argue that they are an adaptive strategic reaction to a particular learning situation, the intensity of which also depends on factors such as the anxiety level of interest and stable styles linked to personality and motivational characteristics. Schmeck (1982) states that they represent the predisposition of the student to adopt a particular learning strategy regardless of the demands of the tasks.

In a broader definition, Alonso et al. (1999) understand learning styles as cognitive, affective and physiological traits that serve as relatively stable indicators of how students perceive, interact and respond to their learning environments. Finally, for Felder (1993), learning styles comprise a characteristic and dominant preference in the way people receive and process information, considering styles as skills that can be developed.

During didactic activities, certain points of observation can be captured by the teacher in the actions performed by the students, which can be considered as vital information in the conduction and improvement of the learning processes. For example, in a group activity, certain students expressing their willingness to work individually or in a purely theoretical activity demonstrate discomfort and dissatisfaction in performing tasks.

Taking into account this context, according to Santos (2007), the teacher who knows the student's learning style, as well as their own style, is able to adopt differentiated and more individualized work strategies, as this attitude will give to their educational practice, more meaning and a motivating element for students. Catholico (2010) and Amaral and Silveira (2014) corroborate with this assertion by clarifying that, once the teacher has such data about the students' learning styles and adopts different and new teaching strategies, the implemented measures make it possible to reach the learning needs present in a group of students.

With regard to the different models present in the identification and interpretation of learning styles, several authors have formulated several proposals, among which we can cite the following: Kolb (1984); Myers and Mccaulley (1986); Felder and Silverman (1988); Honey and Mumford (2000); and Butler (2003). The proposals cited are summarized below, with the exception of the questionnaire of Felder and Soloman, an object used in this research, which will be extensively detailed.

The model of experimental learning proposed by Kolb encompasses two dimensions, "Active-Reflective" and "Theoretical-Concrete", being constructed from these four learning styles, as explained by Flores et al. (2013):

- **Accommodators:** They comprise Concrete and Active dimensions, whose focus is strongly located in the active experimentation with concrete objects;
- **Assimilators:** Located in the Theoretical and Reflexive dimensions, whose focus is inversely centered on what is proposed in the Accommodators;
- **Convergent:** Formed by the Theoretical and Active dimensions, seek to discover the why and the relevance of a given situation;
- **Divergent:** Composed by the Concrete and Reflexive dimensions, its focus is inversely centered on what is proposed in the Convergent.

Regarding the Honey and Mumford model, Mozzaquatro (2010) explains that a questionnaire called "Honey-Alonso Questionnaire of Learning Styles" (CHAEA) was created with the objective of helping students to be attentive to their strengths and weaknesses. In this questionnaire, four different learning styles can be explored: Active, Reflective, Theoretical, and Pragmatic.

According to Mozzaquatro (2010), the questionnaire consists of eighty items, twenty items corresponding to each of the four styles measured. In a proposition similar to that used by Felder and Soloman in their proposal, CHAEA authors have created five preference levels designated by very high preference, high preference, moderate preference, low preference, and very low preference for the student not to be located in only one Learning style and despise others.

In the model developed and called Myers-Briggs (MBTI), the person can be classified on a scale consisting of four dimensions: orientation for life (extroverted / introverted); Perception (sensory / intuitive); Contractual approaches to judgment (reflexive / sentimental); and, orientation towards the external world (judges / perceptual).

Finally, the Butler model uses a questionnaire called the Style Research Questionnaire (SRQ), which encompasses five dimensions of learning styles: Realistic, Analytical, Pragmatic, Personal and Divergent. According to Mozzaquatro (2010), the instrument has fifteen affirmations, with five response options each, which is associated with one of the five proposed style dimensions and the three most probable answers for each sentence, indicated by the order of preference, are selected. Results may indicate dominant, contrasting, or complementary styles.

In this research was used the Felder and Silverman model. As described by Cavellucci (2003), Felder's thinking is that if the teacher uses an approach that favors a particular style of learning, students who do not develop that same skill will tend to be uninterested and will find it difficult to learn. On the other hand, the author explains that if the teacher simply cares about attending each student according to his/her learning style, he will not allow him or her developing other abilities to deal with information, impairing his/her academic and professional performance (Cavellucci, 2003).

Based on these assertions, it is essential that the teacher analyze the profile of his/her class to create the conditions to explore the potential and to meet the needs of the group of students, in accordance with what was interpreted from the analysis of the preferred styles. In this way, resources can be made available in a variety of formats aimed to meet at least part of the needs of each student, as well as providing the development of different skills to deal with information that is not appropriate to their preferences.

Felder (1993) explains that a particular learning style can be defined between pairs representing opposing actions at the time that didactic tasks are performed. In the model proposed by Felder and Salomon it is considered that all individuals present at least a slight inclination in each category, and the balance are considered an ideal point. Preferences are classified as strong, moderate, or weak.

The four dimensions of learning styles are related to the way information is captured, perceived, organized, processed and understood, and Júnior (2005) and Dias et al. (2009) describe the pairs of categories below:

- **Active and Reflective:** Actives tend to better understand through action, discussing, applying, or explaining concepts to others through active experimentation. Reflectors prefer to meditate on the subject, from a time alone to think and reflect on the information obtained.
- **Sensory and Intuitive:** Sensors prefer to deal with concrete data and experiments, learn facts, solve problems with established methods, are thorough and memorize facts very easily. Intuitivist like to discover possibilities and novelties, if bored with repetitions, are good at abstractions, concepts, theories and mathematical formulations, being faster and innovative at work.
- **Visual and Verbal's:** Visuals are those that learn best what they see, for example, using figures, diagrams, flowcharts, and movies. Verbal learners take better advantage of what they hear, of information that is transmitted through words.
- **Sequential and Global:** Sequential learns best in a linear way, in stages with logical sequencing, that is, when the concept is expressed in a continuous form of difficulty and complexity. Already global learn randomly in conceptual leaps and are good at quickly solving complex problems.

From this model, Felder and Soloman (1991) created the ILS (Index of Learning Styles), an instrument that evaluates preferences in four dimensions of the model, excluding the inductive-deductive that had been proposed in the original work of Felder and Silverman. The questionnaire consists of 44 questions, with two alternatives each and the individual's data for the four dimensions are provided at the end. The use of Felder's model in this study is justified by the adequacy to the objectives proposed in this research, being concomitantly essential for the mapping of students' learning trajectories. The diversity of contents that can be inserted in the Virtual World opens the possibility for the teacher to seek to aggregate a greater range of resources that seek to satisfy each student's learning preferences.

IMMERSIVE E-LEARNING ENVIRONMENT TO SCIENCES

This section aims to present the main problems, difficulties and benefits that were identified during the conduction of this experiment, as well as other particularities analyzed in the theoretical survey carried out. The case of study applied and the results obtained are presented, as well as the analysis of the information collected.

ISSUES, CONTROVERSIES AND PROBLEMS

The implementation of virtual worlds involves aspects related to technological and educational focus, as well as to related areas, as is the case in this experiment involving the area of Sciences. The process of building a virtual laboratory requires technological knowledge for the implementation of the resources and development of the simulations.

This finding can be considered a problematic factor, since a predominant portion of teachers who are not included in a technological area, will not be able to manipulate the resources in a virtual world. For building and modeling 3D objects, you need to be knowledgeable in software's for modeling, such as Sketchup and Blender. In addition, to insert animation effects into these objects and create the simulations, it also requires the use of programming resources with the use of scripts. Potkonjak et al. (2016) highlight that this type of environment has not been created to this kind of use (education) and a training is necessary for the users, besides the requests that are imposed to computer resources: dynamic modeling and 3D CAD modeling of objects may be rather complex and requiring.

It is important to note that a teacher outside the technological area will have greater difficulties in creating animated experiments and inserting multimedia resources in the virtual world. Avila et al. (2014) emphasizes that, despite the pedagogical potential that is being found in these tools, teachers still miss skills to handle with and build such resources.

It is important to emphasize that the planning of educational activities and contents used in the subject requires knowledge of the teacher both in the educational area and in the specific area that is, being conducted the experiment, as for example in the area of Sciences. The teacher needs to plan the didactic activities following a well-defined educational approach, which serves as a basis for the articulation of the tasks to be proposed to the students.

Because of the virtual world allows the insertion of different types of multimedia resources, the teacher needs to be attentive when it comes to merge the types of materials and the amount of resources that will be added to an activity. According to the cognitive load theory (Sweller, 1994), when the instructional material is presented in a complex or inconsistent way, they can produce strange cognitive load. This reduces the user's capacity of properly processing the learning activities (i.e., the relevant cognitive load) and hampers the learning process (Merchant et al., 2012).

Wylie and Allport (2000) support this idea by stating that switching from one task to another requires a certain amount of time to cognitively "shift gears," since different parts of the brain and neural circuits are usually required for each separate activity. It is important to balance this aspect to improve the user's assimilation of the content, especially when different types of materials are used to satisfy the individual needs of users regarding their learning styles. This aspect is also directly related to the design and usability of the environment, from the moment its construction should be planned so that the user has a smooth and trouble-free interaction, thus being able to concretely assimilate the available content in the environment.

By virtue of the wide variety of teaching materials available and the high level of interaction provided by the Virtual World, users have at their disposal instigating options to be explored. However, one should be very careful about the different types of learning styles that a group of students can be, highlighting the following question: what types of styles can the Virtual World respond more appropriately and how do other users interact with different styles of proposed activities?

This problem is one of the key points of this study and should be explored appropriately. The Cognitive Load Theory must also be taken into account, since a high number of elements can impair the interaction of users and overload their interaction, leading to unwanted experiences and greater difficulties to assimilate the content presented in the Virtual World.

Jacka (2015) believes there is some common sense that virtual worlds are in a construction process, and there is a lot yet to be done before teachers, students and managers fully adopt virtual worlds as a learning space. Despite some difficulties, Chang e Law (2008) highlight that the creation of virtual laboratories and use of simulations with virtual worlds in the field of sciences, chemistry and physics have special characteristics to be explored. Studies related to these areas are described in the next section to present a clearer view about the scope of this work.

SOLUTIONS AND RECOMMENDATIONS

This section presents and contextualizes the main directions followed by the work done in the areas discussed in this chapter. In line with this analysis, the differences of this proposal compared to the overall scenario described can be highlighted more clearly.

Different researchers have explored the construction of virtual laboratories in areas such as Chemistry and Sciences in recent years, mainly due to the possibility of interaction with 3D objects and representation of chemical and physical phenomena in the environment. Examples of papers that involve research on the impact of the use of simulations to teach more practical contents in the area of Sciences and Chemistry and the effects that such resources can have on student learning can be seen in Kennedy-Clark (2011), Limniou et al. (2008), Merchant et al. (2012) and Rutten et al. (2012).

Aspects related to the study of learning styles in virtual worlds can still be considered scarce, since there is not a high number of works in this scope of research. One justification for this is that the insertion of multimedia resources such as videos, slides, questions, links and texts can be considered complex to implement, which requires a greater knowledge of programming in the environment.

Even with such difficulties and challenges, some works can be seen in Junglas et al. (2007), Jarmon et al. (2009) e Cheng (2014). These works address some alternatives of using teaching environments taking into account the different learning styles of the users, seeking to clarify how an environment can be exploited in a suitable way to satisfy the different needs and preferences of users. However, such studies can be considered as preliminary studies, with a more exploratory and investigative focus, without influencing results.

Another important point to consider is the analysis of aspects related to the usability of the virtual world, whose objective is to improve the quality of interaction of users during the accomplishment of educational activities in the environment. In this aspect, there are several researches related to this aspect, since it may be considered essential to carry out the analysis of the environment to seek to improve the resources made available and consequently to improve the quality of interaction of the users. Examples of works can be seen in Bowman et al. (2002), Virvou and Katsionis (2008), Minocha and Reeves (2010) and Kohler et al. (2011).

These works address how the interaction of users can be performed adequately and satisfactorily, taking into account usability and quality of interaction requirements. The results are instigating, showing that different alternatives are possible to be explored to improve the quality of the proposed activities in these types of environments.

The research presented shows that the points discussed in this chapter can be considered essential when building and implementing a virtual world. This assertion is based on the importance that the diversification of the types of materials can have during an interaction for the students, since it increases the possibility of satisfying the individual needs of the students. Likewise, the usability of the environment can be considered, in which, the arrangement of 3D objects and the form of organization can be seen as important elements in the quality of interaction to the users.

With regard to the work developed in this research, the interconnection of these research topics can be considered as a differential in relation to the other researches presented. Aspects related to the usability of the environment and analysis of learning styles for the teaching of Sciences were important elements for the analysis of the results obtained with the experiment.

CASE OF STUDY

The experiment presented in this chapter sought through a case study with qualitative and quantitative analysis to describe how the learning styles are related to the use of a virtual world geared towards teaching in the area of sciences, interconnecting such points to their evaluation of learning. The case study investigates contemporary phenomena within their real-life context, in situations where the boundaries between phenomenon and context are not clearly established, where multiple sources of evidence are used (Yin, 2010).

The study of this experiment was initiated with the theoretical survey on virtual worlds and learning styles, seeking to improve knowledge on such topics and structure the experiment. Solutions and research initiatives in these areas were also essential to analyse what has been accomplished and how to structure the study.

The experiment lasted one semester between August and November 2016 and was applied in a military college in Brazil. It was chosen the science discipline of elementary school (sixth year) to carry out the experiment, and the teacher in charge was in agreement and helped in the development of resources and contents in the virtual world, as well as taught classes in person during the semester. The contents of the course during the semester were divided into 4 units, as follows:

- Physical and chemical properties of water;
- Water Cycle;
- Water and Sewage Treatment;
- Ecology.

Participants had a weekly lesson totalling 45 minutes in the morning presently, where the teacher with the help of Blackboard and slide presentations displayed the content. The virtual world was used at a different time of the class period, the distance. A set of videos and tutorials in text format was made available so that participants' installation and configuration of the viewer (with the help of their legal guardians) could be performed.

It is important to emphasize that at no time was established as mandatory that they access the virtual world, this interaction being entirely their choice and free will, serving as a complementary activity for learning in the discipline. As a result, the total number of participants who used the virtual world became smaller, totalling eight participants who were actually part of the experiment.

This group consisted of four girls and four boys between the ages of 10 and 14 years old, who had never interacted with virtual worlds before. The justifications for the other students in the course did not use the virtual world were centralized in not being able to access at home due to problems with Internet connection, limitations in hardware, lack of interest in using the virtual world and preference to study in a more traditional way (notes in the classroom).

As a data collection instrument, three questionnaires were applied during the semester with this group of students. The first questionnaire was applied at the beginning of the course, being related the identification of the preferred learning styles of the participants, adopting the test proposed by Felder and Silverman (1991), called the Index of Learning Styles Questionnaire (ILS Questionnaire), and previously described in this chapter.

The second test applied, also at the beginning of the semester, is configured as a pre-test prepared by the teacher of the discipline containing eight objective questions that addressed the four topics covered during the semester. The objective was to quantify the participants' performance at the beginning of the course since none of them had previously seen the content.

Similarly, at the end of the semester, a post-test was also prepared by the teacher, addressing all the content seen, being composed of 24 objective questions. The intention was to evaluate the students at the end of the semester and compare their evolution between the pre-test applied and the post-test, after having studied the contents. Finally, interviews with the participants were conducted with the purpose of evaluating the usability of the environment, identifying possible problems, difficulties and pointing out the advantages and benefits described by them.

Described the conceptual basis of the experiment, it was necessary to articulate the technological structure so that the virtual world was constructed and used by the participants. In this way, it was defined that the Open Simulator virtual worlds platform (OpenSim) would be used to create the environment, since it is a free, open source software with vast documentation in the academic environment and knowledge of the authors of this work. Sketchup software was used to construct and model some 3D objects imported into the virtual world, using the OpenSim Scripted Language (OSSL) language to perform animations on objects arranged in the environment.

A web server has been configured with support for the MySQL database, which stores the data generated by OpenSim. The participants adopted the Singularity viewer for use, as it provides the support necessary for complete and consistent visualization of the objects.

Described the necessary technological structure for the construction of the virtual world and the realization of the experiment, it is described the virtual laboratory created to assist in the teaching of the subject. The laboratory was developed in a region in the virtual world, being partitioned into rooms to better organize the disposition of the resources in the environment. An entrance room has been added to welcome the user and five other rooms have been created to allocate each of the types of features added in the environment: slides, texts, questions, videos, and simulations.

The room of texts and slides is formed by several panels containing the contents covered during the experiment, being imported into the environment in the format of separate images. Figure 1 shows an example panel in the slide room where the user has the option to move the slides forward and backward and to request that the presentation is restarted.

In the video room was available several videos about the contents covered, and these are presented directly on the YouTube site. Figure 2 presents an example of video watched by participants during interaction in the virtual world.

Figure 1. Panel in the slide room

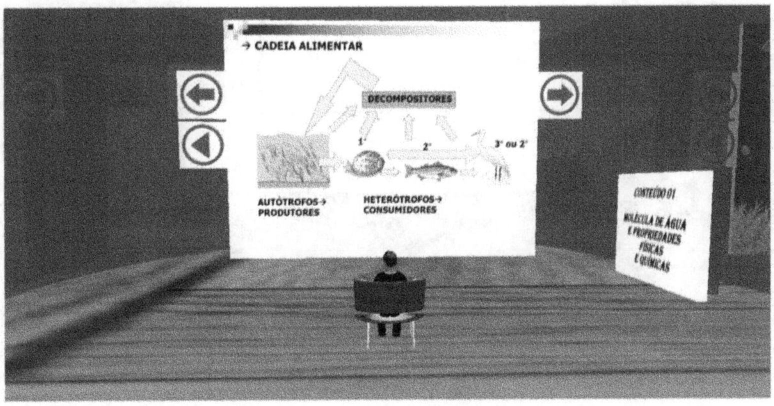

Figure 2. Video being watched directly in the virtual world

The panels with the questions were constructed in the multiple-choice format; however, it is important to note that the questions were added in the image format because of some contained graphs and representations necessary for the student to answer the question.

As can be seen in Figure 3, the question is presented to the student in this image format, with the alternatives made available in the statement itself. The buttons below represent the alternatives that he can point out, and when choosing an alternative, feedback with the hit or error is automatically provided to him. At the end of the questionnaire, his overall performance on the questionnaire is also presented.

With regard to the simulations built for the virtual world, around 20 animated experiments were made encompassing all topics covered in the semester. Figures 4 and 5 present examples of simulations developed in the environment, the representation of molecules being presented in the first illustration, while the second one depicts the complete process performed in a water treatment station.

It is important to emphasize that simulations were developed in two formats: static, in which the user received information about the object he was visualizing, and animated, in which when triggering the

Figure 3. Environment issues panel

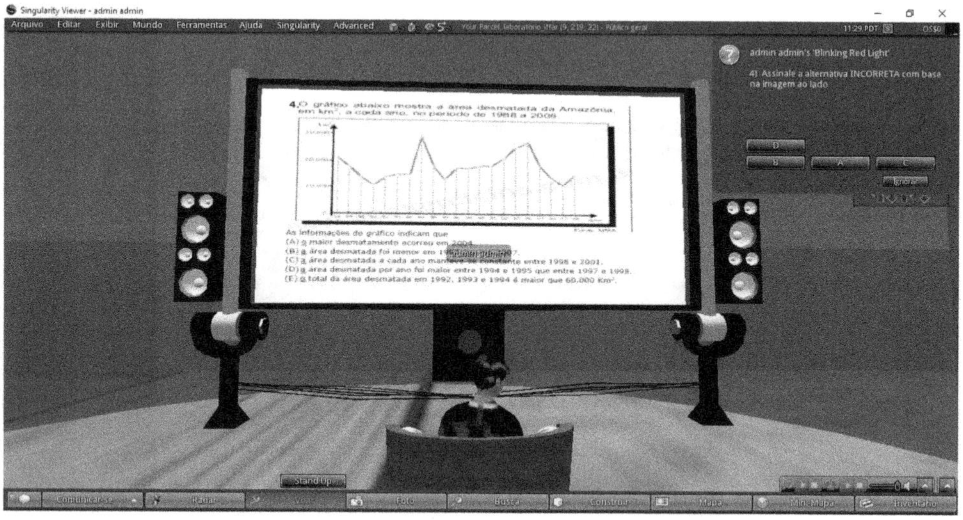

Figure 4. Water molecules represented in the virtual world

Figure 5. Representation of a water treatment plant

experiment, pre-defined actions were performed and presented along with a textual explanation. After describing the laboratory built in the virtual world and the procedures adopted to carry out the case study conducted in this research, the next subsection presents the results obtained.

DISCUSSION OF RESULTS

The construction of the virtual laboratory at OpenSim sought to aggregate a greater diversity of learning materials such as slides, videos, texts, questionnaires, and simulations. This decision was adopted based on the resources that the virtual world allows to insert in the environment and sought to attend to the different preferences related to the learning styles of the participants.

Although the virtual world has as native characteristics, the sensation of immersion and a greater degree of interactivity, which meets the preferences of subjects with more active characteristics, this experiment sought to aggregate different teaching materials to suit all dimensions of the learning styles addressed in the model of Felder and Silverman (1991).

The analysis of the results obtained with the Index of Learning Styles Questionnaire was heterogeneous; there was a greater division among the eight participants in the dimensions of the model. Table 1 presents the results of the analysis of the responses of the questionnaire, in which the trend of each of the participants in the 4 dimensions can be seen.

To perform a more consistent analysis, the students' performance in the assessments made the pre-test at the beginning of the discipline and the post-test at the end of the discipline were performed to verifying the performance improvement. Figure 6 shows the results of the evaluations performed by the eight participants of this experiment.

An important finding to be highlighted is that all participants had a significant improvement in the post-test scores compared to the pre-test applied. This factor can be considered positive since the complementary activities carried out in the virtual world show signs of having helped the students in their learning process and may have influenced the improvement of their performance in the evaluations

Table 1. Result of the analysis of participants' learning styles

ID	Dimensions of Felder & Silverman Learning Styles Model			
	Processing of Information	Perception of Information	Retention of Information	Organization of Information
User 01	Active	Intuitive	Visual	Sequential
User 02	Reflective	Intuitive	Visual	Sequential
User 03	Reflective	Intuitive	Visual	Sequential
User 04	Active	Sensory	Visual	Global
User 05	Active	Sensory	Visual	Global
User 06	Reflective	Intuitive	Visual	Sequential
User 07	Active	Sensory	Visual	Global
User 08	Reflective	Sensory	Visual	Global

carried out. Jonassen (1999) describes the constructivist learning environments, with Virtual Worlds in this context, such as those in which the student plays an active role in the construction of knowledge, being provided situations involving research, experimentation, formulation of hypotheses, and other actions that allow reflection and authorship.

The pre-test had an average grade of 56.25, which can be considered low since it was not above the level of approval required in the course, which was 70. However, the post-test had an average of 92.75, being considered an expressive and positive result; there was an increase of 36.50 in the final average of the participants.

Seeking to provide a clearer and more detailed presentation to the readers of this study, more analyses that are specific were carried out, relating the evaluation and learning styles of the participants, as well as the comments they provided in the interviews. In this way, it was possible to separate the participants into four distinct groups regarding the dimensions of learning styles, as seen in Table 2.

Figure 6. Evaluation results of the participants

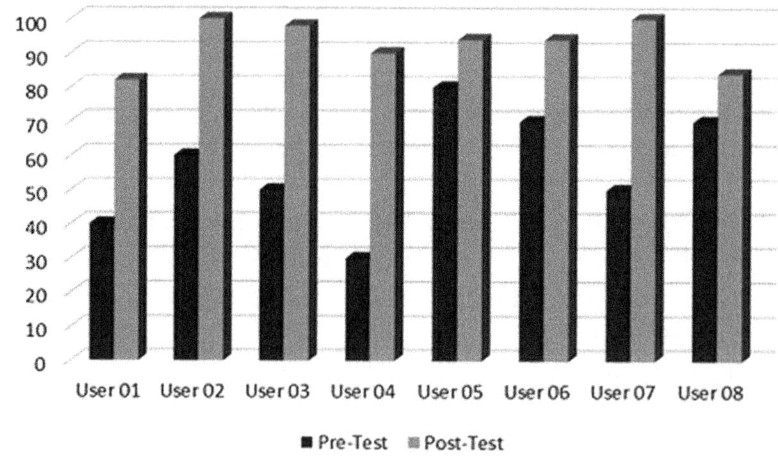

Table 2. Interconnection of grades with learning styles

Group	User's	Dimensions	Post-Test Average
1	User 01	Active, Intuitive, Visual and Sequential	82
2	User 02, 03 and 06	Reflective, Intuitive, Visual and Sequential	97,3
3	User 04, 05 and 07	Active, Sensorial, Visual and Global	94,6
4	User 08	Reflexive, Sensorial, Visual and Global	84

An important common feature in the four groups formed is that they all have a preferred visual style. Machet and Lowe (2013) emphasize that laboratorial work in education is recognized for bringing real benefits to students, and one factor that can enhance these results is the interface used to contextualize laboratory activity, as in Virtual Worlds.

This statement establishes an important connection in the analysis of these groups, where their preference is to use a more visual resource, which consistently reflects the way of interaction that occurs in the virtual world, leading to believe that the students had a sense of being more adequate to use this kind of environment. All diversity that manifests itself in the classroom has a dual character: it prevents the establishment of a standard for the conduct of teaching activities and, at the same time, offers a rich soil so that the diversification of strategies meets the expectations of the students (Júnior, 2005).

The interviewees' comments reinforce this statement, which stated that the virtual world provides visual experience, which helps them to better remember the contents seen in the simulations and to remember more easily when answering the questions in the evaluation. This factor can also be considered as one of the main reasons why the participants chose to use the virtual world since it was an arbitrary choice and it is possible to justify this choice due to the predominant visual style of this group.

The interviews conducted also sought to better understand the user's perception about the Virtual World, in which, they emphasized learning with a more active and practical character, in which they become trainers of their knowledge. Users noted that interaction with simulations reflects this impression well, in that they have the freedom to choose which object to view, as well as having the freedom to access the environment at the time it deems most appropriate.

Regarding the other learning styles, it is important to note that the average of the post-test scores was higher in Group 2, formed by the preferred styles: Reflective, Intuitive, Visual and Sequential. Such a finding can be considered instigating, since the natural tendency would be of a predominance of the Active style, because it has the active experience as one of the pillars guiding this style, which can be considered predominantly related to the style of interaction that is proposed in the virtual world, mainly due to the use of simulations.

The best performance of students who were more reflective may be justified by the fact that the user becomes the owner of their action and trainer of their learning process in the environment, which generates the freedom for him to reflect on the interaction that occurs in the virtual world and perform their actions in the environment according to their will. In line with this note is the preference of the group for the Intuitive style, which can be considered natural, since in the virtual world the user interacts in order to discover new information and possibilities. Oliveira et al. (2016) corroborates this finding, stating that in a Virtual World planned for these educational purposes, multi-users have the possibility to move freely and develop their teaching and learning processes, according to their own demand.

Finally, the Sequential preferential style can be justified by the path travelled by users, where they had the option of freely choosing which features would be visualized in the environment, according to their preference. This allows the user to plan their learning route in a sequential manner, in which it will follow its defined roadmap for as long as it interacts in the virtual world. According to Júnior (2005), the method of measuring the pedagogical trajectory covered by the student during a didactic intervention to estimate the learning trajectory developed is a practice considered as the learning path that the student traverses, with the objective of reaching the necessary knowledge about one or more interrelated concepts through a general topic.

It is important to note that all groups performed positively, even with their differences in preferred learning styles. This observation is reinforced by the comments presented by them, in which they considered the virtual world an important tool to complement the contents seen in the classroom, having a great diversity of learning materials and having the freedom to interact and choose the best path to be followed by each user.

Therefore, it can be considered in a first impression that Virtual Worlds have an important diversification of types of learning materials that can be used during didactic activities. This makes this kind of environment an important tool when it comes to learning styles.

Because they consider different ways of learning, Virtual Worlds can meet varied learning styles, as seen in the analyzes carried out, including some styles that may be considered more distant from the proposal presented in this type of environment. It is also important to point out that despite this, it is not possible to contemplate and adapt the activities for all styles, since many students do not have a more active, exploratory profile that seeks learning in the ways proposed by the Virtual World. Thus, the teacher should explore all the resources provided by this type of environment to suit different learning styles of students, mixing with different techniques and activities outside the environment to satisfy the preferences of all students.

FUTURE RESEARCH DIRECTIONS

The expansion of initiatives in educational areas has been gaining strength in the last decade where different types of educational methods and approaches have been proposed and adapted to be used in conjunction with Information and Communication Technologies. Among the several solutions that have been explored are the virtual worlds, which has gained prominence in recent years with an increasing number of studies in different areas of teaching.

Its use in the educational area has opened a varied field of possibilities to be explored, since its interactivity, collaboration, communication, immersion and 3D representation make its application possible in several areas. A wide variety of experiments have been developed to assist the teaching and learning processes, based on different application topics, among which it is possible to highlight the construction of didactic activities in Virtual Worlds in the following areas:

- Algorithms and Programming (Pellas, 2014) (Amaral, 2015);
- Engineering and Robotics (Symeonidis et al., 2010) (Vivian et al., 2015);
- Mathematics (Bouta et al., 2012) (Tarouco et al., 2013);
- Chemistry (Fang et al., 2010) (Nunes et al., 2014);

- Health (Boulos et al., 2007) (Johnson et al., 2009);
- Foreign Language (Varli, 2009) (Chen and Su, 2011).

It is possible to identify that the research area addressed in this chapter has also been the subject of research by Kennedy-Clark (2011) and Potkonjaka et al. (2016). In addition, work involving the identification of students' learning styles also continues to be explored, since the wide variety of multimedia resources available to users within the virtual world makes it an exciting alternative to seeking to meet the different learning styles of the students.

The presentation of this variety of teaching and research areas represents an instigating sensation of growth of the works realized using the virtual worlds, being considered by the authors of this work as an environment more and more consolidated in the academic environment. Initiatives involving the use of intelligent agents within virtual worlds, their application in areas related to Chemistry, Physics, Sciences and Informatics (mainly in the teaching of Algorithms and Programming) are some of the tendencies visualized after the analysis of the literature of this area in this chapter. The basic areas of teaching are characterized by several contents that require a more visual and practical presentation, which is in line with the characteristics present in a virtual world. It is demonstrated in this chapter that the implementation of different types of simulations is feasible and offers a new vision for the students, in addition to contemplating the different styles of learning preferences existing in a class.

Concerns the teaching of Algorithms and Programming, the environment provides an editor for building codes that can be coupled to 3D objects. Such a factor becomes interesting to be used in teaching programming since students can implement the programming logic and assign an action to the object, which will be seen in real time with its movement.

At the same time, the use of virtual agents can be applied during didactic activities, in which they can be developed to play a virtual tutor role, instigating the student to visualize the contents and asking more general questions. In this way, these are some of the trends identified by the authors of this chapter as instigating and feasible to be explored in future research.

CONCLUSION

Virtual worlds can be considered three-dimensional environments that portray people, objects, and interactions that occur in real life, having a vital importance for the educational area. Its application in this field opens a great diversity of options to be explored by teachers, such as the insertion of interactive, collaborative and authoring activities to be carried out by the students during the classroom period or at a distance, in the format of complementary activity.

The diversity of options available to be inserted in the environment (e.g., videos, slides, texts, questions, simulations, audio, links) opens up an important range of alternatives to be explored by the teacher during a course. At the same time, this type of choice becomes important when considering the learning styles in a group of students, which can be significantly varied.

Despite the difficulties expressed in the course of this work, such as the insertion of multimedia content in the virtual world and the creation of interactive simulations, the teacher has the option to explore the possibility of insertion of these learning materials to propose different types of didactic activities, the varied learning preferences that a group of learners may have. Allied to this possibility is the set of characteristics that are naturally provided by the virtual world, being considered a highly visual and interactive environment in which the student becomes the idealizer of his learning.

The case study described in this research presented important indications that the diversity of possible resources to be inserted in the virtual world does not create limitations on the preferred learning styles in this type of environment. It was possible to notice that individuals with a more visual preference feel more comfortable and safe in using this type of environment, being allowed to choose the most suitable path to be followed by each individual, sequentially or globally, adopting a more active or reflexive posture, both possible to be followed in this environment, according to the learning preference of each individual.

Learning styles can be satisfactorily addressed in the Virtual World, given the diversity of possible resources to be used and their mode of operation, as well as providing ample possibilities for the articulation of didactic activities by the teacher. It is important to emphasize that this type of environment may not be satisfactorily accepted by some users, who have totally adverse styles, and such cases should be adequately addressed by the teacher.

It is important to emphasize that the role of the teacher is fundamental in this process because he is the creator of this diversified amount of learning materials to be inserted in the virtual world, which can be considered laborious and require a lot of hours of work. However, this may be critical to improving students' performance when using this environment, as can be seen in the results obtained in the evaluations carried out and in the diagnosis of the preferred learning styles of the participants in this case study.

As future steps of this research is to carry out new tests in the area of natural sciences, as well as the planning of new experiments in different areas of education. The objective is to determine if the performance associated with the preferred learning styles of individuals in the virtual world has the same pattern of functioning in different areas.

REFERENCES

Alonso, C. M., Gallego, D. J., & Honey, P. (1999). *Los estilos de aprendizage: Procedimientos de diagnóstico y mejora*. Ediciones Mensajero.

Amaral, E. M. H. (2015). Processo de ensino e aprendizagem de algoritmos integrando ambientes imersivos e o paradigma de blocos de programação visual. Academic Press.

Amaral, M. P., & Silveira, I. F. (2014). Estilos de aprendizagem dos alunos do último ano do curso técnico de informática do Centro Federal de Educação Tecnologia de Minas Gerais: Levantamento de um perfil cognitivo dominante. *Rev. Prod. Disc. Educ. Matem., 3*(2), 81–92.

Avila, B. G., Tarouco, L. M. R., Passerino, L. M., Guterer, P. (2014). Autoria nos Mundos Virtuais: um novo desafio ao docente. *Revista Novas Tecnologias na Educação,* 12(2), 1-10.

Bainbridge, W. S. (2010). Online Worlds: Convergence of the Real and the Virtual. Human-Computer Interaction Series.

Banerjee, I., Perera, I., & Choudhury, J. (2013). Introducing Immersive Technologies for Learning. *Sixth International Conference on Contemporary Computing (IC3),* 1– 6.

Bariani, I. C. D. (1998). *Estilos cognitivos de universitários e iniciação cientifica, Tese de Doutorado.* Unicamp.

Bouda, T. (2012). *User-centered Design and Evaluation of Virtual Worlds*. In Experiential Learning in Virtual Worlds: 2nd Global Conference, Prague, Czech Republic.

Boulos, M. N. K., Hetherington, L., & Wheeler, S. (2007). Blackwell Publishing Ltd Second Life: An overview of the potential of 3-D virtual worlds in medical and health education. *Health Information and Libraries Journal*, *24*(4), 233–245. doi:10.1111/j.1471-1842.2007.00733.x PMID:18005298

Bouta, H., Retalis, S., & Paraskeva, F. (2012). Utilizing a collaborative macro-script to enhance student engagement: A mixed method study in a 3D virtual environment. *Computers & Education*, *58*(1), 501–517. doi:10.1016/j.compedu.2011.08.031

Bowman, D. A., Gabbard, J. L., & Hix, D. (2002). A Survey of Usability Evaluation in Virtual Environments: Classification and Comparison of Methods. *Presence (Cambridge, Mass.)*, *11*(4), 404–424. doi:10.1162/105474602760204309

Butler, K. A. (2003). *Estilos de Aprendizagem: as dimensões psicológicas*. Editora da UFRGS.

Catholico, R. A. R. (2010). Mediação da aprendizagem de Feuerstein à luz dos estilos de aprendizagem de Felder. *Revista Eletrônica de Educação e Tecnologia do SENAI-SP*, *4*(8).

Cavellucci, L. C. B. (2003). *Estilos de aprendizagem: em busca das diferenças individuais*. Academic Press.

Chang, M. K., & Law, M. S. P. (2008). Factor Structure for Young's Internet Addiction Test: A confirmatory study. *Computers in Human Behavior*, *24*(6), 2597–2619. doi:10.1016/j.chb.2008.03.001

Chen, H. J., & Su, C. C. (2011). *Constructing a 3D Virtual World for Foreign Language Learning Based on Open Source Freeware*. Edutainment Technologies. Educational Games and Virtual Reality/ Augmented Reality Applications. doi:10.1007/978-3-642-23456-9_10

Cheng, G. (2014). Exploring students' learning styles in relation to their acceptance and attitudes towards using Second Life in education: A case study in Hong Kong. *Computer Education*, *70*, 105–115. doi:10.1016/j.compedu.2013.08.011

Chow, M. (2016). Determinants of presence in 3d virtual worlds: A structural equation modelling analysis. *Australasian Journal of Educational Technology*, *32*(1), 1–18. doi:10.14742/ajet.1939

Clark, R. C., & Mayer, R. E. (2011). e-Learning and the Science of Instruction: Proven Guidelines for Consumers and Designers of Multimedia Learning (3rd ed.). Pfeiffer.

Colin, A., Miller, A., Sturgeon, T., Nicoll, J. R., & Perera, I. (2010). Educationally Enhanced Virtual Worlds. *40th ASEE/IEEE Frontiers in Education Conference*, 1–6.

Dias, C. C. L., Gasparini, I., & Kemczinski, A. (2009). *Identificação dos estilos cognitivos de aprendizagem através da interação em um Ambiente EAD*. Congresso da Sociedade Brasileira de Computação.

Fang, Y., Chang, T., Zhong, Y., Ye, E., & Liu, C. (2010). Improving Public Awareness of Everyday Chemical Pollutants Utilizing a 3-D Immersive Game. *EdMedia: World Conference on Educational Media and Technology*, 1–5.

Felder, R., & Henriques, E. (1995). Learning and Teaching Styles in Foreign and Second Language Education. *Foreign Language Annals*, *28*(1), 21–31. doi:10.1111/j.1944-9720.1995.tb00767.x

Felder, R. M. (1993). Reaching the Second Tier: Learning and teaching styles in college science education. *Journal of College Science Teaching*, *23*(5), 286–290.

Felder, R. M., & Silverman, L. K. (1988). Learning and Teaching Styles in Engineering Education. *Journal of Engineering in Education*, *78*(7), 674–681.

Felder, R. M., & Soloman, B. A. (1991). *Learning styles and strategies*. Available in: http://www4.ncsu.edu/unity/lockers/users/f/felder/public/ILSdir/styles.htm

Flores, M. S., Frozza, R., Bagatini, D., & Cruz, M. E. J. K. D. A. (2013). *Uso de rede neural artificial para determinar o estilo cognitivo do aprendiz*. XXIV Simpósio Brasileiro de Informática na Educação.

Ford, N., & Chen, S. Y. (2001). Matching/ mismatching revised: An empirical study of learning and teaching styles. *British Journal of Educational Technology*, *32*(1), 5–22. doi:10.1111/1467-8535.00173

Geller, M., Tarouco, L. M. R., & Franco, S. R. K. (2004). Educação a Distância e Estilos Cognitivos: Construindo a Adaptação de Ambientes Virtuais. *VII Congresso Iberoamericano de Informática Educativa*, 1–10.

Herpich, F., Nunes, F. B., Voss, G. B., Jardim, R. R., & Medina, R. D. (2014). Ambiente Virtual Imersivo para ensino em Redes de Computadores: uma proposta usando Agentes Inteligentes. *25th Brazilian Symposium on Computer in Education*, 65–69. 10.5753/cbie.sbie.2014.65

Honey, P., & Mumford, A. (2000). *The Learning Styles helper's guide. Maldenhead Berks*. Peter Honey Publications.

Jacka, L. (2015). *Virtual worlds in pre-service teacher education: The introduction of virtual worlds in preservice teacher education to foster innovative teaching-learning processes. Tese de Doutorado*. Southern Cross University.

Jarmon, L., Traphagan, T., Mayrath, M., & Trivedi, A. (2009). Virtual world teaching, experiential learning, and assessment: An interdisciplinary communication course in Second Life. *Computer Education*, *53*(1), 169–182. doi:10.1016/j.compedu.2009.01.010

Johnson, C. M., Vorderstrasse, A., & Shaw, R. (2009). Virtual Worlds in Health Care Higher Education. *Journal of Virtual Worlds Research*, *2*(2), 1–12.

Jonassen, D. (1996). O uso das tecnologias na Educação à Distância e as aprendizagens construtivistas. Em Aberto, 70, 1-19.

Junglas, I. A., Johnson, N. A., Steel, D. J., Abraham, D. A., Loughlin, P. M. (2007). Identity formation, learning styles and trust in virtual worlds. *ACM SIGMIS Database: The DATABASE for Advances in Information Systems archive, 38*(4), 90-96.

Júnior, G. D. C. (2005). *Trajetórias de aprendizagem de alunos de ensino médio: produção de significados em um curso introdutório de física térmica. Dissertação de Mestrado*. UFMG.

Kennedy-Clark, S. (2011). Pre-service teachers' perspectives on using scenario-based virtual worlds in science education. Computer & Education, 57(4), 2224–2235.

Kickmeier-rust, M. D., & Albert, D. (2013). *Learning Analytics to Support the Use of Virtual Worlds in the Classroom*. Human-Computer Interaction and Knowledge Discovery in Complex. doi:10.1007/978-3-642-39146-0_34

Kohler, T., Fueller, J., Matzler, K., Stieger, D., & Füller, J. (2011). Co-Creation in Virtual Worlds: The Design of the User Experience. *Management Information Systems Quarterly*, *35*(3), 773–788. doi:10.2307/23042808

Kolb, D. A. (1984). *Experiential Learning: experience as the source of learning and development*. Englewood Cliffs, NJ: Prentice-Hall.

Konstantinidis, A., Tsiatsos, T., Demetriadis, S., & Pomportsis, A. (2010). Collaborative Learning in OpenSim by Utilizing SLoodle. *Sixth Advanced International Conference on Telecommunications*, 90–95. 10.1109/AICT.2010.75

Kotsilieris, T.; Dimopoulou, N. (2013). The evolution of e-learning in the context of 3D virtual worlds. *Electronic Journal of e-Learning*, *11*(2), 147–167.

Limniou, M., Roberts, D., & Papadopoulos, N. (2008). Full immersive virtual environment CAVETM in chemistry education. Computer & Education, 51(2), 584–593. doi:10.1016/j.compedu.2007.06.014

Machet, T., & Lowe, D. (2013). Issues Integrating Remote Laboratories into Virtual Worlds. In H. Carter, M. Gosper, & J. Hedberg (Eds.), Electric Dreams. Academic Press.

Merchant, Z., Goetz, E. T., Keeney-Kennicutt, W., Kwok, O., Cifuentes, L., Davis, T. J. (2012). The learner characteristics, features of desktop 3D virtual reality environments, and college chemistry instruction: A structural equation modeling analysis. *Computers & Education, 59*, 551–568.

Messick, S. (1984). The Nature of Cognitive Styles: Problems and Prornises in Educational Practice. *Educacional Psychologist*, *19*(2), 59–74. doi:10.1080/00461528409529283

Minocha, S., & Reeves, A. J. (2010). Interaction Design and Usability of Learning Spaces in 3D Multi-user Virtual Worlds. In D. Katre, R. Orngreen, P. Yammiyavar, & T. Clemmensen (Eds.), *Human Work Interaction Design: Usability in Social, Cultural and Organizational Contexts. IFIP Advances in Information and Communication Technology* (Vol. 316). Berlin: Springer. doi:10.1007/978-3-642-11762-6_13

Morgado, L. (2011). *Características e desafios tecnológicos dos mundos virtuais no ensino. Habilitation seminar*. Universidade de Trás-os-Montes e Alto Douro.

Mozzaquatro, P. M. (2010). *Adaptação do Mobile Learning Engine Moodle (MLE MOODLE) aos diferentes estilos cognitivos utilizando Hipermídia Adaptativa*. Dissertação de Mestrado, Universidade Federal de Santa Maria.

Myers, I. B., & Mccaulley, M. H. (1986). *Manual: a guide to the development and use of the Myers-Briggs type indicator* (2nd ed.). Palo Alto, CA: Consulting Psychologist Press.

Nelson, B. C., & Erlandson, B. E. (2012). *Design for Learning in Virtual Worlds.* Library of Congress Cataloging-in-Publication Date. By Swales & Willis Ltd.

Nunes, F. B., Herpich, F., Voss, G. B., Medina, R. D., de Lima, J. V., & Tarouco, L. M. R. (2014). *Laboratório Virtual de Química: uma ferramenta de estímulo à prática de exercícios baseada no Mundo Virtual OpenSim* (pp. 1–10). Simpósio Brasileiro de Informatica na Educacao.

Oliveira, J. D., & Oliveira, V. (2012). Estilos cognitivos divergentes demandam estratégias diferentes no ensino contábil. *Revista de Informação Contábil, 6*(4), 23–41.

Oliveira, L. C., Amaral, M. A., Botelho, S. S. C., Espíndola, D. B., & Barwaldt, R. (2016). Artefato Metodológico de Autoria Aplicado aos Mundos Virtuais para Educação. *Revista Brasileira de Informática na Educação, 24*(3).

Pardo, A. G., Rosa, A., & Camacho, D. (2014). Behaviour-based identification of student communities in Virtual Worlds. *Computer Science and Information Systems, 11*(1), 195–213. doi:10.2298/CSIS130214003G

Pellas, N. (2014). The development of a virtual learning platform for teaching concurrent programming languages in secondary Education: the use of OpenSim and Scratch4OS. *Journal of e-Learning and Knowledge Society, 10*(1).

Potkonjaka, V., Gardner, M., Callaghan, V., Mattila, P., Guetl, C., Petrović, V. M., & Jovanović, K. (2016). Virtual laboratories for education in science, technology, and engineering: A review. *Computers & Education, 95*, 309–327. doi:10.1016/j.compedu.2016.02.002

Riding, R., & Rayner, S. (1998). *Cognitive Styles and Learning Strategies - Understanding style differences in learning and behavior.* David Fulton Publisher London.

Rutten, N., Joolingen, W. R. J., & Veen, J. T. V. (2012). The learning effects of computer simulations in science education. Computer & Education, 58(1), 136–153. doi:10.1016/j.compedu.2011.07.017

Santos, E. M. D. (2007). *Avaliação da influência dos estilos cognitivos no perfil do aluno de educação a distância.* Academic Press.

Schmeck, R. R. (1982). *Inventory of learning processes. NASSP.* Student Learning Styles and Brain Behavior.

Simsek, I., & Can, T. (2016). The Design and Use of Educational Games in 3D Virtual Worlds. In *Society for information technology and teacher education* (pp. 611–617). Savannah, GA: SITE.

Soto, V. J. (2013). Which Instructional Design Models are Educators Using to Design Virtual World Instruction? *MERLOT Journal of Online Learning and Teaching, 9*(3), 1–12.

Sweller, J. (1994). Cognitive load theory, learning difficulty and instructional design. *Learning and Instruction, 4*, 295–312.

Symeonidis, I., Kavadarli, G., Schuller, E., & Peldschus, S. (2010). Simulation of Biomechanical Experiments in OpenSim. *XII Mediterranean Conference on Medical and Biological Engineering and Computing.* 107–110. 10.1007/978-3-642-13039-7_27

Tarouco, L. M. R., Gorziza, B., Correa, Y., Amaral, E. M. H., & Muller, T. (2013). Virtual laboratory for teaching Calculus: An immersive experience. *IEEE Global Engineering Education Conference (EDUCON)*, 774 – 781. 10.1109/EduCon.2013.6530195

Varli, O. (2009). *An Exploration of Three-Dimensional (3D) Virtual Worlds through ESL/EFL Teachers' Perspectives in Second Life*. Academic Press.

Virvou, M., & Katsionis, G. (2008). On the usability and likeability of virtual reality games for education: The case of VR-ENGAGE. *Computer Education, 50*(1), 154–178. doi:10.1016/j.compedu.2006.04.004

Vivian, M., Tagliapietra, L., Sartori, M., & Reggiani, M. (2015). Dynamic Simulation of Robotic Devices Using the Biomechanical Simulator OpenSim. *Intelligent Autonomous Systems, 13*, 1639–1651.

Wilson, P. H., Mojica, G. F., & Confrey, J. (2013). Learning trajectories in teacher education: Supporting teacher's understandings of student's mathematical thinking. *The Journal of Mathematical Behavior, 32*(2), 103–121. doi:10.1016/j.jmathb.2012.12.003

Witkin, H. A., & Goodenough, D. R. (1981). *Cognitive Styles and Learning Strategies - Understanding style differences in learning and behavior*. International Universities Press.

Wylie, G., & Allport, A. (2000). Task switching and the measurement of "switch costs". *Psychological Research, 63*(3-4), 212–233. doi:10.1007004269900003 PMID:11004877

Yin, R. K. (2010). Estudo de caso: planejamento e métodos (2nd ed.). Academic Press.

Zaharias, P., Andreou, I., & Vosinakis, S. (2010). Educational Virtual Worlds, Learning Styles and Learning Effectiveness: an empirical investigation. *Proceedings of the 7th Pan-Hellenic Conference with International Participation «ICT in Education»*, 1-6.

Chapter 7
Improving Learner Experience Within Educational Nooks in Digital Libraries

Desislava Paneva-Marinova
Bulgarian Academy of Sciences, Bulgaria

Radoslav Pavlov
Bulgarian Academy of Sciences, Bulgaria

ABSTRACT

This chapter presents solutions for personalized observation and enhanced learning experience in digital libraries (DLs) by special smart educational nooks. Main factors related to the DLs user experience and content usability issues are considered. During the user experience design, the users' needs, goals, preferences, and interests have been carefully studied and have become the starting point for the new DLs functionality development. This chapter demonstrates several educational nooks or their components, such as learning tools in a digital library for fashion objects, a smart learning corner in an iconographical art digital library, an ontology of learning analysis method, and some educational games for art and culture in which authors are co-developers.

INTRODUCTION

The emergence of knowledge society and knowledge-based economy signifies a new era for education and training - the ubiquitous learning. The ubiquitous learning aims at replacing old-fashioned time / place / content-predetermined learning with a just-in-time / at work-place / customized / on-demand process of learning by new ICT-based tools (Pavlov, Paneva, Pavlova-Draganova, & Draganov, 2007). Moreover, the new educational strategies point to the investigation and the deployment of workable learning methods, approaches and scenarios for better understanding, creative thinking and experience, learning-by-doing and learning-by-authoring, engaging learners in more active participation during the perceiving of knowledge. Many questions are asked:

DOI: 10.4018/978-1-5225-4206-3.ch007

- What tasks could be interesting and attractive and could stimulate learners' desire to work?
- How could learners' creativity be activated and stimulated?
- What contemporary software environments can be used in order to attract learners in more active participation in the learning process?
- How to improve the knowledge understanding by the usage of imperceptible and unobtrusive approaches and tools—desirable for students as well as for teachers?
- How to help the user in exploring the information resources about the chosen learning domain by offering the most suitable tools: provisioning of suitable and necessary services (improved searching and grouping of resources, creative resource usage), providing automatic simultaneous access to the resources of more than a single system (learning management system, digital cultural ecosystems, digital library, repository, archive, *etc.*), flexibility regarding the order of the suggested information objects, resource recommendation, object reuse, analysis and generation of resources, *etc*?
- How to describe the selected resources in a given context and to determine the conditions and use cases – cognitive or educational goals, analysis, creative use, *etc.*?
- How to help the learner not just to view, but to also gain knowledge?
- How to provide knowledge in the most suitable way and form, intuitive and eligible?
- How to adapt the offered information content for each individual learner or group in order to achieve their cognitive goals and tasks, *etc.*

The difficulties in solving these issues are related to the lack of common models and workable solutions regarding the effective and context-dependent usage of the available e-resources, content presentation in the most suitable way for the different learners (content adaptation and customization), necessity for clear definition of the learner's needs, goals, interests, increase and generalisation of user experience in the learning platforms, provisioning of meaningful learning.

The aim of this chapter is to demonstrate some solutions for effective usage of digital libraries (DLs) content for learning purposes through tools and services to improved content observation and enhanced learning experience. Main factors, related to the DLs user experience and content usability issues are considered. Users' cognitive needs, goals, preferences, and interests have been carefully studied and become the starting point for the new DL functionality. This chapter presents several educational nooks or their components, which become applicable learning tools in different digital libraries. Special attention is paid on the modern educational games, providing the learners with a form of fun, motivating learning goals, high interactivity, and active immersion in the virtual learning world.

BACKGROUND

Libraries have always been a valuable source of knowledge resources. Their contemporary technological equivalent - digital libraries also pretend to hold this highly-valued position mainly due to the variety of content resources and the provisioning of easy access to them. A digital library is not just a static digital content repository, but also a system with a dynamic federation of functional units satisfying a wide variety of users' content requests (Arapi, Paneva-Marinova, Pavlov, & Christodoulakis, 2016). Fox et al. (1995) observe that the expression 'Digital Library' evokes a different impression in each person, ranging from the simple computerisation of traditional libraries to a space in which people communicate, share and produce new knowledge and knowledge products. Specifically, these systems range from digital object and metadata repositories, reference-linking systems, archives, and content administration systems (mainly developed by industry) to complex systems that integrate advanced digital library services (Candela, et al., 2007). The digital library mediates between the information needs of its user community and the globally available content. This is achieved by contributions in four areas (Niederée, Steffens, & Hemmje, 2002):

- **Content Pre-Selection:** The library selects high-quality content potentially relevant for the members of its user community;
- **Content Structuring:** The library structures the content according to the predominant domain understanding of its user community;
- **Content Enrichment:** Domain and library experts as well as community members enrich content objects with descriptive and value-adding metadata;
- **Library Services:** Services for content retrieval, access, annotation, *etc.* support the identification of relevant material and facilitate content access.

The DLs flexibility came because of the needs of the market, the emergence of new technologies, and especially from the request for stricter use of the existing resources and adapting their content and services to the needs of different user groups (Paneva-Marinova, Goynov, & Luchev, 2017).

Being desirable sources of knowledge, DLs can become an alternative of the contemporary learning management systems, which currently follow strictly defined learning procedures and rarely include creativity, freedom of thinking, and emergence / instigating of new ideas and inspirations. On the other hand, DLs can provide some non-trivial, but creative learning tasks, for example, to:

- Observe, analyze and study the target domains: find or verify trend/s in the domain, find new trend/s, influence, and problem/s, reach new result/s.
- Make new developments and projects for shared and (or) linked digital assets (DAs); new learning projects, documentaries, performance.
- Content-dependent exploitation of DAs for different purposes, *incl.* interactive virtual exhibition, gaming and gamification, storytelling, mobile applications, study, *etc.*
- Stimulate new research and promotion of innovative usage and user interaction with the target DL domain, *etc.*

Performing these tasks requires a functionality for effective DL content exploitation, context-based usage of the resources, "real-time" integration of different content types according to the users' interests and needs, provisioning of new forms of content presentation, and learning-oriented tools and services.

There is a great interest in the research, applications and innovation search in this field. For example, Yoshinov and al. (2016) present a framework and models for supporting personalized learning services on top of multimedia digital libraries, by a) supporting re-purposing of multimedia digital content / archives to cultural digital objects, learning objects and higher learning units, b) supporting the construction of pedagogy-driven personalized learning experiences on top of multimedia digital archives statically or dynamically. The dynamic construction of the learning experiences takes into account user profiles (the variety of the learners and their individual needs) and pedagogical templates.

Ferrara et al. (2014) present tools providing museum information to be shared with teachers who can reuse and re-contextualize them in their multimedia lessons and create educational environments to improve engagement and student learning. Their educational platform aims mainly to disseminate multimedia cultural content inside of classroom through open access data modality to sharing museum resources and to making multimedia lessons.

Gao et al. (2016) present a personalized learning recommendation system for digital library with which the users spend the least time and energy in accurately finding the information they need, where efficiency is improved to the greatest extent.

Qian et al. (2007) mentioned the "learning-oriented individual digital library" embodying the concept of knowledge economy based on the production exchange and use of knowledge. Authors claim that as a treasury of knowledge, a digital library must conform to the requirement of knowledge economy so as to offer everyone their knowledge of interest timely, precisely and effectively as much as it can. Moreover, it will take the advantage of the advanced cyber technology, will integrate the interesting knowledge bank and will provide precise knowledge guidance to save their corresponding finding time. Facing such a complicated situation, authors argued that offering personalized service has to become the first priority, because it will be the best guidance for users to dive in the knowledge.

Digital libraries are recognised as one of the most significant technological solutions for saving valuable parts of mankind's cultural and historical ancestry. Until recently, however, its potential to be a learning source is being neglected and there are no lots of solutions in this field. The authors actively try to develop workable solutions in this field. Part of them are presented in the next section.

Other modern technology-enhanced strategies are applied games, which are increasingly used as research, teaching or measurement tools helping teachers to stimulate learning by experiencing novelty, curiosity and challenge in development of various skills and competences (Griffiths, 2002). Game-based learning becomes even more and more popular. Games are applied in education boost enjoyment, motivation and engagement of learners by providing an interactive virtual playing environment where the player "always has to struggle against some kind of opposition" (Fabricatore, 2000). Engagement in game-playing (Brockmyer, et al., 2009) indicates the level of immersion, presence inside a virtual environment, flow (describing sense of enjoyment produced at balance between skill and challenge when performing intrinsically rewarding tasks (Csikszentmihalyi & Csikszentmihalyi, 1988)), and psychological absorption. By now, many educational games have been proposed, providing high level of learner's engagement and contributing in great extent to the effectiveness of the teaching process. However, teachers are still unable "to customize an appropriate game, and the game may not completely fit the curriculum content" (Chung-Ho & Ching-Hsue, 2013).

The massive invasion of applied video games for educational purposes is highly correlated with the modern understanding of the need of experiential learning (Kolb, 1984), *viz.* "learning-by-doing". Together with concrete and personalized experiences, video games provide to learners form of fun and structured play, motivating goals, interactivity, outcomes and feedback, win states, challenging competition, creative problem solving, social interaction and visual narrative (Prensky, 2001). These specific characteristics of video games might make game-based learning more effective than traditional teaching approaches regarding students' motivation, engagement, and learning outcomes (Papastergiou, 2009). Connolly et al. (2012) present a systematic literature review comprising articles discussing 82 educational games in various teaching areas, with an analysis of the positive impact of paying on learning achievements of the users.

The chapter presents below educational games for improved understanding of art and culture and the more concrete case of several applied games for *Orthodox iconographical art* and *fairy tales* study. The learners' engagement with appropriate methods and tools is pursued, aiming to provide more active participation of the "players" during the perceiving of knowledge. The role-playing learning method is also involved giving the opportunity to the learner to manage the story.

DLS USER EXPERIENCE AND CONTENT USABILITY

Factors Related to the DLs User Experience: Content Usability Issues

When the DL user is a learner, or has learning purposes in the environment, "one size fits all" solutions are not enough to satisfy his/her needs (Arapi P., Moumoutzis, Mylonakis, & Christodoulakis, 2007). Different DL learners have different learning needs and preferences that (should) affect the learning function outcome. Learners expect from the DL system a "personal facilitator" and not a "classroom" behaviour, where their personality and needs are known and taken into account. Based on Cronbach & Snow (1997), in learning personalization is most generally defined as an adaptation of the learning process and its content to the personal characteristics and preferences of the learner, as much as possible.

There are several benefits of thinking about and trying to understand learning preferences (Centre-Student-Development):

- People learn most effectively when the strategies used are closely matched with their preferred learning style.
- Sometimes we can improve our learning by knowing what our strengths are and then doing more of what we're good at.
- Often we can improve our learning by knowing what our weakness are and trying to enhance our skills in these areas.
- Different situations and learning environments require different learning strategies, so it's best to have a large repertoire from which to draw.

But which are these educational needs and preferences that essentially should be considered as input parameters in personalization processes and what is their role in the construction of a learning plan and the selection of appropriate learning resources (Arapi P., et al., 2008)? Arapi et al. (2008) identify and analyze a number of factors that can influence the extent and outcome of learning such as the learning style, learner goals / objectives, previous knowledge, educational level and difficulty, technical and other preferences (*e.g.* language, *etc.*).

The chapter' authors research practices points to different factors that should affect even more the learning activities and selection and usage of the DL content for learning, such as:

- The space in which learning takes place, its aesthetics and mood, user interfaces, visual elements, input devices, interaction with other learners / mentors, possibility of dynamic changing of the learning place, even its realism.
- Interactivity and the learner immersion in the learning place.
- The "interplay" between the learner and the learning's narrative or the learning place as a whole.

- The learnativity content model - the concept of assembling content into higher-level objects, as it is defined by Wagner (2002).
- The set of challenges the learner will face within the learning space; Synchronization of the challenges with the ability of the learner.
- Keeping interests by:
    - Implementation of multiple difficulty settings for the different learners.
    - Usage of non-trivial learning objects – applied games, puzzles, stories, conundrums, *etc.*
- Transforming the boring learning activities in a fun and adventures. The quality of the learner experience – whether learner enjoy working with the e-system, or whether they find it frustrating.
- Setting awards for the efforts – Reward the learners for skill, imagination, intelligence and dedication.
- Enhancing the motivation by encouragement, diversity, and extended curiosity.
- Eventually, conscious awareness of the learning as a key engine for the future success.

It could be also mentioned the provision of creative experiences, learning-by-doing and role-playing scenarios.

Moreover, a key factor is the proper learner model defining: the "who", or the degree of specialization in defining who is modeled and what the learner history is; the "what", or the cognitive goals, plans, attitudes, capabilities, knowledge, and beliefs of the learner; the "how" the model is to be acquired and maintained; and the "why", including whether to elicit information from the learner, give assistance, provide feedback, or interpret the learner's behavior (Paneva, 2006). Callan et al. (2003) commented in their paper that the DL user models should take into account also the overall information space – the context – including:

- Cognitive abilities, *e.g.* learning styles, perception.
- Individual differences, *e.g.* experience, education, age, gender.
- Individual and group behavior patterns and history.
- Subject domains.
- Work tasks, *e.g.* writing an essay, choosing a movie, planning a holiday.
- Work environments, and
- How all of the above change over time.

Callan et al. (2003) emphasized on investigating methods for building more robust, flexible and portable models of the complexity of users, tasks and contexts to inform the diverse possibilities for personalisation in digital libraries. Targets for this work include being able to develop implicit rather than explicit methods for learning user preferences which form the user models and developing user models that are portable across applications, devices and digital libraries. Perhaps the biggest challenge in this area will involve the development of user models that will drive personalisation and recommender systems, that are rich enough to capture as much of the user's task environment (context, task, situation), history, contribution to communities and individual preferences, as possible while conforming to a person's privacy choices.

Stefanov (2014) discusses a combined adaptability model for digital libraries, actively involving three main components – adaptability, user modelling and user interface modelling. Adaptability is a constant iterative process, continuing during the whole life cycle of the system.

The general concept here is the user personalization. According to the DELOS/NSF Working Group on Personalisation and Recommender Systems (Callan, et al., 2003), "personalization is required to make an increasingly heterogeneous population of digital libraries accessible to an increasingly heterogeneous population of users. It is no longer realistic to expect every user to adapt to every digital library. If a person must be an anthropologist to use an anthropological digital library, the library is available to only a limited community; if the library can tailor its services and materials for a wider range of users, the impact and utility of the library is magnified greatly. The next generation of digital libraries must support a wide range of personalized services that support the activities of a wide range of users".

Concerning to DL usability issues, it could be said that usability plays a vital role for the successful usage of the library and there have been valuable research findings fifteen years ago. As it is well known in the IT sector, the usability testing shows how the system is used by the user and how he/she gets benefits while using it. Buchanan & Salako (2009) offered an integrated measurement framework, derived from the goal, question, metric paradigm, which provides a relatively comprehensive and representative set of system usability and system usefulness attributes and associated measures, which could be adapted and further refined on a case-by-case basis. Blandford & Buchenan (2003) previously discussed some challenges to integrating user perspectives with technical developments, in terms of understanding those user perspectives, developing design processes that adequately accommodate them and ensuring adequate communications between all stakeholders in design. In "Designing digital libraries for usability", Borgman (2003) explores the importance of the relation between the content in a digital library, its design, and the needs of the target audience. Her paper also discusses criteria and evaluation method for digital libraries and emphasizes the importance of discovering "who would use the content, how, and why" (Borgman, 2003, p. 92).

Major problems appeared during the design of the software solutions (services, components, *etc.*), closely capturing the above discussed factors. Some of them concern the communication between the user and the software environment, which are in many cases ambiguous and even unsuited. Other are related with the formal presentation of the subjective issues such as learner' skill, imagination, motivation, intelligence, dedication, *etc.* Moreover, in order to provide effective forms of personalized learner experiences the focus must be on the design of the interaction per se as an integral part of the whole system. There is a need to develop multi-modal mixed initiative interfaces that draw on a range of user information seeking models. The requirement is thus for research to develop theories of interaction which underpin the design of applications and vice versa and which go beyond issues of simple elicitation, presentation and feedback.

DLs Educational Nooks and Components

This section presents several DLs educational nooks or their components improving DLs content usability for learning purposes.

Learning Tools in a Digital Library for Fashion Objects

The *Interactive Environment for Digital Presentation and Preservation of Fashion Objects* (IEFO) is an Internet-based digital library - a place where fashion objects of different kinds (sketches, closed models, fashion shows, clothe details, accessories, *etc.*) and origins (students' work, professional dress designers lines, *etc.*) were documented, classified, and "exhibited" in order to be widely accessible to both dress designers (*incl.* students, learning fashion arts and their mentors) and the wide audience (Luchev, Paneva-Marinova, Pavlova-Draganova, & Pavlov, 2013). Authors define the library as a completely interactive multimedia solution that provides services for registration, access and exploration of a practically unlimited number of fashion objects and knowledge and the users can use this rich knowledge base through its flexible preview, objects complex search, improved selection, grouping and creative usage. The IEFO database is depicted on Figure 1.

IEFO makes direct connection between the practical part of the learning process (widely used in IEFO from the birth of the idea to its realization into a fashion object, collection and a fashion show) and its theoretical preparation necessary for this entire cycle. The creation of an electronic storage, named *Learning Resources* (LR), is realized in order to store the theoretical knowledge. By creating the necessary connections between IEFO and LR, electronic fashion storage would not remain only a passive library, sorting its content in a particular way (Sapundjiev & Luchev, 2016). At every step of the creation of a fashion object, the authors have the easiest and quickest possible access to the theory necessary for that.

Moreover, LR has the capability of working independently as a system for storage of learning materials with the following functionality:

- Centralized access to the learning materials for each professor. The professors have a personal repository at their disposal to which they provide partial or full access to the students (the authors of fashion objects) from each separate study course.

Figure 1. Database of the interactive environment for digital presentation and preservation of fashion objects
Source: Paneva-Marinova, Pavlova, Sapundjiev, & Bogdanova, 2014.

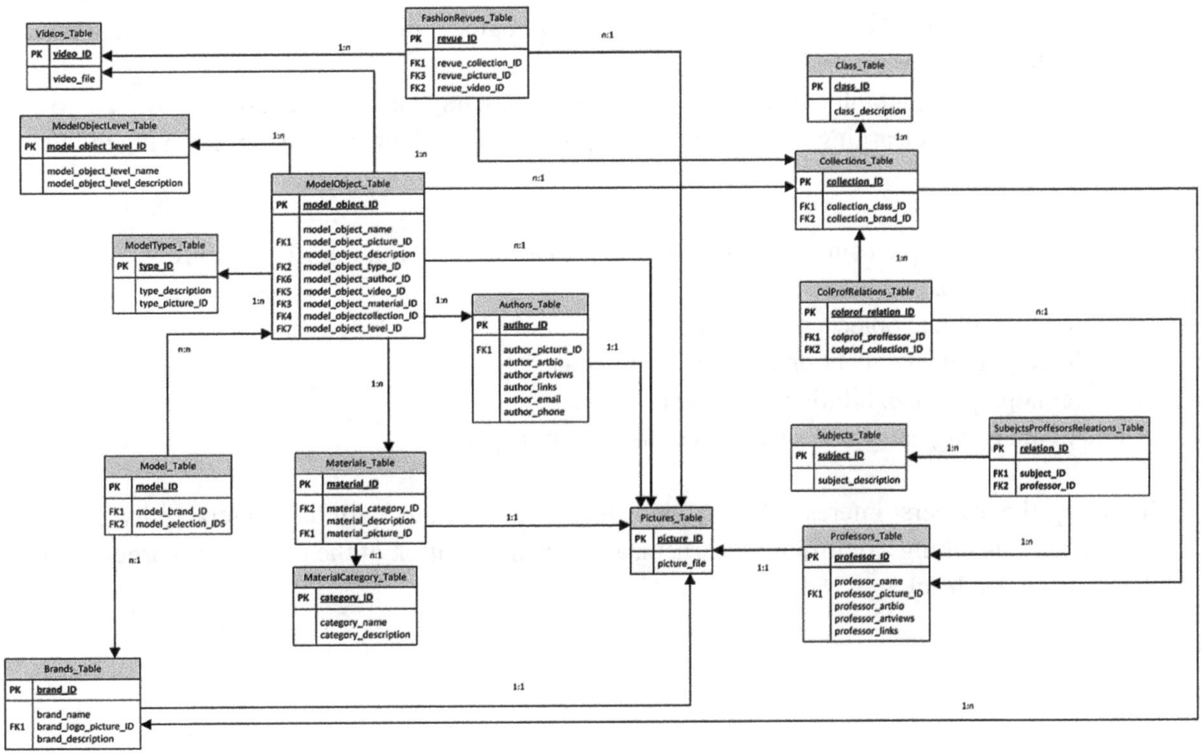

- Capability for sharing the learning content with other colleagues.
- Capability of storing files / resources, search and extraction of information back from it;
- Indexation of the digitalized documents (manual, automatic).
- Sorting and processing of digitalized documents.
- Processing of new documents, adding and uploading to the electronic storage.
- Building of a virtual archive containing the academic articles and publications of the professors, *etc.*

IEFO also provides services for creative e-performances stimulating learners' creative thinking and self-expression. The environment is actively used in the National Art Academy of Bulgaria by students, educated in Master class on "Fashion and Art".

Smart Learning Corner in an Art Digital Library

Classic digital libraries often provide solutions for later or delayed content delivery in order to provide to the user different ways to experience with DLs objects in more creative settings (examples: recommendation panels, content-on-demand services, *etc.*). However, the user's demand is for real time interaction with the content.

The DL smart learning corner (Arapi, Paneva-Marinova, Pavlov, & Christodoulakis, 2016) includes services for "real time" personalized content marking, commenting and analysing. It aims at adjusting the user's individual needs for content study. The solution is borrowed from real work and studying of traditional written content sources (*incl.* books, manuals), where the user mainly performs activities such as underlining the important parts of the content, writing notes and inferences, selecting and marking zones of their interest in pictures, *etc.* This personal work space could be also organized as an separate interactive service, saving the "marked user's content" or could be integrated in the DL content review service by additional "user's working tools".

In the Bulgarian Iconographical Digital Library (Pavlova-Draganova, Paneva-Marinova, Pavlov, & Goynov, 2010) the smart learning corner is now in a process of implementation, covering the following functionalities:

- Sharing, ranking, enclosing, tagging, linking, underlining, outlining, commenting, reviewing, bookmarking, *etc.* of:
  - Iconographical objects or their metadata.
  - Iconographical collections or their metadata.
  - Iconographical exhibitions or their metadata.
- Content analyzing and synthesizing (see the following part).

Observing the learners' interests the authors try to find solutions with high interactivity, learners' immersion, various settings for different learners, and synchronization of the tools with learners' ability and their knowledge level.

Ontology of Learning Analysis Method

Understanding art and culture is not an easy task, but it is important for personal development and growth. It helps individuals to take non-trivial decisions and to think in creative ways in life situations.

The long-term observation of the user's needs in DLs gives us an idea to look at analysis techniques and tools for improved usage of digital cultural assets, mainly for learning purposes. The analysis includes a specific research/study about a particular object or a whole domain, and aims to collect useful information about their properties, characteristics, and integral parts (Paneva-Marinova, Goynov, & Pavlov, 2011) (Paneva-Marinova, Pavlova-Draganova, Draganov, & Georgiev, 2012). The main purpose is finding the most important characteristics about the objects or domain being analysed, their structure, dependencies, internal and external relationships between their constituents, *etc.* Those are revealed by:

- Main trends in the development in the domain, direction and dynamics of the development;
- Discovering the key factors and conditions that directly affect the changes and development in the domain; examining the strength of the degree of their influence upon and the direction of the changes;
- Determining the degree of influence of the domain upon other related domains;
- Identifying new trends in the development of the domain being analyzed;
- Defining current problems, boundaries and limitations in the development of the analyzed domain, as well as problems related to them and possible areas of improvement;
- Evaluating the results in the domain's development.

To implement the analysis method (mainly for learning purposes), the practical research/learning problem is divided into a series of steps, leading to its solution. The steps are defined as a formula (Paneva-Marinova, Pavlova-Draganova, Draganov, & Georgiev, 2012), which combines *actions* with *content units*. The actions are based on the Bloom taxonomy (1956) and its "recommended vocabulary" of actions (called skills by Bloom), leading to results of the learning process (learning objective) in a certain area (Paneva-Marinova & Pavlov, 2011).

For example, the DL user (*i.e.* learner) classifies digital art objects (paintings) according to their author, i.e. he/she performs an action of grouping objects based on certain criteria. The selection could be further arranged according to the time feature and the user can see / discover main trends, direction and dynamics in the author's artwork.

Following a wide variety of concrete learning analysis scenarios (examples are presented in (Pavlova-Draganova, Paneva-Marinova, & Draganov, 2009)), an ontological structure for analysis learning method is developed (Paneva-Marinova, Pavlova-Draganova, Draganov, & Georgiev, 2012).

The ontology includes the base classes: Action, Analysis, Efficiency, Feature, Objective, Purpose, Type and User. The Action class is subclassed by: BreakingDown, Choosing, Classifying, Comparing, Correlating, Diagramming, Differentiating, Discriminating, Distinguishing, Focusing, Illustrating, Inferring, Limiting, Outlining, PointingOut, Prioritizing, Recognizing, Separating and Subdividing, used to describe the types of analysis sub-actions. Efficiency is extended by the two classes Effective and Ineffective. The Purpose class has the following subclasses: Development, Influence, NewTrends, Problems, Results and Trends. A Type is further specified by being: AssessmentAnalysis, CombinedAnalysis, ComparativeAnalysis, DiagnosticAnalysis, PartialAnalysis, ProspectiveAnalysis, QualitativeAnalysis, QuantitiveAnalysis and TemporalAnalysis. We have also the three subclasses of User – Educator, Learner and LearnersGroup, given that Educator and Learner are disjoint. The relations in the ontology are: Analysis hasAction Action, Analysis hasEfficiency Efficiency, Analysis hasFeature Feature, Analysis hasObjective Objective, Analysis hasPurpose Purpose, Analysis hasType Type, Analysis usedBy User, LearnersGroup hasLearner (inverse of partOfGroup) Learner, and Learner partOfGroup (inverse of has-Learner) LearnersGroup. Analysis itself could also be related to several external entities, for example, it solves Learning Task(s), it could be related to other Learning Method(s), and it leads to achieving of Learning Goal(s).

Based on this ontological structure a range of analysis actions are specified. Figure 2 depicts the analysis actions provided to the users (viz. viewers: learner, educator, researcher/professional, tourist, connoisseur, *etc.*; editor; moderator; administrator) of a digital library with cultural content. They are separated into two types: *Standard analysis* and *Specific analysis*. As shown below, the standard analysis actions include the basic functionality for objects/collections search, review, selection and management. The specific analysis actions aim to improve the manipulation activities with DL assets. We regard the

Figure 2. Analysis actions provided to the DL users

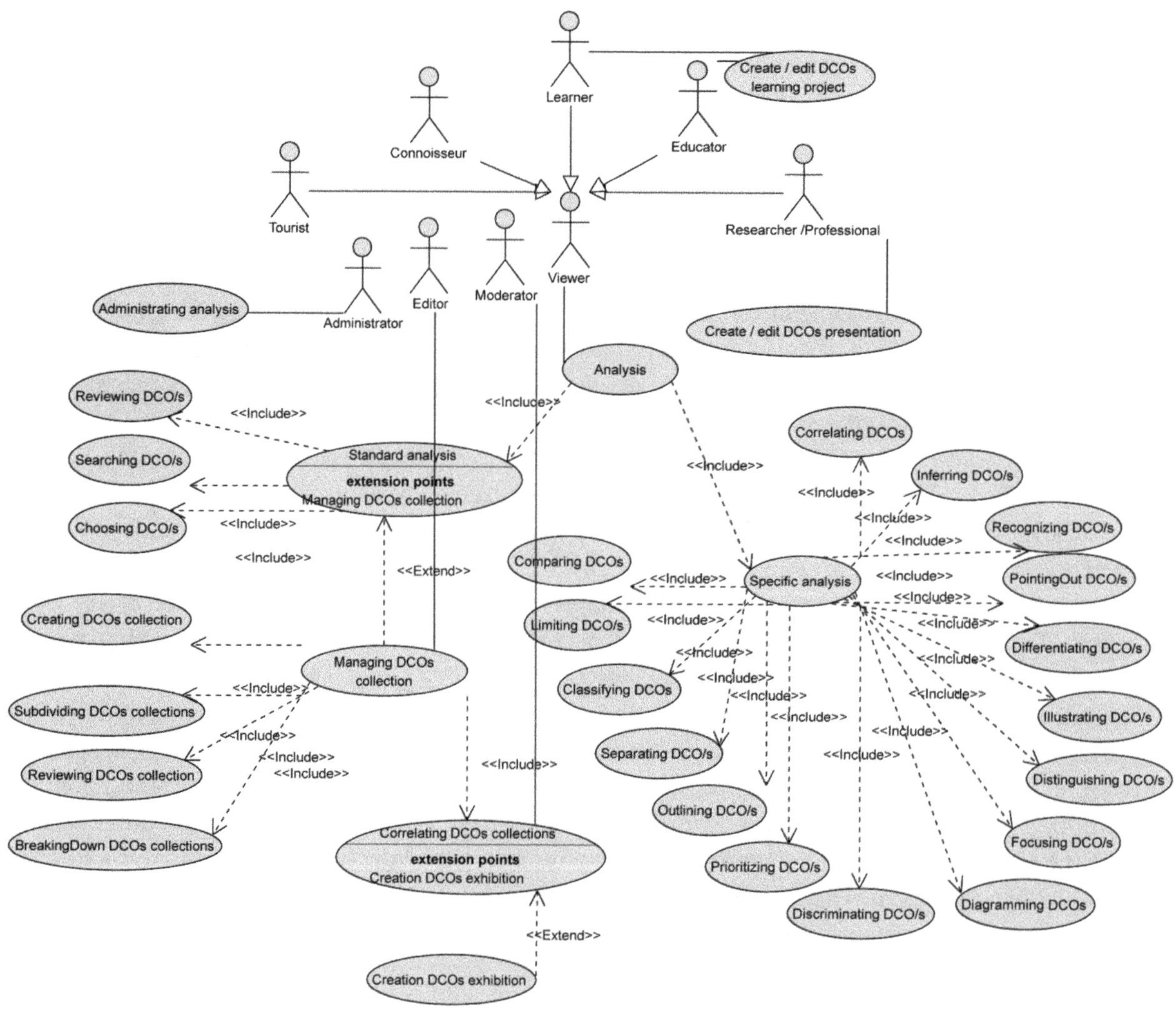

following DL content types: digital cultural object (DCO), DCOs collection (public DCOs collection, private DCOs collection, temporary DCOs group, etc.), DCOs exhibition, DCOs presentation, DCOs learning project.

The next scenario demonstrates a real usage of the DL analysis actions by professionals - the artists.

The analysis actions (or part of them) will, for example, assist the artists in their preliminary preparation (research, analysis) that they make before creating a new piece of artwork. DL will give them possibilities for review and analysis of digital copies of artworks in a specific domain, topic, *etc.*, also displaying additional descriptive information (metadata) about them (if available).

In particular, let the artist (*viz.* an iconographer) plan to paint a specific theme/character - "The Virgin" → *General goal.*

In the DL environment, he/she performs a search by the specified theme/character and review of the found digital art objects → *Task 1* and *Task 2.*

The next step is the additional choice of a specific subset of the main theme, for example, "The Virgin Hodegetria" → *Task 3.*

The selected objects are separated/arranged according to their creation time/period, which brings different characteristics about the objects from iconographic and technological perspective/point of view → *Task 4.*

After that, the system could distinguish digital art objects by a selected school, point out digital art object/s, including components for new artwork and prioritize one or several of them as a main sample/s → *Task 5* and *Task 6.*

The final step is the inferring phase, which aim is to consider and present a conceptual solution/project of the new artwork, using the selected digital objects and their components → *Task 7.*

The presented ontological structure and its real usage aim to improve art literacy of young people by providing technology-enhanced method for art study. Some experiments with the presented learning analysis are done during the SINUS project (SINUS-Project) and Dochev and Agre (2012) have discussed them.

Current and future research work will focus on the improvement of the presented learning analysis issues during the ongoing project "Concepts and Models for Innovation Ecosystems of Digital Cultural Assets" [1], which aim is to develop optimal and feasible conceptual models and methods of analysis, understanding, interpretation, and sharing of content in ecosystems for digital culture in new ways and through innovative means for fuller delivery of knowledge to digital collections and archives of cultural artefacts (CultEcoSys-Project, 2017). The authors will try to find solutions not only to support learning "about heritage" that is preserved in ecosystems for digital culture, but also "learning from cultural heritage", providing context-dependent use of digital resources.

Educational Games for Art and Culture

This part presents several educational games for improved understanding of art and culture.

Bontchev et al. (2016) present a maze video game, called "Educational video game for Bulgarian orthodox iconography", which introduces Bulgarian Orthodox iconographic arts by following specific learning methods for this domain. Game activities for studying Orthodox iconography aim at implementing different art analysis actions, assisting the learners (in particular, the artists) in their preliminary preparation (research, analysis) that they do before creating a new piece of art project (artwork). The game gives them possibilities for interactive review and analysis of digital copies of artworks in a specific domain, topic, *etc.*, also displaying additional descriptive information (metadata) about them, giving motivating learning goals, active immersion in the virtual learning world, *etc.* For realization of an effective game-based learning process, iconography teachers define specific tasks such as an artistic analysis of the development of iconographical objects and scenes in the different iconographical schools through time, tracing the iconographical technology development in different iconographical schools and time periods, technological analysis of a piece of art and restoration manipulations, tracing the authentication of an object, and analysis of the religious meaning of an iconographical image as the object of research (Paneva-Marinova, Pavlova-Draganova, Draganov, & Georgiev, 2012). Main teaching methods involve project-based learning and understanding-by-design, learning-by-doing, learning-by-authoring and creative thinking practices, giving students real painting tasks, which are based on their individual / independent iconographic art observation and study (Draganov et al., 2010).

More specifically, the game presents different images of Jesus Christ – from infant to adult, painted by iconographers from significant Bulgarian iconographic schools, digital copies of rare Orthodox specimens and icons from difficult-to-access storages, distant churches, chapels, and monasteries, objects at risk. The learning content objects are based on the iconographical materials of the "Virtual Encyclopedia of the Bulgarian Icons" multimedia digital library (also called Bulgarian Iconographical Digital Library, BIDL) (Pavlova-Draganova, Paneva-Marinova, Pavlov, & Goynov, 2010). The game labyrinth includes five main rooms connected with tunnels: Introductory room, Room 2: Jesus Christ depicted as a baby, Room 3: Jesus Christ depicted as a child, Room 4: Jesus Christ in images of worship, and Room 5: Jesus in scenes of his life. To give to the user a topic-related challenge every room has corresponding learning task. During the labyrinth passing, the player has to answer several questions, enigmas, puzzles and problems to finish the game and learn the content. Within the maze, the player can play two additional games: a 3D Quiz game for assessment of his/her current knowledge in the domain, and a 3D Zoom game for ordering context-related icons. Both games can be adapted according to the player's emotional state and playing style following the ADAPTIMES player-centric adaptation model (Bontchev, 2016). The presented maze video games are experimentally implemented as a BIDL nook.

Luchev et al. (2016) present a solution integrating Bulgarian Iconographical Digital Library and the tourist mobile application family named as BOOK@HAND BIDL for supporting the learning process of Orthodox iconographical art. Draganov et al. (2015) demonstrate some use cases for technology-enhanced learning on Orthodox iconographical art, combining analysis, collaborative work, mobile learning, discussion, and learning-by-authoring approaches in order to achieve more active participation of the learners during the reception of knowledge and to stimulate their creative thinking. The learners visit famous churches, monasteries, museums, *etc.*, where they can see samples of Bulgarian Iconography supported by m-learning. They rely on the BOOK@HAND BIDL platform containing personalized collections presenting location, historical data, pictures, *etc.* delivered through BIDL. The main goal of the learners is to create their own learning material (or project) by analysing the available resources. Moreover, the BOOK@HAND BIDL application contains several interactive games:

- **Ordering:** The names and locations of some icons are given in random order. The objective of the game is to put the icons in chronological order.
- **Blind Map:** The user should find the source location of the icons on a blind map presenting the provinces of Bulgaria without their names.

- **Memory Game:** Cards containing the pictures and titles of icons are located along a grid. Initially, the cards are laid face down and two cards are flipped face up over each turn. The objective of the game is to turn over pairs of matching pictures and titles.
- **Sliding Puzzle:** The pictures of icons are cut into small square tiles. The starting screen of the puzzle contains the tiles arranged in random order with one tile missing. The objective of the puzzle is to move the tiles to their right position thereby restoring the original picture. Tiles can be moved by using the empty space. The puzzle exists in two sizes with different difficulty levels. The easier version has 3×3 tiles, whereas the more difficult version has 4×4 tiles.

The BOOK@HAND BIDL games seem very simple and easy, but the experiments show that deeper knowledge understanding is achieved.

Slavova-Petkova et al. (2016), mentored by the chapter' authors, discuss a learning scenario for better understanding of fairy tales through applied game using as a core the role-playing method. Role-playing (Nikolova, 2013) gives opportunity to the child to be the main character, whose actions manage the story. In their scenario Slavova-Petkova et al. suppose that the character-child lives through the fairy tale, which seems like a game. Utilizing creative thinking, the child analyses the problem, generates possible decisions, follows a choice and application of the best of these decisions. As a result, an "insight" or "sudden realization" happens or in other words the process of entire comprehension of all connections and possibilities in a given problematic situation and the generation of ideas for solving the latter. This type of generalized learner experience demonstrates that the learners' engagement with appropriate methods and tools could provide more active participation during the perceiving of knowledge.

SOME COMMENTS ON THE PRESENTED FACTORS AND SOLUTIONS

In this chapter, the authors have outlined a range of factors that contribute to the improvement of the DL user' experience and DL content usability for learning purposes. These factors are mainly oriented to better learner – *DL* system interaction and issues related to the context of use. This list is by no means complete. For example, authors have not even mentioned learning content layout or detailed design of learner navigation through data structures; authors have not also mentioned interaction style or design evolution; cognitive issues have not been discussed, the transformation, if any, of the DL content units (digital objects, collections, exhibitions, *etc.*) to learning units (learning objects, learning projects, presentations, packages, *etc.*), the content interoperability problem, *etc.*

The presented educational nooks are only some examples, considered to improve the users' experiences in digital libraries, aiming to satisfy user' content observation and learning needs. Part of the presented solutions are in a stage of development, but they are designed to capture key factors, affecting the learning activities in the DL, mentioned above. The authors do not claim to offer a complete solution but give ideas for future improvements and innovations in this field. Deeper understanding of learner behaviours and learner needs, and learner-oriented design techniques will be necessary. Deeper understanding of the constraints in the design of proper usability and acceptable user experience will be necessary. Measuring and assessing learning experience in the DL will affects its further exploitation and evolution in this direction.

FUTURE RESEARCH DIRECTIONS

The further investigations in the above-discussed domain point to a wide variety of directions:

- To create of workable methods and tools, aiming to increase and generalize the visitor experience in the digital culture platforms (*incl.* digital libraries). Moreover, creative user experiences will support the effective on-line learning through DLs.
- Contextual techniques for personalizing its experience in these platforms.
- Context-dependent use of digital resources in digital culture platforms (for e-learning or e-training purposes).
- To develop of new digital and transmedia storytelling solutions for learning purposes, creation of interactive virtual exhibitions, gaming and gamification, virtual worlds, live simulations, animations, interactive media previews.
- Multimodal interfaces and intelligent visualization of complex information relying on enhanced user experience and usability (*incl.* user-centric visualization and analytics, real-time adaptable and interactive visualization, real-time and collaborative 3D visualization, dynamic clustering of information, *etc.*), *etc.*

Moreover, the design and improvement of the learner' experience in the changing cases would not be restricted by the available technologies, platforms and tools. The field has great potential for innovations especially in our world of active imposition of e-devices, e-literacy, and e-content. The focus will be in the research and exploitation of new or emerging technologies (*e.g.* 3D, augmented and virtual reality, visual computing, smart world, environments and devices, media convergence, social media, *etc.*) for the development of innovative products, tools, applications, and services for creative digital content production, usage and management. The aims is to transform and customize the valuable parts of mankind's cultural and historical ancestry into digital assets, whose integration and reuse through research-lead methods has high commercial and non-commercial potential for learning and cultural institutions, tourism, creative and media industries.

CONCLUSION

Libraries have been used from ancient times to serve as repositories of knowledge and information, which are used to learn new or further improve previously acquired knowledge. Libraries were considered as a major asset for educational institutions and the society as a whole. The technology evolution of the modern age transformed the traditional libraries into digital ones which arose the need of efficient serve of the huge amount of information that now exists in the form of digitized content, as well as the provisioning of new workable applications (*incl.* e-learning, e-research, *etc.*). The focus of this chapter was on the search of innovations especially in areas and subareas relevant to digital library data creative use/re-use and remix, reinterpretation, study, understanding, analysis, personalization, intelligent curation, adaptation, innovative tools for approaching cultural assets, applications and services for better access and exploiting of the rich and diverse digital cultural heritage in a sustainable way, targeting the improvement of the

DLs users' experiences and DLs content usability. The research deals with important issues of handling data directly, affecting education, the public sector (cultural institutions—museums, libraries, galleries, *etc.*), the economy (as presented by creative and re-creative industry), and the society as a whole.

REFERENCES

Arapi, P., Moumoutzis, N., Mylonakis, M., & Christodoulakis, S. (2007). A Pedagogy-driven personalization framework to support adaptive learning experiences. In *Proceedings of the 7th IEEE International Conference on Advanced Learning Technologies (ICALT 2007)* (pp. 96-97). Niigata, Japan: IEEE. 10.1109/ICALT.2007.27

Arapi, P., Moumoutzis, N., Mylonakis, M., Stylianakis, G., Theodorakis, G., & Christodoulakis, S. (2008). Design, implementation and experimental evaluation of a pedagogy-driven framework to support personalised learning experiences. In *2th LOGOS Workshop "Cross-Media and Personalised Learning Applications with Intelligent Content" in Conj. with AIMSA2008 Conference* (pp. 7-25). Varna, Bulgaria: Institute of Information Technologies - BAS.

Arapi, P., Paneva-Marinova, D., Pavlov, R., & Christodoulakis, S. (2016). Techniques to personalized observation and improved learning experience in digital libraries. In *Proceedings of the International Conference on e-Learning'16* (pp. 94-100). Retrieved March 20, 2017, from http://elearning-conf.eu/docs/cp16/paper-14.pdf

Blandford, A., & Buchenan, G. (2003). Usability of digital libraries: a source of creative tensions with technical developments. *IEEE-CS Technical Committee on Digital Libraries' on-line newsletter*. Retrieved March 20, 2017, from http://web4.cs.ucl.ac.uk/uclic/annb/docs/abgbTCDLpreprint.pdf

Bloom, B. S. (1956). *Taxonomy of educational objectives: The classification of educational goals, Book 1. Cognitive domain*. New York, NY: Longman.

Bontchev, B. (2016). Holistic player modelling for controlling adaptation in video games. *Proceedings of 14th International Conference e-Society*, 11-18.

Bontchev, B., Paneva-Marinova, D., & Draganov, L. (2016). Educational video games for Bulgarian Orthodox iconography. In L. G. Chova, A. L. Martínez, & I. C. Torres (Ed.), *ICERI2016 Proceedings 9th Annual International Conference of Education, Research and Innovation* (pp. 1679-1688). Seville, Spain: IATED Academy. 10.21125/iceri.2016.1374

Borgman, C. (2003). Designing digital libraries for usability. In A. Bishop, N. Van House, & B. Buttenfield (Eds.), *Digital Library Use: Social Practice in Design and Evaluation* (pp. 85-118). Cambridge, MA: MIT Press. Retrieved May 18, 2017, from http://works.bepress.com/borgman/307/

Brockmyer, J. H., Fox, C. M., Curtiss, K. A., McBroom, E., Burkhart, K. M., & Pidruzny, J. N. (2009). The development of the game engagement questionnaire: A measure of engagement in video game-playing. *Journal of Experimental Social Psychology*, *45*(4), 624–634. doi:10.1016/j.jesp.2009.02.016

Buchanan, S., & Salako, A. (2009). Evaluating the usability and usefulness of a digital library. *Library Review*, *58*(9), 638–651. doi:10.1108/00242530910997928

Callan, J., Smeaton, A., Beaulieu, M., Borlund, P., Brusilovsky, P., Chalmers, M., . . . Toms, E. (2003). *Personalisation and recommender systems in digital libraries.* Retrieved May 18, 2017, from https://www.ercim.eu/publication/ws-proceedings/Delos-NSF/Personalisation.pdf

Candela, L., Castelli, D., Ferro, N., Ioannidis, Y., Koutrika, G., Meghini, C., . . . Schuldt, H. (2007). *The DELOS Digital Library Reference model. Foundations for digital Libraries.* Version 0.96. Retrieved March 24, 2017, from http://delosw.isti.cnr.it/files/pdf/ReferenceModel/DELOS_DLReferenceModel_096.pdf

Centre-Student-Development. (n.d.). Retrieved March 20, 2017, from https://www.uwo.ca/sdc/learning/selfhelp/skill_building_handouts/PDFs/Memory%20and%20Thinking%20Skills/Learning%20Styles.pdf

Chung-Ho, S., & Ching-Hsue, C. (2013). 3D game-based learning system for improving learning achievement in software engineering curriculum. *TOJET: The Turkish Online Journal of Educational Technology, 12*(2), 1-12. Retrieved March 20, 2017, from http://www.tojet.net/articles/v12i2/1221.pdf

Connolly, T. M., Boyle, E. A., Macarthur, E., Hainey, T., & Boyle, J. M. (2012). A systematic literature review of empirical evidence on computer games and serious games. *Computers & Education, 59*(2), 661–686. doi:10.1016/j.compedu.2012.03.004

Cronbach, L., & Snow, R. (1997). *Aptitudes and instructional methods: A handbook for research on interactions.* New York: Irvington Publishers.

Csikszentmihalyi, M., & Csikszentmihalyi, I. S. (1988). *Optimal experience. Psychological studies of flow in consciousness.* New York, NY: Cambridge University Press. doi:10.1017/CBO9780511621956

CultEcoSys-Project. (2017). *Concepts and models for innovation ecosystems of digital cultural assets, No. DN02/06/15.12.2016 (project web page).* Retrieved March 20, 2017, from http://cultecosys.math.bas.bg

Dochev, D., & Agre, G. (2012). Supporting learning-by-doing situations by Semantic technologies. In D. Stefanoui, & J. Culita (Ed.), *Proceedings of the 17th Annual Conference on Media and Web Technology EUROMEDIA,* (pp. 49-53). Budapest, Hungary: Academic Press.

Draganov, L., Paneva-Marinova, D., Pavlova, L., Luchev, D., Márkus, Z., Szántó, G., & Szkaliczki, T. (2015). Technology-enhanced learning for cultural heritage. In R. Pavlov & P. Stanchev (Eds.), *Proceedings of the 5th International Conference on Digital Presentation and Preservation of Cultural and Scientific Heritage.* Veliko Tarnovo, Bulgaria: Institute of Mathematics and Informatics - BAS. Retrieved March 25, 2017, from http://dipp.math.bas.bg

Fabricatore, C. (2000). Learning and videogames: an unexploited synergy. *2000 Annual Convention of the Association for Educational Communications and Technology (AECT). Workshop: In Search of the Meaning of Learning,* 1-17. Retrieved March 20, 2017, from http://learndev.org/dl/FabricatoreAECT2000.PDF

Ferrara, V., Macchia, A., & Sapia, S. (2014). Cultural heritage open data for developing an educational platform [Abstract]. In *Proceedings of the 5th International Conference on Information, Intelligence, Systems and Applications.* IEEE. doi:10.1109/IISA.2014.6878775

Fox, E., Akscyn, R., Furuta, R., & Leggett, J. (1995). Digital libraries. *Communications of the ACM, 38*(4), 23–28. doi:10.1145/205323.205325

Gao, X., Huang, W., Wang, N., Yang, Y., & Yan, Y. (2016). A top-N algorithm-based personalized learning recommendation system for digital library. *International Journal of Emerging Technologies in Learning, 11*(11), 55–59. doi:10.3991/ijet.v11i11.6256

Griffiths, M. (2002). The educational benefits of videogames. *Education for Health, 20*(3), 47–51. Retrieved from http://sheu.org.uk/sites/sheu.org.uk/files/imagepicker/1/eh203mg.pdf

Kolb, D. (1984). *Experiential learning, experience as the source of learning and development.* Englewood Cliffs, NJ: Prentice Hall.

Luchev, D., Paneva-Marinova, D., Pavlov, R., Kaposi, G., Markus, Z., Szanto, G., . . . Veres, M. (2016). Game-based learning of Bulgarian iconographical art on smart phone application. In *Proceedings of the International Conference on e-Learning* (pp. 195-200). Bratislava, Slovakia: University of Ruse, Bulgaria. Retrieved March 20, 2017, from http://elearning-conf.eu/docs/cp16/paper-30.pdf

Luchev, D., Paneva-Marinova, D., Pavlova-Draganova, L., & Pavlov, R. (2013). New digital fashion world. In B. Rachev, & A. Smrikarov (Ed.), *Proceedings of the 14th International Conference on Computer Systems and Technologies, CompSysTech'13* (vol. 767, pp. 270-275). The Association for Computing Machinery.

Niederée, C., Steffens, U., & Hemmje, M. (2002). Towards digital library mediation for web services. EurAsian conference Workshop Knowledge Foraging for Dynamic Networking of Communities and Economies (EurAsia-ICT 2002), 445-449.

Nikolova, M. (2013). Development of creativity by role playing in the classroom. *Proceedings of the National Conference with international participation "Knowledge – traditions, innovations, perspectives"*, 441-449.

Paneva, D. (2006). Ontology-based student modeling. *Proceedings of the Fourth CHIRON Open Workshop "Ubiquitous Learning Challenges: Design, Experiments and Context Aware Ubiquitous Learning"*, 17-21.

Paneva-Marinova, D., Goynov, M., & Luchev, D. (2017). *Multimedia digital library: Constructive block in ecosystems for digital cultural assets. Basic functionality and services.* Saarbrücken, Germany: LAP LAMBERT Academic Publishing.

Paneva-Marinova, D., Goynov, M., & Pavlov, R. (2011). Content analyzing and synthesizing services in a digital library. *International Journal. Information Technologies and Knowledge, 2*(4), 403–416.

Paneva-Marinova, D., & Pavlov, P. (2011). Educational application of top of digital library for cultural heritage. *Proceedings of the International Conference on e-Learning and the Knowledge Society (E-Learning'11)*, 211-224.

Paneva-Marinova, D., Pavlova, L., Sapundjiev, V., & Bogdanova, M. (2014). Interactive environment for digital preservation and preservation of fashion objects. In R. Pavlov & P. Stanchev (Ed.), *Proceedings of the UNESCO International Conference on Digital Presentation and Preservation of Cultural and Scientific Heritage* (pp. 147-154). Veliko Tarnovo, Bulgaria: Institute of Mathematics and Informatics, BAS. Retrieved April 27, 2017, from http://dipp.math.bas.bg

Paneva-Marinova, D., Pavlova-Draganova, L., Draganov, L., & Georgiev, V. (2012). Ontological presentation of analysis method for technology-enhanced learning. In *Proceedings of the International Conference on Computer Systems and Technologies ComSysTech'12* (pp. 384-390). Ruse, Bulgaria: ACM New York. 10.1145/2383276.2383332

Papastergiou, M. (2009). Digital game-based learning in high school computer science education: Impact on educational effectiveness and student motivation. *Computers & Education, 52*(1), 1–12. doi:10.1016/j.compedu.2008.06.004

Pavlov, R., Paneva, D., Pavlova-Draganova, L., & Draganov, L. (2007). Ubiquitous learning applications on top of iconographic digital library. In L. Dimitrova, & R. Pavlov (Ed.), *Proceedings of the Jubilee International Conference on Mathematical and Computational Linguistics "30 years Department of Mathematical Linguistics"*. Sofia, Bulgaria: Institute of Mathematics and Informatics, Bulgarian Academy of Sciences.

Pavlova-Draganova, L., Paneva-Marinova, D., & Draganov, L. (2009). A use case scenario for technology-enhanced learning through Semantic Web services. *International Journal. Information Technologies & Knowledge, 3*(3), 257–268.

Pavlova-Draganova, L., Paneva-Marinova, D., Pavlov, R., & Goynov, G. (2010). On the wider accessibility of the valuable phenomena of Orthodox iconography through digital library. In M. Ioannides, D. Fellner, A. Georgopoulos, & D. Hadjimitsis (Ed.), *Proceedings of the 3rd International Conference dedicated on Digital Heritage (EuroMed 2010)* (pp. 173-178). Lymassol, Cyprus: ARCHAEOLINGUA.

Prensky, M. (2001). *Digital game-based learning*. McGraw-Hill.

Qian, L., Liu, L., & Hu, Y. (2007). Analysis of personalized information service system for digital libraries. In *Proceedings of the First IEEE International Symposium onInformation Technologies and Applications in Education, ISITAE '07*. Kunming, China: IEEE. doi: 10.1109/ISITAE.2007.4409277

Sapundjiev, V., & Luchev, D. (2016). Interactive environment for creating and preservation of fashion objects integrated with electronic storage of learning resources. In N. Dimitrova (Ed.), *Proceedings of the Doctoral Conference in Mathematics and Informatics, MIDOC 2015* (pp. 116-123). Sofia, Bulgaria: "St. Kliment Ohridski" University Press.

SINUS-Project. (n.d.). *Semantic technologies for Web services and technology enhanced learning, No. D-002-189 (Project web page)*. Retrieved March 20, 2017, from http://sinus.iinf.bas.bg

Slavova-Petkova, S., Dimova, M., & Luchev, D. (2016). Learning scenario for better understanding of fairy tales using role-playing and serious games methods. In R. Pavlov & P. Stanchev (Eds.), *Proceedings of the 6th UNESCO International Conference on Digital Presentation and Preservation of Cultural and Scientific Heritage.* Veliko Tarnovo, Bulgaria: Institute of Mathematics and Informatics - BAS. Retrieved May 10, 2017, from http://dipp.math.bas.bg

Stefanov, K. (2014). Digital libraries as a social media. In *Proceedings of the UNESCO International Conference on Digital Presentationa dn preservation of Cultural and Scientific Heritage* (pp. 26-32). Veliko Tarnovo, Bulgaria: Institute of Mathematics and Informatics, BAS. Retrieved March 25, 2017, from http://dipp.math.bas.bg

Wagner, E. D. (2002). Steps to creating a content strategy for your organization. *The eLearning Developers' Journal*, 1-9. Retrieved April 29, 2017, from http://www.elearningguild.com/pdf/2/102902mgt-h.pdf

Yoshinov, R., Arapi, P., Christodoulakis, S., & Kotseva, M. (2016). Supporting personalized learning experiences on top of multimedia digital libraries. *International Journal of Education and Information Technologies, NAUN*, *10*, 152–158.

KEY TERMS AND DEFINITIONS

Digital Cultural Ecosystem: A system, which virtually assembles various digital collections, archives, virtual museums, digital libraries and cultural heritage sites in order to facilitate the access to their resources, bringing cultural content to new audiences in novel ways.

Educational Nook: User's working tools and services, used mainly for satisfying educational purposes.

Learning Analysis: Specific research/study about particular objects or a whole domain, aiming to collect useful information about their properties, characteristics, and integral parts. The main purpose is finding the most important characteristics about the objects or domain being analyzed, their structure, dependencies, internal and external relationships between their constituents, etc.

Learning by Authoring: A learning approach, which lays down on experiences resulting directly from the learner' authoring actions.

Learning by Doing: A learning approach, which lays down on experiences resulting directly from the learner' own actions.

Learning Service: A functional unit that refers to the management of training activities and/or processes in the software platform.

Personalized Content Observation: A technique for customizing the user content exploration and usage in a software environment.

ENDNOTE

1 The research presented in this chapter is partly funded by the Bulgarian NSF under the research project N°DN02/06/15.12.2016 "Concepts and Models for Innovation Ecosystems of Digital Cultural Assets" under the tasks: T2.1. Research, development and application of new models and tools for analysis, understanding and interpretation of the digital cultural content of digital culture ecosystems and T2.2. Research, adaptation and application of tools for context-dependent use of digital cultural resources by digital culture ecosystems (for training purposes).

Chapter 8
Ensuring Quality of Web Portals Through Accessibility Analysis

Amar Ranjan Dash
Berhampur University, India

Manas Ranjan Patra
Berhampur University, India

ABSTRACT

With the increase in number of electronic services being delivered through web portals, a lot of emphasis is being given to ensure the quality of web portals in terms of contents and associated design aspects. This has led to studies investigating various requirements of web users and to guidelines for quality enhancement in order to make web portals accessible to all irrespective of one's age, physical challenges, ethnicity, and level of literacy. In this chapter, the authors address the accessibility issues of web portals based on ongoing research. They analyze the accessibility in three levels (i.e., at the levels of authoring tool, web component, and user-agent). The contents of this chapter can throw light on the design aspects of web portals, web browsers, and media players to make them more suitable for users in general.

INTRODUCTION

Over the last couple of years, web portals are being considered as excellent means of information dissemination and visibility. At the initial stages web portals were used as a source of information but with the passage of time organizations have begun to extend a plethora of services electronically. Analysis reveals that due to inadequacies in the content, presentation, and online assistance available in those web sites, users are not very much attracted towards web portals. Therefore, we need to understand user requirements to make web portals accessible for all, irrespective of their age, physical challenges, ethnicity, and levels of literacy. The World Wide Web consortium has recommended WCAG 2.0, UAAG 2.0, and ATAG 2.0 guidelines to analyze web portals at web component, user-agent, and authoring tool levels.

Since 1997, the initializations of web accessibility initiatives, the web technology researchers have been carried out some studies to evaluate the accessibility of web portals and user agents. Abanumy, Al-Badi and Mayhew (2005) evaluated the accessibility of the government web portals of Saudi Arabia

DOI: 10.4018/978-1-5225-4206-3.ch008

and Oman, using WCAG 1.0 guidelines and Multiweb, Lynx, and W3C Validation as software tools to find error percentages. They have used Assistive technologies and haptic devices for users having problems like total blindness and mobility. But, they have not addressed the issue of persons with color blindness. Ceaparu and Shneiderman, (2002) analyzed the home pages of 50 US state Web sites. The analysis was done manually and initial recommendations were made with 10 rules which did not include any recommendation for disable people.

Kuzma, Yen and Oestreicher, (2009) examined the accessibility of government web portals from different continent that is European Union, Asia, and Africa with respect to the guidelines of WCAG 1.0 using TAW as software tool. Similarly, Al-Radaideh, Nurser and Wahbeh, (2011) have evaluated 25 Government websites of jordan by considering TAW with respect to WCAG 1.0 Guideline. Similarly, Malaysian researchers, Latif and Masrek, (2010) have used WCAG 1.0 priority 1 and Bobby as automatic tool, to evaluate 9 websites. They have provided only the number of errors of different portals instead of computing the percentage of error. Thus, it doesn't give an exact picture of the overall error percentage which can be used as a comparative measure among different web portals. Carter and Markel, (2001) classify disable peoples into four categories and demonstrate tools made for them by different company.

Kamoun, Mourad and Bataineh, (2013) have made a comparative analysis of web sites in Dubai using both WCAG 1.0 and WCAG 2.0; and recommend the use of WCAG 2.0 for e-Governments. In [Patra, Dash, Mishra, 2014, IJCSEA], the accessibility features of fifteen Indian web portals have been analyzed with respect to the WCAG 2.0 guideline. Accessibility of these web portals have been checked both manually and with the help of some tools. This work has been further extended to analyzing fifteen government web portals of Asian countries in Patra, Dash, Mishra, (2014) ICEGOV. In that work, the accessibility of four embedded media players also have been analyzed using UAAG 2.0.

Ismail and Kuppusamy, (2015) evaluate the accessibility of 302 Indian universities using ACHEKER on the basis of WCAG 2.0. Ismailova and Inal, (2016) analyses the accessibility of government websites of four countries viz, Kyrgyzstan, Azerbaijan, Kazakhstan and Turkey. In Baazeem and Al-Khalifa, (2015) authors investigate 23 accessibility evaluation studies. They analyze different type of methodology and tools used during last five years for analyzing the accessibility of web components.

Till 2004 in most research works the researchers have looked into the accessibility of web components. Then in 2005, Chisholm and Henry, (2005) have classified the web accessibility guidelines into three categories, viz., WCAG (Web Content Accessibility Guideline), ATAG (Authoring Tool Accessibility Guideline), UAAG (User Agent Accessibility Guideline) and describe how these three guidelines can control three different aspects of a web portal. After that the researchers also focus on the accessibility features of the user agents and authoring tools. Gonzalez et al. (2011) and Moreno et al., (2011) have analyzed the accessibility requirements of YouTube, BBC iplayer and CCplayer based on UAAG 2.0 guideline.

Souley and Sambo (2014) analyze Mozilla Firefox, Internet Explorer, Netscape and Opera based on their Performance, Usability, Accessibility and Security. Babu and Sekharaiahm, (2014) have described different types of assistive software and their integration with user agents to make them more accessible for physically challenged people. They have also classified the types of disabilities causing problem in accessing websites. Patra and Dash, (2017) have evaluated accessibility of 10 PC web browsers based on UAAG 2.0. Mahmud, Borodin, and Ramakrishnan, (2007) designed a context driven non-visual web browser "CSurf". Borodin, Mahmud, Ramakrishnan, and Stent, (2007) designed HearSay, a non-visual web browser with cognitive directed browsing with extensible Voice XML dialog. Patra and Dash, (2017) have evaluated accessibility of 15 web browsers used in android mobiles based on UAAG 2.0.

GUIDELINES

Today web portals are major sources of information for varieties of electronic services. Thus, it is necessary that, those should be accessible to all types of users, irrespective of age, level of literacy, physical disability in persons, etc. Accessibility to web portals refers to the degree to which it is available to as many people as possible. In order to achieve this, the World Wide Web Consortium (W3C) has launched Web Accessibility Initiative (WAI) in April 1997. The Web Accessibility Initiatives consist of several working groups (Authoring Tool Accessibility Guide-lines Working Group [ATAG WG, 2015], User Agent Accessibility Guidelines Working Group [UAWG, 2015], Web Content Accessibility Guidelines Working Group [WCAG WG, 2015], etc.) each with their specific focus. The working groups have introduced three standardizations to ensure accessibility of web portals at three levels.

Web Component Accessibility Guideline [WCAG, 2008] has been recommended by the WCAG working group to verify accessibility of web contents. WCAG is an international standard for maintaining and verifying accessibility of the contents of a web portal. The first version of WCAG came out in the form of WCAG 1.0 on 5th May 1999. Subsequently, by adding new features (guidelines needed to be technology-neutral and guidelines needed to be worded as testable) a new version, WCAG 2.0 was recommended by W3C on 11 December 2008. Now, WCAG has been approved by ISO as an international standard (ISO/IEC40500:2012) on October 2012. WCAG 2.0 recommends twelve guidelines based on four basic principles, viz., perceivable, operable, understandable, and robust. A comparative study of WCAG 1.0 and WCAG 2.0 has been done by Termens et al., (2009).

Authoring Tool Accessibility Guideline [ATAG, 2015] has been recommended by the ATAG working group to ensure accessibility of authoring tools. ATAG is an international standard for maintaining and verifying accessibility of authoring tools. The first version of ATAG came out in the form of ATAG 1.0 on 3rd February 2000 and later by adding extra features and removing some of the limitations, a new version of ATAG, ATAG 2.0, was recommended by W3C on 24th September 2015.

User Agent Accessibility Guideline [UAAG, 2013] has been recommended by the UAAG working group to verify accessibility of user agents and assistive technologies. UAAG is an international standard for maintaining and verifying accessibility of different user agents (like web browsers, media players) and assistive technologies (like text to speech synthesizer). The first version of UAAG came out in the form of UAAG 1.0 on 17th December 2002 and later by adding extra features and removing some of the limitations a new version is underway. The last working draft of UAAG (UAAG 2.0) was published by W3C on 15th December 2015 which has 26 guidelines based on five principles, namely, perceivable, operable, understandable, programmatic access, specifications and conventions. A schematic representation of the guidelines included in WCAG 2.0, ATAG 2.0, and UAAG 2.0 is presented in Figure 1.

ACCESSIBILITY OF WEB COMPONENTS

WCAG (Web Component Accessibility Guideline) is an international standard for maintaining accessibility of different web portals. The latest version of WCAG, WCAG 2.0 was recommended by W3C on 11 December 2008.WCAG defines some features to evaluate and maintain the accessibility of different components of websites, considering different disable persons.

Figure 1. A schematic representation of WCAG 2.0, ATAG 2.0, UAAG 2.0

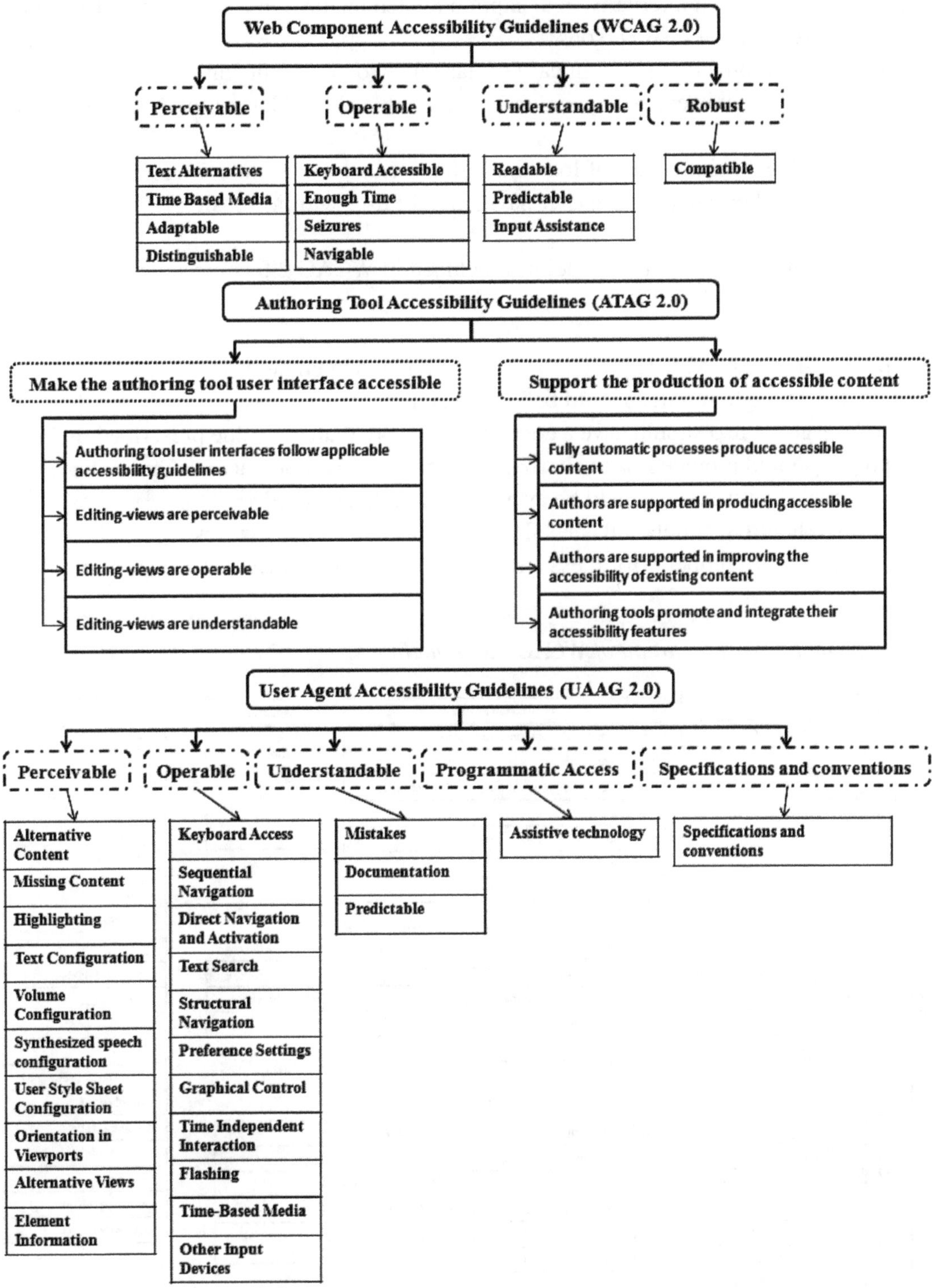

- As WCAG defines some colour contrast features for colour blind peoples.
- WCAG describe the text alternative and caption related features in case of the audio or video files available in websites for deaf persons.
- WCAG point out some restriction in case of flash files to avoid causing seizerus in users.
- WCAG prescribe that every web page, frame, and table should have proper title and headers for better usability.
- WCAG prescribe "maintenance of location", "maintenance of identical web frame", and "different navigational alternatives" for easier navigation of user within website.

A schematic representation of the guidelines included in WCAG 2.0 is presented in Figure 2 which in short describes the following:

- Web portals should provide text alternatives for all non text contents.
- Reading and navigation order should be logical and intuitive.
- Text and images of text should have a contrast ratio more than the value prescribed by WCAG 2.0.
- Web portals should provide image alternatives wherever text contents are hard to understand.
- All functionality of website should be available through keyboard.
- Web portals should not contain flashes/flickering that can cause seizures.
- While filling a form proper error messages should be prompted whenever there is an error.

Figure 2. A schematic representation of WCAG 2.0 guideline

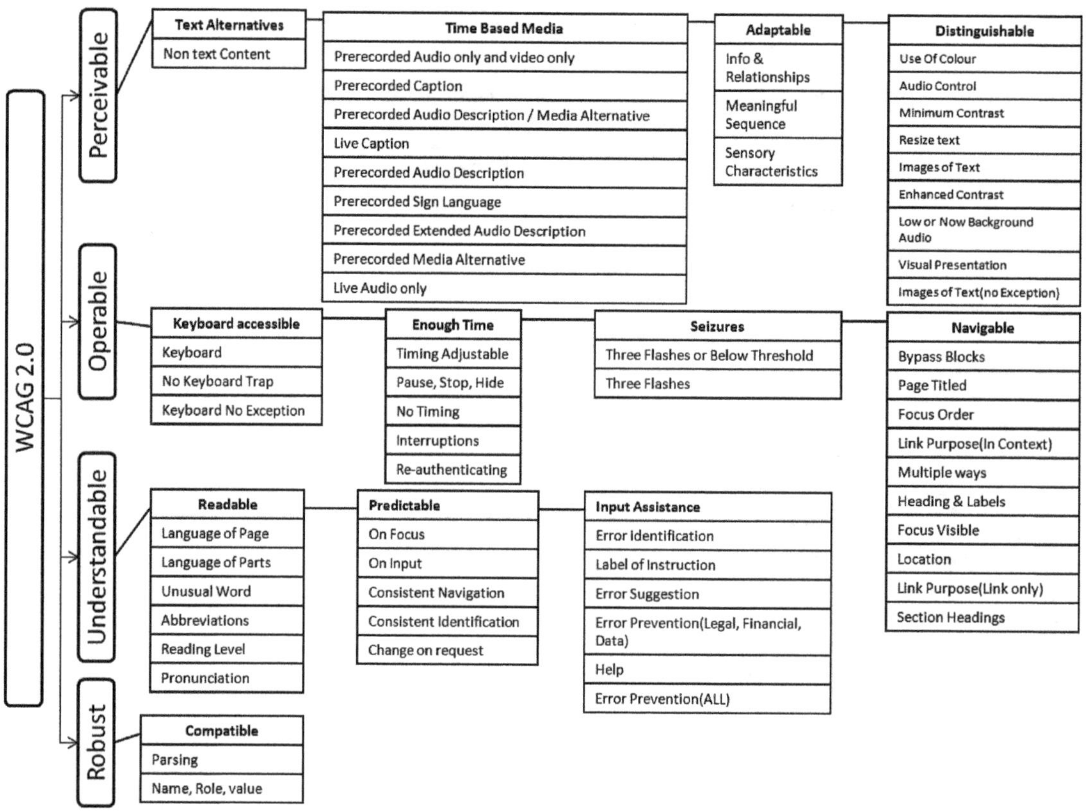

Evaluation of Indian Web Portals

Methodology

In Patra, Dash, Mishra, (2014, IJCSEA), we have considered three different categories of websites for evaluating their accessibility. Under each category we have selected five web portals which are frequently used by the public, thus a total of 15 websites are used in our study. The testing parameters are based on WCAG 2.0 guidelines. The accessibility parameters are checked both manually and by using some tools. Figure 3 indicates the adopted methodology.

Table 1 shows some of the tools used in the measurement of different accessibility parameters in the websites. For checking the colour contrast of links we used "Check my colour". For checking the colour contrast of text and images of text we used two tools. In order to obtain the hexadecimal colour code we used "Colour Scheme studio" and then the colour contrast was checked with the help of the

Figure 3. Methodology adopted for accessibility evaluation of Indian websites

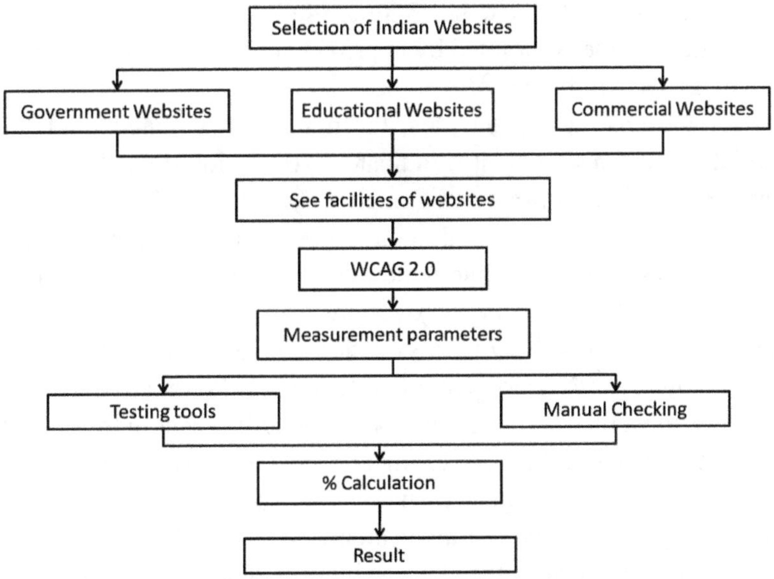

Table 1. List of tools adopted for evaluating accessibility of Indian web portals

SL No.	Target	Tools	URL
1.	Colour Contrast (link)	Check my colour	http://www.checkmycolours.com/
2.	Colour Contrast (image's Text)	Colour Scheme studio	
		Colour Contrast Check	http://snook.ca/technical/colour_contrast/colour.html
3.	Web Browser	Aurora	
		Chomodo Dragon	
		Google Chrome	
4.	Rule Wise Checker	Achecker	http://achecker.ca/checker/index.php

online tool "Colour Contrast Check". Different web browsers like Aurora, Comodo Dragon, and Google Chrome were used for accessing the web sites. We also used the "AChecker" tool for checking some of the parameters as per the WCAG 2.0 Guidelines.

Evaluation

This research is intended to provide an accessibility evaluation of 15 Indian websites based on WCAG 2.0. The data taken for our analysis is gathered during the period 15th Sep 2013 to 9th Oct 2013. Table 2 contains list of Indian web portals selected for evaluation.

Figure 4(a) describes the overall average percentage violation per rule as provided in WCAG 2.0. In the following graph we analyze each accessibility issue for the Indian Government websites. The guideline where the % is 0 it means that either the web component which deals with that guideline is absent or there is no error for that web component.

While analyzing the Perceivable features of the government websites, it is found that the maximum violated guideline is guideline 1.3 (Adaptable) in which government websites indicate 44.20% violation. Violations with respect to guideline 1.1 (Text Alternative), guideline 1.2 (Time Based Media), and guideline 1.4 (Distinguishable) were found to be 23.89%, 34.67%, and 34.23% respectively. Although the percentage is little less but this rule is violated by approximately all websites, so we provide a separate point by point graphical analysis in Figure 4(b).

While evaluating for the Operable principles, the maximum violated guideline is guideline 2.2 (Enough Time) in which government websites indicate 40.00% violation. But, for guideline 2.1 (Keyboard Accessible), guideline 2.3 (Seizures), and guideline 2.4 (Navigable) the violation percentages are 37.00%, 30.00%, and 16.98% respectively. Although the percentage is less but this rule is violated by approximately all websites, so we give a separate point by point graphical analysis in Figure 4(c).

With respect to Understandable principle in government websites, the maximum violated guideline is guideline 3.3 (Input Assistance) with 57.05% violation. Government websites indicate 34.60% and 15.96% violation in guideline 3.1 (Readable) and Guideline 3.2 (Predictable) respectively. This rule is violated by approximately all websites, so we give a separate point by point graphical analysis in Figure 4(d). According to our analysis the Indian Government Websites does not contain Robust error.

Figure 5(a) describes the overall average percentage violation results per each rule of WCAG 2.0. In the following Graph we analyze each accessibility principle in Indian Educational websites. In respect of Perceivable principle in educational websites, the maximum violated guideline is guideline 1.3 (Adaptable) in which educational websites indicate 49.00% violation. Educational websites indicate 18.20%,

Table 2. List of selected Indian web portals

Government Websites	Educational Websites	Commercial Websites
India.gov.in	www.iitb.ac.in	www.irctc.co.in
www.nic.in	www.iitd.ac.in	www.ebay.in
www.csc.gov.in	www.uohyd.ac.in	www.amazon.in
www.incometaxindia.gov.in	www.ugc.ac.in	www.flipkart.com
www.passportindia.gov.in	www.dheorissa.in	www.makemytrip.com

Figure 4. Overall average percentage violation done by selected Indian Government websites with respect to (a) WCAG 2.0, (b) Perceivable principle of WCAG, (c) Operable principle of WCAG, (d) Understandable Principle of WCAG

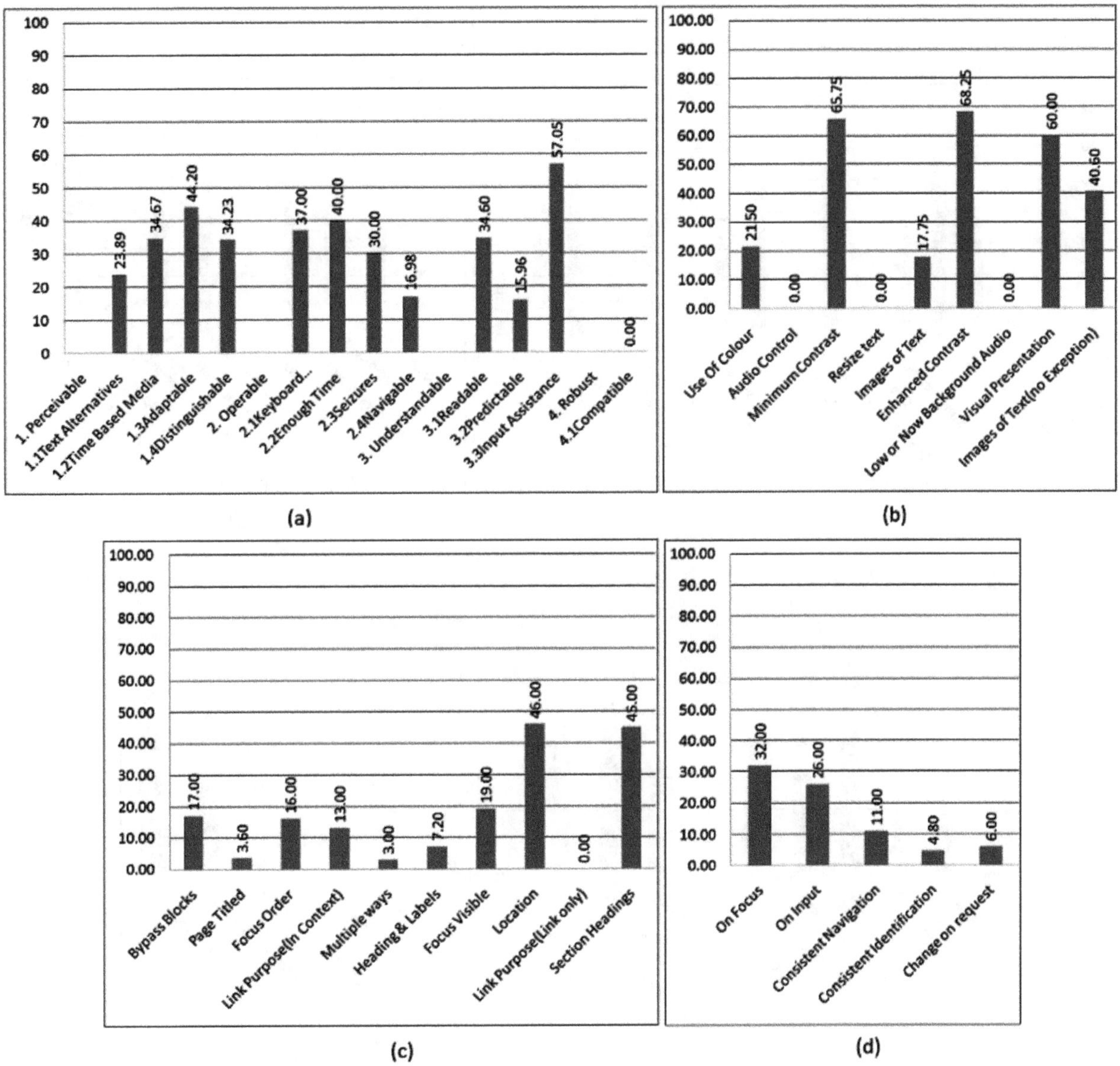

25.00%, and 23.01% violation in respect of guideline 1.1 (Text Alternative), guideline 1.2 (Time Based Media), and guideline 1.4 (Distinguishable) respectively. We represent a separate point by point graphical analysis in Figure 5(b).

While considering Operable principle in educational websites, the maximum violated guideline is guideline 2.1 (Keyboard accessible) in which educational websites indicate 55.00% violation. Educational websites show 6.25%, 35.00%, and 25.61% violation in guideline 2.2 (Enough Time), guideline 2.3 (Seizures), and guideline 2.4 (Navigable) respectively. We represent a point by point graphical analysis in Figure 5(c).

Figure 5. Overall average percentage violation done by selected Indian Educational websites with respect to (a) WCAG 2.0, (b) Perceivable principle of WCAG, (c) Operable principle of WCAG, (d) Understandable Principle of WCAG

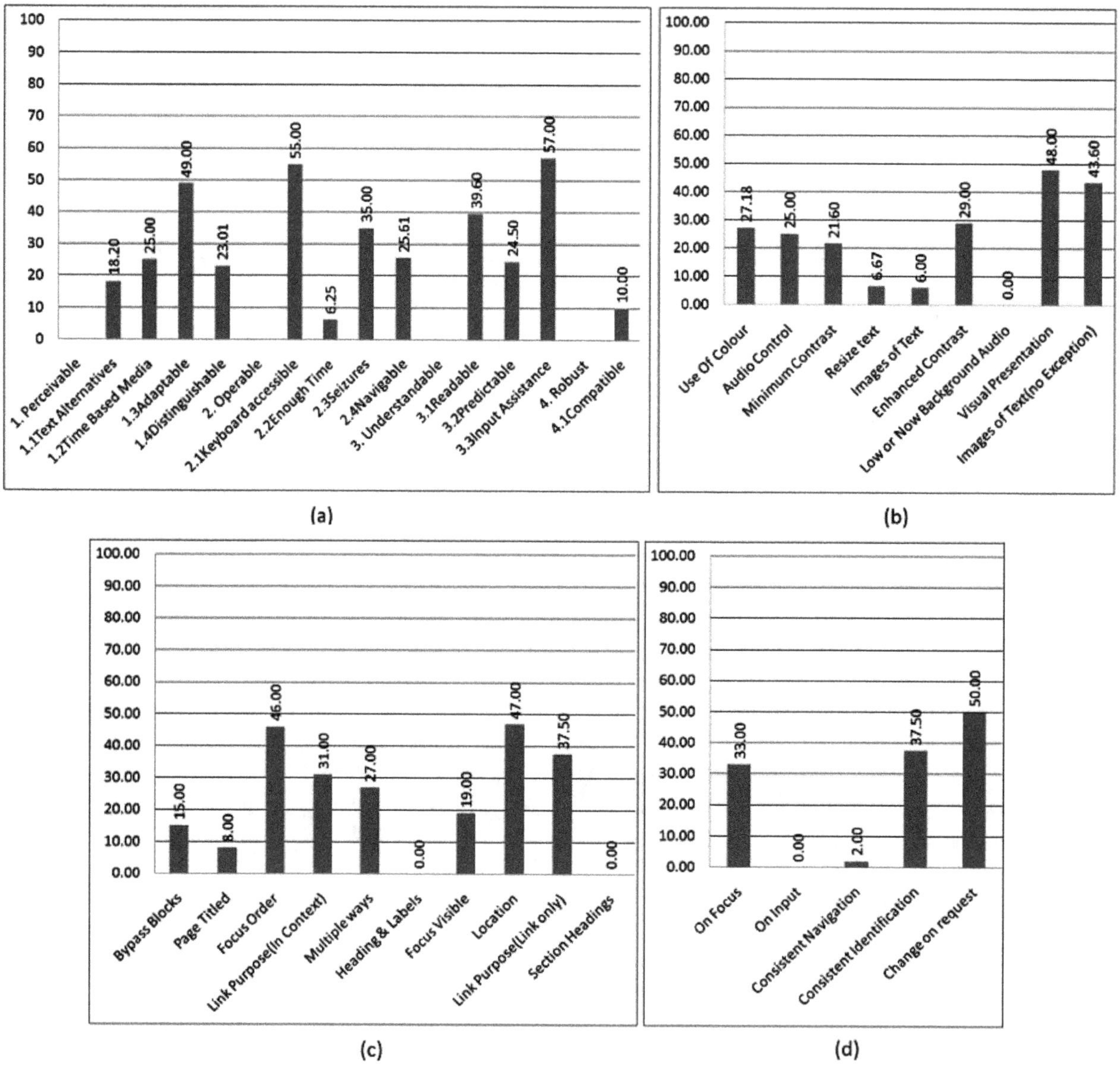

While considering Understandable principle in educational websites, the maximum violated guideline is guideline 3.3 (Input Assistance) in which educational websites indicate 57.00% violation. Educational websites show 39.60% and 24.50% violation in guideline 3.1 (Readable) and Guideline 3.2 (Predictable) respectively. We give a separate point by point graphical analysis in Figure 5(d). According to our analysis the In Indian Educational Websites Guideline 4 (Robust) gives 10.00% violation.

Figure 6(a) describes the overall average percentage violation results for each rule of WCAG 2.0, when applied to some of the Indian Commercial websites. With respect to the Perceivable principle in case of commercial websites, the maximum violated guideline is guideline 1.2 (Time Based Media) in

Figure 6. Overall average percentage violation done by selected Indian Commercial websites with respect to (a) WCAG 2.0, (b) Perceivable principle of WCAG, (c) Operable principle of WCAG, (d) Understandable Principle of WCAG

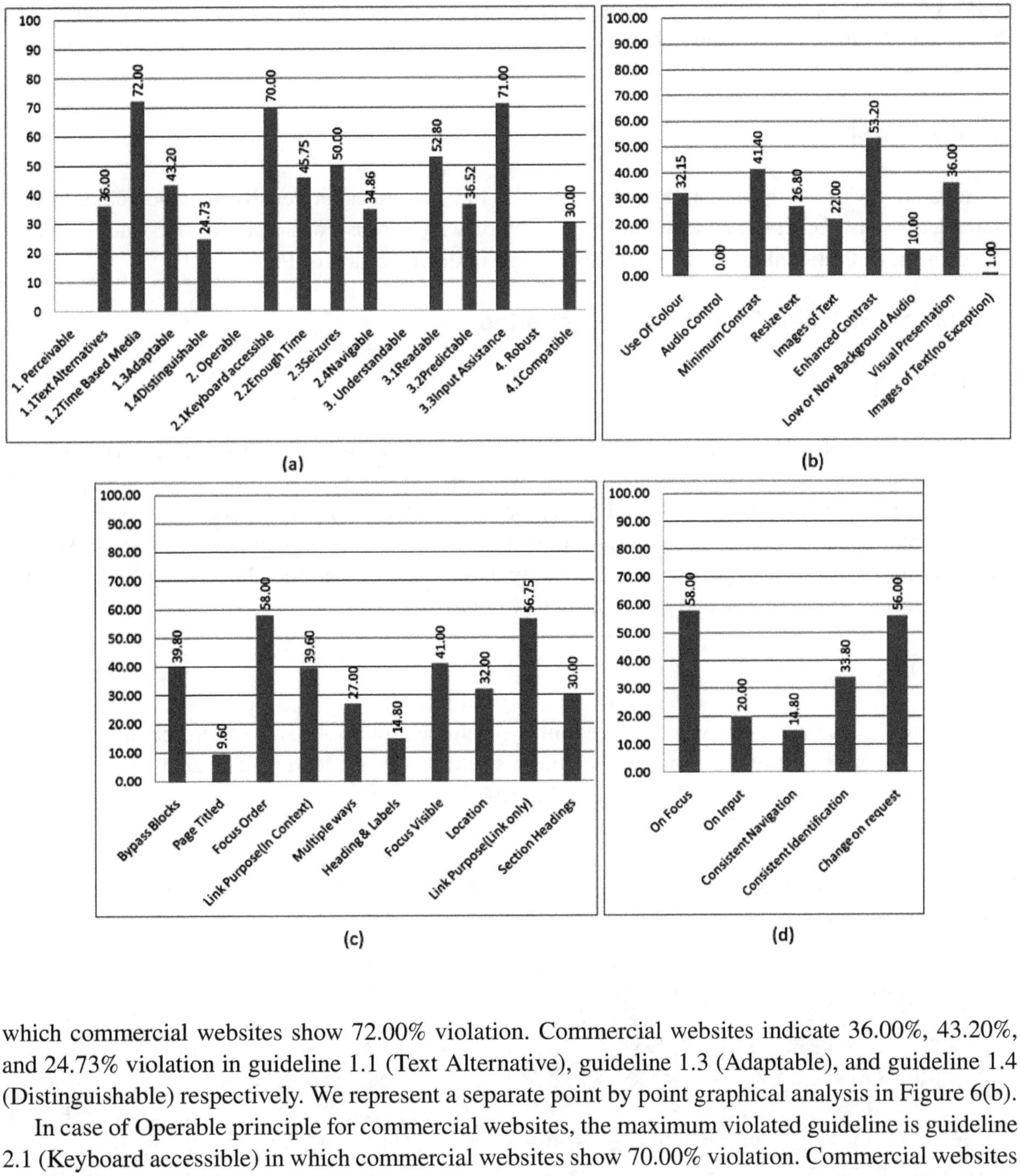

which commercial websites show 72.00% violation. Commercial websites indicate 36.00%, 43.20%, and 24.73% violation in guideline 1.1 (Text Alternative), guideline 1.3 (Adaptable), and guideline 1.4 (Distinguishable) respectively. We represent a separate point by point graphical analysis in Figure 6(b).

In case of Operable principle for commercial websites, the maximum violated guideline is guideline 2.1 (Keyboard accessible) in which commercial websites show 70.00% violation. Commercial websites indicate 45.75%, 50.00%, and 34.86% violation in guideline 2.2 (Enough Time), guideline 2.3 (Seizures), and guideline 2.4 (Navigable) respectively. We introduce a separate point by point graphical analysis in Figure 6(c).

While considering the Understandable principle in commercial websites, the maximum violated guideline is guideline 3.3 (Input Assistance) in which commercial websites show 71.00% violation. Commercial websites indicate 52.80% and 36.52% violation in guideline 3.1 (Readable) and Guideline 3.2 (Predictable) respectively. We represent a separate point by point graphical analysis in Figure 6(d). The Indian Commercial Websites considered in our study indicated 30.00% violation in case of Guideline 4 (Robust).

Result Analysis

A comparative view of the violations with respect to the guidelines on Perceivable, Operable, Understandable, Robust for the three different categories of web portals considered in our study, namely, Government, Educational & commercial is presented in the pie charts of Figure 7.

Evaluation of Asian Government Websites

Methodology

The objective of Patra, Dash, Mishra, (2014, ICEGOV) is to study the accessibility of government web portals of some Asian countries. For our analysis, we have considered three different categories of web portals and five sample portals under each category. Facilities provided by each of the websites are checked both manually and by using certain tools based on the testing parameters as per the WCAG 2.0 guidelines. More or less the same methodology and tools, as described above, have been used for evaluating accessibility of selected government websites.

Evaluation

This research is intended to provide an accessibility evaluation of 15 Asian websites based on WCAG 2.0. Table 3 contains list of Government web portals selected for evaluation. The analysis is based on the data available during 1st May 2014 to 21st June2014.

Figure 7. Percentage of accessibility violation done by websites of different category with respect to four principles of WCAG 2.0

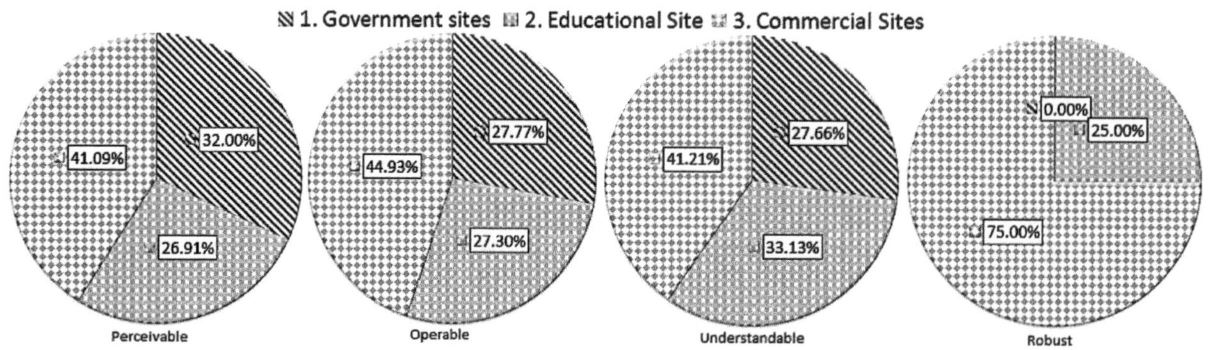

Figure 8. Methodology adopted for accessibility evaluation of Asian Government Websites

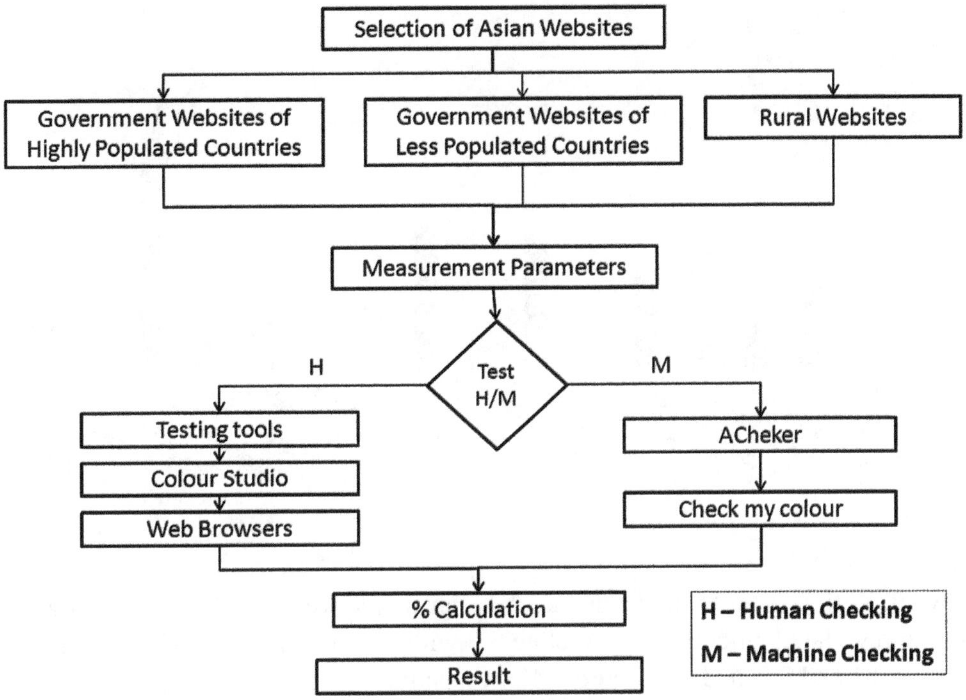

Table 3. List of selected Asian government web portals

Government Websites of Highly Populated Country	Government Websites of Less Populated Country	Government Websites of Rural Countries
http://www.ebeijing.gov.cn/	http://www.southkoreagovernment.com/	http://www.nspafghanistan.org
http://india.gov.in/	https://www.malaysia.gov.my/en	http://www.rmdcnepal.com/front/index.php
http://www.mofa.go.jp/	http://www.saudi.gov.sa/	http://www.bard.gov.bd
http://www.gov.ph/	http://www.taiwan.gov.tw/mp.asp?mp=1	http://www.rrdtc.org/
http://www.thaigov.go.th/en.html	http://www.priu.gov.lk/	http://www.crdt.org.kh/

Figure 9 describes the average percentage of WCAG 2.0 guideline violation in Government websites of highly populated Asian countries. The Perceivable principle states that Web contents should be made available to the senses. While analyzing the Perceivable features of the web portals of this category, it is observed that the maximum violated guideline is guideline 1.3 in which web portals indicates 40% violation. Violations with respect to guideline 1.1, 1.2, and 1.4 were found to be 24.1%, 13.33%, and 30.04% respectively.

The Operable principle states that the interface forms, controls, and navigation should be easily operable. While evaluating the Operable principles, the most violated guidelines are guideline 2.1and 2.3both with 40% violation. But, for guideline 2.2and 2.4 the violation percentages are 6.67% and 18.44% respectively. The Understandable principle requires that Content and interface of web portals are easy to

Figure 9. Violation of guideline in government web portals of highly populated Asian countries

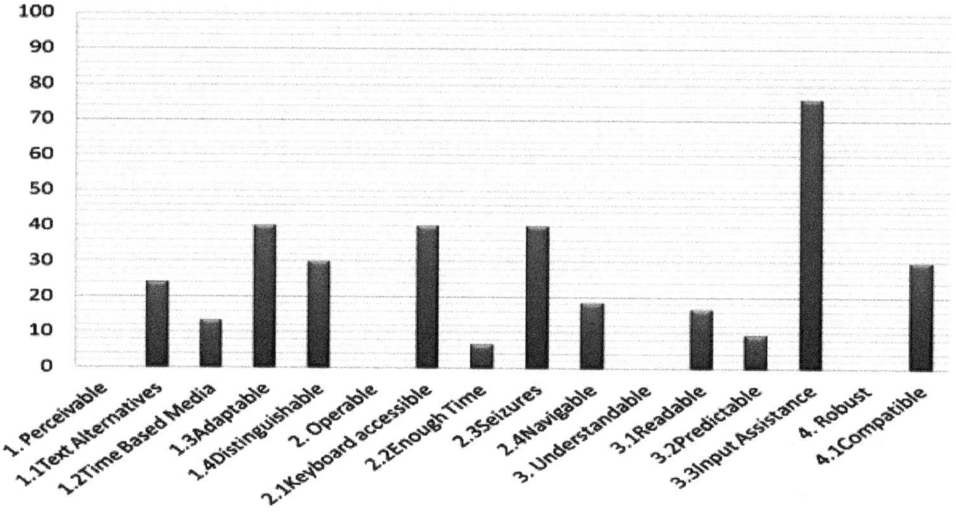

understand by all. With respect to the Understandable principle web portals of this category, we found that the maximum violated guideline is guideline 3.3 with 75.95% violation. Further, the violations in case of guideline 3.1 and 3.2 are16.67% and 9.4% respectively.

The Robust principle requires that content of a web portal can be used reliably by a wide variety of user agents. Our analysis shows that there is 30% violation of guideline 4 is found in web portals of this category. In Figure 10 wherever the web component dealing with a particular guideline is absent in the web site, it is indicated by "-" in the corresponding column and when there is no violation, it is indicated by"0.00%".

Figure 10. Test results of government web portals of highly populated Asian countries

Country	China	India	Japan	Philipines	Thailand	
Websites	www.ebeijing.gov.cn/	india.gov.in/	www.mofa.go.jp/	www.gov.ph/	www.thaigov.go.th/en.html	Avg
1. Perceivable						
1.1. Text Alternatives	16.67%	30.00%	16.67%	28.57%	28.57%	**24.10%**
1.2. Time Based Media	22.22%	0.00%	0.00%	11.11%	33.33%	**13.33%**
1.3. Adaptable	33.33%	50.00%	33.33%	33.33%	50.00%	**40.00%**
1.4. Distinguishable	36.71%	35.56%	29.75%	25.95%	22.26%	**30.04%**
2. Operable						
2.1. Keyboard accessible	75.00%	25.00%	0.00%	75.00%	25.00%	**40.00%**
2.2. Enough Time	33.33%	0.00%	0.00%	0.00%	0.00%	**6.67%**
2.3. Seizures	0.00%	50.00%	50.00%	50.00%	50.00%	**40.00%**
2.4. Navigable	21.83%	20.20%	3.83%	32.83%	13.50%	**18.44%**
3. Understandable						
3.1. Readable	16.67%	50.00%	0.00%	16.67%	0.00%	**16.67%**
3.2. Predictable	20.00%	27.00%	0.00%	0.00%	0.00%	**9.40%**
3.3. Input Assistance	85.71%	85.00%	57.14%	-	-	**75.95%**
4. Robust						
4.1.Compatible	0.00%	0.00%	50.00%	50.00%	50.00%	**30.00%**

Figure 11 shows the average percentage of WCAG 2.0 guidelines violations in Government web portals of less populated Asian countries. While analyzing the Perceivable features of the web portals of this category, it is observed that the maximum violated guideline is guideline 1.3 in which web portals indicates 33.33% violation. Violations with respect to guideline 1.1, 1.2, and 1.4 were found to be 30.82%, 27.78%, and 25.25% respectively.

While evaluating the Operable principles, the maximum violated guideline is guideline 2.3 in which these websites indicate 40.00% violation. But, for guideline 2.1, 2.2, and 2.4 the violation percentages are 30%, 12.22%, and 12.47% respectively.

Figure 11. Violation of guideline in government web portals of less populated Asian countries

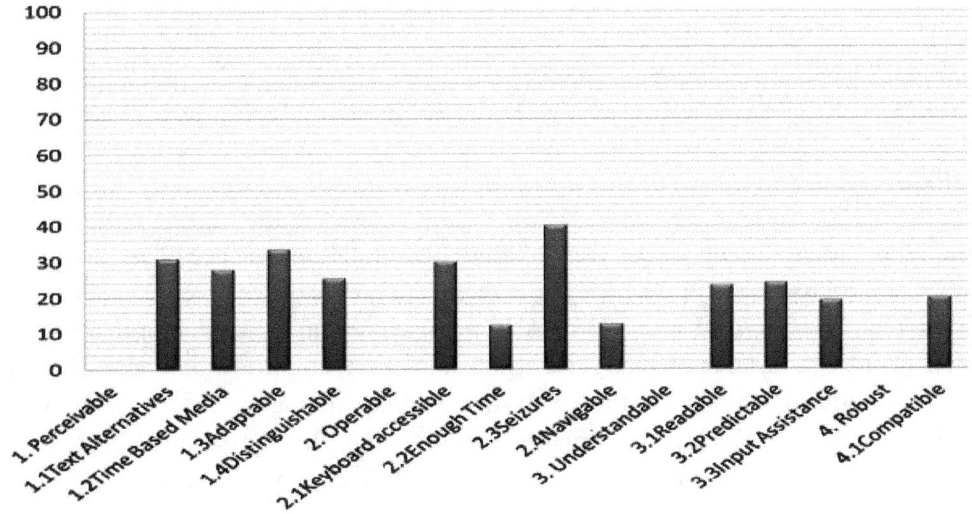

Figure 12. Test results of government web portals of less populated Asian countries

Country	Korea	Malaysia	Saudi Arabia	Taiwan	Srilanka	
Websites	www.southkoreagovernment.com/	www.malaysia.gov.my/en	www.saudi.gov.sa/	www.taiwan.gov.tw/mp.asp?mp=1	www.priu.gov.lk/	Avg
1. Perceivable						
1.1. Text Alternatives	66.00%	16.67%	28.57%	14.28%	28.57%	**30.82%**
1.2. Time Based Media	-	-	33.33%	22.22%	-	**27.78%**
1.3. Adaptable	50.00%	33.33%	16.67%	16.67%	50.00%	**33.33%**
1.4. Distinguishable	14.40%	38.72%	23.28%	24.80%	25.03%	**25.25%**
2. Operable						
2.1. Keyboard accessible	0.00%	0.00%	50.00%	50.00%	50.00%	**30.00%**
2.2. Enough Time	-	0.00%	20.00%	16.67%	-	**12.22%**
2.3. Seizures	50.00%	50.00%	50.00%	50.00%	0.00%	**40.00%**
2.4. Navigable	9.00%	7.50%	9.06%	13.00%	22.95%	**12.47%**
3. Understandable						
3.1. Readable	50.00%	0.00%	0.00%	50.00%	16.67%	**23.33%**
3.2. Predictable	40.00%	20.00%	0.00%	20.00%	40.00%	**24.00%**
3.3. Input Assistance	-	0.00%	0.00%	57.14%	-	**19.05%**
4. Robust						
4.1.Compatible	0.00%	50.00%	50.00%	0.00%	0.00%	**20.00%**

With respect to Understandable principle in these websites, the maximum violated guideline is guideline 3.2 with 24% violation, whereas guideline 3.1 and 3.3 indicate 23.33% and 19.05% violation respectively. According to our analysis we found 20% violations according to guideline 4(Robust) in these government websites.

Figure 13 describes the average percentage of WCAG 2.0 guideline violation in websites pertaining to rural development. While analyzing the Perceivable features of the web portals of this category, it is observed that the maximum violated guideline is guideline 1.3 in which rural websites indicates 35% violation. Violations with respect to guideline 1.1, 1.2, and 1.4 were found to be 16.67%, 17.41%, and 18.99% respectively.

While evaluating the Operable principles, the maximum violated guideline is guideline 2.1 in which rural websites indicate 45% violation. But, for guideline 2.2, 2.3, and 2.4 the violation percentages are 16.67%, 28.33%, and 20.11% respectively.

With respect to Understandable principle in rural websites, the maximum violated guideline is guideline 3.3 with 52.37% violation. Further, rural websites indicate 16.67% and 16% violation in guideline 3.1 and 3.2 respectively. Our analysis shows that the Asian rural websites violate guideline 4 by almost 10%.

Result Analysis

Figure 15 and 16 provides a comparative view of guideline violations in case of perceivable, operable, understandable, and robustness with respect to the three categories of websites.

While evaluating the chosen 15 websites of Asia we observe that there is an urgent need to improve the web portals in order to make them really accessible. However, countries like Japan and Saudi Arabia have already taken initiatives to improve their web sites. The Japanese government has begun its mission since last five years, whereas the Saudi Arabian government has already obtained WAI-A certification (certificate of conformance level A) from W3C (World Wide Web Consortium).

Figure 13. Violation of guideline in government web portals of rural countries

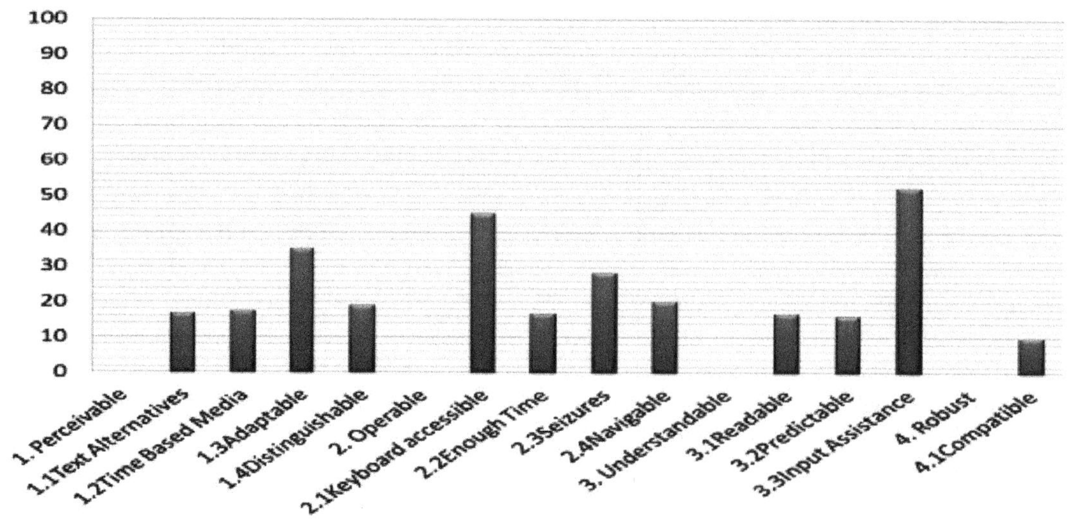

Figure 14. Test results of government web portals of rural countries

Country	Afghanistan	Nepal	Bangladesh	Laos	Cambodia	
Websites	www.nspafghanistan.org	www.rmdcnepal.com/front/index.php	www.bard.gov.bd	www.rrdtc.org/	www.crdt.org.kh/	Avg
1. Perceivable						
1.1. Text Alternatives	16.67%	33.33%	16.67%	0.00%	16.67%	**16.67%**
1.2. Time Based Media	0.00%	-	30.00%	-	22.22%	**17.41%**
1.3. Adaptable	33.33%	50.00%	50.00%	25.00%	16.67%	**35.00%**
1.4. Distinguishable	10.22%	15.74%	21.72%	19.19%	34.07%	**18.99%**
2. Operable						
2.1. Keyboard accessible	0.00%	75.00%	75.00%	0.00%	75.00%	**45.00%**
2.2. Enough Time	0.00%	0.00%	33.33%	-	33.33%	**16.67%**
2.3. Seizures	0.00%	16.67%	50.00%	25.00%	50.00%	**28.33%**
2.4. Navigable	16.53%	28.09%	19.59%	30.00%	15.75%	**20.11%**
3. Understandable						
3.1. Readable	16.67%	16.67%	16.67%	33.33%	0.00%	**16.67%**
3.2. Predictable	20.00%	0.00%	0.00%	0.00%	60.00%	**16.00%**
3.3. Input Assistance	71.40%	-	42.85%	-	42.85%	**52.37%**
4. Robust						
4.1.Compatible	0.00%	0.00%	0.00%	0.00%	50.00%	**10.00%**

Figure 15. Category wise total result analysis Asian government websites

WCAG (Web Content Accessibility Guidelines) 2.0	Pgov	Lpgov	Rural
1. Perceivable			
1.1. Text Alternatives	24.10%	30.82%	16.67%
1.2. Time Based Media	13.33%	27.78%	17.41%
1.3. Adaptable	40.00%	33.33%	35.00%
1.4. Distinguishable	30.04%	25.25%	18.99%
2. Operable			
2.1. Keyboard accessible	40.00%	30.00%	45.00%
2.2. Enough Time	6.67%	12.22%	16.67%
2.3. Seizures	40.00%	40.00%	28.33%
2.4. Navigable	18.44%	12.47%	20.11%
3. Understandable			
3.1. Readable	16.67%	23.33%	16.67%
3.2. Predictable	9.40%	24.00%	16.00%
3.3. Input Assistance	75.95%	19.05%	52.37%
4. Robust			
4.1.Compatible	30.00%	20.00%	10.00%

Pgov : Highly populated government websites
Lpgov : Less populated government websites
Rural : Rural websites

Figure 16. Percentage of accessibility violation done by government websites of different category of countries with respect to four principles of WCAG 2.0

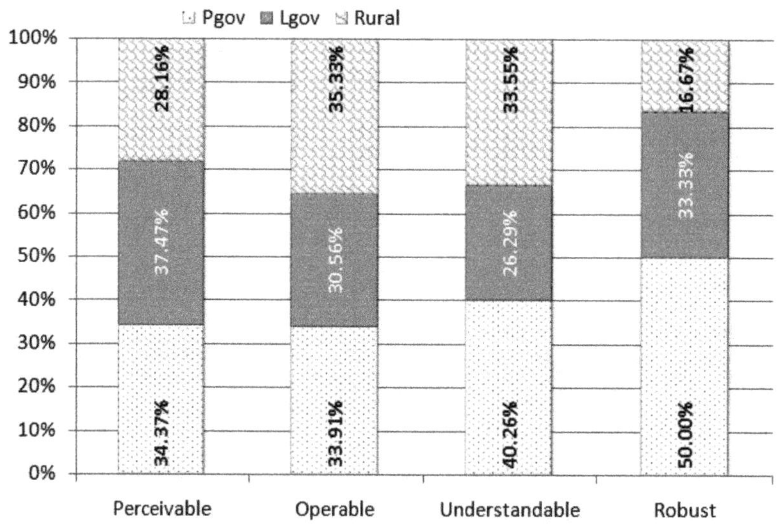

ACCESSIBILITY OF USER AGENTS

Evaluation of PC Web Browsers

According to UAAG, user agents are tools used to access websites (from the client side). Media players and web browsers are examples of such user agents which are widely used to access websites. Besides this, UAAG also provides accessibility guidelines for assistive technologies (like text to speech synthesizers). This research is intended to evaluate the accessibility feature of web browser.

By using an effective web browser we can improve the accessibility of web. When we click by typing an URL of a website in the address bar of the web browser, it only gets the source code of that website from the server, and represents it in its own way taking into account the size of the display and by using DOM (Document Object Model). Thus, a website can be represented in different ways in different web browsers. The following features of a web browser can be evaluated by using UAAG:

- **Colour Contrast:** The colour of the text, link and background can be decided during the creation of a web portal using its source code. But if the colour is not mentioned for text, link and background then it uses the default colour provided by the web browser. Thus, we can control the colour contrast by controlling the colour provided in the web browser.
- **Default Navigation:** Web browser should allow direct and sequential navigation between its elements. A web browser should allow all keyboard accessibility features. It should also allow the hierarchical and structural navigation. User must be able to reverse navigation between web addresses.
- **Controlling and Customizing the Shortcuts:** Web browser should provide the list of keyboard and mouse shortcuts used in it. It should allow customization of shortcuts (except conventional shortcuts).

Figure 17. Effect of colour contrast setting of web browser

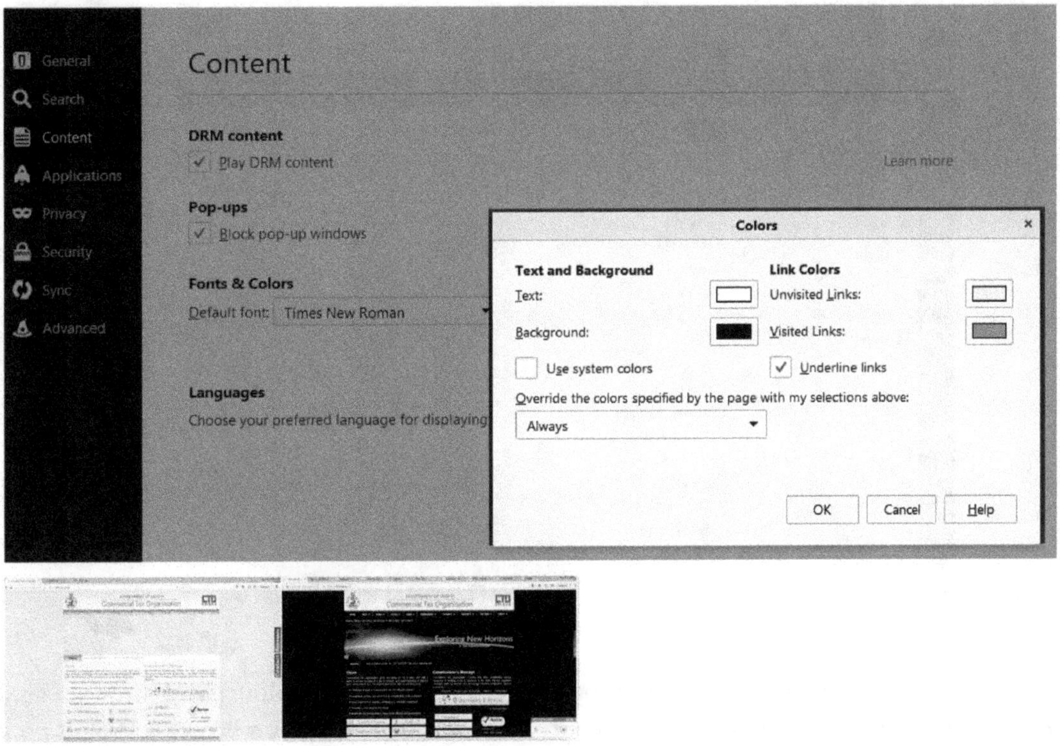

- **Control Focus:** Web browsers should be able to control and restrict the unpredictable change of focus (like pop-up and adware).
- **Controlling the Viewports and Top-Level Viewports:** The websites are represented in the viewports of a web browser. Web browser should allow easy navigation between the view ports (tab) or top-level viewports (window). Web browser should able to control the zooming percentage of the viewport. Viewports should maintain the point of regard of its elements during resizing of the viewport or changing the zoom. Viewport should be able to indicate the position of view and should be able to provide scrollbar. When clicking on a link user should be able to choose whether to open the new link in new viewport or in top-level viewport or in the same viewport. Web browser should be able to control the change of focus during creation of a new viewport or top-level viewport. Viewports should be resizable.
- **Controlling the View:** Web browser should be able to provide the outline view, source view of a web portal. Web browser should be able to show the related element and the element hierarchy in the source code of a website.
- **Default Alternative Contents:** Web browser should be able to provide the alternative text content provided by the source code of the website for respective non-text content (image, video etc). Web browser should also be able to indicate the absence of alternative text.
- **Highlight:** Web browser should be able to differentiate mouse focus, keyboard focus, and activated element. Web browser should be able to customize their highlighting method (by controlling

Figure 18. Shortcut key control menu provide by the web browser

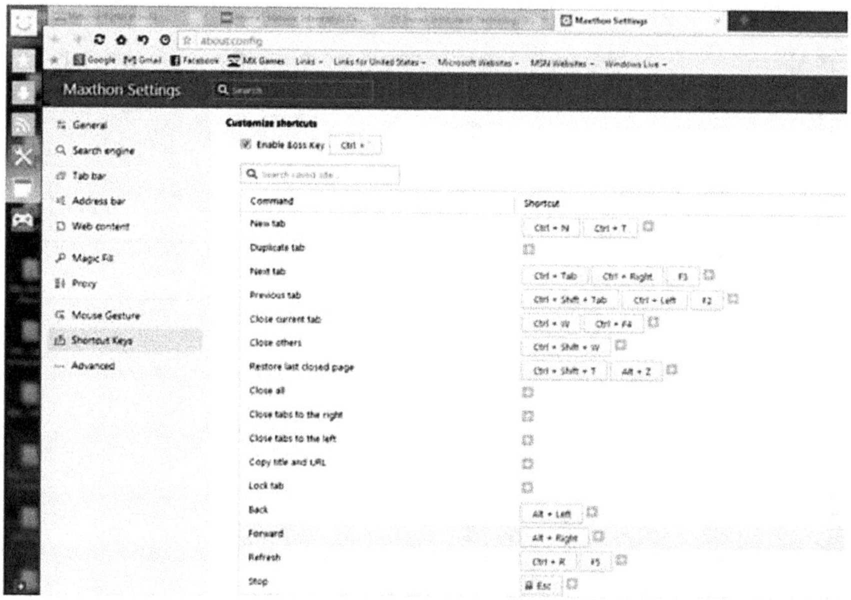

the size, blink rate, and controlling the foreground, back ground colour).Web browser should be able to differentiate the highlighted viewports among other. The web browser should be able to control different methods of highlighting (by colour contrast of highlighted viewport with others, size, specific borders, by any blink rate).

- **Making the Form Usable and Predictable:** Web browser should be able to make the form usable and predictable. Web browser should be able to provide the spelling assistance for editable text. User should be able to reverse recognized navigation between forms (unless there is any authentication). Web browser must be able to store the local version of a website. User should be able to specify whether or not recognized form submissions must be confirmed. Web browser should be able to provide auto fill option for some repeatedly used harmless data.
- **Retrieval Progress:** Web browser should be able to show the state of content retrieval activity.
- **Controlling the Input Devices and Input Methods:** Web browser should be able to interact with any input device, which is able to interact with the platform (the Operating System of the device). Web browser must be able to access and activate different input methods.
- **Controlling the Configuration Settings:** Web browser should be able to confirm or reverse the configuration setting. Settings must be applicable to all viewports.
- **Good Documentation:** A good documentation can help the user to understand the features provided by the web browser. The documentation of the web browser should also contain the assistive features of the web browser. It should contain the version-wise additional features provided by the web browser.
- **Transferable Preferences: Web** browser should allow the user to construct multiple preferences. Web browser should be able to transfer the preference setting between the devices.
- **Controlling the Style Sheets:** Web browser should be able to control and customize different style-sheets.

Methodology

UAAG 2.0 contains the accessibility features for the user agents (media-players and web browsers) and the assistive technologies. The objective of this section is to study the accessibility of web browsers. First of all, we classify the UAAG 2.0 guidelines and choose the accessibility guidelines that are applicable to web browsers. For our analysis, we have considered top ten web browsers commonly used across the world. Facilities provided by each of the web browsers are checked manually based on the testing parameters as specified in the UAAG 2.0 guidelines. We have checked the features of web browsers with the help of 20 top websites that satisfy most of the accessible criteria as per WCAG 2.0. A schematic representation of the methodology adopted in our work is depicted in Figure 19. Table 4 shows the guidelines, which are extracted from UAAG2.0, for accessibility analysis of web-browsers.

Evaluation

This research is intended to provide an accessibility evaluation of 10 Web browsers based on UAAG 2.0. For our analysis, we have considered the latest version of top 10 web browsers, as shown in Table 5. These browsers are the mostly widely used web browsers across the world. The data taken for our analysis is gathered during the period 1st November 2014 to 21st July 2015.

In order to measure all the dictum of UAAG 2.0 for different web browsers, first we check all the elements and features provided by the web browsers. Next, we evaluate the web browsers by browsing varieties of web-sites with different peculiarities (Assistive facilities). We have documented our findings in a tabular form by indicating '✓' when a web browser passes the test, and '✗' when a web browser fails the test. Based on this, we have calculated the error percentage which is a ratio of the number of failed features to the total number of features. The guidelines marked with red colour are violated by all tested web browsers. Similarly, the guidelines marked with green colour are regarded by all tested web browsers.

Table 6(a) provides the result of accessibility evaluation of web browsers with respect to the Perceivable guidelines of UAAG 2.0. According to Perceivable principle of UAAG, a web browser should be able to make its component and websites component available to human senses. During analysis of the perceivable feature, we test the web browser's ability to control text formatting. Web browsers can

Figure 19. Methodology for accessibility analysis of web browsers

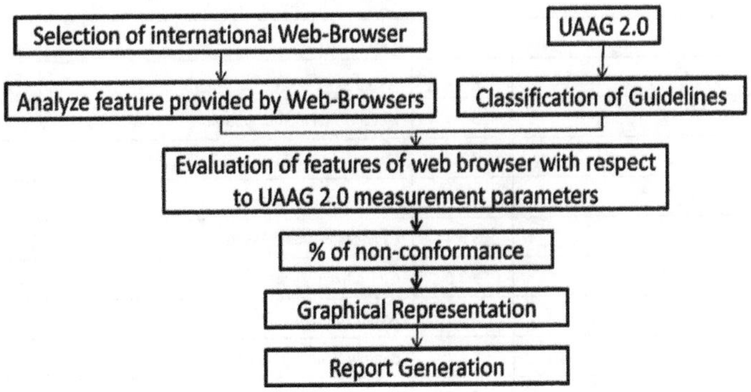

Table 4. Selected guidelines of UAAG 2.0 that are used for accessibility analysis of web-browsers

Guidelines Applicable to Web-Browsers			
1.1.1	Render Alternative Content	2.2.2	Sequential Navigation Between Viewports
1.1.2	Indicate Unrendered Alternative Content	2.2.3	Default Navigation Order
1.1.3	Replace Non-Text Content	2.2.4	Options for Wrapping in Navigation
1.1.4	Provide Configurable Alternative Content Defaults	2.3.1	Allow Direct Navigation to Enabled Elements
1.2.1	Support Repair by Assistive Technologies	2.3.2	Allow Direct Activation of Enabled Elements
1.2.2	Repair Missing Structure	2.3.3	Present Direct Commands from Rendered Content
1.3.1	Highlighted Items	2.3.4	Present Direct Commands in user interface
1.3.2	Highlighting Options	2.3.5	Allow Customized Keyboard Commands
1.4.1	Basic text formatting (Globally)	2.4.1	Text Search
1.4.2	Basic text formatting (by Element)	2.4.2	Search Direction
1.4.3	Blocks of text (Globally)	2.4.3	Match Found
1.4.4	Configured and Reflowed Text Printing	2.4.4	Alert on Wrap or No Match
1.4.5	Advanced text formatting (Globally)	2.4.5	Alternative Content Search
1.7.1	Support User Stylesheets	2.5.1	Show Location in Hierarchy
1.7.2	Apply User Stylesheets	2.5.2	Provide Structural navigation by heading and Within Tables
1.7.3	Disable Author Stylesheets	2.5.3	Configure Structural navigation and Views
1.7.4	Save copies of Stylesheets	2.6.1	Allow Access and activation of input Methods
1.8.1	Highlight Viewport	2.7.1	Allow Persistent Accessibility Settings
1.8.2	Move Viewport to Selection and Focus	2.7.2	Allow Restore All to Default
1.8.3	Provide Viewport Scrollbars	2.7.3	Allow Multiple Sets of Preference Settings
1.8.4	Indicate Viewport position	2.7.4	Allow Preference Changes from outside the user Interface
1.8.5	Allow Zoom	2.7.5	Make Preference Settings Transferable
1.8.6	Maintain Point of Regard	2.8.1	Customize Display of controls for User Interface Commands, Functions, and Extensions
1.8.7	Customize Viewport Highlighting	2.9.1	Adjustable Time Limits
1.8.8	Allow Viewport Resize	2.12.1	Platform Text Input Devices
1.8.9	Provide Viewport History	2.12.2	Operation With Any Devices
1.8.10	Allow Top-Level Viewport Open on Request	2.12.3	Text Input With Any Device
1.8.11	Allow Top-Level Viewport Focus Control	3.1.1	Text Entry Undo
1.8.12	Allow Same User Interface	3.1.2	Settings Changes can be Reversed or confirmed
1.8.13	Multi-Column Text Reflow	3.1.3	Retrieval Progress
1.8.14	Ignore Absolute Layout Dimensions	3.1.4	Spell Check
1.8.15	Linearize Content	3.1.5	Back Button
1.8.16	Provide Web Page Bookmarks	3.1.6	Form Submission Confirm
1.9.1	Outline View	3.1.7	Form Auto-Fill
1.9.2	Source View	3.1.8	Save Form Entries
1.10.1	Show Related Elements	3.2.1	Accessible Documentation
1.10.2	Show Element Hierarchy	3.2.2	Describe Accessibility Features
2.1.1	Provide Full Keyboard Functionality	3.2.3	Document All Features
2.1.2	Show Keyboard Focus	3.2.4	Changes Between Versions
2.1.3	Avoid keyboard Traps	3.2.5	Centralized View
2.1.4	Separate Selection from Activation	3.3.1	Avoid Unpredictable Focus
2.1.5	Follow Text Keyboard Conventions	5.1.1	comply With WCAG
2.1.6	Make Keyboard Access Efficient	5.1.2	Implement Accessibility Features of content Specifications
2.2.1	Sequential Navigation Between Elements	5.1.6	Enable Reporting of user Agent Accessibility Faults

Table 5. List of selected web browsers of Android mobiles

Web Browsers	Source Link
Mozilla Firefox 35.0	http://filehippo.com/download_firefox/59773/
Google Chrome 40.22	http://filehippo.com
Opera 27.0	http://www.androidapksfree.com/apk/opera-27-0-1698-89115-apk-download/
Comodo Dragon 36.1	http://xetbox.com/programs/internet/browsers/673-comodo-dragon
Internet Explorer 8	http://internet-explorer-8.en.softonic.com
Avant 12.5	http://avant-browser.software.informer.com/12.5/
Flock 2.6.1	http://filehippo.com/download_flock/
Safari 5.34.57	http://www.4shared.com/rar/gZ8rCymt/Safari_53457.html?locale_en
SeaMonkey 2.32	http://www.seamonkey-project.org/releases/2.32
Maxthon 4.4	http://maxthon-cloud-browser.software.informer.com/4.4

regulate the text-formatting by operating on text colour, text size, and font of the text. We observe that web browsers are able to control text formatting of rendered text and links, but unable to control it for block of text. Mozilla-Firefox, Flock, and SeaMonkey provide the best text formatting mechanism.

We checked whether the web browsers are able to differentiate between the elements selected by keyboard or mouse and activated element through its highlighting features. We also analyzed the methods provided by the web browsers to customize the highlighting feature. These two accessibility features are well organized by Mozilla-Firefox, Internet-explorer, Flock, and SeaMonkey. Web browser should be able to provide the outline view, source view, and off-line view of a website. This accessibility feature is properly managed by all the web browsers.

We analyzed all features of viewport and top-level viewport of a web browser. The viewports of a web browser should be resizable and contain the zooming and scrolling features. Web browser should be able to control the bookmark features. We also evaluated the web browser's ability for text reflow. All these viewport and top-level viewport related accessibility features are mostly confirmed by Google-Chrome, Opera, and Avant web browsers. We tested the ability of web browsers to control the text alternative for all non-text web components. Web browsers should also be able to find the absence of text alternatives. We analyzed the facilities provided by different web browsers for creating and using user style sheet and also to save copies of author style sheet.

Table 6(b) provides the result of accessibility evaluation of web browsers with respect to the Operable guidelines of UAAG 2.0. According to Operable principle of UAAG, web browsers should be able to make their components and websites components easily operable by users. During analysis of the Operable feature we tested whether web browsers support all functionality of keyboard or not. There should not be any keyboard traps, or loss of keyboard focus.

We analyzed the shortcuts available in web browsers for forward and backward sequential navigation. A web browser should alert the user during wrapping of navigation. We analyzed the commands present in web browser for direct navigation and the method to customize them. We also tested the forward and backward text search. Web browsers should show all match found and should alert on wrap. We also analyzed the navigation of web browsers through different structures of websites. The navigation related accessibility features are mostly confirmed by Mozilla-firefox. We tested different processes provided by

Table 6. Result of accessibility evaluation of web browsers with respect to (a) Perceivable guideline, (b) Operable guideline

	mozilla Firefox 35.0	Google Chrome 40.22	Opera 27.0	Comodo Dragon 36.1	Internet Explorer 8	Avant 12.5	Flock 2.6.1	Safari 5.34.57	SeaMonkey 2.32	Maxthon 4.4
1.1.1	✓	✓	✓	✓	✓	✓	✓	✓	✓	✓
1.1.2	✗	✓	✗	✓	✓	✗	✗	✗	✗	✗
1.1.3	✗	✓	✗	✓	✓	✓	✗	✗	✗	✗
1.1.4	✗	✗	✗	✗	✗	✗	✗	✗	✗	✗
1.2.1	✗	✗	✗	✗	✗	✗	✗	✗	✗	✗
1.2.2	✗	✗	✗	✗	✗	✗	✗	✗	✗	✗
1.3.1	✓	✓	✓	✓	✓	✓	✓	✓	✓	✓
1.3.2	✓	✗	✗	✗	✓	✗	✓	✗	✓	✗
1.4.1	✓	✓	✓	✓	✓	✗	✓	✓	✓	✗
1.4.2	✓	✗	✗	✗	✗	✗	✓	✗	✓	✗
1.4.3	✗	✗	✗	✗	✗	✗	✗	✗	✗	✗
1.4.4	✓	✓	✓	✓	✓	✓	✓	✓	✓	✓
1.4.5	✗	✗	✗	✗	✗	✗	✗	✗	✗	✗
1.7.1	✓	✓	✓	✓	✗	✗	✗	✗	✗	✓
1.7.2	✓	✓	✓	✓	✗	✗	✗	✗	✗	✓
1.7.3	✓	✓	✓	✓	✗	✗	✗	✗	✗	✓
1.7.4	✓	✓	✓	✓	✗	✗	✗	✗	✓	✓
1.8.1	✓	✓	✓	✓	✓	✓	✓	✓	✓	✓
1.8.2	✓	✓	✓	✓	✓	✓	✓	✓	✓	✓
1.8.3	✓	✓	✓	✓	✓	✓	✓	✓	✓	✓
1.8.4	✗	✗	✗	✗	✗	✗	✗	✗	✗	✗
1.8.5	✓	✓	✓	✓	✓	✓	✓	✗	✓	✓
1.8.6	✓	✓	✓	✓	✓	✓	✓	✓	✓	✓
1.8.7	✗	✗	✗	✗	✗	✓	✗	✗	✗	✗
1.8.8	✓	✓	✓	✓	✓	✓	✓	✓	✓	✓
1.8.9	✓	✓	✓	✓	✗	✓	✓	✓	✓	✓
1.8.10	✓	✓	✓	✓	✓	✓	✓	✓	✗	✓
1.8.11	✗	✓	✓	✗	✗	✗	✗	✓	✓	✓
1.8.12	✓	✓	✓	✓	✓	✓	✓	✓	✓	✓
1.8.13	✗	✗	✗	✗	✗	✗	✗	✗	✗	✗
1.8.14	✗	✗	✗	✗	✗	✗	✗	✗	✗	✗
1.8.15	✗	✗	✗	✗	✗	✗	✗	✗	✗	✗
1.8.16	✓	✓	✓	✓	✓	✓	✓	✓	✓	✓
1.9.1	✓	✓	✓	✓	✓	✓	✓	✓	✓	✓
1.9.2	✓	✓	✓	✓	✓	✓	✓	✓	✓	✓
1.10.1	✗	✗	✗	✗	✓	✓	✗	✗	✗	✗
1.10.2	✗	✗	✗	✗	✓	✓	✗	✗	✗	✗

(a)

	mozilla Firefox 35.0	Google Chrome 40.22	Opera 27.0	Comodo Dragon 36.1	Internet Explorer 8	Avant 12.5	Flock 2.6.1	Safari 5.34.57	SeaMonkey 2.32	Maxthon 4.4
2.1.1	✓	✓	✗	✓	✓	✓	✓	✗	✗	✗
2.1.2	✓	✓	✗	✓	✓	✗	✓	✗	✓	✓
2.1.3	✓	✓	✓	✓	✗	✗	✓	✓	✓	✓
2.1.4	✓	✓	✓	✓	✓	✓	✓	✓	✓	✓
2.1.5	✓	✓	✗	✓	✗	✗	✗	✗	✗	✗
2.1.6	✓	✓	✓	✓	✓	✓	✓	✓	✓	✓
2.2.1	✓	✓	✗	✓	✓	✓	✓	✗	✓	✓
2.2.2	✓	✓	✓	✓	✓	✓	✓	✓	✓	✓
2.2.3	✓	✓	✓	✓	✓	✓	✓	✓	✓	✓
2.2.4	✗	✗	✗	✗	✗	✗	✗	✗	✗	✗
2.3.1	✓	✓	✓	✓	✓	✓	✓	✓	✓	✓
2.3.2	✓	✓	✓	✓	✓	✓	✓	✓	✓	✓
2.3.3	✓	✓	✓	✓	✓	✓	✓	✓	✓	✓
2.3.4	✓	✓	✓	✓	✗	✗	✗	✗	✗	✓
2.3.5	✓	✗	✗	✗	✗	✗	✗	✗	✗	✓
2.4.1	✓	✓	✓	✓	✓	✓	✓	✗	✓	✓
2.4.2	✓	✓	✓	✓	✓	✓	✓	✓	✓	✓
2.4.3	✓	✓	✓	✗	✓	✓	✓	✓	✓	✓
2.4.4	✗	✗	✗	✗	✗	✗	✗	✗	✗	✗
2.4.5	✓	✓	✗	✓	✓	✓	✓	✓	✓	✗
2.5.1	✓	✓	✓	✓	✓	✓	✓	✓	✓	✓
2.5.2	✗	✗	✗	✗	✗	✗	✗	✗	✗	✗
2.5.3	✗	✗	✗	✗	✗	✗	✗	✗	✗	✗
2.6.1	✗	✗	✗	✗	✗	✗	✗	✗	✗	✗
2.7.1	✓	✓	✓	✓	✓	✓	✓	✓	✓	✓
2.7.2	✗	✓	✗	✓	✓	✓	✗	✗	✗	✗
2.7.3	✓	✓	✓	✓	✗	✗	✗	✗	✓	✗
2.7.4	✗	✗	✗	✗	✗	✗	✗	✗	✗	✗
2.7.5	✓	✓	✓	✓	✓	✓	✓	✓	✗	✗
2.8.1	✓	✓	✗	✓	✗	✓	✗	✗	✗	✓
2.9.1	✓	✓	✓	✓	✓	✓	✓	✓	✓	✓
2.12.1	✓	✓	✓	✓	✓	✓	✓	✓	✓	✓
2.12.2	✓	✓	✓	✓	✓	✓	✓	✓	✓	✓
2.12.3	✓	✓	✓	✓	✓	✓	✓	✓	✓	✓

(b)

**For a more accurate representation see the electronic version.*

web browsers to access and activate input methods. A web browser should be compatible with all input devices appropriate to its platform. We analyzed the configuration setting of all web browsers and also the persistence and reversibility of web browsers' configuration. We verified whether a web browser allows creating multiple preference settings. The preference settings should be transferable from one device to another. We also analyzed the customize display of controls over the user interface of web browsers.

Table 7 provides the result of accessibility evaluation of web browsers with respect to the Guideline 3 (Understandable) and Guideline 5 (specifications and conventions) of UAAG 2.0. According to Understandable principle of UAAG, web browser should be able to make its contents, interface, documentation, and websites component easily understood by users. We analyzed the effect of web browsers on the form of websites to make it understandable as web browsers can't totally control the forms of websites, but can control and customize specific features. Web browser should provide auto-fill mechanism for specific common fields. Web browsers should be capable to save local versions of web contents. It was found that form related accessibility features are mostly confirmed by Mozilla-Firefox, Comodo-Dragon, and Safari web browsers.

We scrutinized the accessibility of the documentations of web browsers. The document should provide the features of the websites, accessibility features, and the changes between versions. We also tested the web browsers capability to avoid unpredictable focus changes. We also analyzed the feedback features of the web browsers.

Table 7. Result of accessibility evaluation of web browsers with respect to Guideline 3 (Understandable) and Guideline 5 (Specification and conventions)

	mozilla Firefox 35.0	Google Chrome 40.22	Opera 27.0	Comodo Dragon 36.1	Internet Explorer 8	Avant 12.5	Flock 2.6.1	Safari 5.34.57	SeaMonkey 2.32	Maxthon 4.4
3.1.1	✗	✓	✓	✓	✗	✗	✗	✓	✗	✓
3.1.2	✓	✓	✗	✓	✓	✓	✓	✗	✓	✗
3.1.3	✗	✗	✗	✗	✓	✓	✓	✓	✓	✗
3.1.4	✓	✗	✗	✓	✗	✗	✓	✓	✓	✓
3.1.5	✓	✓	✓	✓	✓	✓	✓	✓	✓	✓
3.1.6	✗	✗	✗	✗	✗	✗	✗	✗	✗	✗
3.1.7	✓	✗	✓	✓	✗	✗	✗	✓	✗	✗
3.1.8	✓	✗	✗	✗	✗	✗	✗	✗	✓	✗
3.2.1	✓	✗	✓	✓	✓	✓	✓	✓	✓	✓
3.2.2	✓	✓	✓	✓	✓	✗	✗	✓	✓	✗
3.2.3	✓	✓	✓	✓	✓	✓	✗	✓	✓	✓
3.2.4	✗	✗	✗	✗	✗	✗	✗	✗	✗	✗
3.2.5	✗	✗	✗	✗	✗	✗	✗	✗	✗	✗
3.3.1	✓	✓	✓	✓	✓	✓	✓	✓	✓	✓
5.1.1	✓	✓	✗	✓	✗	✗	✓	✗	✓	✗
5.1.2	✓	✗	✗	✗	✗	✗	✓	✗	✓	✗
5.1.6	✓	✓	✗	✓	✗	✗	✓	✓	✗	✓

**For a more accurate representation see the electronic version.*

Result Analysis

Figure 20 provides the result of accessibility evaluation of individual web browsers with respect to the "perceivable", "operable", "understandable", and "specifications & conventions" principles.

It was observed that the most two accessible web browsers of all are "Mozilla Firefox" and "Comodo Dragon" with an overall violation of 30.68% and 32.95% respectively. Two web browsers that are less accessible among all are "Safari" and "Avant" with an overall violation of 50.00% and 46.59% respectively. The overall accessibility violation of "Google Chrome", "Opera", "Internet Explorer", "Flock", "SeaMonkey", and "Maxthon" are 34.09%, 45.45%, 44.32%, 44.32%, 42.05%, and 44.32% respectively.

Figure 21 represents the Accessibility Evaluation of individual web browsers with respect to different conformance like Conformance A, AA, and AAA. As per the conformance level A, least accessible web browsers is "Safari" with 43.59% violation, similarly most accessible web browsers are "Google Chrome" and "Chomodo Dragon" both with 12.82% violation. According to the conformance level AA least accessible web browsers is "Safari" with 49.35% violation, similarly most accessible web browser is "Mozilla Firefox" with 27.27% violation. As per the conformance level AAA least accessible web browsers is "Safari" with 50.00% violation, similarly most accessible web browser is "Mozilla Firefox" with 30.68% violation.

Figure 20. Accessibility evaluation of individual web browsers with respect to the "Perceivable", "Operable", "Understandable", and "Specifications and conventions" principles of UAAG2.0 guideline

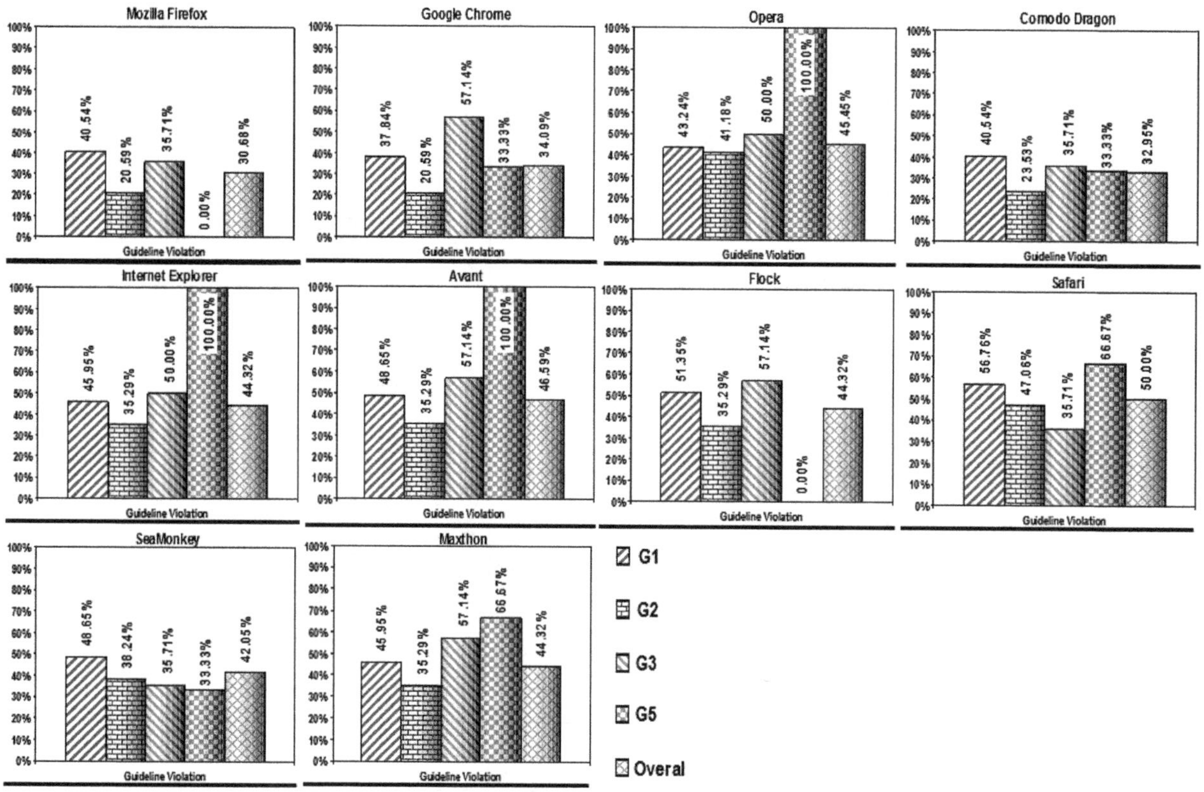

Figure 21. Accessibility evaluation of individual web browsers with respect to three conformance level

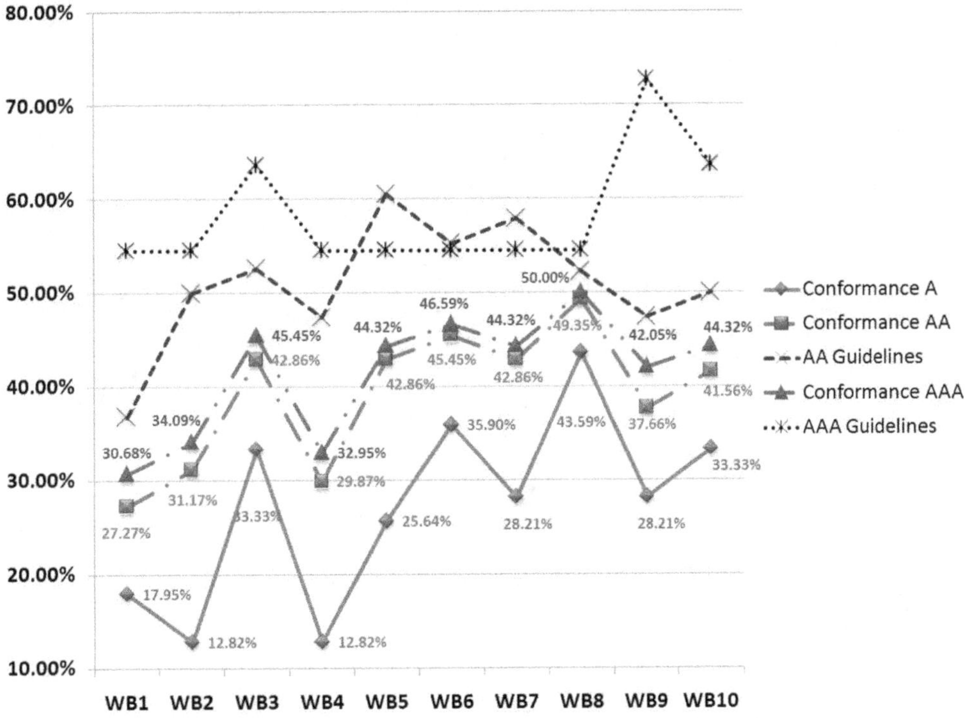

Figure 22 provides a comparative view of guideline violations in case of perceivable, operable, understandable, and robust with respect to different web browsers. During our analysis we observed that most of the web browsers violated the fifth principle of UAAG 2.0 (specifications & conventions) with an average of 53.33% violation. The principle which is less violated by all web browsers is "Operable" with an average of 33.24% violation.

Evaluation of Web Browsers of Android Mobile

Methodology

The objective of this research is to study the accessibility of web browsers available for android mobile phones. The operating environment of mobile phones and personal computers (PC) are different, such as use of keyboard, mouse, touch screens and navigation features. Thus, the applicability of accessibility guidelines on web browsers for PCs differs from that of web browsers meant for mobile phones. First, we classify the UAAG 2.0 guidelines and choose the accessibility guidelines that are applicable to web browsers. Then, we select guidelines that are applicable to web browsers of mobile phones. Figure 23 represents the methodology adopted for evaluating web browsers of android mobiles. Table 8 shows the guidelines, which are extracted from UAAG2.0, for accessibility analysis of web-browsers.

Figure 22. Accessibility violation of principles of UAAG 2.0 with respect to the web browsers

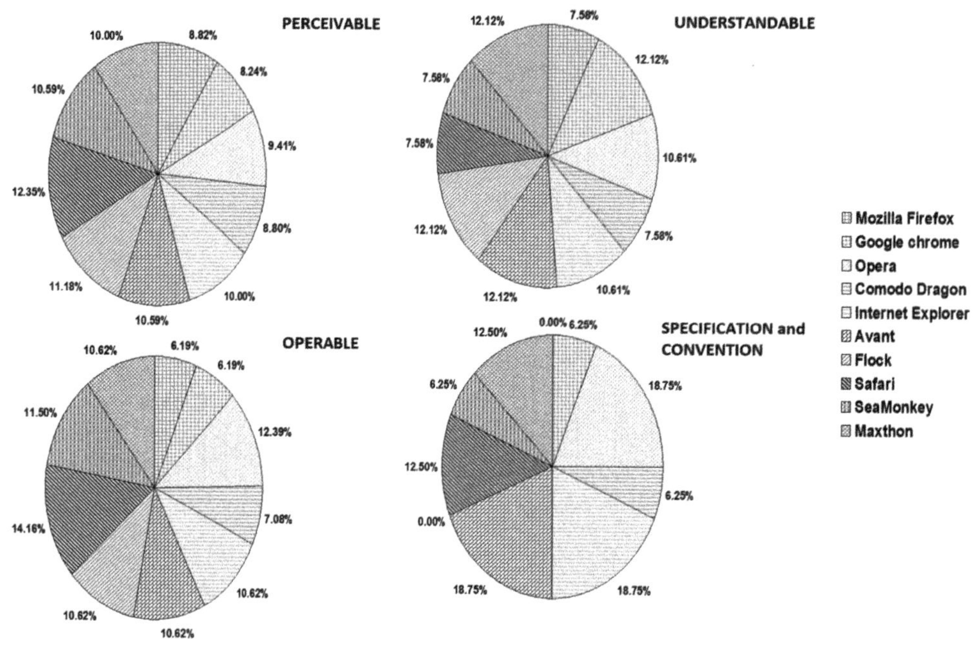

Figure 23. Methodology adopted to analyze the accessibility of web browsers of android mobiles

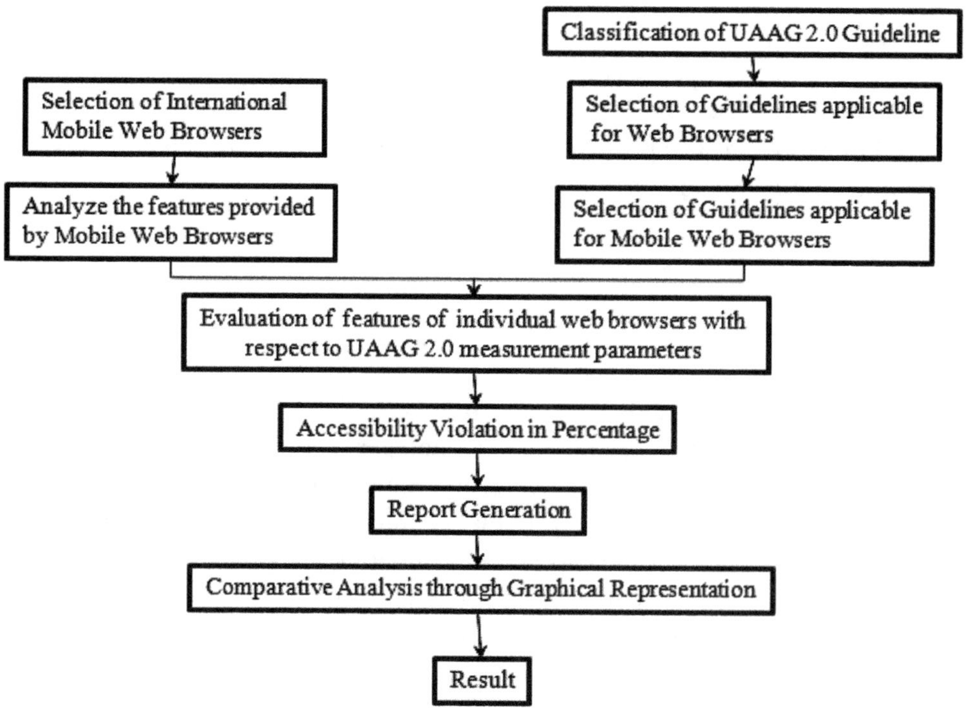

Table 8. Result of accessibility evaluation of web browsers with respect to guideline 3 (understandable) and guideline 5 (specification and conventions)

Guidelines Applicable to Web-Browsers of Mobile			
1.1.1	Render Alternative Content	1.10.2	Show Element Hierarchy
1.1.2	Indicate un-rendered Alternative Content	2.3.1	Allow Direct Navigation to Enabled Elements
1.1.3	Replace Non-Text Content	2.3.2	Allow Direct Activation of Enabled Elements
1.1.5	Provide Configurable Alternative Content Defaults	2.4.1	Text Search
1.3.1	Distinguishable Highlighting	2.4.2	Search Direction
1.3.2	Highlighting Options	2.4.3	Match Found
1.3.4	Distinguishing Enabled Elements from disabled elements	2.4.4	Alert on Wrap or No Match
1.3.5	Distinguishing Visited links from Unvisited links	2.4.5	Alternative Content Search
1.4.1	Basic text formatting (Globally)	2.5.1	Provide Structural navigation by heading and Within Tables
1.4.2	Basic text formatting (By Element)	2.6.1	Allow Persistent Accessibility Settings
1.4.3	Blocks of text (Globally)	2.6.2	Allow Restore All to Default
1.4.4	Configured and Reflowed Text Printing	2.6.3	Allow Multiple Sets of Preference Settings
1.4.5	Default to Platform text strings	2.6.4	Allow Preference Changes from outside the user Interface
1.4.6	Advanced text formatting	2.6.5	Make Preference Settings Transferable
1.8.1	Highlight Viewport	2.7.1	Customize Display of controls for User Interface Commands, Functions, and Add-ons
1.8.2	Move Viewport to Selection and Focus	2.8.1	Adjustable Time Limits
1.8.3	Provide Viewport Scrollbars	3.1.1	Text Entry Undo
1.8.4	Indicate Viewport position	3.1.2	Settings Changes can be Reversed or confirmed
1.8.5	Allow Zoom	3.1.3	Retrieval Progress
1.8.6	Maintain Point of Regard	3.1.4	Spell Check
1.8.7	Customize Viewport Highlighting	3.1.5	Back Button
1.8.9	Provide Viewport History	3.1.6	Form Submission Confirm
1.8.10	Allow Top-Level Viewport Open on Request	3.1.7	Form Auto-Fill
1.8.11	Allow Top-Level Viewport Focus Control	3.1.8	Save Form Entries
1.8.12	Allow Same User Interface	3.2.1	Accessible Documentation
1.8.13	Multi-Column Text Reflow	3.2.2	Describe Accessibility Features
1.8.14	Ignore Fixed Unit Dimensions	3.2.3	Document All Features
1.8.15	Linearize Content	3.2.4	Changes Between Versions
1.8.16	Provide Web Page Bookmarks	3.2.5	Centralized View
1.9.1	Outline View	3.3.1	Avoid Unpredictable Focus
1.9.2	Source View	5.1.6	Enable Reporting of user Agent Accessibility Faults
1.10.1	Show Related Elements		

Evaluation

This research is intended to provide an accessibility evaluation of 15 Web browsers, commonly used in android mobiles, based on UAAG 2.0. For our analysis, we have considered the latest version of top 15 web browsers available for android mobiles. The data taken for our analysis is gathered during the period 1st February 2016 to 21st August 2016. Figure 24 represents the list of selected web browsers.

Figure 25(a) depicts the result of accessibility evaluation of web browsers with respect to the Perceivable guidelines of UAAG 2.0. During analysis of the perceivable feature, we tested the web browser's ability to control text formatting. Web browsers can regulate the text-formatting by operating on text colour, text size, and font of the text. We observe that all web browsers are unable to control text formatting of either rendered text, links or block of text. We also analyzed the methods provided by the web browsers to customize the highlighting feature. This accessibility feature is well organized in case of "Puffin" and "Mercury" web browsers. Web browsers should be able to provide the outline view, source view, and off-line view of a website. This accessibility feature is well-managed by "Mozilla Firefox", "Google Chrome", "Blue Safari", "Pale Moon", "Flash Fox", "Fire Phoenix", and "Puffin" web browsers.

We analyzed all features of viewport and top-level viewport of a web browser. The viewports of a web browser should contain the zooming and scrolling features. Web browser should be able to control the bookmark features. We also evaluated the web browsers' ability for text reflow. All these viewport and top-level viewport related accessibility features are mostly confirmed by "Maxthon", "Dolphin", and "Puffin and Mercury" web browsers. We tested the ability of web browsers to control the text alternative for all non-text web components. Web browsers should also be able to indicate the absence of text alternatives.

Figure 25(b) provides the result of accessibility evaluation of web browsers of mobile phones with respect to the Operable guidelines of UAAG 2.0. A web browser should alert the user during wrapping of navigation. We analyzed the commands present in web browsers for direct navigation and the method to customize them. We also tested the forward and backward text search. Web browsers should show all match found and should alert on wrap. We also analyzed the navigation of web browsers through different structures of websites. The search and navigation related accessibility features are mostly confirmed by "Puffin" web browser. We analyzed the configuration setting of all web browsers and also the persistence and reversibility of web browsers configuration. We verified whether a web browser allows creating multiple preference settings. The preference settings should be transferable from one device to another. We also analyzed the customize display of controls over the user interface of web browsers.

Figure 24. List of Android cell phone web Browsers selected for analysis

Figure 25. Result of accessibility evaluation of web browsers of mobile phones with respect to (a) Guideline 1 (Perceivable),(b) Guideline 2 (Operable), (c) Guideline 3 (Understandable), and Guideline 5 (specification and convention)

	mozilla Firefox	Google Chrome	Opera	Maxthon	Blue safari	Internet Web Exploer	Pale Moon	Flash fox	Fire Phonix	Web Browser & Web Explorer	Web Browser & Explorer	UC browser	Dolphin	Puffin Browser	Mercury browser
1.1.1	✓	✓	✗	✓	✓	✗	✓	✓	✓	✓	✓	✗	✗	✓	✗
1.1.2	✗	✗	✗	✓	✗	✗	✗	✗	✗	✓	✓	✗	✓	✗	✓
1.1.3	✓	✗	✗	✓	✗	✗	✗	✗	✗	✓	✓	✓	✓	✗	✓
1.1.5	✗	✗	✗	✗	✗	✗	✗	✗	✗	✗	✗	✗	✗	✗	✗
1.3.1	✓	✓	✓	✓	✓	✓	✓	✓	✓	✓	✓	✓	✓	✓	✓
1.3.2	✗	✗	✗	✗	✗	✗	✗	✗	✗	✗	✗	✗	✗	✓	✓
1.3.4	✗	✗	✗	✗	✗	✗	✗	✗	✗	✗	✗	✗	✗	✗	✗
1.3.5	✗	✗	✗	✗	✗	✗	✗	✗	✗	✗	✗	✗	✗	✗	✗
1.4.1	✗	✗	✗	✗	✗	✗	✗	✗	✗	✗	✗	✗	✗	✗	✗
1.4.2	✗	✗	✗	✗	✗	✗	✗	✗	✗	✗	✗	✗	✗	✗	✗
1.4.3	✗	✗	✗	✗	✗	✗	✗	✗	✗	✗	✗	✗	✗	✗	✗
1.4.4	✗	✗	✗	✗	✗	✗	✗	✗	✗	✗	✗	✗	✗	✗	✗
1.4.5	✗	✗	✗	✗	✗	✗	✗	✗	✗	✗	✗	✗	✗	✗	✗
1.4.6	✗	✗	✗	✗	✗	✗	✗	✗	✗	✗	✗	✗	✗	✗	✗
1.8.1	✓	✓	✓	✓	✓	✓	✓	✓	✓	✓	✓	✓	✓	✓	✓
1.8.2	✓	✓	✓	✓	✓	✓	✓	✓	✓	✓	✓	✓	✓	✓	✓
1.8.3	✓	✓	✓	✓	✓	✓	✓	✓	✓	✓	✓	✓	✓	✓	✓
1.8.4	✗	✗	✗	✗	✗	✗	✗	✗	✗	✗	✗	✗	✗	✗	✗
1.8.5	✓	✓	✓	✓	✓	✓	✓	✓	✓	✓	✓	✓	✓	✓	✓
1.8.6	✓	✓	✓	✓	✓	✓	✓	✓	✓	✓	✓	✓	✓	✓	✓
1.8.7	✗	✗	✗	✗	✗	✗	✗	✗	✗	✗	✗	✗	✗	✗	✗
1.8.9	✓	✓	✓	✓	✓	✓	✓	✓	✓	✓	✓	✓	✓	✓	✓
1.8.10	✓	✓	✓	✓	✗	✓	✓	✓	✓	✓	✓	✓	✓	✓	✓
1.8.11	✗	✗	✓	✓	✗	✗	✗	✗	✗	✗	✗	✗	✓	✓	✓
1.8.12	✓	✓	✓	✓	✓	✓	✓	✓	✓	✓	✓	✓	✓	✓	✓
1.8.13	✓	✓	✓	✓	✓	✓	✓	✓	✓	✓	✓	✓	✓	✓	✓
1.8.14	✓	✓	✓	✓	✓	✓	✓	✓	✓	✓	✓	✓	✓	✓	✓
1.8.15	✗	✗	✗	✗	✗	✗	✗	✗	✗	✗	✗	✗	✗	✗	✗
1.8.16	✓	✓	✗	✓	✓	✓	✓	✓	✓	✓	✓	✓	✓	✓	✓
1.9.1	✓	✓	✓	✓	✓	✓	✓	✓	✓	✓	✓	✓	✓	✓	✓
1.9.2	✓	✓	✗	✗	✓	✗	✓	✓	✓	✗	✗	✗	✗	✓	✗
1.10.1	✗	✗	✗	✗	✗	✗	✗	✗	✗	✗	✗	✗	✗	✗	✗
1.10.2	✗	✗	✗	✗	✗	✗	✗	✗	✗	✗	✗	✗	✗	✗	✗

(a)

	mozilla Firefox	Google Chrome	Opera	Maxthon	Blue safari	Internet Web Exploer	Pale Moon	Flash fox	Fire Phonix	Web Browser & Web Explorer	Web Browser & Explorer	UC browser	Dolphin	Puffin Browser	Mercury browser
2.3.1	✓	✓	✓	✓	✓	✓	✓	✓	✓	✓	✓	✓	✓	✓	✓
2.3.2	✓	✓	✓	✓	✓	✓	✓	✓	✓	✓	✓	✓	✓	✓	✓
2.4.1	✓	✓	✓	✓	✗	✗	✓	✓	✓	✗	✗	✓	✓	✓	✗
2.4.2	✓	✓	✓	✓	✗	✗	✓	✗	✓	✗	✗	✓	✓	✓	✗
2.4.3	✗	✓	✓	✓	✗	✗	✗	✓	✗	✗	✗	✓	✓	✓	✗
2.4.4	✗	✗	✗	✗	✗	✗	✗	✗	✓	✗	✗	✗	✗	✗	✗
2.4.5	✗	✗	✗	✗	✗	✗	✗	✗	✗	✗	✗	✗	✗	✓	✗
2.5.1	✓	✓	✓	✓	✓	✓	✓	✓	✓	✓	✓	✓	✓	✓	✓
2.6.1	✓	✓	✓	✓	✗	✗	✓	✓	✓	✓	✓	✓	✓	✓	✓
2.6.2	✗	✗	✗	✓	✗	✗	✗	✗	✗	✗	✗	✓	✓	✗	✗
2.6.3	✗	✓	✗	✗	✗	✗	✗	✗	✗	✗	✗	✗	✗	✗	✗
2.6.4	✗	✗	✗	✗	✗	✗	✗	✗	✗	✗	✗	✗	✗	✗	✗
2.6.5	✗	✗	✗	✗	✗	✗	✗	✗	✗	✓	✓	✗	✗	✗	✓
2.7.1	✓	✗	✗	✗	✗	✗	✓	✓	✓	✗	✗	✗	✓	✓	✗
2.8.1	✓	✓	✓	✓	✓	✓	✓	✓	✓	✓	✓	✓	✓	✓	✓

(b)

	mozilla Firefox	Google Chrome	Opera	Maxthon	Blue safari	Internet Web Exploer	Pale Moon	Flash fox	Fire Phonix	Web Browser & Web Explorer	Web Browser & Explorer	UC browser	Dolphin	Puffin Browser	Mercury browser
3.1.1	✗	✗	✗	✗	✗	✗	✗	✗	✗	✗	✗	✗	✗	✗	✗
3.1.2	✓	✓	✓	✓	✓	✓	✓	✓	✓	✓	✓	✓	✓	✓	✓
3.1.3	✓	✓	✓	✓	✓	✓	✓	✓	✓	✓	✓	✓	✓	✓	✓
3.1.4	✗	✗	✗	✗	✗	✗	✗	✗	✗	✗	✗	✗	✗	✗	✗
3.1.5	✓	✓	✓	✓	✓	✗	✗	✓	✓	✓	✓	✓	✓	✓	✓
3.1.6	✓	✓	✓	✓	✓	✓	✓	✓	✓	✓	✓	✓	✓	✓	✓
3.1.7	✓	✓	✓	✗	✓	✓	✗	✓	✓	✓	✓	✓	✓	✓	✓
3.1.8	✓	✓	✓	✓	✓	✓	✓	✓	✓	✓	✓	✓	✓	✓	✓
3.2.1	✓	✗	✓	✗	✗	✗	✓	✓	✓	✗	✗	✗	✓	✓	✓
3.2.2	✓	✗	✗	✗	✗	✗	✗	✗	✗	✗	✗	✗	✗	✗	✗
3.2.3	✓	✓	✗	✗	✗	✗	✗	✗	✗	✗	✗	✗	✗	✗	✗
3.2.4	✓	✓	✓	✓	✓	✓	✓	✓	✗	✓	✓	✓	✓	✓	✓
3.2.5	✗	✗	✗	✗	✗	✗	✗	✗	✗	✗	✗	✗	✗	✗	✗
3.3.1	✓	✓	✓	✓	✗	✗	✓	✓	✓	✗	✗	✓	✓	✓	✓
5.1.5	✓	✓	✓	✓	✗	✗	✗	✗	✓	✗	✗	✓	✓	✓	✓

(c)

Figure 25(c) depicts the result of accessibility evaluation of web browsers of mobile phones with respect to Guideline 3 (Understandable) and Guideline 5 (specifications and conventions) of UAAG 2.0. We analyzed the effect of web browsers on the form of websites to make it understandable as web browsers can't totally control the forms of websites, but can control and customize specific features. Web browsers should provide auto-fill mechanism for specific common fields. Web browsers should be capable to save local versions of web contents. It was found that form related accessibility features are mostly confirmed by all web browsers except "Maxthon" and "Internet Explorer". We verified the accessibility of the documentations of web browsers. A document should provide all the features of a web browser, accessibility features, and the changes between versions. We tested the web browsers' capability to avoid unpredictable focus changes. We also analyzed the feedback features of the web browsers.

Result Analysis

Figure 26 provides the result of accessibility evaluation of individual web browsers of mobile phones with respect to the "perceivable", "operable", "understandable", and "specifications and conventions" principles.

It was observed that the most accessible web browser is "Puffin Web browser" with an overall violation of 41.27%. Similarly, least accessible web browser is "Internet Web Explorer" with an overall violation of 63.49%. The overall accessibility violation of "Mozilla Firefox", "Google Chrome", "Opera", "Maxthon", "Blue Safari", "Pale Moon", "Flash Fox", "Fire Phoenix", "Web Browser & Web Explorer", "Web Browser & Explorer", "UC Browser", "Dolphin", and "Mercury" are 42.86%, 46.03%, 50.79%, 46.03%, 61.90%, 52.38%, 49.21%, 47.62%, 53.97%, 53.97%, 49.21%, 42.86% and 47.62% respectively.

Figure 27 represents the Accessibility Evaluation of individual web browsers with respect to different conformance like Conformance A, AA, and AAA. As per the conformance level A, least accessible web browsers is "Internet Web Explorer" with 62.50% violation, similarly most accessible web browsers are "Maxthon" and "Dolphin" both with 25.00% violation. According to the conformance level AA, least accessible web browsers is "Internet Web Explorer" with 60.00% violation, similarly most accessible web browser are "Dolphin" and "Puffin" both with 38.18% violation. As per the conformance level AAA least accessible web browsers is "Internet Web Explorer" with 63.49% violation, similarly most accessible web browser is "Puffin" with 41.27% violation.

Figure 28 provides a comparative view of guideline violations in case of perceivable, operable, understandable, and robustness with respect to different web browsers of mobile phones. During our analysis we observed that most of the web browsers violated the "Perceivable" principle of UAAG 2.0 with an average of 53.94% violation. The principle which is less violated by all web browsers is "specifications & conventions" with an average of 40.00% violation.

In case of Perceivable guideline, the web browsers which cause most accessibility violation are "Opera", "Blue Safari", and "Internet Web Explorer" each with 7.49% violation. For Operable guideline, the web browsers which cause most accessibility violation are "Blue Safari" and "Internet Web Explorer" each with 9.91% violation. With respect to Understandable guideline, the web browser which causes most accessibility violation is "Internet Web Explorer" with 9.09% violation. As per the "specifications and conventions" guideline, the web browsers which cause most accessibility violation are "Blue Safari", "Internet Web Explorer", "Pale Moon", "Flash Fox", "Web Browser and Web Explorer", and "Web Browser & Explorer" all with 16.67% violation. While evaluating the 15 chosen web browsers it was observed that there is an urgent need to improve the web browsers of mobile phones in order to make them effective for accessing web sites.

Evaluation of Embedded Media Players

Methodology

Here we have considered four media players. Features of each media players are minutely verified. First we extract the set of guideline, which are dealing with the accessibility of media players, form UAAG 2.0 then check each media players. All the features are checked minutely, but the important points are

Figure 26. Accessibility evaluation of web browsers of mobile phones with respect to the "Perceivable", "Operable", "Understandable", and "Specifications and conventions" principles of UAAG2.0 Guideline

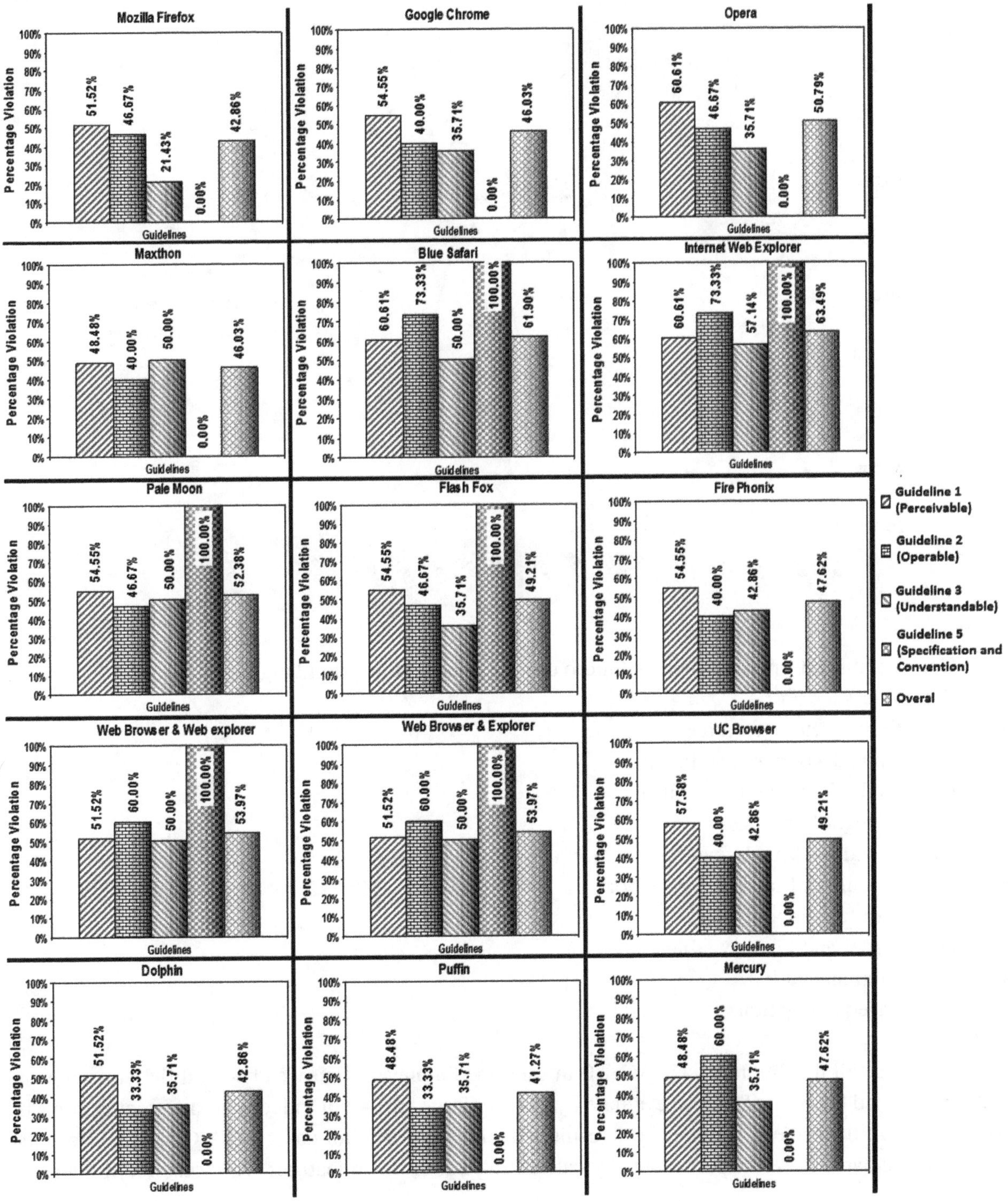

Figure 27. Accessibility evaluation of individual android cell phone web browsers with respect to three conformance level

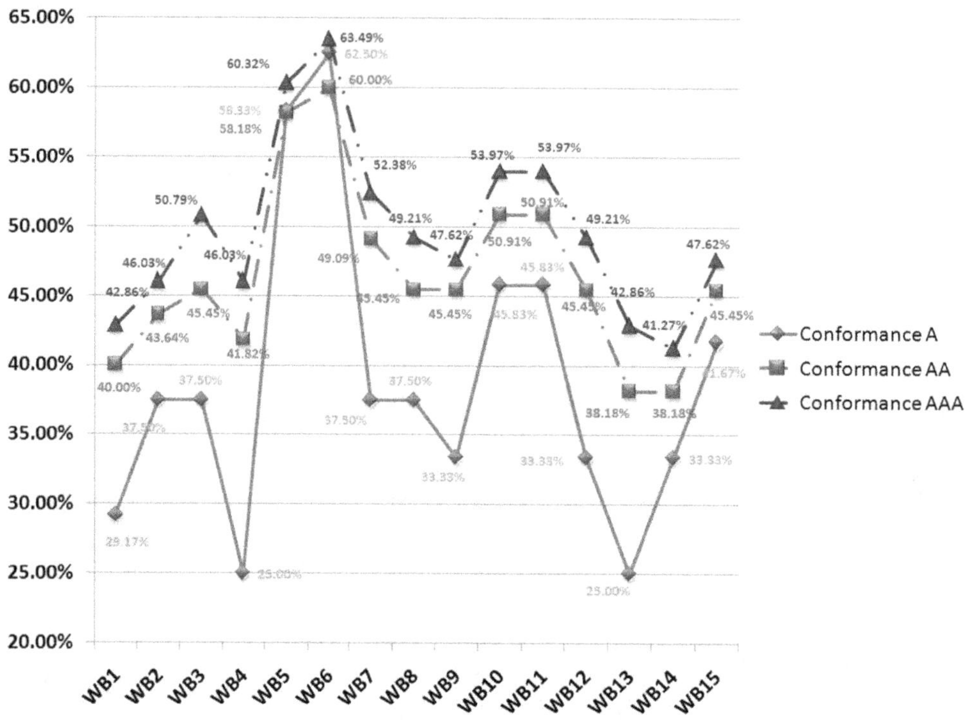

- Configurable alternative contents (audio description, caption, sign language),
- Resizable View Ports,
- Play, Stop, Resume features,
- Zoom in and Zoom out features,
- Local and Global volume control,
- Point of regard of icons,
- History and bookmark features,
- Controllability of top level view port,
- Keyboard functionality,
- Focus order and Focus visible,
- Sequential navigation,
- Time based navigation.

To measure all the dictum of UAAG 2.0 in each media players first we check all the elements and feature provided by them. Then we evaluate by playing large variety of video with different peculiarity (Assistive facilities). We documented the result in a table with '✓' (for pass) and '✗' symbol (for fail). Then we calculated the error percentage by calculating no. of failed features with total no. of features.

Figure 28. Accessibility violation of principles of UAAG 2.0 with respect to web browsers

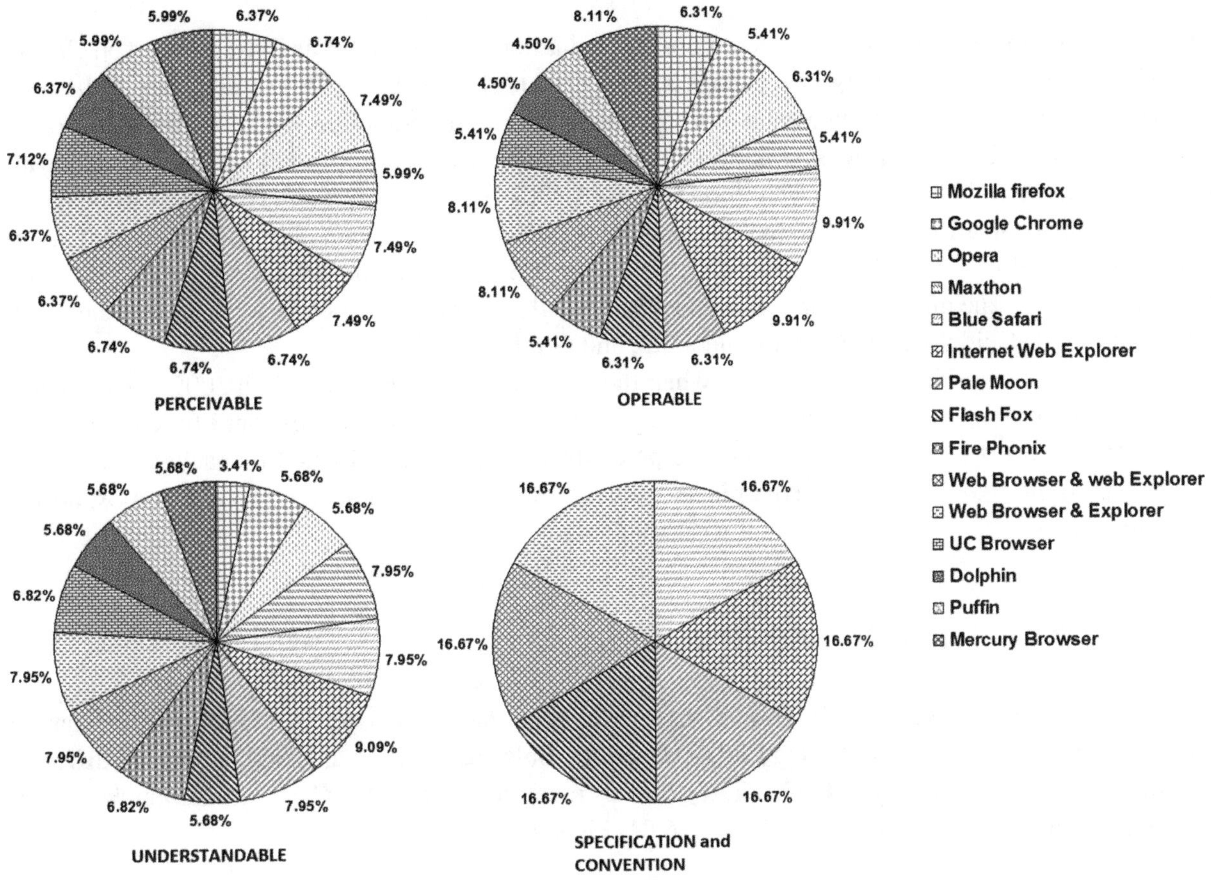

Figure 29. Workflow for accessibility analysis of embedded media players

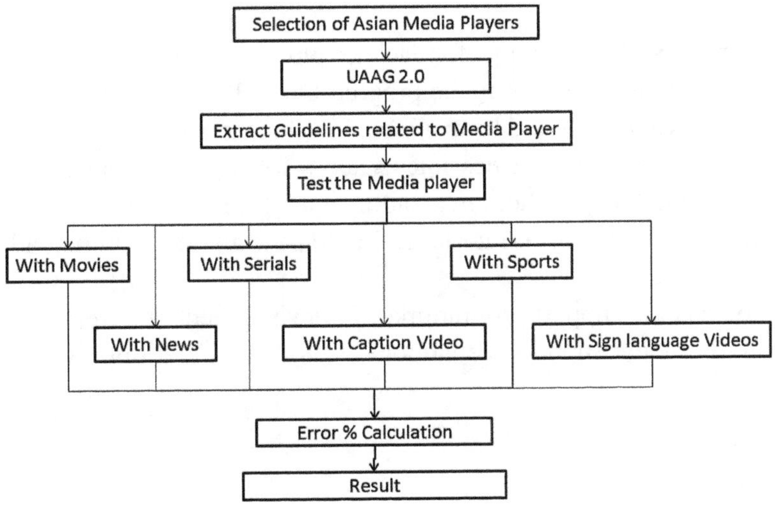

Evaluation

This research is intended to provide an accessibility evaluation of 4 Asian Media Players based on UAAG 2.0. The data taken for our analysis is gathered during the period 1st May 2014 to 21st June 2014.

While analyzing the media players we observe that, maximum guideline violation found in Youku with 57.14% violation, and the least violation found in Youtube with 22.86% violation. The violation with respect to Vimeo and Dailymotion were found to be 51.43%. Figure 30 represents the result of analysis.

During the evaluation we detect that the guidelines, which are not violated by all player are Guideline 1.8.9, Guideline 1.8.12, Guideline 1.8.13, Guideline 1.8.14, Guideline 2.9.1, Guideline 2.11.2, and Guideline 2.11.5. The guidelines, which are violated by all players are Guideline 1.1.6, Guideline 1.3.2, Guideline 1.6.1, Guideline 1.6.3, Guideline 2.2.2, and Guideline 2.11.8.

We studied that in Youku media player when the zooming in reaches more than 300% the elements are not working properly. We studied that in daily motion media player the keyboard functionality are not working properly. Figure 31represents the percentage of guideline violated by each media player. According to the figure Youtube media player has less guideline violation. So Youtube is most accessible than others.

ACCESSIBILITY OF AUTHORING TOOLS

ATAG (Authoring Tool Accessibility Guideline) is an international standard for maintaining and evaluating the accessibility of different authoring tools. Authoring tools are the software used to develop different websites. The latest version of ATAG, ATAG 2.0 was recommended by W3C on 24th September 2015. Following features describe the guidelines of ATAG in short:

- The user interface of authoring tool should be accessible,
- The online user interface of the authoring tool should follow WCAG 2.0 Accessibility features,
- The offline user interface of the authoring tool should follow Platform specific Accessibility features,
- Alternative content should be available for each graphical element of the interface.
- The presentation of editing view should be programmatically determined,
- All keyboard related features should be available in user interface,
- The preview window should be as accessible as accessible as user agents.
- The user interface should help authors in avoiding and correcting mistakes
- A well accessible document, of user interface, should be available including all necessary features of user interface,
- The authoring tool should support programmers in development of accessible web content,
- The authoring tools should support the authors in producing and improving the accessibility of web contents.

Figure 30. Result of analysis of guidelines per embedded Media players

Name		Media Players			
		Youtube	Vimeo	Youku	Dailymotion
UAAG (User Agent Accessibility Guidelines) 2.0					
1.1.4	Provide Configurable Alternative Content Defaults	✓	✗	✓	✓
1.1.5	Facilitate Clear Display of Alternative Content for Time-based Media	✓	✗	✗	✓
1.1.6	Allow Resize and Reposition of Time-based Media Alternatives	✗	✗	✗	✗
1.3.1	Highlighted Items	✓	✗	✗	✗
1.3.2	Highlighting Options	✗	✗	✗	✗
1.5.1	Global Volume	✓	✗	✓	✓
1.6.1	Speech Rate, Volume, and Voice	✗	✗	✗	✗
1.6.3	Advanced Speech Characteristics	✗	✗	✗	✗
1.6.5	Synthesized Speech Language	✓	✗	✗	✗
1.8.1	Highlight Viewport	✓	✗	✓	✓
1.8.5	Allow Zoom	✓	✓	✗	✗
1.8.6	Maintain Point of Regard	✓	✗	✓	–
1.8.9	Allow Viewport Resize	✓	✓	✓	✓
1.8.10	Provide Viewport History	✓	✗	✓	✓
1.8.11	Allow Top-Level Viewport Open on Request	✓	✓	✗	✓
1.8.12	Allow Top-Level Viewport Focus Control	✓	✓	✓	✓
1.8.13	Allow Same User Interface	✓	✓	✓	✓
1.8.14	Provide Webpage Bookmarks	✓	✓	✓	✓
2.1.1	Provide Full Keyboard Functionality	✓	✓	✗	✗
2.1.2	Show Keyboard Focus	✓	✓	✗	✗
2.1.3	Avoid Keyboard Traps	✓	✓	✗	✗
2.1.4	Separate Selection from Activation	✓	✓	✗	✗
2.2.1	Sequential Navigation Between Elements	✓	✓	✗	✗
2.2.2	Sequential Navigation Between Viewports	✗	✗	✗	✗
2.2.3	Default Navigation Order	✓	✓	–	–
2.2.4	Options for Wrapping in Navigation	✗	✗	✗	–
2.9.1	Adjustable Time Limits	✓	✓	✓	✓
2.11.1	Time-Based Media Load-Only	✗	✓	✗	✗
2.11.2	Execution Placeholder	✓	✓	✓	✓
2.11.3	Execution Toggle	✓	✓	–	–
2.11.4	Adjustable Playback Rate for Prerecorded Content	✓	✗	✗	✗
2.11.5	Stop/Pause/Resume Time-Based Media	✓	✓	✓	✓
2.11.6	Navigation of Time-Based media by Time	✓	✗	✓	✓
2.11.7	Navigation of Time-Based Media by Semantics	✓	✗	✗	✗
2.11.8	Video Contrast and Brightness	✗	✗	✗	✗
	Error Percentage	22.86%	51.43%	57.14%	48.57%

RECOMMENDATIONS

Based on our study the following recommendations are made with respect to the design of web portals: text alternatives should be provided for all non-text web content, headers are to be included for each page, section, and table. There should be provision for controlling color contrasts. All keyboard functionalities need to be supported, and all the forms must be well structured and interactive.

On the basis of our analysis the following recommendations are made with respect to the design of web browsers: Web browsers should provide mechanisms to customize different highlighted options,

Figure 31. Percentage of guideline violation in each embedded Media Player

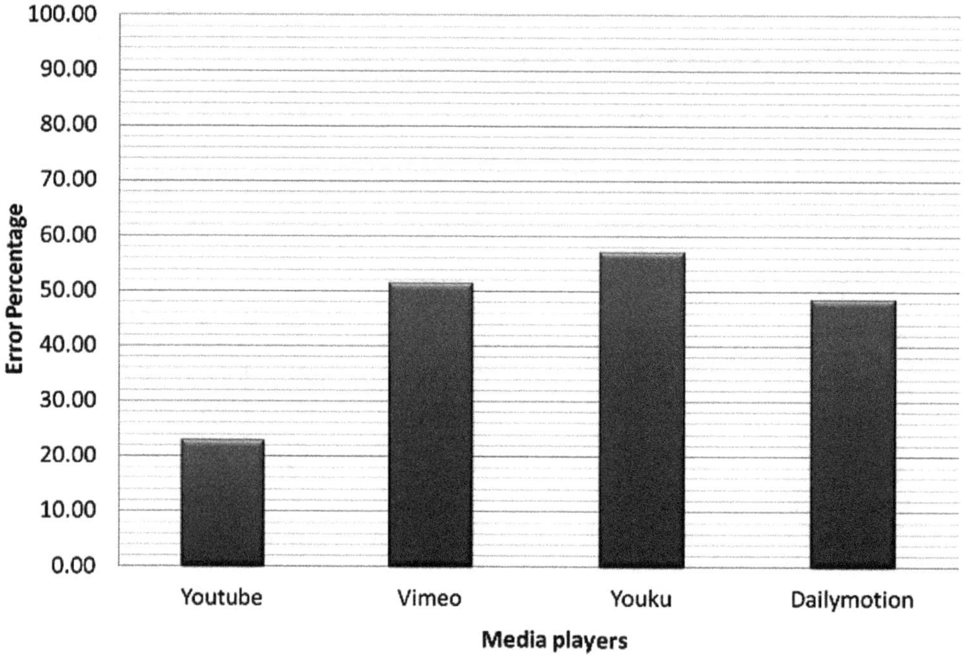

users should be allowed to control the focus during creation of new viewports or top level viewports, the position of view should be indicated in the viewport, text formatting should be provided for blocks of text, wrapping of navigation should be allowed but with a message after completion of one round, customization of keyboard commands should be allowed, alternative content search should be allowed, mechanism should be provided to support and apply user style sheets, there should be mechanisms to activate new input methods, web browsers should provide mechanisms to choose and customize alternative contents, and there should be provision to create and transfer multiple preference settings. These features must be incorporated in web browsers so that web portals can be accessed effectively.

Similarly, the media players should allow resizing and repositioning of media alternatives provided in videos, highlight the options (like foreground and background colors, and resize the indicator when it is an image), allow a user to adjust all speech characteristics provided by the speech synthesizer, allow sequential navigation between viewports, and allow the users to adjust the contrast and brightness of visual time-based media.

CONCLUSION

With the growing number of web portals worldwide, accessibility issues have emerged as a serious concern for web designers. In this chapter we have analyzed the accessibility of web components based on WCAG 2.0 and accessibility of user agents, such as web browsers and media players based on UAAG 2.0. We also describe important features of ATAG. The issues dealt in this chapter can help web developers for effective design of web portals, web browsers, and media players by adhering to the recommendations.

REFERENCES

Abanumy, A., Al-Badi, A., & Mayhew, P. (2005). E-Government Website Accessibility: In-Depth Evaluation of Saudi Arabia and Oman. *The Electronic Journal of eGovernment, 3*(3), 99-106.

Al-Radaideh, M., Nuser, M., & Wahbeh, A. (2011, May). Evaluating Accessibility of Jordanian E-Government Websites for People with Disabilities. *Proceedings of International Conference on Information and Communication Systems*, 127-131.

Arrue, M., Vigo, M., & Abascal, J. (2007). Automatic evaluation of mobile web accessibility. In *Universal Access in Ambient Intelligence Environments*. Springer.

Authoring Tool Accessibility Guidelines (ATAG 2.0). (2017, May 11). Retrieved from http://www.w3.org/TR/ATAG20/

Authoring Tool Accessibility Guidelines Working Group (ATAG WG). (2017, May 11). Retrieved from http://www.w3.org/WAI/AU/

Baazeem, I. S., & Al-Khalifa, H. S. (2015, December). Advancements in Web Accessibility Evaluation Methods: How Far Are We? In *Proceedings of the 17th International Conference on Information Integration and Web-based Applications & Services (IIWAS 2015)*. ACM. doi: 10.1145/2837185.2843850

Babu, J. R., & Sekharaiahm, K. C. (2014). A Panorama of Web Accessibility. *International Journal of Computer Science and Mobile Computing, 3*(8), 311–317.

Bandeira, R., Lopes, R., & Carriço, L. (2010). Towards mobile Web accessibility evaluation. Free and Open Source Software for Accessible Mainstream Applications (FOSS-AMA), colocated with ETAPS (2010), 27-28.

Borodin, Y., Mahmud, J., Ramakrishnan, I. V., & Stent, A. (2007). The HearSay Non-Visual Web Browser. In *Proceedings of the 2007 international cross-disciplinary conference on Web accessibility (W4A 2007)*. ACM. 10.1145/1243441.1243444

Carter, J., & Markel, M. (2001). Web Accessibility for People With Disabilities: An Introduction for Web Developers. *IEEE Transactions on Professional Communication, 44*(4), 225–233. doi:10.1109/47.968105

Ceaparu, I., & Shneiderman, B. (2002). Improving Web-based Civic Information Access: A Case Study of the 50 US States. *International Symposium on Technology and Society (ISTAS 2002), Copyright 2002 IEEE*, 275-282. doi: 10.1109/ISTAS.2002.1013826

Chisholm, W. A., & Henry, S. L. (2005). Interdependent Components of Web Accessibility. In *Proceedings of the 2005 International Cross-Disciplinary Workshop on Web Accessibility (W4A)*. ACM. 10.1145/1061811.1061818

Gandhi, S. K. (2016). India's Jumbo Jump from E-Commerce to Mobile Enabled Services (MES): A Review. *Productivity, 56*(4), 326.

González, M., Moreno, L., Martínez, P., & Iglesias, A. (2011). Web accessibility requirements for media players. In *Human-Computer Interaction–INTERACT 2011*. Springer. doi: .10.1007/978-3-642-23768-3_109

Ismail, A., & Kuppusamy, K. S. (2015). Accessibility of Indian universities' homepages: An exploratory study. Journal of King Saud University – Computer and Information Sciences, 1–11.

Ismailova, R., & Inal, Y. (2016). Web site accessibility and quality in use: a comparative study of government Web sites in Kyrgyzstan, Azerbaijan, Kazakhstan and Turkey. In *Universal Access in the Information Society*. Springer. DOI: 10.1007/s10209-016-0490-z

Kadu, M. V., Bagret, M. V. M., & Verma, M. A. (2015). Transforming from e-Governance to M-Governance. *International Journal of Advanced Research in Computer and Communication Engineering*, *4*(2), 457–462. doi:10.17148/IJARCCE.2015.42103

Kamal, K. K., Kumar, M., Shrivastava, S., & Chourasia, P. (2016). Mobile Seva-Enabling mGovernance in India. In *Proceedings of the 2016 CHI Conference Extended Abstracts on Human Factors in Computing Systems*. ACM. 10.1145/2851581.2851586

Kamal, K. K., Kumar, M., Varyani, B., Shrivastava, S., & Tripathi, P. (2015). Mobile Platform as a Service A Case Study of User Friendly Approach to Mobile Strategy. In *Proceedings of the 13th International Conference on Advances in Mobile Computing and Multimedia (MoMM 2015)*. ACM. 10.1145/2837126.2837163

Kamoun, F., Mourad, B. M. A., & Bataineh, E. (2013). WCAG 1.0 versus WCAG 2.0 Web Accessibility Compliance: A Case Study. In *Proceeding of the International Conference on Digital Information Processing, E-Business and Cloud Computing (DIPECC2013)* (pp. 94-101). The Society of Digital Information and Wireless Communication.

Kuzma, J. M., Yen, D., & Oestreicher, K. (2009). Global e-government Web Accessibility: An Empirical Examination of EU, Asian and African Sites. *Proceeding of 2nd International Conference on Information and Communication Technologies and Accessibility*, 1-6.

Latif, M. H. A., & Masrek, M. N. (2010). Accessibility Evaluation on Malaysian E-Government Websites. Journal of e-Government Studies and Best Practice, 1-11.

Lopes, R., Bandeira, R., Carriço, L., & Isacker, K. V. (2010). Towards Mobile Web Accessibility: Vision And Challenges. *Proceedings of the first International ÆGIS Conference*, 151-158.

Mahmud, J., Borodin, Y., & Ramakrishnan, I. V. (2007). CSurf: A Context-Driven Non-Visual Web-Browser. In *Proceedings of the 16th international conference on World Wide Web, WWW 2007*. ACM. 10.1145/1242572.1242578

Moreno, L., Gonzalez, M., Martínez, P., & Iglesias, A. (2011). A Study of Accessibility Requirements for Media Players on the Web. In *Proceeding of 6th International Conference, UAHCI 2011*. Springer. 10.1007/978-3-642-21672-5_28

Patra, M. R., & Dash, A. R. (2017). Analysis of Android Cell Phone Web-Browsers to Facilitate Accessible m-Governance. *Proceedings of the 10th International Conference on Theory and Practice of Electronic Governance, ICEGOV 2017*, 276-284. 10.1145/3047273.3047279

Patra, M. R., & Dash, A. R. (2017). Accessibility Analysis of Some Indian Educational Web Portals. *International Journal of Computer Science, Engineering and Applications (IJCSEA), 7*(4), 9–24. doi:10.5121/ijcsea.2017.7404

Patra, M. R., & Dash, A. R. (2017). Accessibility analysis of web browsers. *International Journal of Services Technology and Management, 23*(4), 313–330.

Patra, M. R., Dash, A. R., & Mishra, P. K. (2014). A Quantitative Analysis of WCAG 2.0 Compliance for some Indian Web Portals. *International Journal of Computer Science, Engineering and Applications (IJCSEA), 4*(1), 9–24. doi:10.5121/ijcsea.2014.4102

Patra, M. R., Dash, A. R., & Mishra, P. K. (2014). Accessibility Analysis of Government Web Portals of Asian Countries. *Proceedings of the 8th International Conference on Theory and Practice of Electronic Governance, ICEGOV 2014*, 383-386. 10.1145/2691195.2691253

Souley, B., & Sambo, A. S. (2014). A Comparative Performance Analysis of Popular Internet Browsers in Current Web Applications. *West African Journal of Industrial and Academic Research, 4*(1), 62–68.

Termens, M., Ribera, M., Porras, M., Boldú, M., Sulé, A., & Paris, P. (2009). Web Content Accessibility Guidelines: from 1.0 to 2.0. *Proceedings of the 18th international conference on World Wide Web*, 1171-1172. doi: 10.1145/1526709.1526912

Upatkoon, K., Wang, W., & Jamin, S. (2005). WebBee: An Architecture for Web Accessibility for Mobile Devices. *Proceeding of the 10th IFIP International Conference on Personal Wireless Communications*, 1-9. 10.1142/9781860947315_0046

User Agent Accessibility Guideline (UAAG 2.0). (2017, May). Retrieved from http://www.w3.org/TR/UAAG20/

User Agent Accessibility Guidelines Working Group (UAWG). (2017, May 11). Retrieved from http://www.w3.org/WAI/UA/

Vigo, M., Aizpurua, A., Arrue, M., & Abascal, J. (2008). Evaluating web accessibility for specific mobile devices. *Proceedings of the 2008 international cross-disciplinary conference on Web accessibility (W4A)*, 65-72. 10.1145/1368044.1368059

Web Content Accessibility Guidelines (WCAG 2.0). (2017, May 11). Retrieved from http://www.w3.org/TR/ WCAG20/

Web Content Accessibility Guidelines Working Group (WCAG WG). (2017, May 11). Retrieved from http://www.w3.org/ WAI/GL/

Yu, C. H., & Miller, R. C. (2011). Enhancing mobile browsing and reading, *Proceedings of the 2011 annual conference extended abstracts on Human factors in computing systems (CHI EA '11)*, 1783-1788. doi: 10.1145/1979742.1979845

KEY TERMS AND DEFINITIONS

Alternative Contents: Additional text alternative provided with all non-text contents for better understandability of disable persons.

ATAG: An international guideline created by W3C to control and verify the accessibility of authoring tools.

Authoring Tool: Software based on which website is created.

UAAG: An international guideline created by W3C to control and verify the accessibility of user agents and assistive technologies.

User Agent: Software tools, agents, used from client side to access websites.

View Port: An interface through which website has been shown.

WAI: An initiative taken by W3C, some technical steps to make the accessible for all.

WCAG: An international guideline created by W3C to control and verify the accessibility of web components.

Chapter 9
Issues in Web-Based Learning

Hesham Alomyan
University of Petra, Jordan

ABSTRACT

The purpose of this chapter is to review and critically evaluate some issues related to Web-based learning. The chapter begins with an introduction to the importance of using the Web in education; then it examines and evaluates such issues. Suggestions and solutions to these issues are offered. These issues are classified into theoretical and design issues. The theoretical issues include: (1) online interaction, (2) learner control, (3) disorientation and cognitive overload. The design issues include: (1) interface design and (2) content structure. The conclusion section summarizes the chapter and points out the importance of considering individual differences in Web-based learning systems design.

INTRODUCTION

Since its introduction, the Web has demonstrated its potential to transform the processes of teaching and learning. Owing to its networking capability, the Web offers multiple dimensions of use in education. It has been used as a resource, management, communication, assessment, and instructional and learning tool.

Uses of the Web have captured the attention and interest of educational institutions around the world. Schools and universities have already started integrating the Web in their educational systems. Schools from primary levels to high secondary levels are now using the Web to supplement classroom instruction, to give learners the ability to access information, and to deliver learning experience. Likewise, since 1997 a rapid increase of utilising the Web has been witnessed in higher education. At present, obtaining an online degree has become the best ways not only to continue education but also to advance students' career.

Along with this rapid growth and integration of the Web in education, researchers and educators (e.g., Fisher, 2003; Murphy, Walker, & Webb, 2001; Nguyen, 2015; Ruttun & Macredie, 2011; Sutton, 2001) have been trying to improve and use the Web effectively in teaching and learning. Several issues have been raised in the literature on how to design effective Web-based learning systems. Hence, the purpose of this chapter is to review and critically evaluate such issues and suggest possible solutions to address these issues and help develop effective Web-based learning systems.

DOI: 10.4018/978-1-5225-4206-3.ch009

ISSUES RELATED TO WEB-BASED LEARNOING

As shown in Figure 1, there are two types of issues related to Web-based learning: theoretical and design issues. The theoretical issues include: (a) online interaction, (b) learner control, and (c) disorientation and cognitive overload. The design issues include: (a) user interface design and (b) content structure. These issues are discussed in depth in the following sections.

Theoretical Issues

Despite the relative novelty of the Web, researchers have sought to establish a theoretical foundation to guide research and practice pertaining to Web-based learning design. Four issues appear to be related to the use of the Web in teaching and learning. These issues are: online interaction, learner control, disorientation, and cognitive overload.

Online Interaction

Interaction is considered to be a very important aspect of the learning process and students' success in face-to-face instruction. Because Web-based learning cannot offer face-to-face instruction as the traditional classroom does, the concept of interaction has received significant attention in the literature (e.g., Agudo, Iglesias, Conde, & Hernandez, 2014; Duval, 2011; Hill, Wiley, Nelson, & Han, 2004). Wagner (1994) defined interaction as "reciprocal events that require at least two objects and two actions. Interactions occur when these objects and events mutually influence one another" (p. 8). Empirical evidence shows positive correlations among interaction, student course satisfaction, and learning outcomes (Kuo, Walker, & Belland, 2014; Kuo, Walker, & Schroder, 2010; Moallem, Pastore, & Martin, 2013; Zhang & Fulford, 1994; Zirkin & Sumler, 1995). Four types of interaction have been identified in Web-based learning: (a) learner-instructor interaction, (b) learner-learner interaction, (c) learner-content interaction, and (d) learner-interface interaction.

Learner-instructor interaction is a key element that provides dialogue between the learner and the instructor. In this type of interaction the instructor plays the role of expert, mentor, or tutor, providing guidance, feedback or encouragement to the learner (Shackelford & Maxwell, 2012). Also, the instructor takes on other responsibilities like presenting material online, then seeking for and receiving feedback from the learners. In addition, learner-instructor interaction can take a form of one-to-one, as in a private e-mail conversation or an office consultation between the two (Sutton, 2001).

Figure 1. Issues related to Web-based learning

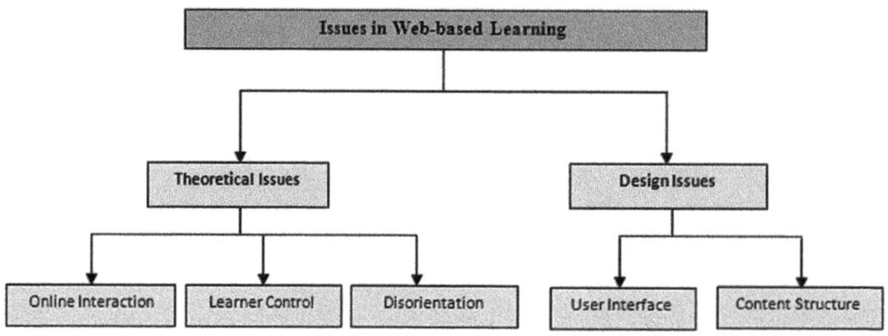

Research shows that instructors are a key element in successful online interaction. For example, Sher (2009) found a significant correlation between student-instructor interaction and student learning and satisfaction. Jiang and Ting (2000) found correlations between perceived interactions with instructors and the average numbers of responses per student that instructors made and the average numbers of responses students themselves made in course discussions. Richardson and Ting (1999) compared the perceptions of two groups of students involved in asynchronous learning. They found that students learning through written correspondence with instructors were more concerned with instructor feedback, whereas students learning online felt that all interactions with instructors mattered. Moore (1989) pointed out that increasing the interaction between learner and instructor could reduce the physical separation and lead to more effective learning.

Learner-learner interaction is the interaction in which two or more learners engage in communication sharing information, ideas, viewpoints, or experiences to create an active learning community (Bonk & Cunningham, 1998). One aspect of learner-learner interaction is collaborative learning (Rhode, 2009). The term "collaborative learning" refers to an instruction method in which students at various performance levels work together in small groups toward a common goal. The Web offers various communication tools that allow collaborative learning to take place online. Online discussion, for example, seems to be the most influential features of collaborative learning (Swan, Shea, Fredericksen, Pickett, Pelz, & Maher, 2000). Harasim (1990) noted students perceive online discussion as more equitable and more democratic than traditional classroom discussions. Perhaps this is true as asynchronous discussion offers participants the opportunity to reflect on their peers' contributions and on their own writing before posting them. Furthermore, a correlation was found between students' perceived learning and the amount of discussion taking place in online courses (Jiang & Ting, 2000; Picciano, 2002). Moreover, peers engagement has been found to be critical to the development of communities of learning (Wenger, McDermott, & Snyder, 2002), allowing learners to develop interpersonal skills, and to investigate tacit knowledge shared by community members. The Web with its sophisticated social tools (Web 2.0, Wiki, Facebook, Tweeter, etc) has now the ability to support peers engagement and development of communities of learning. Future research could be conducted in this area to investigate the role of the social aspects of the Web in learning.

Another important aspect of online interaction is learner-content interaction. Learner-content interaction is defined as "the process of intellectually interacting with content that results in changes in the learner's understanding, the learner's perspective, or the cognitive structures of the learner's mind" (Moore, 1989, p. 2). In this type of interaction, the learners navigate through the content to access the curriculum of the lesson (Wiley, 2002). Berge, Collins, and Dougherty (2000) note that as learners interact with the content, they should be encouraged to apply, assess, analyse, synthesize, evaluate, and reflect on what they learn. Ally and Fahy (2002), referring to the information processing theory, relate that during this stage of interaction learners process the information to transform it from short-term to long-term memory. The higher the level of processing, the more associations are made in long-term memory, which results in higher-level learning. Ally advises that instructional strategies should be devised to facilitate this process.

Various organizational methods and techniques have been proposed for structuring online content and facilitating the process of transforming information. For example, Chalmers, (2003) suggested that advance organizers, graphic organizers, and concept maps should be employed in structuring online materials. These techniques are believed to enable learners to construct a coherent mental representation of what they learn, prompt previous knowledge and give the learners an elaborative tool for new information (MacGregor, 1999). Mayer (2003) proposed a multimedia instructional strategy in which words are integrated with pictures. In his research on instructional design methods across different media, Mayer found that students learn more deeply from well-designed multimedia message where printed words are placed near rather than far from corresponding pictures.

Other researchers (e.g., Ford & Chen, 2000; Gagne, Wager, Golas, & Keller, 2005; Magoulas, Papanikolaou, & Grigoriadou, 2003; Martin, 2003; Riding & Rayner, 1998) suggest that further investigation of whether the above mentioned instructional strategies facilitate learning may be usefully addressed by considering individual differences in learner characteristics. Such researchers tend to argue that individuals do not learn in the same way, thus when it comes to instruction "one size does not fit all". That is, there is no single instructional strategy that is best for all students: The pace, content, and sequencing of instructional materials should be tailored to the individual needs of the learners. One view is that it is now possible for the Internet technology with its capabilities to significantly support tailoring beyond that of traditional stand alone, computer-based learning.

Given the fact that Web-based learning is technology-driven, learner-interface interaction is considered to be another important type of online interaction. Learner-interface interaction describes the interaction between the learner and the computer interface tools needed to access and participate in instruction and communicate with instructors and other learners (Sinha, Khreisat, & Sharma, 2009). This type of interaction can be of a challenge for learners as they do not experience such interaction in traditional classroom education. Lohr (2000) argues that the design and development of an effective instructional interface is a challenging task. Lohr further adds that there is a need for user interface design and this need should be a learner-driven, rather than technically-driven. Beldaglia and Adiguzel (2010) argue that designers of Web-based learning systems are now forced to create adaptive and flexible learning environments with the potential of improving the learner performance. However, Galitz (1997) relates that this kind of adaptation requires understanding learners first, that is, understanding users' characteristics.

Overall, from the literature reviewed, it is apparent that online interaction is important for quality Web-based learning. Although interaction with instructors and interaction with peers have most been investigated to date in the asynchronous online medium, interaction with online content and instructional interface has been less researched particularly from an individual difference perspective. Future research is encouraged to investigate how instructional strategies may help learners with different characteristics interact with interface and content structure.

Learner Control

Learner control refers to the amount of control learners exert over the process or style of instruction they receive (Sizmann, Wisher, Stewart, & Kraiger, 2004; Snow, 1980). Features of the Web including links, non-linear structure, and independence of time and place have given learners more control over their learning than ever. In hypermedia learning environments learners can have more control over the sequence (i.e., learners have the opportunity to choose the content they wish to explore), pace (i.e., learners are not just allowed to adapt instructional pace to their comfort level but also allowed to take a break from instruction and return at a later date or time), and content of their learning (i.e., learners can be granted extensive control over the content) (Sizmann et al., 2004; Snow, 1980). Another type of control is program control where the program makes decisions for each learner in a predetermined manner (Wang & Beasley, 2002).

The learner control issue has triggered a debate among instructional designers and educators as to how much control should a learner have in Web-based learning. Should Web-based learning be an open-ended learning environment in which learners have choices to direct their own learning process? What are the effects of learner control on the effectiveness of learning? When should learners be given control? When should learners not be given control?

Research conducted to address such questions has shown somewhat conflicting results. For example, in examining the effect of learner control on learning in a hypermedia environment, research studies by Behrend and Thompson (2012), Granger and Levine (2010), and Schnackenberg and Sullivan (2000) showed increased effectiveness of learning with learner control. On the other hand, other research studies by Burke, Etnier, and Sullivan (1998), Crooks, Klein, Jones, and Dwyer (1996), and Morrison, Ross, and Baldwin (1992), and Sun and Hsu (2013) showed decreased effectiveness of learning with learner control. Yet, some studies by Carrier, Davidson, Higson, and Williams (1984), and Hannafin (1984) reported no significant effect related to the factor of learner control.

Other studies were more specific in that they examined the effect of learner control on students of varying ability levels. Some of these studies showed achievement gains for higher ability students when learner control is employed while other results showed lower ability students benefited from less learner control and more program control. For example, research by Borsook and Higginbotham, (1991), Williams (2001), and Lawless and Brown (1997) found that lower ability learners benefit from more program control while high achieving learners benefit from a high degree of learner control. However, in a review of the literature, Schnackenbery and Hilliard (1998), concluded that measurements used in past studies of the effect of learner control might be invalid and that learners of both high and low ability achieve more using learner control.

It appears that there is inconsistency in the findings of these studies on the effectiveness of learner control. Wang and Beasley (2002) explained that the reason for this inconsistency might be a result of considering learner control as a single construct. They further explained that there are many other factors that function together with learner control to make it effective. Learner control may be influenced by the learner's characteristics being granted control and the conditions under which it is being granted.

In conclusion, although learner control is assumed to be a beneficial feature of hypermedia learning systems, simply granting potential learner control to any learner without considering his or her individual differences may create problems related to navigation and cognitive load. These problems are discussed in the next section of disorientation and cognitive overload.

Disorientation and Cognitive Overload

One of the important features of hypermedia systems is permitting non-sequential access to information and offer many advantages over plain linear text. However, with this flexibility of accessing information on the Web, it is too easy for users to get off learning experience path and access irrelevant information which leads in most cases to a problem of disorientation (Conklin 1987) and cognitive overload (Nielsen, 1995). In addition to the vast amount of information available, hypermedia-based learning systems often consist of various textual as well as static and dynamic pictorial representations which might become a burden on learner's cognition (Kalyuga & Liu, 2015). Bodemer and Ploetzner (2002) relate that while such multiple representations have the potential to improve learning in specific ways, they also might make specific demands on learners. That is, learners have to process different representations simultaneously to construct a coherent mental representation which might cause learners to experience cognitive overload.

Attempts have been made to overcome these problems. With regard to the disorientation problem, many researchers have endeavoured to provide adaptation mechanisms for Web-based learning systems (Beldaglia & Adiguzela, 2010; Brusilovsky, 2003; Chen & Macredie, 2004; Khan, 1997; Magoulas et al., 2003). According to Brusilovsky, Kobsa and Vassileva (1998) these adaptation mechanisms can be classified into two types: (a) navigational adaptation and (b) content adaptation. Navigational adaptation provides guidance on the available learning paths in a manner that is both pedagogically sound and customised to individual students. It can be implemented as direct guidance, link annotation, adaptive hiding, and map adaptation (Eklund & Sinclair, 2000). On the other hand, content adaptation works at the domain content level. The information can be adapted to various details, difficulty, and media usage to meet users with different needs, background knowledge, interaction style, and cognitive characteristics (Lo, Chan, & Yeh, 2011; Recker, Ram, Shikano, Li, & Stasko, 1995). The goal of these adaptation systems is to both ease the information burden and direct user's paths of exploration.

Another possible solution for cognitive overload comes from researchers (De Jong, 2010; Kalyuga & Liu, 2015; Mayer & Moreno, 2002; Sweller, Chandler, Tierney, & Cooper, 1990) who promote the idea that instructional designers should work from a cognitive theory of learning perspective rather than from an information delivery viewpoint. These researchers emphasize that a crucial design goal is to promote schema construction in the learner. Three cognitive theories are often used in this context: (a) cognitive load theory, (b) dual coding theory, and (c) cognitive theory of multimedia learning.

Cognitive load theory is a theory of instructional design. It describes how the structure of cognition has specific implications for the design of instruction (Sweller, 1999). Cognitive load theory suggests that the central problem is to avoid overloading the learner's cognitive abilities. Overload is seen as negative attribute resulting from instructional element being poorly attuned with learner's mental attributes, notably their working memory capabilities. This theory differentiates between three sources of cognitive load: (a) intrinsic cognitive load which is related to the integral complexity of the application domain and reflects the absolute difficulty of the material to be learnt as well as by the learners' prior-knowledge (Van Merrienboer & Sweller, 2005), (b) extraneous cognitive load is the unnecessary load caused by poorly designed instruction, and (c) germane cognitive load relates to the degree of effort involved in the processing, construction and automation of learning material (Bodemer & Ploetzner, 2002). According to this theory, when the sum of intrinsic and the extraneous loads become high, learning becomes difficult. It is not always possible to change intrinsic load, but it is possible to reduce the extraneous and germane load if well-designed materials are used (Martin & Mendelsohn, 2000).

Dual coding theory of Paivio, is another theory of information processing. This theory suggests that there are two separate processing systems for verbal and nonverbal source of information. Drawing on the dual coding theory, Sweller, Chandler, Tierney, and Cooper (1990) demonstrated in a series of experiments that the physical integration of textual and graphical information can prevent learners from splitting their attention between the two kinds of representations and subsequently reduce cognitive overload. Furthermore, their research showed that presenting information in an integrated format resulted in better learning than in a separated format (e.g., Chandler & Sweller, 1991; Tarmizi & Sweller, 1988). That is, via the simultaneous presentation of related textual and graphical elements, students do not have to expend cognitive resources in the extraneous process of searching for and matching related elements of information.

Based on the cognitive load theory and dual coding theory, Mayer (1997) proposed a cognitive theory of multimedia learning. According to his theory, the learner possesses separate systems for processing verbal and pictorial material (dual channel assumption), that each channel is limited in the amount of material that can be processed at one time (limited-capacity assumption), and that meaningful learning involves cognitive processing including building connections between pictorial and verbal representations (active-processing assumption) (Mayer, 2011b; Mayer & Moreno, 2003).

Mayer argues in his theory that the superiority of presenting information in visual and verbal forms over merely verbal form is that information is encoded in two modalities rather than a single modality. Thus, students have multiple retrieval cues that facilitate the retrieval of information from memory. Mayer (2003) explains that when cognitive load is distributed between the verbal and visual channels, the limited capacity of working memory is effectively expanded. Indeed, several researchers (e.g., Bradshaw & Johari, 2003; Brunken, Plass, & Leutner, 2003; Gyselinck, Ehrlich, Cornoldi, Beni, & Dubois, 2000; Mayer, 1997, 2001; Mayer & Moreno, 1998; Mousavi, Low, & Sweller, 1995; Tindall-Ford, Chandler, & Sweller, 1997) found that learning is improved when images such as diagrams are accompanied with explaining text. Perhaps using visualizations like diagrams provide an external representation of information that has analog properties (Hegarty & Steinhoff, 1997; Moreno, 2003; Zhang, 1997). Shah and Freedman (2003) explain that, because information is depicted in the environment, students do not have to maintain a mental representation of that information or mentally transform it. Consequently, such displays may reduce the cognitive load required to comprehend the information presented.

Other researchers (e.g., Amadieu, Gog, Paas, Tricot, & Marin, 2009; Hu & WU, 2012; Keller, Gerjets, Scheiter, & Garsoffky, 2006; Schnotz & Rasch, 2005) suggested another solution to cognitive overload. They proposed the idea of concept mapping (Ausubel, 1968; Novak, 1976). These researchers argued that concept maps may allow learners to draw inferences very easily on how different information units are related to each other with regard to those attributes that are represented spatially. Concept maps are 2D-diagrams formed by nodes and links and integrate two kinds of coding-verbal and visual. These nodes are connected by labelled lines in order to represent their interrelations. Tergan (2003) relates that concept maps foster processes of knowledge acquisition as these representations provide learners with a better understanding of the structures underlying a domain without imposing high cognitive load on them.

Overall, according to these theoretical considerations it can be hypothesized that integrated presentations (i.e. verbal and visual presentations) and concept maps might have substantial pedagogical potentials in Web-based learning, because they allow deploying cognitive resources available for learning in a way that is more appropriate than it is with conventional representations of large sets of information units. Nevertheless, while cognitive load theory, dual coding theory, and cognitive theory of multimedia present an instructional design framework that has been found useful in solving the cognitive overload problem in hypermedia instruction, such theories have not recognised the importance of considering learner characteristics as moderating variables between cognitive load and instructional design. Therefore, it is important to consider learner characteristics as they alter the nature of an individual's cognitive load and can be used to facilitate learning.

Design Issues

The Web as a medium for delivering instruction relies upon hypertext and hypermedia systems of interaction and design. Some of the issues related to these systems are user interface design and content structure.

User Interface Design

The user interface of a computer program refers to the graphical, textual and auditory information the program presents to the user, and the control sequences the user employs to control the program (Chambers, 2003; Lohr, 2000). The vast majority of the early research into computer interface was technology driven. That is, research was conducted to test out or validate new screen display technologies such as higher resolution monitors and the utility of pointing devices such as the mouse (e.g., Buxton, Will, & Rowley, 1985; Card, English, & Burr, 1978; Foley, Wallace, Victor, & Chan, 1984). However, with the growing number of the end user population with little or no computer expertise, the user interface design has become an important area of study. Research shows that disorientation and cognitive overload are now common problems faced by online users, and caused by badly designed interfaces (Ahuja & Webster, 2001; Chalmers, 2003; Faghih, Azadehfer, & Katebi, 2013). It was found that about 50% of a person's time was wasted as a result of frustrating computer interfaces (Creaparu, Lazar, Bessiere, Robinson, & Shneiderman, 2004).

As the use of the Web is rapidly increasing in our educational systems, the need for *instructional* interface design has become a necessity. Several instructional researchers stress this necessity. For example, Peslak (2005) states that it should be noted that most of the directions available to the designers of an instructional interface falls outside the domain of instructional design in fields long involved in human-computer interaction research. Such fields include cognitive science (Norman, 1988), graphic arts (Mullet & Sano, 1995), and technical communications (Hackos & Redish, 1998). Instructional interfaces are often designed to promote the user's acquisition of new knowledge, skills, and attitudes needed for performance or for understanding. In these learning environments learners build their expertise. Hence, guidelines for the design of an instructional user interface clearly must be based on a set of assumptions different from those based on software users and tasks (Lhor, 2000).

A few attempts have been made to draw guidelines for instructional interface design. For example, Faghih et al., (2013) determined three golden rules to design user interface for instructional software: (1) place the user in control; (2) reduce the user's memory load; (3) make the interface consistent. Chalmers (2003) advises that learning theory (e.g., schema theory, cognitive load theory, and retention theories) should be applied to user interface development when design software screens for education. Other researchers (e.g., Mayer & Moreno, 2002; Sweller, Chandler, Tierney, & Cooper, 1990) agree with Chalmers on linking interface design with cognitive theories claiming that many computer users have trouble learning and remembering information presented on a computer screen. For example, based on cognitive theories, part of the reason for a lack of retention is hypothesized to be the user's inability to form a mental picture, or schemata of the information presented via a computer screen. It is suggested that these problems of the inability to form a schema and disorientation with human interface are worth researching, not only for better retention, but also for increased satisfaction among users.

Oppermann (2001) drew some principles for educational software that are specific to user interface. First, the user of a learning system is a novice. That is, educational software is used by a user for a limited time until he or she has learnt the content of the system. Therefore, the user should not need to learn the interface before starting to learn the domain content. Thus, the user interface of an educational system should be "self-descriptive" and "suitable for learning". Second, an educational system is not under the control of the user as an information system is. Rather, the goals of the educational system and the sequences of the dialogue follow the underlying educational curriculum. However, this does not exclude completely the user controllability but requires much more guidance to communicate the meaning of particular elements and particular sequences of the educational system (Oppermann, 2001).

Lohr (2000) suggested four steps for the development of instructional interfaces, viz,

1. **The Analysis Step:** During the analysis step the interface designer identifies specific design goals focused on environment, teacher, and learner tasks that must be performed or supported by the interface.
2. **The Synthesis Step:** During the synthesis step principles of message design, graphic arts, and information design guide the shaping of interface elements to facilitate the environment, teacher, and student functions identified in the analysis step.
3. **The Evaluation Step:** During evaluation the effectiveness of the form created in the synthesis step is assessed. If the form is not communicating effectively the design process moves to,
4. **The Change Step:** Change step where the goals identified in the analysis step and the form created in the synthesis step are re-evaluated and reshaped. This process continues until satisfactory design of the interface or elements of the interface evolve.

Further, Lohr (2000) explained that designers of software interfaces were encouraged to observe extensively people performing job-related tasks in their work environment prior to user interface development in order to translate the objects and actions (observable events) from the user's environment into interface elements, and develop visual tools that simulate the environment. This task-based approach works for the instructional interface when learning goals relate to specific, observable tasks. However, there are many learning situations where the nature of the task may be predominantly cognitive, and non-observable. In these situations the advice to translate objects from the learner's previous experience into familiar metaphors is often not helpful.

Hence, in this case a suitable approach would be to investigate learner's characteristics to identify their needs and preferences. Adaptive user interfaces can be then created to meet such needs and preferences. Chan and Macredie (2004) stressed in their study the importance of considering a learner's characteristics in user interface design. They found important cognitive differences among the participants that suggest different model components to support Web-based instruction. It seems that different cognitive styles require different approaches to reach these diverse students.

In conclusion, the research into interface design has yet to fully investigate how Web-based information relates to human processing tendencies. In particular, we need to consider the implications of individual differences as one possible factor that could impact upon instructional interface design.

Content Structure

Another issue of concern to educational researchers is ways in which online material should be organised and presented. Educational institutions are now placing more course material online than ever. However, when looking closely, one has to be slightly alarmed because a significant proportion of online material fails badly when judged from teaching and learning perspective (Oliver, 2000). A need for some guidelines for organising and structuring the online material has become important. Oliver (2000) states that while many guidelines have been produced to assist developers of printed-based materials few produced similar sets for designers of Web-based learning. Ally (2000) relates that the development of effective Web-based learning material should be based upon proven and sound learning theories.

By way of overview, it is possible to describe three broad theoretical positions that have contributed toward the psychology of human learning and might have implications for Web-based learning design, viz, behavioural approaches, cognitive theory, and constructivism.

Implications of Behavioural Approaches for Web-Based Learning

This approach is seen more in the way of historical analysis in that it is not represented by any contemporary researchers. However, the impact of behavioural psychology on learning theory was significant as attention was drawn towards many key variables in learning situations. For example, the process of feedback is fundamental to both initial learning and to subsequent corrective learning. Drill and practice is a good implication of such process. *Sequencing* is another key principle of behaviourism. Learning is viewed as a sequence of stimulus and response actions in observable cause and effect relationships (McCormick & Pressley, 1998). According to the sequencing principle, Web-based learning materials could be sequenced appropriately so that learning can be promoted.

Implications of Cognitive Theory for Web-based Learning

Cognitivists describe learning from an information processing perspective. Such approach focuses upon how the human memory system acquires, transforms, compacts, elaborates, encodes, retrieves, and uses information. According to the information processing theory the memory system is divided into three main storage structures: sensory store, short-term memory, and long-term memory (Ally, 2002). Drawing on this analysis several strategies can be implemented in designing a Web-based learning system.

1. Strategies should be used to allow learners to perceive and attend to the information so that it can be easily transferred to working memory. Such strategies might include:
    a. Placing important information in the centre of the screen for reading.
    b. Critical information should be highlighted to attract learners' attention using headings and/or colour. According to the information processing theory a large amount of information impinges on the sensory registers but is quickly lost if not attended to (Moore, Burton & Myers, 2004).
    c. Information should be chunked to prevent overload during processing in working memory. A central notion of information processing theory is that the mental system is remarkably fragile and aspects such as short-term working memory are easily disrupted. In any new situation, the mental chunks the mind uses are necessarily small and limited. For example, learning a new word (e.g., *anopisthography*) uses with perhaps 6 chunks of information at the outset. Later the chunk size will increase, sometime dramatically, such that this word may occupy a fraction of a chunk, and be able to be incorporated into sentences without mental effort.
2. To be recalled from long-term memory, information must be activated to make sense of the new information. Strategies to facilitate the retention and use of existing schema are listed below.
    a. **Advance Organizers:** Advance organizers can be used to link what the learner already knows with what is being learnt (Ausubel, 1968). Mayer (1997) conducted a meta-analysis of advance organizer studies, and found that these strategies were effective when students were learning from text that was presented in an unfamiliar form. Since most courses contain materials that are new to learners, advance organizers should be used to provide the framework for learning.

b. **Concept Maps:** Concept maps are used if there are many concepts in a lesson. A generalized concept map is provided as an overview for the online lesson, and can be linear, hierarchical, or spider-shaped (Chiou, 2008; Holley, Dansereau, McDonald, Garland, & Collins, 1979). As the lesson progresses, each item in the main concept map is presented and broken down into sub-concepts. At the end of the lesson, the main map is shown again, showing the relationships among the concepts illustrated. The advantage of these maps is that they provide the "big picture" to learners, to help them comprehend the details of a lesson and in turn facilitate deep processing. Web-based learning can take advantage of the modern computer capabilities to present concept maps to learners or to ask learners to generate concept maps themselves (Ally, 2001; Puntambekar, Stylianou, & Hubscher, 2003).

3. Different modes of presenting information should be used to accommodate individual differences in processing information and to facilitate transfer to long-term memory. The Web can support multiple modes of representation by being able to incorporate various kinds of media such as text, illustrations, animations, video, audio, and simulations. It is often accepted that these modes can support students with different learning styles (Ally & Fahy, 2002; Mayer, 2011b; Mayer, 2003). According to dual coding theory information received in different modes (verbal and non-verbal) will be processed better than that presented in a single mode (verbal only) (Paivio, 1986).
4. Motivating strategies should be used in Web-based learning systems. Motivation is an essential factor for learners to succeed online even if the online materials were effective. According to Keller model motivation consists of the following elements: Attention, relevance, confidence, and satisfaction (Keller, 1983; Keller & Suzuki, 1988). Instructional designers should take these elements into account when designing Web-based learning materials. Motivation theory argues that relevant experiences satisfy intrinsic needs or goals, encouraging effort and performance.

Implications of Constructivism for Web-Based Learning

The constructivist approach dominates learning theory today. Constructivism considers learners as active builders of their own knowledge rather than the receivers of knowledge. Learners are actively engaged in seeking knowledge and information in their learning process either individually or in small groups (Mayer, 1992; Hendry, 1996). However, two major views appear to be roughly regarded as cognitive constructivism and social constructivism. According to the cognitive constructivism viewpoint, individuals construct new meaning within the context of their current knowledge, experience, and environment (Swan, 2005). On the other hand, social constructivism places more emphasis on the social context of the learning environment. Our learning experiences are a function of social norms and interpretations and knowledge is constructed not by the individual alone but by social groups working in a collaborative learning environment (Vygotsky, 1978).

Based on these two kinds of constructivism and as far as the design of online learning environments concerned, constructivism suggests that we should be concerned with the design of particular kinds of learning environments, namely, learning environments that are learner-centred, and community-centred. In the learner-centred leaning environments, recognition should be given to the importance of building on the conceptual and cultural knowledge that students bring with them to the learning experience, of linking learning to students' experiences, and of accepting and exploring multiple perspectives and divergent understandings (Swan, 2005). Through its characteristics and tools, the Web offers unique affordances to learner-centeredness. For example, tools such as text, audio, video, self-testing, and Internet links, can be used to support learner-centred instruction (Fisher, 2003). Future research should focus on the cognitive aspect of constructivism to support learner-centred learning through using Web tools such as self- testing, Internet external links, and dynamic diagrams. Multimedia presentations and concept maps can be used to assist students in processing information by linking their prior knowledge with incoming information.

Constructivist approaches to learning also emphasize the importance of designing learning environments that enable community-centred (Bransford, Brown, & Cocking, 2000). Constructivism implies that learning is strengthened by environments which support and value the participation of all students, whose social norms encourage collaboration, the negotiation of meaning, and the search for understanding (Swan, 2005). Through its communication tools, the Web has the ability to create community-centred learning environments. One suggestion is that participants in online courses often feel less psychological distance between themselves and their classmates. In addition, relationships between learners' perceptions of social presence and their satisfaction in, and perceived learning from, online courses have been documented (Picciano, 2002). Furthermore, the Web through its new online communication tools (i.e., social-networking sites, wikis, and folksonomies) makes it easy to situate learning in authentic, real world problems and link it to local communities.

To recap, given the complexity of hypermedia and its close relationship to cognitive science, it was helpful to review the learning theories to understand the possible implications of such theories on content structure of Web-based learning systems. These implications are summarised and presented in Figure 2. Furthermore, it must be noted that there is a lack of research that thoroughly investigate theories of learning in the context of hypermedia and multimedia. Therefore, Research is needed to provide foundation from which to design learning environments in the hypermedia arena.

Figure 2. Implications of learning theories for content structure of Web-based learning systems

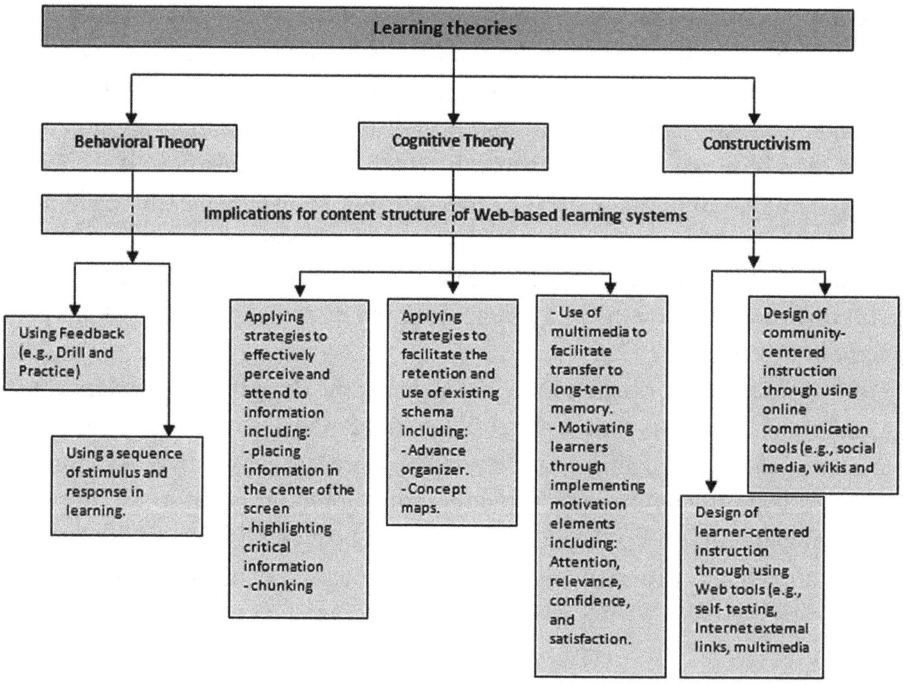

CONCLUSION AND FUTURE RESEARCH DIRECTIONS

The present chapter has identified and discussed issues related to Web-based learning. These issues have been classified into theoretical and design issues. The theoretical issues included: online interaction, learner control, and disorientation and cognitive overload. The design issues included: interface design and content structure. Implications have emerged for Web-based learning design from the review. The discussion of these issues has illustrated the importance and the need of considering individual differences of learners when designing Web-based learning systems.

Future research should be directed at examining and understanding the effect of individual differences on learning in general and on Web-based learning in particular. Selected individual differences that can be examined include: Cognitive style, prior knowledge, motivation, interest, and attitudes.

REFERENCES

Aggarwal, A. K., & Bento, R. (2000). Web-based education. In A. Aggarwal (Ed.), Web-based Learning and Teaching Technologies: Opportunities and Challenges (pp. 2-16). Hershey, PA: Idea Group Publishing. doi:10.4018/978-1-878289-60-5.ch001

Agudo-Peregrina, A. F., Iglesias-Pradas, S., Conde-González, M. A., & Hernandez-Garcia, A. (2014). Can we predict success from log data in VLEs? Classification of interactions for learning analytics and their relation with performance in VLE-supported F2F and online learning. *Computers in Human Behavior, 31*, 542–550. doi:10.1016/j.chb.2013.05.031

Ahuja, J. S., & Webster, J. (2001). Perceived disorientation: An examination of a new measure to assess Web design effectiveness. *Interacting with Computers, 14*(1), 15–29. doi:10.1016/S0953-5438(01)00048-0

Ally, M. (2000). Learning strategies for multimedia instruction. *Proceedings of the annual EdMedia Conference.*

Ally, M. (2002, August). *Designing and managing successful online distance education courses.* Workshop presented at the 2002 World Computer Congress, Montreal, Canada.

Ally, M., & Fahy, P. (2002, August). Using students' learning styles to provide support in distance education. *Proceedings of the 18th Annual Distance Education Conference on Teaching and Learning.*

Amadieu, F., Gog, T., Paas, F., Tricot, A., & Marin, C. (2009). Effects of prior knowledge and concept-map structure on disorientation,cognitive load, and learning. *Learning and Instruction, 19*(5), 376–386. doi:10.1016/j.learninstruc.2009.02.005

Ausubel, D. P. (1968). *Educational psychology: A cognitive view.* New York: Holt, Rinehart and Winston.

Behrend, T. S., & Thompson, L. F. (2012). Using Animated Agents in Learner-Controlled Training: The Effects of Design Control. *International Journal of Training and Development, 16*(4), 263–283. doi:10.1111/j.1468-2419.2012.00413.x

Beldaglia, B., & Adiguzela, T. (2010). Illustrating an ideal adaptive e-learning: A conceptual framework. *Procedia: Social and Behavioral Sciences, 2*(2), 5755–5761. doi:10.1016/j.sbspro.2010.03.939

Berge, Z. L., Collins, M., & Dougherty, K. (2000). Design guidelines for Web-based courses. In B. Abbey (Ed.), *Instructional and cognitive impact of Web-based education* (pp. 32–40). Hershey, PA: Idea Group Publishing. doi:10.4018/978-1-878289-59-9.ch002

Bodemer, D., & Ploetzner, R. (2002). Encouraging the active integration of information during learning with multiple and interactive representations. In R. Ploetzner (Ed), *International workshop on dynamic visualization and learning*. Tubigen, Germany: Knowledge Media Research Center

Bonk, C. J., & Cummings, J. C. (1998). A dozen recommendations for placing the student at the center of Web-based learning. *Educational Media International*, *35*(2), 82–89. doi:10.1080/0952398980350205

Borsook, T. K., & Higginbotham-Wheat, N. (1991). Interactivity: What it is and what it can do for computer-based instruction. *Educational Technology*, *31*, 11–17.

Bradshaw, A. C., & Johari, A. (2003). Effects of an online visual procedure on task completion, time, and attitude. *Journal of Educational Computing Research*, *29*(4), 401–417. doi:10.2190/0KVF-BNYT-7CPW-WWCY

Bransford, J. D., Brown, A. L., & Cocking, R. R. (2000). *How People Learn: Brain, Mind, Experience, and School*. Washington, DC: National Academy Press.

Brunken, R., Plass, J., & Leutner, D. (2003). Direct measurement of cognitive load in multimedia learning. *Educational Psychologist*, *38*(1), 53–61. doi:10.1207/S15326985EP3801_7

Brusilovsky, P. (2003). Developing adaptive educational hypermedia systems: From design models to authoring tools. In T. Murray, S. Blessing, & S. Ainsworth (Eds.), Authoring tools for advanced technology learning environments: Toward cost- effective adaptive, interactive, and intelligent educational software. Ablex.

Brusilovsky, P., Kobsa, A., & Vassileva, J. (Eds.). (1998). *Adaptive Hypertext and Hypermedia*. Dordrecht: Kluwer Academic Publishers. doi:10.1007/978-94-017-0617-9

Burke, P. A., Etnier, J. L., & Sullivan, H. J. (1998). Navigational aids and learner control in hypermedia instructional programs. *Journal of Educational Computing Research*, *18*(2), 183–196. doi:10.2190/HJXT-YH1K-6PDX-5FE4

Buxton, W., Hill, R., & Rowley, P. (1985). Issues and techniques in touch-sensitive tablet input. *Proceedings of SIGGRAPH. Computer Graphics*, *19*(3), 69–85. doi:10.1145/325165.325239

Card, S. K., English, W. K., & Burr, B. J. (1978). Evaluation of mouse, rate-controlled isometric joystick, step keys, and text keys for text selection on a CRT. *Ergonomics*, *21*(8), 601–613. doi:10.1080/00140137808931762

Carrier, C., Davidson, G., Higson, V., & Williams, M. (1984). Selection of options by field independent and dependent children in a computer-based concept lesson. *Journal of Computer-Based Instruction*, *11*, 49–54.

Chalmers, A. P. (2003). The role of cognitive theory in human–computer interface. *Computers in Human Behavior*, *19*(5), 593–607. doi:10.1016/S0747-5632(02)00086-9

Chandler, P., & Sweller, J. (1991). Cognitive load theory and the format of instruction. *Cognition and Instruction*, *8*(4), 293–332. doi:10.12071532690xci0804_2

Chen, S. Y., & Macredie, R. D. (2004). Cognitive Modeling of Student Learning in Web-Based Instructional Programs. *International Journal of Human-Computer Interaction*, *17*(3), 375–402. doi:10.120715327590ijhc1703_5

Chiou, C.-C. (2008). The effect of concept mapping on students' learning achievements and interests. *Innovations in Education and Teaching International*, *45*(4), 375–387. doi:10.1080/14703290802377240

Conklin, J. (1987). Hypertext: An introduction and surveys. *IEEE Computer*, *20*(9), 17–41. doi:10.1109/MC.1987.1663693

Crooks, S. M., Klein, J. D., Jones, E. E. K., & Dwyer, H. (1996). Effects of cooperative learning and learner-control modes in computer-based instruction. *Journal of Research on Computing in Education*, *29*(2), 109–123. doi:10.1080/08886504.1996.10782189

De Jong, T. (2010). Cognitive load theory, educational research, and instructional design: Some food for thought. *Instructional Science*, *38*(2), 105–134. doi:10.100711251-009-9110-0

Duval, E. (2011). Attention please! Learning analytics for visualization and recommendation. *Proceedings of the 1st International Conference on Learning Analytics and Knowledge LAK '11*, 9–17. 10.1145/2090116.2090118

Eklund, J., & Sinclair, K. (2000). An empirical appraisal of adaptive interfaces for instructional systems. *Educational Technology and Society Journal*, *3*, 165–177.

Faghih, B., Azadehfar, M., & Katebi, S. (2013). User Interface Design for E-Learning Software. *The International Journal of Soft Computing and Software Engineering*, *3*(3), 786–794.

Fisher, M. (2003). *Designing courses and teaching on the Web: A "how-to-guide" to proven innovative strategies*. Lanham, MD: Scarecrow Education.

Foley, J. D., Wallace, P. C., & Chen, P. (1984). The human factors of computer graphics interaction techniques. *IEEE Computer Graphics and Applications*, *4*(11), 13–48. doi:10.1109/MCG.1984.6429355

Ford, N., & Chen, S. Y. (2000). Individual differences, hypermedia navigation and learning: An empirical study. *Journal of Educational Multimedia and Hypermedia*, *9*, 281–312.

Galitz, W. O. (1997). *The essential guide to user interface design: An introduction to GUI design principles and techniques*. New York: John Wiley & Sons.

Garner, R., & Gillingham, M. G. (1996). *Internet Communication in Six Classrooms. Conversations Across Time, Space and Culture*. Mahwah, NJ: Erlbaum.

Granger, B. P., & Levine, E. L. (2010). The perplexing role of learner control in e-learning: Will learning and transfer benefit or suffer? *International Journal of Training and Development*, *14*(3), 180–199. doi:10.1111/j.1468-2419.2010.00351.x

Gyselinck, V., Ehrlich, M., Cornoldi, C., Beni, R., & Dubois, V. (2000). Visuospatial working memory in learning from multimedia systems. *Journal of Computer Assisted Learning*, *16*(2), 166–176. doi:10.1046/j.1365-2729.2000.00128.x

Hackos, J. T., & Redish, J. C. (1998). *User and task analysis for interface design*. New York: John Wiley & Sons.

Hannafin, M. J. (1984). Guidelines for using locus of instructional control in the design of computer-assisted instruction. *Journal of Instructional Development*, *7*(3), 6–10. doi:10.1007/BF02905753

Harasim, L. M. (1990). Online education: An environment for collaboration and intellectual amplification. In L. M. Harasim (Ed.), *Online education: perspectives on a new environment* (pp. 39–64). Praeger Publishing.

Hegarty, M., & Just, M. A. (1993). Constructing mental models of machines from text and diagrams. *Journal of Memory and Language*, *32*(6), 717–742. doi:10.1006/jmla.1993.1036

Hill, J. R., Wiley, D., Nelson, L. M., & Han, S. (2004). Exploring research on internet-based learning: From infrastructure to interactions. In D. H. Jonassen (Ed.), *The Handbook of Research on Educational Communications and Technology* (pp. 433–460). Mahwah, NJ: Lawrence Erlbaum Associates.

Hillman, D. C., Willis, D. J., & Gunawardena, C. N. (1994). Learner-interface interaction in distance education: An extension of contemporary models and strategies for practitioners. *American Journal of Distance Education*, *8*(2), 30–42. doi:10.1080/08923649409526853

Holley, C. D., Dansereau, D. F., McDonald, B. A., Garland, J. C., & Collins, K. W. (1979). Evaluation of a hierarchical mapping technique as an aid to prose processing. *Contemporary Educational Psychology*, *4*(3), 227–237. doi:10.1016/0361-476X(79)90043-2

Hu, M., & Wu, M. (2012). The effect of concept mapping on students' cognitive load. *World Transactions on Engineering and Technology Education*, *10*(2), 134–137.

Irani, T. (1998). Communication potential, information richness and attitude: A study of computer mediated communication in the ALN classroom. *ALN Magazine*, *2*, 1–12.

Jamieson, J. (1992). The cognitive styles of reflection/impulsivity and field independence/dependence and ESL success. *Modern Language Journal*, *3*(4), 491–501. doi:10.1111/j.1540-4781.1992.tb05398.x

Jiang, M., & Ting, E. (2000). A study of factors influencing students' perceived learning in a Web-based course environment. *International Journal of Educational Telecommunications*, *6*, 317–338.

Kalyuga, S., & Liu, T. C. (2015). Guest editorial: Managing cognitive load in technology-based learning environments. *Journal of Educational Technology & Society*, *18*(4), 1–8.

Keller, J. M. (1983). Motivational design of instruction. In C. M. Reigeluth (Ed.), *Instructional-design theories and models: An overview of their current status* (pp. 383–434). Hillsdale, NJ: Erlbaum.

Keller, J. M., & Suzuki, K. (1988). Application of the ARCS model to courseware design. In D. H. Jonassen (Ed.), *Instructional Designs for Microcomputer Courseware* (pp. 401–434). New York: Lawrence Erlbaum.

Keller, T., Gerjets, P., Scheiter, K., & Garsoffky, B. (2006). Information visualizations as tools for knowledge acquisition: The impact of dimensionality and color coding. *Computers in Human Behavior*, *22*(1), 43–65. doi:10.1016/j.chb.2005.01.006

Khan, B. H. (1997). *Web-based instruction*. Englewood Cliffs, NJ: Educational Technology.

Khan, B. H. (1998). Web-based instruction: An introduction. *Educational Media International*, *35*(2), 63–71. doi:10.1080/0952398980350202

Kuo, Y.-C., Walker, A., & Schroder, K. (2010, March). *Interaction and other variables as predictors of student satisfaction in online learning environments*. Paper presented at the Society for Information Technology & Teacher Education International Conference, San Diego, CA.

Kuo, Y.-C., Walker, A. E., Schroder, K. E., & Belland, B. R. (2014). Interaction, Internet self- efficacy, and selfregulated learning as predictors of student satisfaction in online education courses. *The Internet and Higher Education*, *20*, 35–50. doi:10.1016/j.iheduc.2013.10.001

Lo, J., Chan, Y., & Yeh, S. (2011). Designing an adaptive web-based learning system based on students' cognitive styles identified online. *Computers & Education*, *58*(1), 209–222. doi:10.1016/j.compedu.2011.08.018

Lohr, L. L. (2000). Designing the instructional interface. *Computers in Human Behavior*, *16*(2), 161–182. doi:10.1016/S0747-5632(99)00057-6

MacGregor, S. K. (1999). Hypermedia navigation profiles: Cognitive characteristics and information processing strategies. *Journal of Educational Computing Research*, *20*(2), 189–206. doi:10.2190/1MEC-C0W6-111H-YQ6A

Magoulas, G. D., Papanikolaou, K. A., & Grigoriadou, M. (2003). Adaptive Web-based learning: Accommodating individual differences through system's adaptation. *British Journal of Educational Technology*, *34*(4), 511–527. doi:10.1111/1467-8535.00347

Martin, A. J. (2003). Boys and motivation. *Australian Educational Researcher*, *30*(3), 43–63. doi:10.1007/BF03216797

Martin-Michiellot, S., & Mendelsohn, P. (2000). Cognitive load while learning with a graphical computer interface. *Journal of Computer Assisted Learning*, *16*(4), 284–293. doi:10.1046/j.1365-2729.2000.00141.x

Mayer, R. E. (1997). Multimedia learning: Are we asking the right questions? *Educational Psychologist*, *32*(1), 1–19. doi:10.120715326985ep3201_1

Mayer, R. E. (2003). The promise of multimedia learning: Using the same instructional design methods across different media. *Learning and Instruction*, *13*(2), 125–139. doi:10.1016/S0959-4752(02)00016-6

Mayer, R. E. (2011b). Instruction based on visualizations. In R. E. Mayer & P. A. Alexander (Eds.), *Handbook of Research on Learning and Instruction*. New York: Routledge.

Mayer, R. E., & Moreno, R. (2002). Aids to computer-based multimedia learning. *Learning and Instruction*, *12*(1), 107–119. doi:10.1016/S0959-4752(01)00018-4

Mayer, R. E., & Moreno, R. (2003). Nine ways to reduce cognitive load in multimedia learning. *Educational Psychologist, 38*(1), 43–52. doi:10.1207/S15326985EP3801_6

McCormack, C., & Jones, D. (1998). *Building a Web-based education system.* New York: Wiley.

Moallem, M., Pastore, R., & Martin, F. (2013, March). *Interaction in Online Learning: A Comparative Study on the Impact of Communication Tools on Student Learning, Motivation, Self- regulation, and Satisfaction.* Paper presented at the Society for Information Technology & Teacher Education International Conference, New Orleans, LA.

Moore, D. M., Burton, J. K., & Myers, R. J. (2004). Multiple-channel communication: The theoretical and research foundations of multimedia. In D. H. Jonassen (Ed.), *Handbook on educational communications and technology* (pp. 981–1006). Mahwah, NJ: Lawrence Erlbaum.

Moore, M. G. (1989). Editorial: Three types of interaction. *American Journal of Distance Education, 3*, 1–6.

Morrison, G. R., Ross, S. M., & Baldwin, W. (1992). Learner control of context and instructional support in learning elementary school mathematics. *Educational Technology Research and Development, 40*(1), 5–13. doi:10.1007/BF02296701

Mousavi, S. Y., Low, R., & Sweller, J. (1995). Reducing cognitive load by mixing auditory and visual presentation loads. *Journal of Educational Psychology, 87*(2), 319–334. doi:10.1037/0022-0663.87.2.319

Mullet, K., & Sano, D. (1995). *Designing visual interfaces-communication oriented techniques.* Englewood Cliffs, NJ: Prentice Hall.

Nguyen, T. (2015). The effectiveness of online learning: Beyond no significant difference and future horizons. *Journal of Online Learning and Teaching / MERLOT, 11*(2), 309.

Nielsen, J. (1995). *Multimedia and Hypertext – The Internet and Beyond.* Academic Press Inc.

Norman, D. A. (1988). *The psychology of everyday things.* New York: Basic Books Inc.

Novak, J. D. (1976). Understanding the learning process and effectiveness of teaching methods in the classroom, laboratory, and field. *Science Education, 60*(4), 493–512. doi:10.1002ce.3730600410

Oliver, R. (2017). *When Teaching Meets Learning: Design Principles and Strategies for Web-based Learning Environments that Support Knowledge Construction.* School of Communications and Multimedia. Retrieved April 10, 2017, from https://pdfs.semanticscholar.org/959c/4c063a1215cb5a99c4f6177d3e6c95b11843.pdf

Oppermann, R. (2001). User-interface design. In Handbook on Information Technologies for Education and Training (pp. 233–248). Berlin: Springer-Verlag.

Owston, R. O. (1997). The World Wide Web: A technology to enhance teaching and learning. *Educational Researcher, 26*, 27–33.

Paivio, A. (1971). *Imagery and verbal processes.* New York: Holt, Rinehart & Winston.

Papert, S. (1980). *Mindstorms: Children, computers, and powerful ideas*. New York: Basic Books.

Peslak, A. (2005). A Framework and implementation of user interface and human-computer interaction instruction. *Journal of Information Technology Education*, *4*, 189–205. doi:10.28945/272

Picciano, A. G. (2002). Beyond student perceptions: Issues of interaction, presence, and performance in an online course. *Journal of Asynchronous Learning Networks*, *6*, 21–40.

Puntambekar, S., Stylianou, A., & Hübscher, R. (2003). Improving navigation and learning in hypertext environments with navigable concept maps. *Human-Computer Interaction*, *18*(4), 395–426. doi:10.1207/S15327051HCI1804_3

Recker, M., Ram, A., Shikano, T., Li, G., & Stasko, J. (1995). Cognitive media types for multimedia information access. *Journal of Educational Multimedia and Hypermedia*, *4*, 183–210.

Rhode, J. F. (2009). Interaction equivalency in self-paced online learning environments: An exploration of learner preferences. *International Review of Research in Open and Distance Learning*, *10*(1), 1–23. doi:10.19173/irrodl.v10i1.603

Richardson, J., & Ting, E. (1999). *Making the most of interaction: What instructors do that most affect students' perceptions of their learning*. Paper presented at the 5th International Conference on Asynchronous Learning, College Park, MD.

Riding, R. J., & Rayner, S. (1998). *Cognitive styles and learning strategies: Understanding style differences in learning and behaviour*. London: David Fulton.

Riel, M. (1996). The Internet: A land to settle rather than an ocean to surf. *Telecommunications in Education News*, *7*, 10–17.

Ruttun, R. D., & Macredie, R. D. (2011). The effects of individual differences and visual instructional aids on disorientation, learning performance and attitudes in a Hypermedia Learning System. *Computers in Human Behavior*, *28*(6), 2182–2198. doi:10.1016/j.chb.2012.06.026

Schnackenberg, H. L., & Hilliard, A. W. (1998, February). *Learner ability and learner control: A 10 year literature review 1987-1997*. Paper presented at the annual meeting of the Association for Educational Communications and Technology, St. Louis, MO.

Schnotz, W., & Rasch, T. (2005). Enabling, facilitating, and inhibiting effects of animations in multimedia learning: Why reduction of cognitive load can have negative results on learning. *Educational Technology Research and Development*, *53*(3), 47–58. doi:10.1007/BF02504797

Seal, K. C., & Przasnyski, Z. H. (2001). Using the World Wide Web for teaching improvement. *Computers & Education*, *36*(1), 33–40. doi:10.1016/S0360-1315(00)00049-X

Shackelford, J., & Maxwellm, M. (2012). Contribution of Learner–Instructor Interaction to Sense of Community in Graduate Online Education. *Journal of Online Learning and Teaching / MERLOT*, *8*(4), 248–260.

Shah, P., & Freedman, E. (2003). Visuospatial thinking in e-learning. *Journal of Educational Computing Research*, *29*(3), 315–324. doi:10.2190/QYVJ-Q59L-VE7C-EHUV

Sher, A. (2009). Assessing the relationship of student-instructor and student-student interaction to student learning and satisfaction in Web-based online learning environment. *Journal of Interactive Online Learning*, *8*(2), 102–120.

Shyu, H. S., & Brown, S. W. (1992). Learner control versus program control in interactive videodisc instruction: What are the effects in procedural learning? *International Journal of Instructional Media*, *19*, 85–96.

Sinha, N., Khreisat, L., & Sharma, K. (2009). Learner-Interface Interaction for TechnologyEnhanced Active Learning. *Innovate: Journal of Online Education.*, *5*(3), 1–7.

Sitzmann, T., Wisher, R., Stewart, D., & Kraiger, K. (2005). Moderators of the effectiveness of web-based instruction. In *20th Annual Conference on Distance Teaching and Learning* (p. 6). The Board of Regents of the University of Wisconsin System.

Snow, E. R. (1980). Aptitude, learner control, and adaptive instruction. *Educational Psychologist*, *15*(3), 151–158. doi:10.1080/00461528009529223

Sun, J., & Hsu, Y. (2013). Effect of interactivity on learner perceptions in Web-based instruction. *Computers in Human Behavior*, *29*(1), 171–184. doi:10.1016/j.chb.2012.08.002

Sutton, L. A. (2001). The principle of vicarious interaction in computer-mediated communications. *International Journal of Educational Telecommunications*, *7*, 223–242.

Swan, K. (2005). A constructivist model for thinking about learning online. In J. Bourne & J. C. Moore (Eds.), *Elements of Quality Online Education: Engaging Communities*. Needham, MA: Sloan-C.

Swan, K., Shea, P., Fredericksen, E., Pickett, A., Pelz, W., & Maher, G. (2000). Building knowledge building communities: Consistency, contact and communication in the virtual classroom. *Journal of Educational Computing Research*, *23*(4), 389–413. doi:10.2190/W4G6-HY52-57P1-PPNE

Sweller, J. (1999). *Instructional design in technical areas*. Camberwell, Australia: Australian Council for Educational Research.

Sweller, J., Chandler, P., Tierney, P., & Cooper, G. (1990). Cognitive load as a factor in the structuring of technical material. *Journal of Experimental Psychology. General*, *119*(2), 176–192. doi:10.1037/0096-3445.119.2.176

Tarmizi, R. A., & Sweller, J. (1988). Guidance during mathematical problem-solving. *Journal of Educational Psychology*, *80*(4), 424–436. doi:10.1037/0022-0663.80.4.424

Tergan, S. O. (2003). Managing knowledge with computer-based mapping tools. In D. Lassner & C. M. Naught (Eds.), *Proceedings of the ed-media 2003 world conference on educational multimedia, hypermedia & telecommunication* (pp. 2514-2517). Honolulu, HI: University of Honolulu.

Tindall-Ford, S., Chandler, P., & Sweller, J. (1997). When two sensory modes are better than one. *Journal of Experimental Psychology. Applied*, *3*(4), 257–287. doi:10.1037/1076-898X.3.4.257

Van Merrienboer, J. J. G., & Sweller, J. (2005). Cognitive load theory and complex learning: Recent developments and future directions. *Educational Psychology Review*, *17*(2), 147–177. doi:10.100710648-005-3951-0

Vygotsky, L. S. (1978). *Mind in Society*. Cambridge, MA: Harvard University Press.

Wang, L., & Beasley, W. (2002). Effects of learner control and hypermedia preference on cyber-students performance in a Web-based learning environment. *Journal of Educational Multimedia and Hypermedia*, *11*, 71–91.

Wenger, E., McDermott, R., & Snyder, W. (2002). *Cultivating communities of practice: A guide to managing knowledge*. Cambridge, MA: Harvard Business School Press.

Williams, M. E. (2001). *The effects of conceptual model provision and cognitive style on problem- solving performance of learners engaged in an exploratory learning environment* (Doctoral Dissertation). University of Oklahoma.

Zhang, C., & Fulford, S. (1994). Are interaction time and psychological interactivity the same thing in the distance learning television classroom? *Educational Technology*, *34*, 58–64.

Zirkin, B., & Sumler, D. (1995). Interactive or non-interactive? That is the question! An annotated bibliography. *Journal of Distance Education*, *10*, 95–112.

Chapter 10
Student Learning and Engagement in a Blended Environment:
A Mixed Methods Study

Lijia Lin
East China Normal University, China

ABSTRACT

The chapter investigated students' behavioral, emotional, and cognitive engagement, as well as their learning in a blended environment. A convergent mixed methods research design was used in which quantitative data (face-to-face attendance, online system login, and survey) were collected from 71 undergraduate students, and qualitative data (focus group interview) were collected from six of these students. These data were further analyzed and integrated. The quantitative results showed that students' online login, the behavioral engagement indicator, had a positive impact on their learning, which was supported by qualitative findings. Further analysis revealed the mixture of students' engagement, such as confusion vs. interesting feelings to online discussions and frustration vs. not much effort using the online system.

INTRODUCTION

Blended learning emerged with the uprising of online learning. This form of learning integrates both online learning and face-to-face learning, and is intended to overcome the weaknesses of online learning and face-to-face learning (Osguthorpe & Graham, 2003). It is believed that blended learning has the potential to transform higher education, as it can engage learners in the learning community (Garrison & Kanuka, 2004; Rovai & Jordan, 2004). Some practical guidelines have been proposed (Kim, Baylen, Leh, & Lin, 2015), and some higher education institutions have implemented blended learning at various stages (Graham, Woodfield, & Harrison, 2013). The current study fills in the existing research gap by utilizing mixed methods approach to directly address students' engagement and learning in a blended environment

DOI: 10.4018/978-1-5225-4206-3.ch010

Blended Learning

Blended learning has shown its pedagogical values despite the fact that it still faces long-standing and newly emerged challenges (Kim et al., 2015). For the past several decades, scholars and educators have been conducting research in order to shed lights on issues regarding research and practice of blended learning. Drysdale, Graham, Spring and Halverson (2013) and Halverson et al. (2014) conducted thematic analysis on journal articles, book chapters, and books, as well as graduate theses and dissertations with respect to blended learning since 2000. They found that blended learning research covers a wide range of topics including instructional design, learner disposition, learning outcomes, comparison of different modes, technology, and interaction. Moreover, their analysis revealed that there is a variety of theoretical models in the existing blended learning literature. Some theories and models are used to guide design (e.g., Kerres & De Witt, 2003), some are used as an evaluation tool or instructional model (e.g., Lewis & Orton, 2006; Laurillard, 2007), and some explore specific type of blended learning (e.g., Jung & Suzuki, 2006). As a relatively new form of learning, blended learning is not inferior to other two forms of learning—online learning and traditional face-to-face learning. The results of a meta-analysis showed that blended learning was not significantly different from synchronous distance education or asynchronous distance education in terms of achievement (Bernard, Abrami, Borokhovski, Wade, Tamim, Surkes, & Bethel, 2009). Further meta-analysis revealed that blended learning was actually superior to classroom instruction (Bernard, Borokhovski, Schmid, Tamim, & Abrami, 2014). There are also research studies reported in the literature that specifically demonstrate blended learning's pedagogical values by comparing it to online learning and face-to-face learning (Al-Qahtani & Higginst, 2013; Ginns, Ellis, 2007; Olapiriyakul, & Scher, 2006; Rovai & Jordan, 2004; Tuckman, 2002). For instance, Al-Qahtani and Higginst (2013) compared university students' achievement in an Islamic Culture course. These students were randomly assigned into three conditions—learning from face-to-face format, learning online via Moodle, or learning via a blended format. The results showed that participating learners in the blended learning condition had significantly higher achievement scores than their counterparts in the face-to-face learning condition and the online learning condition. Rovai and Jordan (2004) also compared students' sense of community in online, face-to-face and blended settings and found similar results: students in the blended learning setting had the highest scores on two variables concerning the sense of community—perceived connectedness and perceived learning.

In addition to comparing different formats of learning, researchers also empirically studied potential factors that influence learning in blended environments. The results of some research indicate that students' perceived usefulness (Lin & Wang, 2012), students' motivation (Xie & Ke, 2010), and interaction with the online system (Lee, Yeh, Kung, & Hsu, 2007; Wei, Peng, & Chou, 2015) have significant impacts on their learning outcomes. For instance, Wei et al. (2015) investigated the relationship between learners' performance and their behaviors of interaction with an e-learning system by collecting data from students who were enrolled in a general-education asynchronous online course in Taiwan. The results of their research revealed that those learners' number of logins and the number of postings in discussion board positively impacted their online discussion quality. Also, these two types of behaviors, as well as the number of reading online learning materials, were positive predictors of students' achievement.

Engagement: Conceptualization and Measurement

One issue that is crucial to students' learning in blended environments is engagement. Based on a thematic analysis of the decade-ago publications in blended learning, Halverson, Graham, Spring, Drysdale and Henrie (2014) found that approximately half of their reviewed publications mentioned the term *engagement*. Their findings also revealed that, despite the popular use of the term, very rarely had studies directly addressed engagement in blended learning.

The current literature with respect to engagement is quite diverse and spans multiple disciplines and theories (Boekaerts, 2016; Eccles, 2016). This status quo has led some scholars to theorize a multidimensional model of engagement (Fredricks, 2011; Fredicks, Blumenfeld, & Paris, 2004; Fredicks, Filsecker, Lawson, 2016). According to this theoretical model, engagement is multi-facets, which may include behavioral, emotional and cognitive aspects (Fredricks & McColskey, 2012; Sinatra, Heddy, & Lombardi, 2015). According to Fredicks et al. (2004), behavioral engagement emphasizes participation, persistence and involvement in academic activities. Emotional engagement focuses on the positive and negative reactions to peers, teachers and schools, as well as values and appreciation of learning outcomes. In terms of cognitive engagement, it encompasses learner's investment of effort to understand and comprehend.

There are a variety of approaches for measuring engagement, including students' self-report, log files, and interviews. Self-report measures have the advantages of being easy to implement with low cost (Fredricks & McColskey, 2012), being able to assess constructs that are not directly observable by researchers (Appleton, Christenson, Kim, & Reschly, 2006), and preventing disruptions of the learning flow in the classroom (Sinatra et al., 2015). However, self-report measures are unable to capture the engagement process (Azevedo, 2015; Greene, 2015). Also, due to the diverse conceptualizations and theoretical perspectives of engagement, there are substantial variations of self-report measures, some being general items and the other being context-specific items (Fredricks & McColskey, 2012; Greene, 2015). Furthermore, researchers need to make inferences about students' engagement from self-report measures, which could result in problematic data interpretation (Gobert, Baker, & Wixon, 2015). Compared to subjective measures, log files from electronic learning management systems can provide more objective and contextual information, such as how many times a student will log into the system. Although researchers have been focusing on log files for different purposes, rarely have they utilized these files to study engagement or disengagement. Only recently did Gobert, Baker and Wixon (2015) develop algorithms to detect disengagement in an online inquiry science learning environment. Therefore, other approaches, such as interviews, have their own advantages. Researchers can use the interview technique to obtain in-depth information about why students engage or disengage in certain activities, why students differ in their engagement behaviors, and the contextual factors that could lead to students' engagement or disengagement (Fredricks & McColskey, 2012). For instance, Fredricks et al. (2016) interviewed 106 students and 34 teachers to explore engagement and disengagement in science, technology, engineering, and mathematics (STEM). Their results revealed not only behavioral, emotional, and cognitive facets of engagement, but also some additional engagement indicators. However, interview data are subject to bias from the interviewer and may suffer from reliability and validity issues. Taken into account the fact that each measurement approach has its own pros and cons, a number of researchers have recommended using multiple methods to measure engagement (Fredricks & McColskey, 2012; Gobert et al., 2015; Greene, 2015).

Overview of the Study

As engagement has rarely been addressed in blended learning (Halverson, Graham, Spring, Drysdale, & Henrie, 2014), it is necessary to fill the existing gap by further investigate engagement in this specific context. The purpose of the current study was to investigate student learning and engagement in a blended learning environment from the lens of mixed methods. The overwhelming majority of the empirical studies investigating engagement have used purely quantitative or qualitative methods. Except Fredricks et al. (2016), rarely did researchers use the mixed methods approach, despite the fact that there tends to be a consensus on the multi-dimensionality of engagement and researchers are becoming aware the pros and cons of the existing measurement tools. In the current study, the researcher utilized mixed methods to collect, analyze and integrate multiple data sources in order to obtain a full picture of students' engagement in the blended learning context.

Mixed methods research design has existed in various forms throughout social science and behavior research disciplines for the past few decades. Mixed methods can be defined in various ways. Tashakkori and Creswell (2007) have explained mixed methods research as "research in which the investigator collects and analyzes data, integrates the findings, and draws inferences in a single study or a program of inquiry." More recently, this form of inquiry has gained popularity and in tandem has earned praiseworthy titles such as, "the third methodological movement," and "third research paradigm" (Johnson & Onwuegbuzie, 2004; Tashakkori & Teddlie, 2003). A convergent mixed methods design was used in the current study, in which both quantitative and qualitative data were collected, analyzed and finally integrated.

The study addressed the following research questions by collecting self-report data, interview data, class attendance records, and online system log files:

1. Do students' behavioral, emotional and cognitive engagement impact their learning?
2. From the students' perspective, what are the factors that potentially contribute to their learning and engagement?

METHOD

Participants and Design

A total of 71 undergraduate students (60 females and 11 males) voluntarily participated in the study. All of them were from the School of Psychology in a public university in Shanghai. They were enrolled in a semester-long statistics course as part of their required program of study. Very few of them (i.e., four individuals) had prior experience of using the Sakai learning management system or similar systems before.

The study used a convergent mixed methods design, in which quantitative and qualitative data were collected and analyzed separately and compared for convergence and differences (Creswell & Clark, 2011).

Context and Procedure

The study was conducted in the spring semester in an undergraduate statistic course, which was offered to undergraduate psychology-major students in a public university in Shanghai. The Sakai learning management system was used for the course (see Figure 1). Students had access to a variety of learning resources hosted in the Sakai system, including PowerPoint slides, static and animated visualizations, video demonstrations, and Word documents. The course was offered in a blended format. Each week students attended lectures in a face-to-face format. In the face-to-face class, the instructor explained statistical concepts using PowerPoint slides and visuals, and allocated time for responding to students' questions emerged in solving the practice problems. For the online part, students were required to watch the online video demos showing procedures of how to use SPSS to conduct certain statistical analysis, such as the independent samples *t* test. They were also instructed to solve practice problems that were contained in those Word documents in the Sakai system, and to discuss with their peers online in the Sakai's discussion forum. The online activities were asynchronous, meaning students had the choice of when to study online. However, they were expected to study online each week. In addition to practice problems, there were a mid-term project and two assignments, as well as a final exam. The instructor provided assignment links for students to submit their assignments to Sakai. But students could also submit assignments via the drop box in Sakai.

At the end of the semester, the researcher administered the online survey via SoJump, an online survey tool, and conducted a focus group interview with selected students. The study was approved by the university's Institutional Review Board, and consent for participation in a research study was obtained from every student who was enrolled in the course.

Measures and Data Sources

Behavioral engagement, emotional engagement and cognitive engagement were measured using a variety of methods (see Table 1). Behavioral engagement was measured through students' attendance records of the face-to-face classes and their records of online login. The researcher obtained these data

Figure 1. The Sakai course management system used in the study

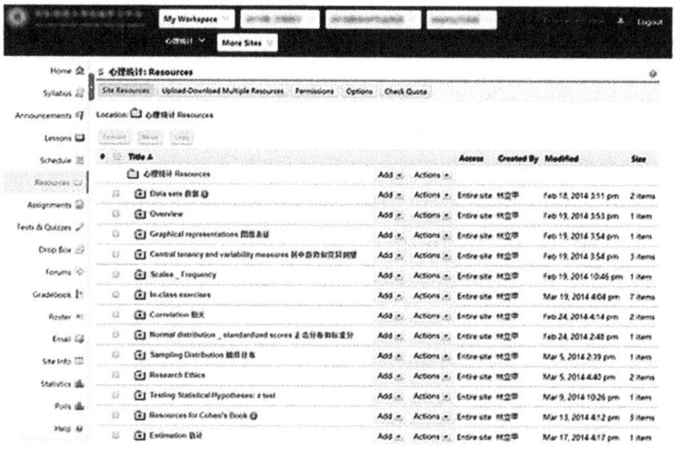

Table 1. Types of engagement and data sources

Type of Engagement	Data Sources	Quantitative or Qualitative
Behavioral engagement	Attendance in face-to-face classes	Quantitative
	Login to the Sakai online system	Quantitative
Emotional engagement	Intrinsic motivation items	Quantitative
	Interview	Qualitative
Cognitive engagement	Effort item	Quantitative
	Interview	Qualitative

from the course instructor's record sheet and log files. The instructor marked each student's attendance as "attended" or "not attended" from Week 2 to Week 11 in a 16-week-long semester. Therefore, the researcher selected students' login data from the log files during that period.

Emotional engagement was measured both quantitatively (via survey) and qualitatively (via interview). The survey was distributed online at the end of the semester to all of the students enrolled. It included six self-report engagement items that were implemented on a 7-point Likert scale (see Table 2), along with two demographic items (gender and prior experience with learning management systems). These engagement items were adapted from intrinsic motivation measures that were used in the previous research (Lin, Atkinson, Savenye, & Nelson, 2016). Negatively worded items were reverse-scored so that higher scores reflect more positive attitude. The Cronbach's alpha for these items was .76.

The interview was conducted at the end of the semester in a focus group format. The researcher selected six enrolled students and conducted a semi-structural interview with this focus group. Three of these six students were high achievers and the remaining three were low achievers according to their final exam scores. The interview lasted approximately 40 minutes and permission was obtained from all interviewees to have the whole process audio recorded. The questions serving as the interview guidelines included:

- What do you like most about this course?
- What do you like least about the course?
- What factors do you think influence your learning?

Table 2. Self-report measures of engagement

	Item	Mean (Standard Deviation)
Emotional Engagement	I enjoyed the course's blended format very much.	4.59 (1.25)
	I believe that it was very interesting to interact with my classmates in both face-to-face and online formats.	4.55 1.35)
	I believe that the course's blended format had value to me.	4.79 (1.16)
	I believe that I was able to use the Sakai online system very well.	5.0 1.22)
	I felt very anxious about the course's blended format. (R)	5.14 (1.52)
	I believe that the blended course format was helpful for me to learn statistical concepts, techniques and software.	5.00 (1.37)
Cognitive Engagement	I put a lot of effort learning how to use the online system. (R)	5.37 (1.14)

Note. R = reverse coded.

Cognitive engagement was measured via a self-report item, which was adapted from the mental effort item in the cognitive load literature (Paas & van Merrienboer, 1994). This item was also reverse coded so that higher scores reflect more positive attitude.

Students' learning was measured by a paper-based final exam. This two-hour exam was administered in a face-to-face format and it tested both conceptual and procedural knowledge. The exam score had a maximum of 100 points with no partial credit.

RESULTS

Quantitative Results

Each student's emotional engagement was computed by averaging their responses on the six self-report items. Then, a regression analysis was conducted to assess the impact of emotional engagement, behavioral engagement (face-to-face attendance and online system login) and cognitive engagement (effort) on learning (final exam), controlling for the effects of gender and prior experience with online learning management systems. The results revealed that the linear regression model can account for approximately 14% of the variance of cognitive engagement, adjusted $R^2 = .10$. But the model was not significant, $F(6, 64) = 1.73, p = .13$. Students' login significantly predicted their learning, $t(64) = 2.24, p = .03, \beta = .26$, indicating that more frequent login tended to result in higher final exam scores. The impact of other predictors were non-significant, all $ps > .21$. Bivariate correlations are presented in Table 3.

Qualitative Results

Audio recordings collected from the focus group interview were transcribed into the verbal format. Thematic analysis was conducted on the qualitative transcripts and three themes emerged in the data analysis. All example responses reported below were translated from Chinese.

Table 3. Bivariate correlation matrix

	Gender	Prior Experience	Attendance	Login	Emotional Engagement	Cognitive Engagement	Final Exam
Gender	1.00						
Prior Experience	-.04	1.00					
Attendance	-.14	.07	1.00				
Login	-.05	.12	.08	1.00			
Emotional Engagement	.10	.12	.06	.10	1.00		
Cognitive Engagement	-.11	-.03	-.02	.07	.13	1.00	
Final Exam	-.12	.15	-.06	.29*	.17	.05	1.00

Note. * indicates $p < .05$.

The Use of the Online Learning System Was Helpful

All interviewed students mentioned that they benefited from the use of the Sakai online system. In addition, some of them mentioned specific features of the online system that they thought were helpful for their learning. For example:

Those videos are very helpful for learning SPSS. I can also get clear instructions about homework and assignments, as well as each deadline for homework submission.

I find it very easy to learn SPSS by watching those videos. Also, submitting my homework through the online system is very convenient.

It is quite helpful to look at the online resources after the lecture.

Confusion About Online Discussion

The interviewed students expressed confusion about the online discussion activity. Neither did they understand the purpose of the online discussion, nor were they clear about what should be discussed. Example responses were:

It seems that there is no use for the discussion forum.

No need for online discussion because the teacher will talk about it in class.

Technological Issues

Although all students enrolled in the course had access to the internet, technological difficulties seem to become the barriers for the blended learning format. These difficulties included internet issues and the use of the online system. Example responses were:

Sometimes the internet speed influences learning online.

I didn't know where to upload my assignment at first. It was frustrating!

Integration of Quantitative and Qualitative Results

A close examination of both the quantitative and qualitative data revealed convergent and divergent results about students' learning and engagement (see Table 4).

One of the themes revealed from the qualitative analysis was that the students found the online system useful, which is consistent with the quantitative results. One of the survey items asked students to rate the statement "I believe that the blended course format was helpful for me to learn statistical concepts, techniques and software." on the 7-point Likert scale. Students' responses (*Mean* = 5.00, *SD* = 1.37) also implied the usefulness of the online system and the blended learning format. Their perceived use-

Table 4. Integration of quantitative and qualitative results

	Quantitative Results	Qualitative Results
Converged Results	Perceived usefulness of the blended learning format. Frequent login to the online system led to the increase of learning.	The use of the online system was useful. Video demos were helpful for learning software to conduct statistical analysis.
Divergent Results	Students perceived the interaction in both face-to-face and online formats quite interesting.	Students had confusions about online discussion activities.
	Students did not put much effort using the online system.	Students felt frustrated uploading their assignments in the online system.

fulness could lead to their frequent login to the online system and the increase of their learning, which was demonstrated in the regression analysis. Moreover, the qualitative data further pointed out some specific features of the online system that turned out to be helpful for students and led them to frequently use the system, such as the video demonstrations that showed them step-by-step how to use software of conduct statistical analysis.

Despite the convergence of the quantitative and qualitative analysis, a couple of results showed somewhat mixed findings. First, one of the quantitative emotional engagement items asked students to rate whether "it was very interesting to interact with my classmates in both face-to-face and online formats." The mean ratings of this item was 4.55 on a 7-point Likert scale with a standard deviation (SD) of 1.25, suggesting that students perceived the interaction with their peers was quite interesting in both face-to-face and online formats. However, qualitative analysis indicated that students had confusions about the online discussion activities, which was one way for students to interact online. To put these results in the engagement framework, the quantitative results indicated that students were emotionally engaged in a positive manner, whereas the qualitative results implied that they were negatively engaged in some online activities. This mixture of both positive and negative engagement was also shown from the results related to the use of the online system. The quantitative survey asked whether students "put a lot of effort learning how to use the online system." The mean rating of this reversely coded item was 5.37 with a SD of 1.14, a piece of evidence showing the easy use of the online system. In addition, students' ratings on another item "I was able to use the Sakai online system very well" were also quite high with a mean of 5.00 and a SD of 1.22. However, qualitative analysis indicated students' frustration when using the system to upload their assignments.

CONCLUSION AND DISCUSSION

There has been ambiguity in terms of the conceptualization of engagement (Boekaerts, 2016). Decades of research shows that engagement is a multi-dimensional construct that incorporates behavioral, emotional and cognitive engagement (Fredricks et al., 2004; Fredricks et al., 2016). Researchers recently have pointed out the need for using diverse tools to measure engagement (Gobert et al., 2015; Greene, 2015), which leads to this mixed methods study that investigated engagement using a variety of data sources to reflect behavioral, emotional and cognitive engagement.

Do Students' Behavioral, Emotional and Cognitive Engagement Impact Their Learning?

The quantitative analysis revealed that only behavioral engagement, particularly the students' login to the online system, had a positive impact on learning, which is consistent with the findings in the literature (e.g., Wei et al., 2015). Integrating the qualitative results with this quantitative finding provides one plausible explanation: students who enrolled in this statistics course found resources hosted in the online system useful for their study, which could result in their increased login behaviors that lead to their enhanced learning. Another behavioral engagement indicator—the face-to-face class attendance—was not a significant predictor. This is probably due to the lack of variability of this variable (i.e., students attended almost every face-to-face class). Taken into account the divergent quantitative and qualitative results that some students were positively engaged and some others were negatively engaged, it is not surprising to find in the regression analysis that emotional engagement and cognitive engagement did not have significant impacts on learning. Due to some technological issues, especially those issues related to the Sakai online system, at least some students did not enjoy using the system or find it useful. Rather, they were experiencing frustrations and might invest a substantial amount of effort fixing the technological issues. This negative emotional engagement could hurt students' motivation (Xie & Ke, 2010) and further prevent them from taking advantage of the resources and useful features of the online system. Nevertheless, confusion could benefit learning (D'Mello, Lehman, Pekrun, & Grasser, 2015). Therefore, it is unclear about the role and impact of students' confusion revealed in the study. Future research could further look into this issue.

From the Students' Perspective, What Are the Factors That Potentially Contribute to Their Learning and Engagement?

Based on the analysis, the main factors could be frequent use to the online system in blended learning environment, easy use of the system, and easy access to technical support. It is of note that the online presence of teachers or instructors did not emerge as a factor from the data analysis. In online learning, teaching presence has shown a significant impact on students' learning and engagement (Zhang, Lin, Zhan, & Ren, 2016). This could be the unique characteristic of blended learning: course instructors do not need to maintain a substantial level of presence online, as they have the opportunity to be physically present in the face-to-face settings. According to the analysis, even students' online activities could be reduced if they have sufficient time to meet in the face-to-face settings (e.g., once a week in the current study). This is different from the findings in the literature (Wei et al., 2015) that needs researchers' further attention.

This study has both methodological values and substantive implications. The use of the convergent mixed methods design is an attempt to investigate engagement in blended learning from multiple data sources, which rarely have been used by sustentative researchers. This study is a starting point for further research that utilizes mixed methods in blended learning research and engagement research. This study is also an example to show Chinese students' learning and engagement, which is rare in the literature. Moreover, the integration of quantitative and qualitative data enables stronger interpretation and more convincing inferences from the results than pure quantitative or qualitative research methods.

This study also bears limitations. Students' frequent login could be due to the novelty effect, because the majority of students did not have the prior experience of blended learning or using the online learning management systems. However, the study did not incorporate any measures to account for the novelty effect. Another limitation is that the sample size was relatively small, as these students were enrolled in one course in one semester. Future research could consider comparing data from two semesters.

REFERENCES

Al-Qahtani, A. A. Y., & Higginst, S. E. (2013). Effects of traditional, blended and e-learning on students' achievement in higher education. *Journal of Computer Assisted Learning*, *29*(3), 220–234. doi:10.1111/j.1365-2729.2012.00490.x

Appleton, J. J., Christenson, S. L., Kim, D., & Reschly, A. L. (2006). Measuring cognitive and psychological engagement: Validation of the Student Engagement Instrument. *Journal of School Psychology*, *44*, 427–445. doi: .2006.04.00210.1016/j.jsp

Azevedo, R. (2015). Defining and measuring engagement and learning in science: Conceptual, theoretical, methodological, and analytical issues. *Educational Psychologist*, *50*(1), 84–94. doi:10.1080/00461520.2015.1004069

Bernard, R. M., Abrami, P. C., Borokhovski, E., Wade, C. A., Tamim, R. M., Surkes, M. A., & Bethel, E. C. (2009). A meta-analysis of three types of interaction treatments in distance education. *Review of Educational Research*, *79*(3), 1243–1289. doi:10.3102/0034654309333844

Bernard, R. M., Borokhovski, E., Schmid, R. F., Tamim, R. M., & Abrami, P. C. (2014). A meta-analysis of blended learning and technology use in higher education: From the general to the applied. *Journal of Computing in Higher Education*, *26*(1), 87–122. doi:10.100712528-013-9077-3

Boekaerts, M. (2016). Engagement as an inherent aspect of the learning process. *Learning and Instruction*, *43*, 65–83. doi:10.1016/j.learninstruc.2016.02.001

Campbell, A. J. (2007). Always have a plan B: student response to an e-learning program under challenging conditions in China. *Proceedings of E-Learn 2007, World Conference on e-learning in Corporate Government, Healthcare and Higher Education*, 689-695.

Chen, P. S. D., Lambert, A. D., & Guidry, K. R. (2010). Engaging online learners: The impact of Web-based learning technology on college student engagement. *Computers & Education*, *54*(4), 1222–1232. doi:10.1016/j.compedu.2009.11.008

Creswell, J. W., & Plano-Clark, V. L. (2010). *Designing and conducting mixed methods research*. Thousand Oaks, CA: Sage.

D'Mello, S., Lehman, B., Pekrun, R., & Grasser, A. (2015). Confusion can be beneficial for learning. *Learning and Instruction*, *29*, 153–170. doi:10.1016/j.learninstruc.2012.05.003

Doymus, K. (2008). Teaching chemical equilibrium with the jigsaw technique. *Research in Science Education*, *38*(2), 249–260. doi:10.100711165-007-9047-8

Drysdale, J. S., Graham, C. R., Spring, K. J., & Halverson, L. R. (2013). An analysis of research trends in dissertations and theses studying blended learning. *The Internet and Higher Education*, *2*(17), 90–100. doi:10.1016/j.iheduc.2012.11.003

Eccles, J. (2016). Engagement: Where to next? *Learning and Instruction*, *43*, 71–75. doi:10.1016/j.learninstruc.2016.02.003

Fredicks, J. A., Blumenfeld, P. C., & Paris, A. H. (2004). School engagement: Potential of the concept, state of the evidence. *Review of Educational Research*, *74*(1), 59–109. doi:10.3102/00346543074001059

Fredicks, J. A., Filsecker, M., & Lawson, M. A. (2016). Student engagement, context, and adjustment: Addressing definitional, measurement, and methodological issues. *Learning and Instruction*, *43*, 1–4. doi:10.1016/j.learninstruc.2016.02.002

Fredricks, J. A. (2011). Engagement in school and out-of-school contexts: A multidimensional view of engagement. *Theory into Practice*, *50*(4), 327–335. doi:10.1080/00405841.2011.607401

Fredricks, J. A., & McColskey, W. (2012). The measurement of student engagement: a comparative analysis of various methods and student self-report instruments. In S. Christenson, A. L. Reschy, & C. Wylie (Eds.), *Handbook of research on student engagement* (pp. 319–339). New York: Springer. doi:10.1007/978-1-4614-2018-7_37

Fredricks, J. A., Wang, M., Schall, J., Hokfkens, T., Parr, A., & Snug, H. (2016). Using qualitative methods to develop a measure of math and science engagement. *Learning and Instruction*, *43*, 5–15. doi:10.1016/j.learninstruc.2016.01.009

Garrison, D. R., Anderson, T., & Archer, W. (2001). Critical thinking, cognitive presence, and computer conferencing in distance education. *American Journal of Distance Education*, *15*(1), 7–23. doi:10.1080/08923640109527071

Garrison, D. R., & Kanuka, H. (2004). Blended learning: Uncovering its transformative potential in higher education. *The Internet and Higher Education*, *7*(2), 95–105. doi:10.1016/j.iheduc.2004.02.001

Giacumo, L. A., Savenye, W., & Smith, N. (2012). Facilitation prompts and rubrics on higher-order thinking skill performance found in undergraduate asynchronous discussion boards. *British Journal of Educational Technology*, *44*(5), 774–794. doi:10.1111/j.1467-8535.2012.01355.x

Ginns, P., & Ellis, R. (2007). Quality in blended learning: Exploring the relationships between on-line and face-to-face teaching and learning. *The Internet and Higher Education*, *10*(1), 53–64. doi:10.1016/j.iheduc.2006.10.003

Gobert, J. D., Baker, R. S., & Wixon, M. B. (2015). Operationalizing and detecting disengagement within online science microworlds. *Educational Psychologist*, *50*(1), 43–57. doi:10.1080/00461520.2014.999919

Graham, C. R., Woodfield, W. W., & Harrison, J. B. (2013). A framework for institutional adoption and implementation of blended learning in higher education. *The Internet and Higher Education*, *18*, 4–14. doi:10.1016/j.iheduc.2012.09.003

Greene, B. A. (2015). Measuring cognitive engagement with selfreport scales: Reflections from over 20 years of research. *Educational Psychologist*, *50*(1), 14–30. doi:10.1080/00461520.2014.989230

Halverson, L. R., Graham, C. R., Spring, K. J., Drysdale, J. S., & Henrie, C. R. (2014). A thematic analysis of the most highly cited scholarship in the first decade of blended learning research. *The Internet and Higher Education*, *20*, 20–34. doi:10.1016/j.iheduc.2013.09.004

Hung, M.-L., & Chou, C. (2015). Students' perceptions of instructors' roles in blended and online learning environments: A comparative study. *Computers & Education*, *81*, 315–325. doi:10.1016/j.compedu.2014.10.022

Johnson, R. B., & Onwuegbuzie, A. J. (2004). Mixed methods research: A research paradigm whose time has come. *Educational Researcher*, *33*(7), 14–26. doi:10.3102/0013189X033007014

Jung, I., & Suzuki, K. (2006). Blended learning in Japan and its application in liberal arts education. In C. J. Bonk & C. R. Graham (Eds.), *The handbook of blended learning: Global perspectives, local designs* (pp. 267–280). San Francisco, CA: Pfeiffer.

Kerres, M., & De Witt, C. (2003). A didactical framework for the design of blended learning. *Journal of Educational Media*, *28*(2), 101–113. doi:10.1080/1358165032000165653

Kim, J. H., Baylen, D., Leh, A., & Lin, L. (2015). Blended learning in teacher education: Uncovering its transformative potential for teacher preparation programs. In N. P. Ololube & P. J. Kpolovie (Eds.), Enhancing Teacher Education with Advanced Instructional Technologies. Hershey, PA: IGI Global.

Laird, N. T. F., & Kuh, G. D. (2005). Student experiences with information technology and their relationship to other aspects of student engagement. *Research in Higher Education*, *46*(2), 211–233. doi:10.100711162-004-1600-y

Laurillard, D. (2007). Modelling benefits-oriented costs for technology enhanced learning. *Higher Education*, *54*(1), 21–39. doi:10.100710734-006-9044-2

Lee, C.-H., Yeh, D., Kung, R. J., & Hsu, C.-S. (2007). The Influences of learning portfolios and attitudes on learning effects in blended e-learning for mathematics. *Journal of Educational Computing Research*, *37*(4), 331–350. doi:10.2190/EC.37.4.a

Lewis, N. J., & Orton, P. Z. (2006). Blending learning for business impact: IBM's case for learning success. In C. J. Bonk & C. R. Graham (Eds.), *The handbook of blended learning: Global perspectives, local designs* (pp. 61–75). San Francisco, CA: Pfeiffer.

Lin, L., Atkinson, R. K., Savenye, W. C., & Nelson, B. C. (2016). The effects of visual cues and self-explanation prompts: Empirical evidence in a multimedia environment. *Interactive Learning Environments*, *24*(4), 799–813. doi:10.1080/10494820.2014.924531

Lin, W., & Wang, C.-H. (2012). Antecedences to continued intentions of adopting e-learning system in blended learning instruction: A contingency framework based on models of information system success and task-technology fit. *Computers & Education*, *58*(1), 88–99. doi:10.1016/j.compedu.2011.07.008

Olapiriyakul, K., & Scher, J. M. (2006). A guide to establishing hybrid learning courses: Employing information technology to create a new learning experience, and a case study. *The Internet and Higher Education*, *9*(4), 287–301. doi:10.1016/j.iheduc.2006.08.001

Osguthorpe, R. T., & Graham, C. R. (2003). Blended learning environments: Definitions and Directions. *The Quarterly Review of Distance Education*, *4*, 227–233.

Paas, F. G. W. C., van Merrienboer, J. J. G., & Adam, J. J. (1994). Measurement of cognitive load in instructional research. *Perceptual and Motor Skills*, *79*(1), 419–430. doi:10.2466/pms.1994.79.1.419 PMID:7808878

Rovai, A. P., & Jordan, H. M. (2004). Blended learning and sense of community: A comparative analysis with traditional and fully online graduate courses. *International Review of Research in Open and Distance Learning*, *5*(2), 1–13. doi:10.19173/irrodl.v5i2.192

Ruey, S. (2010). A case study of constructivist instructional strategies for adult online learning. *British Journal of Educational Technology*, *41*(5), 706–720. doi:10.1111/j.1467-8535.2009.00965.x

Sinatra, G. M., Heddy, B. C., & Lombardi, D. (2015). The challenges of defining and measuring student engagement in science. *Educational Psychologist*, *50*(1), 1–13. doi:10.1080/00461520.2014.1002924

Singh, H. (2003). Building effective blended learning programs. *Educational Technology*, *43*(6), 51–54.

Tashakkori, A., & Creswell, J. (2007). The new era of mixed methods. *Journal of Mixed Methods*, *1*(1), 3–7. doi:10.1177/2345678906293042

Tashakkori, A., & Teddlie, C. (2003). The past and future of mixed methods research: From data triangulation to mixed model designs. In A. Tashakkori & C. Teddlie (Eds.), *Handbook of Mixed Methods in Social & Behavioral Research* (pp. 671–701). Thousand Oaks, CA: Sage.

Tham, K., & Tham, C. (2011). Blended learning—A focus study on Asia. *International Journal of Computer Science Issues*, *8*, 136–142.

Tuckman, B. (2002). Evaluating ADAPT: A hybrid instructional model combining Web-based and classroom components. *Computers & Education*, *39*(3), 261–269. doi:10.1016/S0360-1315(02)00045-3

Vatrapu, R., & Suthers, D. (2007). Culture and computers: A review of the concept of culture and implications for intercultural collaborative online learning. In T. Ishida, S. R. Fussell, & P. T. J. M. Vossen (Eds.), *Intercultural Collaboration* (Vol. 4568, pp. 260–275). Berlin: Springer Berlin Heidelberg. doi:10.1007/978-3-540-74000-1_20

Wei, H.-C., Peng, H., & Chou, C. (2015). Can more interactivity improve learning achievement in an online course? Effects of college students' perception and actual use of a course-management system on their learning achievement. *Computers & Education*, *83*, 10–21. doi:10.1016/j.compedu.2014.12.013

Xie, K., & Ke, F. (2010). The role of students' motivation in peer-moderated asynchronous online discussions. *British Journal of Educational Technology*, *42*(6), 916–930. doi:10.1111/j.1467-8535.2010.01140.x

Xie, K., Yu, C., & Bradshaw, A. C. (2014). Impacts of role assignment and participation in asynchronous discussions in college-level online classes. *The Internet and Higher Education*, *20*, 10–19. doi:10.1016/j.iheduc.2013.09.003

Zhang, H., Lin, L., Zhan, Y., & Ren, Y. (2016). The impact of teaching presence on online engagement behaviors. *Journal of Educational Computing Research*, *54*(7), 887–900. doi:10.1177/0735633116648171

Compilation of References

Abanumy, A., Al-Badi, A., & Mayhew, P. (2005). E-Government Website Accessibility: In-Depth Evaluation of Saudi Arabia and Oman. *The Electronic Journal of eGovernment, 3*(3), 99-106.

Ackerman, G. (2012). *Measuring technology acceptance: Adapting an instrument.* Paper presented at the New England Educational Research Organization Annual Conference, Portsmouth, NH.

Ackerman, G. (2017). Strategies to increase technology acceptance. In M. Grassetti & S. Brookby (Eds.), *Advancing next-generation elementary teacher education through digital tools and applications.* Hershey, PA: IGI Global, Inc. doi:10.4018/978-1-5225-0965-3.ch001

ACRL. (2004). *Information literacy competency standards for higher education.* Retrieved fromwww.ala.org/acrl/standards/informationlit?PMU ?eracycompetency#ilassess

Aggarwal, A. K., & Bento, R. (2000). Web-based education. In A. Aggarwal (Ed.), Web-based Learning and Teaching Technologies: Opportunities and Challenges (pp. 2-16). Hershey, PA: Idea Group Publishing. doi:10.4018/978-1-878289-60-5.ch001

Agudo-Peregrina, A. F., Iglesias-Pradas, S., Conde-González, M. A., & Hernandez-Garcia, A. (2014). Can we predict success from log data in VLEs? Classification of interactions for learning analytics and their relation with performance in VLE-supported F2F and online learning. *Computers in Human Behavior, 31*, 542–550. doi:10.1016/j.chb.2013.05.031

Ahuja, J. S., & Webster, J. (2001). Perceived disorientation: An examination of a new measure to assess Web design effectiveness. *Interacting with Computers, 14*(1), 15–29. doi:10.1016/S0953-5438(01)00048-0

Akilli, G. K. (2007). Games and Simulations: A New Approach in Education? In D. Gibson, C. Aldrich, & M. Prensky (Eds.), *Games and simulations in online learning. Research and development frameworks* (pp. 1–20). Hershey, PA: Information Science Publishing. doi:10.4018/978-1-59904-304-3.ch001

Akputu, K. O., Seng, K. P., & Lee, Y. L. (2013). Facial Emotion Recognition for Intelligent Tutoring Environment. *2nd International Conference on Machine Learning and Computer Science (IMLCS'2013)*, 9–13. Available at: http://scholar.google.com.my/scholar?hl=en&q=oryina+Kingsley+Akputu&btnG=&as_sdt=1%252C5&as_sdtp=

Albers, J. (2006). *Interaction of color.* New Haven, CT: Yale University Press.

Aljohani, N. R., & Davis, H. C. (2012). *Learning Analytics in Mobile and Ubiquitous Learning Environments.* Academic Press.

Ally, M. (2002, August). *Designing and managing successful online distance education courses.* Workshop presented at the 2002 World Computer Congress, Montreal, Canada.

Ally, M. (2000). Learning strategies for multimedia instruction. *Proceedings of the annual EdMedia Conference.*

Ally, M., & Fahy, P. (2002, August). Using students' learning styles to provide support in distance education. *Proceedings of the 18th Annual Distance Education Conference on Teaching and Learning.*

Alonso, C. M., Gallego, D. J., & Honey, P. (1999). *Los estilos de aprendizage: Procedimientos de diagnóstico y mejora.* Ediciones Mensajero.

Al-Qahtani, A. A. Y., & Higginst, S. E. (2013). Effects of traditional, blended and e-learning on students' achievement in higher education. *Journal of Computer Assisted Learning, 29*(3), 220–234. doi:10.1111/j.1365-2729.2012.00490.x

Al-Radaideh, M., Nuser, M., & Wahbeh, A. (2011, May). Evaluating Accessibility of Jordanian E-Government Websites for People with Disabilities. *Proceedings of International Conference on Information and Communication Systems*, 127-131.

Amadieu, F., Gog, T., Paas, F., Tricot, A., & Marin, C. (2009). Effects of prior knowledge and concept-map structure on disorientation,cognitive load, and learning. *Learning and Instruction, 19*(5), 376–386. doi:10.1016/j.learninstruc.2009.02.005

Amaral, E. M. H. (2015). Processo de ensino e aprendizagem de algoritmos integrando ambientes imersivos e o paradigma de blocos de programação visual. Academic Press.

Amaral, M. P., & Silveira, I. F. (2014). Estilos de aprendizagem dos alunos do último ano do curso técnico de informática do Centro Federal de Educação Tecnologia de Minas Gerais: Levantamento de um perfil cognitivo dominante. *Rev. Prod. Disc. Educ. Matem., 3*(2), 81–92.

Anderson, K., & May, F. (2010). Does the method of instruction matter? An experimental examination of information literacy instruction in the online, blended, and face-to-face classrooms. *Journal of Academic Librarianship, 36*(6), 495–500. doi:10.1016/j.acalib.2010.08.005

Annetta, L. A., & Bronack, S. (2011). *Serious Educational Game Assessment: Practical Methods and Models for Educational Games, Simulations and Virtual Worlds: Practical Methods and Models for Educational Games, Simulations and Virtual Worlds.* Springer Science & Business Media.

Apache Software Foundation. (2017). *Licenses.* Retrieved March 28, 2017, from https://www.apache.org/licenses/

Appleton, J. J., Christenson, S. L., Kim, D., & Reschly, A. L. (2006). Measuring cognitive and psychological engagement: Validation of the Student Engagement Instrument. *Journal of School Psychology, 44*, 427–445. doi:.2006.04.00210.1016/j.jsp

Arapi, P., Paneva-Marinova, D., Pavlov, R., & Christodoulakis, S. (2016). Techniques to personalized observation and improved learning experience in digital libraries. In *Proceedings of the International Conference on e-Learning'16* (pp. 94-100). Retrieved March 20, 2017, from http://elearning-conf.eu/docs/cp16/paper-14.pdf

Arapi, P., Moumoutzis, N., Mylonakis, M., & Christodoulakis, S. (2007). A Pedagogy-driven personalization framework to support adaptive learning experiences. In *Proceedings of the 7th IEEE International Conference on Advanced Learning Technologies (ICALT 2007)* (pp. 96-97). Niigata, Japan: IEEE. 10.1109/ICALT.2007.27

Arapi, P., Moumoutzis, N., Mylonakis, M., Stylianakis, G., Theodorakis, G., & Christodoulakis, S. (2008). Design, implementation and experimental evaluation of a pedagogy-driven framework to support personalised learning experiences. In *2th LOGOS Workshop "Cross-Media and Personalised Learning Applications with Intelligent Content" in Conj. with AIMSA2008 Conference* (pp. 7-25). Varna, Bulgaria: Institute of Information Technologies - BAS.

Armstrong, A., & Georgas, H. (2006). Using interactive technology to teach information literacy concepts to undergraduate students. *RSR. Reference Services Review, 34*(4), 491–497. doi:10.1108/00907320610716396

Armstrong, H. (2009). *Graphic design theory: Readings from the field.* New York: Princeton Architectural Press.

Arnab, S., Lim, T., Carvalho, M. B., Bellotti, F., Freitas, S., Louchart, S., ... De Gloria, A. (2015). 'Mapping learning and game mechanics for serious games analysis', *British Journal of Educational Technology. Wiley Online Library, 46*(2), 391–411.

Arnold, P., Kilian, L., Thillosen, A., & Zimmer, G. (Eds.). (2011). *Handbuch E-Learning. Lehren und Lernen mit digitalen Medien*. Bielefeld, Germany: Bertelsmann.

Arntson, A. E. (2011). *Graphic design basics*. Fort Worth, TX: Harcourt Brace College Publishers.

Arroyo, I., Woolf, B. P., Burelson, W., Muldner, K., Rai, D., & Tai, M. (2014). A Multimedia Adaptive Tutoring System for Mathematics that Addresses Cognition, Metacognition and Affect. *International Journal of Artificial Intelligence in Education, 24*(4), 387–426. doi:10.100740593-014-0023-y

Arrue, M., Vigo, M., & Abascal, J. (2007). Automatic evaluation of mobile web accessibility. In *Universal Access in Ambient Intelligence Environments*. Springer.

Association of College & Research Libraries Board. (2016). *Framework for Information Literacy for Higher Education*. Retrieved from http://www.ala.org/acrl/standards/ilframework

Austin, T., & Doust, R. (2007). *New media design*. London, UK: Laurence King Publishing.

Ausubel, D. P. (1968). *Educational psychology: A cognitive view*. New York: Holt, Rinehart and Winston.

Authoring Tool Accessibility Guidelines (ATAG 2.0). (2017, May 11). Retrieved from http://www.w3.org/TR/ATAG20/

Authoring Tool Accessibility Guidelines Working Group (ATAG WG). (2017, May 11). Retrieved from http://www.w3.org/WAI/AU/

Avila, B. G., Tarouco, L. M. R., Passerino, L. M., Guterer, P. (2014). Autoria nos Mundos Virtuais: um novo desafio ao docente. *Revista Novas Tecnologias na Educação,* 12(2), 1-10.

Azevedo, R. (2015). Defining and measuring engagement and learning in science: Conceptual, theoretical, methodological, and analytical issues. *Educational Psychologist, 50*(1), 84–94. doi:10.1080/00461520.2015.1004069

Baalsrud Hauge, J., Berta, R., Fiucci, G., Fernandez Manjon, B., Padrón-Nápoles, C., Westra, W., & Nadolski, R. (2014). Implications of learning analytics for serious game design. *Advanced Learning Technologies (ICALT), 2014 IEEE 14th International Conference on*, 230–232.

Baazeem, I. S., & Al-Khalifa, H. S. (2015, December). Advancements in Web Accessibility Evaluation Methods: How Far Are We? In *Proceedings of the 17th International Conference on Information Integration and Web-based Applications & Services (iiwas 2015)*. ACM. DOI: 10.1145/2837185.2843850

Babich, N. (2017). *Accessibility for visual design*. Retrieved from http://www.uxbooth.com/articles/accessibility-visual-design/

Babu, J. R., & Sekharaiahm, K. C. (2014). A Panorama of Web Accessibility. *International Journal of Computer Science and Mobile Computing, 3*(8), 311–317.

Bader, J. (2015). *Functional e-learning design*. Unpublished manuscript, Boise State University.

Bahreini, K., Nadolski, R., & Westera, W. (2014b). Towards multimodal emotion recognition in e-learning environments. In Interactive Learning Environments. Taylor & Francis.

Bahreini, K., Nadolski, R., & Westera, W. (2014a). *Multimodal Emotion Recognition for Assessment of Learning in a Game-Based Communication Skills Training*. Springer International Publishing.

Bahreini, K., Nadolski, R., & Westera, W. (2015). *Towards real-time speech emotion recognition for affective e-learning. In Education and Information Technologies* (pp. 1–20). Springer.

Bainbridge, W. S. (2010). Online Worlds: Convergence of the Real and the Virtual. Human-Computer Interaction Series.

Baker, R., D'Mello, S. K., Rodrigo, M. M. T., & Graesser, A. C. (2010). Better to be frustrated than bored: The incidence, persistence, and impact of learners' cognitive--affective states during interactions with three different computer-based learning environments. *International Journal of Human-Computer Studies*, *68*(4), 223–241.

Baker, F. (2017). An alternative approach: Openness in education over the last 100 years. *TechTrends*, *61*(2), 130–140. doi:10.100711528-016-0095-7

Baker, R. S., Corbett, A. T., Koedinger, K. R., & Wagner, A. Z. (2004). Off-task behavior in the cognitive tutor classroom: when students game the system. *Proceedings of the SIGCHI conference on Human factors in computing systems*, 383–390. 10.1145/985692.985741

Banda, N., & Robinson, P. (2011). Multimodal affect recognition in intelligent tutoring systems. *Affective Computing and Intelligent Interaction (ACII'11)*, 200–207. Available at: http://link.springer.com/chapter/10.1007/978-3-642-24571-8_21

Bandeira, R., Lopes, R., & Carriço, L. (2010). Towards mobile Web accessibility evaluation. Free and Open Source Software for Accessible Mainstream Applications (FOSS-AMA), colocated with ETAPS (2010), 27-28.

Bandura, A. (1977). Self-efficacy: Toward a unifying theory of behavioral change. *Psychological Review*, *84*(2), 191–215. doi:10.1037/0033-295X.84.2.191 PMID:847061

Banerjee, I., Perera, I., & Choudhury, J. (2013). Introducing Immersive Technologies for Learning. *Sixth International Conference on Contemporary Computing (IC3)*, 1– 6.

Baran, E., & Correia, A.-P. (2014). A professional development framework for online teaching. *TechTrends*, *58*(5), 95–101. doi:10.100711528-014-0791-0

Bariani, I. C. D. (1998). *Estilos cognitivos de universitários e iniciação cientifica, Tese de Doutorado*. Unicamp.

Barik, N., & Karforma, S. (2012). Risks and Remedies in E-Learning System. *International Journal of Network Security & Its Applications*, *4*(1), 51–59. doi:10.5121/ijnsa.2012.4105

Barnett, R. (1997). *Higher education: A critical business*. Maidenhead, UK: Open University Press.

Becla, A. (2012). Information Society and Knowledge-based Economy – Development Level and the Main Barriers – some Remarks. *Economia e Sociologia (Evora, Portugal)*, *5*(1), 125–132.

Beeson, E. (2001). Rural schools: Facing unique challenges. *Principal*, *8*(1), 22–24.

Behrend, T. S., & Thompson, L. F. (2012). Using Animated Agents in Learner-Controlled Training: The Effects of Design Control. *International Journal of Training and Development*, *16*(4), 263–283. doi:10.1111/j.1468-2419.2012.00413.x

Behrens, R. (1998). Art, design and gestalt theory. *Leonardo*, *31*(4), 299–303. doi:10.2307/1576669

Beldaglia, B., & Adiguzela, T. (2010). Illustrating an ideal adaptive e-learning: A conceptual framework. *Procedia: Social and Behavioral Sciences*, *2*(2), 5755–5761. doi:10.1016/j.sbspro.2010.03.939

Benassi, V., Overson, C., & Hakala, C. (2014). *Applying science of learning in education: Infusing psychological science into the curriculum.* Retrieved from the Society for the Teaching of Psychology web site: http://teachpsych.org/ebooks/asle2014/index.php

Benkler, Y. (2006). *The wealth of networks: how social production transforms markets and freedom*. New Haven, CT: Yale University Press.

Bereiter, C. (2002). *Education and mind in the knowledge age*. Mahwah, NJ: L. Erlbaum Associates.

Berge, Z. L., Collins, M., & Dougherty, K. (2000). Design guidelines for Web-based courses. In B. Abbey (Ed.), *Instructional and cognitive impact of Web-based education* (pp. 32–40). Hershey, PA: Idea Group Publishing. doi:10.4018/978-1-878289-59-9.ch002

Bernard, M., Lida, B., Riley, S., Hackler, T., & Janzen, K. (2002). *A comparison of popular online fonts: Which size and type is best?* Retrieved from http://goo.gl/7uiHk2

Bernard, R. M., Abrami, P. C., Borokhovski, E., Wade, C. A., Tamim, R. M., Surkes, M. A., & Bethel, E. C. (2009). A meta-analysis of three types of interaction treatments in distance education. *Review of Educational Research*, *79*(3), 1243–1289. doi:10.3102/0034654309333844

Bernard, R. M., Borokhovski, E., Schmid, R. F., Tamim, R. M., & Abrami, P. C. (2014). A meta-analysis of blended learning and technology use in higher education: From the general to the applied. *Journal of Computing in Higher Education*, *26*(1), 87–122. doi:10.100712528-013-9077-3

Bernsen, N. O., & Dybkjær, L. (2010). Usability data analysis and evaluation. In *Multimodal Usability* (pp. 351–385). Springer. doi:10.1007/978-1-84882-553-6_16

Bevan, N. (2009). *What is the difference between the purpose of usability and user experience evaluation methods*. Paper presented at UXEM'09Workshop, INTERACT 2009, Uppsala, Sweden.

Beyer, H., & Holtzblatt, K. (2016). *Contextual design: Defining customer-centered systems* (2nd ed.). San Francisco: Morgan Kaufmann.

Bhaskar, N. U., & Govindarajulu, P. (2008). Context exploration for requirements elicitation in mobile learning application development. *IJCSNS International Journal of Computer Science and Network Security*, *8*(8), 292–299.

Blandford, A., & Buchenan, G. (2003). Usability of digital libraries: a source of creative tensions with technical developments. *IEEE-CS Technical Committee on Digital Libraries' on-line newsletter*. Retrieved March 20, 2017, from http://web4.cs.ucl.ac.uk/uclic/annb/docs/abgbTCDLpreprint.pdf

Blauvelt, A. (1998). Remaking theory, remaking practice. In S. Heller (Ed.), *The education of a graphic designer* (pp. 71–77). New York: Allworth Press.

Bloom, B. S. (1956). *Taxonomy of educational objectives: The classification of educational goals, Book 1. Cognitive domain*. New York, NY: Longman.

Blumenfeld, P., Kempler, T., & Krajcik, J. (2006). Motivation and cognitive engagement in learning environments. In R. Keith Sawyer (Ed.), *The Cambridge Handbook of Learning Science* (pp. 475–488). New York: Cambridge University Press.

Blumschein, P., & Fischer, M. (2006). *Didactic Design of E-Learning Measures. E-learning in Vocational Education and Training*. Bonn, Germany: Capacity Building International, on behalf of Federal Ministry for Economic Cooperation and Development.

Bodemer, D., & Ploetzner, R. (2002). Encouraging the active integration of information during learning with multiple and interactive representations. In R. Ploetzner (Ed), *International workshop on dynamic visualization and learning*. Tubigen, Germany: Knowledge Media Research Center

Boekaerts, M. (2016). Engagement as an inherent aspect of the learning process. *Learning and Instruction*, *43*, 65–83. doi:10.1016/j.learninstruc.2016.02.001

Bolter, J. D., & Grusin, R. A. (1999). *Remediation: Understanding new media*. Cambridge, MA: MIT Press.

Bonk, C. J., & Cummings, J. C. (1998). A dozen recommendations for placing the student at the center of Web-based learning. *Educational Media International*, *35*(2), 82–89. doi:10.1080/0952398980350205

Bonsignore, E., Ahn, J., Clegg, T., Guha, M. L., & Yip, J. C. (2013). Embedding Participatory Design into Design for Learning: An Untapped Interdisciplinary Resource? In CSCL 2013 Proceedings (pp. 549-556). Madison, WI: Academic Press.

Bontchev, B., Paneva-Marinova, D., & Draganov, L. (2016). Educational video games for Bulgarian Orthodox iconography. In L. G. Chova, A. L. Martínez, & I. C. Torres (Ed.), *ICERI2016 Proceedings 9th Annual International Conference of Education, Research and Innovation* (pp. 1679-1688). Seville, Spain: IATED Academy. 10.21125/iceri.2016.1374

Bontchev, B. (2016). Holistic player modelling for controlling adaptation in video games. *Proceedings of 14th International Conference e-Society*, 11-18.

Borgman, C. (2003). Designing digital libraries for usability. In A. Bishop, N. Van House, & B. Buttenfield (Eds.), *Digital Library Use: Social Practice in Design and Evaluation* (pp. 85-118). Cambridge, MA: MIT Press. Retrieved May 18, 2017, from http://works.bepress.com/borgman/307/

Borodin, Y., Mahmud, J., Ramakrishnan, I. V., & Stent, A. (2007). The HearSay Non-Visual Web Browser. In *Proceedings of the 2007 international cross-disciplinary conference on Web accessibility (W4A 2007)*. ACM. 10.1145/1243441.1243444

Borsook, T. K., & Higginbotham-Wheat, N. (1991). Interactivity: What it is and what it can do for computer-based instruction. *Educational Technology*, *31*, 11–17.

Bosch, N., Chen, H., Baker, R., Shute, V., & D'Mello, S. (2015). Accuracy vs. Availability Heuristic in Multimodal Affect Detection in the Wild. *Proceedings of the 17th International Conference on Multimodal Interaction*. 10.1145/2818346.2820739

Bosch, N., Hall, F., & Dame, N. (2015). *Multimodal Affect Detection in the Wild : Accuracy*. Availability, and Generalizability. doi:10.1145/2818346.2823316

Bostick, S. L. (1992). *The development and validation of the library anxiety scale* (Order No. 9310624). Available from ProQuest Dissertations & Theses Global. (304002616)

Bouda, T. (2012). *User-centered Design and Evaluation of Virtual Worlds*. In Experiential Learning in Virtual Worlds: 2nd Global Conference, Prague, Czech Republic.

Boudewijnse, G. (2012). Gestalt theory and Bauhaus: A correspondence. *Gestalt Theory*, *34*(1), 81–98.

Boulos, M. N. K., Hetherington, L., & Wheeler, S. (2007). Blackwell Publishing Ltd Second Life: An overview of the potential of 3-D virtual worlds in medical and health education. *Health Information and Libraries Journal*, *24*(4), 233–245. doi:10.1111/j.1471-1842.2007.00733.x PMID:18005298

Bouta, H., Retalis, S., & Paraskeva, F. (2012). Utilizing a collaborative macro-script to enhance student engagement: A mixed method study in a 3D virtual environment. *Computers & Education*, *58*(1), 501–517. doi:10.1016/j.compedu.2011.08.031

Bowman, D. A., Gabbard, J. L., & Hix, D. (2002). A Survey of Usability Evaluation in Virtual Environments: Classification and Comparison of Methods. *Presence (Cambridge, Mass.)*, *11*(4), 404–424. doi:10.1162/105474602760204309

Bracke, P. J., & Dickstein, R. (2002). Web tutorials and scalable instruction: Testing the waters. *RSR. Reference Services Review*, *30*(4), 330–337. doi:10.1108/00907320210451321

Braden, R. A. (1996). Visual literacy. In D. H. Johanssen (Ed.), *Handbook of research for educational communications and technology* (pp. 491–520). New York: Simon & Schuster.

Bradshaw, A. C., & Johari, A. (2003). Effects of an online visual procedure on task completion, time, and attitude. *Journal of Educational Computing Research*, *29*(4), 401–417. doi:10.2190/0KVF-BNYT-7CPW-WWCY

Bransford, J. D., Brown, A. L., & Cocking, R. R. (2000). *How People Learn: Brain, Mind, Experience, and School*. Washington, DC: National Academy Press.

Bratteteig, T., Bødker, K., Dittrich, Y., Mogensen, P. H., & Simonsen, J. (2013). Participatory Design: an introduction. In J. Simonsen & T. Robertson (Eds.), *Routledge international handbook of participatory design* (pp. 117–144). New York, NY: Routledge.

Bringhurst, R. (2002). *The elements of typographic style*. Point Roberts, WA: Hartley & Marks.

Brockmyer, J. H., Fox, C. M., Curtiss, K. A., McBroom, E., Burkhart, K. M., & Pidruzny, J. N. (2009). The development of the game engagement questionnaire: A measure of engagement in video game-playing. *Journal of Experimental Social Psychology*, *45*(4), 624–634. doi:10.1016/j.jesp.2009.02.016

Brown, A. L. (1992). Design experiments: Theoretical and methodological challenges in creating complex interventions in classroom settings. *Journal of the Learning Sciences*, *2*(2), 141–178. doi:10.120715327809jls0202_2

Brown, L., & Howard, A. M. (2014). *Assessment of Engagement for Intelligent Educational Agents: A Pilot Study with Middle School Students*. Georgia Institute of Technology.

Brunken, R., Plass, J., & Leutner, D. (2003). Direct measurement of cognitive load in multimedia learning. *Educational Psychologist*, *38*(1), 53–61. doi:10.1207/S15326985EP3801_7

Brusilovsky, P. (2003). Developing adaptive educational hypermedia systems: From design models to authoring tools. In T. Murray, S. Blessing, & S. Ainsworth (Eds.), Authoring tools for advanced technology learning environments: Toward cost- effective adaptive, interactive, and intelligent educational software. Ablex.

Brusilovsky, P., Kobsa, A., & Vassileva, J. (Eds.). (1998). *Adaptive Hypertext and Hypermedia*. Dordrecht: Kluwer Academic Publishers. doi:10.1007/978-94-017-0617-9

Buchanan, R. (1992). Wicked problems in design thinking. *Design Issues*, *8*(2), 5–21. doi:10.2307/1511637

Buchanan, R., Manzini, E., Vanlaethem, F., & Ambasz, E. (1990). Metaphors, narratives, and fables in new design thinking. *Design Issues*, *7*(1), 78–82. doi:10.2307/1511474

Buchanan, S., & Salako, A. (2009). Evaluating the usability and usefulness of a digital library. *Library Review*, *58*(9), 638–651. doi:10.1108/00242530910997928

Burelli, P., Triantafyllidis, G., & Patras, I. (2014). Non-invasive player experience estimation from body motion and game context. *Computational Intelligence and Games (CIG), 2014 IEEE Conference on*, 1–7. 10.1109/CIG.2014.6932871

Burgstahler, S. (2004). *Real connections: Making distance learning accessible to everyone*. Retrieved from https://goo.gl/aQ2DaP

Burke, P. A., Etnier, J. L., & Sullivan, H. J. (1998). Navigational aids and learner control in hypermedia instructional programs. *Journal of Educational Computing Research*, *18*(2), 183–196. doi:10.2190/HJXT-YH1K-6PDX-5FE4

Burmester, M., & Hassenzahl, M. (2013). *Benutzerzentrierte Softwaregestaltung*. Retrieved March 25, 2017, from http://www.ergo-online.de/site.aspx?url=html/software/software_entwicklung_prototyp/benutzerzentrierte_softwarege.htm

Butler, K. A. (2003). *Estilos de Aprendizagem: as dimensões psicológicas*. Editora da UFRGS.

Buxton, W., Hill, R., & Rowley, P. (1985). Issues and techniques in touch-sensitive tablet input. *Proceedings of SIGGRAPH. Computer Graphics, 19*(3), 69–85. doi:10.1145/325165.325239

Byun, J. H., Loh, C. S., & Zhou, T. (2014). 'Assessing play-learners' performance in serious game environments by using in situ data: Using eye tracking for Serious Game Analytics. In *Annual Conference of the Association for Educational Communications and Technology*. Jacksonville, FL: AECT. Retrieved from http://www. csloh. com/research/publications/

Callan, J., Smeaton, A., Beaulieu, M., Borlund, P., Brusilovsky, P., Chalmers, M., . . . Toms, E. (2003). *Personalisation and recommender systems in digital libraries.* Retrieved May 18, 2017, from https://www.ercim.eu/publication/ws-proceedings/Delos-NSF/Personalisation.pdf

Campbell, A. J. (2007). Always have a plan B: student response to an e-learning program under challenging conditions in China. *Proceedings of E-Learn 2007, World Conference on e-learning in Corporate Government, Healthcare and Higher Education*, 689-695.

Candela, L., Castelli, D., Ferro, N., Ioannidis, Y., Koutrika, G., Meghini, C., . . . Schuldt, H. (2007). *The DELOS Digital Library Reference model. Foundations for digital Libraries.* Version 0.96. Retrieved March 24, 2017, from http://delosw.isti.cnr.it/files/pdf/ReferenceModel/DELOS_DLReferenceModel_096.pdf

Cao, J. (2015, January 26). *How & why prototypes are mandatory for good design*. Retrieved from https://goo.gl/NdGVZR

Card, S. K., English, W. K., & Burr, B. J. (1978). Evaluation of mouse, rate-controlled isometric joystick, step keys, and text keys for text selection on a CRT. *Ergonomics, 21*(8), 601–613. doi:10.1080/00140137808931762

Carrier, C., Davidson, G., Higson, V., & Williams, M. (1984). Selection of options by field independent and dependent children in a computer-based concept lesson. *Journal of Computer-Based Instruction, 11*, 49–54.

Carter, M. (2014). *My life in typefaces* [Video file]. Retrieved from https://www.ted.com/talks/matthew_carter_my_life_in_typefaces

Carter, J., & Markel, M. (2001). Web Accessibility for People With Disabilities: An Introduction for Web Developers. *IEEE Transactions on Professional Communication, 44*(4), 225–233. doi:10.1109/47.968105

Catholico, R. A. R. (2010). Mediação da aprendizagem de Feuerstein à luz dos estilos de aprendizagem de Felder. *Revista Eletrônica de Educação e Tecnologia do SENAI-SP, 4*(8).

Cavellucci, L. C. B. (2003). *Estilos de aprendizagem: em busca das diferenças individuais*. Academic Press.

Ceaparu, I., & Shneiderman, B. (2002). Improving Web-based Civic Information Access: A Case Study of the 50 US States. *International Symposium on Technology and Society (ISTAS 2002), Copyright 2002 IEEE*, 275-282. DOI: 10.1109/ISTAS.2002.1013826

Cennamo, K., & Brandt, C. (2012). The "right kind of telling": Knowledge building in the academic design studio. *Educational Technology Research and Development, 60*(5), 839–858. doi:10.100711423-012-9254-5

Centre-Student-Development. (n.d.). Retrieved March 20, 2017, from https://www.uwo.ca/sdc/learning/selfhelp/skill_building_handouts/PDFs/Memory%20and%20Thinking%20Skills/Learning%20Styles.pdf

Chaiyama, N. (2015). The development of blended learning management model in developing information literacy skills (BL-ILS Model). *International Journal of Information and Education Technology (IJIET)*, *5*(7), 483–489. doi:10.7763/IJIET.2015.V5.554

Chalmers, A. P. (2003). The role of cognitive theory in human–computer interface. *Computers in Human Behavior*, *19*(5), 593–607. doi:10.1016/S0747-5632(02)00086-9

Chandler, P., & Sweller, J. (1991). Cognitive load theory and the format of instruction. *Cognition and Instruction*, *8*(4), 293–332. doi:10.12071532690xci0804_2

Chang, M. K., & Law, M. S. P. (2008). Factor Structure for Young's Internet Addiction Test: A confirmatory study. *Computers in Human Behavior*, *24*(6), 2597–2619. doi:10.1016/j.chb.2008.03.001

Chaouachi, M., Jraidi, I., & Frasson, C. (2015). MENTOR: A Physiologically Controlled Tutoring System. In *User Modeling, Adaptation and Personalization* (pp. 56–67). Springer. doi:10.1007/978-3-319-20267-9_5

Cheng, G. (2014). Exploring students' learning styles in relation to their acceptance and attitudes towards using Second Life in education: A case study in Hong Kong. *Computer Education*, *70*, 105–115. doi:10.1016/j.compedu.2013.08.011

Chen, H. J., & Su, C. C. (2011). *Constructing a 3D Virtual World for Foreign Language Learning Based on Open Source Freeware*. Edutainment Technologies. Educational Games and Virtual Reality/Augmented Reality Applications. doi:10.1007/978-3-642-23456-9_10

Chen, P. S. D., Lambert, A. D., & Guidry, K. R. (2010). Engaging online learners: The impact of Web-based learning technology on college student engagement. *Computers & Education*, *54*(4), 1222–1232. doi:10.1016/j.compedu.2009.11.008

Chen, S. Y., & Macredie, R. D. (2004). Cognitive Modeling of Student Learning in Web-Based Instructional Programs. *International Journal of Human-Computer Interaction*, *17*(3), 375–402. doi:10.120715327590ijhc1703_5

Cheock, M. L., & Wong, S. L. (2015). Predictors of E-Learning Satisfaction in Teaching and Learning for School Teachers: A Literature Review. *International Journal of Instruction*, *8*(1), 75–90. doi:10.12973/iji.2015.816a

Chiou, C.-C. (2008). The effect of concept mapping on students' learning achievements and interests. *Innovations in Education and Teaching International*, *45*(4), 375–387. doi:10.1080/14703290802377240

Chisholm, W. A., & Henry, S. L. (2005). Interdependent Components of Web Accessibility. In *Proceedings of the 2005 International Cross-Disciplinary Workshop on Web Accessibility (W4A)*. ACM. 10.1145/1061811.1061818

Chow, M. (2016). Determinants of presence in 3d virtual worlds: A structural equation modelling analysis. *Australasian Journal of Educational Technology*, *32*(1), 1–18. doi:10.14742/ajet.1939

Christmann, U., Groeben, N., & Schreier, M. (1999). Subjektive Theorien: Rekonstruktion und Dialog-Konsens. *Siegener Periodikum zur Internationalen Empirischen Literaturwissenschaft: SPIEL*, *18*(1), 138–154.

Chung-Ho, S., & Ching-Hsue, C. (2013). 3D game-based learning system for improving learning achievement in software engineering curriculum. *TOJET: The Turkish Online Journal of Educational Technology, 12*(2), 1-12. Retrieved March 20, 2017, from http://www.tojet.net/articles/v12i2/1221.pdf

Clark College Libraries. (2015). *IRIS*. Retrieved from http://www.clark.edu/Library/iris/ index.shtml

Clark, R. C., & Mayer, R. E. (2011). e-Learning and the Science of Instruction: Proven Guidelines for Consumers and Designers of Multimedia Learning (3rd ed.). Pfeiffer.

Clark, R. C., & Mayer, R. E. (2016). e-Learning and the science of instruction: Proven guidelines for consumers and designers of multimedia learning. Hoboken, NJ: Wiley.

Colin, A., Miller, A., Sturgeon, T., Nicoll, J. R., & Perera, I. (2010). Educationally Enhanced Virtual Worlds. *40th ASEE/ IEEE Frontiers in Education Conference*, 1–6.

Collins, A. (1990). *Toward a design science of education*. New York, NY: Center for Technology in Education. Retrieved from http://cct2.edc.org/ccthome/reports/tr1.html

Conati, C., & Gutica, M. (2016). Interaction with an Edu-Game: A Detailed Analysis of Student Emotions and Judges' Perceptions. *International Journal of Artificial Intelligence in Education*, *26*(4), 975–1010.

Conati, C. (2004). *How to evaluate models of user affect? In Affective dialogue systems* (pp. 288–300). Springer.

Conati, C., & Maclaren, H. (2009). Modeling user affect from causes and effects. *International Conference on User Modeling, Adaptation, and Personalization*, 4–15. 10.1007/978-3-642-02247-0_4

Conklin, J. (1987). Hypertext: An introduction and surveys. *IEEE Computer*, *20*(9), 17–41. doi:10.1109/MC.1987.1663693

Connolly, T. M., Boyle, E. A., Macarthur, E., Hainey, T., & Boyle, J. M. (2012). A systematic literature review of empirical evidence on computer games and serious games. *Computers & Education*, *59*(2), 661–686. doi:10.1016/j.compedu.2012.03.004

Constantin, J. (2013, May). Typographic design patterns and current practice. *Smashing Magazine*. Retrieved from https://www.smashingmagazine.com/2013/05/typographic-design-patterns-practices-case-study-2013/

Cook, D. L. (2002). Ship to shore: An online information literacy tutorial using BlackBoard distance education software. *Journal of Library Administration*, *37*(1), 177–187. doi:10.1300/J111v37n01_16

Council of Writing Program Administrators. (2008). *WPA outcomes statement for first-year composition*. WPA.

Cowley, B., Fantato, M., Jennett, C., Ruskov, M., & Ravaja, N. (2014). Learning When Serious: Psychophysiological Evaluation of a Technology-Enhanced Learning Game. *Journal of Educational Technology & Society*, *17*(1), 3–16.

Cowley, B., Ravaja, N., & Heikura, T. (2013). Cardiovascular physiology predicts learning effects in a serious game activity. *Computers & Education. Elsevier*, *60*(1), 299–309. doi:10.1016/j.compedu.2012.07.014

Creative Commons. (n.d.). *Creative Commons—Attribution-ShareAlike 3.0 Unported—CC BY-SA 3.0*. Retrieved March 28, 2017 from https://creativecommons.org/licenses/by-sa/3.0/

Creswell, J. W. (2013). *Qualitative inquiry and research design: Choosing among five approaches* (3rd ed.). Thousand Oaks, CA: Sage.

Creswell, J. W., & Plano-Clark, V. L. (2010). *Designing and conducting mixed methods research*. Thousand Oaks, CA: Sage.

Cronbach, L., & Snow, R. (1997). *Aptitudes and instructional methods: A handbook for research on interactions*. New York: Irvington Publishers.

Crooks, S. M., Klein, J. D., Jones, E. E. K., & Dwyer, H. (1996). Effects of cooperative learning and learner-control modes in computer-based instruction. *Journal of Research on Computing in Education*, *29*(2), 109–123. doi:10.1080/08886504.1996.10782189

Crow, D. (2016). *Visible signs: An introduction to semiotics in the visual arts* (3rd ed.). London: Bloomsbury.

Crow, K. L. (2008). Four types of disabilities: Their impact on online learning. *TechTrends*, *52*(1), 51–55. doi:10.100711528-008-0112-6

Csikszentmihalyi, M., & Csikszentmihalyi, I. S. (1988). *Optimal experience. Psychological studies of flow in consciousness*. New York, NY: Cambridge University Press. doi:10.1017/CBO9780511621956

CultEcoSys-Project. (2017). *Concepts and models for innovation ecosystems of digital cultural assets, No. DN02/06/15.12.2016 (project web page)*. Retrieved March 20, 2017, from http://cultecosys.math.bas.bg

Cyr, D. (2013). Website design, trust and culture: An eight country investigation. *Electronic Commerce Research and Applications*, *12*(6), 373–385. doi:10.1016/j.elerap.2013.03.007

D'Mello, S., Lehman, B., Pekrun, R., & Grasser, A. (2015). Confusion can be beneficial for learning. *Learning and Instruction*, *29*, 153–170. doi:10.1016/j.learninstruc.2012.05.003

Dabrowski, A., & Lodge, J. (2017). Pedagogy, practice, and the allure of open online courses: Implications for schools and their students. In A. Marcus-Quinn & T. Hourigan (Eds.), *Handbook on digital learning for K-12 schools* (pp. 443–454). Cham, Switzerland: Springer International Publishing. doi:10.1007/978-3-319-33808-8_27

Davis, F. (1989). Perceived usefulness, perceived ease of use, and user acceptance of information technology. *Management Information Systems Quarterly*, *13*(3), 319–340. doi:10.2307/249008

De Jong, T. (2010). Cognitive load theory, educational research, and instructional design: Some food for thought. *Instructional Science*, *38*(2), 105–134. doi:10.100711251-009-9110-0

Dede, C. (2010). Comparing frameworks for 21st century skills. In J. Bellanca & R. Brandt (Eds.), 21st century skills: Rethinking how students learn (pp. 51-76). Bloomington, IN: Solution Tree Press.

Dennis, M. R., Murphey, R. M., & Rogers, K. (2011). Assessing information literacy comprehension in first-year students. *Practical Academic Librarianship: The International Journal of the SLA, 1*(1), 1-15.

Deuze, M. (2006). Participation, Remediation, Bricolage: Considering Principal Components of a Digital Culture. *The Information Society*, *22*(2), 63–75. doi:10.1080/01972240600567170

Dewey, J. (2005). Art as experience. New York: Berkley.

Dias, C. C. L., Gasparini, I., & Kemczinski, A. (2009). *Identificação dos estilos cognitivos de aprendizagem através da interação em um Ambiente EAD*. Congresso da Sociedade Brasileira de Computação.

DIN EN ISO 9241-210. (n.d.). In *Standards of NA 023*. Retrieved from http://www.din.de/en/getting-involved/standards-committees/naerg/standards/wdc-beuth:din21:135399380

Dochev, D., & Agre, G. (2012). Supporting learning-by-doing situations by Semantic technologies. In D. Stefanoui, & J. Culita (Ed.), *Proceedings of the 17th Annual Conference on Media and Web Technology EUROMEDIA*, (pp. 49-53). Budapest, Hungary: Academic Press.

Don, A., & Petrick, J. (2003). User Requirements. In B. Laurel (Ed.), *Design research: Methods and perspectives* (pp. 70–80). Cambridge, MA: MIT Press.

Doymus, K. (2008). Teaching chemical equilibrium with the jigsaw technique. *Research in Science Education*, *38*(2), 249–260. doi:10.100711165-007-9047-8

Drachen, A., Nacke, L. E., Yannakakis, G., & Pedersen, A. L. (2010). Correlation between heart rate, electrodermal activity and player experience in first-person shooter games. *Proceedings of the 5th ACM SIGGRAPH Symposium on Video Games - Sandbox '10*, 49–54. 10.1145/1836135.1836143

Draganov, L., Paneva-Marinova, D., Pavlova, L., Luchev, D., Márkus, Z., Szántó, G., & Szkaliczki, T. (2015). Technology-enhanced learning for cultural heritage. In R. Pavlov & P. Stanchev (Eds.), *Proceedings of the 5th International Conference on Digital Presentation and Preservation of Cultural and Scientific Heritage*. Veliko Tarnovo, Bulgaria: Institute of Mathematics and Informatics - BAS. Retrieved March 25, 2017, from http://dipp.math.bas.bg

Drever, E. (2006). *Using semi-structured interviews in small-scale research: a teacher's guide*. Glasgow, UK: The SCRE Centre.

Drysdale, J. S., Graham, C. R., Spring, K. J., & Halverson, L. R. (2013). An analysis of research trends in dissertations and theses studying blended learning. *The Internet and Higher Education*, *2*(17), 90–100. doi:10.1016/j.iheduc.2012.11.003

Duval, E. (2011). Attention please! Learning analytics for visualization and recommendation. *Proceedings of the 1st International Conference on Learning Analytics and Knowledge LAK '11*, 9–17. 10.1145/2090116.2090118

Eccles, J. (2016). Engagement: Where to next? *Learning and Instruction*, *43*, 71–75. doi:10.1016/j.learninstruc.2016.02.003

Economides, A. A. (2009). Adaptive context-aware pervasive and ubiquitous learning. *International Journal of Technology Enhanced Learning*, *1*(3), 169–192.

Edmonds, C. D. (2004). Providing access to students with disabilities in online distance education: Legal and technical concerns for higher education. *American Journal of Distance Education*, *18*(1), 51–62. doi:10.120715389286ajde1801_5

Ehrlinger, J., Johnson, K., Banner, M., & Kruger, J. (2008). Why the unskilled are unaware: Further explorations of (absent) self-insight among the incompetent. *Organizational Behavior and Human Decision Processes*, *105*(1), 98–121. doi:10.1016/j.obhdp.2007.05.002 PMID:19568317

Eklund, J., & Sinclair, K. (2000). An empirical appraisal of adaptive interfaces for instructional systems. *Educational Technology and Society Journal*, *3*, 165–177.

Eom, S. B., Wen, H. J., & Ashill, N. (2006). The Determinants of Students' Perceived Learning Outcomes and Satisfaction in University Online Education: An Empirical Investigation. *Decision Sciences Journal of Innovative Education*, *4*(2), 215–235. doi:10.1111/j.1540-4609.2006.00114.x

Ezen-can, A., Grafsgaard, J. F., Lester, J. C., & Boyer, K. E. (n.d.). *Classifying Student Dialogue Acts with Multimodal Learning Analytics Categories and Subject Descriptors*. Academic Press.

Fabricatore, C. (2000). Learning and videogames: an unexploited synergy. *2000 Annual Convention of the Association for Educational Communications and Technology (AECT). Workshop: In Search of the Meaning of Learning*, 1-17. Retrieved March 20, 2017, from http://learndev.org/dl/FabricatoreAECT2000.PDF

Faghih, B., Azadehfar, M., & Katebi, S. (2013). User Interface Design for E-Learning Software. *The International Journal of Soft Computing and Software Engineering*, *3*(3), 786–794.

Fain, M. (2011). Assessing information literacy skills development in first year students: A multi-year study. *Journal of Academic Librarianship*, *37*(2), 109–119. doi:10.1016/j.acalib.2011.02.002

Fang, Y., Chang, T., Zhong, Y., Ye, E., & Liu, C. (2010). Improving Public Awareness of Everyday Chemical Pollutants Utilizing a 3-D Immersive Game. *EdMedia: World Conference on Educational Media and Technology*, 1–5.

Farkas, M. (2017). Information literacy toolkits: Creating better resources for instructors. *American Libraries*, *45*(5), 54.

Felder, R. M., & Soloman, B. A. (1991). *Learning styles and strategies*. Available in: http://www4.ncsu.edu/unity/lockers/users/f/felder/public/ILSdir/styles.htm

Felder, R. M. (1993). Reaching the Second Tier: Learning and teaching styles in college science education. *Journal of College Science Teaching*, *23*(5), 286–290.

Felder, R. M., & Silverman, L. K. (1988). Learning and Teaching Styles in Engineering Education. *Journal of Engineering in Education*, *78*(7), 674–681.

Felder, R., & Henriques, E. (1995). Learning and Teaching Styles in Foreign and Second Language Education. *Foreign Language Annals*, *28*(1), 21–31. doi:10.1111/j.1944-9720.1995.tb00767.x

Ferrara, V., Macchia, A., & Sapia, S. (2014). Cultural heritage open data for developing an educational platform [Abstract]. In *Proceedings of the 5th International Conference on Information, Intelligence, Systems and Applications*. IEEE. doi:10.1109/IISA.2014.6878775

Findeli, A. (2001). Rethinking design education for the 21st century: Theoretical, methodological, and ethical discussion. *Design Issues*, *17*(1), 5–17. doi:10.1162/07479360152103796

Fisher, M. (2003). *Designing courses and teaching on the Web: A "how-to-guide" to proven innovative strategies*. Lanham, MD: Scarecrow Education.

Flick, U. (Ed.). (2014). *An Introduction to Qualitative Research* (5th ed.). Los Angeles, CA: Sage Pub.

Flores, M. S., Frozza, R., Bagatini, D., & Cruz, M. E. J. K. D. A. (2013). *Uso de rede neural artificial para determinar o estilo cognitivo do aprendiz*. XXIV Simpósio Brasileiro de Informática na Educação.

Fogg, B. (2003). Conceptual designs. In B. Laurel (Ed.), *Design Research: Methods and Perspectives* (pp. 201–211). Cambridge, MA: MIT Press.

Foley, J. D., Wallace, P. C., & Chen, P. (1984). The human factors of computer graphics interaction techniques. *IEEE Computer Graphics and Applications*, *4*(11), 13–48. doi:10.1109/MCG.1984.6429355

Ford, N., & Chen, S. Y. (2000). Individual differences, hypermedia navigation and learning: An empirical study. *Journal of Educational Multimedia and Hypermedia*, *9*, 281–312.

Ford, N., & Chen, S. Y. (2001). Matching/ mismatching revised: An empirical study of learning and teaching styles. *British Journal of Educational Technology*, *32*(1), 5–22. doi:10.1111/1467-8535.00173

Fox, E., Akscyn, R., Furuta, R., & Leggett, J. (1995). Digital libraries. *Communications of the ACM*, *38*(4), 23–28. doi:10.1145/205323.205325

Fredicks, J. A., Blumenfeld, P. C., & Paris, A. H. (2004). School engagement: Potential of the concept, state of the evidence. *Review of Educational Research*, *74*(1), 59–109. doi:10.3102/00346543074001059

Fredicks, J. A., Filsecker, M., & Lawson, M. A. (2016). Student engagement, context, and adjustment: Addressing definitional, measurement, and methodological issues. *Learning and Instruction*, *43*, 1–4. doi:10.1016/j.learninstruc.2016.02.002

Fredricks, J. A. (2011). Engagement in school and out-of-school contexts: A multidimensional view of engagement. *Theory into Practice*, *50*(4), 327–335. doi:10.1080/00405841.2011.607401

Fredricks, J. A., & McColskey, W. (2012). The measurement of student engagement: a comparative analysis of various methods and student self-report instruments. In S. Christenson, A. L. Reschy, & C. Wylie (Eds.), *Handbook of research on student engagement* (pp. 319–339). New York: Springer. doi:10.1007/978-1-4614-2018-7_37

Fredricks, J. A., Wang, M., Schall, J., Hokfkens, T., Parr, A., & Snug, H. (2016). Using qualitative methods to develop a measure of math and science engagement. *Learning and Instruction*, *43*, 5–15. doi:10.1016/j.learninstruc.2016.01.009

Free Software Foundation. (2016, November 18). Retrieved March 28, 2017, from https://www.gnu.org/licenses/gpl.html

Fu, F.-L., & Yu, S.-C. (2008). Three layered thinking model for designing web-based educational games. *International Conference on Web-Based Learning*, 265–274. 10.1007/978-3-540-85033-5_26

Fylan, F. (2005). Semi-structured interviewing. In D. Miles & P. Gilbert (Eds.), *A Handbook of Research Methods for Clinical and Health Psychology* (pp. 65–78). New York: Oxford University Press.

Galarneau, L., & Zibit, M. (2007). Online Game for 21st Century Skills. In D. Gibson, C. Aldrich, & M. Prensky (Eds.), *Games and simulations in online learning. Research and development frameworks* (pp. 59–88). Hershey, PA: Information Science Publishing. doi:10.4018/978-1-59904-304-3.ch004

Galitz, W. O. (1997). *The essential guide to user interface design: An introduction to GUI design principles and techniques* (3rd ed.). Medford, MA: Wiley.

Gandhi, S. K. (2016). India's Jumbo Jump from E-Commerce to Mobile Enabled Services (MES): A Review. *Productivity, 56*(4), 326.

Ganster, L. A., & Walsh, T. R. (2008). Enhancing library instruction to undergraduates: Incorporating online tutorials into the curriculum. *College & Undergraduate Libraries, 15*(3), 314–333. doi:10.1080/10691310802258232

Gao, X., Huang, W., Wang, N., Yang, Y., & Yan, Y. (2016). A top-N algorithm-based personalized learning recommendation system for digital library. *International Journal of Emerging Technologies in Learning, 11*(11), 55–59. doi:10.3991/ijet.v11i11.6256

Garfield, S. (2010). *Just my type*. New York: Gotham.

Garner, R., & Gillingham, M. G. (1996). *Internet Communication in Six Classrooms. Conversations Across Time, Space and Culture*. Mahwah, NJ: Erlbaum.

Garreta-Domingo, M., & Mor, E. (2007). *User Centered Design in E-Learning Environments: from Usability to Learner Experience.* Retrieved March 13, 2017, from https://www.researchgate.net/publication/43669285_User_Centered_Desing_in_E-Learning_Environments_from_Usability_to_Learner_Experience

Garrison, D. R., Anderson, T., & Archer, W. (2001). Critical thinking, cognitive presence, and computer conferencing in distance education. *American Journal of Distance Education, 15*(1), 7–23. doi:10.1080/08923640109527071

Garrison, D. R., & Kanuka, H. (2004). Blended learning: Uncovering its transformative potential in higher education. *The Internet and Higher Education, 7*(2), 95–105. doi:10.1016/j.iheduc.2004.02.001

Garris, R., Ahlers, R., & Driskell, J. E. (2002). Games, motivation, and learning: A research and practice model. *Simulation & Gaming, 33*(4), 441–467. doi:10.1177/1046878102238607

Gee, D., Chu, M.-W., Blimke, S., Rockwell, G., Gouglas, S., Holmes, D., & Lucky, S. (2014). Assessing Serious Games: The GRAND Assessment Framework. *Digital Studies/Le champ num{é}rique*.

Geis, T. (2010a). Neue ISO 9241-210 "Prozess zur Gestaltung gebrauchstauglicher Systeme" ersetzt die ISO 13407. Retrieved March 3 from http://www.procontext.com/aktuelles/2010/03/iso-9241210-prozess-zur-entwicklung-gebrauchstauglicher-interaktiver-systeme-veroeffentlicht.html

Geis, T. (2010b). Usability und User Experience unterscheiden. Retrieved March 31 from http://www.procontext.com/aktuelles/2010/03/usability-und-user-experience-unterscheiden.html

Geller, M., Tarouco, L. M. R., & Franco, S. R. K. (2004). Educação a Distância e Estilos Cognitivos: Construindo a Adaptação de Ambientes Virtuais. *VII Congresso Iberoamericano de Informática Educativa*, 1–10.

Germek, G. (2011). Empowered library eLearning: Capturing assessment and reporting with ease, efficiency, and effectiveness. *RSR. Reference Services Review, 40*(1), 90–102. doi:10.1108/00907321211203658

Getty, N. K., Burd, B., Burns, S. K., & Piele, L. (2000). Using courseware to deliver library instruction via the Web: Four examples. *RSR. Reference Services Review, 28*(4), 349–359. doi:10.1108/00907320010359678

Giacumo, L. A., Savenye, W., & Smith, N. (2012). Facilitation prompts and rubrics on higher-order thinking skill performance found in undergraduate asynchronous discussion boards. *British Journal of Educational Technology, 44*(5), 774–794. doi:10.1111/j.1467-8535.2012.01355.x

Gibson, J. J. (1979). *The ecological approach to visual perception.* Boston: Houghton Mifflin.

Gilbert, S. (2015). *Designing Gamified Systems: Meaningful Play in Interactive Entertainment, Marketing and Education.* CRC Press.

Ginns, P., & Ellis, R. (2007). Quality in blended learning: Exploring the relationships between on-line and face-to-face teaching and learning. *The Internet and Higher Education, 10*(1), 53–64. doi:10.1016/j.iheduc.2006.10.003

Glaser, B. (1965). The constant comparative method of qualitative analysis. *Social Problems, 12*(4), 436–445. doi:10.2307/798843

Göbel, S., de Carvalho Rodrigues, A., Mehm, F., & Steinmetz, R. (2009). Narrative game-based learning objects for story-based digital educational games. *Narrative, 14*, 16. Available at: http://www.eightydays.eu/Paper/GdCMS09.pdf

Göbel, S., Gutjahr, M., & Hardy, S. (2013). *Evaluation of Serious Games.* Serious Games and Virtual Worlds in Education, Professional Development, and Healthcare.

Göbel, S., Gutjahr, M., & Steinmetz, R. (2011). What Makes a Good Serious Game--Conceptual Approach Towards a Metadata Format for the Description and Evaluation of Serious Games. *Proceedings of the European Conference on Games Based Learning*, 202–210.

Gobert, J. D., Baker, R. S., & Wixon, M. B. (2015). Operationalizing and detecting disengagement within online science microworlds. *Educational Psychologist, 50*(1), 43–57. doi:10.1080/00461520.2014.999919

Gomes, J., Yassine, M., Worsley, M., & Blikstein, P. (2013). Analysing Engineering Expertise of High School Students Using Eye Tracking and Multimodal Learning Analytics. Educational Data Mining 2013.

Gómez, S., Zervas, P., Sampson, D. G., & Fabregat, R. (2014). Context-aware adaptive and personalized mobile learning delivery supported by UoLmP. *Journal of King Saud University-Computer and Information Sciences, 26*(1), 47–61.

González, M., Moreno, L., Martínez, P., & Iglesias, A. (2011). Web accessibility requirements for media players. In *Human-Computer Interaction–INTERACT 2011*. Springer.DOI: .10.1007/978-3-642-23768-3_109

Grafsgaard, J. F., Wiggins, J. B., Boyer, K. E., Wiebe, E. N., & Lester, J. C. (2014). *Predicting Learning and Affect from Multimodal Data Streams in Task-Oriented Tutorial Dialogue. In Proceedings of the 7th International Conference on Educational Data Mining* (pp. 122–129). EDM. Available at http://research.csc.ncsu.edu/learndialogue/pdf/LearnDialogue-Grafsgaard-EDM-2014.pdf

Grafsgaard, J. F., Wiggins, J. B., Boyer, K. E., Wiebe, E. N., & Lester, J. C. II. (2013). Embodied affect in tutorial dialogue. *16th International Conference on Artificial Intelligence in Education, AIED 2013.*

Graham, C. R., Woodfield, W. W., & Harrison, J. B. (2013). A framework for institutional adoption and implementation of blended learning in higher education. *The Internet and Higher Education, 18*, 4–14. doi:10.1016/j.iheduc.2012.09.003

Granger, B. P., & Levine, E. L. (2010). The perplexing role of learner control in e-learning: Will learning and transfer benefit or suffer? *International Journal of Training and Development, 14*(3), 180–199. doi:10.1111/j.1468-2419.2010.00351.x

Greenbaum, J. (1993). A design of One's Own: Towards Participatory Design in the United States. In D. Schuler & A. Namioka (Eds.), *Participatory Design: Principles and Practices* (pp. 27–40). Hillsdale, NJ: Lawrence Erlbaum Associates, Inc., Publishers.

Greene, B. A. (2015). Measuring cognitive engagement with selfreport scales: Reflections from over 20 years of research. *Educational Psychologist, 50*(1), 14–30. doi:10.1080/00461520.2014.989230

Griffiths, M. (2002). The educational benefits of videogames. *Education for Health, 20*(3), 47–51. Retrieved from http://sheu.org.uk/sites/sheu.org.uk/files/imagepicker/1/eh203mg.pdf

Gros, B. (2016). The design of smart educational environments. *Smart Learning Environments, 15*(3). doi:10.118640561-016-0039x

Gross, M., & Latham, D. (2007). Attaining information literacy: An investigation of the relationship between skill level, self-estimates of skill, and library anxiety. *Library & Information Science Research, 29*(3), 332–353. doi:10.1016/j.lisr.2007.04.012

Gross, M., & Latham, D. (2012). What's skills got to do with it?: Information literacy skills and self-views of ability among first-year college students. *Journal of the American Society for Information Science and Technology, 63*(3), 574–583. doi:10.1002/asi.21681

Gustavson, A., Whitehurst, A., & Hisle, D. (2011). Laying the information literacy foundation: A multiple-media solution. *Library Hi Tech, 29*(4), 725–740. doi:10.1108/07378831111189796

Gutica, M., & Conati, C. (2013). Student emotions with an edu-game: a detailed analysis. *Affective Computing and Intelligent Interaction (ACII), 2013 Humaine Association Conference on*, 534–539. 10.1109/ACII.2013.94

Gyselinck, V., Ehrlich, M., Cornoldi, C., Beni, R., & Dubois, V. (2000). Visuospatial working memory in learning from multimedia systems. *Journal of Computer Assisted Learning, 16*(2), 166–176. doi:10.1046/j.1365-2729.2000.00128.x

Hackos, J. T., & Redish, J. C. (1998). *User and task analysis for interface design*. New York: John Wiley & Sons.

Hagen, P., Collin, P., Metcalf, A., Nicholas, M., Rahilly, K., & Swainston, N. (2012). *Participatory Design of evidence-based online youth mental health promotion, prevention early intervention and treatment*. Melbourne: Young and Well Cooperative Research Centre.

Halverson, E. (2012). Participatory media spaces: A design perspective on learning with media and technology in the 21st Century. In C. Steinkuehler, K. Squire, & S. Barab (Eds.), *Games learning & society: Learning and meaning in a digital age* (pp. 244–270). New York: Cambridge University Press. doi:10.1017/CBO9781139031127.020

Halverson, L. R., Graham, C. R., Spring, K. J., Drysdale, J. S., & Henrie, C. R. (2014). A thematic analysis of the most highly cited scholarship in the first decade of blended learning research. *The Internet and Higher Education, 20*, 20–34. doi:10.1016/j.iheduc.2013.09.004

Hannafin, M. J. (1984). Guidelines for using locus of instructional control in the design of computer- assisted instruction. *Journal of Instructional Development, 7*(3), 6–10. doi:10.1007/BF02905753

Harasim, L. M. (1990). Online education: An environment for collaboration and intellectual amplification. In L. M. Harasim (Ed.), *Online education: perspectives on a new environment* (pp. 39–64). Praeger Publishing.

Hasiah, M. O., & Azizah, J. (2010). Challenges in the evaluation of educational computer games. *2010 International Symposium in Information Technology (ITSim)*, 15–17.

Hassenzahl, M., Burmester, M., & Koller, F. (2008). Der User Experience (UX) auf der Spur: Zum Einsatz von attrakdiff.de. In H. Brau, S. Diefenbach, M. Hassenzahl, F. Koller, M. Peissner, & K. Röse (Eds.), *Usability Professionals 2008* (pp. 78–82). Stuttgart, Germany: German Chapter der Usability Professionals Association.

Hegarty, M., & Just, M. A. (1993). Constructing mental models of machines from text and diagrams. *Journal of Memory and Language*, *32*(6), 717–742. doi:10.1006/jmla.1993.1036

Heller, S., & Fernandez, T. (1999). *Becoming a graphic designer*. New York: Wiley.

Herpich, F., Nunes, F. B., Voss, G. B., Jardim, R. R., & Medina, R. D. (2014). Ambiente Virtual Imersivo para ensino em Redes de Computadores: uma proposta usando Agentes Inteligentes. *25th Brazilian Symposium on Computer in Education*, 65–69. 10.5753/cbie.sbie.2014.65

Herrington, J., Oliver, R., & Reeves, A. (2013). Authentic learning environments. In Handbook of research on educational communications and technology (4th ed., pp. 401-412). New York, NY: Springer New York.

Herrington, J., Reeves, T. C., & Oliver, R. (2006). Authentic tasks online: A synergy among learner, task, and technology. *Distance Education*, *27*(2), 233–247. doi:10.1080/01587910600789639

Hew, K., & Brush, T. (2007). Integrating technology into K-12 teaching and learning: Current knowledge gaps and recommendations for future research. *Educational Technology Research and Development*, *55*(3), 223–252. doi:10.100711423-006-9022-5

Hill, J. R., Wiley, D., Nelson, L. M., & Han, S. (2004). Exploring research on internet-based learning: From infrastructure to interactions. In D. H. Jonassen (Ed.), *The Handbook of Research on Educational Communications and Technology* (pp. 433–460). Mahwah, NJ: Lawrence Erlbaum Associates.

Hillman, D. C., Willis, D. J., & Gunawardena, C. N. (1994). Learner-interface interaction in distance education: An extension of contemporary models and strategies for practitioners. *American Journal of Distance Education*, *8*(2), 30–42. doi:10.1080/08923649409526853

Holden, H., & Rada, R. (2011). Understanding the influence of perceived usability and technology self-efficacy on teachers' technology acceptance. *Journal of Research on Technology in Education*, *43*(4), 343–367. doi:10.1080/15391523.2011.10782576

Holley, C. D., Dansereau, D. F., McDonald, B. A., Garland, J. C., & Collins, K. W. (1979). Evaluation of a hierarchical mapping technique as an aid to prose processing. *Contemporary Educational Psychology*, *4*(3), 227–237. doi:10.1016/0361-476X(79)90043-2

Honey, P., & Mumford, A. (2000). *The Learning Styles helper's guide. Maldenhead Berks*. Peter Honey Publications.

Hsieh, M., Dawson, P., Hofmann, M., Titus, M., & Carlin, M. (2014). Four pedagogical approaches in helping students learn information literacy skills. *Journal of Academic Librarianship*, *40*(3/4), 234–246. doi:10.1016/j.acalib.2014.03.012

Huang, Y.-T. (2015). Participatory Design to Enhance ICT Learning and Community Attachment: A Case Study in Rural Taiwan. *Future Internet*, *7*(1), 50–66. doi:10.3390/fi7010050

Hu, M., & Wu, M. (2012). The effect of concept mapping on students' cognitive load. *World Transactions on Engineering and Technology Education*, *10*(2), 134–137.

Hung, M.-L., & Chou, C. (2015). Students' perceptions of instructors' roles in blended and online learning environments: A comparative study. *Computers & Education*, *81*, 315–325. doi:10.1016/j.compedu.2014.10.022

Hu, P., Clark, T., & Ma, W. (2003). Examining technology acceptance by school teachers: A longitudinal study. *Information & Management, 41*(2), 227–241. doi:10.1016/S0378-7206(03)00050-8

HusbyO. (2014). *The function utopia*. Retrieved from http://www.oysteinhusby.com/function-utopia-form-follows-function/

Hussy, W., Schreier, M., & Echterhoff, G. (Eds.). (2013). *Forschungsmethoden in Psychologie und Sozialwissenschaften für Bachelor* (2nd ed.). Berlin: Springer. doi:10.1007/978-3-642-34362-9

Ibrahim, R., & Jaafar, A. (2009). Educational Games (EG) design framework: Combination of game design, pedagogy and content modeling. *Electrical Engineering and Informatics, 2009. ICEEI'09. International Conference on*, 293–298. 10.1109/ICEEI.2009.5254771

Insight, A. (2013). *International eLearning Market Research*. Academic Press.

Irani, T. (1998). Communication potential, information richness and attitude: A study of computer mediated communication in the ALN classroom. *ALN Magazine, 2*, 1–12.

Ireland, C. (2003). The changing role of research. In B. Laurel (Ed.), *Design research: Methods and perspectives* (pp. 22–29). Cambridge, MA: MIT Press.

Ismail, A., & Kuppusamy, K. S. (2015). *Accessibility of Indian universities' homepages: An exploratory study. Journal of King Saud University – Computer and Information Sciences,* 1–11.

Ismailova, R., & Inal, Y. (2016). Web site accessibility and quality in use: a comparative study of government Web sites in Kyrgyzstan, Azerbaijan, Kazakhstan and Turkey. In *Universal Access in the Information Society*. Springer. DOI: 10.1007/s10209-016-0490-z

Itten, J. (2003). *The elements of color*. New York: John Wiley and Sons.

Itten, J. (2004). *The art of color: The subjective experience and objective rationale of color*. New York: John Wiley and Sons.

Ivanitskaya, L., Laus, R., & Casey, A. M. (2004). Research Readiness Self-Assessment. *Journal of Library Administration, 41*(1/2), 167–183. doi:10.1300/J111v41n01_13

Jacka, L. (2015). *Virtual worlds in pre-service teacher education: The introduction of virtual worlds in preservice teacher education to foster innovative teaching-learning processes. Tese de Doutorado*. Southern Cross University.

Jaguszewski, J., & Williams, K. (2013). *New Roles for New Times: Transforming Liaison Roles in Research Libraries.* Association of Research Libraries. Retrieved from the University of Minnesota Digital Conservancy, http://hdl.handle.net/11299/169867

Jamieson, J. (1992). The cognitive styles of reflection/impulsivity and field independence/dependence and ESL success. *Modern Language Journal, 3*(4), 491–501. doi:10.1111/j.1540-4781.1992.tb05398.x

Jarmon, L., Traphagan, T., Mayrath, M., & Trivedi, A. (2009). Virtual world teaching, experiential learning, and assessment: An interdisciplinary communication course in Second Life. *Computer Education, 53*(1), 169–182. doi:10.1016/j.compedu.2009.01.010

Jenkins, H. (2009). *Confronting the challenges of participatory culture: media education for the 21st century*. Cambridge, MA: The MIT Press.

Jetter, H.-C., & Gerken, J. (2007). A Simplified Model of User Experience for Practical Application. In *Proceeding of 2nd COST294-MAUSE International Open Workshop* (pp. 106-111). Oslo, Norway: Academic Press.

Jiang, M., & Ting, E. (2000). A study of factors influencing students' perceived learning in a Web-based course environment. *International Journal of Educational Telecommunications*, *6*, 317–338.

Jitsi [Computer Software]. (n.d.). Retrieved from https://jitsi.org/

Johnson, C. M., Vorderstrasse, A., & Shaw, R. (2009). Virtual Worlds in Health Care Higher Education. *Journal of Virtual Worlds Research*, *2*(2), 1–12.

Johnson, R. B., & Onwuegbuzie, A. J. (2004). Mixed methods research: A research paradigm whose time has come. *Educational Researcher*, *33*(7), 14–26. doi:10.3102/0013189X033007014

Jonassen, D. (1996). O uso das tecnologias na Educação à Distância e as aprendizagens construtivistas. Em Aberto, 70, 1-19.

Julier, G. (2008). *The culture of design*. Los Angeles, CA: Sage.

Jung, I., & Suzuki, K. (2006). Blended learning in Japan and its application in liberal arts education. In C. J. Bonk & C. R. Graham (Eds.), *The handbook of blended learning: Global perspectives, local designs* (pp. 267–280). San Francisco, CA: Pfeiffer.

Junglas, I. A., Johnson, N. A., Steel, D. J., Abraham, D. A., Loughlin, P. M. (2007). Identity formation, learning styles and trust in virtual worlds. *ACM SIGMIS Database: The DATABASE for Advances in Information Systems archive*, *38*(4), 90-96.

Júnior, G. D. C. (2005). *Trajetórias de aprendizagem de alunos de ensino médio: produção de significados em um curso introdutório de física térmica. Dissertação de Mestrado*. UFMG.

Kadu, M. V., Bagret, M. V. M., & Verma, M. A. (2015). Transforming from e-Governance to M-Governance. *International Journal of Advanced Research in Computer and Communication Engineering*, *4*(2), 457–462. doi:10.17148/IJARCCE.2015.42103

Kai, S., Paquette, L., Baker, R. S., Bosch, N., D'Mello, S., Ocumpaugh, J., ... Ventura, M. (2015). *A Comparison of Video-based and Interaction-based Affect Detectors in Physics Playground*. EDM.

Kalyuga, S., & Liu, T. C. (2015). Guest editorial: Managing cognitive load in technology-based learning environments. *Journal of Educational Technology & Society*, *18*(4), 1–8.

Kamal, K. K., Kumar, M., Shrivastava, S., & Chourasia, P. (2016). Mobile Seva-Enabling mGovernance in India. In *Proceedings of the 2016 CHI Conference Extended Abstracts on Human Factors in Computing Systems*. ACM. 10.1145/2851581.2851586

Kamal, K. K., Kumar, M., Varyani, B., Shrivastava, S., & Tripathi, P. (2015). Mobile Platform as a Service A Case Study of User Friendly Approach to Mobile Strategy. In *Proceedings of the 13th International Conference on Advances in Mobile Computing and Multimedia (MoMM 2015)*. ACM. 10.1145/2837126.2837163

Kamoun, F., Mourad, B. M. A., & Bataineh, E. (2013). WCAG 1.0 versus WCAG 2.0 Web Accessibility Compliance: A Case Study. In *Proceeding of the International Conference on Digital Information Processing, E-Business and Cloud Computing (DIPECC2013)* (pp. 94-101). The Society of Digital Information and Wireless Communication.

Karabeg, D. (2003). Designing information design. *Information Design Journal*, *11*(1), 82–90. doi:10.1075/idj.11.1.12kar

Karjaluoto, E. (2014). *The design method: A philosophy and process for functional visual communication*. San Francisco: New Riders.

Keefe, P. A. O., Letourneau, S. M., Homer, B. D., Schwartz, R. N., & Plass, J. L. (2014). *Computers in Human Behavior Learning from multiple representations: An examination of fixation patterns in a science simulation*. Academic Press.

Keller, J. M. (1983). Motivational design of instruction. In C. M. Reigeluth (Ed.), *Instructional-design theories and models: An overview of their current status* (pp. 383–434). Hillsdale, NJ: Erlbaum.

Keller, J. M., & Suzuki, K. (1988). Application of the ARCS model to courseware design. In D. H. Jonassen (Ed.), *Instructional Designs for Microcomputer Courseware* (pp. 401–434). New York: Lawrence Erlbaum.

Keller, T., Gerjets, P., Scheiter, K., & Garsoffky, B. (2006). Information visualizations as tools for knowledge acquisition: The impact of dimensionality and color coding. *Computers in Human Behavior, 22*(1), 43–65. doi:10.1016/j.chb.2005.01.006

Kellum, K., Mark, A. E., & Riley-Huff, D. A. (2011). Development, assessment and use of an on-line plagiarism tutorial. *Library Hi Tech, 29*(4), 641–654. doi:10.1108/07378831111189741

Kendall, M. (2005). Tackling student referencing errors through an online tutorial. *Aslib Proceedings, 57*(2), 131–145. doi:10.1108/00012530510589100

Kennedy-Clark, S. (2011). Pre-service teachers' perspectives on using scenario-based virtual worlds in science education. Computer & Education, 57(4), 2224–2235.

Kerres, M. (2016). E-Learning vs. Digitalisierung der Bildung: Neues Label oder neues Paradigma? In A. Hohenstein & K. Wilbers (Eds.), *Handbuch E-Learning (61. Ergänzungslieferung)*. Köln, Germany: Fachverlag Deutscher Wirtschaftsdienst.

Kerres, M., & De Witt, C. (2003). A didactical framework for the design of blended learning. *Journal of Educational Media, 28*(2), 101–113. doi:10.1080/1358165032000165653

Khan, B. H. (1997). *Web-based instruction*. Englewood Cliffs, NJ: Educational Technology.

Khan, B. H. (1998). Web-based instruction: An introduction. *Educational Media International, 35*(2), 63–71. doi:10.1080/0952398980350202

Khine, M. S. (2011). *Learning to play: exploring the future of education with video games*. Peter Lang. doi:10.3726/978-1-4539-0084-0

Kickmeier-rust, M. D., & Albert, D. (2013). *Learning Analytics to Support the Use of Virtual Worlds in the Classroom*. Human-Computer Interaction and Knowledge Discovery in Complex. doi:10.1007/978-3-642-39146-0_34

Kiel, S., Burclaff, N., & Johnson, C. (2015). Learning by doing: Developing a baseline information literacy assessment. *portal. Libraries and the Academy, 15*(4), 747–766. doi:10.1353/pla.2015.0049

Kiili, K., Lainema, T., de Freitas, S., & Arnab, S. (2014). Flow framework for analyzing the quality of educational games. *Entertainment Computing. Elsevier, 5*(4), 367–377. doi:10.1016/j.entcom.2014.08.002

Kim, J. H., Baylen, D., Leh, A., & Lin, L. (2015). Blended learning in teacher education: Uncovering its transformative potential for teacher preparation programs. In N. P. Ololube & P. J. Kpolovie (Eds.), Enhancing Teacher Education with Advanced Instructional Technologies. Hershey, PA: IGI Global.

Kimball, M. A. (2013). Visual design principles: An empirical study of design lore. *Journal of Technical Writing and Communication, 43*(1), 3–41. doi:10.2190/TW.43.1.b

Kimmons, R. (2015). Open online system adoption in K-12 as a democratising factor. *Open Learning: The Journal of Open. Distance and E-Learning, 30*(2), 138–151. doi:10.1080/02680513.2015.1077109

Klemme, B., & Siegmann, G. (Eds.). (2006). *Clinical Reasoning. Therapeutische Denkprozesse lernen*. Stuttgart: Georg Thieme Verlag.

Kohler, T., Fueller, J., Matzler, K., Stieger, D., & Füller, J. (2011). Co-Creation in Virtual Worlds: The Design of the User Experience. *Management Information Systems Quarterly*, *35*(3), 773–788. doi:10.2307/23042808

Kolb, D. (1984). *Experiential learning, experience as the source of learning and development*. Englewood Cliffs, NJ: Prentice Hall.

Kolb, D. A. (1984). *Experiential Learning: experience as the source of learning and development*. Englewood Cliffs, NJ: Prentice-Hall.

Konstantinidis, A., Tsiatsos, T., Demetriadis, S., & Pomportsis, A. (2010). Collaborative Learning in OpenSim by Utilizing SLoodle. *Sixth Advanced International Conference on Telecommunications*, 90–95. 10.1109/AICT.2010.75

Kort, B., & Reilly, R. (2002). Analytical models of emotions, learning and relationships: towards an affect-sensitive cognitive machine. *Conference on virtual worlds and simulation (VWSim 2002)*.

Korucu, A. T., & Alkan, A. (2011). Differences in m-learning (mobile learning) and e-learning, basic terminology and usage of m-learning in education. *Procedia: Social and Behavioral Sciences*, *15*, 1925–1930. doi:10.1016/j.sbspro.2011.04.029

Kotsilieris, T.; Dimopoulou, N. (2013). The evolution of e-learning in the context of 3D virtual worlds. *Electronic Journal of e-Learning, 11*(2), 147–167.

Kraemer, E., Lombardo, S., & Lepkowski, F. (2007). The librarian, the machine, or a little of both: A comparative study of three information literacy pedagogies at Oakland University. *College & Research Libraries*, *68*(4), 330–342. doi:10.5860/crl.68.4.330

Kristian Kiili Harri Ketamo, M. D. K.-R. (2014). Eye Tracking in Game-based Learning Research and Game Design. *International Journal of Serious Games*, 1.

Kruger, J., & Dunning, D. (1999). Unskilled and unaware of it: How difficulties in recognizing one's own incompetence lead to inflated self-assessments. *Journal of Personality and Social Psychology*, *77*(6), 1121–1134. doi:10.1037/0022-3514.77.6.1121 PMID:10626367

Krug, S. (2000). *Don't make me think!: A common sense approach to Web usability*. Indianapolis, IN: New Riders.

Kuo, Y.-C., Walker, A., & Schroder, K. (2010, March). *Interaction and other variables as predictors of student satisfaction in online learning environments*. Paper presented at the Society for Information Technology & Teacher Education International Conference, San Diego, CA.

Kuo, Y.-C., Walker, A. E., Schroder, K. E., & Belland, B. R. (2014). Interaction, Internet self- efficacy, and selfregulated learning as predictors of student satisfaction in online education courses. *The Internet and Higher Education*, *20*, 35–50. doi:10.1016/j.iheduc.2013.10.001

Kurbanoglu, S. (2010). *Self-efficacy: An alternative approach to the evaluation of information literacy*. QQML 2009: Qualitative and Quantitative Methods in Libraries, *International Conference*, Chania, Greece.

Kurbanoglu, S., Akkoyunlu, B., & Umay, A. (2006). Developing the information literacy self-efficacy scale. *The Journal of Documentation*, *62*(6), 730–743. doi:10.1108/00220410610714949

Kuzma, J. M., Yen, D., & Oestreicher, K. (2009). Global e-government Web Accessibility: An Empirical Examination of EU, Asian and African Sites. *Proceeding of 2nd International Conference on Information and Communication Technologies and Accessibility*, 1-6.

Laird, N. T. F., & Kuh, G. D. (2005). Student experiences with information technology and their relationship to other aspects of student engagement. *Research in Higher Education*, *46*(2), 211–233. doi:10.100711162-004-1600-y

Landa, R. (2014). *Graphic design solutions*. Boston: Wadsworth.

Lapidus, M., McCord, S. K., McCloskey, W. W., & Kostka-Rokosz, M. (2012). Combined use of online tutorials and hands-on group exercises in bibliographic instruction for pharmacy students. *Medical Reference Services Quarterly, 31*(4), 383–399. doi:10.1080/02763869.2012.724277 PMID:23092416

Latif, M. H. A., & Masrek, M. N. (2010). Accessibility Evaluation on Malaysian E-Government Websites. Journal of e-Government Studies and Best Practice, 1-11.

Latourelle, R. (2015). *Sensing the future: Moholy-Nagy, media and the arts* [e-flux online editorial]. Retrieved from http://goo.gl/Jg9Gt3

Laurillard, D. (2007). Modelling benefits-oriented costs for technology enhanced learning. *Higher Education, 54*(1), 21–39. doi:10.100710734-006-9044-2

Law, E. L.-C., Roto, V., Hassenzahl, M. Vermeeren, A. P. O. S., & Kort, J. (2009). Understanding, Scoping and Defining UsereXperience: A Survey Approach. In *Proceedings of the 27th International Conference on Human Factors in Computing Systems, CHI 2009* (pp. 719-728). Boston, MA: Association for Computing Machinery (ACM). 10.1145/1518701.1518813

Lee, C.-H., Yeh, D., Kung, R. J., & Hsu, C.-S. (2007). The Influences of learning portfolios and attitudes on learning effects in blended e-learning for mathematics. *Journal of Educational Computing Research, 37*(4), 331–350. doi:10.2190/EC.37.4.a

Lewis, N. J., & Orton, P. Z. (2006). Blending learning for business impact: IBM's case for learning success. In C. J. Bonk & C. R. Graham (Eds.), *The handbook of blended learning: Global perspectives, local designs* (pp. 61–75). San Francisco, CA: Pfeiffer.

Liang, C., Chou, W.-S., Hsu, Y.-L., & Yang, C.-C. (2009). A User-Centered Design Approach to Develop a Web-Based Instructional Resource System for Homeland Education. *Knowledge Management & E-Learning: An International Journal, 1*(1), 67–80.

Lidwell, W., Butler, J., & Holden, K. (2010). Universal principles of design: 125 ways to enhance usability, influence perception, increase appeal, make better design decisions, and teach through design. Beverly, MA: Rockport.

Li, J.-S., Han, Y.-X., & Liu, S. (2014). Physiological Evaluation of the Players' Emotions in Different Educational Games. *American Journal of Educational Research, 2*(9), 735–739.

Limniou, M., Roberts, D., & Papadopoulos, N. (2008). Full immersive virtual environment CAVETM in chemistry education. Computer & Education, 51(2), 584–593. doi:10.1016/j.compedu.2007.06.014

Lindauer, B. G. (2004). The three arenas of information literacy assessment. *Reference and User Services Quarterly, 44*(2), 122–129.

Lindsay, E. B., Cummings, L., Johnson, C. M., & Scales, B. J. (2006). If you build it, will they learn? Assessing online information literacy tutorials. *College & Research Libraries, 67*(5), 429–445. doi:10.5860/crl.67.5.429

Lin, L., Atkinson, R. K., Savenye, W. C., & Nelson, B. C. (2016). The effects of visual cues and self-explanation prompts: Empirical evidence in a multimedia environment. *Interactive Learning Environments, 24*(4), 799–813. doi:10.1080/10494820.2014.924531

Lin, W., & Wang, C.-H. (2012). Antecedences to continued intentions of adopting e-learning system in blended learning instruction: A contingency framework based on models of information system success and task-technology fit. *Computers & Education, 58*(1), 88–99. doi:10.1016/j.compedu.2011.07.008

Lockwood, D. L. (1979). *Library instruction: A bibliography*. Westport, CT: Greenwood Press.

Loh, C. S., Sheng, Y., & Ifenthaler, D. (2015). Serious games analytics: Theoretical framework. In *Serious Games Analytics* (pp. 3–29). Springer. doi:10.1007/978-3-319-05834-4_1

Lohr, L. (2008). *Creating graphics for learning and performance: Lessons in visual literacy*. Columbus, OH: Pearson.

Lohr, L. L. (2000). Designing the instructional interface. *Computers in Human Behavior, 16*(2), 161–182. doi:10.1016/S0747-5632(99)00057-6

Lo, J., Chan, Y., & Yeh, S. (2011). Designing an adaptive web-based learning system based on students' cognitive styles identified online. *Computers & Education, 58*(1), 209–222. doi:10.1016/j.compedu.2011.08.018

Lopes, R., Bandeira, R., Carriço, L., & Isacker, K. V. (2010). Towards Mobile Web Accessibility: Vision And Challenges. *Proceedings of the first International ÆGIS Conference*, 151-158.

Lowenthal, P. R., & White, J. W. (2009). Enterprise model. In P. Rogers, G. Berg, J. Boettcher, C. Howard, L. Justice, & K. Schenk (Eds.), *Encyclopedia of distance and online learning* (2nd ed., pp. 932-936). Hershey, PA: IGI Global. doi:10.4018/978-1-60566-198-8.ch130

Lowe, S. M., Booth, C., Tagge, N., & Stone, S. (2014). Integrating an information literacy quiz into the learning management system. *Communications in Information Literacy, 8*(1), 115–130. doi:10.15760/comminfolit.2014.8.1.156

Luchev, D., Paneva-Marinova, D., Pavlov, R., Kaposi, G., Markus, Z., Szanto, G., . . . Veres, M. (2016). Game-based learning of Bulgarian iconographical art on smart phone application. In *Proceedings of the International Conference on e-Learning* (pp. 195-200). Bratislava, Slovakia: University of Ruse, Bulgaria. Retrieved March 20, 2017, from http://elearning-conf.eu/docs/cp16/paper-30.pdf

Luchev, D., Paneva-Marinova, D., Pavlova-Draganova, L., & Pavlov, R. (2013). New digital fashion world. In B. Rachev, & A. Smrikarov (Ed.), *Proceedings of the 14th International Conference on Computer Systems and Technologies, CompSysTech'13* (vol. 767, pp. 270-275). The Association for Computing Machinery.

Lupton, E. (2010). Thinking with type: A critical guide for designers, writers, editors, & students. New York: Princeton Architectural Press.

Lupton, E. (2009). Forward. In H. Armstrong (Ed.), *Graphic design theory: Readings from the field* (pp. 6–7). New York: Princeton Architectural Press.

Lupton, E. (2014). *Type on screen: A guide for designers, developers, writers, and students*. New York: Princeton Architectural Press.

Lupton, E., & Miller, J. A. (2006). *The ABC's of ▲■●: The Bauhaus and design theory*. London: Thames and Hudson.

Lyons, S., & Warlick, T. (2012). Health sciences information literacy in CMS environments: Learning from our peers. *The Electronic Library, 31*(6), 770–780. doi:10.1108/EL-06-2012-0063

Macario, J. W. (2009). *Graphic design essentials: Skills, software, and creative solutions*. Upper Saddle River, NJ: Pearson.

MacGregor, S. K. (1999). Hypermedia navigation profiles: Cognitive characteristics and information processing strategies. *Journal of Educational Computing Research, 20*(2), 189–206. doi:10.2190/1MEC-C0W6-111H-YQ6A

Machet, T., & Lowe, D. (2013). Issues Integrating Remote Laboratories into Virtual Worlds. In H. Carter, M. Gosper, & J. Hedberg (Eds.), Electric Dreams. Academic Press.

Madonna University Library. (2014). *Tip quiz.* Retrieved from http://library. madonna.edu/pages/InfoLit-TipQuiz/generalform.cfm

Magoulas, G. D., Papanikolaou, K. A., & Grigoriadou, M. (2003). Adaptive Web-based learning: Accommodating individual differences through system's adaptation. *British Journal of Educational Technology, 34*(4), 511–527. doi:10.1111/1467-8535.00347

Mahara [Computer Software]. (n.d.). Retrieved from https://mahara.org/

Mahmud, J., Borodin, Y., & Ramakrishnan, I. V. (2007). CSurf: A Context-Driven Non-Visual Web-Browser. In *Proceedings of the 16th international conference on World Wide Web, WWW 2007*. ACM. 10.1145/1242572.1242578

Malamed, C. (2009). *Visual language for designers: Principles for creating graphics that people understand.* Beverly, MA: Rockport Publishing.

Mandryk, R. L., & Atkins, M. S. (2007). A fuzzy physiological approach for continuously modeling emotion during interaction with play technologies. *International Journal of Human-Computer Studies, 65*(4), 329–347.

Manovich, L. (2000). *The language of new media.* Cambridge, MA: MIT Press.

Manovich, L. (2017). Aesthetics. In L. Ouellette & J. Gray (Eds.), *Keywords for media studies* (pp. 9–11). New York: NYU Press.

Manzini, E. (1989). *The materials of invention: Materials and design.* Cambridge, MA: MIT Press.

Marcus, A., & Gould, E. W. (2000). CROSSCURRENTS. Cultural Dimensions and Global Web-User Interface Design. *Interaction, 7*(4), 32–46. doi:10.1145/345190.345238

Marczak, R., & Schott, G. R. (2015). Audio visual analysis of player experience: feedback-based gameplay metrics. Game Research Methods, 207–230.

Margolin, V., & Margolin, S. (2002). A "social model" of design: Issues of practice and research. *Design Issues, 18*(4), 24–30. doi:10.1162/074793602320827406

Marks, K. (2016). How the web became unreadable. *Wired Magazine.* Retrieved from https://www.wired.com/2016/10/how-the-web-became-unreadable/

Marne, B., Wisdom, J., Huynh-Kim-Bang, B., & Labat, J.-M. (2012). The six facets of serious game design: a methodology enhanced by our design pattern library. *European Conference on Technology Enhanced Learning*, 208–221. 10.1007/978-3-642-33263-0_17

Martin, A. J. (2003). Boys and motivation. *Australian Educational Researcher, 30*(3), 43–63. doi:10.1007/BF03216797

Martin-Michiellot, S., & Mendelsohn, P. (2000). Cognitive load while learning with a graphical computer interface. *Journal of Computer Assisted Learning, 16*(4), 284–293. doi:10.1046/j.1365-2729.2000.00141.x

Massironi, M. (2010). *The psychology of graphic images: Seeing, drawing, communicating.* Mahwah, NJ: L. Erlbaum. (Original work published 1937)

Mayer, R. E. (1997). Multimedia learning: Are we asking the right questions? *Educational Psychologist, 32*(1), 1–19. doi:10.120715326985ep3201_1

Mayer, R. E. (2003). The promise of multimedia learning: Using the same instructional design methods across different media. *Learning and Instruction, 13*(2), 125–139. doi:10.1016/S0959-4752(02)00016-6

Mayer, R. E. (2011b). Instruction based on visualizations. In R. E. Mayer & P. A. Alexander (Eds.), *Handbook of Research on Learning and Instruction*. New York: Routledge.

Mayer, R. E., & Moreno, R. (2002). Aids to computer-based multimedia learning. *Learning and Instruction, 12*(1), 107–119. doi:10.1016/S0959-4752(01)00018-4

Mayer, R. E., & Moreno, R. (2003). Nine ways to reduce cognitive load in multimedia learning. *Educational Psychologist, 38*(1), 43–52. doi:10.1207/S15326985EP3801_6

Mayring, P. (2000). Qualitative Content Analysis. *Forum Qualitative Social Research, 2*(1). Retrieved from http://www.qualitative-research.net/index.php/fqs/article/view/1089/2385

McCormack, C., & Jones, D. (1998). *Building a Web-based education system*. New York: Wiley.

McKenney, S., & Reeves, T. (2012). *Conducting educational design research*. New York: Routledge.

McKenney, S., & Reeves, T. (2014). Educational design research. In J. M. Spector, M. D. Merrill, J. Elen, & M. J. Bishop (Eds.), *Handbook of research on educational communications and technology* (pp. 131–140). New York, NY: Springer New York. doi:10.1007/978-1-4614-3185-5_11

Medina, J. (2008). *Brain rules: 12 principles for surviving and thriving at work, home, and school*. Seattle, WA: Pear Press.

Mehm, F., Göbel, S., & Steinmetz, R. (2012). *Authoring of serious adventure games in storytec*. Springer. doi:10.1007/978-3-642-33466-5_16

Meinel, C., & Leifer, L. (2011). Design thinking research. In H. Plattner, C. Meinel, & L. Leifer (Eds.), *Design thinking: Understand - improve - apply* (pp. xiii–xxi). Berlin: Springer. doi:10.1007/978-3-642-13757-0

Mellon, C. A. (1986). Library anxiety: A grounded theory and its development. *College & Research Libraries, 47*(3), 160–165. doi:10.5860/crl_47_02_160

Merchant, Z., Goetz, E. T., Keeney-Kennicutt, W., Kwok, O., Cifuentes, L., Davis, T. J. (2012). The learner characteristics, features of desktop 3D virtual reality environments, and college chemistry instruction: A structural equation modeling analysis. *Computers & Education, 59*, 551–568.

Messick, S. (1984). The Nature of Cognitive Styles: Problems and Prornises in Educational Practice. *Educacional Psychologist, 19*(2), 59–74. doi:10.1080/00461528409529283

Metros, S. E. (2008). The educator's role in preparing visually literate learners. *Theory into Practice, 47*(2), 102–109. doi:10.1080/00405840801992264

Michalak, R., & Rysavy, M. (2016). Information literacy in 2015: International graduate students' perceptions of information literacy compared to test-assessed skills. *Journal of Business & Finance Librarianship, 21*(2), 152–174. doi:10.1080/08963568.2016.1145787

Michalak, R., Rysavy, M., & Wessel, A. (2017). Students' perceptions of their information literacy skills: The confidence gap between male and female international graduate students. *Journal of Academic Librarianship, 43*(2), 100–104. doi:10.1016/j.acalib.2017.02.003

Miller, L. (2012). Situating the rural teacher labor market in the broader context: A descriptive analysis of the market dynamics of New York state. *Journal of Research in Rural Education, 27*(13), 1–31.

Miller, V. (2011). *Understanding digital culture*. Los Angeles, CA: SAGE.

Mills, M. (2006). Appendix: Gender of the universal. In E. Lupton & J. A. Miller (Eds.), *The ABC's of ▲■ ●: The Bauhaus and design theory* (pp. 46–49). London: Thames and Hudson.

Minocha, S., & Reeves, A. J. (2010). Interaction Design and Usability of Learning Spaces in 3D Multi-user Virtual Worlds. In D. Katre, R. Orngreen, P. Yammiyavar, & T. Clemmensen (Eds.), *Human Work Interaction Design: Usability in Social, Cultural and Organizational Contexts. IFIP Advances in Information and Communication Technology* (Vol. 316). Berlin: Springer. doi:10.1007/978-3-642-11762-6_13

Mirza-Babaei, P., Wallner, G., McAllister, G., & Nacke, L. E. (2014). Unified Visualization of Quantitative and Qualitative Playtesting Data. *Proceedings of CHI EA 2014*, 1363–1368. 10.1145/2559206.2581224

Mitgutsch, K., & Alvarado, N. (2013). Purposeful by Design? A Serious Game Design Assessment Framework. Academic Press.

Moallem, M., Pastore, R., & Martin, F. (2013, March). *Interaction in Online Learning: A Comparative Study on the Impact of Communication Tools on Student Learning, Motivation, Self- regulation, and Satisfaction.* Paper presented at the Society for Information Technology & Teacher Education International Conference, New Orleans, LA.

Mohamed, H., & Jaafar, A. (2012). Analyzing critical usability problems in educational computer game (UsaECG). *Proceedings of the IASTED International Conference on Human-Computer Interaction, HCI 2012*, 162–168. 10.2316/P.2012.772-038

Mohamed, O., & Jaafar, A. (2011). Usability of Educational Computer Game Usa _ ECG: Applying Analytic Hierarchy Process. *Advances in Visual Informatics, 2011*, 147–156.

Moodle [Computer Software]. (2014). Retrieved from http://www.moodle.org

Moore, D. M., Burton, J. K., & Myers, R. J. (2004). Multiple-channel communication: The theoretical and research foundations of multimedia. In D. H. Jonassen (Ed.), *Handbook on educational communications and technology* (pp. 981–1006). Mahwah, NJ: Lawrence Erlbaum.

Moore, M. G. (1989). Editorial: Three types of interaction. *American Journal of Distance Education, 3*, 1–6.

Moreno-Ger, P., Torrente, J., Hsieh, Y. G., & Lester, W. T. (2012). Usability Testing for Serious Games: Making Informed Design Decisions with User Data. *Advances in Human-Computer Interaction, 2012*, 1–13. doi:10.1155/2012/369637

Moreno, L., Gonzalez, M., Martínez, P., & Iglesias, A. (2011). A Study of Accessibility Requirements for Media Players on the Web. In *Proceeding of 6th International Conference, UAHCI 2011*. Springer. 10.1007/978-3-642-21672-5_28

Morgado, L. (2011). *Características e desafios tecnológicos dos mundos virtuais no ensino. Habilitation seminar.* Universidade de Trás-os-Montes e Alto Douro.

Morrison, G. R., Ross, S. M., & Baldwin, W. (1992). Learner control of context and instructional support in learning elementary school mathematics. *Educational Technology Research and Development, 40*(1), 5–13. doi:10.1007/BF02296701

Moser, F. (2007). Faculty adoption of education technology: Educational technology support plays a critical role in helping faculty add technology to their teaching. *EDUCAUSE Quarterly, 30*(1), 66–69.

Mousavi, S. Y., Low, R., & Sweller, J. (1995). Reducing cognitive load by mixing auditory and visual presentation loads. *Journal of Educational Psychology, 87*(2), 319–334. doi:10.1037/0022-0663.87.2.319

Mozzaquatro, P. M. (2010). *Adaptação do Mobile Learning Engine Moodle (MLE MOODLE) aos diferentes estilos cognitivos utilizando Hipermídia Adaptativa.* Dissertação de Mestrado, Universidade Federal de Santa Maria.

Muir, M., & Conati, C. (2012). Understanding student attention to adaptive hints with eye-tracking. In *Advances in User Modeling* (pp. 148–160). Springer. doi:10.1007/978-3-642-28509-7_15

Mullet, K., & Sano, D. (1995). *Designing visual interfaces: Communication oriented techniques*. Englewood Cliffs, NJ: Prentice Hall.

Mullet, K., & Sano, D. (1995). *Designing visual interfaces-communication oriented techniques*. Englewood Cliffs, NJ: Prentice Hall.

Myers, I. B., & Mccaulley, M. H. (1986). *Manual: a guide to the development and use of the Myers-Briggs type indicator* (2nd ed.). Palo Alto, CA: Consulting Psychologist Press.

Nacke, L. E., Stellmach, S., & Lindley, C. (2010). Electroencephalographic Assessment of Player Experience: A Pilot Study in Affective Ludology. *Simulation & Gaming*, *42*(5), 632–655. doi:10.1177/1046878110378140

Neilsen, J. (1993). *Usability engineering*. Boston: Academic Press.

Nelson, B. C., & Erlandson, B. E. (2012). *Design for Learning in Virtual Worlds*. Library of Congress Cataloging-in-Publication Date. By Swales & Willis Ltd.

Nesbitt, K., Blackmore, K., Hookham, G., Kay-Lambkin, F., & Walla, P. (2015). Using the Startle Eye-Blink to Measure Affect in Players. In *Serious Games Analytics* (pp. 401–434). Springer. doi:10.1007/978-3-319-05834-4_18

Ngampornchai, A., & Adams, J. (2016). Students' acceptance and readiness for E-learning in Northeastern Thailand. *International Journal of Educational Technology in Higher Education*, *13*(34). doi:10.118641239-016-0034-x

Nguyen, T. (2015). The effectiveness of online learning: Beyond no significant difference and future horizons. *Journal of Online Learning and Teaching / MERLOT*, *11*(2), 309.

Nichols, J., Shaffer, B., & Shockey, K. (2003). Changing the face of instruction: Is online or in-class more effective? *College & Research Libraries*, *64*(5), 378–388. doi:10.5860/crl.64.5.378

Niederée, C., Steffens, U., & Hemmje, M. (2002). Towards digital library mediation for web services. EurAsian conference Workshop Knowledge Foraging for Dynamic Networking of Communities and Economies (EurAsia-ICT 2002), 445-449.

Niederhelman, M. (2001). Education through design: Review of the "Re-inventing design education in the university" conference. *Design Issues*, *17*(3), 83–87. doi:10.1162/074793601750357222

Nielsen, J. (1995). *Multimedia and Hypertext – The Internet and Beyond*. Academic Press Inc.

Nikolova, M. (2013). Development of creativity by role playing in the classroom. *Proceedings of the National Conference with international participation "Knowledge – traditions, innovations, perspectives"*, 441-449.

Noble, I., & Bestley, R. (2016). *Visual research: An introduction to research methods in graphic design*. London: Bloomsbury.

Nogueira, P. a., Aguiar, R., Rodrigues, R., Oliveira, E., & Nacke, L. E. (2014). *Fuzzy Affective Player Models: A Physiology-Based Hierarchical Clustering Method. In Proceedings of the Tenth Artificial Intelligence and Interactive Digital Entertainment Conference* (pp. 132–138). Aiide. Available at http://www.aaai.org/ocs/index.php/AIIDE/AIIDE14/paper/view/8947

Norgaard, N. (2009). The semiotics of typography in literary texts: A multimodal approach. *Orbis Litterarum*, *64*(2), 141–160. doi:10.1111/j.1600-0730.2008.00949.x

Norman, D. A. (1988). *The psychology of everyday things*. New York: Basic Books Inc.

Norman, D. A. (1990). *The design of everyday things.* New York: Doubleday.

Novak, J. D. (1976). Understanding the learning process and effectiveness of teaching methods in the classroom, laboratory, and field. *Science Education, 60*(4), 493–512. doi:10.1002ce.3730600410

Nunes, F. B., Herpich, F., Voss, G. B., Medina, R. D., de Lima, J. V., & Tarouco, L. M. R. (2014). *Laboratório Virtual de Química: uma ferramenta de estímulo à prática de exercícios baseada no Mundo Virtual OpenSim* (pp. 1–10). Simpósio Brasileiro de Informatica na Educacao.

Nunez Castellar, E., Oksanen, K., & Van Looy, J. (2014). Assessing game experience: Heart rate variability, in-game behavior and self-report measures. *Quality of Multimedia Experience (QoMEX), 2014 Sixth International Workshop on,* 292–296. 10.1109/QoMEX.2014.6982334

O'regan, K. (2003). Emotion and e-learning. *Journal of Asynchronous Learning Networks, 7*(3), 78–92.

Oakleaf, M. (2009). The information literacy instruction assessment cycle. *The Journal of Documentation, 65*(4), 539–560. doi:10.1108/00220410910970249

Olapiriyakul, K., & Scher, J. M. (2006). A guide to establishing hybrid learning courses: Employing information technology to create a new learning experience, and a case study. *The Internet and Higher Education, 9*(4), 287–301. doi:10.1016/j.iheduc.2006.08.001

Oliveira, L. C., Amaral, M. A., Botelho, S. S. C., Espíndola, D. B., & Barwaldt, R. (2016). Artefato Metodológico de Autoria Aplicado aos Mundos Virtuais para Educação. *Revista Brasileira de Informática na Educação, 24*(3).

Oliveira, J. D., & Oliveira, V. (2012). Estilos cognitivos divergentes demandam estratégias diferentes no ensino contábil. *Revista de Informação Contábil, 6*(4), 23–41.

Oliver, R. (2017). *When Teaching Meets Learning: Design Principles and Strategies for Web-based Learning Environments that Support Knowledge Construction.* School of Communications and Multimedia. Retrieved April 10, 2017, from https://pdfs.semanticscholar.org/959c/4c063a1215cb5a99c4f6177d3e6c95b11843.pdf

Olsen, T., Procci, K., & Bowers, C. (2011). Serious games usability testing: How to ensure proper usability, playability, and effectiveness. *International Conference of Design, User Experience, and Usability*, 625–634. 10.1007/978-3-642-21708-1_70

On Course Workshop. (n.d.). *The 67 worst teaching mistakes.* Retrieved from http://oncourseworkshop.com/table-contents/67-worst-teaching-mistakes/

Ondrusek, A., Dent, V. F., Bonadie-Joseph, I., & Williams, C. (2005). A longitudinal study of the development and evaluation of an information literacy test. *RSR. Reference Services Review, 33*(4), 388–417. doi:10.1108/00907320510631544

Oppermann, R. (2001). User-interface design. In Handbook on Information Technologies for Education and Training (pp. 233–248). Berlin: Springer-Verlag.

Osguthorpe, R. T., & Graham, C. R. (2003). Blended learning environments: Definitions and Directions. *The Quarterly Review of Distance Education, 4*, 227–233.

Oviatt, S., Cohen, A., & Weibel, N. (2013). Multimodal learning analytics: Description of math data corpus for ICMI grand challenge workshop. *Proceedings of the 15th ACM on International conference on multimodal interaction*, 563–568. 10.1145/2522848.2533790

Owston, R. O. (1997). The World Wide Web: A technology to enhance teaching and learning. *Educational Researcher, 26*, 27–33.

Paas, F. G. W. C., van Merrienboer, J. J. G., & Adam, J. J. (1994). Measurement of cognitive load in instructional research. *Perceptual and Motor Skills*, *79*(1), 419–430. doi:10.2466/pms.1994.79.1.419 PMID:7808878

Paivio, A. (1971). *Imagery and verbal processes*. New York: Holt, Rinehart & Winston.

Paneva, D. (2006). Ontology-based student modeling. *Proceedings of the Fourth CHIRON Open Workshop "Ubiquitous Learning Challenges: Design, Experiments and Context Aware Ubiquitous Learning"*, 17-21.

Paneva-Marinova, D., Pavlova, L., Sapundjiev, V., & Bogdanova, M. (2014). Interactive environment for digital preservation and preservation of fashion objects. In R. Pavlov & P. Stanchev (Ed.), *Proceedings of the UNESCO International Conference on Digital Presentation and Preservation of Cultural and Scientific Heritage* (pp. 147-154). Veliko Tarnovo, Bulgaria: Institute of Mathematics and Informatics, BAS. Retrieved April 27, 2017, from http://dipp.math.bas.bg

Paneva-Marinova, D., Pavlova-Draganova, L., Draganov, L., & Georgiev, V. (2012). Ontological presentation of analysis method for technology-enhanced learning. In *Proceedings of the International Conference on Computer Systems and Technologies ComSysTech'12* (pp. 384-390). Ruse, Bulgaria: ACM New York. 10.1145/2383276.2383332

Paneva-Marinova, D., Goynov, M., & Luchev, D. (2017). *Multimedia digital library: Constructive block in ecosystems for digital cultural assets. Basic functionality and services*. Saarbrücken, Germany: LAP LAMBERT Academic Publishing.

Paneva-Marinova, D., Goynov, M., & Pavlov, R. (2011). Content analyzing and synthesizing services in a digital library. *International Journal. Information Technologies and Knowledge*, *2*(4), 403–416.

Paneva-Marinova, D., & Pavlov, P. (2011). Educational application of top of digital library for cultural heritage. *Proceedings of the International Conference on e-Learning and the Knowledge Society (E-Learning'11)*, 211-224.

Papastergiou, M. (2009). Digital game-based learning in high school computer science education: Impact on educational effectiveness and student motivation. *Computers & Education*, *52*(1), 1–12. doi:10.1016/j.compedu.2008.06.004

Papert, S. (1980). *Mindstorms: Children, computers, and powerful ideas*. New York: Basic Books.

Paquette, L., Mott, B., Brawner, K., Rowe, J., Lester, J., Sottilare, R., ... Georgoulas, V. (2015). Sensor-Free or Sensor-Full: A Comparison of Data Modalities in Multi-Channel Affect Detection. *Proceedings of the 8th International Conference on Educational Data Mining.*

Pardo, A. G., Rosa, A., & Camacho, D. (2014). Behaviour-based identification of student communities in Virtual Worlds. *Computer Science and Information Systems*, *11*(1), 195–213. doi:10.2298/CSIS130214003G

Pârgaru, I., Gherghina, R., & Duca, I. (2009). The role of education in the knowledge-based society during the economic crisis. *Annales Universitatis Apulensis Series Oeconomica*, *11*(2), 646–651.

Paris. M. B., Bakkes, S., Tan, C. T., Whiteson, S., Roijers, D., Valenti, R., & Gevers, T. (2014). Towards Personalised Gaming via Facial Expression Recognition. *Proceedings of Tenth AAAI Conference on Artificial Intelligence and Interactive Digital Entertainment*, 30–36.

Parrish, P. E. (2009). Aesthetic principles for instructional design. *Educational Technology Research and Development*, *57*(4), 511–528. doi:10.100711423-007-9060-7

Parrish, P., Wilson, B. G., & Dunlap, J. C. (2011). Learning experience as transaction: A framework for instructional design. *Educational Technology*, *51*(2), 15–22.

Patra, M. R., & Dash, A. R. (2017). Accessibility Analysis of Some Indian Educational Web Portals. International Journal of Computer Science, Engineering and Applications (IJCSEA), *7*(4), 9–24. doi:10.5121/ijcsea.2017.7404

Patra, M. R., & Dash, A. R. (2017). Accessibility analysis of web browsers. *International Journal of Services Technology and Management, 23*(4), 313–330.

Patra, M. R., & Dash, A. R. (2017). Analysis of Android Cell Phone Web-Browsers to Facilitate Accessible m-Governance. *Proceedings of the 10th International Conference on Theory and Practice of Electronic Governance, ICEGOV 2017*, 276-284. 10.1145/3047273.3047279

Patra, M. R., Dash, A. R., & Mishra, P. K. (2014). A Quantitative Analysis of WCAG 2.0 Compliance for some Indian Web Portals. *International Journal of Computer Science, Engineering and Applications (IJCSEA), 4*(1), 9–24. doi:10.5121/ijcsea.2014.4102

Patra, M. R., Dash, A. R., & Mishra, P. K. (2014). Accessibility Analysis of Government Web Portals of Asian Countries. *Proceedings of the 8th International Conference on Theory and Practice of Electronic Governance, ICEGOV 2014*, 383-386. 10.1145/2691195.2691253

Patsis, G., Sahli, H., Verhelst, W., & De Troyer, O. (2013). Evaluation of attention levels in a tetris game using a brain computer interface. In *User Modeling, Adaptation, and Personalization* (pp. 127–138). Springer. doi:10.1007/978-3-642-38844-6_11

Pavlova-Draganova, L., Paneva-Marinova, D., Pavlov, R., & Goynov, G. (2010). On the wider accessibility of the valuable phenomena of Orthodox iconography through digital library. In M. Ioannides, D. Fellner, A. Georgopoulos, & D. Hadjimitsis (Ed.), *Proceedings of the 3rd International Conference dedicated on Digital Heritage (EuroMed 2010)* (pp. 173-178). Lymassol, Cyprus: ARCHAEOLINGUA.

Pavlova-Draganova, L., Paneva-Marinova, D., & Draganov, L. (2009). A use case scenario for technology-enhanced learning through Semantic Web services. *International Journal. Information Technologies & Knowledge, 3*(3), 257–268.

Pavlov, R., Paneva, D., Pavlova-Draganova, L., & Draganov, L. (2007). Ubiquitous learning applications on top of iconographic digital library. In L. Dimitrova, & R. Pavlov (Ed.), *Proceedings of the Jubilee International Conference on Mathematical and Computational Linguistics "30 years Department of Mathematical Linguistics"*. Sofia, Bulgaria: Institute of Mathematics and Informatics, Bulgarian Academy of Sciences.

Pechuel, R., & Beutner, M. (2013). Task based authentic Serious Game in vocational and further education and the PVEC – Paderborn Vocational Education Concept for e-learning: The Copy Job – A Bid Comparison of Suppliers. *Proceedings of E-Learn: World Conference on E-Learning in Corporate, Government, Healthcare, and Higher Education, 2013*, 931–939.

Pekrun, R. (2006). The control-value theory of achievement emotions: Assumptions, corollaries, and implications for educational research and practice. *Educational Psychology Review, 18*(4), 315–341.

Pekrun, R., Frenzel, A. C., Goetz, T., & Perry, R. P. (2007). *The control-value theory of achievement emotions: An integrative approach to emotions in education*. Academic Press.

Pekrun, R., Goetz, T., Frenzel, A. C., Barchfeld, P., & Perry, R. P. (2011). Measuring emotions in students' learning and performance: The Achievement Emotions Questionnaire (AEQ). *Contemporary Educational Psychology, 36*(1), 36–48.

Pellas, N. (2014). The development of a virtual learning platform for teaching concurrent programming languages in secondary Education: the use of OpenSim and Scratch4OS. *Journal of e-Learning and Knowledge Society, 10*(1).

Pentak, S., & Lauer, D. (2015). *Design basics* (9th ed.). Thousand Oaks, CA: Wadsworth.

Pentak, S., & Roth, R. (2003). *Color basics*. Thousand Oaks, CA: Wadsworth.

Perry, G. T., Kulpa, C. C., Pinheiro, E. T., & Eichler, M. L. (2012). Lessons from an educational game usability evaluation. *International Journal of Interactive Mobile Technologies*, *6*(2).

Peslak, A. (2005). A Framework and implementation of user interface and human-computer interaction instruction. *Journal of Information Technology Education*, *4*, 189–205. doi:10.28945/272

Picard, R. W., & Daily, S. B. (2005). Evaluating affective interactions: Alternatives to asking what users feel. *CHI Workshop on Evaluating Affective Interfaces: Innovative Approaches*, 2119–2122.

Picciano, A. G. (2002). Beyond student perceptions: Issues of interaction, presence, and performance in an online course. *Journal of Asynchronous Learning Networks*, *6*, 21–40.

Pinelle, D., Wong, N., & Stach, T. (2008). Heuristic evaluation for games: usability principles for video game design. *Proceedings of the SIGCHI Conference on Human Factors in Computing Systems*, 1453–1462. 10.1145/1357054.1357282

Plass, J. L., Homer, B. D., & Kinzer, C. K. (2014). *Playful Learning: An Integrated Design Framework*. White Paper.

Porayska-Pomsta, K., Mavrikis, M., D'Mello, S., Conati, C., & Baker, R. S. J. D. (2013). Knowledge elicitation methods for affect modelling in education. *International Journal of Artificial Intelligence in Education*, *22*(3), 107–140. doi:10.3233/JAI-130032

Potkonjaka, V., Gardner, M., Callaghan, V., Mattila, P., Guetl, C., Petrović, V. M., & Jovanović, K. (2016). Virtual laboratories for education in science, technology, and engineering: A review. *Computers & Education*, *95*, 309–327. doi:10.1016/j.compedu.2016.02.002

Prager, P. (2006). Back to the future: Interactivity and associational narrativity at the Bauhaus. *Digital Creativity*, *17*(4), 195–204. doi:10.1080/14626260601073195

Prensky, M. (2001). *Digital game-based learning*. McGraw-Hill.

Puntambekar, S., Stylianou, A., & Hübscher, R. (2003). Improving navigation and learning in hypertext environments with navigable concept maps. *Human-Computer Interaction*, *18*(4), 395–426. doi:10.1207/S15327051HCI1804_3

Qian, L., Liu, L., & Hu, Y. (2007). Analysis of personalized information service system for digital libraries. In *Proceedings of the First IEEE International Symposium onInformation Technologies and Applications in Education, ISITAE '07*. Kunming, China: IEEE. doi: 10.1109/ISITAE.2007.4409277

Rana, H., Singh, R., & Lal, M. (2014). E-learning: Issues and Challenges. *International Journal of Computers and Applications*, *97*(5), 20–24. doi:10.5120/17004-7154

Rand, P. (1985). *Paul Rand, a designer's art*. New Haven, CT: Yale University Press.

Rand, P. (2014). *Thoughts on design*. San Francisco: Chronicle Books.

Range, B., Pijanowski, J., Duncan, H., Scherz, S., & Hvidston, D. (2014). An analysis of instructional facilitators' relationships with Teachers and Principals. *Journal of School Leadership*, *24*(2), 253.

Ravaja, N., Saari, T., Salminen, M., Laarni, J., & Kallinen, K. (2006). Phasic emotional reactions to video game events: A psychophysiological investigation. *Media Psychology. Taylor & Francis*, *8*(4), 343–367. doi:10.12071532785xmep0804_2

Recker, M., Ram, A., Shikano, T., Li, G., & Stasko, J. (1995). Cognitive media types for multimedia information access. *Journal of Educational Multimedia and Hypermedia*, *4*, 183–210.

Resnis, E., Gibson, K., Hartsell-Gundy, A., & Misco, M. (2010). Information literacy assessment: A case study at Miami University. *New Library World*, *111*(7/8), 287–301. doi:10.1108/03074801011059920

Rhode, J. F. (2009). Interaction equivalency in self-paced online learning environments: An exploration of learner preferences. *International Review of Research in Open and Distance Learning*, *10*(1), 1–23. doi:10.19173/irrodl.v10i1.603

Richardson, J., & Ting, E. (1999). *Making the most of interaction: What instructors do that most affect students' perceptions of their learning.* Paper presented at the 5th International Conference on Asynchronous Learning, College Park, MD.

Riding, R. J., & Rayner, S. (1998). *Cognitive styles and learning strategies: Understanding style differences in learning and behaviour*. London: David Fulton.

Riding, R., & Rayner, S. (1998). *Cognitive Styles and Learning Strategies - Understanding style differences in learning and behavior*. David Fulton Publisher London.

Riel, M. (1996). The Internet: A land to settle rather than an ocean to surf. *Telecommunications in Education News*, *7*, 10–17.

Rittel, H. W. J., & Webber, M. M. (1973). Dilemmas in a general theory of planning. *Policy Sciences*, *4*(2), 155–169. doi:10.1007/BF01405730

Robson, M. (2002). *Problem-solving in groups*. Aldershot, UK: Gower.

Rodrigo, M. M. T., & Baker, R. (2011). 'Comparing learners' affect while using an intelligent tutor and an educational game. *Research and Practice in Technology Enhanced Learning*, *6*(1), 43–66.

Rovai, A. P., & Jordan, H. M. (2004). Blended learning and sense of community: A comparative analysis with traditional and fully online graduate courses. *International Review of Research in Open and Distance Learning*, *5*(2), 1–13. doi:10.19173/irrodl.v5i2.192

Rowland, G. (2003). *A little ambiguity can go a long way*. Presented at Association for Educational Communications and Technology Annual Conference, Anaheim, CA.

Ruey, S. (2010). A case study of constructivist instructional strategies for adult online learning. *British Journal of Educational Technology*, *41*(5), 706–720. doi:10.1111/j.1467-8535.2009.00965.x

Rutten, N., Joolingen, W. R. J., & Veen, J. T. V. (2012). The learning effects of computer simulations in science education. Computer & Education, 58(1), 136–153. doi:10.1016/j.compedu.2011.07.017

Ruttun, R. D., & Macredie, R. D. (2011). The effects of individual differences and visual instructional aids on disorientation, learning performance and attitudes in a Hypermedia Learning System. *Computers in Human Behavior*, *28*(6), 2182–2198. doi:10.1016/j.chb.2012.06.026

Salmeron-majadas, S., Santos, O. C., & Boticario, J. (2013). Affective State Detection in Educational Systems through Mining Multimodal Data Sources. *Proceedings of the 6th International Conference on Educational Data Mining*, 348–349. Available at: http://www.educationaldatamining.org/EDM2013/papers/rn_paper_75.pdf

Salmeron-majadas, S. (2014). Affective standards-based modeling in educational contexts from mining multimodal data sources State of the art. *CEUR Workshop Proceedings*.

Samson, S., & Granath, K. (2004). Reading, writing, and research: Added value to university first-year experience programs. *RSR. Reference Services Review*, *32*(2), 142–156. doi:10.1108/00907320410537667

San Pedro, M. O. Z., Baker, R. S. J., & Rodrigo, M. M. T. (2014). Carelessness and Affect in an Intelligent Tutoring System for Mathematics. *International Journal of Artificial Intelligence in Education*, *24*(2), 189–210.

Sanchez, E. (2011). *Key criteria for game design. A framework*. Academic Press.

Santa-Rosa, J. G. (2012). Participatory design in the project of virtual learning environments of histology. *Work (Reading, Mass.), 41*(Suppl. 1), 1157–1159. doi:10.3233/WOR-2012-0296-1157 PMID:22316875

Santos, E. M. D. (2007). *Avaliação da influência dos estilos cognitivos no perfil do aluno de educação a distância.* Academic Press.

Sapundjiev, V., & Luchev, D. (2016). Interactive environment for creating and preservation of fashion objects integrated with electronic storage of learning resources. In N. Dimitrova (Ed.), *Proceedings of the Doctoral Conference in Mathematics and Informatics, MIDOC 2015* (pp. 116-123). Sofia, Bulgaria: "St. Kliment Ohridski" University Press.

Saunders, L. (2009). The future of information literacy in academic libraries: A Delphi study. *portal. Library and the Academy, 9*(1), 99–114. doi:10.1353/pla.0.0030

Sawyer, K. (2008). Optomising learning: Implications of learning sciences research. In *Innovating to learn, learning to innovate* (pp. 45–65). Organisation for Economic Co-operation and Development Publishing. doi:10.1787/9789264047983-4-en

Scheele, B., & Groeben, N. (2017). *Dialog-Konsens-Methodik.* Retrieved June 6, 2017, from https://portal.hogrefe.com/dorsch/dialog-konsens-methodik/

Scheele, B., & Groeben, N. (1988). *Dialog-Konsens-Methoden zur Rekonstruktion Subjektiver Theorien: die Heidelberger Struktur-Lege-Technik (SLT), konsensuale Ziel-Mittel-Argumentation und kommunikative Flußdiagramm-Beschreibungen von Handlungen.* Tübingen, Germany: Francke.

Schmeck, R. R. (1982). *Inventory of learning processes. NASSP.* Student Learning Styles and Brain Behavior.

Schnackenberg, H. L., & Hilliard, A. W. (1998, February). *Learner ability and learner control: A 10 year literature review 1987-1997.* Paper presented at the annual meeting of the Association for Educational Communications and Technology, St. Louis, MO.

Schnotz, W., & Rasch, T. (2005). Enabling, facilitating, and inhibiting effects of animations in multimedia learning: Why reduction of cognitive load can have negative results on learning. *Educational Technology Research and Development, 53*(3), 47–58. doi:10.1007/BF02504797

Schön, D. A. (1984). *The reflective practitioner: How professionals think in action.* New York: Basic Books.

Schön, D. A. (1987). *Educating the reflective practitioner: Toward a new design for teaching and learning in the professions.* San Francisco: Jossey-Bass.

Schrader, P. G., & McCreery, M. (2012). Are All Games the Same? In D. Ifenthaler, D. Eseryel, & X. Ge (Eds.), *Assessment in game-based learning. Foundations, innovations, and perspectives* (pp. 11–28). New York: Springer. doi:10.1007/978-1-4614-3546-4_2

Schwartz, B. (2004). *The paradox of choice: Why more is less.* New York: Ecco.

Schwier, R., & Misanchuk, E. (1993). *Interactive multimedia instruction.* Englewood Cliffs, NJ: Educational Technology Publications.

Seal, K. C., & Przasnyski, Z. H. (2001). Using the World Wide Web for teaching improvement. *Computers & Education, 36*(1), 33–40. doi:10.1016/S0360-1315(00)00049-X

Seeker. (2016, September 25). *How your brain simplifies complex reality* [Video file]. Retrieved from https://www.youtube.com/watch?v=YmDqJniyK6U

Seif El-Nasr, M., Desurvire, H., Nacke, L., Drachen, A., Calvi, L., Isbister, K., & Bernhaupt, R. (2012). Game user research. CHI' 12 Extended Abstracts on Human Factors in Computing Systems, 2679–2682. doi:10.1145/2212776.2212694

Seigel, D. (2006). Designing Our Own Graves. In H. Armstrong (Ed.), *Graphic design theory: Readings from the field* (pp. 115–118). New York: Princeton Architectural Press.

Shackelford, J., & Maxwellm, M. (2012). Contribution of Learner–Instructor Interaction to Sense of Community in Graduate Online Education. *Journal of Online Learning and Teaching / MERLOT*, *8*(4), 248–260.

Shaer, O., Horn, M., & Jacob, R. J. K. (2009). Tangible user interface laboratory: Teaching tangible interaction design in practice. *Artificial Intelligence for Engineering Design, Analysis and Manufacturing*, *23*(03), 251–261. doi:10.1017/S0890060409000225

Shah, P., & Freedman, E. (2003). Visuospatial thinking in e-learning. *Journal of Educational Computing Research*, *29*(3), 315–324. doi:10.2190/QYVJ-Q59L-VE7C-EHUV

Shaker, N., Shaker, M., Abuabdallah, I., Zonjy, M., & Sarhan, M. H. (2013). A Quantitative Approach for Modeling and Personalizing Player Experience in First-Person Shooter Games. *2013 Conference on User Modeling, Adaptation and Persolization*. Available at: http://citeseerx.ist.psu.edu/viewdoc/summary?doi=10.1.1.416.371

Shaker, N., & Shaker, M. (2014). Towards Understanding the Nonverbal Signatures of Engagement in Super Mario Bros. In *User Modeling, Adaptation, and Personalization* (pp. 423–434). Springer. doi:10.1007/978-3-319-08786-3_38

Shedroff, N. (2003). Research methods for designing effective experiences. In B. Laurel (Ed.), *Design research: Methods and perspectives* (pp. 155–163). Cambridge, MA: MIT Press.

Shen, L., Leon, E., Callaghan, V., & Shen, R. M. (2007). Exploratory research on an Affective e-Learning Model. *Proceedings of Workshop on Blended Learning*, 267–278.

Sher, A. (2009). Assessing the relationship of student-instructor and student-student interaction to student learning and satisfaction in Web-based online learning environment. *Journal of Interactive Online Learning*, *8*(2), 102–120.

Shi, K., & Ali, K. (2012). GetJar Mobile Application Recommendations with Very Sparse Datasets. In *Proceedings of the 18th ACM SIGKDD International Conference on Knowledge Discovery and Data Mining*. New York, NY: ACM. 10.1145/2339530.2339563

Shoukry, L., Göbel, S., & Steinmetz, R. (2014b). Towards Mobile Multimodal Learning Analytics. *Proceedings of the Learning Analytics for and in Serious Games Workshop at EC-TEL.*

Shoukry, L., Caserman, P., Göbel, S., & Steinmetz, R. (2015). Blitzmerker: learning idioms with a mobile game. *Joint International Conference on Serious Games*, 77–88. 10.1007/978-3-319-19126-3_7

Shoukry, L., & Gobel, S. (2017). *Reasons and Responses: A Multimodal Serious Games Evaluation Framework. IEEE Transactions on Emerging Topics in Computing.*

Shoukry, L., Göbel, S., Galal-Edeen, G. H., & Sturm, C. (2014). Conducting Evaluation Studies of Mobile Games with Preschoolers. *CEUR Workshop Proceedings*, *1227*, 262–269.

Shoukry, L., Göbel, S., & Steinmetz, R. (2014a). Learning analytics and serious games: Trends and considerations. *Proceedings of the 2014 ACM International Workshop on Serious Games*, 21–26. 10.1145/2656719.2656729

Shoukry, L., Reuter, C., & Mehm, F. (2014). StoryTec and StoryPlay as Tools for Adaptive Game-Based Learning Research. In *Games for Training, Education, Health and Sports* (pp. 195–198). Springer. doi:10.1007/978-3-319-05972-3_21

Shoukry, L., Sturm, C., & Galal-Edeen, G. H. (2015). Pre-MEGa: A Proposed Framework for the Design and Evaluation of Preschoolers' Mobile Educational Games. In *Innovations and Advances in Computing, Informatics, Systems Sciences, Networking and Engineering* (pp. 385–390). Springer. doi:10.1007/978-3-319-06773-5_52

Shumaker, D. (2012). *Distinctive Roles: Engagement, Innovation, and the Liaison Model*. Medford, NJ: Information Today.

Shute, V. J. (2011). Stealth assessment in computer-based games to support learning. *Computer Games and Instruction, 55*(2), 503–524. Available at: http://myweb.fsu.edu/vshute/pdf/shute

Shyu, H. S., & Brown, S. W. (1992). Learner control versus program control in interactive videodisc instruction: What are the effects in procedural learning? *International Journal of Instructional Media, 19*, 85–96.

Siemens, G., & Long, P. (2011). Penetrating the Fog: Analytics in Learning and Education. *EDUCAUSE Review, 46*(5), 30.

Silver, S. L., & Nickel, L. T. (2007). Are online tutorials effective? A comparison of online and classroom library instruction methods. *Research Strategies, 20*(4), 389–396. doi:10.1016/j.resstr.2006.12.012

Simsek, I., & Can, T. (2016). The Design and Use of Educational Games in 3D Virtual Worlds. In *Society for information technology and teacher education* (pp. 611–617). Savannah, GA: SITE.

Sinatra, G. M., Heddy, B. C., & Lombardi, D. (2015). The challenges of defining and measuring student engagement in science. *Educational Psychologist, 50*(1), 1–13. doi:10.1080/00461520.2014.1002924

Singh, G., & Hardaker, G. (2014). Barriers and enablers to adoption and diffusion of eLearning: A systematic review of the literature – a need for an integrative approach. *Education + Training, 56*(2/3), 105–121. doi:10.1108/ET-11-2012-0123

Singh, H. (2003). Building effective blended learning programs. *Educational Technology, 43*(6), 51–54.

Sinha, N., Khreisat, L., & Sharma, K. (2009). Learner-Interface Interaction for TechnologyEnhanced Active Learning. *Innovate: Journal of Online Education., 5*(3), 1–7.

SINUS-Project. (n.d.). *Semantic technologies for Web services and technology enhanced learning, No. D-002-189 (Project web page)*. Retrieved March 20, 2017, from http://sinus.iinf.bas.bg

Sitzmann, T., Wisher, R., Stewart, D., & Kraiger, K. (2005). Moderators of the effectiveness of web-based instruction. In *20th Annual Conference on Distance Teaching and Learning* (p. 6). The Board of Regents of the University of Wisconsin System.

Slavova-Petkova, S., Dimova, M., & Luchev, D. (2016). Learning scenario for better understanding of fairy tales using role-playing and serious games methods. In R. Pavlov & P. Stanchev (Eds.), *Proceedings of the 6th UNESCO International Conference on Digital Presentation and Preservation of Cultural and Scientific Heritage*. Veliko Tarnovo, Bulgaria: Institute of Mathematics and Informatics - BAS. Retrieved May 10, 2017, from http://dipp.math.bas.bg

Smale, M. A., & Regalado, M. (2009). Using blackboard to deliver library research skills assessment. *Communications in Information Literacy, 3*(2), 142–157. doi:10.15760/comminfolit.2010.3.2.77

Smarkola, C. (2007). Technology acceptance predictors among student teachers and experienced classroom teachers. *Journal of Educational Computing Research, 37*(1), 65–82. doi:10.2190/J3GM-3RK1-2907-7U03

Smith, A., Dunckley, L., French, T., Minocha, S., & Chang, Y. (2004). A process model for using cross-cultural websites. *Interacting with Computers, 16*(1), 63–91. doi:10.1016/j.intcom.2003.11.005

Snow, E. R. (1980). Aptitude, learner control, and adaptive instruction. *Educational Psychologist, 15*(3), 151–158. doi:10.1080/00461528009529223

Solomon, G. (1994). *Interaction of media, cognition and learning*. Mahwah, NJ: Lawrence Erlbaum.

Soto, V. J. (2013). Which Instructional Design Models are Educators Using to Design Virtual World Instruction? *MERLOT Journal of Online Learning and Teaching, 9*(3), 1–12.

Souley, B., & Sambo, A. S. (2014). A Comparative Performance Analysis of Popular Internet Browsers in Current Web Applications. *West African Journal of Industrial and Academic Research, 4*(1), 62–68.

Spinuzzi, C. (2005). The Methodology of Participatory Design. *Technical Communication (Washington), 52*(2), 163–174.

Stefaniak, J. (2015). Promoting learner-centered instruction through the design of contextually relevant experiences. In B. Hokanson, G. Clinton, & M. W. Tracey (Eds.), *The design of learning experience* (pp. 49–62). Cham, Switzerland: Springer International Publishing. doi:10.1007/978-3-319-16504-2_4

Stefanov, K. (2014). Digital libraries as a social media. In *Proceedings of the UNESCO International Conference on Digital Presentationa dn preservation of Cultural and Scientific Heritage* (pp. 26-32). Veliko Tarnovo, Bulgaria: Institute of Mathematics and Informatics, BAS. Retrieved March 25, 2017, from http://dipp.math.bas.bg

Stokes, D. (1997). *Pasteur's quadrant: basic science and technological innovation*. Washington, DC: Brookings Institution Press.

Straub, E. (2009). Understanding technology adoption: Theory and future directions for informal learning. *Review of Educational Research, 79*(2), 625–649. doi:10.3102/0034654308325896

Sullivan, L. H. (1896). *The tall office building artistically considered.* Retrieved from https://archive.org/details/tallofficebuildi00sull

Sun, J., & Hsu, Y. (2013). Effect of interactivity on learner perceptions in Web-based instruction. *Computers in Human Behavior, 29*(1), 171–184. doi:10.1016/j.chb.2012.08.002

Susskind, R., & Susskind, D. (2015). *The future of the professions: how technology will transform the work of human experts*. Oxford, UK: Oxford University Press.

Sutton, L. A. (2001). The principle of vicarious interaction in computer-mediated communications. *International Journal of Educational Telecommunications, 7*, 223–242.

Svensson, P. (2003). Interdisciplinary design research. In B. Laurel (Ed.), *Design Research: Methods and Perspectives* (pp. 193–200). Cambridge, MA: MIT Press.

Swan, K. (2005). A constructivist model for thinking about learning online. In J. Bourne & J. C. Moore (Eds.), *Elements of Quality Online Education: Engaging Communities*. Needham, MA: Sloan-C.

Swan, K., Shea, P., Fredericksen, E., Pickett, A., Pelz, W., & Maher, G. (2000). Building knowledge building communities: Consistency, contact and communication in the virtual classroom. *Journal of Educational Computing Research, 23*(4), 389–413. doi:10.2190/W4G6-HY52-57P1-PPNE

Sweller, J. (1994). Cognitive load theory, learning difficulty and instructional design. *Learning and Instruction, 4*, 295–312.

Sweller, J. (1999). *Instructional design in technical areas*. Camberwell, Australia: Australian Council for Educational Research.

Sweller, J., Chandler, P., Tierney, P., & Cooper, G. (1990). Cognitive load as a factor in the structuring of technical material. *Journal of Experimental Psychology. General, 119*(2), 176–192. doi:10.1037/0096-3445.119.2.176

Symeonidis, I., Kavadarli, G., Schuller, E., & Peldschus, S. (2010). Simulation of Biomechanical Experiments in OpenSim. *XII Mediterranean Conference on Medical and Biological Engineering and Computing*. 107–110. 10.1007/978-3-642-13039-7_27

Szabo, M., & Kanuka, H. (1999). Effects of violating screen design principles of balance, unity, and focus on recall learning, study time, and completion rates. *Journal of Educational Multimedia and Hypermedia, 8*, 23–42.

Tarmizi, R. A., & Sweller, J. (1988). Guidance during mathematical problem-solving. *Journal of Educational Psychology, 80*(4), 424–436. doi:10.1037/0022-0663.80.4.424

Tarouco, L. M. R., Gorziza, B., Correa, Y., Amaral, E. M. H., & Muller, T. (2013). Virtual laboratory for teaching Calculus: An immersive experience. *IEEE Global Engineering Education Conference (EDUCON)*, 774 – 781. 10.1109/EduCon.2013.6530195

Tashakkori, A., & Creswell, J. (2007). The new era of mixed methods. *Journal of Mixed Methods, 1*(1), 3–7. doi:10.1177/2345678906293042

Tashakkori, A., & Teddlie, C. (2003). The past and future of mixed methods research: From data triangulation to mixed model designs. In A. Tashakkori & C. Teddlie (Eds.), *Handbook of Mixed Methods in Social & Behavioral Research* (pp. 671–701). Thousand Oaks, CA: Sage.

Taylor, L., & Atwong, C. (2008). Integrating information literacy into business education: A successful case of faculty-librarian collaboration. *Journal of Business & Finance Librarianship, 13*(4), 433–449. doi:10.1080/08963560802202227

Teine, M., & Beutner, M. (2016). Conceptualizing an M-Learning System for Seniors. In *Proceedings of the 12 International Conference on Mobile Learning 2016* (pp. 85-88). Academic Press.

Teo, T. (2011). Technology acceptance research in education. In T. Teo (Ed.), *Technology acceptance in education: Research and issues* (pp. 1–5). Rotterdam, The Netherlands: Sense Publishers. doi:10.1007/978-94-6091-487-4_1

Tergan, S. O. (2003). Managing knowledge with computer-based mapping tools. In D. Lassner & C. M. Naught (Eds.), *Proceedings of the ed-media 2003 world conference on educational multimedia, hypermedia & telecommunication* (pp. 2514-2517). Honolulu, HI: University of Honolulu.

Termens, M., Ribera, M., Porras, M., Boldú, M., Sulé, A., & Paris, P. (2009). Web Content Accessibility Guidelines: from 1.0 to 2.0. *Proceedings of the 18th international conference on World Wide Web*, 1171-1172. DOI: 10.1145/1526709.1526912

Tham, K., & Tham, C. (2011). Blended learning—A focus study on Asia. *International Journal of Computer Science Issues, 8*, 136–142.

The Board of Trustees of the Leland Stanford Junior University. (2009). *Stanford's key to information literacy*. Retrieved fromhttp://skil.stanford.edu/intro/index.html

Tholkes, R., & Sederberg, C. (1990). Economies of scale and rural schools. *Journal of Research in Rural Education, 7*, 9–15.

Thompson, M. E. (1994). Design considerations of visuals. In D. M. Moore & F. M. Dwyer (Eds.), *Visual literacy: A spectrum of visual learning* (pp. 165–182). Englewood Cliffs, NJ: Educational Technology Publishing.

Thomson, M. E., Sharun, S., Knoch, J., & Goebel, N. (2014). Institutions collaborating on an information literacy assessment tool. *Library Management, 35*(8/9), 538–546. doi:10.1108/LM-03-2014-0035

Tindall-Ford, S., Chandler, P., & Sweller, J. (1997). When two sensory modes are better than one. *Journal of Experimental Psychology. Applied, 3*(4), 257–287. doi:10.1037/1076-898X.3.4.257

Trail, M. A., Gutierrez, C., & Lechner, D. (2006). Reconsidering a traditional instruction technique: Reassessing the print workbook. *Journal of Academic Librarianship, 32*(6), 632–640. doi:10.1016/j.acalib.2006.07.003

Tronstad, B., Phillips, L., Garcia, J., & Harlow, M. A. (2009). Assessing the TIP online information literacy tutorial. *RSR. Reference Services Review, 37*(1), 54–64. doi:10.1108/00907320910934995

Tuckman, B. (2002). Evaluating ADAPT: A hybrid instructional model combining Web-based and classroom components. *Computers & Education, 39*(3), 261–269. doi:10.1016/S0360-1315(02)00045-3

Tufte, E. R. (1990). *Envisioning information.* Cheshire, CT: Graphics Press.

U.S. Department of Education, National Center for Education Statistics, Institute of Education Sciences. (2011). *Learning at a distance: Undergraduate enrollment in distance education courses and degree programs (NCES 2012–154).* Retrieved from http://nces.ed.gov/pubs2012/2012154.pdf

Upatkoon, K., Wang, W., & Jamin, S. (2005). WebBee: An Architecture for Web Accessibility for Mobile Devices. *Proceeding of the 10th IFIP International Conference on Personal Wireless Communications*, 1-9. 10.1142/9781860947315_0046

User Agent Accessibility Guideline (UAAG 2.0). (2017, May). Retrieved from http://www.w3.org/TR/UAAG20/

User Agent Accessibility Guidelines Working Group (UAWG). (2017, May 11). Retrieved from http://www.w3.org/WAI/UA/

Vali, I. (2013). The role of education in the knowledge-based society. *Procedia Social and Behavioral Sciences, 76*, 388-392. doi: 101016/j.sbspro.2013.04.133

Valtolina, S., Barricelli, B. R., Mesiti, M., & Ribaudo, M. (2012). User-Centered Design of E-Learning Tools for Users with Special Needs: The VisualPedia Case Study. *Interaction Design and Architecture(s). Journal, 13-14*, 47–55.

Van Allen, P. (2011). *Prototyping for interaction design.* Retrieved July 14, 2017, from https://www.slideshare.net/pvanallen/prototyping-for-interaction-design

van den Hoogen, W. M., IJsselsteijn, W. A., de Kort, Y. A. W., & Poels, K. (2008). *Toward real-time behavioral indicators of player experiences: Pressure patterns and postural responses. In Proceedings of Measuring Behaviour 2008* (pp. 100–101). Citeseer.

Van Leeuwen, T. (2006). Towards a semiotics of typography. *Informational Design Journal & Document Design, 14*(2), 139–155. doi:10.1075/idj.14.2.06lee

Van Merrienboer, J. J. G., & Sweller, J. (2005). Cognitive load theory and complex learning: Recent developments and future directions. *Educational Psychology Review, 17*(2), 147–177. doi:10.100710648-005-3951-0

Van Staalduinen, J.-P., & de Freitas, S. (2011). A game-based learning framework: Linking game design and learning. *Learning to play: exploring the future of education with video games, 53*, 29.

Varli, O. (2009). *An Exploration of Three-Dimensional (3D) Virtual Worlds through ESL/EFL Teachers' Perspectives in Second Life*. Academic Press.

Vatrapu, R., & Suthers, D. (2007). Culture and computers: A review of the concept of culture and implications for intercultural collaborative online learning. In T. Ishida, S. R. Fussell, & P. T. J. M. Vossen (Eds.), *Intercultural Collaboration* (Vol. 4568, pp. 260–275). Berlin: Springer Berlin Heidelberg. doi:10.1007/978-3-540-74000-1_20

Venkatesh, V., Morris, M., Davis, G., & Davis, F. (2003). User Acceptance of Information Technology: Toward a Unified View. *Management Information Systems Quarterly*, *27*(3), 425–478. doi:10.2307/30036540

Verbeek, P. P. (2015). Beyond interaction: A short introduction to mediation theory. *Interaction*, *22*(3), 26–31. doi:10.1145/2751314

Vigo, M., Aizpurua, A., Arrue, M., & Abascal, J. (2008). Evaluating web accessibility for specific mobile devices. *Proceedings of the 2008 international cross-disciplinary conference on Web accessibility (W4A)*, 65-72. 10.1145/1368044.1368059

Virvou, M., & Katsionis, G. (2008). On the usability and likeability of virtual reality games for education: The case of VR-ENGAGE. *Computer Education*, *50*(1), 154–178. doi:10.1016/j.compedu.2006.04.004

Vivian, M., Tagliapietra, L., Sartori, M., & Reggiani, M. (2015). Dynamic Simulation of Robotic Devices Using the Biomechanical Simulator OpenSim. *Intelligent Autonomous Systems*, *13*, 1639–1651.

Vygotsky, L. S. (1978). *Mind in Society*. Cambridge, MA: Harvard University Press.

Wagner, E. D. (2002). Steps to creating a content strategy for your organization. *The eLearning Developers' Journal*, 1-9. Retrieved April 29, 2017, from http://www.elearningguild.com/pdf/2/102902mgt-h.pdf

Wang, L., & Beasley, W. (2002). Effects of learner control and hypermedia preference on cyber-students performance in a Web-based learning environment. *Journal of Educational Multimedia and Hypermedia*, *11*, 71–91.

Wang, R. (2016). Assessment for one-shot library instruction: A conceptual approach. *Portal (Baltimore, Md.)*, *16*(3), 619–648. doi:10.1353/pla.2016.0042

Web Content Accessibility Guidelines (WCAG 2.0). (2017, May 11). Retrieved from http://www.w3.org/TR/ WCAG20/

Web Content Accessibility Guidelines Working Group (WCAG WG). (2017, May 11). Retrieved from http://www.w3.org/ WAI/GL/

WebAIM. (2013). *Visual disabilities.* Retrieved from http://webaim.org/articles/visual/

Weber, B. G., John, M., Mateas, M., & Jhala, A. (2011). Modeling Player Retention in Madden NFL 11. IAAI.

Wei, H.-C., Peng, H., & Chou, C. (2015). Can more interactivity improve learning achievement in an online course? Effects of college students' perception and actual use of a course-management system on their learning achievement. *Computers & Education*, *83*, 10–21. doi:10.1016/j.compedu.2014.12.013

Weiner, S. A., Pelaez, N., Chang, K., & Weiner, J. (2011). Biology and nursing students' perceptions of a web-based information literacy tutorial. *Communications in Information Literacy*, *5*(2), 187–201. doi:10.15760/comminfolit.2012.5.2.112

Wenger, E., & White, N., Smith, J. (2009). *Digital habitats: Stewarding technology for communities.* Portland. OR: CPSquare.

Wenger, E., McDermott, R., & Snyder, W. (2002). *Cultivating communities of practice: A guide to managing knowledge.* Cambridge, MA: Harvard Business School Press.

Williams, M. E. (2001). *The effects of conceptual model provision and cognitive style on problem- solving performance of learners engaged in an exploratory learning environment* (Doctoral Dissertation). University of Oklahoma.

Williams, B., & Stimatz, L. R. (2005). The origins of graphic screen design principles: Theory or rhetoric? *International Journal of Instructional Media, 32*, 181–194.

Williams, R. (1996). *Beyond the Mac is not a typewriter*. Berkeley, CA: Peachpit Press.

Williams, R. (2004). *The non-designer's design book: Design and typographic principles for the visual novice*. Berkeley, CA: Peachpit Press.

Wilson, B. G. (Ed.). (1996). *Constructivist learning environments: Case studies in instructional design*. Englewood Cliffs, NJ: Educational Technology Publications.

Wilson, P. H., Mojica, G. F., & Confrey, J. (2013). Learning trajectories in teacher education: Supporting teacher's understandings of student's mathematical thinking. *The Journal of Mathematical Behavior, 32*(2), 103–121. doi:10.1016/j.jmathb.2012.12.003

Winn, B. (2008). The design, play, and experience framework. In Handbook of research on effective electronic gaming in education. IGI Global.

Witzel, A. (2000). The Problem-Centered Interview. *Forum Qualitative Social Research, 1*(1). Retrieved from http://www.qualitative-research.net/index.php/fqs/article/viewArticle/1132/2521

Wokurka, G., Banschback, Y., Houlder, D., & Jolly, R. (2017). Digital culture: Why strategy and culture should eat breakfast together. In G. Oswald & M. Kleinemeir (Eds.), *Shaping the Digital Enterprise* (pp. 109–120). Springer International Publisher. doi:10.1007/978-3-319-40967-2_5

Wylie, G., & Allport, A. (2000). Task switching and the measurement of "switch costs". *Psychological Research, 63*(3-4), 212–233. doi:10.1007004269900003 PMID:11004877

Xie, K., & Ke, F. (2010). The role of students' motivation in peer-moderated asynchronous online discussions. *British Journal of Educational Technology, 42*(6), 916–930. doi:10.1111/j.1467-8535.2010.01140.x

Xie, K., Yu, C., & Bradshaw, A. C. (2014). Impacts of role assignment and participation in asynchronous discussions in college-level online classes. *The Internet and Higher Education, 20*, 10–19. doi:10.1016/j.iheduc.2013.09.003

Yau, J. Y.-K., & Joy, M. (2010). An adaptive context-aware mobile learning framework based on the usability perspective. *International Journal of Mobile Learning and Organisation, 4*(4), 378–390.

Yin, R. K. (2010). Estudo de caso: planejamento e métodos (2nd ed.). Academic Press.

Yip, J. (2017). Participatory Design. In A. A. Carr-Chellman & G. Rowland (Eds.), *Issues in Technology, Learning, and Instructional Design. Classic and contemporary dialogues* (pp. 202–209). New York: Routledge.

Yoshinov, R., Arapi, P., Christodoulakis, S., & Kotseva, M. (2016). Supporting personalized learning experiences on top of multimedia digital libraries. *International Journal of Education and Information Technologies, NAUN, 10*, 152–158.

You, S., Kim, M., & Lim, Y. (2016). Value of culturally oriented information design. *Universal Access in the Information Society, 15*(3), 369–391. doi:10.100710209-014-0393-9

Yu, C. H., & Miller, R. C. (2011). Enhancing mobile browsing and reading, *Proceedings of the 2011 annual conference extended abstracts on Human factors in computing systems (CHI EA '11)*, 1783-1788. DOI: 10.1145/1979742.1979845

Zaharias, P., Andreou, I., & Vosinakis, S. (2010). Educational Virtual Worlds, Learning Styles and Learning Effectiveness: an empirical investigation. *Proceedings of the 7th Pan-Hellenic Conference with International Participation «ICT in Education»,* 1-6.

Zain, N. H. M., Razak, F. H. A., Jaafar, A., & Zulkipli, M. F. (2011). Eye tracking in educational games environment: evaluating user interface design through eye tracking patterns. In *Visual Informatics: Sustaining Research and Innovations* (pp. 64–73). Springer. doi:10.1007/978-3-642-25200-6_7

Zhang, C., & Fulford, S. (1994). Are interaction time and psychological interactivity the same thing in the distance learning television classroom? *Educational Technology*, *34*, 58–64.

Zhang, H., Lin, L., Zhan, Y., & Ren, Y. (2016). The impact of teaching presence on online engagement behaviors. *Journal of Educational Computing Research*, *54*(7), 887–900. doi:10.1177/0735633116648171

Zirkin, B., & Sumler, D. (1995). Interactive or non-interactive? That is the question! An annotated bibliography. *Journal of Distance Education*, *10*, 95–112.

About the Contributors

Gary Ackerman has extensive experience designing technology-based curriculum and teaching and learning. He has held many positions in K-12 and community college public education, and he applies research methods to his practice. He currently serves as the Flexible Pathways Coordinator at the Windsor (Vermont) School.

Hesham Alomyan is an assistant professor of instructional technology at the University of Petra, Jordan. He received his Ph.D in instructional technology from the University of South Australia where he taught subjects related to ICTs and education from 2003 to 2007. He currently teaches at undergraduate and graduate levels across a number of courses including computers in education, computer skills, educational technology, and design and production of instructional aids. His current research interests include Web-based learning design, developing online instructional strategies, and the use of digital and mobile technologies in learning. Dr Alomyan was the director of the Academic Development Center, Petra University from 2012 to 2016 with his expertise being in the utilisation of ICTs to enhance academic staff teaching at the University of Petra

Fabiano Antunes has a Master degree in Animal Biology from Federal University of Rio Grande do Sul. Biology and Natural Science teacher - Military School of Porto Alegre.

Amar Ranjan Dash has obtained his B. Tech. degree from Biju Patnaik University of Technology, India and M. Tech. degree from Berhampur University, India. Currently, he is pursuing his doctoral research. He has 7 research publications to his credit. His research interests include Web Accessibility, Web Service Choreography, Cloud Computing, and Optimization of CPU Scheduling. He is a member of ACM.

José Valdeni De Lima is a professor at the Federal University of Rio Grande do Sul - UFRGS. He holds a PhD in Computer Science from Joseph Fourier University - Grenoble I - France (1990), a Master in Computer Science from the PPGC-UFRGS (1982) and a Bac Data Processing from the Federal University of Ceará - UFC in 1978 His fields of interest are multimedia information systems, e-learning, databases and applications that support the use of Computer Science in Education, specifically Adaptive Learning Trajectories. He has published more than 200 articles, supervised more than 20 PhD theses, and more than 45 master research.

Sérgio Franco holds a degree in Psychology and Philosophy, a Masters and a Doctorate in Education from the Federal University of Rio Grande do Sul - UFRGS (1990 and 2000). He is a Full Professor of the Faculty of Education of UFRGS and professor of the Postgraduate programs in Education and Computer Science in Education. He was a member of the National Council of Education (CNE) and Vice-President of the Board of Higher Education of this Council. He was President of the National Commission for the Evaluation of Higher Education (CONAES) of the Ministry of Education. He was Dean of Graduation, Secretary of Distance Education, Director of the Faculty of Education, Director of the Interdisciplinary Center for New Technologies in Education at UFRGS. He was the Director of Distance Education Policies of the Ministry of Education's Secretariat for Distance Education. Research the areas of learning and higher education.

Kelly Hannel is a Doctor in Informatics in Education by the Federal University of Rio Grande do Sul (UFRGS) in 2017. She did her master degree in Computer Science at the Post Graduation Program of Informatics at the Federal University of Rio Grande do Sul (2008). Her research interests include Virtual Learning Environments, Distance Education, and Learning Trajectories. Currently, she works as Lieautenant at Brazilian Army in Military College of Porto Alegre, where her position is Information Technology Analyst and her main responsibilities are: modeling and support Web systems; network administration, support and maintenance; besides infrastructure and management of the park of machines. In the educational area, she works as a teacher in Estácio de Sá University, giving classes such as: system modeling, software engineering, software testing and information systems management. As future directions, she intend to increase the research about Virtual Learning Environments mainly MOODLE and Khan Academy.

Kevin Hunt is Assistant Professor and Chair of the Arts and Sciences Department at Goldey-Beacom College, where he directs the first-year writing program.

Johannes Konert is professor for Web Engineering at Beuth University of Applied Sciences in Berlin since 2015. Prior to that he studied computer science at the Karlsruhe Institute of Technology (KIT), founded a social media company and became a scholarship as Ph.D. student of the DFG research training group "Feedback-based Quality Management in E-learning" while working as research assistant at Multimedia Communication Lab (KOM) at Technische Universität Darmstadt, Germany. In his Ph.D. thesis he focused on the development of solutions to use social media concepts for knowledge transfer between peers in serious games. Currently, his research builds on these outcomes and concentrates on optimization of individual learning experiences in social media-based learning applications and serious games. He is co-author of various book chapters and publications in the field of technology enhanced learning (TEL), involved as co-chair and board member of various academic conferences and journals. Since 2016 he is elected to be the representative for support of young scientists as a steering board member of the SIG E-Learning of the German chapter of ACM (g.i. e.V.).

Lijia Lin is an Associate Professor in the School of Psychology and Cognitive Science at East China Normal University in Shanghai, China. His research focuses on using a variety of digital technologies and instructional strategies to enhance learning. His work has been widely published in journals such as Computers & Education, Journal of Educational Computing Research, Interactive Learning Environments, Journal of Experimental Education, and Educational Technology Research & Development. He has also made dozens of presentations at the international conferences, such as the American Educational Research Association's annual meeting. He is currently serving as an ad hoc reviewer for 12 international journals and a regular proposal reviewer for American Educational Research Association. He obtained his Ph.D. from the Educational Technology Program at Arizona State University in the United States.

Patrick Lowenthal is an Associate Professor at Boise State University. Prior to that he was an Instructional Designer at Boise State University. Before that he was an Academic Technology Coordinator at CU Online at the University of Colorado Denver. He completed his doctoral studies on instructional design and technology in the School of Education and Human Development. His research interests focus on instructional communication, with a specific focus on social and teaching presence, in online and face-to-face environments. In addition, he often writes about issues and problems of practice related to post-secondary education. He has an MA in Instructional Design and Technology as well as an MA in the Academic Study of Religion. Patrick has been teaching and designing instruction since 1998 and teaching online since 2003.

Russell Michalak, MLIS, joined Goldey-Beacom College (GBC) in 2010. As Director of Library & Learning Center/Assistant Professor, he oversees all operations of the library including the annual budget, In addition, he supervises and hires librarians, tutors, paraprofessionals, as well as manages the delivery of research, information, and instructional services as well as the operations of the tutoring center. His research agenda focuses on information literacy-related topics, with an emphasis on utilizing online training modules to increase international information literacy skills.

Felipe Nunes has Doctoral at the Post Graduation Program of Informatics in Education (PPGIE) at the Federal University of Rio Grande do Sul (UFRGS). Master in Computer Science from the Post Graduation Program in Informatics (PPGI) of the Federal University of Santa Maria (UFSM) (2014). Has experience with Virtual Worlds, Pedagogical Agents, Virtual Learning Environments, Distance Education, Mobile and Ubiquitous Computing, Context and Quality of Context, Learning Trajectories. Currently, I work with Virtual Worlds and Intelligent Agents applied in education in different areas of teaching. As future directions, I intend to continue in this area of research and expand the scope of work to research involving serious games applied in education using Unity.

Radoslav Palvov (http://mdl.cc.bas.bg/radko) - Professor at the Institute of Mathematics and Informatics at the Bulgarian Academy of Sciences (IMI—BAS), Deputy director of IMI—BAS (2007 – 2017), PhD (Informatics, 1977), Head of the Department of Mathematical Linguistics at IMI—BAS (1984-2016). Senior Researcher within the same organization. His major research interests are in the fields of Human Language Technologies, Knowledge Technologies and Management, Semantic WEB services, Software Platform Evaluation, Semantic Information Processing, Digital Libraries and Content Management Systems, Algorithmics, e-Learning. In the latest years he was the site leader of 10 national and international projects. Prof. Pavlov published 5 books, more than 170 chapters in monographs, journal and conference peer-reviewed papers, and have more than 250 citations.

Desislava Paneva-Marinova (http://mdl.cc.bas.bg/dessi) - Associate Professor at the Institute of Mathematics and Informatics at the Bulgarian Academy of Sciences (IMI—BAS) (2013), PhD (Informatics, 2008), Head of the Department of Mathematical Linguistics at IMI—BAS (2016-present). Her major research interests are in the fields Multimedia Digital Libraries, Knowledge and Semantic Web Technologies, eLearning, Information Systems, Personalization, Advance Gamification. Participant in more than 10 research projects of IMI—BAS. Author or co-author of two books and more than 70 journal and conference peer-reviewed papers; More than 200 citations.

Manas Ranjan Patra holds a Ph.D. Degree in Computer Science from the Central University of Hyderabad. He is a Professor in the Department of Computer Science, Berhampur University, India and has been teaching Computer Science for the last 30 years. He was a United Nations Fellow at IIST/UNU, Macao. He has more than 170 research publications to his credit. His research interests include Service Oriented Computing, Applications of Data mining and e-Governance. He has extensively traveled to many countries for presenting research papers, chairing technical sessions and delivering invited talks. He has been a member of Editorial Boards and Programme Committees of many International journals and conferences. He is a member of ACM, CSI and ISTE.

Monica D. T. Rysavy, Ph.D., is the Director of Institutional Research and Training for Goldey-Beacom College in Wilmington, Delaware. In this role she leads all institutional research and data analysis projects for the College. Her office provides faculty and staff training support by developing new training offerings (asynchronous and synchronous face-to-face and online programs) on a variety of instructional technology, survey research, and data management/interpretation topics. Her current research agenda focuses on information literacy-related topics, with an emphasis on utilizing online training modules to increase international students' information literacy skills.

Laila Shoukry is an adjunct research associate and PhD student at the Multimedia Communications Lab (KOM) at the Technical University of Darmstadt. Her research interests lie in Serious Games evaluation, Learning Analytics and Mobile Sensing.

Matthias Teine holds a Master's degree in Business and Human Resource Education from the Paderborn University. Following to his studies, he stayed at the Chair for Human Resource Education and Evaluation Research to participate in different international research projects. Here, he was concerned with the conceptualization and implementation of digital learning application for varying target groups and educational contexts. Concurrent to his actual employment as an expert for IT-based learning at an industrial leading company, he is an external doctoral candidate at the Paderborn University. Within his doctoral thesis, he focuses on the conceptualization, development, and evaluation processes of digital learning applications but pedagogical and didactical concerns of innovative learning measures as well.

Manuel Zunguze holds a degree in Physics from Pedagogical University - Mozambique, a Master's of Science in Information Technology from Punjab Technical University - India and a PhD in Informatics in Education from the Federal University of Rio Grande do Sul - Brazil. He currently teaches Technology, Learning and Complexity at Pedagogical University. He develops research on adaptive learning, creative learning and virtual worlds.

Index

L

M

O

P

Q

R

S

T

U

V

W

www.ingramcontent.com/pod-product-compliance
Lightning Source LLC
LaVergne TN
LVHW062144300926
849161LV00010B/2619